Computational Logic and Set Theory

Jacob T. Schwartz • Domenico Cantone •
Eugenio G. Omodeo

# Computational Logic and Set Theory

## Applying Formalized Logic to Analysis

Foreword by Martin Davis

Springer

Prof. Dr. Jacob T. Schwartz
(January 9, 1930–March 2, 2009)
New York University
New York, NY
USA

Prof. Domenico Cantone
Dept. of Mathematics & Computer Science
University of Catania
Viale Andrea Doria 6
95125 Catania
Italy
cantone@dmi.unict.it

Prof. Eugenio G. Omodeo
Dept. of Mathematics & Computer Science
University of Trieste
Via Valerio 12/1
34127 Trieste,
Italy
eomodeo@units.it

ISBN 978-1-4471-6018-2 ISBN 978-0-85729-808-9 (eBook)
DOI 10.1007/978-0-85729-808-9
Springer London Dordrecht Heidelberg New York

British Library Cataloguing in Publication Data
A catalogue record for this book is available from the British Library



*Cover design*: VTeX UAB, Lithuania

Printed on acid-free paper

Springer is part of Springer Science+Business Media (www.springer.com)

*To Diana*

*To Maria Pia and Riccardo*

*To Paola, Pietro, and Sara*

Jacob Theodore "Jack" Schwartz (January 9, 1930–March 2, 2009), courtesy of Diana Robinson Schwartz

# Foreword

Jack Schwartz, the principal, but alas posthumous, author of this book, turned his serious attention to computer science in the mid 1960s. At the time he had already been recognized as a brilliant young mathematician, and the two volumes of the magisterial Dunford–Schwartz *Linear Operators* already in print were widely admired. Jack saw that computers were going to have a revolutionary effect and that the expansions of their use would give rise to many fundamental problems, and he wanted to be part of that. He realized that as software became more complex the question of how its correctness could be ensured would become ever more critical. Moreover he saw formal logic embodied in computer programs as an important part of the answer.

A substantial part of Jack's research program in computer science derived from his appreciation of the possibility of expressing mathematical discourse in the language of set theory. In much the same way that the seventeenth century work of Descartes and Fermat had shown that propositions of Euclid's geometry could be regarded as statements in the language of algebra, so the twentieth century contributions of Russell, Zermelo, and von Neumann showed how propositions of the various branches of mathematics could be regarded as statements in the language of set theory. This appreciation led him in three directions:

1. He designed SETL, a general purpose high level programming language based on the language of set theory. The need to achieve acceptable performance from software written in a language that made no concessions to the vagaries of computer architecture led to work on compiler optimization in fruitful collaboration with researchers from IBM.
2. After studying Heinrich Behmann's algorithm for the decision problem of second order monadic predicate calculus, Jack saw that these methods could be extended to yield algorithms for decidable fragments of set theory. Over a period of decades, working with a group of collaborators almost all from Italy, who were first students at New York University and then became distinguished scientists in their own right, a surprising collection of non-trivial mathematics was found to lie within the scope of such algorithms.

3. Working with some of these same Italian researchers, a computer program was designed and implemented (at least as a prototype) that could verify the correctness of mathematical proofs presented in the language of set theory. Jack proposed to use this verifier to certify the correctness of a substantial body of the fundamentals of mathematical analysis. This was to include proofs of the basic properties of the real and complex number systems defined in set-theoretic terms, the fundamental properties of limits, continuity and the differential and integral calculus, and was to culminate in a proof of the Cauchy Integral Theorem of complex analysis.

The present volume is concerned with this verifier, its use and its context. However this context is to be understood in an extremely broad sense. Some of the work on decidable fragments of set theory is presented in a context that includes other algorithms from various sources for branches of logic as well. The main metamathematical theorems covered in a modern course in mathematical logic are here: the completeness theorem and the two incompleteness theorems of Gödel. Such topics as reflection principles and large cardinals are here as well. Those familiar with Jack Schwartz's mode of thought and with his way of putting his own stamp on a field will have no trouble hearing his voice in this important thought-provoking book.

Martin Davis

Professor Emeritus, Courant Institute, New York University
Visiting Scholar, University of California, Berkeley

# Preface

In June 2000, the third named author visited New York University and was invited by Jack Schwartz to read what he called the ("common shared") *scenario*: a wide, carefully assembled sequence of definitions, theorems, and proofs, leading from the bare rudiments of set theory to the beginning of mathematical analysis. Proofs began to be gappy after a few hundred pages, and then totally absent, but the flow of definitions and theorems went on, to culminate in the definition of complex line integral and finally in the celebrated Cauchy integral theorem of complex analysis.

With an implementation appearing all but imminent, Jack had cast a significant piece of mathematics in rigorous formal detail, honestly asking himself whether a computer program could conceivably process and validate every single step. The resulting large-scale proof scenario was meant—in Jack's own words—"to serve as an essential part of the feasibility study that must precede the development of any ambitious proof-checker". Eventually, it would also serve as a testing-bench for the concrete implementation of the proof-checker.

The conception of this book on computational logic began then. According to our initial plans, the book would have described the structure of a proof verifier rooted in set theory and would also have surveyed a twenty-year long stream of results on decidable fragments of set theory.

One year later, the second named author visited New York in his turn; at his request Jack advanced the implementation work, speedily bringing into existence the proof-checker Referee, also known as Ref, or as ÆtnaNova. This is still a prototype, but it is reliable and fast enough to give us the possibility of debugging our proof scenarios. Some, though not all, of the content of this book is thus related to concrete experience, which we are now pleased to share with our readers.

A very large proof scenario is available today as a LaTeX-generated PDF-file. But given its size (over a thousand pages), it seems appropriate to publish it on the web (and eventually as a CD) rather than to print it. As for the proof verifier, it is usable on the web, but it depends on a SETL2 implementation. Since there is hardly anyone maintaining the SETL system today, Jack undertook with us a re-implementation of the proof verifier in a currently more popular language. But this will take some time; it should not be permitted to delay the publication of this book.

This is a posthumous publication, as its principal author passed away on March 2, 2009. In spite of his long illness, until the end of his life, Jack showed unbelievable resources of energy in the preparation of this book, in implementing and debugging Ref, and in drafting and writing the scenario. With the inspirer of this work gone, the book may not have achieved the degree of perfection that had been Jack Schwartz's goal; nevertheless we believe that the material he left behind will attract many readers and that its publication will be an appropriate tribute to a distinguished scientist.

## *A Word on the Audience for Whom This Book Is Intended*

Any technical book must, by emphasizing certain details and leaving others unspoken, make definite assumptions about the prior knowledge of the reader.

This book assumes that the reader has a good knowledge of standard programming techniques, particularly of string manipulation and parsing, and also a general familiarity with those parts of mathematics that are analyzed in detail in the main series of definitions and proof scenarios to which much of the book is devoted.

On the other hand, little knowledge of formal logic is assumed. For this reason we try to present what is needed from logic in a reasonably self-contained way, emphasizing concepts likely to be important in continuations of the work begun here, rather than technicalities. Foundational issues, for example consideration of the strength or necessity of axioms, or the precise relationship of our formalism to other weaker or stronger formalisms studied in the literature, are neglected.

Because we expect our readers to be programmers of some sophistication, syntactic details of the kind that often appear early in books on logic are underplayed, and we repeatedly assume that anything programmable with relative ease can be taken as routine, and that the properties of such programmable operations can be proved when necessary to some theoretical discussion. This reflects our feeling that understanding develops top-down, focusing on details only as these become necessary.

We believe that too much detail is more likely to impede than to promote understanding. Who reads, or would want to read, the Whitehead–Russell *Principia*, or could testify that its hundreds of formula-filled pages are without error? But since we ask this question, why do we include hundreds of formula-filled pages in this book, which would not exist without the pioneering work of Whitehead and Russell? The reason lies in the fact that our formal proof text is, to a large extent, computer-checked. Though relatively useless to the human reader unless their correctness can be verified mechanically, long lists of formulae become useful once such verification becomes possible.

## *Content of This Book*

Chapter 1 gives rapid overviews of the authors' approach to automated proof verification and of the large-scale formalized proof scenario whose development has accompanied the writing of this book.

Chapter 2 prepares for an extensive account of our proof verifier ÆtnaNova, by surveying three traditional branches of logic: propositional calculus, first-order predicate calculus, set theory. Completeness proofs are provided for the first two of these deductive systems; the much-debated issue of the consistency of Zermelo–Fraenkel set theory and of some of its proposed extensions is highlighted.

Chapter 3 provides an extended survey of inference mechanisms. Some of these belong to the initial endowment of ÆtnaNova, others are candidates for inclusion in that endowment should our proof verifier be re-implemented or enhanced. In some cases efficiency considerations show that an inference mechanism cannot be applied at its fullest; notwithstanding we present it because of the mathematical insight it provides. Two classics of the automated deduction field, Robinson's resolution principle and the Knuth–Bendix equational method, are also surveyed in this chapter.

Chapter 4 describes our verifier and its underlying design in more detail. In Chapter 5 we expand a broad survey of main definitions and theorems, showing the salient steps of a formalized proof scenario leading toward the (as yet) unachieved goal of proving the Cauchy integral theorem.

In Chapter 6, for completeness sake and to enjoy the intellectual insight that these results provide, we derive several of the main classical results on undecidability and unsolvability; in particular, Chaitin's theorem and the two celebrated Gödel's incompleteness theorems.

To convey the character of a scenario verifiable by means of our ÆtnaNova system, we conclude with Chapter 7 showing formalized proofs of many facts about ordinals, of various properties of the transitive closure operation, of finite and transfinite induction principles, and of Zorn's lemma.

## *Acknowledgements*

We are grateful to Martin Davis, to Alfredo Ferro, and to Alberto Policriti for encouraging, through decades of scientific interaction with the authors, the maturation of many ideas in this book; to Salvatore Paxia, who enabled us to keep the ÆtnaNova system alive; to Alexandru Ioan Tomescu, who contributed to the development of proof scenarios. Various results reported in this book stem from joint work with Gianluca Cincotti, Piero Ursino, and Calogero Zarba; Emanuele Giaquinta gave us precious advice concerning LaTeX.

Diana Robinson Schwartz gave us major support throughout the preparation of this book.

This research was partially funded by MIUR/PRIN project 2006/2007 "*Large-scale development of certified mathematical proofs*" No. 2006012773, and by INdAM/GNCS (Istituto Nazionale di Alta Matematica "F. Severi", Gruppo Nazionale per il Calcolo Scientifico).

Catania, Italy — Domenico Cantone
Trieste, Italy — Eugenio G. Omodeo

# Contents

# Chapter 1
# Introduction

[⋯] *This then is the advantage of our method: that immediately* [⋯] *guided only by characters in a safe and really analytic way, we bring to light truths that others have barely achieved by an immense effort of mind and by chance. And therefore we are able to present results within our century which otherwise would hardly be attained in the course of millennia.* (Gottfried Wilhelm Leibniz, 1679)

## 1.1 Loomings

Logic begins with Aristotle's systematic enumeration of the forms of syllogism, as an attempt to improve the rigor of philosophical (and possibly also political) reasoning. Euclid then demonstrated that reasoning at Aristotle's syllogistic level of rigor could cover a substantial body of knowledge, namely the whole of geometry as known in his day. Subsequent mediaeval work, first in the Islamic world and later in Europe, began to uncover new algebraic forms of symbolic reasoning. Fifteen centuries after Euclid, Leibniz proposed that algebra be extended to a larger symbolism covering all rigorous thought. So two basic demands, for rigor and for extensive applicability, are fundamental to logic.

Leibniz did little to advance his proposal, which only began to move forward with the much later work of Boole (on the algebra of propositions), the 1879 Concept-Notation (*Begriffsschrift*) of Frege, and Peano's axiomatization of the foundations of arithmetic. This stream of work reached a pinnacle in Whitehead and Russell's 1910 demonstration that the whole corpus of mathematics could be covered by an improved Frege-like logical system.

Developments in mathematics had meanwhile prepared the ground for the Whitehead–Russell work. Mathematics can be seen as the combination of two forms of thought. Of these, the most basic is intuitive, and, as shown by geometry (or more primitively by arithmetic), often inspired by experience with the physical world which it captures and abstracts. But mathematics works on this material by systematically manipulating collections of statements about it. Thus the second face of mathematics is linguistic and formal. Mathematics attains rigor by demanding


DOI 10.1007/978-0-85729-808-9_1, 

that the statement sequences which it admits as proofs conform to rigid formal constraints. For this to be possible, the pre-existing, intuition-inspired content of mathematics must be progressively resolved into carefully formalized concepts, and thus ultimately into sentences which a Leibniz-like formal logical language can cover. A major step in this analysis was Descartes' reduction, via his coordinate method, of 2- and 3-dimensional geometry to algebra. To complete this, it became necessary to solve a nagging technical problem, the 'problem of the continuum', concerning the system of numbers used. An intuition basic to certain types of geometric reasoning is that no continuous curve can cross from one side of a line to another without intersecting the line in at least one point. To capture this principle in an algebraic model of the whole of geometry one must give a formal definition of the system of 'real' numbers which models the intuitively conceived real axis, must top this by giving a formal definition of the notion of continuity, and must use this definition to prove the fundamental theorem that a continuous function cannot pass from a positive to a negative value without becoming zero somewhere between.

This work was accomplished gradually during the 19th century. The necessary definition of continuity appeared in Cauchy's *Cours d'Analyse* of 1821. A formal definition of the system of 'real' numbers rigorously completing Cauchy's work was given in Dedekind's 1872 study *Continuity and Irrational Numbers*. Together these two efforts showed that the whole of classical calculus could be based on the system of fractions, and so, by a short step, on the whole numbers. What remained was to analyze the notion of number itself into something more fundamental. Such an analysis, of the notion of number into that of sets of arbitrary objects standing in 1-1 correspondence, appeared in Frege's 1884 *Foundations of Arithmetic*, was generalized and polished in Cantor's transfinite set theory of 1895, and was approached in alternative, more conventionally axiomatic terms by Peano in his 1894 *Mathematical Formulary*. Like Whitehead and Russell's *Principia Mathematica*, the series of definitions and theorems found later in this work walks the path blazed by Cauchy, Dedekind, Frege, Cantor, and Peano.

As set theory evolved, its striving for ultimate generality came to be limited by certain formal paradoxes, which become unavoidable if the doors of formal set-theoretic definition are opened too widely. These arise very simply. Suppose, for example, that we allow ourselves to consider 'the set of all sets that are not members of themselves'. In a formal notation very close to that continually used below, this is simply $s = \{x \mid x \notin x\}$. But now consider the proposition $s \in s$. On formal grounds this is equivalent to $s \in \{x \mid x \notin x\}$, and so, by the very definition of set membership, to the proposition $s \notin s$. So in these few formal steps we have derived the proposition

$$s \in s \leftrightarrow s \notin s,$$

a situation around which no coherent logical system can be built. The means adopted to avoid this immediate collapse of the formal structure that one wants to build is to restrict the syntax of the set formers which can legally be written, in a way which forbids constructions like $\{x \mid x \notin x\}$ without ruling out the similar but somewhat more limited expressions needed to express the whole of standard mathematics.

These fine adjustments to the formal structure of logic were worked out, first by Whitehead and Russell, later and a bit differently by their successors.

A higher technical polish was put on all this work by 20th century efforts. Cantor's work was extended, and began to be formalized, by Zermelo in 1908, and more completely formalized by Fraenkel in 1923. The axiomatization of set theory at which they arrived is called Zermelo–Fraenkel set theory. Starting in 1905 the great German mathematician David Hilbert began the influential series of studies of the algebra of logic, later summarized in his 1939 work *Foundations of Mathematics* (with Paul Bernays). First in his 1925 paper 'An Axiomatization of Set Theory', and then in a fuller 1928 version, John von Neumann elegantly recast the Zermelo–Fraenkel set formalism, along with Frege's analysis of the concept of number, by encoding the integers set-theoretically: the number 0 as the empty set, 1 as the singleton-set {0}, 2 as the set {0, 1}, and, more generally, each integer $n$ as the $n$-element set $\{0, 1, \ldots, n-1\}$. A corresponding, equally elegant definition of the notions of ordinal and cardinal numbers (both finite and infinite) was given in von Neumann's carefully honed formalism, from which the more computer-oriented exposition found later in the present work derives very closely.

Especially at first, Hilbert's logical studies stood in a positive relation to the program proposed by Leibniz, since it was hoped that close analysis of the algebra of logic might in principle lead to a set of algorithms allowing any mathematical statement to be decided by a suitable calculation. But the radical attack on the intuitive soundness of non-constructive Cantorian reasoning and of the conventional foundations of mathematics published by the Dutch mathematician L.E.J. Brouwer in 1918 led Hilbert's work in a different direction. Hilbert hoped that the 'metamathematical' tools he was developing could be used to reply to Brouwer's critique. For this reply, a combinatorial analysis of the algebra of logic, to which Brouwer could have no objections since only constructive arguments would be involved, would be used metamathematically to demonstrate formal limits on what could be proved within standard mathematics, and in particular to show that no contradiction could follow from any standard proof. Once done, this would demonstrate the formal consistency of standard mathematics within a Brouwerian framework. But things turned out differently. In a startling and fundamentally new development, the metamathematical techniques pioneered by the Hilbert school were used in 1931 by Kurt Gödel to show that Hilbert's program was certainly unrealizable, since no logical system of the type considered by Hilbert could be used to prove its own consistency. The brilliance of this result changed the common professional view of logic, which came to be seen, not as a Leibnizian engine for the formal statement and verification of ordinary mathematics, but as a negatively-oriented tool for proving various qualitative and quantitative limits on the power of formalized mathematical systems.

In the late 1940s the coming of the computer brought in new influences. Expression in a rigorously defined system of formulae makes mathematics amenable to computer processing, and daily work with computer programs makes the absolute rigor of formalized mathematical systems obvious. The possibility of using computer assistance to lighten the tedium (so evident in Whitehead and Russell) of fully formalized proof began to make the Leibniz program seem more practical. (Initially it was even hoped that suitably pruned computer searches could be used rather directly to find many of the ordinary proofs used in mathematics.) The fact that the methods of formalized proof could be used to check and verify the correctness of computer programs gave economic importance to what would otherwise remain an esoteric endeavor. Computerized proof-verifier systems, emphasizing various styles of proof and potential application areas, began to appear in the 1960s. The system described in the present text belongs to this stream of work.

A fully satisfactory formal logical system should be able to digest 'the whole of mathematics', as this develops by progressive extension of mathematics-like reasoning to new domains of thought. To avoid continual reworking of foundations, one wants the formal system taken as basic to remain unchanged, or at any rate to change only by extension as such efforts progress. In any fundamentally new area, work and language will initially be controlled more by guiding intuitions than by precise formal rules, as when Euclid and his predecessors first realized that the intuitive properties of geometric figures in 2 and 3 dimensions, and also some familiar properties of whole numbers could be covered by modes of reasoning more precise than those used in everyday life. Similarly, the initially semiformal languages that developed around studies of the 'complex' and 'imaginary' roots of algebraic equations, the 'infinitesimal' quantities spoken of in early versions of the calculus, the 'random' quantities of the probabilist, and the physicist's 'Dirac delta functions', all need to be absorbed into a single formal system. This is done by modeling the intuitively grasped objects appearing in important semiformalized languages by precisely defined objects of the formal system, in a way that maps all the useful statements of the imprecise initial language into corresponding formulae. If less than vital, statements of the initial language that do not fit into its formalized version can then be dismissed as 'misunderstandings'.

The mathematical developments surveyed in the preceding discussion succeeded in re-expressing the intuitive content of geometry, arithmetic, and calculus ('analysis') in set-theoretic terms. The geometric notion of 'space' maps into 'set of all pairs (or triples) of real numbers', preparing the way for consideration of the 'set of all $n$-tuples of real numbers' as '$n$-dimensional space', and of more general related constructs as 'infinite dimensional' and 'functional' spaces. The 'figures' originally studied in geometry map, via the 'locus' concept, into sets of such pairs, triples, etc. The next necessary step is to analyze the notion of real number into something more basic, the essential technical requirement for this being to ensure that no function roots (e.g. Pythagoras' square root of 2) are 'missing'. As noted above, this was accomplished by Dedekind, who reduced 'real number $x$' to 'nonempty set $x$ of rational numbers, bounded above, such that every rational not in $x$ is larger than every rational in $x$'. To eliminate everything but set theory from the formal foundations of mathematics, it only remains (since 'fractions' can be seen as pairs of numbers) to reduce the notion of 'integer' to set-theoretic terms. This was done by Cantor and Frege: an integer is the class of all finite sets in 1-1 correspondence with any one such set. None of the other important mathematical developments enumerated in the preceding paragraph required fundamental extension of the set-theoretic foundation thereby attained. Gauss realized that the 'complex' numbers used in algebra could be modeled as pairs of real numbers, Kolmogorov modeled 'random' variables as functions defined on an implicit set-theoretic measure space, and Laurent Schwartz interpreted the initially puzzling 'delta functions' in terms of a broader notion of generalized function defined systematically in set-theoretic terms. So all of these concepts were digested without forcing any adjustment of the set-theoretic foundation constructed for arithmetic, analysis, and geometry. This foundation also supports all the more abstract mathematical constructions elaborated in such 20th century fields as topology, abstract algebra, and category theory. Indeed, these were expressed set-theoretically from their inception. So (if we ignore a few ongoing explorations whose significance remains to be determined) set theory currently stands as a comfortable and universal basis for the whole of mathematics.

It can even be said that set theory captures a set of reality-derived intuitions more fundamental than such basic mathematical ideas as that of number. Arithmetic would be very different if the real-world process of counting did not return the same result each time a set of objects was counted, or if a subset of a finite set $S$ of objects proved to have a larger count than $S$. So, even though Peano showed how to characterize the integers and derive many of their properties using axioms free of any explicit set-theoretic content, his approach robs the integers of much of their intuitive significance, since in his reduced context they cannot be used to count anything. For this and the other reasons listed above, we will work with a thoroughly set-theoretic formalism, contrived to mimic the language and procedures of standard mathematics closely.

### *1.1.1 The Special Nature of Mathematical Reasoning Within Human Reason in General*

The syllogistic patterns characteristic of mathematical reasoning derive from, and thus often reappear in, other reasoned forms of human discourse, for example in arguments offered by lawyers and philosophers. Mathematical reasoning is distinguished within this world of reason by its rigorous adherence to the pattern originally set by Euclid. Some fixed set of statements, the *axioms*, perhaps carrying some insight about an observed or intuited world, must be firmly set down. Certain named predicates (and perhaps also function symbols) will appear in these axioms. The ensuing discourse (which may be lengthy) must work exclusively with properties of these predicates (and symbols) which follow formally from the axioms, precisely as if these predicates had no meaning other than that which the axioms give them. When new vocabulary is introduced (as will generally be necessary to provide intellectual variety and sustain interest) this must be by formal definition in terms of predicates (and function symbols) which either are those found in the axioms or which appear earlier in the discourse. Such extensions of vocabulary are subject to rules which ensure that all new symbols introduced can be regarded as tools of art which add nothing fundamental to the axioms. That is, mathematics' rules of definition ensure that allowed extensions of vocabulary cannot make it possible to prove any statement made in the original vocabulary that could not be proved, in the axioms' original vocabulary, from the axioms. This rule, which insists that definitions must be devoid of all hidden axiomatic content, is fundamental to mathematics. It will appear in our later technical discussions as the *conservative extension principle.*

Legal, philosophical, and scientific reasoning commonly fail to observe the rules which restrict mathematical discourse, since these styles of argument allow new terms with explicitly or implicitly assumed properties to be introduced far more freely. Science cannot avoid this, since it is dedicated to exploration of the world in all its variety, and must therefore speak of what it finds as best it can. But unconstrained introduction, into a line of reasoning, of even a few new terms having implicitly assumed properties can readily become an engine of deception (and of self-deception). Science tries to avoid such self-deception by taking all of its reasoned outcomes as provisional subject to comparison with observed reality. If observation conflicts with the outcome of a line of scientific reasoning, the assumptions and informal definitions entering into it will be adjusted until better agreement is attained. Legal and philosophical reasoning, lacking this mechanism, remain more permanently able to be used as engines of deception (perhaps deliberate) or of self-deception (which has its intellectual delights).

## 1.2 Proof Verifiers

A *Proof verifier* is an interactive program for manipulation of the state of a mathematical discourse. It allows computer checking of such discourse in full detail, and collection of the resulting theorems for subsequent re-use. It must

(a) only allow theorems to be derived;
(b) allow all theorems to be derived.

Besides their theoretical interest, proof verifiers have one potential practical use: Program Verification. To adapt a proof verifier to this use, we can simply annotate (ordinary procedural) programs with assertions $A_i$ breaking every loop in their control flow. Then, for every path forward through the annotated program $P$ and its assignments

$$x_1 := expn(x_1, \dots, x_n)$$

running from an assertion $A_1$ immediately before such an assignment to an assertion $A_2$ immediately after the assignment we must show that

$$\big(\forall x_1, \dots, x_n \mid A_1(x_1, \dots, x_n) \to A_2\big(expn(x_1, \dots, x_n), x_2, \dots, x_n\big)\big)$$

holds. Once this has been done systematically throughout the program, we can be sure that the program is correct.

To give proofs acceptable to a programmed verifier, i.e. proofs every one of whose details can be checked by a computer, we must 'walk in shackles'; but then we want these shackles to be as light as possible. That is, we want the ordinary small steps of mathematical discourse to remain small, rather than expanding into tedious masses of detail. We aim for a formalized interactive conversation with the computer whose general 'feel' resembles that of ordinary mathematical exposition. The better we succeed in achieving this, the closer the verifier comes to passing the 'Turing test', at least in the restricted mathematical setting in which it is designed to operate. So the internal structure of a successful proof verifier can be seen as a model both of mathematics and of mathematical intelligence, which is an important, albeit limited, form of intelligence in general.

## 1.3 Informal Introduction to the Formalism in which We Will Work

A proof verifier must provide various tools. First of all, it must allow the elementary steps of proofs to be expressed by formulae in some agreed-on system. These formulae become the elementary steps which the system allows. The system-provided tools, which embody the system's 'deduction rules', must allow manipulation of these formulae in ways which mimic the normal flow of a mathematical discourse.

The collection of proofs presented to a verifier for validation is expressed as a sequence of logical formulae, to which we may attach formalized annotations to guide the action of the verifier. Given such a sequence of formulae, the verifier first checks all the statements presented to it for syntactic legality, and then goes on to verify the successive statements of each proof. As in ordinary proof, the verifier's user aims to guide discourse along paths which bring designated target theorems into the collection of proved statements. This is done by arranging the formulae (proof steps) of the discourse in such a way as to ensure that each step encountered satisfies the conditions required for it to be accepted as a consequence of what has gone before. This will be the case in various situations, each corresponding to one of the basic deduction rules which the system allows. Broadly speaking, these are as follows.

### *1.3.1 (A) Immediate Deduction*

The collection of statements already accepted as proved are always included in a 'penumbra' $D$ of additional statements which follow from them as elementary consequences. The verifier as programmed is able to check that each statement in $D$ follows immediately from statements already accepted. Some well-known examples are as follows:

(a) If a formula $F$ in a proof is preceded by an (already accepted) formula $G$, and by a second (already accepted) formula of the form $G \to F$, where '$\to$' is the operator sign designating implication, then $F$ will be accepted.

(b) If a formula $x \in E$ in a proof is preceded by an (already accepted) formula $x \in H$, and by a second (already accepted) formula $E \supseteq H$, where '$\supseteq$' is the operator sign designating set-theoretic inclusion, then $x \in E$ will be accepted.
(c) If (c.1) we are given a formula having the syntactic structure $P(e)$, where $P(x)$ is a formula containing a variable $x$, and $P(e)$ is the result of replacing each of the occurrences of $x$ in $P$ with an occurrence of the (syntactically well-formed) subexpression $e$; (c.2) the formula $P(e)$ is preceded by an (already accepted) formula $(\forall x \mid P(x))$, where the symbol '$\forall$' designates the 'universal quantifier' construct of logic, then $P(e)$ will be accepted.

The more we can enlarge the available family of immediate deductions by extending a verifier's immediate-deduction algorithms, the more we will succeed in reducing the number of steps needed to reach our target theorems. Means for doing this are explored later in this chapter, and then more systematically in Chap. 3.

### 1.3.2 (B) Proof by 'Supposition' and 'Discharge' ('Natural Deduction')

At any point in a proof, any syntactically well-formed statement $S$ can be introduced for provisional use by including a verifier directive of the form

$$\textsf{Suppose} \Longrightarrow S.$$

Conclusions can be drawn from such statements in the normal way, but such conclusions are not accepted as having been definitively proved, but only as having been 'provisionally proved', subject to the 'assumption' expressed by $S$. However, if such an assumption $S$ can be shown to lead to the impossible conclusion 'false', then $S$ can be 'discharged', i.e. its negation $\neg S$ can be accepted as a definitely proved formula. This manner of proceeding mimics the familiar method of 'proof by contradiction' (also called '*reductio ad absurdum*') of ordinary mathematical discourse.

### 1.3.3 (C) Use of Definitions

Statements which introduce entirely new constant or function names can be true 'by definition'. Suppose, for example, that constants $b$ and $c$, and a dyadic function symbol $f$, have already been introduced into a discourse, and that $d$ is a name not previously used. Then the statement

$$d = f\big(b, f(c, b)\big)$$

can be accepted immediately, since it merely *defines* $d$, i.e. makes an initial reference to an object $d$ concerning which we know nothing else. Such definitions are subject to rules which serve to ensure that the new symbols introduced by such definitions imply only those properties of previously introduced symbols which are entailed by our previous knowledge concerning them. For example, a statement like

$$b = f(b, f(d,b))$$

is not a valid definition for a new constant $d$, since at the very least it implies that there exists some $x$ for which $b = f(b, f(x,b))$ (and this may be false).

Definitions serve various purposes. At their simplest they are merely abbreviations which concentrate attention on interesting constructs by assigning them names which shorten their syntactic form. (But of course the compounding of such abbreviations can change the appearance of a discourse completely, transforming what would otherwise be an exponentially lengthening welter of bewildering formulae into a sequence of sentences which carry helpful intuitions.) Beyond this, definitions serve to 'instantiate', that is, to introduce the objects whose special properties are crucial to an intended argument. Like the selection of crucial lines, points, and circles from the infinity of geometric elements that might be considered in a Euclidean argument, definitions of this kind often carry a proof's most vital ideas.

As explained in more detail below, we use the dictions of set theory, in particular its general *set formers*, as an essential means of instantiating new objects. As we will show later by writing a hundred or so short statements which define all the essential foundations of standard mathematics, set theory gives us a very flexible and powerful tool for making definitions.

Our system allows four forms of definition. The first of these is definition using set formers (or 'algebraic constructions' more generally), as exemplified by

$$\bigcup s =_{\mathrm{Def}} \{y : x \in s,\ y \in x\}$$

(which defines 'the set of all elements of elements of $s$', i.e. 'the union of all elements of $s$'), and assigns it the symbol '$\bigcup$' (which must never have been used previous to this definition). A second example is

$$\mathsf{less\_usual}(s) =_{\mathrm{Def}} \{y : x \in s,\ y \in x\} \setminus s$$

(which defines 'the set of all elements of elements of $s$ which are not directly elements of $s$').

The second form of definition allowed generalizes this kind of set-theoretic definition in a less commonly used but very powerful way. In ordinary definitions, the symbol being defined can only appear on the left-hand side of the definition, not on its right. This standard rule prohibits 'circular' definitions. In a *recursive definition* this rule is relaxed. Here the symbol being defined, which must designate a function of one or more variables, can also appear on the right of the definition, but only in a special way. More specifically, we allow function definitions like

$$f(s,t) =_{\mathrm{Def}} d(\{g(f(x, h_1(t)),\ s, t) : x \in s \mid P(x,\ f(x, h_2(t)),\ s, t)\}),$$

where it is assumed that $d, g, h_1, h_2$, and $P$ are previously defined symbols and that $f$ is the symbol being defined by the formula displayed. Here circularity is avoided by the fact that the value of $f(s,t)$ can be calculated from values $f(x,t')$ for which we can be sure that $x$ is a member of $s$, so $x$ must come before $s$ in the implicit (possibly infinite) sequence of steps which build sets up from their members, starting with the empty set as the only necessary foundation object for the so-called 'pure' theory of sets.

'Transfinite recursive' definitions like that displayed above give us access to the sledgehammer technique called 'transfinite induction', which like other sledgehammers we use occasionally to break through key obstacles, but generally set aside.

The third and fourth forms of definition allowed, 'Skolemization' and use of 'theories', are explained later.

## 1.4 More About Our Formalism

Any formalism begins with some initial '*endowment*', i.e. system of allowed formulae and built-in rules for the derivation of new formulae from old. If one intends to use such a formalism as a basis for metamathematical reasoning, one may aim to simplify the implied combinatorial analyses of the formalism by minimizing this endowment. But we intend to use our formalism to track ordinary mathematical reasoning as closely and comfortably as we can; hence we streamline the endowment of formulae and formula transformations with which our system begins, but try to maximize its power. Accordingly, the system we propose incorporates various very powerful means for definition of objects and proof of their properties.

### *1.4.1 Propositional and Predicate Calculus*

First consider what is most necessary, which we will handle in entirely standard ways. The apparatus of Boolean reasoning is needed if we are to make such statements as '$a$ and $b$ are both true', '$a$ or $b$ is true', '$a$ implies $b$', etc. The '*propositional calculus*' required for this is elementary, and easily automated. We simply adopt this calculus, writing its operators as '&' (conjunction), '$\vee$' (disjunction), '$\neg$' (negation), '$\rightarrow$' (implication), '$\leftrightarrow$' (logical equivalence). Our system is *decidable*, in the sense it includes an algorithm able to detect statements which are universally true by virtue of their propositional form. This will, for example, automatically detect that

$$(p \rightarrow q) \rightarrow \big((\neg q) \rightarrow (\neg p)\big)$$

and

$$\big(F(x+y) = F\big(F(x)\big) \rightarrow F\big(F(x)\big) = 0\big) \rightarrow \big(F\big(F(x)\big) \neq 0 \rightarrow F(x+y) \neq F\big(F(x)\big)\big)$$

are both always true. The first of these formulae belongs directly to the propositional calculus. Automatic treatment of the second formula uses a fundamental internal system operation called '*blobbing*', which works by reducing formulae to skeletal forms legal in some tractable sublanguage of the full set-theoretic language in which we work. Applied to the second formula displayed above, blobbing sees it to have a Boolean skeleton identical to that of the first. More is said about this important technique below.

Statements of the form 'for all ...' and 'there exists ...', as in 'for all integers $n$ greater than 2 there exists a unique non-decreasing sequence of prime integers whose product is $n$', are obviously needed for mathematics. To handle these, we adopt the standard apparatus of the '*predicate calculus*' (or more properly 'first-order predicate calculus'). This extends the propositional calculus by allowing its proposition-symbols $p, q, \ldots$ to be replaced by predicate subformulae constructed recursively out of the following.

1. *Constants* $c$ and *variables* $x$ denoting specified or arbitrary objects drawn from some (implicit) '*universe*' $\mathcal{U}$ of objects.
2. Named *predicates*, e.g. $\mathsf{P}(x, y)$, $\mathsf{Ord}(x)$, $\mathsf{Between}(x, c, z)$, depending on some given number of constants and variables, which for each combination $\mathbf{x}, \mathbf{y}, \ldots$ chosen from the 'universe' $\mathcal{U}$ yield some true/false (i.e. Boolean) value.
3. Named *function symbols*, e.g. $f(x), g(x, y), h(x, c, z)$, depending on some given number of constants and variables, which for each combination $\mathbf{x}, \mathbf{y}, \ldots$ chosen from the 'universe' $\mathcal{U}$ yield an object belonging to this same universe.
4. Two '*quantifiers*',
$$\big(\forall x \mid P(x)\big) \quad \text{and} \quad \big(\exists x \mid P(x)\big),$$
respectively, representing the *universal* quantification construct 'for all possible values of the variable $x$, $P(x)$ (the statement which follows the vertical bar) is true' and the *existential* quantification construct 'there exists some value of the variable $x$ for which $P(x)$ (the statement which follows the vertical bar) is true'. For example, to express the condition that at least one of the predicates $P(x)$ and $Q(x)$ is true for each possible value of the variable $x$, we write
$$\big(\forall x \mid P(x) \vee Q(x)\big).$$
To state that exactly one of these conditions is true for every possible value of the variable $x$, we can write
$$\big(\forall x \,\big|\, \big(P(x) \vee Q(x)\big) \,\&\, \big(\neg\big(P(x) \,\&\, Q(x)\big)\big)\big).$$
To state that for each possible value of the variable $x$ having the property $P(x)$ there exists a value standing in the relationship $R(x, y)$ to it, we can write
$$\big(\forall x \mid P(x) \rightarrow \big(\exists y \mid R(x, y)\big)\big), \tag{1.1}$$
or equivalently
$$\big(\forall x \,\big|\, \big(\exists y \mid P(x) \rightarrow R(x, y)\big)\big). \tag{1.2}$$

It should be plain that this predicate notation allows us to write universally and existentially quantified statements generally, provided only that names are available for all the multivariable predicates in which we are interested.

Intuitively speaking, a universally quantified (resp. existentially quantified) formula represents the conjunction (resp. disjunction) of all possible cases of the formula; e.g., $(\forall x \mid P(x))$ can be regarded as a formalized abbreviation for the 'infinite conjunction' that might be written informally as

$$P(\mathbf{x}_1)\ \&\ P(\mathbf{x}_2)\ \&\ P(\mathbf{x}_3)\ \&\ \cdots,$$

where $\mathbf{x}_1, \mathbf{x}_2, \mathbf{x}_3, \ldots$ is an enumeration of all the values which the variable $x$ can assume. Similarly, an existentially quantified statement like $(\exists x \mid P(x))$ can be regarded as a formalized abbreviation for the 'infinite disjunction' that might be written as

$$P(\mathbf{x}_1) \vee P(\mathbf{x}_2) \vee P(\mathbf{x}_3) \vee \cdots.$$

This shows us why the two predicate formulae (1.1) and (1.2) displayed above are equivalent, namely this informal style of interpretation explicates

$$\big(\forall x \mid P(x) \to \big(\exists y \mid R(x, y)\big)\big)$$

as

$$\big(P(\mathbf{x}_1) \to \big(\exists y \mid R(\mathbf{x}_1, y)\big)\big)\ \&\ \big(P(\mathbf{x}_2) \to \big(\exists y \mid R(\mathbf{x}_2, y)\big)\big)\ \&\ \cdots$$

and hence as

$$\begin{aligned}&\big(P(\mathbf{x}_1) \to \big(R(\mathbf{x}_1, \mathbf{x}_1) \vee R(\mathbf{x}_1, \mathbf{x}_2) \vee R(\mathbf{x}_1, \mathbf{x}_3) \vee \cdots\big)\big)\\ &\qquad \&\ \big(P(\mathbf{x}_2) \to \big(R(\mathbf{x}_2, \mathbf{x}_1) \vee R(\mathbf{x}_2, \mathbf{x}_2) \vee R(\mathbf{x}_2, \mathbf{x}_3) \vee \cdots\big)\big)\ \&\ \cdots. \qquad (1.3)\end{aligned}$$

Expansion of $(\forall x \mid (\exists y \mid P(x) \to R(x, y)))$ in exactly the same way results in

$$\begin{aligned}&\big(\big(P(\mathbf{x}_1) \to R(\mathbf{x}_1, \mathbf{x}_1)\big) \vee \big(P(\mathbf{x}_1) \to R(\mathbf{x}_1, \mathbf{x}_2)\big) \vee \big(P(\mathbf{x}_1) \to R(\mathbf{x}_1, \mathbf{x}_3)\big) \vee \cdots\big)\\ &\ \&\ \big(\big(P(\mathbf{x}_2) \to R(\mathbf{x}_1, \mathbf{x}_1)\big) \vee \big(P(\mathbf{x}_2) \to R(\mathbf{x}_1, \mathbf{x}_2)\big) \vee \big(P(\mathbf{x}_2) \to R(\mathbf{x}_1, \mathbf{x}_3)\big) \vee \cdots\big)\\ &\qquad\qquad \&\ \cdots. \qquad (1.4)\end{aligned}$$

Applying the standard propositional reduction of the implication operator $p \to q$ to $(\neg p) \vee q$, we can rewrite the first line of (1.3) as

$$\big(\neg P(\mathbf{x}_1)\big) \vee \big(R(\mathbf{x}_1, \mathbf{x}_1) \vee R(\mathbf{x}_1, \mathbf{x}_2) \vee R(\mathbf{x}_1, \mathbf{x}_3) \vee \cdots\big)$$

and the first line of (1.4) as

$$\big(\neg P(\mathbf{x}_1) \vee R(\mathbf{x}_1, \mathbf{x}_1)\big) \vee \big(\neg P(\mathbf{x}_1) \vee R(\mathbf{x}_1, \mathbf{x}_2)\big) \vee \big(\neg P(\mathbf{x}_1) \vee R(\mathbf{x}_1, \mathbf{x}_3)\big) \cdots,$$

respectively, and similarly for all later lines. But then, using the associativity and commutativity of the disjunction operator $\vee$, and since disjunction is idempotent, i.e.

$$p \vee p \vee p \vee \cdots$$

is exactly equivalent to $p$, the two propositional expansions seen above are equivalent. Hence the claimed equivalence of

$$\big(\forall x \mid P(x) \rightarrow \big(\exists y \mid R(x, y)\big)\big) \quad \text{and} \quad \big(\forall x \big| \big(\exists y \mid P(x) \rightarrow R(x, y)\big)\big)$$

is intuitively apparent. We will explain later how the predicate calculus manages to handle all of this formally.

### *1.4.2 Set Theory: The Third Main Ingredient of Our Formalism*

We view set theory as the established language of mathematics and take a rich version of it as fundamental. In particular, the language with which we will work includes a full sublanguage of *set formers*, constrained just enough to avoid paradoxical constructions like the $\{x \mid x \notin x\}$ set former discussed above. Set-former expressions like

$$\big\{e(x) : x \in s \mid P(x)\big\},$$
$$\big\{e(x, y) : x \in s(y) \mid P(x, y)\big\},$$
$$\big\{e(x, y, z) : x \in s(z),\ y \in s'(x, z) \mid P(x, y, z)\big\},$$

and even

$$\big\{e(x, y, z, w) : x \in s(w),\ y \in s'(x, w),\ z \in s''(x, y, w) \mid P(x, y, z, w)\big\},$$

are all allowed, as are

$$\big\{e(x) : x \subseteq s \mid P(x)\big\},$$
$$\big\{e(x, y) : x \subseteq s(y) \mid P(x, y)\big\},$$
$$\big\{e(x, y, z) : x \subseteq s(z),\ y \subseteq s'(x, z) \mid P(x, y, z)\big\},$$

and

$$\big\{e(x, y, z, w) : x \subseteq s(w),\ y \in s'(x, w),\ z \subseteq s''(x, y, w) \mid P(x, y, z, w)\big\},$$

which use the sign '⊆' designating set inclusion in place of one or more occurrences of the sign '∈' (designating set membership).

Set formers have several crucial advantages as language elements. First of all, they give us very powerful means for defining most mathematical objects of strategic interest. This allows the very succinct series of mathematical definitions given later, which lead in roughly 100 lines from rudimentary set-theoretic concepts to core statements in analysis (e.g. the Cauchy integral theorem). A second advantage of set formers traces back to the fact that the human mind is 'perception dominated', in the sense that we all depend heavily upon many innate perceptual abilities, which operate rapidly and subconsciously, and by which the conscious (and reasoning) abilities of the mind are largely limited. Perceivable things and relationships can be dealt with rapidly. Where direct perception fails, we must fall back on more tortuous processes of reconstruction and detection, slowing progress by orders of magnitude. Hence the importance of notations, diagrams, graphs, animations, and scientific visualization techniques generally (e.g. the Arabic numerals, algebra, calculus, 'commutative diagrams' in topology, etc.). Among innate perceptual abilities we count the ability to decode spoken and written language, to remember phrases and simple relationships among them, and to recognize various language-like but somewhat more abstract syntactic structures. From this point of view, much of the importance of set theory and its set-former notations lies in the fact that their syntax reveals various simplifications and relationships with which the mind operates comfortably. These include:

(i) Various algebraic transformations of set formers, of which

$$\bigl\{e(x) : x \in \bigl\{e'(y) : y \in s \mid Q(y)\bigr\} \mid P(x)\bigr\} \\ = \bigl\{e\bigl(e'(y)\bigr) : y \in s \mid P\bigl(e'(y)\bigr) \mathbin{\&} Q(y)\bigr\}$$

and

$$\bigl\{e(x) : x \in \bigl\{e'(y,z) : y \in s_1,\ z \in s_2 \mid Q(y,z)\bigr\} \mid P(x)\bigr\} \\ = \bigl\{e\bigl(e'(y,z)\bigr) : y \in s_1,\ z \in s_2 \mid P\bigl(e'(y,z)\bigr) \mathbin{\&} Q(y,z)\bigr\}$$

are typical.

(ii) Set-former expressions make various important monotonicity and domination relationships visible. For example, a glance at

$$\bigl\{e(x) : x \in s \mid F(x) \in s \setminus t\bigr\}$$

tells us that this expression is monotone increasing in $s$ and monotone decreasing in $t$. From this, a statement like

$$\bigl(g(a) \supseteq g(b) \mathbin{\&} h(a) \subseteq h(b)\bigr) \\ \rightarrow \bigl(\bigl\{e(x) : x \in s \mid F(x) \in g(a)\setminus h(a)\bigr\} \supseteq \bigl\{e(x) : x \in s \mid F(x) \in g(b)\setminus h(b)\bigr\}\bigr)$$

is obvious by elementary reasoning concerning set unions, differences, and inclusions, which an algorithm can handle very adequately.

Deductions like this are frequent in the long sequence of steps which we will use to verify the standard mathematical material at which this text aims. Hence the stress we lay on deduction methods like that just explained, which we make available within our system under such names as ELEM ('elementary set-theoretic deduction', expanded as much as we dare), SIMPLF (deduction methods based on algebraic simplification), etc. Hence also the special methods provided to deal with set-theoretic, predicate, and algebraic monotonicity.

The set-former constructs described above, and the other elementary operations of set theory, play two roles. On the one hand, they define operations on finite sets which can be implemented explicitly, for example by programming them systematically so as to create a full programming language which allows free use of finite sets as data objects. On the other hand, they define a language in which one can talk about a much larger universe of infinite sets, even though such sets can have no explicit representation other than the formulae used to speak of them. Since the formulae used to speak of infinite sets are the same as those used for finite sets, and since much the same axioms are assumed for sets of both kinds, many of the properties deduced for infinite sets stand in analogy to the more directly visible properties of finite sets.

#### 1.4.2.1 A Few Simple but Basic Set Constructs

The operation $\{x, y\}$ which forms the (unordered) *pair* of two sets is an important but entirely elementary set operation. For this we have

$$z \in \{x, y\} \leftrightarrow (z = x \lor z = y).$$

Then plainly $\{x, x\}$ satisfies $z \in \{x, x\} \leftrightarrow z = x$, so $\{x, x\}$ is the *singleton* $\{x\}$ whose only member is $x$.

The set-former expression

$$\bigcup x =_{\text{Def}} \{z : y \in x, z \in y\}$$

defines the set of all $z$ which are elements of some element of $x$. This is the so-called '*general union set*' of $x$, which can be thought of as 'the union of all elements of $x$'. Since we have

$$z \in \bigcup \{x, y\} \leftrightarrow (z \in x \lor z \in y),$$

$\bigcup \{x, y\}$ is the set of all $z$ which are either members of $x$ or of $y$. This very commonly used operation is generally written as $x \cup y$. Given any two sets $x$ and $y$, it gives us a way of constructing a set at least as large as either of them, of which both are subsets.

We can use the union operator to define the sets having three, four, etc. given elements by writing

$$\{x, y, z\} = \{x, y\} \cup \{z\}, \qquad \{x, y, z, w\} = \{x, y, z\} \cup \{w\}, \ldots.$$

It is easily proved from these definitions that

$$u \in \{x, y, z\} \leftrightarrow (u = x \vee u = y \vee u = z),$$
$$u \in \{x, y, z, w\} \leftrightarrow (u = x \vee u = y \vee u = z \vee u = w),$$

etc. The *intersection* operator, which gives the common part of two sets $s$ and $t$, can be defined directly by a set former:

$$s \cap t =_{\mathrm{Def}} \{x : x \in s \mid x \in t\}.$$

The *powerset* operator, which gives the set of all subsets of a set $s$, can also be defined by a set-former expression:

$$\mathscr{P}(s) =_{\mathrm{Def}} \{x : x \subseteq s\}.$$

#### 1.4.2.2 The Choice Operator 'arb'

The less elementary *'choice' operation* $\mathsf{arb}(s)$ reflects the intuition, verifiably true in the hereditarily finite case discussed in Sects. 2.4.2.1 and 4.3.10 that all sets can be constructed in an order in which all the elements of set $s$ are constructed before $s$ itself is constructed. Since, as we shall see, a finite string representation is available for each hereditarily finite set, we can arrange such sets in order of the length of their string representations. Then $\mathsf{arb}(s)$ can be defined for each finite set as the first member of $s$, in this standard order. We complete this definition for the one special case in which $s$ has no members, i.e. is the null set, by agreeing that $\mathsf{arb}(\emptyset) = \emptyset$. Then, for each nonempty set $s$, $\mathsf{arb}(s)$ must be disjoint from $s$, since if $x$ were a common member of $s$ and $\mathsf{arb}(s)$, $x$ would have to be an element of $s$ coming earlier than $\mathsf{arb}(s)$ in standard order, contradicting our definition of $\mathsf{arb}(s)$ as the first element of $s$ in this order. Hence, whenever this notion of 'construction in some standard order' applies, we can expect the 'arb' operator, defined in the manner just explained, to satisfy

$$\big(\forall s \mid \big(s = \emptyset \;\&\; \mathsf{arb}(s) = \emptyset\big) \vee \big(\mathsf{arb}(s) \in s \;\&\; \mathsf{arb}(s) \cap s = \emptyset\big)\big).$$

This statement, intuitively justified in the manner just explained, is taken as an axiom in the version of set theory used in this book. It is assumed to apply to all sets, whether finite or infinite. In conventional terms, this axiom states a very strong form of the so-called 'axiom of choice': $\mathsf{arb}$ chooses a first element from each nonempty set, 'first' in the sense that there exists no other element of $s$ which is also an element of $\mathsf{arb}(s)$.

It follows that there can exist no set $x$ for which $x \in x$. For if there were, we would have $\mathsf{arb}(\{x\}) = x$, and so $x$ would be a common element of $\{x\}$ and $\mathsf{arb}(\{x\})$, contradicting our assumption concerning 'arb'. It follows similarly that there can exist no 'membership cycle', i.e. no sequence $x_1, x_2, \ldots, x_n$ of sets of which each is a member of the next and for which the last is a member of the first. For if there were, we would have $\mathsf{arb}(\{x_1, x_2, \ldots, x_n\}) = x_j$ for some $j$, and then either $x_{j-1}$ or $x_n$ would be a common element of $\mathsf{arb}(\{x_1, x_2, \ldots, x_n\})$ and $\{x_1, x_2, \ldots, x_n\}$. Much the same argument shows that there can exist no infinite sequence $x_1, x_2, \ldots, x_n, \ldots$ for which each $x_{j+1}$ is a member of $x_j$. Note, however, that $x, \{x\}, \{\{x\}\}, \ldots$ is always a sequence each of whose components is an element of the next following component.

#### 1.4.2.3 The 'arb' Operator as the Basis for Proofs by Transfinite Induction

The standard (Peano) principle of *mathematical induction* is equivalent to the statement that every nonempty set $s$ of integers contains a smallest element $n_0$. For suppose that $P(n)$ is a predicate, defined for integers, for which the implication

$$\big(\forall n \mid \big(\forall m \mid (m < n) \rightarrow P(m)\big) \rightarrow P(n)\big)$$

has been established, that is, for which $P(n)$ must be true for a given $n$ if it is true for all smaller $m$. Then $P(n)$ must be true for all integers $n$. For if not, the set of all integers $n$ such that $P(n)$ is false will be nonempty, and so will contain a smallest integer $n_0$. But then $P(m)$ is clearly true for all $m < n_0$, implying that $P(n_0)$ is true, contrary to assumption.

Use of the 'arb' operator allows us to extend this very convenient style of inductive reasoning to entirely general sets, irrespective of whether they are finite or infinite. Suppose, more specifically, that $P(s)$ is a predicate, defined for sets, for which the implication

$$\big(\forall s \mid \big(\forall t \mid (t \in s) \rightarrow P(t)\big) \rightarrow P(s)\big)$$

has been established. That is, we suppose that $P(s)$ must be true for a given $s$ if it is true for all members of $s$. Then $P(s)$ must be true for all sets $s$. For if not, then $P(s)$ must be false for some member $s_1$ of $s$. Repeating this argument, we see that there must exist a member $s_2$ of $s_1$ for which $P(s_2)$ is false, then a member $s_3$ of $s_2$ for which $P(s_3)$ is false, and so forth. This gives us an infinite sequence $s = s_0, s_1, s_2, \ldots, s_n, \ldots$, each component of which is a member of the preceding component, which we have seen to be impossible.

This very broad generalization of the ordinary principle of mathematical induction is called the *principle of transfinite induction*. It plays much the same role for the infinite ordinals discussed in the next section that the ordinary principle of mathematical induction plays for integers.

#### 1.4.2.4 Ordered Pairs

We need, in many situations, not the unordered pair construct $\{x, y\}$ described above, but rather an *ordered pair* construct $[x, y]$. The only properties of $[x, y]$ that we require are: (i) $[x, y]$ is defined for any two sets $x, y$ and is itself a set; (ii) the pair $[x, y]$ defines its two components $x$ and $y$ uniquely, i.e. there exist operations $z^{[1]}$ and $z^{[2]}$ such that $[x, y]^{[1]} = x$ and $[x, y]^{[2]} = y$ for all $x$ and $y$. It is not necessary to add these statements as additional set-theoretic axioms, since the necessary pairing operations can be defined using the unordered pair construct $\{x, y\}$ and the arb operator, in any number of (artificial) ways (none of them having any particular significance). For example, we can use the definition

$$[x, y] =_{\mathrm{Def}} \{\{x\}, \{\{x\}, \{\{y\}, y\}\}\}.$$

Then $\mathsf{arb}([x, y]) = \{x\}$, since the only other element of $\{\{x\}, \{\{x\}, \{\{y\}, y\}\}\}$ has the element $\{x\}$ in common with $[x, y]$. Thus the expression $\mathsf{arb}(\mathsf{arb}([x, y]))$ always reconstructs $x$ from $[x, y]$. Moreover

$$\{\{x\}, \{\{x\}, \{\{y\}, y\}\}\} \setminus \{\{x\}\} = \{\{\{x\}, \{\{y\}, y\}\}\},$$

so

$$\mathsf{arb}\big(\mathsf{arb}\big([x, y] \setminus \{\mathsf{arb}([x, y])\}\big) \setminus \{\mathsf{arb}([x, y])\}\big) = \{\{y\}, y\},$$

and therefore the expression $\mathsf{arb}(\mathsf{arb}(\mathsf{arb}([x, y] \setminus \{\mathsf{arb}([x, y])\}) \setminus \{\mathsf{arb}([x, y])\}))$ reconstructs $y$ from $[x, y]$. The reader is invited to amuse him/herself by inventing other like constructions having similar properties.

Once ordered pairs and the operators which extract their components have been defined in this way, it is easy to define the general set-theoretic notion of 'relationship' and the associated notions of 'single-valued mapping', 'inverse relationship', and '1-1 relationship'. A *relationship* or *mapping*, or just *map*, is simply a set of ordered pairs. To formalize this, we have only to write

$$\mathsf{Is\_map}(f) =_{\mathrm{Def}} \big(f = \{[x^{[1]}, x^{[2]}] : x \in f\}\big).$$

The domain and range of a relationship are then defined in the usual way as

$$\mathsf{domain}(f) =_{\mathrm{Def}} \{x^{[1]} : x \in f\}$$

and

$$\mathsf{range}(f) =_{\mathrm{Def}} \{x^{[2]} : x \in f\},$$

respectively. A relationship is *single-valued* if the first component $u$ of each pair $[u, v]$ in it defines the associated second component $v$ uniquely. Formally this is

$$\mathsf{Svm}(f) \leftrightarrow_{\mathrm{Def}} \mathsf{Is\_map}(f) \mathbin{\&} \big(\forall x \in f \mid \big(\forall y \in f \mid \big(x^{[1]} = y^{[1]}\big) \rightarrow (x = y)\big)\big).$$

The *inverse* of a relationship is defined by

$$f^{-1} =_{\text{Def}} \{[x^{[2]}, x^{[1]}] : x \in f\}.$$

A relationship is 1-1 if it and its inverse are both single-valued:

$$\mathsf{1\_1}(f) \leftrightarrow_{\text{Def}} \mathsf{Svm}(f) \,\&\, \mathsf{Svm}(f^{-1}).$$

Other standard constructs involving mappings, for example the composition of two mappings, are equally easy to define.

#### 1.4.2.5 Integers and Ordinal Numbers in Set Theory

As noted above, John von Neumann suggested that the fundamental mathematical notion of '*integer*' be expressed set-theoretically by encoding $0, 1, \ldots, n, \ldots$ as $\emptyset, \{0\}, \ldots, \{0, 1, \ldots, n-1\}, \ldots$. The set $\mathbb{N}$ of all integers is then

$$\{0, 1, \ldots, n, \ldots\}.$$

All of these sets $s$, including the infinite set $\mathbb{N}$, have the following properties:

(i) any member of a member of $s$ is also a member of $s$;
(ii) given any two distinct members $x$, $y$ of $s$, one of $x$ and $y$ must (come earlier in the sequence in which we have enumerated the members of $s$, and so must) be a member of the other.

Von Neumann then realized that sets having these two properties had exactly the properties of '*ordinal numbers*' as originally defined by Cantor, so that (i) and (ii) can be taken as the definition of the notion of ordinal number. Besides its striking directness and simplicity, this definition has the advantage (over Cantor's original definition) of representing each ordinal number by a unique set. Moreover, all the basic operations on infinite ordinals which Cantor introduced take on simple set-theoretic forms if ordinals are defined in this way. For example, for the integers in their von Neumann representation, each integer $m$ less than an integer $n$ is a member of $n$; hence the arithmetic relationship $m < n$ can be defined $m \in n$, i.e. by the simplest of all set-theoretical relationships. We use this definition, i.e. '$s$ less than $t$' means simply $s \in t$, for arbitrary ordinals $s$.

#### 1.4.2.6 Instantiation and Proof by Use of 'Theories'

The 'theory' mechanism which our system provides relates to logical proof in something like the way in which the use of 'procedures' relates to programming practice. It facilitates introduction of symbol groups or single symbols (like the standard mathematical summation operator $\sum$ and the rather similar product operator $\prod$) which derive from previously defined functions and constants ('+' and '0' in the case of $\sum$, multiplication and '1' in the case of $\prod$), that have the properties required for definition of the new symbols. As these examples indicate, our 'theory' mechanism eases an important class of instantiations which need to be justified by supporting theorems. It adds a touch of second-order logic capability to the first-order system in which we work.

The syntax used to work with 'theories' is described by the following procedure-like template:

THEORY *theory_name( list_of_assumed_symbols )*
*assumptions*
$\Longrightarrow$ ( *list_of_defined_symbols* )
*conclusions*
END *theory_name.*

The formal description of the important 'theory of Sigma', which we will use as a running example, illustrates the way in which we set up and use theories. This theory captures a construction, ubiquitous in mathematical practice, which is normally written using 'three dots' notation, e.g. as $f_1 + f_2 + \cdots + f_k$.

THEORY Sigma_theory( s, $u \oplus v$, e )
$\mathsf{e} \in \mathsf{s}\ \&\ \big(\forall x \in \mathsf{s} \mid (\forall y \in \mathsf{s} \mid x \oplus y \in \mathsf{s})\big)$
$(\forall x \in \mathsf{s} \mid x \oplus \mathsf{e} = x)$
$\big(\forall x \in \mathsf{s} \mid (\forall y \in \mathsf{s} \mid x \oplus y = y \oplus x)\big)$
$\big(\forall x \in \mathsf{s} \big| \big(\forall y \in \mathsf{s} \mid \big(\forall z \in \mathsf{s} \mid (x \oplus y) \oplus z = x \oplus (y \oplus z)\big)\big)\big)$
$\Longrightarrow (\Sigma_\Theta)$ -- *$\Sigma_\Theta(f)$ is about being defined for any finite*
-- *single-valued mapping $f$ with values in* s
$\big(\forall f \,\big|\, \big(\mathsf{Finite}(f)\ \&\ \mathsf{Svm}(f)\ \&\ \mathsf{range}(f) \subseteq \mathsf{s}\big) \rightarrow$
$\big(\Sigma_\Theta(f) \in \mathsf{s}\ \&\ \Sigma_\Theta(\emptyset) = \mathsf{e}\ \&$
$\big(\forall x, y \mid f = \{[x,\, y]\} \rightarrow \Sigma_\Theta(f) = y\big)\ \&$
$\big(\forall t \mid \Sigma_\Theta(f) = \Sigma_\Theta(f_{|t}) \oplus \Sigma_\Theta(f_{|\mathsf{domain}(f)\setminus t})\big)\ \&$
$\big(\forall x \in \mathsf{domain}(f) \mid \Sigma_\Theta(f) = \Sigma_\Theta(f_{|\mathsf{domain}(f)\setminus\{x\}}) \oplus \mathsf{arb}\big(f\{x\}\big)\big)\ \&$
$\big(\forall g \,\big|\, \big(\mathsf{Svm}(g)\ \&\ \mathsf{domain}(f) = \mathsf{domain}(g)\big) \rightarrow$
$\Sigma_\Theta(f) = \Sigma_\Theta\big(\big\{\big[y,\, \Sigma_\Theta(f_{|g^{-1}\{y\}})\big] : y \in \mathsf{range}(g)\big\}\big)\big)\big)\big)$
END Sigma_theory.

(The final conclusion displayed encapsulates a general 'rearrangement of sums' principle.) The *assumed_symbols* of this theory are $s$, $\oplus$, and e, and its only *defined_symbol* is $\Sigma_\Theta$, to which we are attaching the $\Theta$ subscript to stress that $\Sigma_\Theta$ is, in a sense, a 'formal output-parameter' of the theory. 'Finite' and 'Svm' are standard set-theoretic predicates, which we assume to have been defined prior to the introduction of the theory displayed: 'Finite($f$)' states that $f$ is finite, and 'Svm($f$)' states that $f$ is a single-valued map. Similarly, 'domain($f$)' and 'range($f$)' denote the domain and range of $f$, respectively, '$f_{|d}$' denotes the restriction of $f$ to $d$

(namely the largest possible map which is included in $f$ and whose domain is included in $d$), '$g \,^{\shortmid}\!\!\upharpoonleft \{y\}$' denotes the set of all elements of the domain of $g$ which $g$ maps into the element $y$, '$f\{x\}$' designates the range of $f$ on the set $\{x\}$, and '$\mathsf{arb}(f\{x\})$' the unique element of this range, i.e. the image of $x$ under the single-valued mapping $f$.

Were the mechanisms of *second-order* predicate calculus available to us, the meaning of the theory could be rendered precisely by

$$
\begin{array}{l}
(\forall s \mid (\forall \oplus \mid (\forall e \mid (\exists \Sigma \mid \\
\quad (e \in s \;\& \\
\quad\quad (\forall x \in s \mid (\forall y \in s \mid x \oplus y \in s)) \;\& \\
\quad\quad (\forall x \in s \mid x \oplus e = x) \;\& \\
\quad\quad (\forall x \in s \mid (\forall y \in s \mid x \oplus y = y \oplus x)) \;\& \\
\quad\quad (\forall x \in s \mid (\forall y \in s \mid (\forall z \in s \mid (x \oplus y) \oplus z = x \oplus (y \oplus z)))) \\
\rightarrow \\
\quad (\forall f \mid (\mathsf{Finite}(f) \;\&\; \mathsf{Svm}(f) \;\&\; \mathsf{range}(f) \subseteq s) \rightarrow \\
\quad\quad (\Sigma(f) \in s \;\&\; \Sigma(\emptyset) = e \;\& \\
\quad\quad (\forall x, y \mid f = \{[x, y]\} \rightarrow \Sigma_{\Theta}(f) = y) \;\& \\
\quad\quad (\forall t \mid \Sigma(f) = \Sigma(f_{|t}) \oplus \Sigma(f_{|\mathsf{domain}(f)\setminus t})) \;\& \\
\quad\quad (\forall x \in \mathsf{domain}(f) \mid \Sigma(f) = \Sigma(f_{|\mathsf{domain}(f)\setminus\{x\}}) \oplus \mathsf{arb}(f\{x\})) \;\& \\
\quad\quad (\forall g \mid (\mathsf{Svm}(g) \;\&\; \mathsf{domain}(f) = \mathsf{domain}(g)) \rightarrow \\
\quad\quad\quad \Sigma(f) = \Sigma(\{[y, \Sigma(f_{|g^{\shortmid}\!\upharpoonleft\{y\}})] : y \in \mathsf{range}(g)\}))))))))).
\end{array}
$$

Informally speaking, this second-order formula states that given any set $s$ and commutative-associative operator defined on it, there must exist a monadic function $\Sigma$ which relates to them in the manner stated in the conclusion of the quantified formula displayed. If our formalism allowed the second-order mechanisms (of quantification over function and relation symbols, which it does not) seen here, and were this second-order formula proved, we could substitute any three actual symbols for which the hypotheses of the formula had been proved for the three universally quantified function symbols $s$, $\oplus$, and $e$ which appear, thereby obtaining the existentially quantified conclusion

$$
\begin{array}{l}
(\exists \Sigma \mid \\
\quad (e \in s \;\& \\
\quad\quad (\forall x \in s \mid (\forall y \in s \mid x \oplus y \in s)) \;\& \\
\quad\quad (\forall x \in s \mid x \oplus e = x) \;\& \\
\quad\quad (\forall x \in s \mid (\forall y \in s \mid x \oplus y = y \oplus x)) \;\& \\
\quad\quad (\forall x \in s \mid (\forall y \in s \mid (\forall z \in s \mid (x \oplus y) \oplus z = x \oplus (y \oplus z))))
\end{array}
$$

$$\begin{array}{l}\rightarrow\\ \quad (\forall f \mid (\mathsf{Finite}(f)\ \&\ \mathsf{Svm}(f)\ \&\ \mathsf{range}(f)\subseteq s)\rightarrow\\ \qquad (\Sigma(f)\in s\ \&\ \Sigma(\emptyset)=e\ \&\\ \qquad (\forall x,y \mid f=\{[x,y]\}\rightarrow \Sigma_\Theta(f)=y)\ \&\\ \qquad (\forall t \mid \Sigma(f)=\Sigma(f_{|t})\oplus\Sigma(f_{|\mathsf{domain}(f)\backslash t}))\ \&\\ \qquad (\forall x\in\mathsf{domain}(f) \mid \Sigma(f)=\Sigma(f_{|\mathsf{domain}(f)\backslash\{x\}})\oplus\mathsf{arb}(f\{x\}))\ \&\\ \qquad (\forall g \mid (\mathsf{Svm}(g)\ \&\ \mathsf{domain}(f)=\mathsf{domain}(g))\rightarrow\\ \qquad\quad \Sigma(f)=\Sigma(\{[y,\Sigma(f_{|g^{\uparrow}\{y\}})] : y\in\mathsf{range}(g)\}))))).\end{array}$$

This last statement (still second-order, since it is quantified over the function symbol $\Sigma$) would allow us to introduce a new symbol $\Sigma_\Theta$ for which

$$\begin{array}{l}(e\in s\ \&\\ \quad (\forall x\in s \mid (\forall y\in s \mid x\oplus y\in s))\ \&\\ \quad (\forall x\in s \mid x\oplus e=x)\ \&\\ \quad (\forall x\in s \mid (\forall y\in s \mid x\oplus y=y\oplus x))\ \&\\ \quad (\forall x\in s \mid (\forall y\in s \mid (\forall z\in s \mid (x\oplus y)\oplus z=x\oplus(y\oplus z)))))\\ \rightarrow\\ \quad (\forall f \mid (\mathsf{Finite}(f)\ \&\ \mathsf{Svm}(f)\ \&\ \mathsf{range}(f)\subseteq s)\rightarrow\\ \qquad (\Sigma_\Theta(f)\in s\ \&\ \Sigma_\Theta(\emptyset)=e\ \&\\ \qquad (\forall x,y \mid f=\{[x,y]\}\rightarrow \Sigma_\Theta(f)=y)\ \&\\ \qquad (\forall t \mid \Sigma_\Theta(f)=\Sigma_\Theta(f_{|t})\oplus\Sigma_\Theta(f_{|\mathsf{domain}(f)\backslash t}))\ \&\\ \qquad (\forall x\in\mathsf{domain}(f) \mid \Sigma_\Theta(f)=\Sigma_\Theta(f_{|\mathsf{domain}(f)\backslash\{x\}})\oplus\mathsf{arb}(f\{x\}))\ \&\\ \qquad (\forall g \mid (\mathsf{Svm}(g)\ \&\ \mathsf{domain}(f)=\mathsf{domain}(g))\rightarrow\\ \qquad\quad \Sigma_\Theta(f)=\Sigma_\Theta(\{[y,\Sigma_\Theta(f_{|g^{\uparrow}\{y\}})] : y\in\mathsf{range}(g)\}))))\end{array}$$

is known. This final statement is now first-order.

The second-order mechanisms needed to proceed in just the manner explained are not available in our first-order setting. The theory mechanism that is provided serves as a partial but adequate substitute for it.

After these introductory remarks we return to a detailed consideration of the general theory template displayed at the start of this section. In it, '*theory_name*' names the theory in which we are interested. A theory's '*list_of_assumed_symbols*' is analogous to the parameter list of a procedure. It is a comma-separated list of symbol names, which stand for other symbols which must replace the '*assumed_symbols*' whenever the theory is *applied*. The members of the list of '*assumptions*' which follow must be formulae which, aside from basic predicate and set-theoretic constructions (quantifiers and set formers), involve only elements of the '*list_of_assumed_symbols*', possibly along with other symbols that have been defined previously to introduction of the theory, in the context in which the theory is introduced. The formal description of the 'theory of Sigma' given above illustrates these rules.

The '*conclusions*' which follow the syntactic delimiter '$\Longrightarrow$' in the general template must be formulae which, aside from basic predicate and set-theoretic constructions, involve only elements of the '*list_of_assumed_symbols*' and the '*list_of_defined_symbols*', along with other symbols that have previously been defined in the context in which the theory is introduced. The elements of the (comma-delimited) '*list_of_defined_symbols*' are symbol names (usually carrying the $\Theta$ subscript), which must be defined within the theory, more precisely as part of a proof (given within the theory), of the theory's stated conclusions. Each '*defined_symbol*' is replaced with a previously unused symbol whenever the theory is *applied*.

Once a theory has been introduced in the manner just explained, and before it can be used, a sequence of theorems and definitions culminating in those which appear as the conclusions of the theory must be proved in the theory. The syntax used to begin this process, which temporarily 'enters' the theory, is simply

ENTER_THEORY *theory_name*.

This statement creates a subordinate proof context in which the '*assumed_symbols*' of the theory, together with all its stated assumptions, are available. Then, using these assumptions, one must give definitions of all the theory's '*defined_symbols*', and proofs of all its conclusions. Once this has been done, one can return from the subordinate logical context to the parent context from which it was entered by executing another ENTER_THEORY command, which now must name the parent theory to which we are returning. (Proof always begins in a top-level context named 'Set_theory'.) After return, the theory's conclusions become available for application. Note also that theories previously developed in the parent context of a new theory **T** are available for application during the construction of **T**.

The syntax (analogous to that for 'calling' procedures) used to apply theories is

APPLY(*defined_symbol_of_theory* : *new_symbol*, ...)
*theory_name*( *list_of_replacements_for_assumed_symbols* ).

As indicated, the keyword 'APPLY' is followed by a comma-delimited sequence of colon-separated pairs which associates each '*defined_symbol*' of the theory with a previously unused symbol, which then replaces the '*defined_symbol*' in the set of conclusions that results from successful application of the theory. Next there must follow a comma-delimited list of symbols defined previously, equal in length to the theory's list of '*assumed_symbols*', which specifies the symbols which are to replace the '*assumed_symbols*' at the point of application. Our verifier replaces all the '*assumed_symbols*' appearing in the theory's assumptions with these replacement symbols, and searches the logical context available at the point of theory application for theorems identical with the resulting formulae. If any of these is missing, the requested theory application is refused. If all are found, then the conclusions of the theory are turned into theorems by replacing every occurrence of the theory's defined symbols by the corresponding '*new_symbol*' and every occurrence of the theory's assumed symbols by its specified replacement symbol.

Assume, for example, that the 'SIGMA_theory' displayed above has been made available (in the way explained above), and that theorems

$$
\begin{aligned}
&0 \in \mathbb{N},\\
&(\forall x \in \mathbb{N} \mid (\forall y \in \mathbb{N} \mid x+y \in \mathbb{N})),\\
&(\forall x \in \mathbb{N} \mid x+0=x),\\
&(\forall x \in \mathbb{N} \mid (\forall y \in \mathbb{N} \mid x+y=y+x)),\\
&(\forall x \in \mathbb{N} \mid (\forall y \in \mathbb{N} \mid (\forall z \in \mathbb{N} \mid (x+y)+z=x+(y+z))))
\end{aligned}
$$

have been proved (separately from the theory) for the integers $\mathbb{N}$, and integer addition. Then the verifier instruction

$$\text{APPLY}(\Sigma_\Theta : \mathsf{SIG})\ \mathsf{SIGMA\_theory}(\mathbb{N}, +, 0)$$

makes the symbol SIG (which must not have been defined previously) available, and gives us the theorem

$$
\begin{aligned}
&(\forall f \mid (\mathsf{Finite}(f)\ \&\ \mathsf{Svm}(f)\ \&\ \mathsf{range}(f) \subseteq \mathbb{N}) \rightarrow\\
&\quad(\mathsf{SIG}(f) \in \mathbb{N}\ \&\ \mathsf{SIG}(\emptyset) = 0\ \&\\
&\quad(\forall x, y \mid f = \{[x, y]\} \rightarrow \mathsf{SIG}(f) = y)\ \&\\
&\qquad(\forall t \mid \mathsf{SIG}(f) = \mathsf{SIG}(f_{|t}) + \mathsf{SIG}(f_{|\mathsf{domain}(f)\setminus t}))\ \&\\
&\quad(\forall x \in \mathsf{domain}(f) \mid \mathsf{SIG}(f) = \mathsf{SIG}(f_{|\mathsf{domain}(f)\setminus x}) + \mathsf{arb}(f\{x\}))\ \&\\
&\quad(\forall g \mid (\mathsf{Svm}(g)\ \&\ \mathsf{domain}(f) = \mathsf{domain}(g)) \rightarrow\\
&\qquad\mathsf{SIG}(f) = \mathsf{SIG}(\{[y, \mathsf{SIG}(f_{|g^{-1}\{y\}})] : y \in \mathsf{range}(g)\}))))
\end{aligned}
$$

without further proof.

The theory of equivalence classes is a second important 'theory' example.

$$
\begin{aligned}
&\text{THEORY}\ \mathsf{equiv\_classes}(\mathsf{E}(u, v), \mathsf{s})\\
&\quad(\forall x \in \mathsf{s} \mid \mathsf{E}(x, x))\\
&\quad(\forall x \in \mathsf{s} \mid (\forall y \in \mathsf{s} \mid (\forall z \in \mathsf{s} \mid \mathsf{E}(x, y) \rightarrow (\mathsf{E}(y, z) \leftrightarrow \mathsf{E}(z, x)))))\\
&\Longrightarrow (\mathsf{Eqc}_\Theta, \mathsf{f}_\Theta)\ \text{-- } \textit{'quotient'-set and globalized 'canonical embedding'}\\
&\quad(\forall x \in \mathsf{s} \mid \mathsf{f}_\Theta(x) \in \mathsf{Eqc}_\Theta)\\
&\quad(\forall y \in \mathsf{Eqc}_\Theta \mid \mathsf{arb}(y) \in \mathsf{s}\ \&\ \mathsf{f}_\Theta(\mathsf{arb}(y)) = y)\\
&\quad(\forall x \in \mathsf{s} \mid (\forall y \in \mathsf{s} \mid \mathsf{E}(x, y) \leftrightarrow (\mathsf{f}_\Theta(x) = \mathsf{f}_\Theta(y))))\\
&\quad(\forall x \in \mathsf{s} \mid \mathsf{E}(x, \mathsf{arb}(\mathsf{f}_\Theta(x))))\\
&\quad(\forall x \in \mathsf{s} \mid x \in \mathsf{f}_\Theta(x))\\
&\text{END}\ \mathsf{equiv\_classes}.
\end{aligned}
$$

This states that any dyadic 'equivalence relation' $\mathsf{E}(x, y)$ can be represented in the form $\mathsf{E}(x, y) \leftrightarrow (\mathsf{f}_\Theta(x) = \mathsf{f}_\Theta(y))$ by some monadic function $\mathsf{f}_\Theta$. (Conventionally, one speaks of $\mathsf{f}_\Theta(x)$ as the equivalence class of $x$; notice, however, that we are deliberately 'hiding' such secondary facts as $\emptyset \notin \mathsf{Eqc}_{\Theta}$, $\mathsf{s} = \bigcup \mathsf{Eqc}_{\Theta}$, and $(\forall y \in \mathsf{Eqc}_{\Theta}, x \in y \mid \mathsf{f}_{\Theta}(x) = y))$.

The theory of equivalence classes is one of a family of easy but widely applicable results which represent various kinds of monadic relationships in terms of elementary relationships which are especially easy to work with (often because decision algorithms apply to them). For example, one can easily show that any partial ordering on set elements $x, y$ can be represented in the form $\mathsf{g}_{\Theta}(x) \subseteq \mathsf{g}_{\Theta}(y)$. Results of this kind lend particular importance to the relationships to which they apply.

## 1.5 An Informal Overview of the Sequence of Formal Set-Theoretic Proofs to Be Given Later

This text culminates in the sequence of definitions and theorems found in Chap. 5, of which we offer a brief overview here. There, theorems will be stated without proofs, even though very many proofs have already been set up to be verifiable by our system—a sample of them will be shown in Chap. 7. In this section some of the theorems surveyed are accompanied by semiformal proofs, which can serve as intuitive guides to the larger mass of detail appearing in their completely formalized versions.

The theorems found in Chap. 5 fall into the following categories.

### *1.5.1 Basic Elementary Results*

**(i)** Definition and basic properties of ordered pairs. These are fundamental to many of the following definitions, e.g. of maps and of the Cartesian product.

**(ii)** Definition of the notions of map, single-valued map, 1-1-map, map restriction, domain, range, map product, etc. and derivation of the ubiquitous elementary properties of maps, as a long series of elementary theorems. Some of these properties of maps are captured for convenience in a theory called 'fcn_symbol' which can be used to prove basic properties of set formers defining single-valued maps.

### *1.5.2 Ordinals*

**(iii)** Definition of the notion of '*ordinal*', and proof of the basic properties of ordinals. Completely formal proofs of all the basic properties of ordinal numbers will be given in Sects. 7.3.2 and 7.3.5 of Chap. 7. But to make these proofs more comprehensible it is well to translate some of them, and some of the key definitions used in them, into the more comfortable language of ordinary mathematics. We follow von

Neumann in defining an ordinal as a set (I) properly ordered by membership,[1] and for which (II) members of members are also members. The key results proved are: (a) the collection of all ordinals is itself properly ordered by membership, and members of ordinals are ordinals, but (b) the collection of all ordinals is not a set. Also, (c) proceeding recursively in the manner explained in Sect. 1.5.3, we define a standard enumeration for every set and show that this puts the members of the set in 1-1 correspondence with an ordinal. This is the 'enumerability principle' fundamental to our subsequent work with cardinal numbers.

The von Neumann representation ties the ordinal concept very directly to the most basic concepts of set theory, allowing the properties of ordinals to be established by reasoning that uses only elementary properties of sets and set formers, with occasional use of transfinite induction. (For ease of use, statement and proof of this general principle are captured as a theory called 'transfinite_induction': the principle follows very directly from our strong form of the axiom of choice.)

For example, in the von Neumann representation, the *next* ordinal after an ordinal $s$ is simply $s \cup \{s\}$. To see that $s' = s \cup \{s\}$ must be an ordinal, note first that each member of a member of $s'$ is either a member of a member of $s$, or directly a member of $s$; and hence in any case a member of $s'$; thus $s'$ has property (II). The proof that $s'$ also has property (I) is equally elementary and is left to the reader. Together these show that $s'$ is an ordinal. Other equally elementary results concerning ordinals, whose proof is also left to the reader are:

a. The intersection $s \cap t$ of any two ordinals is an ordinal.
b. Any member $t$ of an ordinal $s$ is an ordinal.

Let $s$ be an ordinal. Since any member of a member $t$ of $s$ is a member of $s$ by (II), any member $t$ of $s$ is a subset of $s$. Thus for ordinals the membership relation $t \in s$ implies the inclusion relation $t \subseteq s$. On the other hand, if $t$ is also an ordinal and $t \subseteq s$, then either $t = s$ or $t \in s$. To prove this, suppose that $t \neq s$, and consider the element $x = \mathsf{arb}(s \setminus t)$. Any element $y$ of $t$ is also an element of $s$, so by (I) we have either $y \in x$, $y = x$, or $x \in y$. Both $y = x$ and $x \in y$ would imply $x \in t$ which is impossible. Thus we must have $y \in x$ whenever $y \in t$, i.e. $t \subseteq x$. But $x \setminus t$ must be null. Indeed, let $z \in x \setminus t$. Then $z \in x$, but also $z \in s \setminus t$, contradicting the fact that $x = \mathsf{arb}(s \setminus t)$ is disjoint from $s \setminus t$. Hence $x = t$, i.e. $t$ is an element of $s$, proving our assertion that any subset $t$ of $s$ which is also an ordinal must either be identical to $s$ or must be a member of $s$. That is, for ordinals the relationship '$\subseteq s$' is equivalent to the condition 'is a member of $s$ or is equal to $s$.'

Next we show that, given any two distinct ordinals $s$ and $t$, one is a member of the other. Suppose that this is not the case. Then if $s = s \cap t$ then $s$ is a subset of $t$, and hence, by the result just proved, is a member of $t$. Similarly, if $t = s \cap t$ then $t$ is a member of $s$. So it follows that $s \neq s \cap t$ and $t \neq s \cap t$. Since $s \cap t$ is an ordinal and a subset of $s$, it follows by the result just proved that $s \cap t \in s$; similarly $s \cap t \in t$, so $s \cap t \in s \cap t$, which is impossible since the membership operator can admit no cycles. This proves our claim.

[1] By *proper order*, we mean strict and total order.

It follows that if $s$ and $t$ are both ordinals, the intersection $s \cap t$ is the smaller of $s$ and $t$, while the union $s \cup t$ is the larger of $s$ and $t$. If $O$ is any non-empty set of ordinals, then $x = \mathsf{arb}(O)$ is a member of $O$ and hence an ordinal. By definition of arb, $x$ must be disjoint from $O$. Hence if $y$ is any other member of $O$, $y \in x$ is impossible so $x \in y$ must be true. That is, $\mathsf{arb}(O)$ must be the smallest of all the elements of $O$. Moreover the union $\bigcup O$ of all the elements of $O$ must be an ordinal, since if $x \in \bigcup O$ and $y \in x$ then there is an $s \in O$ such that $x \in s$, from which it follows that $y \in s$ and so $y \in \bigcup O$, proving that $\bigcup O$ has property (II). Moreover if $x \in \bigcup O$ and $y \in \bigcup O$, then there must exist $s \in O$ and $t \in O$ such that $x \in s$ and $y \in t$. Then one of $s$ and $t$, say $s$, must include the other, and so $x$ and $y$ must both be members of $s$. Since $s$ is an ordinal and therefore has property (I), it follows that either $x \in y$, $x = y$, of $y \in x$. Hence $\bigcup O$ also has property (I). This shows that the union $\bigcup O$ of any set of ordinals must itself be an ordinal, which is easily seen to be the smallest ordinal including all the members of $O$.

Using the statements just proved it is easy to show that if $s$ is an ordinal, then $s' = s \cup \{s\}$ is the least ordinal greater than $s$. Indeed, we have shown above that $s'$ is an ordinal. Moreover $s \in s'$, so $s'$ is larger than $s$ in the ordering of ordinals. If $t$ is any ordinal larger than $s$, i.e. $s \in t$, then either $s' \in t$, $s' = t$, or $t \in s'$ by what has been proved above. But $t \in s'$ is impossible, since it would imply that either $t \in s$ or $t = s$, and so in either case would lead to an impossible membership cycle. Therefore either $s' \in t$ or $s' = t$, i.e. $t$ is no smaller than $s'$, proving that $s'$ is the least ordinal greater than $s$, as asserted. It is therefore reasonable to write $s \cup \{s\}$ as $\mathsf{next}(s)$.

Any ordinal $s$ which is greater than every integer $n$ must have all such $n$ as members, proving that the set $\mathbb{N}$ of all integers must be a subset of the set $s$. Hence $\mathbb{N}$ must be the smallest ordinal which is greater than every integer $n$. Therefore the smallest members of the collection of all ordinals can be written as

$$0,\ 1,\ \ldots,\ n,\ \ldots,\ \mathbb{N},\ \mathsf{next}(\mathbb{N}),\ \mathsf{next}\big(\mathsf{next}(\mathbb{N})\big),\ \ldots$$

in their natural order (of membership). In his initial series of papers on ordinals Georg Cantor introduced a variety of constructions for ordinals which generalize various arithmetic constructions for ordinary integers and which allow the sequence of ordinal notations shown above to be extended systematically.

### *1.5.3 Well Ordering: The Principle of Transfinite Enumerability*

The ordinal numbers, as we (or von Neumann, or Cantor) have defined them, capture an abstract notion of sequential enumeration, even for sets which are not restricted to be finite. A crucial property of the ordinals is that they allow any set $s$ to be enumerated, irrespective of whether $s$ is finite or infinite. This is the so-called *Well-Ordering Theorem*. This famous result is not hard to prove given the very generous variant of set theory which we allow, which as explained earlier lets us write very general recursive definitions in set-theoretic notation, and also admits free use of the choice operator 'arb'.

To prove the well-ordering theorem, we first show that the collection Ord of all ordinals is not a set, i.e. that there is no set $O$ such that $s$ is an ordinal if and only if $s \in O$. For otherwise $s = \bigcup O$ would be an ordinal by what we have just proved, and so as shown above $s \cup \{s\}$ would also be an ordinal, implying that $s$ is a member of a member of $O$, and so $s \in s$, which is impossible.

Next define a function enum$(X, S)$ of two parameters by writing

$$\begin{aligned}\mathsf{enum}(X,S) =_{\mathrm{Def}} \ & \textbf{if } S \subseteq \big\{\mathsf{enum}(y,S) : y \in X\big\} \textbf{ then } S \\ & \textbf{else } \mathsf{arb}\big(S \setminus \big\{\mathsf{enum}(y,S) : y \in X\big\}\big) \textbf{ end if}.\end{aligned}$$

That is, we define enum$(X, S)$ to be the element of $S \setminus \{\mathsf{enum}(y, S) : y \in X\}$ chosen by 'arb' if $\{\mathsf{enum}(y, S) : y \in X\}$ differs from $S$; otherwise enum$(X, S)$ is simply $S$. This definition implies that the elements

$$\mathsf{enum}(0, S),\ \ \mathsf{enum}(1, S),\ \ \mathsf{enum}(2, S),\ \ \ldots\ ,\ \ \mathsf{enum}(\mathbb{N}, S),\ \ \ldots$$

have the following values:

$$\begin{aligned}\mathsf{enum}(0,S) &= \mathsf{arb}(S),\\ \mathsf{enum}(1,S) &= \mathsf{arb}\big(S \setminus \big\{\mathsf{arb}(S)\big\}\big),\\ \mathsf{enum}(2,S) &= \mathsf{arb}\big(S \setminus \big\{\mathsf{arb}(S), \mathsf{enum}(1,S)\big\}\big),\\ &\ \ \cdots\\ \mathsf{enum}(\mathbb{N},S) &= \mathsf{arb}\big(S \setminus \big\{\mathsf{arb}(S), \mathsf{enum}(1,S), \mathsf{enum}(2,S), \ldots\big\}\big),\\ &\ \ \cdots\end{aligned}$$

The crucial fact, proved in the next paragraph, is that the elements enum$(x, S)$ remain distinct, for distinct ordinals $x$, as long as $\{\mathsf{enum}(y, S) : y \in x\}$ is a proper subset of $S$. Note also that as the ordinal $x$ increases, so does the set $\{\mathsf{enum}(y, S) : y \in x\}$.

It is easy to prove that enum$(x, S)$ and enum$(y, S)$ must be distinct if $x$ and $y$ are distinct ordinals and both enum$(x, S)$ and enum$(y, S)$ are different from $S$. Indeed, one of $x$ and $y$, say $y$, must be a member of the other, and then by definition we must have $\mathsf{enum}(x, S) = \mathsf{arb}(S \setminus \{\mathsf{enum}(z, S) : z \in x\})$, so $\mathsf{enum}(x, S) \in S \setminus \{\mathsf{enum}(z, S) : z \in x\}$, while $\mathsf{enum}(y, S) \in \{\mathsf{enum}(z, S) : z \in x\}$. It follows from this that there must exist an ordinal $x$ for which $S = \{\mathsf{enum}(z, S) : z \in x\}$. For if this is false, then by what we have just proved the mapping $z \mapsto \mathsf{enum}(z, S)$ maps the collection of all ordinals in 1-1 fashion into a subset of the set $S$. But an axiom of set theory (the so-called 'Axiom of Replacement', detailed below) tells us that every collection which can be put in 1-1 correspondence with a set must itself be a set. Hence it would follow that the collection of all ordinals is a set, contradicting what has been proved above.

Since we have just shown that there exists an ordinal $x$ such that $\{\mathsf{enum}(z, S) : z \in x\} = S$, there must exist a least such ordinal $y$, which we can define as

$$\mathsf{arb}\big(\{y \in \mathsf{next}(x) \mid S = \{\mathsf{enum}(z, S) : z \in y\}\}\big).$$

It is easily seen (we leave details to the reader) that $z \mapsto \mathsf{enum}(z, S)$ maps this $y$ in 1-1 fashion onto $S$, completing our proof of the Well-Ordering Theorem.

### *1.5.4 Cardinal Numbers*

**(iv)** Definition of '*cardinality*' and of the operator $\#s$ which gives the (possibly infinite) number of members of a set $s$. The cardinality of a set is defined as the smallest ordinal which can be put into 1-1 correspondence with the set, and it is proved that (a) there is only one such ordinal, and (b) this is also the smallest ordinal which can be mapped onto $s$ by a single-valued map.

The proof of the Well-Ordering Theorem puts us in position to introduce the notion of *cardinal number* and to prove the basic elementary properties of these numbers. We define the cardinals as a subcollection of the ordinals; an ordinal $x$ is called a *cardinal* if $x$ cannot be put into 1-1 correspondence with any smaller ordinal. By the Well-Ordering Theorem, any set $s$ can be put in 1-1 correspondence with some ordinal, and arguing as above it follows that $s$ can be put in 1-1 correspondence with some smallest ordinal $x$. Since the composition of two 1-1 mappings is itself 1-1, it follows that this unique $x$ must itself be a cardinal. We call this cardinal the *cardinality of* $s$, and write it (using the standard number sign) as $\#s$.

In this section we also define the notions of cardinal sum and product of two sets $a$ and $b$. These are, respectively, defined as $\#(copy\_a \cup copy\_b)$, where $copy\_a$ and $copy\_b$ are disjoint copies of $a$ and $b$, and the cardinality of the Cartesian product $a \times b$ of $a$ and $b$. Using these definitions, it is easy to prove the associative and distributive laws of cardinal arithmetic. We also prove a few basic properties of the $\#s$ operator, e.g. its monotonicity.

**(v)** A set $s$ is then defined to be *finite* if it has no 1-1 mapping into a proper subset of itself, or, equivalently, is not the single-valued image of any such proper subset. We prove that the null set and any singleton are finite, and (using transfinite induction) that the collection of finite sets is closed under the union, Cartesian product, and power set operators. It is proved that $s$ is finite if and only if its cardinality $\#s$ is finite. We then prepare for the introduction of signed integer arithmetic by proving all the basic arithmetic properties of unsigned integers and then defining the cardinal subtraction operator $a - b$ and showing that for finite cardinals subtraction has its expected properties. We also prove that integer division with remainder is always possible. These results are proved with the help of a modified version of the principle of induction which is demonstrated for finite sets: given any predicate $P(x)$ not true for all finite sets, there exists a finite set $s$ for which $P(s)$ is false, but $P(s')$ is true for all proper subsets of $s$. Like the rather similar transfinite induction, this principle is captured for convenience in a theory.

**(vi)** Sets which are not finite are said to be *infinite*. By considering the cardinality $\#\mathsf{s}_\infty$ of the infinite set $\mathsf{s}_\infty$ whose existence is assumed in an axiom of infinity, we prove that there exists an infinite cardinal, and so can define the set $\mathbb{N}$ of integers as *the least infinite ordinal*, and show that this is a cardinal, and is in fact the set of all finite cardinals. The set $\mathbb{N}$ of all integers is infinite, since the 1-1 correspondence $n \mapsto \mathsf{next}(n)$ maps $\mathbb{N}$ to a subset of itself (the zero integer, i.e. $\emptyset$, is not in the range of '$\mathsf{next}$'). It is not hard to see that if the set $s$ is finite, so is $\mathsf{next}(s) = s \cup \{s\}$. Indeed, if $s \cup \{s\}$ is infinite, there exists a 1-1 mapping $f$ of $s \cup \{s\}$ to a proper subset of itself. The range of the mapping $f$ must therefore omit some element of $s \cup \{s\}$, i.e. must either omit $s$ or some element $x$ of $s$. Consider the latter of these two cases. We can plainly construct a 1-1 mapping $g$ of $s \cup \{s\}$ onto itself which interchanges $x$ and $s$. Then the composition of $f$ and $g$ is a 1-1 mapping of $s \cup \{s\}$ into itself whose range omits the value $s$. This shows that if $\mathsf{next}(s)$ is infinite, there must always exist a 1-1 mapping $f$ of $\mathsf{next}(s)$ into $s$, but then $f$ maps $s$ into $s \setminus \{f(s)\}$, so $s$ is also infinite. I.e., $s$ is infinite if $\mathsf{next}(s)$ is infinite, implying that $\mathsf{next}(s)$ is finite if $s$ is finite.

It follows that all the integers $0 = \emptyset$, $1 = \mathsf{next}(0)$, $2 = \mathsf{next}(1), \ldots$ are finite, and so each of these ordinals must also be a cardinal. Moreover, the infinite ordinal $\mathbb{N}$ must also be a cardinal. Indeed, if this is not the case, there would exist a 1-1 mapping $f$ of $\mathbb{N}$ into a smaller ordinal, i.e. to some integer $n \in \mathbb{N}$. But then $f$ would also map the subset $\mathsf{next}(n)$ of $\mathbb{N}$ into its proper subset $n$, implying that $\mathsf{next}(n)$ is infinite, which we have seen to be impossible. Thus $\mathbb{N}$ is not only the smallest infinite ordinal but also the smallest infinite cardinal. This implies that

$$\#0 = 0, \quad \#1 = 1, \; \#2 = 2, \; \ldots, \; \#\mathbb{N} = \mathbb{N}$$

(every cardinal is its own cardinality, and every ordinal less than or equal to $\mathbb{N}$ is a cardinal). On the other hand, the cardinality of $\mathsf{next}(\mathbb{N}) = \mathbb{N} \cup \{\mathbb{N}\}$ is simply $\mathbb{N}$. Indeed, we have seen that there exists a 1-1 mapping $f$ of $\mathbb{N}$ into itself whose range omits the integer 0; this can plainly be extended to a 1-1 mapping of $\mathbb{N} \cup \{\mathbb{N}\}$ into $\mathbb{N}$. This same argument shows that if $\#s = \mathbb{N}$ then $\#\mathsf{next}(s) = \mathbb{N}$ also. Therefore the sequence of cardinalities of the ordinals

$$0, \; 1, \; 2, \; \ldots, \; \mathbb{N}, \; \mathsf{next}(\mathbb{N}), \; \mathsf{next}\big(\mathsf{next}(\mathbb{N})\big), \; \mathsf{next}\big(\mathsf{next}\big(\mathsf{next}(\mathbb{N})\big)\big), \; \ldots$$

is

$$0, \; 1, \; 2, \; \ldots, \; \mathbb{N}, \; \mathbb{N}, \; \mathbb{N}, \; \mathbb{N}, \; \ldots.$$

That is, all the infinite ordinals displayed, though distinct, have the same cardinality. Any set $s$ whose cardinality $\#s$ is $\mathbb{N}$ is said to be *denumerable*, or *countably infinite*; and a set which is either finite or denumerable is said to be *countable*. Our next question is: how can we be sure that *uncountable* sets, namely sets whose cardinality exceeds $\mathbb{N}$, actually exist?

**(vii)** Another idea is plainly needed if we are to show that there exist any cardinals larger than $\mathbb{N}$. As a digression, we prove that the sum and product of any two infinite cardinals degenerates to their maximum (hence there are no more rational numbers than there are integer numbers), but (Cantor's Theorem) that *the power set of any cardinal always has a larger cardinality*. Cantor noted that for any set $s$, the set $\mathscr{P}(s)$ of all subsets of $s$ must have cardinality larger than that of $s$. For suppose the contrary, i.e. suppose that there exists a 1-1 mapping $f$ of $s$ onto $\mathscr{P}(s)$. Then consider the subset $\{x : x \in s \mid x \notin f(x)\}$ of $s$. This must have the form $f(y)$ for some $y \in s$; hence $f(y) = \{x : x \in s \mid x \notin f(x)\}$. But then $y \in f(y)$ is equivalent to $y \in \{x : x \in s \mid x \notin f(x)\}$, i.e. to $y \notin f(y)$, which is impossible. (Incidentally, since a 1-1 correspondence between reals and $\mathscr{P}(\mathbb{N})$ can be found, this implies that real numbers form an uncountable set.)

Since $s$ always has a 1-1 embedding into $\mathscr{P}(s)$ (we can simply map each $x$ in $s$ into the singleton $\{x\}$), the cardinality of $s$ is never greater than that of $\mathscr{P}(s)$. The theorem of Cantor proved in the preceding paragraph shows that in fact we always have $\#s < \#\mathscr{P}(s)$, i.e. $\#s \in \#\mathscr{P}(s)$. Hence $\#\mathscr{P}(\mathbb{N})$ is an infinite cardinal which is definitely larger than $\mathbb{N}$; similarly $\#\mathscr{P}(\#\mathscr{P}(\mathbb{N}))$ is larger than $\#\mathscr{P}(\mathbb{N})$ and so forth, proving that there must exist infinitely many infinite cardinals. In fact, we can easily prove that there exists a 1-1 correspondence between the collection of all ordinals and the collection of all cardinals. For this, we simply need to make the transfinite inductive definition

$$\mathsf{alph}(x) =_{\mathrm{Def}} \mathsf{arb}\Big(\Big\{z : z \in \Big(\mathsf{next}\Big(\#\mathscr{P}\Big(\bigcup\{\mathsf{alph}(y) : y \in x\}\Big)\Big) \setminus \{\mathsf{alph}(y) : y \in x\}\Big) \mid \mathsf{Is\_cardinal}(z)\Big\}\Big),$$

where '$\mathsf{Is\_cardinal}$' is the predicate, easily expressible in elementary set-theoretic terms, which states that its argument $y$ is a cardinal number. Since all the occurrences of '$\mathsf{alph}$' on the right-hand side of this definition lie in the scope of constraints of the form '$y \in x$', this is a legal transfinite definition according to the rule stated earlier. For each ordinal $x$, this formula defines $\mathsf{alph}(x)$ to be the smallest cardinal (if any) which is not more than $\#\mathscr{P}(\bigcup\{\mathsf{alph}(y) : y \in x\})$ but is not one of the cardinals $\mathsf{alph}(y)$ for any ordinal $y$ less than $x$. Since we have seen above that $u = \bigcup\{\mathsf{alph}(y) : y \in x\}$ is an ordinal at least as large as any of the $\mathsf{alph}(y)$ for $y \in x$, and also that $\#\mathscr{P}(u)$ is larger than $u$, the set $\mathsf{next}(\#\mathscr{P}(u)) \setminus \{\mathsf{alph}(y) : y \in x\})$ must be nonempty, and so $\mathsf{alph}(x)$ must indeed be the smallest cardinal greater than all of the cardinals $\mathsf{alph}(y)$ for any ordinal $y \in x$. It is easily seen (details are left to the reader) that $\mathsf{alph}(y) < \mathsf{alph}(z)$ if $y < z$. Hence the function '$\mathsf{alph}$' is a 1-1, monotone increasing map of the collection of all ordinals to the collection of all cardinals. It is not hard to prove that every cardinal must appear as one of the $\mathsf{alph}(y)$. Thus '$\mathsf{alph}$' actually puts the collection of all ordinals in 1-1 correspondence with the collection of all cardinals. For small ordinals we have

$$\mathsf{alph}(0) = 0, \quad \mathsf{alph}(1) = 1, \quad \mathsf{alph}(2) = 2, \quad \ldots, \quad \mathsf{alph}(\mathbb{N}) = \mathbb{N}.$$

A mystery, first encountered by Cantor, occurs at the very next position in this sequence. $\mathsf{alph}(\mathsf{next}(\mathbb{N}))$ is the smallest cardinal greater than $\mathbb{N}$. We have seen that the cardinal number $\#\mathscr{P}(\mathbb{N})$ is larger than $\mathbb{N}$; hence $\mathsf{alph}(\mathsf{next}(\mathbb{N})) \leqslant \#\mathscr{P}(\mathbb{N})$. But is this inequality actually an equality, or does there exist a cardinal number between $\mathbb{N}$ and $\#\mathscr{P}(\mathbb{N})$? Indeed, do there exist infinitely many cardinal numbers in this range? This is the so-called 'Continuum problem', originally stated by Cantor. Its very surprising resolution, ultimately achieved by Kurt Gödel and Paul Cohen, required over 60 years of penetrating work: the statement $\mathsf{alph}(\mathsf{next}(\mathbb{N})) = \#\mathscr{P}(\mathbb{N})$ is independent of the axioms of set theory, which admit both of models in which this statement is true and of many structurally distinct models in which it is false.

### *1.5.5 Survey of the Major Sequence of Definitions and Proofs Considered in This Text*

**(viii)** The set of *signed integers* is then introduced as the set of pairs $[x, 0]$ (representing the positive integers) and $[0, x]$ (representing the integers of negative sign). $[0, 0]$ is the 'signed integer' 0, and the 1-1 mapping $x \mapsto [x, 0]$, whose inverse is simply $y \mapsto y^{[1]}$, embeds $\mathbb{N}$ into the set of signed integers, in a manner allowing easy extension of the addition, subtraction, multiplication, and division operators to signed integers. In preparation for introduction of the set of rational numbers, it is proved that the set of signed integers is an 'integral domain'. At this point, we are well on the royal road of standard mathematics.

**(ix)** Next we introduce two important 'theories' mentioned above: the theory of *equivalence classes* and the theory of *Sigma*. As previously noted, the theory of Sigma is a formal substitute for the common but informal mathematical use of 'three dot' summation (and product) notations like

$$a_1 + a_2 + \cdots + a_n \quad \text{and} \quad a_1 * a_2 * \cdots * a_n.$$

The theory of equivalence classes characterizes the dyadic predicates $R(x, y)$ which can be represented in terms of the equality predicate using a monadic function, i.e. as $R(x, y) \leftrightarrow (f(x) = f(y))$. These $R$ are the so-called 'equivalence relationships', and for each such $R$ defined for all $x$ belonging to a set $s$, the theory of equivalence classes constructs $f$ (for which $\mathsf{arb}$ turns out to be an inverse), and the set into which $f$ maps $s$. This range is the 'family of equivalence classes' defined by the dyadic predicate $R$. The construction seen here, which traces back to Gauss, is ubiquitous in 20th century mathematics.

**(x)** Next the family $\mathbb{Q}$ of *rational numbers* is defined as the set of equivalence classes arising from the set of all pairs $[n, m]$ of signed integers for which $m \neq 0$. To do this we consider the equivalence relationship

$$\mathsf{Same\_frac}([n, m], [n', m']) \leftrightarrow_{\mathrm{Def}} n * m' = n' * m.$$

The mapping $n \mapsto [n,1]$, whose inverse is simply $x^{[1]}$, embeds the signed integers into the rationals in a manner preserving all elementary algebraic operations, and also preserving order. From the fact that the set of signed integers is an ordered integral domain we easily prove that the rationals are an ordered field.

**(xi)** Our next step, following Cantor, is to define *real numbers* as equivalence classes of 'Cauchy sequences' $s_i$ of rationals. Here, a sequence is a *Cauchy sequence* if it satisfies[2]

$$\big(\forall \varepsilon \in \mathbb{Q} \,\big|\, \big(\exists n \in \mathbb{N} \,\big|\, \big(\forall i, j \in \mathbb{N} \mid (\epsilon > 0 \,\&\, i > n \,\&\, j > n) \rightarrow |s_i - s_j| < \epsilon\big)\big)\big).$$

The equivalence relation used is

$$\mathsf{Same\_real}(s,t) \leftrightarrow_{\mathrm{Def}} \big(\forall \varepsilon \in \mathbb{Q} \,\big|\, \big(\exists n \in \mathbb{N} \,\big|\, \big(\forall i \in \mathbb{N} \mid (\varepsilon > 0 \,\&\, i > n) \rightarrow |s_i - t_i| < \varepsilon\big)\big)\big).$$

Arithmetic operations for these equivalence classes are easily derived from the corresponding functions for rationals, and the 'completeness' of the set of real numbers, a key goal of early 19th century foundational work on analysis, can be proved without difficulty.

Since it is required for the elementary discussion of complex numbers, we prove the existence and basic properties of the square root, which is shown to exist for any non-negative real number.

**(xii)** Next the *complex numbers* are introduced as pairs of real numbers, and their elementary properties are established. In particular, they are shown to constitute a field, within which the field of real numbers has a natural embedding. The *modulus* of a complex number is defined and its basic properties demonstrated.

**(xiii)** This completes our preliminary work. What remains is to give the formal details of those parts of standard mathematical analysis needed to state and prove our assigned target result, the *Cauchy integral theorem*. For this, various familiar results concerning differentiation and integration are needed, first for functions of a real variable, then for functions of a complex variable. Our approach is as follows. The space of all *real functions* of a real variable is defined, along with the (pointwise) operations of addition, subtraction, and multiplication for functions, function comparison, the positive part of a function, and the least upper bound of a set of functions. Various elementary facts concerning this space of functions are established. In particular, it is shown that they form a ring under addition and multiplication. This allows application of the previously developed 'theory of Sigma' to define the sum of an arbitrary finite sequence of real functions. In preparation for the definition of

[2]Conciser, but less classical, characterizations of Cauchy sequences and of equivalence between them will be seen in Sect. 4.1.4.

the (ordinary Lebesgue) integral, the sum of an *absolutely convergent series* of positive real numbers is defined, and the basic properties of such sums are established. This prepares for definition of the sum of an absolutely convergent series of positive real functions, and for a proof of a few basic properties of such series.

In more direct preparation for definition of the integral, we define 'block' functions as real-valued functions of a real variable which are constant inside some finite interval of the real axis, and zero outside this interval. The integral of such a function is simply the area under its graph, which is an elementary rectangular block.

The greatest lower bound of a set of real numbers bounded below is then defined. This is immediately used to define the (Lebesgue) 'upper' integral of an arbitrary non-negative real function of a real variable. This is the greatest lower bound of the sum the integrals of all infinite sequences of non-negative block functions, extended over all such sequences whose (pointwise) sum exceeds the value $f(x)$ at each real point $x$. Using this, we can define the integral of an arbitrary real function $f$ (which now can have values of both signs) as the difference of the upper integrals of its positive and negative parts.

A function $f$ of a real value is defined to be *continuous* if it satisfies the standard 'epsilon–delta' condition. To define the derivative of such functions by the technique we adopt, the extension of this definition to the space of real-valued functions of two real variables is needed. To set this up, we first define $n$-dimensional Euclidean space as the set of all real-valued maps whose domain is the set of integers less than $n$. The standard Euclidean distance function is defined in this space and its basic properties are proved. Once this has been done, the space of continuous real-valued functions on a Euclidean space of any number of dimensions can be defined by extending the 'epsilon–delta' formulation to this slightly more general setting. We can then define a real-valued function $f$ of one real variable to be (continuously) differentiable if there exists a real-valued function $g$ of two real variables such that $(x - y) * g(x, y) = f(x) - f(y)$ for all real $x$ and $y$. We prove that if such a $g$ exists it is unique, in which case we define the *derivative* of $f$ as the function $h$ of one variable satisfying $h(x) = g(x, x)$.

Next this whole discussion is carried over to complex functions of a complex variable. We successively define the space of all such functions, the complex Euclidean space of $n$ dimensions with its norm, and the sum, difference, and product for complex-valued functions, either of a single complex variable, or of a point in complex Euclidean space. The 'epsilon–delta' definition of continuity is extended to the complex case for both these classes of functions. This allows direct extension of the notion of derivative, and of its elementary properties, to complex-valued functions of a complex variable.

A set of points in the complex plane is defined to be *open* if it is the union of the interiors of a set of circles, and a complex function defined in such a set is defined to be *analytic* if it is differentiable within the set.

Next we define the complex *exponential* function $\mathsf{cexp}$ as the unique complex function analytic everywhere in the complex plane and satisfying the equations $\mathsf{Dcexp} = \mathsf{cexp}$ and $\mathsf{cexp}([0, 0]) = [1, 0]$, where $\mathsf{Dcexp}$ denotes the derivative of $\mathsf{cexp}$. The constant $\pi$ is then defined as the smallest positive real root of $\mathsf{cexp}([0, x]) = [-1, 0]$.

Directly after this, we define the notion of a continuous complex function of a real variable by extending the 'epsilon–delta' formulation to this case in the obvious way. A similar extension of the construction used in the real case gives us the notion of a differentiable complex-valued function of a real variable (i.e. of a smooth curve in the complex plane), and of its derivative. The complex line integral of a complex function $g$ defined on such a curve is then taken to be the ordinary integral of the complex product of $g$ by $Df$ (where as before $Df$ is the derivative of $f$); the integral of the complex-valued function $h = g * Df$ (which is a function of a single real variable) is by definition obtained by adding the real integrals of the real and imaginary parts of $h$. We show that the line integrals of an analytic function $g$ over any two curves lying in its domain of analyticity are the same, provided that the two curves lie sufficiently close to one another. Using this, we show that the line integral over the periphery of the unit circle of the quotient function $f/(z - w)$ is $2 * \pi * \mathrm{i} * f[w]$ for every function $f$ analytic in an open set including the unit circle and its interior, and for every point interior to the unit circle.

Satisfied with this somewhat special form of the Cauchy integral theorem, we rest from our labors.

# Chapter 2
# Propositional- and Predicate-Calculus Preliminaries

This chapter prepares for the extensive account of our verifier system given in Chap. 4 by describing and analyzing two of the system's basic ingredients, the *propositional calculus*, from which we take all necessary properties of the logical operations &, $\vee$, $\neg$, $\rightarrow$, and $\leftrightarrow$, and the (first-order) *predicate calculus*, which to these propositional mechanisms adds compound functional and predicate constructions and the two quantifiers $\forall$ and $\exists$. Then we will show the axioms of a classical specification of *set theory* in predicate calculus; to end, we will highlight the much-debated issue of the consistency of this Zermelo–Fraenkel–Skolem theory and of some of its proposed extensions.

**Why Predicate Calculus?** Our aim is to develop a mechanism capable of ensuring that the logical formulae in which we are interested are universally valid. Since, as we shall see in Chap. 6, there can exist no algorithm capable of making this determination in all cases, we must use the mechanism of *proof*. This embeds the formulae in which we are interested in some system of sequences of formulae, within which we can define a property Is_a_proof($p$) capable of being verified by an algorithm, such that we can be certain that the final component $t$ of any sequence $p$ satisfying Is_a_proof($p$) is universally valid. Then we can use intuition freely to find aesthetically pleasing sequences $p$, the proofs, leading to interesting end goals $t$, the *theorems*. In principle, any system of formulae and sequences of formulae having this property is acceptable. The propositional/predicate calculus and set theory in which we work is merely one such formalism, of interest because of its convenience and wide use, and because much effort has gone into ensuring its reliability.

## 2.1 The Propositional Calculus

The propositional calculus constitutes the 'bottom-most' part of the full logical formalism with which we will work in this book. It provides only the operations &, $\vee$, $\neg$, $\rightarrow$, and $\leftrightarrow$ and the two constants 'true' and 'false', all other symbolic con-

J.T. Schwartz et al., *Computational Logic and Set Theory*,
DOI 10.1007/978-0-85729-808-9_2, © Springer-Verlag London Limited 2011

structions being reduced ('blobbed') down to single letters when propositional deductions must be made. An example given earlier, i.e. the formula

$$\big(F(x+y)=F\big(F(x)\big)\to F\big(F(x)\big)=0\big)\to\big(F\big(F(x)\big)\neq 0\to F(x+y)\neq F\big(F(x)\big)\big)$$

whose 'blobbed' propositional skeleton is

$$(p\to q)\to\big((\neg q)\to(\neg p)\big),$$

illustrates what is meant.

*Formulae* of the propositional calculus are built starting with string names designating propositional variables and combining them using the dyadic infix operators '&', '∨', '→', and '↔' and the monadic operator '¬'. Parentheses are used to group the subparts of formulae. The only precedence relation supported is the rule that '&' binds more tightly than '∨', so parentheses must normally be used rather liberally. Syntactically, the propositional calculus is a simple operator language, whose (syntactically valid) formulae parse unambiguously into syntax trees, each of whose internal nodes is marked either with one of the allowed infix operators, in which case it has two descendants, or with the monadic operator '¬', in which case it has one descendant. Each leaf of such a tree is marked either with the name of a propositional variable or with one of the two allowed constant symbols 'true' and 'false'.

An example is

$$(\mathsf{pan}\to\mathsf{quack})\to\big((\neg\mathsf{quack})\to(\neg\mathsf{true})\big).$$

Here the propositional variables which appear are 'pan' and 'quack', and the constant 'true' also appears.

Since the derivation of the syntax tree of a propositional formula from its string form ('parsing') and of the string form from the syntax tree ('unparsing') are both standard programming operations, we generally regard these two structures as being roughly synonymous and use whichever is convenient without further ado.

As in other logical systems we can think of our formulae either in terms of the values of functions which they represent, or as statements deducible from one another under certain circumstances, and so as the ingredients of some system of formalized proof. We begin with the first approach. In this way of looking at things, each propositional variable represents one of the truth values 1 or 0, which the propositional operators combine in standard ways. The following more formal definition captures this idea:

**Definition 2.1** An *assignment* for a collection of propositional formulae is a single-valued function $A$ mapping each of its constants and variables into one of the two values 1 and 0. Each assignment is required to map 'true' into 1 and 'false' into 0. The assignment is said to *cover* each of the formulae in the collection.

Given any such assignment $A$, and a formula $F$ which it covers, the value $\mathsf{Val}(A,F)$ *of the assignment A for the expression F* is the Boolean value defined in the following recursive way.

(i) If the formula $F$ is just a variable $x$ or is one of the constants 'true' and 'false', then $\mathsf{Val}(A, F) = A(F)$.
(ii) If the formula $F$ has the form '$G \,\&\, H$', then $\mathsf{Val}(A, F)$ is the minimum of $\mathsf{Val}(A, G)$ and $\mathsf{Val}(A, H)$.
(iii) If the formula $F$ has the form '$G \vee H$', then $\mathsf{Val}(A, F)$ is the maximum of $\mathsf{Val}(A, G)$ and $\mathsf{Val}(A, H)$.
(iv) If the formula $F$ has the form '$\neg G$', then $\mathsf{Val}(A, F) = 1 - \mathsf{Val}(A, G)$.
(v) If the formula $F$ has the form '$G \to H$', then $\mathsf{Val}(A, F) = \mathsf{Val}(A, \text{'}(\neg G) \vee H\text{'})$.
(vi) If the formula $F$ has the form '$G \leftrightarrow H$', then

$$\mathsf{Val}(A, F) = \mathsf{Val}\big(A, \text{'}(G \,\&\, H) \vee \big((\neg G) \,\&\, (\neg H)\big)\text{'}\big).$$

**Definition 2.2** A propositional formula $F$ is a *tautology* if $\mathsf{Val}(A, F) = 1$ for all the assignments $A$ covering it.

So tautologies are propositional formulae which evaluate to true no matter what truth values are assigned to their variables. Examples are

$$p \vee (\neg p), \qquad q \to (p \to q), \qquad p \to \big(q \to (p \,\&\, q)\big),$$

and many others, some listed below. These are the propositional formulae which possess 'universal logical validity'.

Since the number of possible assignments $A$ for a propositional formula $F$ is at most $2^n$, where $n$ is the number of variables in the formula, we can determine whether $F$ is a tautology by evaluating $\mathsf{Val}(A, F)$ for all such $A$. An alternative approach is to establish a system of proof by singling out some initial collection of tautologies (which we will call 'axioms') from which all remaining tautologies can be derived using rules of inference, which must also be defined. (This is the 'logical system' approach.) The axioms and rules of inference can be chosen in many ways. Though not at all the smallest possible set, the following collection has a familiar and convenient algebraic flavor.

(i) $(p \,\&\, q) \leftrightarrow (q \,\&\, p)$
(ii) $((p \,\&\, q) \,\&\, r) \leftrightarrow (p \,\&\, (q \,\&\, r))$
(iii) $(p \,\&\, p) \leftrightarrow p$
(iv) $(p \vee q) \leftrightarrow (q \vee p)$
(v) $((p \vee q) \vee r) \leftrightarrow (p \vee (q \vee r))$
(vi) $(p \vee p) \leftrightarrow p$
(vii) $(\neg(p \,\&\, q)) \leftrightarrow ((\neg p) \vee (\neg q))$
(viii) $(\neg(p \vee q)) \leftrightarrow ((\neg p) \,\&\, (\neg q))$
(ix) $((p \vee q) \,\&\, r) \leftrightarrow ((p \,\&\, r) \vee (q \,\&\, r))$
(x) $((p \,\&\, q) \vee r) \leftrightarrow ((p \vee r) \,\&\, (q \vee r))$
(xi) $(p \leftrightarrow q) \to ((p \,\&\, r) \leftrightarrow (q \,\&\, r))$
(xii) $(p \leftrightarrow q) \to ((p \vee r) \leftrightarrow (q \vee r))$

(xiii) $(p \leftrightarrow q) \rightarrow ((\neg p) \leftrightarrow (\neg q))$
(xiv) $(p \leftrightarrow q) \rightarrow (q \rightarrow p)$
(xv) $(p \rightarrow q) \leftrightarrow ((\neg p) \vee q)$
(xvi) $(p \leftrightarrow q) \leftrightarrow ((p \rightarrow q) \,\&\, (q \rightarrow p))$
(xvii) $(p \,\&\, q) \rightarrow p$
(xviii) $(p \leftrightarrow q) \rightarrow ((q \leftrightarrow r) \rightarrow (p \leftrightarrow r))$
(xix) $(p \leftrightarrow q) \rightarrow (q \leftrightarrow p)$
(xx) $(p \leftrightarrow p)$
(xxi) $(p \,\&\, (\neg p)) \leftrightarrow \mathsf{false}$
(xxii) $(p \vee (\neg p)) \leftrightarrow \mathsf{true}$
(xxiii) $(\neg(\neg p)) \leftrightarrow p$
(xxiv) $(p \,\&\, \mathsf{true}) \leftrightarrow p$
(xxv) $(p \,\&\, \mathsf{false}) \leftrightarrow \mathsf{false}$
(xxvi) $(p \vee \mathsf{true}) \leftrightarrow \mathsf{true}$
(xxvii) $(p \vee \mathsf{false}) \leftrightarrow p$
(xxviii) $(\neg \mathsf{true}) \leftrightarrow \mathsf{false}$
(xxix) $(\neg \mathsf{false}) \leftrightarrow \mathsf{true}$
(xxx) $\mathsf{true}$

The preceding are to be understood as axiom 'templates' or 'schemas', in the sense that all formulae resulting from one of them by substitution of syntactically legal propositional formulae $P, Q, \ldots$ for the letters $p, q, \ldots$ occurring in them are also axioms. For example,

$$\big(((p \vee q) \vee (r \rightarrow r)) \,\&\, ((p \vee q) \vee (r \rightarrow r))\big) \leftrightarrow \big((p \vee q) \vee (r \rightarrow r)\big)$$

is a substituted instance of (iii) and therefore is also regarded as an axiom.

The reader can verify that all of the axioms listed are in fact tautologies.

In the presence of this lush collection of axioms we need only one rule of inference (namely the '*modus ponens*' of mediaeval logicians). From any two formulae of the form $p$ and $p \rightarrow q$ this allows us to deduce $q$. As with the axioms, this rule is to be understood as a template, covering all of its substituted instances.

To ensure that the tautologies are exactly the derivable propositional formulae we must prove *soundness*, namely that (I) only tautologies can be derived, and *completeness*, namely that (II) all tautologies can be derived. (I) is easy. We reason as follows. All the axioms are tautologies. Moreover, since

$$\mathsf{Val}(A,\ p \rightarrow q) = \max\big(1 - \mathsf{Val}(A, p),\ \mathsf{Val}(A, q)\big),$$

it follows that if $\mathsf{Val}(A, p \rightarrow q)$ and $\mathsf{Val}(A, p)$ are both 1, so is $\mathsf{Val}(A, q)$. So if '$p \rightarrow q$' and $p$ are both tautologies, then so is $q$. This proves our claim (I).

Proving claim (II) takes a bit more work, whose general pattern is much like that used to reduce multivariate polynomials to their canonical form. Starting with any syntactically well-formed propositional formula $F$, we can proceed in the following way to derive a chain of formulae equivalent to $F$ (via an explicit chain of equivalences $F_i \leftrightarrow F_{i+1}$). Note that axioms (xviii–xx) ensure that the equivalence relator

'$\leftrightarrow$' has the same transitivity, symmetry, and reflexivity properties as equality, while (xi–xiii) allow us to replace any subexpression of an expression formed using only the three operators &, $\vee$, $\neg$ by any equivalent subexpression.

Using these facts and (xv–xvi) we first descend recursively through the syntax tree of $F$, replacing any occurrence of one of the operations $\rightarrow$, $\leftrightarrow$ by an equivalent expression involving only &, $\vee$, $\neg$. This reduces $F$ to an equivalent formula involving only the operators &, $\vee$, $\neg$. Then, using (vii–viii) and (x), we systematically push '$\neg$' and '$\vee$' operators down in the syntax tree, moving '&' operators up. Subformulae of the form $(\neg(\neg p))$ are simplified to $p$ using axiom (xxiii). Axioms (xxiv–xxix) can be used to simplify expressions containing the constants 'true' and 'false'. When this work is complete $F$ will been have reduced to an equivalent formula $F'$ which is either one of the constants 'true' or 'false' or has the form $a_1 \mathbin{\&} \cdots \mathbin{\&} a_k$, where each $a_j$ is a disjunction of the form

$$b_1 \vee \cdots \vee b_h,$$

each $b_m$ being either a propositional variable or the negation of a propositional variable. (ii) and (v) allow us to think of these conjunctions and disjunctions without worrying about how they are parenthesized. Then (iv) and (vi) can be used to bring all the $b_m$ involving a particular propositional variable together within each $a_j$.

Now assume that $F$ is a tautology, so that every one of the formulae to which we have reduced it must also be a tautology (since the substitutions performed all convert tautologies to tautologies), and so our final formula $F'$ is a tautology. We will now further reduce $F'$, so that it becomes the formula 'true'. Unless $F'$ is already 'true', in each $a_j$, there must occur at least one pair $b_m$, $b_n$ of disjuncts such that $b_m$ is a propositional variable of which $b_n$ is the negation, '$\neg b_m$'. Indeed, if this is not the case, then any propositional variable which occurs in $a_j$ will occur either negated or non-negated, but not both. Given this, we can assign the value 0 to each non-negated variable and the value 1 to each negated variable. Then every $b_m$ in $a_j$ will evaluate to 0, so the whole expression $b_1 \vee \cdots \vee b_h$ will evaluate to 0, that is, $a_j$ will evaluate to 0. But as soon as this happens the whole formula $a_1 \mathbin{\&} \cdots \mathbin{\&} a_k$ will evaluate to 0. This shows that there exists an assignment $A$ such that $\mathsf{Val}(A, F') = 0$, contradicting the fact that $F'$ is a tautology. This contradiction proves our claim that each $a_j$ must contain at least one pair $b_m$, $b_n$ of disjuncts which agree except for the presence of a negation operator in one but not in the other.

Given this fact, (xxii) tells us that '$b_m \vee b_n$' simplifies to 'true', so that (xxvi) can be used repeatedly to simplify $a_j$ to 'true'. Since this is the case for each $a_j$, repeated use of (xxiv) allows us to reduce any tautology to 'true' using a chain of equivalences. Since this chain of equivalences can as well be traversed in the reverse direction, we can equally well expand the axiom 'true' (axiom (xxx)) into our original formula $F$ using a chain of equivalences. Then (xiv) can be used to convert this chain of equivalences into a chain of implications, giving us a proof of $F$, by repeated uses of modus ponens.

Any set of axioms from which all the statements (i–xxx) can be derived as theorems can clearly be used as an axiomatic basis for the propositional calculus. This allows much leaner sets of axioms to be used. We refrain from exploring this point, which lacks importance for the rest of our discussion.

However, it is worth embedding the notion of 'tautology' in a wider, relativized, set of ideas. Suppose that we write

$$\models F$$

to indicate that the formula $F$ is a tautology, and

$$\vdash F$$

to indicate that $F$ is a provable formula of the propositional calculus. The preceding discussion shows that $\models F$, and $\vdash F$, are equivalent conditions. This result can be generalized as follows. Let $S$ designate any finite set of syntactically well-formed formulae of the propositional calculus. We can then write

$$S \models F$$

to indicate that, for each assignment $A$ covering both $F$, and all the formulae in $S$, we have $\mathsf{Val}(A, F) = 1$ whenever $\mathsf{Val}(A, G) = 1$ for all $G$ in $S$. Also, we write

$$S \vdash F$$

to indicate that $F$ follows by propositional proof if the statements in $S$ are added to the axioms of propositional calculus (each of them acting as an individual axiom, not as a template). Then it is easy to show that

$$S \models F \quad \text{if and only if} \quad S \vdash F.$$

To show this, first suppose that $S \models F$. Let $C$ designate the conjunction

$$G_1 \,\&\, \cdots \,\&\, G_k$$

of all the formulae in $S$. Then since $\mathsf{Val}(A, H_1 \,\&\, H_2) = \min(\mathsf{Val}(A, H_1), \mathsf{Val}(A, H_2))$ for any two formulae $H_1, H_2$, it follows that $\mathsf{Val}(A, C) = 1$ if and only if $\mathsf{Val}(A, G) = 1$ for all $G$ in $S$. We have

$$\mathsf{Val}(A,\ C \to F) = \mathsf{Val}\big(A,\ (\neg C) \vee F\big) = \max\big(1 - \mathsf{Val}(A, C),\ \mathsf{Val}(F)\big)$$

for all assignments $A$ covering $C \to F$, (i.e. covering both $F$, and all the formulae in $S$). It follows that for each assignment $A$ covering both $F$, and all the formulae in $S$, we have $\mathsf{Val}(A, C \to F) = 1$, since if $1 - \mathsf{Val}(A, C) \neq 1$ then $\mathsf{Val}(A, C)$ must be 1 and so $\mathsf{Val}(F)$ must be 1. Thus

$$\models C \to F,$$

and so it follows that $\vdash C \to F$, i.e. $C \to F$ can be proved from the axioms of propositional calculus alone. But then if the statements in $S$ are added as additional axioms we can prove $F$, by first proving $C \to F$, and then using the statements in $S$ to prove the conjunction $C$. This shows that $S \models F$ implies $S \vdash F$.

Next suppose that $S \vdash F$, and let $A$ be an assignment covering both $F$, and all the formulae in $S$ so that $\mathsf{Val}(A, G) = 1$ for every statement $G$ in $S$. Then $\mathsf{Val}(A, G) = 1$ for every statement $G$ that can be used as an axiom in the proof of $F$, from the standard axioms of propositional calculus and the statements in $S$ as additional axioms. But we have seen above that if $\mathsf{Val}(A, p \to q)$ and $\mathsf{Val}(A, p)$ are both 1, so is $\mathsf{Val}(A, q)$. Since derivation of $q$ from $p$ and $p \to q$ is the only inference step allowed in propositional calculus proofs, it follows that $S \models F$, completing our proof that the conditions $S \models F$, and $S \vdash F$, are equivalent.

We shall see that similar statements apply to the much more general predicate calculus studied in the following section. In that section, we will need the following extension of the preceding results to countably infinite collections of propositional formulae.

**Definition 2.3** A (finite or infinite) collection $S$ of formulae of the propositional calculus is said to be *consistent* if the proposition '$\mathsf{false}$' cannot be deduced from $S$, i.e.

$$S \vdash \mathsf{false}$$

is false. We say that $S$ *has a model* $A$ if there exists some assignment $A$ covering all the formulae of $S$ such that $\mathsf{Val}(A, F) = 1$ for every $F$ in $S$.

**Theorem 2.1** (Compactness) *Let $S$ be a denumerable collection of formulae of the propositional calculus. Then the following three conditions are equivalent*:

(i) *$S$ is consistent.*
(ii) *Every finite subset of $S$ is consistent.*
(iii) *$S$ has a model.*

*Proof* Since subsets of a consistent $S$ are plainly consistent, (i) implies (ii). On the other hand, any proof of '$\mathsf{false}$' from the statements of $S$ is of finite length by definition, and so uses only a finite number of the statements of $S$. Thus (ii) implies (i), so (ii) and (i) are equivalent.

Next suppose that $S$ is not consistent, so that '$\mathsf{false}$' can be proved from some finite subset $S'$ of the statements in $S$. Let $C$ be the conjunction of all the statements in $S'$. It follows from the discussion immediately preceding the statement of the present theorem that $\vdash C \to \mathsf{false}$, and so $\mathsf{Val}(A, `C \to \mathsf{false}') = 1$ for any assignment $A$ covering all the propositional symbols in $S$. This gives $\mathsf{Val}(A, C) = 0$ for all such $A$, so that $S$ has no model. This proves that (iii) implies (i).

Next we show that (i) implies (iii). For this, let $\{S_j\}$ be an increasing sequence of finite subsets of $S$ whose union is all of $S$. Each $S_j$ is plainly consistent, so

$$S_j \vdash \mathsf{false}$$

is false for each $j$, and therefore

$$S_j \models \text{false}$$

is false, since we have shown above that these two conditions are equivalent for finite $S_j$. That is, for each $j$ there must exist an assignment $A_j$ covering all the variables appearing in any formula of $S_j$, such that $\mathsf{Val}(A_j, S_j) = 1$. Let $v_1, v_2, v_3, \ldots$ be an enumeration of all the variables appearing in any of the formulae of $S$. Then each $v_k$ must be in the domain of all $A_j$ for all $j$ beyond a certain point $j = j_k$.

Let $I_0$ designate the sequence of all integers. Since $A_j(v_1)$ must have one of the two values 0 and 1, there must exist an infinite subsequence $I_1$ of $I_0$ for all $j$ of which $A_j(v_1)$ has the same value. Call this value $B(v_1)$. Arguing in the same way we see that here must exist an infinite subsequence $I_2$ of $I_1$ and a Boolean value $B(v_2)$ such that

$$B(v_2) = A_j(v_2) \quad \text{for all } j \text{ in } I_2.$$

Arguing repeatedly in this way we eventually construct values $B(v_k)$ for each $k$ such that for each finite $m$, there exist infinitely many $j$ such that

$$B(v_n) = A_j(v_n) \quad \text{for all } n \text{ from 1 to } m.$$

Now consider any of the formulae $G$ of $S$. Since $G$ can involve only finitely many propositional variables $v_j$, all its variables will be included in the set $\{v_1, \ldots, v_k\}$ for each sufficiently large $k$. Take any $A_j$ for which $B(v_n) = A_j(v_n)$ for all $n$ from 1 to $k$. Then it is clear that for some $i$ greater than $j$, we have

$$\mathsf{Val}(B, G) = \mathsf{Val}(A_i, G) = 1.$$

Hence $\mathsf{Val}(B, G) = 1$ for all $G$ in $S$, so that $B$ is a model of $S$, proving that (i) implies (iii), and thereby completing the proof of our theorem. □

Using the Compactness Theorem, we can show that the conditions $S \vdash F$, and $S \models F$, are equivalent even in the case in which $S$ is an infinite set of propositional formulae.

To show this, first assume that $S \models F$. Then the set $S \cup \{\neg F\}$ of propositions is plainly not consistent, and so by the Compactness Theorem $S$ must contain some finite subset $S_0$ such that $S_0 \cup \{\neg F\}$ is not consistent. Then plainly $S_0 \models F$, so we have $S_0 \vdash F$. This clearly implies $S \vdash F$; so $S \vdash F$, follows from $S \models F$.

But, as noted at the end of the proof of the Compactness Theorem, $S \models F$ follows from $S \vdash F$, even if $S$ is infinite, completing the proof of our claim.

## 2.2 The Predicate Calculus

The predicate calculus constitutes the next main part of the logical formalism used in this book. This calculus enlarges the propositional calculus, preserving all its operations but also allowing compound functional and predicate terms and the two quantifiers ∀ and ∃. An example is the formula

$$\big((\forall x, y \mid F(x+y) = F\big(F(x)\big)\big) \to F\big(F(x)\big) = 0\big)$$
$$\to \big((\exists x \mid F\big(F(x)\big) \neq 0\big) \to \big(F(x+y) \neq F\big(F(x)\big)\big)\big).$$

*Formulae* of the predicate calculus are built starting with string names of three kinds, respectively, designating 'individual' variables, function symbols, and predicate symbols. These are combined into '*terms*', '*atomic formulae*', and '*formulae*' using the following recursive syntactic rules.

(i) Any variable name is a term. (We assume variable names to be alphanumeric and to start with lower case letters.)

(ii) Each function symbol has some fixed finite number $k$ of arguments. If $f$ is a function symbol of $k$ arguments, and $t_1, \ldots, t_k$ are any $k$ terms, then $f(t_1, \ldots, t_k)$ is a term. (We assume function names to be alphanumeric and to start with lower case letters.)

(iii) Each predicate symbol has some fixed finite number $k$ of arguments. If $P$ is a predicate symbol of $k$ arguments, and $t_1, \ldots, t_k$ are any $k$ terms, then $P(t_1, \ldots, t_k)$ is an atomic formula. (We assume predicate names to be alphanumeric and to start with upper case letters.)

(iv) Formulae are formed starting from atomic formulae and using the operators and syntactic rules of the propositional calculus and the two quantifiers ∀ and ∃. More precisely, if $e$ and $f$ are any two predicate formulae and $v_1, \ldots, v_n$ are any $n$ variable names, with $n > 0$, then the following expressions are predicate formulae:

$$e \,\&\, f, \qquad e \vee f, \qquad \neg e,$$
$$e \to f, \qquad e \leftrightarrow f,$$
$$(\forall v_1, \ldots, v_n \mid e), \qquad (\exists v_1, \ldots, v_n \mid e).$$

Like propositional formulae, the formulae of predicate calculus parse unambiguously into syntax trees each of whose internal nodes is marked either (i) with one of the propositional operators, and then has as many descendants as the corresponding propositional node, or (ii) with a function or predicate symbol, in which case its descendants correspond to the arguments of the function or predicate symbol; (iii) a quantifier ∀ or ∃ involving $n$ variable names, in which case the node has $n+1$ descendants, the first $n$ marked with the $n$ variable names appearing in the quantifier and the $n+1$-st which is the syntax tree of the expression $e$ that is being quantified. Each leaf of such a tree is marked either with the name of an individual variable or a function symbol of zero arguments. (Such function symbols are called 'constants'.)

Each occurrence of a variable $v$ at a leaf of the syntax tree of a valid predicate formula is either *free* or *bound*. A variable $v$ is considered to be bound if it appears as the descendant of some syntax tree node which is marked with a quantifier in whose associated list of variables $v$ occurs; otherwise the occurrence is a free occurrence. These notions clearly translate back into corresponding notions for variable occurrences in the unparsed string forms of the same formulae. For example, in the predicate formula

$$(\forall x, z, x \mid F(x+y+z)) \vee (\exists y, y \mid F(x+y))$$

the first three occurrences of $x$ are bound, but the fourth occurrence of $x$ is free. Likewise the last three occurrences of $y$ are bound, but its first occurrence is free. Note that, as this example shows, repeated occurrences of a variable in the list following one of the quantifier symbols $\forall$ or $\exists$ are legal. However, we will see, when we come to define the semantics of predicate formulae, that such repetitions are always superfluous since any variable occurrence repeated later in the list following a quantifier symbol can simply be dropped. For example, the formula shown above has the same meaning as

$$(\forall z, x \mid F(x+y+z)) \vee (\exists y \mid F(x+y)).$$

Bound variables are considered to belong to the *scope* of the nearest ancestor quantifier in whose list of variables they appear; this quantifier is said to *bind* them. For example, in

$$(\forall x \mid F(x) \vee (\exists x \mid G(x)) \vee H(x))$$

the first, second, and final occurrences of $x$ are in the scope of the first quantifier '$\forall$', but the third and fourth occurrences are in the scope of the second quantifier '$\exists$'.

As was the case for the propositional calculus, we can think of predicate formulae either as representing certain functions, or as the ingredients of a system of formalized proof. Again we begin with the first approach. Here the required definitions are a bit trickier.

**Definition 2.4** An *interpretation framework* for a collection PF of predicate formulae is a triple $(\mathcal{U}, I, A)$ such that

(i) $\mathcal{U}$ is a nonempty set, called the *universe* or *domain* of the interpretation framework. We write $\mathcal{U}^k$ for the $k$-fold Cartesian product of $\mathcal{U}$ with itself.

(ii) $I$ is a single-valued function, called an *interpretation*, which maps each of the function and predicate symbols occurring in the collection in accordance with the following rules:

  (ii.a) Each function symbol $f$ of $k$ arguments occurring in the collection of formulae is mapped into a function $I(f)$ which sends $\mathcal{U}^k$ into $\mathcal{U}$.

  (ii.b) Each predicate symbol $P$ of $k$ arguments occurring in the collection of formulae is mapped into a function $I(P)$ which sends $\mathcal{U}^k$ into the set $\{0, 1\}$ of values.

(iii) $A$ is a single-valued function, called an *assignment*, which maps each of the individual variables occurring freely in the collection PF of formulae into an element of $\mathcal{U}$.

As previously we speak of such an interpretation framework as *covering* the collection PF of predicate formulae.

Suppose that we are given any such interpretation $I$ and assignment $A$ with universe $\mathcal{U}$, and an expression $F$ which they cover. (Note that $F$ can be either a term or a predicate formula.) Then the value $\mathsf{Val}(I, A, F)$ *of the assignment for the expression* is the value defined in the following recursive way.

(i) If $F$ is just an individual variable $x$, then $\mathsf{Val}(I, A, F) = A(x)$.

(ii) If $F$ is a term having the form $g(t_1, \ldots, t_k)$, and $G$ is the corresponding mapping $I(g)$ from $\mathcal{U}^k$ to $\mathcal{U}$, then $\mathsf{Val}(I, A, F) = G(\mathsf{Val}(I, A, t_1), \ldots, \mathsf{Val}(I, A, t_k))$.

(iii) If $F$ is an atomic formula having the form $P(t_1, \ldots, t_k)$, and $p$ is the corresponding mapping $I(P)$ from $\mathcal{U}^k$ to $\{0, 1\}$, then $\mathsf{Val}(I, A, F)$ is the 0/1 value $p(\mathsf{Val}(I, A, t_1), \ldots, \mathsf{Val}(I, A, t_k))$.

(iv) If $F$ is a formula having the form $G \,\&\, H$, then $\mathsf{Val}(I, A, F)$ is the minimum of $\mathsf{Val}(I, A, G)$ and $\mathsf{Val}(I, A, H)$.

(v) If $F$ is a formula having the form $G \vee H$, then $\mathsf{Val}(I, A, F)$ is the maximum of $\mathsf{Val}(I, A, G)$ and $\mathsf{Val}(I, A, H)$.

(vi) If $F$ is a formula having the form $\neg G$, then $\mathsf{Val}(I, A, F) = 1 - \mathsf{Val}(I, A, G)$.

(vii) If $F$ is a formula having the form $G \rightarrow H$, then $\mathsf{Val}(I, A, F) = \mathsf{Val}(I, A,$ '$(\neg G) \vee H$').

(viii) If $F$ is a formula having the form $G \leftrightarrow H$, then $\mathsf{Val}(I, A, F) = \mathsf{Val}(I, A,$ '$(G \,\&\, H) \vee ((\neg G) \,\&\, (\neg H))$').

(ix) If $F$ is a formula having the form $(\forall v_1, \ldots, v_n \mid e)$, then $\mathsf{Val}(I, A, F)$ is the minimum of $\mathsf{Val}(I, A', e)$, extended over all assignments $A'$ such that $A'$ covers the formula $e$ and $A'(x) = A(x)$ for every variable $x$ not in the list $v_1, \ldots, v_n$.

(x) If $F$ is a formula having the form $(\exists v_1, \ldots, v_n \mid e)$, then $\mathsf{Val}(I, A, F)$ is the maximum of $\mathsf{Val}(I, A', e)$, extended over all assignments $A'$ such that $A'$ covers the formula $e$ and $A'(x) = A(x)$ for every variable $x$ not in the list $v_1, \ldots, v_n$.

Since, as seen in (ix) and (x) above, the variables appearing in the lists following quantifier symbols '∀' and '∃' merely serve to mark occurrences of the same variables in the quantifier's scope as being 'bound' and hence subject to minimization/maximization when values $\mathsf{Val}(I, A, F)$ are calculated, it follows that these variables can be replaced with any others provided that this replacement is made uniformly over the entire scope of each quantifier, and that no variable occurring freely in the original formula thereby becomes bound. For example, the formula

$$\big(\forall x \mid F(x) \vee \big(\exists x \mid G(x)\big) \vee H(x)\big)$$

appearing above can as well be written as

$$\big(\forall x \mid F(x) \vee \big(\exists y \mid G(y)\big) \vee H(x)\big)$$

or as

$$\big(\forall y \mid F(y) \vee \big(\exists x \mid G(x)\big) \vee H(y)\big).$$

A convenient way of performing this kind of 'bound variable standardization' is as follows. We make use of some standard list $L$ of bound variable names, reserved for this purpose and used for no other. We work from the leaves of a formula's syntax tree up toward its root, processing all quantifiers more distant from the root before any quantifier closer to the root is processed. Suppose that a quantifier like

$$(\forall v_1, \ldots, v_n \mid e)$$

or

$$(\exists v_1, \ldots, v_n \mid e)$$

is encountered at a tree node $Q$ during this process. We then take the first $n$ variables $b_1, \ldots, b_n$ from the list $L$ that do not already appear in any descendant of the node $Q$, replace $v_1, \ldots, v_n$ by $b_1, \ldots, b_n$, respectively, and make the same replacements for every free occurrence of any of the $v_1, \ldots, v_n$ in $e$.

This standardization will for example transform

$$\big(\forall y \,\big|\, (\forall y \,|\, F(y) \vee (\exists x \mid G(x))) \vee H(y)\big)$$

into

$$\big(\forall b_3 \,\big|\, (\forall b_1 \,|\, F(b_1) \vee (\exists b_2 \mid G(b_2))) \vee H(b_3)\big).$$

Such standardization of bound variables makes it easier to see what quantifier each bound variable occurrence relates to. It also uncovers identities between quantified subexpressions that might otherwise be missed, and so is a valuable preliminary to examination of the propositional structure of predicate formulae.

It also follows from (ix) and (x) that the value assigned to any quantified formula

$$(\forall v_1, v_2, \ldots, v_n \mid e) \tag{2.1}$$

is exactly the same as that assigned to

$$\big(\forall v_1 \,\big|\, \big(\forall v_2 \,\big|\, \big(\forall \cdots \mid (\forall v_n \mid e) \cdots\big)\big)\big) \tag{2.2}$$

and, likewise, the value assigned to any quantified formula

$$(\exists v_1, v_2, \ldots, v_n \mid e) \tag{2.3}$$

is exactly the same as that assigned to

$$\big(\exists v_1 \,\big|\, \big(\exists v_2 \,\big|\, \big(\exists \cdots \mid (\exists v_n \mid e) \cdots\big)\big)\big). \tag{2.4}$$

Accordingly, we shall regard (2.1) and (2.3) as abbreviations for (2.2) and (2.4). This allows us to assume (wherever convenient) that each quantifier examined in the following discussion involves only a single variable.

**Definition 2.5** A predicate formula $F$ is *universally valid* if $\mathsf{Val}(I, A, F) = 1$ for every interpretation framework $(\mathcal{U}, I, A)$ covering it.

In predicate calculus, universally valid formulae are those which evaluate to true no matter what 'meanings' are assigned to the variables, function symbols, and predicate symbols that occur within them. Examples are

$$P(x, y) \vee (\neg P(x, y)),$$
$$(\forall ya \mid Q(x) \rightarrow (P(x, y) \rightarrow Q(x))),$$
$$(\forall x \mid P(x, y) \rightarrow (\exists y \mid (Q(x) \rightarrow (P(x, y) \,\&\, Q(x))))).$$

However, the problem of determining whether a given predicate formula is universally valid is of a much higher order of difficulty than the problem of recognizing propositional tautologies, since the collection of interpretation frameworks that must be considered is infinite rather than finite. There is no longer any reason for believing that this determination can be made algorithmically, and indeed it cannot, as we shall see in Chap. 6. Thus we have little alternative to setting up the predicate calculus as a logical system in which universally valid formulae are found by proof. We now begin to do this, starting with a special subclass of universally valid formulae, the *predicate tautologies*, which are defined as follows.

**Definition 2.6** A predicate formula $F$ is a *tautology* if it reduces to a propositional tautology by descending through its syntax tree and reducing each node not marked with a propositional operator to a single propositional variable, identical subnodes always being reduced to the same propositional variable. (In what follows we will call this latter formula the *propositional blobbing* of $F$.)

As an example, note that the indicated reduction sends

$$P(x, y) \vee (\neg P(x, y)) \text{ into } A \vee (\neg A),$$
$$(\forall y \mid Q(x) \rightarrow (P(x, y) \rightarrow Q(x))) \text{ into } B,$$
$$P(x, y) \rightarrow (\exists y \mid (Q(x) \rightarrow (P(x, y) \,\&\, Q(x)))) \text{ into } A \rightarrow C.$$

Thus the first of these three formulae is a predicate tautology, but the two others are not.

The recursive computation of $\mathsf{Val}(I, A, F)$ assigns some $0/1$ value to each subtree of the syntax tree of $F$, and plainly assigns the same value to identical subtrees of the syntax tree of $F$. This makes it clear that every predicate tautology is universally valid. But there are other basic forms of universally well-formed predicate formulae, of which the most crucial are listed in the following definition.

**Definition 2.7** A formula is an *axiom of the predicate calculus* if it is either

(i) any predicate tautology;
(ii) any formula of the form

$$((\forall y \mid P \rightarrow Q) \,\&\, (\forall y \mid P)) \rightarrow (\forall y \mid Q);$$

(iii) any formula of the form

$$(\neg(\forall y \mid \neg P)) \leftrightarrow (\exists y \mid P);$$

(iv) any formula of the form $P \leftrightarrow (\forall y \mid P)$, where the variable $y$ does not occur in $P$ as a free variable;

(v) any formula of the form $(\forall y \mid P) \rightarrow P(y \hookrightarrow e)$, where $P(y \hookrightarrow e)$ is the formula obtained from $P$ by substituting the syntactically well-formed term $e$ for each free occurrence of the variable $y$ in $P$, provided that no variable free in $e$ is bound at the point of occurrence of any such $y$ in $P$.

We can easily see that all of these predicate axioms are universally valid. Given a formula $P$ of the predicate calculus, let $P'$ designate its propositional blobbing. Predicate tautologies are universally valid since the final stages of computation of $\mathsf{Val}(I, A, P)$ always use the values assigned to certain basic subformulae of $P$ in the same way that values assigned to corresponding propositional variables are used in the propositional computation of $\mathsf{Val}(I, A, P')$. To see that (iii) is universally valid, we have only to note that for 0/1 valued functions $f$ of any number of arguments we always have

$$\max(f) = 1 - \min(1 - f).$$

(iv) is universally valid because if $y$ does not occur in $P$ as a free variable, we have

$$\mathsf{Val}\big(I, A, \text{`}(\forall y \mid P)\text{'}\big) = \mathsf{Val}(I, A, P)$$

for every interpretation $I$ and assignment $A$ covering $P$.

(v) is universally valid because any interpretation $I$ and assignment $A$ covering $P(y \hookrightarrow e)$ will assign some value $a_0$ to $e$, and then $\mathsf{Val}(I, A, P(y \hookrightarrow e)) = \mathsf{Val}(I, A', P)$, where $A'$ is the assignment identical to $A$ except that it assigns the value $a_0$ to $y$. Since $\mathsf{Val}(I, A', (\forall y \mid P))$ is by definition the minimum of $\mathsf{Val}(I, B, P)$ extended over all assignments $B$ which are identical to $A$ except on the variable $y$, it follows that $\mathsf{Val}(I, A, \text{`}(\forall y \mid P)\text{'}) = 1$ implies $\mathsf{Val}(I, A, P(y \hookrightarrow e)) = 1$, so that

$$\max\big(1 - \mathsf{Val}\big(I, A, \text{`}(\forall y \mid P)\text{'}\big), \mathsf{Val}\big(I, A, P(y \hookrightarrow e)\big)\big)$$

is identically 1, i.e. $(\forall y \mid P) \rightarrow P(y \hookrightarrow e)$ is universally valid.

To show that (ii) is universally valid, note that for any interpretation $I$ and assignment $A$ covering (ii)

$$\mathsf{Val}\big(I, A, \text{`}(\forall y \mid P \rightarrow Q)\text{'}\big)$$

and

$$\mathsf{Val}\big(I, A, \text{`}(\forall y \mid P)\text{'}\big)$$

are, respectively, the minimum of $\max(1 - \mathsf{Val}(I, A', P), \mathsf{Val}(I, A', Q))$ and of $\mathsf{Val}(I, A', P)$, extended over all assignments $A'$ which are identical to $A$ except on the variable $y$. If both of these minima are 1, then $1 - \mathsf{Val}(I, A', P)$ must be 0 for all such $A'$, so $\mathsf{Val}(I, A', Q)$ must be 1 for all such $A'$, proving that $\mathsf{Val}(I, A, `(\forall y \mid Q)\text{'}) = 1$. This implies the universal validity of (ii), completing our proof that all predicate axioms are universally valid.

### 2.2.1 Proof Rules of the Predicate Calculus

The predicate calculus has just two proof rules. The first is identical with the modus ponens rule of propositional calculus. The second is the *Rule of Generalization*, which states that if $P$ is any previously proved result, then

$$(\forall x \mid P)$$

can be deduced.

A stronger variant of the Rule of Generalization, which turns out to be very useful in practice, allows us to deduce the formula

$$P \rightarrow (\forall x \mid Q)$$

from $P \rightarrow Q$, provided that the variable $x$ does not occur free in $P$. This variant can be justified as follows. Let us assume that the formula $P \rightarrow Q$ has been derived and that $x$ is a variable which does not have free occurrences in $P$. By generalization and as instance of the predicate axiom (ii) we can derive the formulae

$$(\forall x \mid P \rightarrow Q), \ \ \big((\forall x \mid P \rightarrow Q) \,\&\, (\forall x \mid P)\big) \rightarrow (\forall x \mid Q).$$

By propositional reasoning these imply the formula

$$(\forall x \mid P) \rightarrow (\forall x \mid Q).$$

Since we are assuming that the variable $x$ does not occur free in $P$, we can derive the formula

$$P \leftrightarrow (\forall x \mid P)$$

using predicate axiom (iv), and it follows by propositional reasoning that

$$P \rightarrow (\forall x \mid Q),$$

which establishes the strong form of the rule of generalization that we have stated.

In what follows we will not always distinguish between the two variants of the rule of generalization and we will use whichever version is more convenient for the purposes at hand. The argument given above shows that any proof which uses the strong variant of the Rule of Generalization can be transformed mechanically into a proof which uses only the standard form of this Rule.

We can easily see that any formula deduced from universally valid formulae using the two proof rules just explained must also be universally valid. For the modus ponens rule this follows as in the propositional case. For the rule of generalization we reason as follows. If $\mathsf{Val}(I, A, P) = 1$ for every interpretation $I$ and assignment $A$ covering $P$, then since for every assignment $B$ covering $(\forall x \mid P)$ the value $v = \mathsf{Val}(I, B, \text{‘}(\forall x \mid P)\text{’})$ is the minimum of $\mathsf{Val}(I, A, P)$ extended over all assignments $A$ which give the same value as $B$ to all variables other than $x$, it follows that $v = 1$ also.

In analogy with the case of the propositional calculus we write

$$\models F$$

to indicate that the formula $F$ is a universally valid formula of the predicate calculus, and write

$$\vdash F$$

to indicate that $F$ is a provable formula of the predicate calculus.

The following very important theorem is the predicate analog of the statement that a propositional formula is a tautology if and only if it is provable.

### 2.2.2 *The Gödel Completeness Theorem*

For any predicate formula, the conditions

$$\models F \quad \text{and} \quad \vdash F$$

are equivalent.

Half of this theorem is just as easy to prove as in the propositional case. Specifically, suppose that $\vdash F$. Then since all the axioms of predicate calculus are universally valid and the predicate-calculus rules of inference preserve universal validity, $F$ must be universally valid, i.e. $\models F$.

The other, more difficult half of this theorem will be proved later, after some preparation. Much as in the case of the propositional calculus, this result can be generalized as follows. Let $S$ designate any set of syntactically well-formed formulae of the predicate calculus. Write

$$S \models F$$

to indicate that, for each interpretation $I$ and assignment $A$ covering both $F$ and all the formulae in $S$, we have $\mathsf{Val}(I, A, F) = 1$ whenever $\mathsf{Val}(I, A, G) = 1$ for all $G$ in $S$. Also, write

$$S \vdash F$$

to indicate that $F$ follows by predicate proof if the statements in $S$ are added to the axioms of predicate calculus. Suppose that none of the formulae in $S$ contain any free variables (formulae with this property are usually called *sentences*). Then for any predicate formula, the conditions

$$S \models F \quad \text{and} \quad S \vdash F$$

are equivalent. (An easy example, given below, shows that we cannot omit the condition 'none of the formulae in $S$ contain any free variables'.) The derivation of this from the more restricted result given by the Gödel completeness theorem is almost the same as the corresponding propositional proof. For the moment we will consider only the case in which $S$ is finite. Suppose first that $S \models F$ and let $C$ designate the conjunction

$$G_1 \,\&\, \cdots \,\&\, G_k$$

of all the formulae in $S$. Let $I$ and $A$ be, respectively, an interpretation and an assignment which cover $C \to F$ (i.e. cover both $F$ and all the formulae in $S$). Then as in the propositional case it follows that $\mathsf{Val}(I, A, C) = 1$ if and only if $\mathsf{Val}(I, A, G) = 1$ for all $G$ in $S$. Hence

$$\begin{aligned}\mathsf{Val}(I, A, C \to F) &= \mathsf{Val}\big(I, A, (\neg C) \vee F\big) \\ &= \max\big(1 - \mathsf{Val}(I, A, C), \mathsf{Val}(I, A, F)\big) = 1,\end{aligned}$$

for all such $I$ and $A$. Hence

$$\models C \to F$$

follows using the Gödel Completeness Theorem, as stated above, and so it follows that

$$\vdash C \to F,$$

i.e. $C \to F$ can be proved from the axioms of predicate calculus alone. But then if the statements in $S$ are added as additional axioms we can prove $F$ by first proving $C \to F$, then using the statements in $S$ to prove the conjunction $C$, and finally proving $F$ by modus ponens from $C \to F$ and $C$. This shows that $S \models F$ implies $S \vdash F$.

Next suppose that there exists a formula $F$ such that $S \vdash F$, but that $S \models F$ is false. Let $F$ be such a formula with the shortest possible proof from $S$, and let $I$ and $A$ be, respectively, any interpretation and assignment $A$ covering both $F$ and all the formulae in $S$ such that $\mathsf{Val}(I, A, G) = 1$ for every statement $G$ in $S$, but $\mathsf{Val}(I, A, F) = 0$. The final step of a shortest proof of $F$ from $S$ cannot be either the citation of an axiom or the citation of a statement of $S$, since in both these cases we would have $\mathsf{Val}(I, A, F) = 1$. Hence this final step is either a modus ponens inference from two formulae $p$, $p \to F$ appearing earlier in the proof, or a generalization inference from one such formula $p$. In the modus ponens case we must have $S \models p$, $S \models p \to F$ by inductive assumption. Hence $\mathsf{Val}(I, A, p \to F)$ and $\mathsf{Val}(I, A, p)$ are both 1, and therefore so is $\mathsf{Val}(I, A, F)$, a contradiction.

In the remaining case, i.e. that of a generalization inference, we must have $S \models p$, where $F$ has the form $(\forall x \mid p)$, for some predicate variable $x$. Since the statements in $S$ have no free variables we have $\mathsf{Val}(I, A', G) = 1$ for every statement $G$ in $S$ and every assignment $A'$ which is identical to $A$ except on the variable $x$, so that $\mathsf{Val}(I, A', p) = 1$. But then

$$\mathsf{Val}\big(I, A, \text{`}(\forall x \mid p)\text{'}\big)$$

is the minimum of $\mathsf{Val}(I, A', p)$, taken over all such $A'$, and therefore it follows that $\mathsf{Val}(I, A, \text{`}(\forall x \mid p)\text{'}) = 1$, i.e. $\mathsf{Val}(I, A, F) = 1$, which is again a contradiction. This shows that $S \vdash F$ implies $S \models F$, completing our proof that the conditions $S \models F$ and $S \vdash F$ are equivalent, at least in the case in which $S$ is finite. We will see later that the condition that the set $S$ is finite can be dropped. In fact, we can notice right away that the derivation given above of $S \models F$ from $S \vdash F$ holds also in the case in which $S$ is infinite. Thus, in order to fully establish the generalization of the Gödel completeness theorem, we are only left with proving that $S \models F$ implies $S \vdash F$, for every infinite set $S$ of predicate formulae none of which has occurrences of free variables.

We conclude this subsection by noting that the result just stated fails if the formulae in $S$ are allowed to contain free variables. To see this, consider the simple case in which $S$ consists of the single formula $P(x)$. If this formula were added to the set of axioms of the predicate calculus, we could give the proof

| | |
|---|---|
| $P(x)$ | [axiom] |
| $\big(\forall x \mid P(x)\big)$ | [generalization] |
| $\big(\forall x \mid P(x)\big) \rightarrow P(y)$ | [predicate axiom (v)] |
| $P(y)$ | [modus ponens] |

Hence we could have $\{P(x)\} \vdash P(y)$. But $\{P(x)\} \models P(y)$ is false, since we can set up a 2-point universe $\mathcal{U} = \{a, b\}$, the assignment $A(x) = a$, $A(y) = b$, and the interpretation $I$ such that $I(P)(a) = 1$ and $I(P)(b) = 0$.

### 2.2.3 Working with Universally Valid Predicate Formulae. A Few Simple Examples of Predicate Proof

A few basic theorems of predicate calculus are needed for later use. One such is

$$\big((\forall x \mid P \rightarrow Q) \;\&\; (\exists x \mid P)\big) \rightarrow (\exists x \mid Q).$$

The following proof of this statement, and two other sample proofs given later in this section, illustrate some of the techniques of direct, fully detailed predicate proof. By predicate axiom (v) we have

$$(\forall x \mid P \rightarrow Q) \rightarrow (P \rightarrow Q),$$

and from this by purely propositional reasoning we have

$$(\forall x \mid P \to Q) \to \big((\neg Q) \to (\neg P)\big).$$

By the (strong) rule of generalization this gives

$$(\forall x \mid P \to Q) \to \big(\forall x \,\big|\, \big((\neg Q) \to (\neg P)\big)\big).$$

Axiom (ii) now tells us that

$$\big(\big(\forall x \,\big|\, \big((\neg Q) \to (\neg P)\big)\big) \,\&\, \big(\forall x \mid (\neg Q)\big)\big) \to \big(\forall x \mid (\neg P)\big),$$

so by propositional reasoning we have

$$(\forall x \mid P \to Q) \to \big(\big(\forall x \mid (\neg Q)\big) \to \big(\forall x \mid (\neg P)\big)\big),$$

and also

$$(\forall x \mid P \to Q) \to \big(\big(\neg\big(\forall x \mid (\neg P)\big)\big) \to \big(\neg\big(\forall x \mid (\neg Q)\big)\big)\big).$$

Since by predicate axiom (iii) we have

$$\big(\neg\big(\forall x \mid (\neg P)\big)\big) \leftrightarrow (\exists x \mid P)$$

and

$$\big(\neg\big(\forall x \mid (\neg Q)\big)\big) \leftrightarrow (\exists x \mid Q),$$

our target statement

$$\big((\forall x \mid P \to Q) \,\&\, (\exists x \mid P)\big) \to (\exists x \mid Q)$$

now follows propositionally.

The following is a useful general principle of the predicate calculus whose universal validity is readily understood intuitively, and which can also be proved formally within the predicate calculus.

Suppose that a predicate formula of the form

$$A \leftrightarrow B$$

has been proved and that $F$ is a syntactically legal predicate formula such that $A$ appears as a subformula of $F$. Let $G$ be the result of replacing some such occurrence of $A$ in $F$ by an occurrence of $B$. Then $F \leftrightarrow G$ is also a theorem.

To show this, note that $F$ can be built up starting from $A$ by steps, each of which either joins subformulae together using a propositional operator, or quantifies a formula. Hence it is enough to show that if

$$H_2 \leftrightarrow H_3 \tag{2.5}$$

has already been proved, then

(a) $(H_1 \mathbin{\&} H_2) \leftrightarrow (H_1 \mathbin{\&} H_3)$
(b) $(H_1 \vee H_2) \leftrightarrow (H_1 \vee H_3)$
(c) $(H_1 \leftrightarrow H_2) \leftrightarrow (H_1 \leftrightarrow H_3)$
(d) $(H_1 \rightarrow H_2) \leftrightarrow (H_1 \rightarrow H_3)$
(e) $(H_2 \rightarrow H_1) \leftrightarrow (H_3 \rightarrow H_1)$
(f) $(\neg H_2) \leftrightarrow (\neg H_3)$
(g) $(\forall x \mid H_2) \leftrightarrow (\forall x \mid H_3)$
(h) $(\exists x \mid H_2) \leftrightarrow (\exists x \mid H_3)$

can be proved as well. Notice that (a)–(f) follow readily from (2.5) by propositional reasoning. So to prove our claim we have only to establish that (g) and (h) follow from (2.5) too. This can be shown as follows. By propositional reasoning and the predicate rule of generalization, statement (2.5) yields

$$(\forall x \mid H_2 \rightarrow H_3).$$

By axiom (ii) we have

$$\big((\forall x \mid H_2 \rightarrow H_3) \mathbin{\&} (\forall x \mid H_2)\big) \rightarrow (\forall x \mid H_3),$$

so by propositional reasoning we get

$$(\forall x \mid H_2) \rightarrow (\forall x \mid H_3).$$

The formula

$$(\forall x \mid H_3) \rightarrow (\forall x \mid H_2)$$

can be derived in the same way, and so we have

$$(\forall x \mid H_2) \leftrightarrow (\forall x \mid H_3).$$

Since (2.5) yields

$$(\neg H_2) \leftrightarrow (\neg H_3)$$

by propositional reasoning, it follows in the same way that

$$\big(\forall x \mid (\neg H_2)\big) \leftrightarrow \big(\forall x \mid (\neg H_3)\big)$$

and so

$$\big(\neg(\forall x \mid (\neg H_2))\big) \leftrightarrow \big(\neg(\forall x \mid (\neg H_3))\big).$$

It follows by predicate axiom (iii) and propositional reasoning that

$$(\exists x \mid H_2) \leftrightarrow (\exists x \mid H_3),$$

completing the proof of our claim.

The following 'change of bound variables' law is still another rule of obvious universal validity, which as usual can be proved formally within the predicate calculus.

Let $F$ be a syntactically well-formed predicate formula containing $x$ as a free variable, let $y$ be a variable not occurring in $F$, and let $F(x \hookrightarrow y)$ be the result of replacing every free occurrence of $x$ by an occurrence of $y$. Then

$$(\forall x \mid F) \leftrightarrow \big(\forall y \mid F(x \hookrightarrow y)\big)$$

and

$$(\exists x \mid F) \leftrightarrow \big(\exists y \mid F(x \hookrightarrow y)\big)$$

are universally valid predicate formulae. To show this, we first use predicate axiom (v) to get

$$(\forall x \mid F) \rightarrow F(x \hookrightarrow y),$$

and so

$$(\forall x \mid F) \rightarrow \big(\forall y \mid F(x \hookrightarrow y)\big)$$

follows by the (strong) rule of generalization, since $y$ does not occur freely in $(\forall x \mid F)$.

Since replacing each free occurrence of $x$ in $F$ by $y$ and then each $y$ by $x$ brings us back to the original $x$, we have

$$F(x \hookrightarrow y)(y \hookrightarrow x) = F.$$

Thus the argument just given can be used again to show that

$$\big(\forall y \mid F(x \hookrightarrow y)\big) \rightarrow (\forall x \mid F),$$

and so it results propositionally that

$$\big(\forall y \mid F(x \hookrightarrow y)\big) \leftrightarrow (\forall x \mid F).$$

Applying the same argument to '$\neg F$' we can get

$$\big(\neg(\forall y \mid \neg F(x \hookrightarrow y))\big) \leftrightarrow \big(\neg(\forall x \mid \neg F)\big),$$

and so

$$\big(\exists y \mid F(x \hookrightarrow y)\big) \leftrightarrow (\exists x \mid F),$$

using predicate axiom (iii).

The observations just made allow any predicate formula $F$ to be transformed, via a sequence of formulae all provably equivalent to each other, into an equivalent formula $G$ all of whose quantifiers appear to the extreme left of the formula. To achieve this, we must also use the following auxiliary group of predicate rules, which apply if the variable $x$ does not occur freely in $Q$:

(a) $(\forall x \mid P \vee Q) \leftrightarrow ((\forall x \mid P) \vee Q)$
(b) $(\forall x \mid P \,\&\, Q) \leftrightarrow ((\forall x \mid P) \,\&\, Q)$

(c) $(\forall x \mid P \rightarrow Q) \leftrightarrow ((\exists x \mid P) \rightarrow Q)$
(d) $(\forall x \mid Q \rightarrow P) \leftrightarrow (Q \rightarrow (\forall x \mid P))$
(e) $(\exists x \mid P \vee Q) \leftrightarrow ((\exists x \mid P) \vee Q)$
(f) $(\exists x \mid P \,\&\, Q) \leftrightarrow ((\exists x \mid P) \,\&\, Q)$
(g) $(\exists x \mid P \rightarrow Q) \leftrightarrow ((\forall x \mid P) \rightarrow Q)$
(h) $(\exists x \mid Q \rightarrow P) \leftrightarrow (Q \rightarrow (\exists x \mid P))$.

These rules can be proved as follows. Predicate axiom (v) gives

$$(\forall x \mid P) \rightarrow P,$$

and so by propositional reasoning from the tautology

$$\big((\forall x \mid P) \rightarrow P\big) \rightarrow \Big(\big((\forall x \mid P) \vee Q\big) \rightarrow (P \vee Q)\Big),$$

we get

$$\big((\forall x \mid P) \vee Q\big) \rightarrow (P \vee Q).$$

Since $x$ does not occur freely in $((\forall x \mid P) \vee Q)$, generalization now gives

$$\big((\forall x \mid P) \vee Q\big) \rightarrow (\forall x \mid P \vee Q).$$

Conversely we get

$$(\forall x \mid P \vee Q) \rightarrow (P \vee Q)$$

from predicate axiom (v), and so

$$\big((\forall x \mid P \vee Q) \,\&\, (\neg Q)\big) \rightarrow P.$$

Since $x$ does not occur freely in $((\forall x \mid P \vee Q) \,\&\, (\neg Q))$, by generalization we get

$$\big((\forall x \mid P \vee Q) \,\&\, (\neg Q)\big) \rightarrow (\forall x \mid P),$$

and then

$$(\forall x \mid P \vee Q) \rightarrow \big((\forall x \mid P) \vee Q\big),$$

so altogether

$$(\forall x \mid P \vee Q) \leftrightarrow \big((\forall x \mid P) \vee Q\big),$$

proving (a).

To prove (b) we reason as follows.

$$(\forall x \mid P \,\&\, Q) \rightarrow (P \,\&\, Q)$$

by axiom (v), so

$$(\forall x \mid P \,\&\, Q) \rightarrow P$$

by propositional reasoning. Since $x$ does not occur freely in $(\forall x \mid P \,\&\, Q)$, by generalization we derive

$$(\forall x \mid P \,\&\, Q) \to (\forall x \mid P)$$

from this. Thus, by propositional reasoning, we obtain

$$(\forall x \mid P \,\&\, Q) \to \big((\forall x \mid P) \,\&\, Q\big).$$

Conversely, since

$$\big((\forall x \mid P) \,\&\, Q\big) \to (\forall x \mid P)$$

we have

$$\big((\forall x \mid P) \,\&\, Q\big) \to P$$

by axiom (v) and propositional reasoning. Since

$$\big((\forall x \mid P) \,\&\, Q\big) \to Q$$

is propositional, we get

$$\big((\forall x \mid P) \,\&\, Q\big) \to (P \,\&\, Q),$$

and now

$$\big((\forall x \mid P) \,\&\, Q\big) \to (\forall x \mid P \,\&\, Q)$$

follows by generalization, since $x$ does not occur freely in $(\forall x \mid P) \,\&\, Q$. Altogether this gives

$$\big((\forall x \mid P) \,\&\, Q\big) \leftrightarrow (\forall x \mid P \,\&\, Q),$$

i.e. (b).

Statement (c) now follows via the chain of equivalences

$$\begin{aligned}(\forall x \mid P \to Q) &\leftrightarrow \big(\forall x \mid (\neg P) \vee Q\big)\\ &\leftrightarrow \big((\forall x \mid (\neg P)) \vee Q\big)\\ &\leftrightarrow \big((\neg(\forall x \mid (\neg P))) \to Q\big)\\ &\leftrightarrow \big((\exists x \mid P) \to Q\big).\end{aligned}$$

Similarly statement (d) follows via the chain of equivalences

$$\begin{aligned}(\forall x \mid Q \to P) &\leftrightarrow \big(\forall x \mid (\neg Q) \vee P\big)\\ &\leftrightarrow \big((\neg Q) \vee (\forall x \mid P)\big)\\ &\leftrightarrow \big(Q \to (\forall x \mid P)\big).\end{aligned}$$

The proofs of (e–h) are left to the reader.

### 2.2.4 The Prenex Normal Form of Predicate Formulae

The prenex normal form of a predicate formula $F$ is a logically equivalent formula in which quantifiers $\forall$ and $\exists$ appear only at the very start of the formula. Rules (a–h) can now be used iteratively in the following way to put an arbitrary formula $F$ into prenex normal form. We first change bound variables, using the equivalences derived above for this purpose, to ensure that all bound variables are distinct and that no bound variable is the same as any variable occurring freely. Then we use equivalences

$$(P \leftrightarrow Q) \leftrightarrow \big((P \rightarrow Q) \,\&\, (Q \rightarrow P)\big)$$

to replace all '$\leftrightarrow$' operators in our formula with combinations of implication and conjunction operators. After this, we search the syntax tree of the formula, looking for all quantifier nodes whose parent nodes are not already quantifier nodes, and moving them upward in a manner to be described. If there are no such nodes, then all the quantifiers occur in an unbroken sequence starting at the tree root, and so in the unparsed form of the formula they all occur at the left of the formula. The quantifier node moved at any moment should always be one that is as close as possible to the root of the syntax tree. Given that the parent of this quantifier is not itself a quantifier node, the parent must be marked with one of the Boolean operators &, $\vee$, $\rightarrow$, $\neg$. If the operator at the parent node is '$\neg$', we use one of the equivalences

$$(\forall x_1, \ldots, x_k \mid \neg P) \leftrightarrow \big(\neg(\exists x_1, \ldots, x_k \mid P)\big)$$

and

$$(\exists x_1, \ldots, x_k \mid \neg P) \leftrightarrow \big(\neg(\forall x_1, \ldots, x_k \mid P)\big)$$

to interchange the positions of the '$\neg$' operator and the quantifier. In the remaining cases we use one of the equivalences (a–h) to achieve a like interchange. When this process, each of whose steps transforms our original formula into an equivalent formula, can no longer continue, the formula that remains will clearly be in prenex normal form.

### 2.2.5 The Deduction Theorem

The Deduction Theorem of predicate calculus, which will be useful below, states that (provided that neither $F$ or any of the statements in $S$ contain any free variables) the implication $F \rightarrow G$ can be proved from a set $S$ of predicate axioms if and only if $G$ can be proved if $F$ is added to the set $S$ of axioms. Note that this is an easy consequence of the Gödel Completeness Theorem in the generalized form discussed at the start of this section. But in what follows we need to know that this result can be proved directly. This will now be shown.

**Theorem 2.2** (Deduction) *Let $S$ be a collection of predicate formulae with no free variables and let $S'$ be obtained from $S$ by adding to it a predicate formula $F$ with no free variables. Then*

$$S \vdash F \to G \quad \text{if and only if} \quad S' \vdash G,$$

*for any predicate formula $G$.*

*Proof* Let $S$, $S'$, $F$, and $G$ be as above. First assume that $S \vdash F \to G$ holds and let

$$H_1, H_2, \ldots, H_n,$$

with $H_n = F \to G$, be a proof of $F \to G$ from $S$. Then it follows immediately that

$$H_1, H_2, \ldots, H_n, F, G$$

is a proof of $G$ from $S'$.

Conversely, assume that $S' \vdash G$ and let

$$H_1, H_2, \ldots, H_n, \tag{2.6}$$

with $H_n = G$, be a proof of $G$ from $S'$. We can suppose without loss of generality that this proof does not use the strong variant of the rule of generalization stated earlier, but only the weaker form of this rule. Consider the sequence of predicate formulae

$$F \to H_1, \quad F \to H_2, \quad \ldots, \quad F \to H_n. \tag{2.7}$$

We will show that by inserting suitable auxiliary formulae into this sequence we can turn it into a proof from $S$ of $F \to G$. Indeed, for each $i = 1, 2, \ldots, n$ one of the following cases will apply:

(i) $H_i$ may be a predicate axiom or $H_i$ may be an element of $S$. In this case we insert the formulae

$$H_i$$
$$H_i \to (F \to H_i)$$

(of which the latter is a tautology) into (2.7) just before the formula $F \to H_i$.

(ii) $H_i$ may follow from $H_j$ and $H_k = H_j \to H_i$ by modus ponens step. In this case we insert the formulae

$$(F \to H_j) \to \big((F \to (H_j \to H_i)) \to (F \to H_i)\big)$$
$$\big(F \to (H_j \to H_i)\big) \to (F \to H_i)$$

(of which the former is a tautology) into (2.7) just before the formula $F \to H_i$.

(iii) In the remaining possible cases, namely if $H_i$ is derived from some earlier statement of (2.6) by the rule of generalization, or if $H_i = F$, we need not add any formula to (2.7).

Let

$$K_1, K_2, \ldots, K_m$$

be the sequence of predicate formulae generated in the manner just described. It is easy to check that this sequence constitutes a proof of $K_m = F \to G$ from $S$, provided that we now allow use of the strong variant of the rule of generalization. Since, as shown above, any such proof can be transformed into one in which all uses of the strong variant of the rule of generalization have been eliminated and only the weak form of this rule is used, it follows that $S \vdash F \to G$, concluding our proof of the deduction theorem. □

The deduction theorem admits the following semantic version, whose proof is left to the reader.

**Theorem 2.3** *Let $S$, $S'$, $F$, and $G$ be as in the statement of the deduction theorem. Then*

$$S \models F \to G \quad \textit{if and only if} \quad S' \models G.$$

### 2.2.6 *Definitions in Predicate Calculus; the Notion of 'Conservative Extension'*

Since the use of definitions to introduce new predicate and function symbols is fundamental to ordinary mathematical practice, it is important to understand the sense in which the predicate calculus accommodates this notion. The simplest definitions are algebraic, i.e. they simply introduce names for compound expressions written in terms of previously defined predicate and function symbols. Such definitions are unproblematical, since any use of them can be eliminated by expanding the new name back into the underlying expression which it abbreviates. But another, less trivial kind of definition is also essential. This is known as *definition by introduction of Skolem functions*. More specifically, once we have proved a formula of the form

$$\bigl(\forall y_1, \ldots, y_n \bigm| \bigl(\exists z \mid P(y_1, \ldots, y_n, z)\bigr)\bigr) \tag{2.8}$$

using the axioms of predicate calculus and some set $S$ of additional axioms (none of which should have any free variables), we can introduce any desired new, never previously used function name $f$ and add the statement

$$\bigl(\forall y_1, \ldots, y_n \mid P\bigl(y_1, \ldots, y_n, f(y_1, \ldots, y_n)\bigr)\bigr) \tag{2.9}$$

to $S$. The point is that, although this added statement clearly allows us to prove new statements concerning the newly introduced symbol $f$, it does not make it possible to prove any statement *not involving* $f$ that could not have been proved without its introduction.

This very important result can be called the *fundamental principle of definition*. To prove it we argue as follows. (But note that the following proof uses the Gödel Completeness Theorem, and so is entirely nonconstructive, i.e. it does not tell us how to produce the definition-free proof whose existence it asserts.) Let $P$, $S$, and $f$ be as above, and let $S'$ be obtained from $S$ by adjoining the formula (2.9) to $S$. Let $F$ be a formula not involving the symbol $f$, and suppose that $S' \vdash F$. Then we have $S' \models F$ by the Gödel completeness theorem (as extended above). Our goal is to show that $S \vdash F$. By the Gödel completeness theorem it is enough to show that $S \models F$. To this purpose, let $(\mathcal{U}, I, A)$ be an interpretation framework covering $F$ and the statements in $S$ and such that $\mathsf{Val}(I, A, G) = 1$ for each $G$ in $S$. Then we must show that $\mathsf{Val}(I, A, F) = 1$.

Introduce an auxiliary Boolean function $p(u_1, \ldots, u_n, u_{n+1})$, mapping the Cartesian product $\mathcal{U}^{n+1}$ of $n+1$ copies of $\mathcal{U}$ into $\{0, 1\}$, by setting

$$p(u_1, \ldots, u_n, u_{n+1}) = \mathsf{Val}\big(I, A(u_1, \ldots, u_n, u_{n+1}),\ `P(y_1, \ldots, y_n, z)'\big),$$

where $A(u_1, \ldots, u_n, u_{n+1})$ is the assignment which agrees with $A$ everywhere except on the variables $y_1, \ldots, y_n$ and $z$, for which variables we take

$$\begin{aligned} A(u_1, \ldots, u_n, u_{n+1})(y_1) &= u_1, \\ \vdots \quad & \quad \vdots \\ A(u_1, \ldots, u_n, u_{n+1})(y_n) &= u_n, \\ A(u_1, \ldots, u_n, u_{n+1})(z) &= u_{n+1}. \end{aligned}$$

Since

$$S \vdash \big(\forall y_1, \ldots, y_n \,\big|\, (\exists z \mid P(y_1, \ldots, y_n, z))\big),$$

we have

$$S \models \big(\forall y_1, \ldots, y_n \,\big|\, (\exists z \mid P(y_1, \ldots, y_n, z))\big)$$

and therefore

$$\begin{aligned} 1 &= \mathsf{Val}\big(I, A, \big(\forall y_1, \ldots, y_n \,\big|\, (\exists z \mid P(y_1, \ldots, y_n, z))\big)\big) \\ &= \min_{u_1, \ldots, u_n}\big(\max_{u_{n+1}}\big(\mathsf{Val}\big(I, A(u_1, \ldots, u_n, u_{n+1}), P(y_1, \ldots, y_n, z)\big)\big)\big) \\ &= \min_{u_1, \ldots, u_n}\big(\max_{u_{n+1}}\big(p(u_1, \ldots, u_n, u_{n+1})\big)\big), \end{aligned}$$

where the minima and maxima over the subscripts seen extend over all values in $\mathcal{U}$. Hence there exists a function $h$ from $\mathcal{U}^n$ into $\mathcal{U}$ such that

$$p\big(u_1, \ldots, u_n, h(u_1, \ldots, u_n)\big) = 1$$

for all $u_1, \ldots, u_n$ in $\mathcal{U}$. Let $I'$ be an interpretation which agrees with $I$ everywhere except on the function symbol $f$ and such that $I'(f)$ is the function $h$ just defined (which is, as required, a mapping from $\mathcal{U}^n$ to $\mathcal{U}$). Hence

$$\begin{aligned}1 &= \min_{u_1,\dots,u_n}\big(p\big(u_1,\dots,u_n,h(u_1,\dots,u_n)\big)\big)\\ &= \min_{u_1,\dots,u_n}\big(\mathsf{Val}\big(I', A(u_1,\dots,u_n),\ P\big(y_1,\dots,y_n,f(y_1,\dots,y_n)\big)\big)\big)\\ &= \mathsf{Val}\big(I', A, \big(\forall y_1,\dots,y_n \mid P\big(y_1,\dots,y_n,f(y_1,\dots,y_n)\big)\big)\big),\end{aligned}$$

where $A(u_1,\dots,u_n)$ is the assignment which agrees with $A$ everywhere except on the variables $y_1,\dots,y_n$, for which variables we take

$$\begin{aligned}A(u_1,\dots,u_n)(y_1) &= u_1,\\ &\vdots\\ A(u_1,\dots,u_n)(y_n) &= u_n.\end{aligned}$$

Since no formula $G$ in $S$ involves the function symbol $f$, we have

$$\mathsf{Val}(I', A, G) = \mathsf{Val}(I, A, G) = 1, \quad \text{for all } G \text{ in } S.$$

Therefore

$$\mathsf{Val}(I', A, F) = 1,$$

since, as observed above, $S' \models F$. But since the formula $F$ does not involve the function symbol $f$, we have

$$\mathsf{Val}(I, A, F) = 1,$$

proving that $S \models F$, and so $S \vdash F$. This concludes our proof of the fundamental principle of definition.

The central notion implicit in the preceding argument is worth capturing formally.

**Definition 2.8** Let $S$ be a set of predicate formulae not involving any free variables, and let $S'$ be a larger such set (possibly involving function and predicate symbols that do not occur in $S$). Then $S'$ is called a *conservative extension* of $S$ if

$$S' \vdash F \quad \text{implies} \quad S \vdash F,$$

for every formula $F$ involving no predicate or function symbols not present in one of the formulae of $S$.

The argument just given shows that the addition of formula (2.9) to any set $S$ of formulae not containing free variables for which (2.8) can be proved yields a conservative extension.

### 2.2.7 Proof of the Gödel Completeness Theorem

Now we come to the proof of the Gödel completeness theorem. To prove it we first show, without using it, that the theorem holds for a certain very limited form of Skolem definition, namely if we introduce a single new constant symbol $C$ (i.e. function symbol of 0 arguments) satisfying $P(C)$, provided that we have previously proved a predicate formula of the form

$$(\exists z \mid P(z)).$$

These constants are traditionally called *Henkin constants*, after Leon Henkin, who introduced the technique that we will use. Our first key lemma is as follows.

**Lemma 2.1** *Let $S$ be a collection of (syntactically well-formed) predicate formulae without free variables and let $C$ be a constant symbol not appearing in any of the formulae of $S$. For each formula $H$, let $H(C \hookrightarrow x)$ denote the result of replacing each occurrence of $C$ in $H$ by an occurrence of $x$, where $x$ designates a variable not otherwise used. Then, if $S \vdash H$, we have*

$$S \vdash H(C \hookrightarrow x).$$

In intuitive terms, this lemma tells us that if the axioms $S$ can be used to prove some statement about a constant which they never mention, they can be used to prove the same statement in which $C$ is replaced by a variable.

*Proof* Suppose that Lemma 2.1 fails for some $H$. Then, proceeding inductively, we can suppose that Lemma 2.1 holds for all statements having proofs shorter than that of $H$. Without loss of generality, we can assume that the variable $x$ is not used in the proof of $H$. Consider the final step in the proof of $H$. This must either be (i) a citation of a predicate axiom; (ii) a citation of some statement in $S$; (iii) a modus ponens step involving two formulae $G$ and $G \to H$ proved earlier; (iv) a generalization step from a formula $G$ proved earlier. Concerning case (i), if $H$ is a predicate axiom so is $H(C \hookrightarrow x)$. In case (ii), namely if $H$ is a member of $S$, $H$ cannot involve the constant $C$, so that $H(C \hookrightarrow x) = H$ and therefore we plainly have $S \vdash H(C \hookrightarrow x)$.

Next consider case (iii). Since in this case $G$ and $G \to H$ both have shorter proofs than that of $H$, it follows by inductive assumption that $S \vdash G(C \hookrightarrow x)$ and $S \vdash (G \to H)(C \hookrightarrow x)$, i.e. $S \vdash G(C \hookrightarrow x) \to H(C \hookrightarrow x)$. Therefore it follows by a modus ponens step that $S \vdash H(C \hookrightarrow x)$.

Finally we consider case (iv). In this case $G$ has a shorter proof than that of its generalization $H = (\forall z \mid G)$. Hence by inductive assumption $S \vdash G(C \hookrightarrow x)$, so that, by the rule of generalization, $S \vdash (\forall z \mid G(C \hookrightarrow x))$ and therefore $S \vdash H(C \hookrightarrow x)$, since

$$H(C \hookrightarrow x) = (\forall z \mid G)(C \hookrightarrow x) = \big(\forall z \mid G(C \hookrightarrow x)\big),$$

proving our claim in case (iv) and thus completing our proof of Lemma 2.1. □

Next we prove the following consequence of Lemma 2.1.

**Lemma 2.2** *Let $S$ be a collection of (syntactically well-formed) predicate formulae without free variables. Let $F$ be a predicate formula involving the one free variable $y$. Let $C$ be a constant symbol not appearing in any of the formulae of $S$ or in $F$, and let $F(y \hookrightarrow C)$ denote the formula obtained from $F$ by replacing each occurrence of $y$ by an occurrence of $C$. Suppose that*

$$S \vdash (\exists y \mid F).$$

*Let $S'$ be the union of $S$ and the statement $F(y \hookrightarrow C)$. Then $S'$ is a conservative extension of $S$.*

*Proof* Let $H$ be a formula involving only the symbols appearing in $S$, so that in particular the constant $C$ does not occur in $H$. Suppose that $S' \vdash H$. By the Deduction Theorem we have

$$S \vdash F(y \hookrightarrow C) \rightarrow H.$$

By Lemma 2.1 this last formula yields

$$S \vdash \big(F(y \hookrightarrow C) \rightarrow H\big)(C \hookrightarrow x),$$

where $x$ is a variable not otherwise used. Therefore

$$S \vdash F(y \hookrightarrow x) \rightarrow H,$$

since $F(y \hookrightarrow C)(C \hookrightarrow x) = F(y \hookrightarrow x)$ and $H(C \hookrightarrow x) = H$. Applying the rule of generalization we obtain

$$S \vdash \big(\forall x \mid F(y \hookrightarrow x) \rightarrow H\big).$$

We have shown above that

$$\big(\big(\forall x \mid F(y \hookrightarrow x) \rightarrow H\big) \,\&\, \big(\exists x \mid F(y \hookrightarrow x)\big)\big) \rightarrow (\exists x \mid H)$$

and

$$(\exists y \mid F) \leftrightarrow \big(\exists x \mid F(y \hookrightarrow x)\big)$$

are universally valid. Thus, by propositional reasoning,

$$S \vdash (\exists x \mid H).$$

But since the variable $x$ does not occur freely in $H$, we have

$$\vdash \big(\forall x \mid (\neg H)\big) \leftrightarrow (\neg H)$$

by predicate axiom (iv), and so it follows propositionally that

$$\vdash \neg\big(\forall x \mid (\neg H)\big) \leftrightarrow H.$$

Predicate axiom (iii) then gives

$$\vdash (\exists x \mid H) \leftrightarrow H$$

and so $S \vdash H$, proving that $S'$ is a conservative extension of $S$. □

#### 2.2.7.1 The Remainder of the Proof: Predicate Consistency Principle

We will now complete our proof of the Gödel completeness theorem. For this, it is convenient to restate it in the following way.

**Predicate consistency principle** *Let S be a set of formulae, none containing free variables, such that S is* consistent, *i.e.* $S \vdash \mathsf{false}$ *is false. Then there exists a* model *for S, i.e. an interpretation framework* $(\mathcal{U}, I, A)$ *covering all the predicate and function symbols appearing in S, such that* $\mathsf{Val}(I, A, F) = 1$ *for each F in S. Conversely if there is a model for S then S is consistent.*

This is simply the statement that $S \vdash \mathsf{false}$ is false iff $S \models \mathsf{false}$ is false. For '$S \models \mathsf{false}$ is false' means that there is an interpretation framework $(\mathcal{U}, I, A)$ covering all the statements $F$ in $S$ such that $\mathsf{Val}(I, A, F) = 1$ for each $F$ in $S$, but nonetheless satisfying the (required) condition that $\mathsf{Val}(I, A, \mathsf{false}) = 0$.

It is an easy matter to see that the predicate consistency principle implies that for every set $S$ of predicate formulae with no free variables and for every predicate formula $F$ the following condition holds:

$$\textbf{if } S \models F \textbf{ then } S \vdash F. \tag{2.10}$$

Indeed, assume that $S \models F$ holds and that $S \vdash F$ is false. Then $S \vdash (\forall v_1, \ldots, v_n \mid F)$, where $v_1, \ldots, v_n$ are the free variables of $F$, must also be false, because otherwise by repeated use of axiom (v) and the rule of modus ponens $S \vdash F$ would follow. Let $S'$ be the set of predicate formulae obtained by adding the formula $\neg(\forall v_1, \ldots, v_n \mid F)$ to $S$. Then $S' \vdash \mathsf{false}$ must be false, because otherwise by the deduction theorem

$$S \vdash \neg(\forall v_1, \ldots, v_n \mid F) \rightarrow \mathsf{false}$$

would hold and therefore, by propositional reasoning, $S \vdash (\forall v_1, \ldots, v_n \mid F)$ would hold. Therefore the predicate consistency principle implies that $S'$ has a model, namely there exists an interpretation framework $(\mathcal{U}, I, A)$ covering all the statements $G$ of $S'$ and such that $\mathsf{Val}(I, A, G) = 1$ for all such $G$. Thus, in particular, we have $\mathsf{Val}(I, A, C) = 1$ for all the formulae $C$ in $S$ and $\mathsf{Val}(I, A, \neg(\forall v_1, \ldots, v_n \mid F)) = 1$. This last statement implies that there exists an assignment $A'$ such that $\mathsf{Val}(I, A', F) = 0$. Since all formulae in $S$ have no free variables, it follows that $\mathsf{Val}(I, A', C) = \mathsf{Val}(I, A, C) = 1$ for each formula $C$ in $S$, thus contradicting our initial assumption that $S \models F$ holds, and thereby proving statement (2.10).

But the statement (2.10) implies, and indeed is a bit more general than, the Gödel completeness theorem. This shows that the Gödel completeness theorem will follow if we can prove the predicate consistency principle.

*Proof* To this end assume first that $S$ is not consistent. Then $S \vdash$ **false** holds. But then, as was shown earlier, $S \models$ **false** follows, so that $S$ cannot have any model.

For the converse, assume that $S$ is consistent, in which case we must show that $S$ has a model. We can and shall suppose that all our formulae are in prenex normal form, since we have seen that given any set of formulae there is an equivalent set of prenex normal formulae. We proceed in a kind of 'algorithmic' style, to generate a steadily increasing collection of formulae known to be consistent. At the end of this process it will be easy to construct a model of the set $S$ of statements using these formulae and a bit of purely propositional reasoning. The idea of the proof is to introduce enough new constants $C$ to ensure that, for each original existentially quantified formula

$$(\exists x \mid F),$$

there exists a $C$ for which

$$F(x \hookrightarrow C)$$

is known to be true. To this end, we maintain the following lists and sets of formulae, along with one set of auxiliary constants. These lists and sets can be (countably) infinite and will steadily grow larger. In order to be certain that there exist only finitely many constants with names below any given length, it will be convenient for us to suppose that all constants have names like '$C$', '$CC$', '$CCC$', .... The lists and sets we maintain are then:

SC: the set of all constants introduced so far.
SUF: the set of all universally quantified formulae generated so far.
SNQ: the set of all formulae containing no quantifiers generated so far.
LEF: the list of all existentially quantified formulae generated so far. This list is always kept in order of increasing length of the formulae on it. Formulae of the same length are arranged in alphabetical order. Each formula on the list LEF is marked either as 'processed' or 'unprocessed'.

These data objects are initialized as follows. SC initially contains all the constants appearing in functions of $S$. SUF contains all the formulae of $S$ which start with a universal quantifier. SNQ contains all the formulae of $S$ which contain no quantifiers. LEF contains all the formulae of $S$ which start with an existential quantifier. These are arranged in the order just described. All the formulae on LEF are originally marked 'unprocessed'.

The auxiliary set FS consists of all function symbols appearing in formulae of $S$.

The following processing steps are repeated as often as they apply, causing our four data objects to grow steadily. Note that SC is always finite, becoming infinite only in the limit, but that SUF, SNQ, and LEF can be infinite during the process that we now describe.

(a) Whenever new constants are added to SC or new universally quantified formulae to SUF, all the constants on SC are combined in all possible ways with function symbols of FS to create new terms, and these terms are substituted in all possible ways for initial universally quantified variables in formulae of SUF (all the variables up to the first existentially quantified variable, if any), thereby generating new formulae, some starting with existential quantifiers (these are added to LEF if not already there, following which LEF is rearranged into its required order), others with no quantifiers at all (these are added to SNQ if not already there).
(b) After each step (a), or if no step (a) is needed, we examine LEF to find the first formula $(\exists x \mid F)$ on it not yet marked 'processed'. For this formula, we generate a new constant symbol $C$, build the formula $F(x \hookrightarrow C)$ produced by replacing each free occurrence of $x$ in $F$ by $C$, and add this formula to SUF or LEF or SNQ, depending on whether it starts with a universal quantifier, starts with an existential quantifier, or has no quantifiers at all, and finally add the new constant $C$ to SC. It is understood that the list LEF must always be maintained in lexicographic order. Finally, the formula $(\exists x \mid F)$ on LEF is then marked 'processed'.

Processing begins as if the set of constants appearing in the formulae of $S$ have just been added to SC, and so with step (a). (If there are no such constants, we must generate one initial constant symbol $C$ to start processing.)

At the end of this (perhaps infinitely long) sequence of processing steps, we may have generated a countably infinite list of constants as SC, and put infinitely many formulae into both of the sets SUF and SNQ and on the list LEF. But we can be sure that it is never possible to prove a contradiction from our set of formulae. For otherwise a contradiction would result from some finite set of formulae, all of which would have been added to our collection at some stage in the process we have described. But by assumption our formulae are consistent to begin with. Moreover no step of type (a) can spoil consistency, since only predicate consequences of previously added formulae are added during such steps. Nor can steps of type (b) spoil consistency, since it was proved above that steps of this kind yield conservative extensions of the set of formulae previously present.

It follows that at the end of the process we have described the set SNQ of unquantified formulae that results is consistent, i.e. that every finite subset of this set of formulae is consistent. We have proved above that this implies that SNQ has a propositional model, i.e. that we can assign a 0/1 value $\mathsf{Va}(T)$ to each atomic formula $T$ appearing in any of the formulae $F$ of SNQ, in such a way that each such $F$ evaluates to 'true' if the atomic formulae appearing in it are replaced by these values, and the standard rules for calculating Boolean truth values of propositional combinations are then applied. Note for use below that each of the atomic formulae $T$ of the set AT of all such formulae appearing in any $F$ has the form $P(t_1, \ldots, t_k)$, where $P$ is a predicate symbol and $t_1, \ldots, t_k$ are 'constant' terms (i.e. terms devoid of variables).

Now we show that there exists a model whose universe is the set CT of all constant terms generated by applying the function symbols in FS to the constants in

SC in all possible ways. (The resulting set of terms is the so called *free universe* FU generated by these constants and the function symbols in FS.) Each $k$-adic function symbol $f$ in $FS$ is trivially associated with a mapping $I(f)$ from the Cartesian product $\mathsf{FU}^k$ of $k$ copies of FU into FU, namely we can put

$$I(f)(t_1, \ldots, t_k) = f(t_1, \ldots, t_k)$$

for all lists $t_1, \ldots, t_k$ of terms. For this $I$ and every possible assignment $A$ it is immediate that

$$\mathsf{Val}(I, A, t) = t$$

for each term $t$ in FU. A 0/1 valued function on $\mathsf{FU}^k$ can now be associated with each predicate symbol $P$ appearing in a formula of $S$, namely we can write

$$I(P)(t_1, \ldots, t_k) = \mathsf{Va}\big(P(t_1, \ldots, t_k)\big)$$

for each atomic formula $P(t_1, \ldots, t_k)$ appearing in one of the formulae of SNQ, and define $I(P)(t_1, \ldots, t_k)$ arbitrarily for all other atomic formulae; here 'Va' is the Boolean assignment of truth values described in the preceding paragraph. It is then immediate that for every assignment $A$ we have

$$\mathsf{Val}(I, A, F) = 1,$$

for each formula of SNQ. It remains to be shown that we must have $\mathsf{Val}(I, A, F) = 1$ for the quantified formulae of SUF and LEF also and for every assignment $A$. Suppose that this is not the case. Then there exists a formula $F$ with $n > 0$ quantifiers for which $\mathsf{Val}(I, A, F) = 0$. Proceeding inductively, we may suppose that $n$ is the smallest number of quantifiers for which this is possible. If $F$ belongs to LEF, then it has the form $(\exists x \mid G)$, and by construction we will have added a formula of the form $G(x \hookrightarrow C)$, with some constant symbol $C$, to our collection. Since $G(x \hookrightarrow C)$ has fewer quantifiers than $n$, we must have $\mathsf{Val}(I, A, G(x \hookrightarrow C)) = 1$, and so $\mathsf{Val}(I, A, F)$, which is the maximum over a collection of values including $\mathsf{Val}(I, A, G(x \hookrightarrow C))$, must be 1 also.

It only remains to consider the case in which $F$ belongs to SUF, and so has the form

$$(\forall x_1, \ldots, x_m \mid G)$$

for some $G$. In this case, all formulae $G(x_1 \hookrightarrow t_1, \ldots, x_m \hookrightarrow t_m)$, where $t_1, \ldots, t_m$ are any terms in our universe, namely the set TERM of all constant terms generated by applying the function symbols in FS to the constants in SC in all possible ways, will have been added to our collection. All these formulae have fewer quantifiers than $n$, and so we must have

$$\mathsf{Val}\big(I, A, G(x_1 \hookrightarrow t_1, \ldots, x_m \hookrightarrow t_m)\big) = 1$$

for all these terms. Hence the minimum of all these values, namely

$$\mathsf{Val}\big(I, A, (\forall x_1, \ldots, x_m \mid G)\big)$$

must also have the value 1. This completes our proof of the predicate consistency principle and in turn of the Gödel completeness theorem. □

The argument just given clearly leads to the following slightly stronger result.

**Corollary 2.1** *Let S be a set of formulae in prenex normal form, and let SNQ be the set of all unquantified formulae generated by the process described above. Then S is consistent, i.e. it has a model, if and only if SNQ, regarded as a collection of propositions whose propositional symbols are the atomic formulae appearing in SNQ, is propositionally consistent.*

*Proof* As shown above, the set of statements in SNQ must be consistent if *S* is consistent. The argument given above establishes the converse, i.e. it shows that *S* has a model if SNQ is propositionally consistent. □

#### 2.2.7.2 Immediate Consequences of the Gödel Completeness Theorem

The preceding corollary implies that in situations in which we can be sure that the procedure described in the proof of the predicate consistency principle will produce sets SC, SUF, SNQ, and a list LEF all of which remain finite, this procedure can be used as an algorithm to decide in a finite number of steps whether or not a given finite set *S* of prenex normal formulae (none of which involves free variables) is consistent. One case in which this remark applies is that of pure '$\exists \cdots \exists \forall \cdots \forall$' formulae, as defined by the following conditions:

i. *S* is a finite set of formulae in prenex normal form not involving free variables.
ii. No formula in *S* involves function symbols of arity greater than zero (i.e., the only terms allowed in these formulae are variables and constant terms). Of course, any number of predicate symbols can be used.
iii. No existential quantifier can follow a universal quantifier in any formula of *S*.

Note that the condition iii, implies that the sequence of quantifiers prefixed to any '$\exists \cdots \exists \forall \cdots \forall$' formula has the form

$$(\exists y_1, \ldots, y_m \mid (\forall x_1, \ldots, x_n \mid \cdots$$

To see why in this case the procedure described in the proof of the predicate consistency principle must converge after a finite number of steps, note first of all that since there are no function symbol the only terms substituted for universally quantified variables in step (a) of that procedure are constants. These constants must either be present in our initial formulae or be generated in some step of the procedure described. But since all existential quantifiers precede all universal quantifiers, the aforesaid step (a) will never generate any new formula containing existential quantifiers. Hence the number of constants generated is no greater than the number of existential quantifiers contained in our original collection of formulae, and substitution of these for all the universally quantified variables present will generate no more than a finite set of formulae.

**Decidability for the Bernays–Schönfinkel Sentences** An interesting special case of the foregoing is that when we are given a finite set $S$ of pure '$\exists \ldots \exists \forall \ldots \forall$' formulae, involving no free variables, as described above, and one additional formula $F$ of the same kind and in which no universal quantifier follows an existential quantifier, and we want to determine whether $S \vdash F$ holds. Let $S'$ be the set of formulae obtained by adding the formula '$\neg F$' to $S$. Then we know that $S \vdash F$ holds if and only $S'$ is inconsistent. But by moving the connective $\neg$ in '$\neg F$' across the quantifier prefix of $F$, we obtain another set $S^*$ which is equivalent to $S'$ and is still a finite set of pure '$\exists$-$\forall$' formulae, whose consistency can be tested algorithmically in the manner just explained.

**The Löwenheim–Skolem Theorem** The argument given in the proof of the predicate consistency principle allows us to derive another interesting fact, known as the Löwenheim–Skolem Theorem. This states that any consistent countable set of sentences has a countable model. Indeed, if $S$ is countable (as was implicitly assumed in our proof of the predicate consistency principle) then all the sets SC, SUF, SNQ, FS, and the list LEF maintained by the process described in the proof of the predicate consistency principle are countable at each stage, and so must also be countable in the limit. Therefore the model constructed from SNQ using the technique seen above must also be countable.

**The Compactness Theorem** A set $S$ of predicate formulae is said to be *satisfiable* if it has a model. The Compactness Theorem states that if $S$ is a set of predicate sentences such that every finite subset of $S$ is satisfiable, then the whole infinite set $S$ is satisfiable. This theorem is an easy consequence of the predicate consistency principle. Indeed, let $S$ be a set of predicate sentences such that every finite subset of $S$ has a model, and assume that $S$ is not satisfiable. Then $S \models \mathsf{false}$ holds, so that by the predicate consistency principle we have $S \vdash \mathsf{false}$ also, i.e. there exists a proof of '$\mathsf{false}$' from $S$. Since any proof from $S$ can involve at most finitely many formulae of $S$, there must exist a finite subset $S'$ of $S$ such that $S' \vdash \mathsf{false}$ holds, and so by the predicate consistency principle $S' \models \mathsf{false}$ must hold. That is, $S'$ is not satisfiable, contradicting our initial hypothesis that every finite subset of $S$ is satisfiable.

### 2.2.7.3 Some Other Consequences of the Gödel Completeness Theorem

**Skolem Normal Form** Let $S$ be a countable (i.e. finite or denumerable) collection of syntactically well-formed predicate sentences. Putting each of these formulae into prenex normal form gives an equivalent set $S'$ of formulae, so that if $S$ has a model (i.e. it is consistent) so does $S'$. We will now describe a second normal form, called the *Skolem normal form*, into which the formulae of $S'$ can be put. We will see that if $S^{**}$ denotes the set of formulae in Skolem normal form derived from $S'$, then $S^{**}$ is consistent if and only if $S'$ (and $S$) is consistent. However, the formulae of $S^{**}$ are generally not equivalent to the formulae of $S'$ from which they derive. Thus $S^{**}$ and $S'$ (and $S$) are only *equiconsistent*, not *equivalent*.

By definition, a formula in prenex normal form is in Skolem normal form if and only if its prefixed list of quantifiers contains no existential quantifiers. To derive the Skolem normal form of a formula $F$ in $S'$, which must already be in prenex normal form, suppose that $F$ has the form

$$(\forall x_1, \ldots, x_k \mid (\exists y \mid G)). \tag{2.11}$$

Introduce a new function symbol $f$ of $k$ variables, along with a statement of the form

$$(\forall x_1, \ldots, x_k \mid G(y \hookrightarrow e)), \tag{2.12}$$

where $G(y \hookrightarrow e)$ is derived from $G$ by replacing every free appearance of the variable $y$ in $G$ by an appearance of the subexpression $e = f(x_1, \ldots, x_k)$. Let $S_1$ be the result of adding (2.12) to $S'$. We have seen above that $S_1$ is a conservative extension of $S'$. Hence if $S' \vdash$ **false** is false, so is $S_1' \vdash$ **false**, and conversely. That is, $S'$ and $S_1$ are equiconsistent.

Let $S^*$ be the set of statements obtained by dropping (2.11) from $S_1$. We shall show that $S'$ and $S^*$ are equiconsistent. But in $S^*$ the existentially quantified statement (2.11) has been replaced by (2.12) which has one fewer existential quantifier. It should be clear that by repeating this step as often as necessary, we can eliminate all existential quantifiers from our original set of statements, introducing function symbols in their stead. The resulting set of statements is the Skolem normal form of our original set. To prove that $S'$ and $S^*$ are equiconsistent, note first of all that, as we have already noted, $S^*$ is consistent if $S'$ is consistent. Suppose conversely that $S^*$ is consistent. We can deduce $G(y \hookrightarrow e)$ from (2.12) by $k$ successive applications of predicate axiom (v) and the rule of modus ponens. More specifically, we have

$$(\forall x_1, \ldots, x_k \mid G(y \hookrightarrow e)) \vdash G(y \hookrightarrow e).$$

But since

$$\vdash (\forall y \mid \neg G) \rightarrow (\neg G(y \hookrightarrow e))$$

by the same axiom (v), it follows that

$$(\forall x_1, \ldots, x_k \mid G(y \hookrightarrow e)) \vdash \neg(\forall y \mid \neg G).$$

Thus by predicate axiom (iii) we have

$$(\forall x_1, \ldots, x_k \mid G(y \hookrightarrow e)) \vdash (\exists y \mid G)$$

and so, by repeated application of the rule of generalization, we obtain

$$(\forall x_1, \ldots, x_k \mid G(y \hookrightarrow e)) \vdash (\forall x_1, \ldots, x_k \mid (\exists y \mid G)).$$

The deduction theorem now implies

$$\vdash (\forall x_1, \ldots, x_k \mid G(y \hookrightarrow e)) \rightarrow (\forall x_1, \ldots, x_k \mid (\exists y \mid G))$$

so that

$$S^* \vdash (\forall x_1, \ldots, x_k \mid (\exists y \mid G)).$$

This implies that exactly the same formulae can be derived from $S_1$ and $S^*$, so that these two sets of formulae are equiconsistent. Hence $S'$ and $S^*$ are equiconsistent, as required.

**The Herbrand Theorem** Herbrand's theorem, which gives a *semi-decision procedure* for the satisfiability of sets of predicate formulae given in Skolem normal form, can be stated as follows.

**Theorem 2.4** (Herbrand) *Let $S$ be a countable collection of predicate sentences, all having Skolem normal form. Let $D$ be the set of all function symbols appearing in the formulae of $S$. Let $SC$ be the set of individual constants (function symbols of zero variables) appearing in the formulae of $S$. (If there are no such constants, let $SC$ consist of just one artificially introduced individual constant, distinct from all the other symbols in $D$.) Let $T$ be the set of all terms which can be generated from the constants in $SC$ using the function symbols appearing in formulae of $S$. Let $S'$ be the set of formulae generated from $S$ by stripping off their quantifiers and substituting terms in $T$ for the variables of the resulting formulae in all possible ways. Then the set $S$ is consistent if and only if every finite subset of $S'$ is consistent when regarded as a collection of propositional formulae in which two atomic formulae correspond to the same propositional variable if and only if they are syntactically identical.*

*Proof* This is just the Corollary of the Gödel completeness theorem stated above, in the special case in which the formulae of $S$ have Skolem normal form, i.e. they contain no existential quantifiers. For in this case the construction we have used to prove that Theorem and Corollary generates no new constant symbols. □

Herbrand's theorem is often used as a technique for searching automatically for predicate-calculus proofs. If none of the formulae concerned have any free variables, we can show that a predicate formula $F$ follows from a set $S$ of such formulae by adjoining the negative of $F$ to $S$, then putting all the resulting formulae into Skolem normal form, and finally searching for the propositional contradiction of whose existence Herbrand's theorem assures us.

As a very simple example, consider the predicate theorem

$$\big(\exists y \,\big|\, (\forall x \mid P(x, y))\big) \to \big(\forall x \,\big|\, (\exists y \mid P(x, y))\big) \tag{2.13}$$

whose negation is

$$\big(\exists y \,\big|\, (\forall x \mid P(x, y))\big) \,\&\, \big(\exists x \,\big|\, (\forall y \mid \neg P(x, y))\big), \tag{2.14}$$

or, in Skolem normal form,

$$\big(\forall x \mid P(x, B)\big) \,\&\, \big(\forall y \mid \neg P(A, y)\big).$$

A substitution then gives the propositional contradiction $P(A, B) \,\&\, (\neg P(A, B))$, showing the impossibility of the negated statement (2.14), and so confirming the universal validity of (2.13).

A very large literature has developed concerning optimization of searches of this kind. Some of the resulting search techniques will be reviewed in Chap. 4.

## 2.3 Predicate Calculus with Equality as a Built-in

The simplicity of the equality relationship and its continual occurrence in mathematical arguments make it appropriate to extend the predicate calculus as defined above to a slightly larger version in which equality is a built-in. Syntactically we have only to make '=' a reserved symbol; semantically we need to introduce axioms for equality strong enough for the Gödel completeness theorem to remain valid. The following axioms suffice.

The axioms of the *equality-extended predicate calculus* are all the axioms of the (ordinary) predicate calculus (cf. Definition 2.7), plus

(vi) Any formula of the form

$$(\forall x, y, z \mid x = x \,\&\, \big((x = y) \to (y = x)\big) \,\&\, \big((x = y \,\&\, y = z) \to (x = z)\big)\big).$$

(vii) Any formula of the form

$$\big(\forall x, y \mid (x = y) \to \big(f(x_j \hookrightarrow x) = f(x_j \hookrightarrow y)\big)\big),$$

where $f$ is a $k$-adic functional expression $f(x_1, \ldots, x_k)$, and $f(x_j \hookrightarrow x)$ (resp. $f(x_j \hookrightarrow y)$) is the result of replacing the $j$th variable in it by an occurrence of $x$ (resp. $y$).

(viii) Any formula of the form

$$\big(\forall x, y \mid (x = y) \to \big(P(x_j \hookrightarrow x) \leftrightarrow P(x_j \hookrightarrow y)\big)\big),$$

where $P$ is a $k$-adic predicate expression $P(x_1, \ldots, x_k)$, and $P(x_j \hookrightarrow x)$ (resp. $P(x_j \hookrightarrow y)$) is the result of replacing the $j$th variable in it by an occurrence of $x$ (resp. $y$).

No new rules of inference are added.

The notion of 'model' is extended to this slightly enlarged version of the predicate calculus by agreeing that

(xi) If the formula $F$ is of the form '$t_1 = t_2$', then

$$\mathsf{Val}(I, A, F) = \textbf{if } \mathsf{Val}(I, A, t_1) = \mathsf{Val}(I, A, t_2) \textbf{ then } 1 \textbf{ else } 0 \textbf{ end if},$$

for every interpretation framework $(\mathscr{U}, I, A)$.

That is, the predicate which models the equality sign is simply the standard predicate of equality.

As before we want to show that the added predicate axioms evaluate to 1 in every model. This is clear for (vi), since it simply states the standard properties of equality. Similarly, since replacement of the arguments of any set-theoretic mapping by an equal argument never changes the map value, (vii) and (viii) must evaluate to 1 in any model.

Additionally we can show that the Gödel completeness theorem carries over to our extended predicate calculus. For this, we argue as follows. If $(\mathcal{U}, I, A)$ is an interpretation framework covering a set $S$ of sentences in our extended calculus, then it follows as previously that if $\mathsf{Val}(I, A, F) = 1$ for each $F$ in $S$, then $\mathsf{Val}(I, A, G) = 1$ for every $G$ such that $S \vdash G$. Hence, as previously, if such a set $S$ has a model it is consistent. Suppose conversely that $S$ is consistent. Add the equality axioms (vi–viii) to $S$ (this preserves consistency since only axioms are added to $S$) and proceed as above to build the sets SC, SUF, SNQ, and the list LEF. Then the collection of statements in SNQ must be propositionally consistent, and so must have a propositional model $V$ for which every statement in SNQ takes on the value 'true'. It was seen above that this gives a model $(\mathcal{U}, I, A)$ of all the statements in our collection, with universe $\mathcal{U}$ equal to the set of all terms formed from the constants in SC using the function symbols appearing in formulae of $S$. This is not quite a model of $S$ in the sense required when we take '=' as a built-in predicate symbol which must be modeled by the standard equality operator, since there may well exist formulae of the form $t_1 = t_2$ such that $\mathsf{Val}(I, A, t_1 = t_2) = 1$ even though $t_1$ and $t_2$ are syntactically distinct. However, the binary relationship

$$R(t_1, t_2) = \big(\mathsf{Val}(I, A, t_1 = t_2) = 1\big) \tag{2.15}$$

between terms of $\mathcal{U}$ must be an equivalence relation, since whenever terms $t_1$, $t_2$ and $t_3$ are generated we will have added all the assertions

$$t_1 = t_1 \;\&\; \big((t_1 = t_2) \to (t_2 = t_1)\big) \;\&\; \big((t_1 = t_2 \;\&\; t_2 = t_3) \to (t_1 = t_3)\big)$$

to our collection. Moreover, since in the same situation statements like

$$\big(t_1 = t_2 \to \big(f(\cdots t_1 \cdots) = f(\cdots t_2 \cdots)\big)\big)$$

and

$$\big(t_1 = t_2 \to \big(P(\cdots t_1 \cdots) \leftrightarrow P(\cdots t_2 \cdots)\big)\big)$$

will have been added to our collection for all function and predicate symbols, the terms must always be equivalent whenever their lead function symbols are the same and their arguments are equivalent, and also we must have $\mathsf{Val}(I, A, P(\cdots t_1 \cdots)) = \mathsf{Val}(I, A, PP(\cdots t_2 \cdots))$ for atomic formulae when their lead function symbols are the same and their arguments are equivalent. Therefore we can form a model of our set of statements by replacing the universe $\mathcal{U}$ by the set $\mathcal{U}'$ of equivalence classes on it defined by the equivalence relation (2.15), and in this new model the symbol '=' is represented by the standard equality operation. This concludes our proof that the Gödel completeness theorem carries over to our extended predicate calculus.

## 2.4 Set Theory as an Axiomatic Extension of Predicate Calculus

In most of the present book we take a rather free version of set theory (perhaps this should be called 'brutal' set theory) as basic, and use it to hurry onward to our main goal of proving the long list of theorems found in Chap. 5. The standard treatment of set theory ties it more carefully to predicate calculus. Specifically, to ensure applicability of the foundational results presented earlier in this chapter, set theory is cast as a collection of predicate axioms. In this form it is customarily referred to as Zermelo–Fraenkel set theory (ZF) if no version of the axiom of choice is necessarily included, or ZFC if an axiom of choice is present. Here is the standard list of ZFC axioms.

### 2.4.1 Zermelo–Fraenkel Theory with the Axiom of Choice

(1) **(Axiom of extension)** $(\forall s, t \mid (s = t) \leftrightarrow (\forall x \mid (x \in s) \leftrightarrow (x \in t)))$.

(2) **(Axioms of elementary sets)** There is an empty set $\emptyset$; for each set $t$ there is a set $\mathsf{Singleton}(t)$ whose only member is $t$; if $s$ and $t$ are sets then there is a set $\mathsf{Unordered\_pair}(s, t)$ whose only members are $s$ and $t$. That is, we have

$$\big(\forall s \mid \neg(s \in \emptyset)\big),$$
$$\big(\forall t, u \mid \big(u \in \mathsf{Singleton}(t)\big) \leftrightarrow (u = t)\big),$$
$$\big(\forall s, t, u \,\big|\, \big(u \in \mathsf{Unordered\_pair}(s, t)\big) \leftrightarrow \big((u = s) \vee (u = t)\big)\big).$$

(3) **(Axiom of power set)** To every set $A$ there corresponds a set $\mathcal{P}(A)$ whose members are precisely the subsets of $A$:

$$\big(\forall s, t \,\big|\, \big(s \in \mathcal{P}(t)\big) \leftrightarrow \big(\forall x \mid (x \in s) \leftrightarrow \big(\forall y \mid (y \in x) \to (y \in t)\big)\big)\big).$$

(4) **(Axiom of union)** To every set $A$ there corresponds a set $\bigcup A$ whose members are precisely those elements belonging to elements of $A$:

$$\left(\forall s, t \,\middle|\, \left(s \in \bigcup t\right) \leftrightarrow \big(\exists x \mid (x \in t)\ \&\ (s \in x)\big)\right).$$

(5) **(Axiom of infinity)** There is at least one set $\mathsf{Inf}$ such that

$$(\emptyset \in \mathsf{Inf})\ \&\ \big(\forall s \mid (s \in \mathsf{Inf}) \to \big(\mathsf{Singleton}(s) \in \mathsf{Inf}\big)\big).$$

(6) **(Axiom of regularity)**

$$\neg\big(\exists x \mid (x \neq \emptyset)\ \&\ \big(\forall y \mid (y \in x) \to \big(\exists z \mid (z \in x)\ \&\ (z \in y)\big)\big)\big).$$

(7) **(Axiom schema of subsets)** If $F(y, z_1, \ldots, z_n)$ is any syntactically valid formula of the language of ZF that has no free variables other than those shown, and neither $x$ nor $z$ occur in the list $y, z_1, \ldots, z_n$, then

$$\big(\exists z \mid \big(\forall y \mid (y \in z) \leftrightarrow \big((y \in x)\ \&\ F(y, z_1, \ldots, z_n)\big)\big)\big)$$

is an axiom. Here and below, a formula is said to be a formula of the language of ZF if it is formed using only the built-in symbols of predicate calculus (i.e. the propositional operators, $\forall, \exists, =$) plus the membership operator. (Note that in stating this axiom, we mean to assert the formula which results by quantifying it universally over all the free variables $z_1, \ldots, z_n$.)

(8) **(Axiom schema of replacement)** If $F(u, v, z_1, \ldots, z_n)$ is any syntactically valid formula of the language of ZF that has no free variables other than those shown, and neither $u$ nor $v$ occur in the list $z_1, \ldots, z_n$, then

$$\big(\forall u, v_1, v_2 \,\big|\, \big((F(u, v_1, z_1, \ldots, z_n) \,\&\, F(u, v_2, z_1, \ldots, z_n)) \to (v_1 = v_2)\big)\big)$$
$$\to \big(\forall b \,\big|\, \big(\exists c \,\big|\, \big(\forall y \mid (y \in c) \leftrightarrow \big(\exists x \mid (x \in b) \,\&\, F(x, y, z_1, \ldots, z_n)\big)\big)\big)\big)$$

is an axiom. (Here again, in stating this axiom, we mean to assert the formula which results by quantifying it universally over all the free variables $z_1, \ldots, z_n$.)

This statement is obscure enough for a brief clarifying discussion of its equivalent in our informal version of set theory to be helpful. In that less formal system we would proceed by defining an auxiliary 'Skolem' function $h$ satisfying

$$\big(\forall x, z_1, \ldots, z_n \,\big|\, \big(\exists y \mid F(x, y, z_1, \ldots, z_n)\big)$$
$$\leftrightarrow F\big(x, h(x, z_1, \ldots, z_n), z_1, \ldots, z_n\big)\big).$$

Then, since the replacement axiom assumes that $F(x, y, z_1, \ldots, z_n)$ defines $y$ uniquely in terms of $x$ and $z_1, \ldots, z_n$, we have

$$\big(\forall x, y, z_1, \ldots, z_n \mid F(x, y, z_1, \ldots, z_n) \to \big(y = h(x, z_1, \ldots, z_n)\big)\big),$$

and so the set $c$ whose existence is asserted by the axiom of replacement can be written in our 'working' version of set theory as

$$\big\{h(x, z_1, \ldots, z_n) : x \in b \mid F\big(x, h(x, z_1, \ldots, z_n), z_1, \ldots, z_n\big)\big\}.$$

This 'set-former' expression is the form in which such constructs will almost always be written.

(9) **(Axiom of choice)**

$$\big(\forall x \,\big|\, \big(\exists f \mid \mathsf{Svm}(f) \,\&\, \big(\mathsf{domain}(f) = x\big)$$
$$\&\, \big(\forall y \,\big|\, ((y \in x) \,\&\, (y \neq \emptyset)) \to \big(f[y] \in y\big)\big)\big)\big).$$

Note that this form of the axiom of choice is weaker than the assumption concerning 'arb' which our 'brutal' set theory uses in its place. Specifically, while 'arb' is a universal choice function applicable to any non-null set, the axiom of choice just stated provides a separate such choice function for each set of sets.

Most axioms appear in Skolemized version in the above list. Other authors prefer to write those in unskolemized form, e.g. to write our axiom $(\forall s \mid \neg(s \in \emptyset))$ in the form

$$(\exists z \mid (\forall s \mid \neg(s \in z))).$$

Similarly the axiom of union will often be written as

$$(\forall t \mid (\exists u \mid (\forall s \mid (s \in u) \leftrightarrow (\exists x \mid (x \in t) \,\&\, (s \in x))))).$$

The main respects in which the ZFC formulation of set theory differs from our 'brutal' version is that no built-in set-former construct is provided, nor are 'transfinite recursive' definitions like those freely allowed in our version of set theory. An issue of relative consistency therefore arises: can our version of set theory be reduced to ZFC in some standard way, or, if ZFC is assumed to be consistent, can it be demonstrated that our 'brutal' version is consistent also?

## *2.4.2 Concerning the Consistency of ZFC and Various Interesting Extensions of It*

To open a discussion of this problem we first consider the general question of consistency for set-theoretic axioms like the ZFC axioms. Since equality can be treated as an operator of logic, these axioms involve only one non-logical symbol, the predicate symbol '$\in$'. The Gödel completeness theorem tells us that the ZFC axioms are consistent if and only if they have a model. How can such models be found? Are there many of them having an interesting variety of properties, or just a few? Since von Neumann's 1928 paper on the axioms of set theory and Gödel's 1938 work on the continuum hypothesis, many profound studies have addressed these questions. We can get some initial idea of the issues involved by looking a bit more closely at the hereditarily finite sets. We will see that these are of interest in the present context since they model all the axioms of set theory other than the axiom of infinity.

### 2.4.2.1 Basic Facts Concerning Hereditarily Finite Sets

In intuitive terms, the '*hereditarily finite*' sets $s$ are those which can be constructed by using the pair formation operation $\{x, y\}$ and union operation $x \cup y$ repeatedly, starting from the null set $\{\}$ (same as $\emptyset$). Any such set has a string representation $r$ consisting of a properly matched arrangement of opening brackets '{' and closing brackets '}', 'properly matched' in the sense that there are equally many opening and closing brackets, and that no initial substring of $r$ contains more closing than opening brackets. Moreover, the string representation $r$ of any such set is indecomposable, in the sense that no initial substring of $r$ is properly matched. Three examples are

$$\{\} \qquad \{\{\}\} \qquad \{\{\}\{\{\}\}\}.$$

The 'height' of any such set is one less than the maximum depth of bracket nesting in its string representation. For example, the three sets just displayed have heights 0, 1, and 2, respectively. The general transfinite induction techniques described in the preceding section make it possible to prove that the hereditarily finite sets are precisely those sets which are finite and all of whose elements are themselves hereditarily finite; this point is discussed in greater detail in Sect. 4.3.10 and in Chap. 6.

Hereditarily finite sets can be represented in many ways by computer data structures which allow the basic operations on them, namely $\{x, y\}$, $x \cup y$, and $x \in y$, to be realized by simple code fragments, and therefore allow translation of set-former expressions and recursive function definitions of all kinds into computer programs. One way of doing this is to make direct use of string representations like those just displayed. To this end, note that each properly matched arrangement of brackets is a concatenation of one or more indecomposable properly matched arrangements of brackets, and that every indecomposable arrangement has the form $\{s\}$ where $s$ itself is properly matched. Moreover the decomposition of any properly matched arrangement of brackets into indecomposable properly matched substrings is unique. (The reader is invited to prove these elementary facts, and to describe an algorithm for separating any properly matched arrangement of brackets into its indecomposable parts.)

It follows from the facts just stated that each hereditarily finite set $t$ has a string representation, itself indecomposable, of the form

$$\{s_1 s_2 \cdots s_m\}, \qquad (2.16)$$

where each of the $s_j$ is properly matched and indecomposable, and where all these $s_j$, which are simply the string representations of the elements of $t$, are distinct. We can make this string representation unique by insisting that the $s_j$ be arranged in order of increasing length, members having string representations of the same length then being arranged in alphabetical order of their representations. We can call a string representation (2.16) having these properties at every recursive level (and in which all the $s_j$ are distinct at every level) a 'nicely arranged' properly matched arrangement of brackets.Then every hereditarily finite set has a unique string representation of this kind, and conversely every nicely arranged properly matched arrangement of brackets represents a unique set. Hence these arrangements give an explicit, 1-1 representation of the family of all hereditarily finite sets.

In this representation, the two elementary operations $\{x, y\}$ and $x \cup y$ which suffice for construction of all such sets have the following simple implementations. The representation of $\{x, y\}$ is obtained by taking the representations $s_x$ and $s_y$ of $x$ and $y$, respectively, checking them for equality and eliminating one of them if they are equal, arranging them in order of length (or alphabetically if their lengths are equal), and forming the string $\{s_x s_y\}$ (or simply $\{s_x\}$ if $s_x$ and $s_y$ are identical). To compute the standard string representation of $x \cup y$, let $\{s_1 s_2 \cdots s_m\}$ and $\{t_1 t_2 \cdots t_n\}$ be the standard string representations of $x$ and $y$, respectively. Then form the concatenation

$$s_1 s_2 \cdots s_m t_1 t_2 \cdots t_n,$$

rearrange its indecomposable parts in the standard order described above, eliminate duplicates, and enclose the result in an outermost final pair of brackets.

In this, or any other convenient representation, it is easy to construct a code fragment which will calculate the value of any set former of the type we allow, for example

$$\{e(x) : x \in s \mid P(x)\},$$

provided that $s$ is hereditarily finite, and that $e$ is any set-valued expression and $P(x)$ any predicate expression which can be calculated by procedures which have already been constructed. For this, we have only to set up an iterative loop over all the elements of $s$, and use an operation which calculates $e(x)$ for each element $x$ of $s$ satisfying $P(x)$ and then inserts all such elements into an initially empty set, eliminating duplicates.

The powerset operation $\mathcal{P}(s)$ (set of all subsets of $s$) satisfies the recursive relationship

$$\begin{aligned}\mathcal{P}(s) = \mathbf{if}\ s = \emptyset\ \mathbf{then}\ \{\emptyset\}\\ \mathbf{else}\ \mathcal{P}(s \setminus \{\mathsf{arb}(s)\}) \cup \{x \cup \{\mathsf{arb}(s)\} : x \in \mathcal{P}(s \setminus \{\mathsf{arb}(s)\})\}\\ \mathbf{end\ if}\end{aligned}$$

which can be used to calculate $\mathcal{P}(s)$ recursively for each hereditarily finite $s$. This makes it possible to calculate set formers of the second allowed form

$$\{e(x) : x \subseteq s \mid P(x)\},$$

by translating them into

$$\{e(x) : x \in \mathcal{P}(s) \mid P(x)\}.$$

Set formers involving multiple bound variables, for example

$$\{e(x, y, z) : x \in s,\ y \in a(x),\ z \in b(x, y) \mid P(x, y, z)\},$$

can be calculated in much the same way using multiply nested loops, provided that all the sets which appear are hereditarily finite and that $e$, $a$, and $b$ are set-valued expressions, and $P(x, y, z)$ a predicate expression, which can be calculated by procedures which have already been constructed. Similar loops can be used to calculate existentially and universally quantified expressions like

$$(\forall x \in s,\ y \in a(x),\ z \in b(x, y) \mid P(x, y, z))$$

and

$$(\exists x \in s,\ y \in a(x),\ z \in b(x, y) \mid P(x, y, z)),$$

or such simpler quantifiers as

$$(\forall x \in s \mid P(x)) \quad \text{and} \quad (\exists x \in s \mid P(x)).$$

Note, however, that the predicate calculus in which we work also allows quantifiers involving bound variables not subject to any explicit limitation, for example

$$(\forall x \mid P(x)) \quad \text{and} \quad (\exists x \mid P(x)).$$

Since translation of expressions of this form into a programmed loop would require iteration over the infinite collection of all hereditarily finite sets, we can no longer claim that the values of these unrestricted iterators are effectively calculable. Thus they represent a first step into the more abstract world of the actually infinite, where symbolic reasoning must replace explicit calculation.

All the kinds of definition we allow translate just as readily into computer codes as long as only hereditarily finite sets are considered. Algebraic definitions like

$$\bigcup x =_{\text{Def}} \{z : y \in x \,\&\, z \in y\}$$

translate directly into procedures whose body consists of a single nested iteration. Recursive definitions like

$$\begin{aligned} \mathsf{enum}(X,S) =_{\text{Def}} \textbf{if} \quad & S \subseteq \{\mathsf{enum}(y,S) : y \in X\} \quad \textbf{then} \;\; S \\ \textbf{else} \; & \mathsf{arb}(S \setminus \{\mathsf{enum}(y,S) : y \in X\}) \;\; \textbf{end if} \end{aligned}$$

translate just as directly into recursive procedures. Thus, as long as we confine ourselves to hereditarily finite sets, the whole of the set theory in which we work (excepting only unrestricted quantifiers of the kind shown above) can be thought of both as a language for the description of mathematical relationships and as an implementable (indeed, implemented) programming language for actual manipulation of a convenient class of finite objects. This parallelism between language of deduction and language of computation will be explored more deeply in Chaps. 4 and 6.

We can summarize the preceding discussion in the following way. All hereditarily finite sets can be given explicit finite representations, so that these sets constitute a 'universe of computation' in which all of the properties we assume for sets can be checked by explicit computation, at least in individual cases. We will see below that the collection of hereditarily finite sets models all the axioms of set theory, save one: there is no infinite set, for example no hereditarily finite set $t$ having the property

$$t \neq \emptyset \;\;\&\;\; (\forall x \in t \mid \{x\} \in t)$$

which we will use as our axiom of infinity. By including this statement in our collection of axioms we cross from the world of computation defined by the hereditarily finite sets into a more abstract world of objects which can no longer be enumerated explicitly but which are known only through the statements about them that we can deduce formally, i.e. as elements of a world of formal computation, whose main elementary property is simply its formal consistency. Nevertheless, mathematical experience has shown that the statements that we can prove about the objects of this abstract world are both beautiful and extremely useful tools for deriving many properties of hereditarily finite sets which it would be harder or impossible to prove if we refused to enlarge our universe of discourse to allow free reference to infinite sets.

#### 2.4.2.2 Hereditarily Finite Sets: Formal Definition Within General Set Theory

Hereditarily finite sets can be defined formally in either of two ways: either as all sets satisfying a predicate Is_HF, or as all the members of a set HF. The predicate Is_HF is defined in the following recursive way (we continue to designate the set of all integers by $\mathbb{N}$):

$$\mathsf{Is\_HF}(x) \leftrightarrow_{\mathrm{Def}} \big((\#x \in \mathbb{N})\ \&\ \big(\forall y \in x \mid \mathsf{Is\_HF}(y)\big)\big).$$

To define the corresponding set HF (thereby showing that the collection of all $x$ satisfying Is_HF($x$) is really a set), a bit more work is needed. We proceed as follows. Begin with the following recursive definition (informally speaking, this defines the collection of all sets of 'rank $x$'):

$$\mathsf{HF\_}(x) =_{\mathrm{Def}} \textbf{if } x = \emptyset \textbf{ then } \emptyset \textbf{ else } \bigcup\big\{\mathscr{P}\big(\mathsf{HF\_}(y)\big) : y \in x\big\} \textbf{ end if}.$$

It is easily proved by induction that

$$\big(\forall y \in \mathsf{HF\_}(x) \mid \mathsf{HF\_}(x) \supseteq y\big).$$

Indeed, if there exists an $x$ for which '$\mathsf{HF\_}(x) \supseteq z$' is false for some $z$ in $\mathsf{HF\_}(x)$, there exists a smallest such $x$, which, after renaming, we can take to be $x$ itself. Then there is a $u$ such that $z \in \mathsf{HF\_}(x)$, $u \in z$, $u \notin \mathsf{HF\_}(x)$. Since $z \in \mathsf{HF\_}(x)$, we have

$$z \in \bigcup\big\{\mathscr{P}\big(\mathsf{HF\_}(y)\big) : y \in x\big\},$$

so $z \in \mathscr{P}(\mathsf{HF\_}(y))$ for some $y \in x$, i.e. $z \subseteq \mathsf{HF\_}(y)$ for some $y \in x$. Then $u \in \mathsf{HF\_}(y)$ for some $y \in x$. Since $x$ has no member $y$ for which

$$\big(\forall w \in \mathsf{HF\_}(y) \mid \mathsf{HF\_}(y) \supseteq w\big)$$

is false, it follows that $\mathsf{HF\_}(y) \supseteq u$, so $u \in \mathscr{P}(\mathsf{HF\_}(y))$, and therefore

$$u \in \bigcup\big\{\mathscr{P}\big(\mathsf{HF\_}(y)\big) : y \in x\big\},$$

i.e. $u \in \mathsf{HF\_}(x)$, proving our claim. Note also that the function HF_ is increasing in its parameter, in the sense that if $y \in x$, then $\mathsf{HF\_}(x) \supseteq \mathsf{HF\_}(y)$. Indeed if $u$ is an element of $\mathsf{HF\_}(y)$, then $\{u\} \in \mathscr{P}(\mathsf{HF\_}(y))$, so

$$\{u\} \in \bigcup\big\{\mathscr{P}\big(\mathsf{HF\_}(y)\big) : y \in x\big\},$$

and therefore $\{u\} \in \mathsf{HF\_}(x)$, so by what we have just proved $u \in \mathsf{HF\_}(x)$.

In what follows we also need the fact that

$$\big(\forall n \in \mathbb{N} \mid \#\mathsf{HF\_}(n) \in \mathbb{N}\big),$$

i.e. that all the sets $\mathsf{HF\_}(n)$ are themselves finite. To prove this, suppose that it fails for some smallest $n$. Then

$$\mathsf{HF\_}(n) = \bigcup\{\mathscr{P}(\mathsf{HF\_}(m)) : m \in n\},$$

all the sets $\mathsf{HF\_}(m)$ for which $m \in n$ are finite, and so are their power sets. Thus $\mathsf{HF\_}(n)$ is the union of a sequence of sets, each of finite cardinality, over a domain of cardinality less than $\mathbb{N}$ (i.e. of finite cardinality). Hence $\mathsf{HF\_}(n)$ is itself finite, i.e. $\#\mathsf{HF\_}(n)$ belongs to $\mathbb{N}$, as asserted.

Now we can define the set HF by

$$\mathsf{HF} =_{\mathrm{Def}} \bigcup\{\mathsf{HF\_}(n) : n \in \mathbb{N}\}. \tag{2.17}$$

To come to the desired goal we must prove that

$$(\forall y \mid \mathsf{Is\_HF}(y) \leftrightarrow y \in \mathsf{HF}).$$

This can be done as follows. Suppose that $y \in \mathsf{HF}$. Then we have $y \in \mathsf{HF\_}(n)$ for some $n \in \mathbb{N}$. To prove that $\mathsf{Is\_HF}(y)$, suppose that this is false, and, proceeding inductively, that $n$ is the smallest element of $\mathbb{N}$ for which $\mathsf{HF\_}(n)$ has an element $y$ such that $\mathsf{Is\_HF}(y)$ is false. Then, since

$$y \in \bigcup\{\mathscr{P}(\mathsf{HF\_}(m)) : m \in n\},$$

we have $y \in \mathscr{P}(\mathsf{HF\_}(m))$ for some $m \in n$. All the elements $u$ of $y$ are therefore elements of $\mathsf{HF\_}(m)$, and so satisfy $\mathsf{Is\_HF}(u)$. We have also proved that $\mathsf{HF\_}(m)$ is finite, so all its subsets are finite, and therefore $\#y \in \mathbb{N}$, proving that $\mathsf{Is\_HF}(y)$, a contradiction implying that

$$(y \in \mathsf{HF}) \rightarrow \mathsf{Is\_HF}(y)$$

for all $y$.

Suppose conversely that $\mathsf{Is\_HF}(x)$, and that $x \notin \mathsf{HF}$. Proceeding inductively, we can suppose that $x$ is a minimal element with these properties, i.e. that $y \in \mathsf{HF}$ for each $y \in x$. Then it follows from (2.17) that for each $y$ in $x$ there is an $n = n(y)$ in $\mathbb{N}$ for which $y \in \mathsf{HF\_}(n(y))$. But then since $x$ is finite by definition of $\mathsf{Is\_HF}(x)$, the maximum $m$ of all these $n(y)$ is finite, so every $y$ in $x$ belongs to $\mathsf{HF\_}(m)$ since the sets $\mathsf{HF\_}(m)$ clearly increase with their parameter $m$. Therefore $x \in \mathscr{P}(\mathsf{HF\_}(m))$, $x \in \mathsf{HF\_}(m+1)$, and $x \in \mathsf{HF}$, a contradiction implying that

$$\mathsf{Is\_HF}(y) \rightarrow (y \in \mathsf{HF})$$

for all $y$, which leads to the desired conclusion.

It is easily seen that HF is a model of all the ZFC axioms *other than the axiom of infinity*. To show this, we simply need to check that all these axioms remain valid if we interpret all quantifiers as extending over the set HF rather than over the 'universe of all sets' that the initial ZFC axioms assume. This can be done as follows.

(1) The axiom of extension remains true since HF is *transitive*, i.e. every member of a member of HF belongs to HF. (2) The null set, singleton, and unordered pair constructions take elements of HF into themselves since they construct finite sets all of whose elements are drawn from HF. (3) The power set axiom remains valid since every subset of an hereditarily finite set is hereditarily finite, and for $s$ in HF, $\mathscr{P}(s)$ consists only of such elements and also is finite. (4) The union set axiom remains valid since every member of a member of $\bigcup s$, where $s$ is an hereditarily finite set, is hereditarily finite, and for $s \in \mathsf{HF}$, $\bigcup s$ is the union of finitely many sets and so is finite. (5) The axiom of infinity fails. (6) The axiom of regularity clearly remains true, since each $z \in \mathsf{HF}$ has the same members as an element of HF that it does as a set. (7) The axiom schema of subsets, which in informal terms asserts the existence of the set $y = \{u : u \in x \mid F(x, z_1, \ldots, z_n)\}$ for every $x$ and $z_1, \ldots, z_n$, remains true since the $y$ whose existence it asserts is a subset of the $x$ which it assumes, and so must be hereditarily finite if $x$ is hereditarily finite. (8) In informal terms, the axiom schema of replacement asserts the existence of the set $y = \{u : x \in b \mid F(x, u, z_1, \ldots, z_n)\}$ for every $b$ and $z_1, \ldots, z_n$ if the predicate $F$ defines $u$ uniquely in terms of $x$ and $z_1, \ldots, z_n$. This remains true if only hereditarily finite sets are allowed, since if $b$ is finite and each $u$ is required to be hereditarily finite the set of whose existence it asserts is a finite set of elements, each of which is hereditarily finite, and so must be hereditarily finite. (9) The axiom of choice remains true since the $f$ whose existence it asserts is a single-valued map whose pairs have their first components in $x$ and their second components in $\bigcup x$: assuming that $x \in \mathsf{HF}$, each such pair plainly belongs to HF and therefore, since $f$ consists of finitely many such pairs, we conclude that $f \in \mathsf{HF}$. (If $\emptyset \in x$, we can carry out a similar argument, after replacing the image $f(\emptyset)$ by $\emptyset$.)

#### 2.4.2.3 Large Cardinal Axioms

The preceding observations concerning the set HF suggest that it may be possible to find a model of set theory, which would imply the consistency of set theory, by replacing $\mathbb{N}$, the smallest infinite cardinal, by something larger in the crucial formula (2.17) seen above. If this is done, the argument that we have given can be shown to go through almost without change for any cardinal having the two properties of $\mathbb{N}$ used in the argument. The following definition gives names to these properties:

**Definition 2.9** A non-null cardinal number $N$ is *inaccessible* if (a) Any set of cardinals, all less than $N$, which has a cardinality smaller than $N$ also has a supremum less than $N$. (Cardinals having this property are called *regular* cardinals.) (b) If $M$ is a cardinal less than $N$, then $2^M$ (which is $\#\mathscr{P}(M)$ by definition) is less than $N$. (Cardinals which have this property are called *strong limit* cardinals.)

Note that the set $\mathbb{N}$ of integers is inaccessible according to this definition. Intuitively speaking, a cardinal number $N$ is inaccessible if it cannot be constructed from smaller cardinals using any 'explicit' set-theoretic operation, so that the very existence of $N$ would seem to involve some new assumption, in the same way that assuming the existence of an infinite set takes a step beyond anything that follows from the properties of hereditarily finite sets $x \in \mathsf{HF}$.

If we make the following quite straightforward definition, which simply generalizes the preceding construction of HF to arbitrary cardinal numbers $N$,

**Definition 2.10** $\mathscr{H}(N) =_{\text{Def}} \bigcup\{\mathsf{HF\_}(n) : n \in N\}$ for every cardinal number $N$,

then the preceding discussion shows that

**Theorem 2.5** *If $N$ is an inaccessible cardinal larger than $\mathbb{N}$, then $\mathscr{H}(N)$ is a model of the ZFC axioms of set theory.*

**Corollary 2.2** *It there exists any inaccessible cardinal larger than $\mathbb{N}$, then the ZFC axioms have a model, and so are consistent.*

A theorem of Gödel to be proved in Chap. 6 shows that no system having at least the expressive power and proof capability of HF can be used to prove its own consistency. Thus the corollary just stated implies the following additional result:

**Corollary 2.3** *Adding the assumption that there exists an inaccessible cardinal larger than $\mathbb{N}$ to the ZFC axioms allows us to construct a model of the ZFC axioms and hence implies that these axioms are consistent. Therefore the ZFC axioms cannot suffice to prove that there exists an inaccessible cardinal larger than $\mathbb{N}$.*

The situation described by this last corollary is much like that seen in the case of HF. The ZFC axioms, which include the axioms of infinity, allow us to define the infinite cardinal number $\mathbb{N}$ and so the model HF of the theory of hereditarily finite sets. The theory of hereditarily finite sets can be formalized by dropping the axiom of infinity (keeping the other axioms of ZFC, and adding a suitable principle of induction); but the resulting set of 'HF axioms' do not suffice to prove the existence of even one infinite set.

The technique for forming models of set theory seen in the preceding discussion, namely identification of some transitive set $\mathscr{H}$ in which the ZFC axioms remain true if we redefine all quantifiers to extend over the set $\mathscr{H}$ only, does not change the definition of ordinal numbers, since an element $t$ of $s$ is an ordinal (in the overall ZFC theory) iff its members are totally ordered by membership and each member of a member of $t$ is a member of $t$. Since the collection of members of $t$ remains the same in $\mathscr{H}$, this definition is plainly invariant. Thus the ordinal numbers of the model $\mathscr{H}$, seen from the vantage point of the overall ZFC universe, are just those ordinals which are members of $\mathscr{H}$. But the situation is different for cardinal numbers, which are defined as those ordinals $O$ which cannot be mapped to smaller ordinals by a 1-1 mapping, i.e. those which do not satisfy

$$\mathsf{not\_cardinal}(O) \leftrightarrow_{\text{Def}} \big(\exists f \mid \mathsf{1\_1}(f) \;\&\; \mathsf{domain}(f) = O \;\&\; \mathsf{range}(f) \in O\big).$$

When we cut the whole ZFC universe of sets down to the set $\mathscr{H}$, the collection of ordinals will grow smaller, but so will the set of 1-1 mappings ('1_1s') $f$ appearing in the formula seen above, making it unclear how the collection of cardinals (relative to $\mathscr{H}$), or the structure of this set, will change. The power set operation can also change, since for $s \in \mathscr{H}$ the power set relative to $\mathscr{H}$ is the set $\mathscr{P}(s) \cap \mathscr{H}$ of the ZFC universe. Thus properties and statements involving the power set can change meaning also. But the union set $\bigcup s$ retains its meaning. (Note also that if $f$ is a member of $\mathscr{H}$, then the property 1_1($f$) holds relative to $\mathscr{H}$ if and only if it holds in the ZFC universe, since it is defined by a formula quantified over the members of $f$, and these are the same in both contexts.)

However, in the particularly simple case in which we restrict our universe of sets to $\mathscr{H}(N)$ where $N$ is an inaccessible cardinal, the property 'not_cardinal' does not change. This is because any 1_1 in the ZFC universe for which domain($f$) $\in \mathscr{H}(N)$ & range($f$) $\in \mathscr{H}(N)$ must itself belong to $\mathscr{H}(N)$, since it is a set of ordered pairs of elements all belonging to $\mathscr{H}(N)$, whose cardinality is at most that of domain($f$), and so is less than $N$. It readily follows that the cardinals of $\mathscr{H}(N)$ are simply those cardinals of the ZFC universe which lie below $N$; likewise for the regular, strong limit, and inaccessible cardinals.

It follows that ZFC, plus the assumption that there are two inaccessible cardinals, allows us to construct a set $\mathscr{H}(N)$ in which there is one inaccessible cardinal (namely we take $N$ to be the second inaccessible cardinal), and so implies the consistency of ZFC plus the axiom that there is at least one inaccessible cardinal. Generally speaking, axioms which imply the existence of many and large inaccessible cardinals imply the consistency of ZFC as extended by statements only implying the existence of fewer and smaller inaccessible cardinals, but not conversely. Thus the addition of stronger and stronger axioms concerning the existence of large cardinal numbers exemplifies a basic consequence of the incompleteness theorems presented in Chap. 6, namely that no fixed set of axioms can exhaust all of mathematics, so that significant extension of consistent systems by the addition of new axioms will always remain possible. The fact that large cardinal axioms can be formulated independently of any detailed reference to the syntax of the language of set theory makes them interesting in this regard, and so has encouraged the study of axioms which imply the existence of more and more, larger and larger, cardinal numbers.

It is worth reviewing a few of the key definitions that have appeared in such studies:

**Definition 2.11** Let $S$ be a set of cardinal numbers all of whose members are less than a fixed cardinal number $N$.

(i) $S$ is said to be *closed relative to* $N$ if the union of every sequence of elements of $S$ whose length is less than $N$ is a member of $S$.
(ii) $S$ is said to be *unbounded in* $N$ if every cardinal less than $N$ is also less than some member of $S$.
(iii) $S$ is said to be *thin in* $N$ if there exists a closed unbounded set relative to $N$ which does not intersect $S$.

**Definition 2.12** A nonempty set $F$ of nonempty subsets of a set $S$ is called a *filter* on $S$ if the intersection of any two elements of $F$ is an element of $F$ and any superset, included in $S$, of an element of $F$ is an element of $S$. A filter $F$ is an *ultrafilter* if whenever the union of finitely many subsets of $S$ belongs to $F$, one of these subsets belongs to $F$. Given a cardinal number $N$, a filter $F$ is said to be *$N$-complete* if whenever the union of fewer than $N$ subsets of $S$ belongs to $F$, one of these subsets belongs to $F$. An ultrafilter $F$ is said to be *nontrivial* if it is not the collection of all sets having a given point $p$ as member.

Note that if $F$ is an $N$-complete filter on $S$, the intersection $IT$ of any collection $T$ of sets in $F$ such that $\#T$ is less than $N$ belongs to $F$. Indeed, $S$ belongs to $F$, and if $G$ belongs to $F$ then $S \setminus G$ is not in $F$, since otherwise $F$ would contain the null set $G \cap (S \setminus G)$. But now $S$ is the union of $IT$ and the collection of all complements $S \setminus G$ for $G \in T$, and since $\#T$ is less than $N$ and $F$ is $N$-complete, the union of all these complements must lie outside $F$, so $IT$ must belong to $F$.

The following definition lists two of the various kinds of large cardinal numbers that have been considered in the literature.

**Definition 2.13**

(i) A cardinal number $N$ is a *Mahlo* cardinal if it is inaccessible and the set of regular cardinals less than $N$ is not thin.

(ii) A cardinal number $N$ is *measurable* if there is a nontrivial $N$-complete ultrafilter for $N$.

Note that if there is a Mahlo cardinal $N$, then the number of inaccessible cardinals below $N$ must be at least $N$. For if there were fewer, then since $N$ is inaccessible the supremum $M$ of all these cardinals would also be less than $N$. But then the set SLC of all strong limit cardinals between $M$ and $N$ is unbounded and closed, contradicting the assumption that $N$ is Mahlo. Indeed, for each $K$ between $M$ and $N$, the supremum of the sequence $2^K$, $2^{2^K}$, ... must be a strong limit cardinal, showing that SLC is unbounded in $N$. Also the supremum $L$ of any collection of strong limit cardinals must itself be a strong limit cardinal, since any $L_1$ less than $L$ must plainly be less than some cardinal of the form $2^K$. This shows that SLC is closed. Now, no member $K$ of SLC can be regular, since if it were it would be inaccessible, contradicting the fact that $M$ is the largest inaccessible below $N$. This shows that the set of regular cardinals below $N$ is thin, contradicting the assumption that $N$ is Mahlo, and so completes our proof of the fact that every Mahlo cardinal $N$ must be the $N$th inaccessible.

It follows that the assumption that there is a Mahlo cardinal is much stronger than the assumption that there is an inaccessible cardinal, since it implies that there are inaccessibly many inaccessible cardinals.

Suppose next that the cardinal number $N$ is measurable, and let $F$ be an $N$-complete nontrivial ultrafilter on $N$. Then any set consisting of just one point $p$ must lie outside $F$ (or else $F$ would be the trivial ultrafilter consisting of all sets having $p$ as member). Since $F$ is $N$-complete, it follows that every subset of $N$ having fewer than $N$ points lies outside $F$, and therefore so does every union of fewer than $N$ such sets. Hence every measurable cardinal is regular. We will now show that if $K$ is a cardinal less than $N$, then $2^K$ is less than $N$ also, showing that every measurable cardinal is inaccessible. Suppose the contrary, so that there exists a collection CF of binary-valued functions $f(j)$ defined for all $j$ in $K$, but having cardinality $N$, and so standing in 1-1 correspondence with $N$. This correspondence maps $f$ to an $N$-complete nontrivial ultrafilter $F'$ on CF. For each $j$ in $K$, let $a(j)$ be that one of the two Boolean values $\{0, 1\}$ for which the set of functions $\{f \in S \mid f(j) = a(j)\}$ belongs to $F'$. Then, since $F'$ is $N$-complete, it follows, as was shown above, that the intersection of all the sets $\{f \in S \mid f(j) = a(j)\}$ must belong to $F'$, and so $F'$ contains a singleton and must therefore be trivial, contrary to assumption.

This proves that any measurable cardinal $N$ is inaccessible. Thomas Jech (whose [Jec97] is a general reference for this area of set theory) proves the much stronger result (Lemma 28.7 and Corollary, p. 313) that $N$ must be Mahlo, and in fact must be the $N$th Mahlo cardinal. He goes on to define yet a third class of cardinals, the *supercompact* cardinals (p. 408), and to show that each supercompact cardinal $N$ must be measurable, and in fact must be the $N$th measurable cardinal (Lemma 33.10 and Corollary, p. 410).

In light of the preceding, we can say that various axioms implying the existence of very many large inaccessible cardinals have been considered in the literature, with some hope that they can be used to define consistent extensions of the axioms of set theory.

The preceding discussion suggests the following transfinite recursive definition, which generalizes some of the properties of very large cardinals considered above:

$$\begin{aligned} P_x(N) \leftrightarrow_{\text{Def}} &\ \textbf{if } x = \emptyset \ \textbf{ then } \mathsf{Is\_inaccessible}(N) \\ &\ \textbf{else } \big(\forall y \in x \mid \#\{M : M \in N \mid P_y(M)\} = N\big)\, \textbf{end if}\,. \end{aligned} \tag{2.18}$$

Thus $P_0(N)$ is true iff $N$ is inaccessible, $P_1(N)$ is true iff $N$ is the $N$th inaccessible (which we have seen to be true for Mahlo cardinals), $P_2(N)$ is true iff $N$ is the $N$th cardinal having property $P_1$ (which we have seen to be true for measurable cardinals), etc. So the axiom

$$\big(\forall x \mid \mathsf{Ord}(x) \to \big(\exists N \mid P_x(N)\big)\big)$$

implies the existence of many and very large cardinals. And, if one likes, one can repeat this construction after replacing the predicate '$\mathsf{Is\_inaccessible}$' in (2.18) by

$$\big(\exists K \,\big|\, \big(\forall x \in K \mid \mathsf{Ord}(x) \to \big(\exists N \mid P_x(N)\big)\big)\big).$$

These particular statements do not seem to have been studied enough for surmises concerning their consistency or inconsistency to have developed. But if they are all consistent, there will exist *inner models* of set theory, in the sense described in the next section, in which any finite collection of them are true. This will allow theories containing such axioms to be covered by 'axioms of reflection' of the kind that will be discussed in Sect. 6.3. Of course, all of this resembles the play of children with large numbers: '*a thousand trillion gazillion* ***plus one***'.

#### 2.4.2.4 More General 'Inner' Models of Set Theory

A predicate model of the Zermelo–Fraenkel axioms must provide some set $\mathcal{U}$ as universe and assign a two-variable Boolean function $E$ on $\mathcal{U}$ to represent the non-logical symbol '$\in$'. The most direct (but of course not the only) way of doing this is to choose a set $\mathcal{U}$ having appropriate properties and simply to define $E$ as

$$E(x, y) = \textbf{if } x \in y \textbf{ then } 1 \textbf{ else } 0 \textbf{ end if},$$

which can be written more simply as

$$E(x, y) \leftrightarrow (x \in y)$$

if we agree to represent predicates by true/false-valued, rather than 0/1-valued, functions. (An element $A(x)$ of $\mathcal{U}$ must be assigned to each free variable $x$ appearing in a term or formula whose value is to be calculated.) Using this convention, and noting that the ZFC axioms involve no function symbols and so they do not require formation of any terms, we can write our previous recursive rules for calculating the value associated with each predicate expression $F$ (cf. Sect. 2.2) in the following slightly specialized way:

(i) If the expression $F$ is just an individual variable $x$, then $\mathsf{Val}(A, F) = A(x)$.

(ii) If $F$ is an atomic formula having the form '$x \in y$', then $\mathsf{Val}(A, F)$ is the Boolean value $A(x) \in A(y)$.

(iii) If $F$ is a formula having the form $(\forall v_1, \ldots, v_k \mid e)$, then $\mathsf{Val}(A, F)$ is

$$\big(\forall x_1, \ldots, x_k \mid (x_1 \in \mathcal{U} \,\&\, \cdots \,\&\, x_k \in \mathcal{U}) \rightarrow \mathsf{Val}\big(A(x_1, \ldots, x_k), e\big)\big),$$

where $A(x_1, \ldots, x_k)$ assigns the same value as $A$ to every free variable of $e$, but assigns the value $x_j$ to each $v_j$, for $j$ from 1 to $k$.

(iv) If $F$ is a formula having the form $(\exists v_1, \ldots, v_k \mid e)$, then $\mathsf{Val}(A, F)$ is

$$\big(\exists x_1, \ldots, x_k \mid (x_1 \in \mathcal{U} \,\&\, \cdots \,\&\, x_k \in \mathcal{U}) \,\&\, \mathsf{Val}\big(A(x_1, \ldots, x_k), e\big)\big),$$

where $A(x_1, \ldots, x_k)$ assigns the same value as $A$ to every free variable of $e$, but assigns the value $x_j$ to each $v_j$, for $j$ from 1 to $k$.

(v) If the formula $F$ has the form '$G \,\&\, H$', then $\mathsf{Val}(A, F)$ is $\mathsf{Val}(A, G) \,\&\, \mathsf{Val}(A, H)$.

(vi) If the formula $F$ has the form '$G \vee H$', then $\mathsf{Val}(A, F)$ is $\mathsf{Val}(A, G) \vee \mathsf{Val}(A, H)$.

(vii) If the formula $F$ has the form '$\neg G$', then

$$\mathsf{Val}(A, F) = \big(\neg \mathsf{Val}(A, G)\big).$$

(viii) If the formula $F$ has the form '$G \rightarrow H$', then $\mathsf{Val}(A, F)$ is

$$\mathsf{Val}(A, G) \rightarrow \mathsf{Val}(A, H).$$

(ix) If the formula $F$ has the form '$G \leftrightarrow H$', then $\mathsf{Val}(A, F)$ is

$$\mathsf{Val}(A, G) \leftrightarrow \mathsf{Val}(A, H).$$

The set $\mathcal{U}$ defines a model of ZFC if and only if each of the ZFC axioms evaluates to 'true' under these rules. We shall pinpoint in Sect. 6.3 conditions on $\mathcal{U}$ sufficient for this to be the case.

We will generally suppose that $\mathcal{U}$ is *transitive*, i.e. that each member of a member of $\mathcal{U}$ is also a member of $\mathcal{U}$. Then axiom (1) of ZFC evaluates to

$$\big(\forall s, t \mid (s \in \mathcal{U} \;\&\; t \in \mathcal{U}) \rightarrow \big(s = t \leftrightarrow \big(\forall x \mid (x \in \mathcal{U}) \rightarrow \big((x \in s) \leftrightarrow (x \in t)\big)\big)\big)\big).$$

This formula clearly has the value $\mathsf{true}$. Indeed, if $s = t$, then $(x \in s) \leftrightarrow (x \in t)$ for every $x \in \mathcal{U}$, so clearly

$$\big(\forall x \mid (x \in \mathcal{U}) \rightarrow \big((x \in s) \leftrightarrow (x \in t)\big)\big) \tag{2.19}$$

must be true. Suppose conversely that $s \neq t$. Then by the ZFC axiom of extensionality, one of these sets, say $s$, has a member $x$ that is not in the other. Since $\mathcal{U}$ is transitive we have $x \in \mathcal{U}$, so (2.19) must be false.

ZFC axiom (6) (axiom of regularity) evaluates to

$$\neg\big(\exists x \mid (x \in \mathcal{U}) \;\&\; (x \neq \emptyset)$$
$$\&\; \big(\forall y \,\big|\, \big((y \in \mathcal{U}) \;\&\; (y \in x)\big) \rightarrow \big(\exists z \mid (z \in \mathcal{U}) \;\&\; (z \in x) \;\&\; (z \in y)\big)\big)\big),$$

and this also must be true. Indeed, if $x$ in $\mathcal{U}$ is non-null, then by the ZFC axiom of regularity it must have an element $y$ which is disjoint from it, and since $\mathcal{U}$ is transitive this $y$ is also in $\mathcal{U}$.

## References

[Jec97] Jech, T.J.: Set Theory, 2nd edn. Perspectives in Mathematical Logic. Springer, Berlin (1997)

# Chapter 3
# A Survey of Inference Mechanisms

In this chapter we provide an extended survey of inference mechanisms which are candidates for inclusion in the verifier's initial *endowment*, and note the efficiency considerations which limit the complexity of the sets of statements to which each inference mechanism can be applied.

In addition to discourse-manipulation mechanisms that will be described in Sects. 4.1 and 4.4, the verifier depends critically on a collection of routines which work by combinatorial search. These are able to examine certain limited classes of logical and set-theoretic formulae and determine their logical validity or invalidity directly. Together they constitute the verifier's inferential core. In the following paragraphs we will examine a variety of candidate algorithms of this kind. While all of these (plus many others too complex to be described here) are interesting in their own right, not all are worth including in the verifier's initial endowment of deduction procedures, since some are too inefficient to be practical, while others are too specialized to be applied more than rarely in ordinary mathematical discourse. The selection actually made in the verifier will be detailed once the collection of candidates that suggest themselves has been reviewed. We begin this review by discussing one of the most elementary but important decision procedures, the *Davis–Putnam–Logemann–Loveland* technique for deciding the validity of sets of propositional formulae [DP60].

## 3.1 The Davis–Putnam Propositional Decision Algorithm

The Davis–Putnam algorithm works on collections $C$ of propositional formulae, each supposed to be a disjunction of the form

$$P_1 \vee P_2 \vee \cdots \vee P_n \tag{3.1}$$

with $n \geqslant 1$, where each $P_j$ is either a propositional symbol or its opposite. It determines, for each such collection, whether it is *satisfiable*, i.e. whether there exists an

J.T. Schwartz et al., *Computational Logic and Set Theory*,
DOI 10.1007/978-0-85729-808-9_3, © Springer-Verlag London Limited 2011

assignment of truth values to the propositional symbols appearing in the statements of $C$ which makes all these statements true, or unsatisfiable.

The flavor of the collections of propositional formulae (3.1) which the Davis–Putnam procedure takes as input can best be understood by moving all the negated symbols $P_j = (\neg Q_j)$ to the left side of each formula and then rewriting it as

$$(Q_1 \,\&\, Q_2 \,\&\, \cdots \,\&\, Q_k) \rightarrow (P_{k+1} \vee \cdots \vee P_n), \tag{3.2}$$

where now all propositional symbols are non-negated. This allows us to recognize Davis–Putnam input disjunctions (3.1) as implications in which multiple conjoined hypotheses $Q_j$ imply one of several alternate conclusions $P_i$. We see at once that sets of clauses of this type are quite typical for ordinary mathematical discourse, and that most typically they will contain just one conclusion $P_i$ rather than several alternative conclusions. We also are forewarned that if many of the clauses in our input set $C$ contain multiple alternative conclusions, the argument necessary to analyze $C$'s satisfiability will probably involve inspection of an exponentially growing set of possible cases.

The Davis–Putnam procedure is designed to work very efficiently on sets of clauses which can be written as implications containing no or few alternative conclusions. It works as follows in a set of input formulae (3.1).

(1) If possible, find a formula $F$ in $C$ consisting of just one propositional atom $Q$, either negated (i.e. $F$ is '$\neg Q$') or non-negated (i.e. $F$ is $Q$). Assign $Q$ the value 'false' if it occurs negated; otherwise assign it the value 'true'.

(2) If step (1) succeeds, remove $F$ from $C$, along with every formula $G$ in which $Q$ occurs with the same sign as in $F$. This reflects the fact that all these $G$ are already satisfied, since '$H \vee$ true' is propositionally equivalent to 'true' for every proposition $H$. Also, remove the negation of $F$ from every formula $G$ in which $Q$ occurs with sign opposite to that seen in $F$. This reflects the fact that '$H \vee$ false' is propositionally equivalent to $H$, for every proposition $H$.

If step (2) ever generates an empty set of propositions, then the whole initial set is clearly satisfied by the sequence of truth values assigned. If it ever generates an empty disjunction (resulting from the fact that two opposed propositions $Q$ and '$\neg Q$' have been seen), then the search ends in failure, since a propositional contradiction has been found.

(3) If step (1) fails, we can find no propositional symbol whose truth value is immediately evident. In this case, we proceed nondeterministically, by choosing some symbol $Q$ that appears in one of the formulae remaining in $C$, and guessing it to have one of the two possible truth values 'true' and 'false'. Guessing that $Q$ is true amounts to adding to $C$ the formula $F$ consisting of $Q$ alone, and guessing that $Q$ is false amounts to inserting the negation of $Q$ into $C$. Thus, in either case, the recursive execution of step (1) is enabled. If this eventually leads to truth values satisfying all the remaining propositions of $C$ we are done; otherwise we backtrack to the (last) point at which we have made a nondeterministic guess, and try the opposite guess. If both guesses fail, then we fail overall. A chain of failures back to the point of our very first guess implies that the input set $C$ of propositions in not satisfiable.

It is easily seen that if we think of a set of Davis–Putnam input clauses as having the form (3.2), then the maximum number of nondeterministic trials that can occur in steps (3) is at most the product $K$ of the numbers $n - k$ of possible alternative conclusions appearing in clauses of the input. Although this can be exponentially large in the worst possible case, it will not be large in typical mathematical situations. Thus we can generally rely on the Davis–Putnam algorithm to handle the propositional side of our verifier's work very effectively.

The Davis–Putnam algorithm can easily be adapted to generate the set of *all* truth-value assignments which satisfy a given set $C$ of input clauses. For this, we search as above, until a satisfying assignment is found, then collect this assignment into a set of all such assignments, but signal the algorithm to behave as if search has failed, so that it will backtrack in the manner described above until it has found the next possible assignment. When no more satisfying assignments can be found, we have collected the set TVA of all truth-value assignments which satisfy all the clauses in $C$. Note that the argument given in the previous paragraph shows that the number of elements in TVA can be no larger than the product $K$ considered there.

If we are using the Davis–Putnam algorithm simply to search for one truth-value assignment satisfying the set of clauses $C$, rather than searching for the set of all such assignments, then it can be improved by including the following step (2b) immediately after the step (2) seen above:

(2b) If any propositional symbol $Q$ occurs in all remaining statements of $C$ with the same sign (that is, either always negated or always non-negated), then give $Q$ the corresponding truth-value (i.e. 'false' if it always occurs negated, 'true' otherwise), and remove all the clauses containing $Q$ from $C$.

This must work since if our clauses have any satisfying assignment, we can change the assignment to give $Q$ the truth value specified by rule (2b), since all clauses not containing $Q$ will clearly still be satisfied, but equally clearly the clauses not containing $Q$ will be satisfied also.

### 3.1.1 Horn Formulae and Sets of Formulae

A propositional formula

$$P_1 \vee P_2 \vee \cdots \vee P_n$$

is called a *Horn formula* if at most one of the propositional symbols in it occurs non-negated, and a set $C$ of such formulae is called a *Horn set.* It is easily seen that any such set $C$ which does not contain (either the empty disjunction or) at least one 'linked' positive 'unit' formula $A$ (i.e. a formula consisting of just the single propositional symbol $A$ that also occurs negated in some other formula) must be satisfiable. For clearly if we give the value 'true' to every symbol $A$ that appears as a positive unit clause of $C$, and 'false' to every symbol that occurs negated in a formula of $C$, all the formulae in $C$ will be satisfied. It follows from this that in the case of an unsatisfiable set $C$ of Horn clauses the Davis–Putnam algorithm will never run out of unit clauses before deducing an empty clause, and so need never use its recursive step (3). In this case, the algorithm will run in time linear in the total length of its input.

For later use it is worth noting that we can look at such 'Horn' cases in a different, somewhat more 'algebraic', way. The non-negated unit formulae $A$ can be considered to be 'inputs', and the formulae

$$(\neg B_1) \vee (\neg B_2) \vee \cdots \vee (\neg B_m)$$

which only consist of negated propositional symbols to be 'goals'. The remaining clauses, which must all have the form

$$(A_1 \ \& \ A_2 \ \& \cdots \& \ A_n) \rightarrow B,$$

can be seen as 'multiplication rules' which allow collections $A_1, A_2, \ldots, A_n$ of inputs to be combined to generate new inputs $B$. Proof of unsatisfiability results once a sequence of multiplications leading to the opposites $B_j$ of all constituents '$\neg B_j$' of a goal formula is found. Note that this observation shows that a Horn set is unsatisfiable if and only if some one of its subsets obtained by dropping all but one of its goal formulae is unsatisfiable.

## 3.1.2 Reducing Collections of Propositional Formulae to Collections of Standardized Disjunctions

Since ordinary mathematical statements generally have the form

$$multiple\_hypotheses \rightarrow single\_conclusion,$$

most of the propositional inferences arising in ordinary mathematical practice convert very readily into the disjunctive Horn form favourable for application of the Davis–Putnam algorithm as soon as their non-propositional elements are reduced ('blobbed down') to propositional symbols. Other formulae can be converted into collections of disjunctions using the following straightforward procedure:

1. Express all other propositional operators in the given collection of propositional formulae by their expressions in terms of the operators '&', '$\vee$', and '$\neg$'.
2. Move all the negations down in the syntax trees of these formulae by using de Morgan's rules: '$\neg(a \ \& \ b)$' is equivalent to '$(\neg a) \vee (\neg b)$', etc. Use the rule $(\neg(\neg a)) \leftrightarrow a$ to eliminate all double negations.
3. Use the fact that disjunction is distributive over conjunction to 'multiply out' wherever a disjunction of conjunctions is encountered, thereby reducing each formula to a conjunction of disjunctions, each such disjunction involving only propositional atoms and their opposites.

Although in most cases encountered in ordinary mathematical practice this recipe will work well, in some cases its third step can expand one of the initial formulae into exponentially many conjunctions. This will, for example, be the case if we multiply out a formula of the form

$$(a_1 \,\&\, b_1) \vee (a_2 \,\&\, b_2) \vee \cdots \vee (a_n \,\&\, b_n)\,.$$

In such cases we can use an alternative, equally easy, approach, which, however, replaces our original set of propositional formulae, not by logically equivalent formulae, but by equisatisfiable formulae (since new variables are introduced). This alternative method is guaranteed to increase the length of our original collection by no more than a constant factor. It works as follows: after applying the above steps (1) and (2), progressively reduce the syntax tree of each of the resulting collection of formulae by working progressively upwards in the tree, replacing each conjunction '$a \,\&\, b$' and each disjunction '$a \vee b$' introducing a new variable $c$ which replaces '$a \,\&\, b$' (resp. '$a \vee b$'), along with a conjoined clause '$c \leftrightarrow (a \,\&\, b)$' (resp. '$c \leftrightarrow (a \vee b)$'), which we can write as

$$\big((\neg a) \vee (\neg b) \vee c\big) \,\&\, \big((\neg c) \vee a\big) \,\&\, \big((\neg c) \vee b\big)$$

in the first case and as

$$\big((\neg c) \vee a \vee b\big) \,\&\, \big((\neg a) \vee c\big) \,\&\, \big((\neg b) \vee c\big)$$

in the second. After elimination of double negatives, the resulting collection of formulae clearly has the asserted properties, proving our claim.

A reduction technique very similar to this reappears in the following discussion of the decidability of the elementary unquantified theory of Boolean set operators, where it will be called *secondary decomposition*.

## 3.2 Elementary Boolean Theory of Sets

Now we move on from the easily decidable statements of the purely propositional calculus to a somewhat larger but still practicable case, namely that of statements formed using the propositional operators plus the elementary Boolean operators and comparators of set theory: $\cap$, $\cup$, $\setminus$, $\supseteq$, $\subseteq$, and '$=$'. It is convenient to allow the null set $\emptyset$, as a constant. Simple examples of statements that can be formed using these operators are

$$(a \supseteq b \,\&\, b \supseteq c) \rightarrow (a \supseteq c)$$

and

$$(a \supseteq b \,\&\, b \cap c = \emptyset) \rightarrow (a \setminus c \supseteq b),$$

both of which are universally valid.

Statements of this general form can be considered in either of two possible settings, that in which quantifiers are forbidden (as in the examples seen above), and that in which quantifiers are allowed, as in the example

$$\big(\forall a \mid \big(\neg(a \cap b = \emptyset)\big) \to (a \supseteq b)\big).$$

If quantifiers are forbidden we describe the language which confronts us as being *unquantified*; in the opposite case we speak of the *quantified* case. Both cases are decidable, but unsurprisingly the quantified case (which is analyzed in a later section of this chapter) is substantially more complex. Indeed, the last formula displayed is readily seen to be equivalent to $\#b = 1 \vee \#b = 0$. This hints at the fact that analysis of such quantified statements must involve consideration of the number of elements in the sets which appear, a perception which we will see to be true when we come to analyze this case. For this reason we confine ourselves in this section to the much more elementary unquantified case.

This case is quite easy, and can be handled in any one of a number of ways. With an eye on what is to follow, we choose to pursue an approach based on the notion of *place*, which can be described as follows. Given a collection of unquantified statements formed using propositional connectives and the elementary set operators and comparators listed above, and having the goal of testing these statements for satisfiability, we can begin by using the Davis–Putnam algorithm (or any other propositional-level algorithm of the same kind) to determine all the propositional-level truth-value assignments which would verify all the statements in our collection. Each of these truth-value assignments gives rise to some collection of negated and non-negated atomic formulae of our language, no longer containing any propositional operators. These collections of formulae must then be tested for satisfiability. If any such collection is found to be satisfiable, then so are our original formulae. If no truth-value pattern satisfying our original formulae at the propositional level gives rise to a collection of atomic formulae which can be satisfied at the underlying set-theoretic level, then our original formula collection is plainly unsatisfiable. We shall refer to this preliminary propositional level step as *decomposition at the propositional level*.

We can equally readily eliminate all compound expressions such as $a \cup (b \cap c)$ formed using the available operators $\cap$, $\cup$, $\setminus$, by introducing new auxiliary variables $t$ and equalities like $t = b \cap c$, which allows compound expressions like $a \cup (b \cap c)$ to be rewritten as $a \cup t$. Similarly, inequalities like $\neg(a = b \cup c)$ can be reduced to inequalities of the simpler form $\neg(a = t)$ by introducing auxiliary variables $t$ and replacing $\neg(a = b \cup c)$ by the equisatisfiable pair of statements $t = b \cup c$, $\neg(a = t)$. Once simplifications of this second kind, which we will call *secondary decomposition*, have been applied systematically, what remains is a collection of literals, each having one of the forms

$$x = y \cap z,\ x = y \cup z,\ x = y \setminus z,\ x = \emptyset,\ x = y,\ x \supseteq y,\ \neg(x = y), \qquad (3.3)$$

where $x, y, z$ stand for set-valued variables. Note that all uses of the comparator $\subseteq$ can be eliminated, since '$x \subseteq y$' is just '$y \supseteq x$'.

Next we make use of the following concept.

**Definition 3.1** A *place* $p$ for a collection $C$ of literals of the forms (3.3), formed using the null set constant $\emptyset$ and the operators and comparators $\cap$, $\cup$, $\setminus$, $\supseteq$, and '$=$', is a Boolean-valued map $p(x)$ defined on all of the set-valued variables appearing in propositions of $C$ for which we have

- $p(x) \leftrightarrow (p(y) \,\&\, p(z))$ whenever $x = y \cap z$ appears in $C$,
- $p(x) \leftrightarrow (p(y) \vee p(z))$ whenever $x = y \cup z$ appears in $C$,
- $p(x) \leftrightarrow (p(y) \,\&\, (\neg p(z)))$ whenever $x = y \setminus z$ appears in $C$,
- $p(x) \leftrightarrow p(y)$ whenever $x = y$ appears in $C$,
- $p(x) \leftrightarrow \mathsf{false}$ whenever $x = \emptyset$ appears in $C$,
- $p(y) \rightarrow p(x)$ whenever $x \supseteq y$ appears in $C$.

Note that this notion depends only on the subcollection of non-negated formulae in $C$. We also observe that the number of distinct places for $C$ is bounded by $2^m$, where $m$ is the number of the distinct variables occurring in the propositions of $C$.

**Definition 3.2** A collection $S$ of places for $C$ is *ample* if, for each negated statement $\neg(x = y)$ in $C$, there exists a $p$ in $S$ such that $\neg(p(x) \leftrightarrow p(y))$.

**Theorem 3.1** *A collection $C$ of literals of the forms* (3.3), *formed using the operators and comparators $\cap$, $\cup$, $\setminus$, $\supseteq$, and '$=$', and the null set constant $\emptyset$ is satisfiable if and only if it has an ample set $A$ of places.*

*Proof* First suppose that $C$ is satisfiable, so that it has a model $\mathcal{M}$, i.e. there exists an assignment $\mathcal{M}(a)$ of an actual set to each variable $a$ appearing in the statements of $C$, such that replacement of each of these variables by the corresponding set $\mathcal{M}(a)$ makes all the statements of $C$ true. Let $\mathcal{U}$ be the 'universe' of this model, i.e. the union of all the sets $\mathcal{M}(a)$, and let $x$ range over the variables appearing in the statements of $C$. Then, for each point $u$ in $\mathcal{U}$, the formula

$$p_u(x) \leftrightarrow \big(u \in \mathcal{M}(x)\big) \tag{3.4}$$

defines a place. Indeed, if $x = y \cap z$ appears in $C$, we have $\mathcal{M}(x) = \mathcal{M}(y) \cap \mathcal{M}(z)$, so $p_u(x) \leftrightarrow (p_u(y) \,\&\, p_u(z))$, and similarly if $x = y \cup z$ appears in $C$, etc. For negated statement in $C$ like '$\neg(x = y)$' we must have $\mathcal{M}(x) \neq \mathcal{M}(y)$, and so there must exist a point $u$ in $\mathcal{U}$ such that $u \in \mathcal{M}(x)$ and $u \in \mathcal{M}(y)$ have different truth values, that is, $\neg(p_u(x) \leftrightarrow p_u(y))$. Hence the set of places deriving from $\mathcal{M}$ via the formula (3.4) is ample.

Conversely let $A$ be an ample set of places. Then we can build a model $\mathcal{M}$ with universe $A$ by setting

$$\mathcal{M}(x) = \big\{p : p \in A \mid p(x)\big\}.$$

The conditions on places displayed above clearly imply that $\mathcal{M}$ is a model of all the positive statements in $C$. But since $A$ is ample, we have $\mathcal{M}(x) \neq \mathcal{M}(y)$ whenever a statement '$\neg(x = y)$' is present in $C$, so that the negative statements in $C$ are modelled correctly also. □

The preceding result implies easily the decidability of the elementary Boolean theory of sets, since the number of distinct places for each collection of literals of the forms (3.3) is exponentially bounded, as observed earlier.

Note that the places $p$ deriving via formula (3.4) from a model $\mathscr{M}$ of any set $C$ of statements serve to classify the points $u$ in the universe of the model into nonempty pairwise disjoint subsets

$$s_p = \{ u \in \mathscr{U} \mid p_u = p \}$$

which are either contained in or disjoint from each of the sets $\mathscr{M}(x)$: in fact, these are the nonempty regions of the Venn diagram of the sets $\mathscr{M}(x)$. Conversely if we assign nonempty disjoint sets $M_p$ to the places $p$ in an ample set $A$ of places in any way, then the union set

$$\mathscr{M}(x) = \bigcup \{ M_p : p \in A \mid p(x) \} \qquad (3.5)$$

is a model of the statements in $C$. Hence altogether, we see that all models of statements in $C$ have this form. This observation will be applied just below.

The technique used in this section, of simplifying collections of statements whose satisfiability is to be determined, first by removing all propositional operators using a preliminary decomposition step, and then reducing all compound expressions by introducing auxiliary variables, will be used repeatedly and implicitly in what follows.

### 3.2.1 *Elementary Boolean Theory of Sets, Plus the Predicates* 'Finite' *and* 'Countable'

We now generalize the unquantified language considered in the preceding section by allowing two additional predicates on sets, namely $\mathsf{Finite}(s)$, which states that $s$ is finite, and $\mathsf{Countable}(s)$, which states that $s$ is either finite or denumerably infinite. (As usual this allows us to write the corresponding negated predicates '$\neg\mathsf{Finite}(x)$' and '$\neg\mathsf{Countable}(x)$'.) In this expanded language we can test candidate statements like

$$\big(a \cup b \supseteq c \;\&\; \mathsf{Countable}(a) \;\&\; \mathsf{Countable}(b)\big) \rightarrow \mathsf{Countable}(c) \qquad (3.6)$$

for satisfiability.

To see how statements in this expanded language can be tested for satisfiability, we have only to use the formula (3.5) shown above. We saw above that any model $\mathscr{M}$ of a collection $C$ of statements involving only Boolean operators and comparators can be analyzed into this form. Let *fi* (resp. *co*) be the set of all places $p$ for which $M_p$ is finite (resp. countably infinite), and let *Fi* and *Co* be the two union sets

$$Fi = \bigcup \{ M_p : p \in fi \},$$

$$Co = \bigcup \{ M_p : p \in fi \cup co \}.$$

Then, plainly, for any variable $x$ for which a statement Finite($x$) (resp. Countable($x$)) is present in $C$, the statement

$$Fi \supseteq \mathscr{M}(x) \quad (\text{resp. } Co \supseteq \mathscr{M}(x))$$

must hold. Also, for any variable $x$ for which a statement '¬Finite($x$)' (resp. '¬Countable($x$)') is present in $C$, the statement

$$\neg\big(Fi \supseteq \mathscr{M}(x)\big) \quad (\text{resp. } \neg(Co \supseteq \mathscr{M}(x)))$$

must hold.

Conversely, suppose that we are given any collection of statements $C$ involving Boolean operators and comparators only, along with assertions of the forms Finite($x$), Countable($x$), ¬Finite($x$), and ¬Countable($x$) for some of the sets $x$ mentioned in the statements of $C$. Introduce two new variables Fi and Co, and for these variables introduce the following statements:

Co ⊇ Fi;
for each $x$ for which a statement Finite($x$) is present,
  a statement Fi ⊇ $x$;
for each $x$ for which a statement Countable($x$) is present,
  a statement Co ⊇ $x$; (3.7)
for each $x$ for which a statement ¬Finite($x$) is present,
  a statement ¬(Fi ⊇ $x$);
for each $x$ for which a statement ¬Countable($x$) is present,
  a statement ¬(Co ⊇ $x$).

Then drop from $C$ all statements of the forms

Finite($x$), Countable($x$), ¬Finite($x$), ¬Countable($x$).

It is plain from what was said above that if our original collection of statements has a model, so does our modified collection. Conversely, if this modified collection has a model, then we can assign disjoint sets $M_p$ to the places $p$ associated with this model according to the following rule:

if $p$(Fi), then let $M_p$ be some single element set;
otherwise, if $p$(Co), then let $M_p$ be some countably infinite set;
otherwise, let $M_p$ be some uncountable set.

It then follows from the collection of statements (3.7) that $\mathscr{M}(x)$ is finite (resp. countable) for each variable $x$ for which a statement 'Finite($x$)' (resp. 'Countable($x$)') was originally present. Moreover if a statement '¬Finite($x$)' was originally present, we must have ¬(Fi ⊇ $x$), so there must exist a place $p$ for which $p$(Fi) is false and $p(x)$ is true, and then plainly $\mathscr{M}(x)$ is not finite. Since much the same argument can be used to handle statements '¬Countable($x$)' originally present, it follows that our original set of statements has a model if and only if the modified version described above has a model. As an example, note that the negative of the statement

$$\big(a \cup b \supseteq c \;\&\; \mathsf{Countable}(a) \;\&\; \mathsf{Countable}(b)\big) \rightarrow \mathsf{Countable}(c)$$

considered above is

$$a \cup b \supseteq c \;\&\; \mathsf{Countable}(a) \;\&\; \mathsf{Countable}(b) \;\&\; \big(\neg\mathsf{Countable}(c)\big).$$

The procedure we have described transforms this into

$$a \cup b \supseteq c \;\&\; Co \supseteq a \;\&\; Co \supseteq b \;\&\; \big(\neg(\mathsf{Co} \supseteq c)\big).$$

Since this is clearly unsatisfiable, the universal validity of our original statement follows.

### 3.2.2 Elementary Boolean Operators on Sets, with the Cardinality Operator and Additive Arithmetic on Integers

We will now generalize the results described above in this Sect. 3.2 by allowing in addition to set-valued variables also a different type of variables $i$, now denoting non-negative integers, and a set-to-integer operation $\#x$. For variables $i, j$ of integer type we allow the operations $i + j$ (integer addition) and $i - j$ (integer subtraction); also, the integer comparators $i > j$ and $i = j$ and two constants designating the integers 0 and 1 are allowed. A simple example of a statement that can be formed using these operators is

$$\big(\#x = 1 \;\&\; \neg(x \cap y = \emptyset)\big) \rightarrow (y \supseteq x),$$

which is universally valid.

By means of decomposition steps of the kind described earlier (decomposition at the propositional level and secondary decomposition), the satisfiability problem for collections of unquantified statements involving

- the null set constant $\emptyset$,
- the set operators and comparators $\cap$, $\cup$, $\setminus$, $\supseteq$, and '$=$',
- the integer constant 0,
- the integer operators and comparators $\#(\cdot)$, $+$, $-$, '$>$', and '$=$'

can be reduced to the satisfiability problem for collections of literals of the forms

$$x = y \cap z,\; x = y \cup z,\; x = y \setminus z,\; x = \emptyset,\; x = y,\; x \supseteq y,\; \neg(x = y), \tag{3.8}$$

$$i = \#x,\; i = j + k,\; i > j,\; i = 0, \tag{3.9}$$

where $x, y, z$ stand for set-valued variables and $i, j, k$ stand for integer-valued variables. Note that all uses of integer subtraction can be eliminated, because we regard '$i = j - k$' as being equivalent to '$j = i + k$'.

Let $C$ be a collection of literals of the forms (3.8) and (3.9) and let $A$ be an ample set of places for $C$. For each place $p$ in $A$, we introduce a new integer-valued variable $i_p$, which is supposed to denote the (finite) cardinality of the set to be later assigned to $p$. It is convenient to associate to $C$ and $A$ the following system $B_{C,A}$ of arithmetic conditions over the integer-valued variables occurring in the statements of $C$ plus the new variables $i_p$. To begin with, we place in $B_{C,A}$ all statements in $C$ of type

$$i = j + k,\ i > j,\ i = 0.$$

Then, for each literal $i = \#x$ in $C$, we add to $B_{C,A}$ the equation

$$i = i_{p_1} + \cdots + i_{p_k},$$

where $p_1, \ldots, p_k$ are all the places $p$ in $A$ such that $p(x) = \mathsf{true}$. Finally, for each statement $\neg(x = y)$ in $C$, we place in $B_{C,A}$ the inequality

$$i_{q_1} + \cdots + i_{q_\ell} > 0,$$

where $q_1, \ldots, q_\ell$ are all the places $q$ in $A$ such that $\neg(q(x) \leftrightarrow q(y))$.

**Theorem 3.2** *A collection $C$ of literals of the forms* (3.8) *and* (3.9) *is satisfiable if and only if it has an ample set $A$ of places such that the system $B_{C,A}$ of arithmetic conditions associated with $C$ and $A$ admits a non-negative integer solution.*

*Proof* Assume first that $C$ is satisfiable and let $\mathcal{M}$ be a model for $C$ with universe $\mathcal{U}$. Let $A$ be the collection of all places $p_u$ defined by (3.4), for $u \in \mathcal{U}$. By arguing as in the proof of Theorem 3.1, it follows that the set of places $A$ is ample, when restricted to set-valued variables. It remains to extend $\mathcal{M}$ over the integer-valued variables $i_p$, for $p$ in $A$. As above, for each place $p$ in $A$, we let

$$s_p = \{u \in \mathcal{U} \mid p_u = p\}.$$

Then, if $s_p$ is finite we put

$$\mathcal{M}(i_p) = \#s_p,$$

otherwise we leave $\mathcal{M}(i_p)$ undefined, as in the latter case the variable $i_p$ does not occur in any arithmetic condition in the system $B_{C,A}$.

It is an easy matter to verify that the restriction to the integer-valued variables of the assignment $\mathcal{M}$ so extended is a solution for the system $B_{C,A}$ of arithmetic conditions associated to $C$ and $A$.

Conversely, let $A$ be an ample set of places for $C$, and let us assume that the system $B_{C,A}$ of arithmetic conditions associated with $C$ and $A$ admits a non-negative integer solution $\mathscr{M}$. We assign disjoint sets $M_p$ to the places $p$ in $A$ so as to satisfy the condition

$$\#M_p = \mathscr{M}(i_p).$$

Then for each set-valued variable $x$ occurring in some statement of $C$ we put

$$\mathscr{M}(x) = \bigcup \{ M_p : p \in A \mid p(x) \}.$$

It can easily be verified that the assignment $\mathscr{M}$ so extended is a model for $C$. For instance, let $\neg(x = y)$ be a statement in $C$ and let $q_1, \ldots, q_\ell$ be all the places $q$ in $A$ such that $\neg(q(x) \leftrightarrow q(y))$. Since $A$ is ample, $\ell \geqslant 1$. By construction, the system $B_{C,A}$ of arithmetic conditions associated with $C$ and $A$ must contain the inequality

$$i_{q_1} + \cdots + i_{q_\ell} > 0,$$

and therefore

$$\mathscr{M}(i_{q_1}) + \cdots + \mathscr{M}(i_{q_\ell}) > 0$$

holds. Without loss of generality, we can therefore assume that $\mathscr{M}(i_{q_1}) > 0$ holds, so that $M_{q_1} \neq \emptyset$. Since

$$\mathscr{M}(x) \supseteq M_{q_1} \quad \text{if and only if} \quad \mathscr{M}(y) \not\supseteq M_{q_1},$$

we can conclude that $\mathscr{M}(x) \neq \mathscr{M}(y)$, proving that $\mathscr{M}$ satisfies the statement $\neg(x = y)$. Similarly it can be shown that $\mathscr{M}$ satisfies also all statements in $C$ of the remaining types, concluding the proof of the theorem. □

Solvability of systems of arithmetic conditions of the types present in $B_{C,A}$ can be tested algorithmically by a method originally developed by M. Presburger in [Pre30]. Therefore the above result readily entails the decidability of the elementary Boolean theory of sets with the cardinality operator and additive arithmetic on integers. Presburger's decision method will be reviewed in detail in Sect. 3.8.1.

### 3.2.3 *Quantified Predicate Formulae Involving Predicates of One Argument Only*

Quantified formulae of the predicate calculus involving only predicates of a single argument and no function symbols can be decided rather easily as for satisfiability by relating them to elementary set-theoretic formulae of the kind considered above. This can be done as follows. Let $F$ be any such formula. First remove all propositional '$\rightarrow$' and '$\leftrightarrow$' operators by replacing them with appropriate combinations of the operators '&', '$\vee$', and '$\neg$'. Then introduce a set name $p$ for each predicate name $P$ appearing in the original formula, and using these rewrite each atomic formula $P(x)$ as '$x \in p$'. This step is justified since if the original formula has a model

$\mathcal{M}$ with universe $\mathcal{U}$, then $\mathcal{M}$ will associate a Boolean-valued function $\mathcal{M}(P)$ with each predicate name $P$ appearing in $F$, and we can simply interpret each corresponding $p$ as the set

$$\{u : u \in \mathcal{U} \mid \mathcal{M}(P)(u)\}.$$

Next, working upward in the syntax tree from its twigs toward its root, process successive quantifiers in the following way, so as to remove them. (The approach we are using is accordingly known as *quantifier elimination*.)

(i) Rewrite universal quantifiers '$(\forall x \mid \cdots)$' as the corresponding existential quantifiers '$\neg(\exists x \mid \neg \cdots)$'.

(ii) Use the algebraic rules for the operators '&', '$\vee$', '$\neg$' to rewrite the *body* of each existential $(\exists x \mid \cdots)$ (i.e. the part of it following the sign '$\mid$') as a disjunction of conjunctions, that is, in the form

$$(A_1 \,\&\, A_2 \,\&\cdots\&\, A_i) \vee (B_1 \,\&\, B_2 \,\&\cdots\&\, B_j) \vee \cdots,$$

where each elementary subpart $A, B, \ldots$ which appears is either of the form '$x \in p$', or of the negated form '$\neg(x \in p)$', or is a subformula not involving $x$ as a free variable. Then use the predicate rules

$$\big(\exists x \mid A(x) \vee B(x)\big) \leftrightarrow \big(\big(\exists x \mid A(x)\big) \vee \big(\exists x \mid B(x)\big)\big)$$

and

$$\big(\exists x \mid A(x) \,\&\, C\big) \leftrightarrow \big(\big(\exists x \mid A(x)\big) \,\&\, C\big)$$

(where $x$ has no free occurrences in $C$) to reduce the existential quantifier being processed to the form

$$(\exists x \mid A_1 \,\&\, A_2 \,\&\cdots\&\, A_n),$$

where each $A_i$ appearing is either of the form '$x \in p$' or '$x \notin p$'.[1] This confronts us with an existential formula of the form

$$(\exists x \mid x \in p_1 \,\&\cdots\&\, x \in p_m \,\&\, x \notin p_{m+1} \,\&\cdots\&\, x \notin p_n),$$

which we can rewrite as

$$\big(p_1 \cap \cdots \cap p_m \cap (\mathcal{U} \setminus p_{m+1}) \cap \cdots \cap (\mathcal{U} \setminus p_n)\big) \neq \emptyset$$

($s_1 \neq s_2$ is short for $\neg(s_1 = s_2)$).

It is clear that we can apply this procedure until no quantifiers remain, at which point we will have derived a formula $F'$ of the unquantified language of elementary

[1] $x \notin p$ is short for $\neg(x \in p)$.

Boolean-set operations considered previously which is equisatisfiable with our initial quantified formula $F$. By testing $F'$ for satisfiability using the method described above, we therefore can determine whether $F$ is satisfiable. Note that clauses

$$\mathcal{U} \supseteq p_j$$

and a clause $\mathcal{U} \neq \emptyset$ implying that the universe $\mathcal{U}$ is non-null and includes all the other sets which appear in our formula must be added just before the final satisfiability check is applied.

Note also that this procedure converts our original collection of quantified formulae into a collection of purely Boolean statements about the sets $\{u : u \in \mathcal{U} \mid P(u)\}$, which can, however, involve arbitrary intersections of these sets and their complements.

As an example of this procedure, consider the formula

$$\big(\exists x \mid (\exists y \mid P(y)) \rightarrow P(x)\big) \tag{3.10}$$

examined in an earlier section. The negation of this is

$$\neg\big(\exists x \mid \big(\neg(\exists y \mid P(y))\big) \vee P(x)\big).$$

Processing this as above we get

$$\neg(p = \emptyset \vee p \neq \emptyset) \ \&\ \mathcal{U} \supseteq p \ \&\ \mathcal{U} \neq \emptyset,$$

which is clearly unsatisfiable. Hence (3.10) is universally valid.

Various somewhat more general quantified cases can be reduced to the case just treated. For example, suppose that as above we take quantified formulae of the predicate calculus involving only predicates of a single argument, but now also allow function symbols of a single variable. If the function symbols sometimes appear compounded within predicates, as in the example $P(f(g(h(x))))$, we can introduce auxiliary new predicate symbols $P^f$ and $P^{fg}$ along with defining clauses

$$\big(\forall x \mid P^f(x) \leftrightarrow P\big(f(x)\big)\big) \ \&\ \big(\forall x \mid P^{fg}(x) \leftrightarrow P^f\big(g(x)\big)\big),$$

and then rewrite $P(f(g(h(x))))$ as $P^{fg}(h(x))$.

Suppose that there exists a model $\mathcal{M}$ with universe $\mathcal{U}$ of the collection of statements, which must therefore model all the predicates $P$ and functions $f$ in such a way as to make all the quantified statements in our original collection $C$ of statements true. Associate the set

$$S_P = \big\{u \in \mathcal{U} \mid \mathcal{M}(P)(u)\big\}$$

with each predicate $P$, and the set

$$S_{Pf} = \big\{u \in \mathcal{U} \mid \mathcal{M}(P)\big(\mathcal{M}(f)(u)\big)\big\}$$

with each predicate symbol $P$ and function symbol $f$. Then $S_{Pf}$ is the inverse image of $S_P$ under the map $\mathcal{M}(f)$ modelling $f$. Let $P_1, \ldots, P_n$ be all the predicate symbols inside of which $f$ appears (as $P_j(f(x))$ for some variable $x$), let

$$S_{P_1} \cap S_{P_2} \cap \cdots \cap S_{P_k} \setminus (S_{P_{k+1}} \cup \cdots \cup S_{P_n}) \tag{3.11}$$

be some intersection of the sets $S_{P_j}$ and their complements, and let

$$S_{P_1 f} \cap S_{P_2 f} \cap \cdots \cap S_{P_k f} \setminus (S_{P_{k+1} f} \cup \cdots \cup S_{P_n f}) \tag{3.12}$$

be the corresponding intersection of the sets $S_{P_j f}$.

It follows that if the first of these sets is empty so is the other, and conversely. Hence, if a model $\mathcal{M}$ for our collection of quantified statements exists, there must exist a model for the collection of sets $S_{P_j}$ and $S_{P_j f}$ which satisfies all the conditions

$$\begin{aligned} &S_{P_1} \cap S_{P_2} \cap \cdots \cap S_{P_k} \setminus (S_{P_{k+1}} \cup \cdots \cup S_{P_n}) = \emptyset \\ &\quad \leftrightarrow S_{P_1 f} \cap S_{P_2 f} \cap \cdots \cap S_{P_k f} \setminus (S_{P_{k+1} f} \cup \cdots \cup S_{P_n f}) = \emptyset. \end{aligned} \tag{3.13}$$

Earlier in this section we developed a systematic method for converting every collection of quantified statements involving only predicates of the form $P(x)$ to an equisatisfiable collection $C'$ of statements about the sets $S_P = \{x \mid P(x)\}$, together with their intersections and complements. If we employ this procedure in the present case, we get a collection $C''$ of statements about the sets $S_P = \{x \mid P(x)\}$ and $S_{Pf} = \{x \mid P(f(x))\}$, together with their intersections and complements, which must be satisfied even if the conditions (3.13) are added. Conversely, suppose that we can find a set-theoretic model for the collection of statements $C''$ plus all statements of type (3.13). Then we can define the predicates $P(x)$ as '$x \in S_P$', and the predicates $P(f(x))$ as '$x \in S_{Pf}$'. To be sure that these predicates can derive from some model of these same predicates in which there do exist maps for which '$x \in S_{Pf} \leftrightarrow f(x) \in S_P$', we can argue as follows. In the assumed model $\mathcal{M}'$ of the sets $S_P$, any two sets of the form (3.11) will be disjoint if the pattern of intersections and complements defining them are different. Hence we can map the whole of each non-null set (3.11) into some selected point $p$ of the (also non-null) set (3.12). This plainly maps each set $S_P$ into the set $S_{Pf}$, establishing that we do have a model of the original collection of quantified statements.

The following formula illustrates the technique just described:

$$\begin{pmatrix} (\forall x \mid (P(x) \,\&\, P(f(x))) \to P(f'(x))) \\ \&\, (\forall x \mid P(f(x)) \to P(x)) \\ \&\, (\exists x \mid P(f(x))) \end{pmatrix} \to (\exists x \mid P(f'(x))). \tag{3.14}$$

The negative of this is the conjoined collection of formulae

$$\begin{gathered} (\forall x \mid (P(x) \,\&\, P(f(x))) \to P(f'(x))), \\ (\forall x \mid P(f(x)) \to P(x)), \end{gathered}$$

$$\big(\exists x \mid P(f(x))\big),$$
$$\neg\big(\exists x \mid P(f'(x))\big).$$

The transformed set $C'$ of formulae derived from this in the manner described above is

$$\big(\forall x \mid (P(x) \,\&\, P_f(x)) \rightarrow P_{f'}(x)\big),$$
$$\big(\forall x \mid P_f(x) \rightarrow P(x)\big),$$
$$\big(\exists x \mid P_f(x)\big),$$
$$\neg\big(\exists x \mid P_{f'}(x)\big).$$

If we now consider the predicate symbols to designate sets, this gives

$$p_{f'} \supseteq p \cap p_f \,\&\, p \supseteq p_f \,\&\, p_f \neq \emptyset \,\&\, p_{f'} = \emptyset. \tag{3.15}$$

Here there appear two sets $p_f$ and $p_{f'}$ derived from predicate terms involving function symbols, one for each of the function symbols $f$ and $f'$. The additional conditions which need to be added to guarantee equisatisfiability are

$$p = \emptyset \leftrightarrow p_f = \emptyset, \qquad \mathscr{U} \setminus p = \emptyset \leftrightarrow \mathscr{U} \setminus p_f = \emptyset,$$
$$p = \emptyset \leftrightarrow p_{f'} = \emptyset, \qquad \mathscr{U} \setminus p = \emptyset \leftrightarrow \mathscr{U} \setminus p_{f'} = \emptyset,$$

together with conditions stating that all other sets are included in $\mathscr{U}$ and that $\mathscr{U}$ is non-null, so that $\mathscr{U}$ must designate the universe of any model. Since the conjunction of all these Boolean conditions is clearly unsatisfiable (in fact, the conjunction (3.15) by itself is already unsatisfiable), formula (3.14) must be universally valid.

We can allow the use of both the MLSS constructs defined in the next section, namely membership statements '$x \in y$' and singleton terms '$\{x\}$', and of quantified predicates $P(x)$, $Q(y)$ of a single variable, under the very restrictive but easy-to-check condition that no quantified variable $x$ can appear in any set-theoretic expression or relationship other than atomic expressions of one of the forms

$$x = e \text{ or } x \in e \text{ or } P(x),$$

where the expression $e$ does not involve any quantified variable. As explained above, a nominal set $p$ can be associated with each predicate $P$, and $P(x)$ then written as $x \in p$. The reductions described above apply easily to the somewhat generalized statements that result. Note that a quantified expressions like

$$(\exists x \mid x = e \,\&\, x \in p_1 \,\&\, \cdots \,\&\, x \in p_m \,\&\, x \notin p_{m+1} \,\&\, \cdots \,\&\, x \notin p_n)$$

can be rewritten as

$$e \in p_1 \cap \cdots \cap p_m \cap (\mathscr{U} \setminus p_{m+1}) \cap \cdots \cap (\mathscr{U} \setminus p_n),$$

while

$$(\exists x \mid (\neg(x=e)) \,\&\, x \in p_1 \,\&\, \cdots \,\&\, x \in p_m \,\&\, x \notin p_{m+1} \,\&\, \cdots \,\&\, x \notin p_n)$$

can be rewritten as

$$(\mathscr{U} \setminus \{e\}) \cap p_1 \cap \cdots \cap p_m \cap (\mathscr{U} \setminus p_{m+1}) \cap \cdots \cap (\mathscr{U} \setminus p_n) \neq \emptyset,$$

so that removal of quantifiers in the manner explained always generates statements belonging to MLSS.

Certain limited classes of statements involving set formers reduce to the kinds of statements considered above. For example, the inclusion

$$\{x \in s \mid P(x)\} \supseteq \{e(y) : y \in t \mid Q(y)\}$$

can be written as

$$(\forall y \mid (y \in t \,\&\, Q(y)) \rightarrow (e(y) \in s \,\&\, P(e(y)))).$$

On the other hand, the converse inclusion

$$\{x \in s \mid P(x)\} \subseteq \{e(y) : y \in t \mid Q(y)\}$$

translates into

$$(\forall x \mid (\exists y \mid (x \in s \,\&\, P(x)) \rightarrow (x = e(y) \,\&\, y \in t \,\&\, Q(y))))$$

which involves the binary equality operator and so is not covered by the preceding discussion. This indicates that statements involving set formers can only be handled by the method just described in particularly favourable cases.

## 3.3 MLSS: Multilevel Syllogistic with Singletons

MLSS is the (unquantified) extension of the elementary Boolean theory of sets obtained by allowing the membership relator '$x \in y$' and the singleton operator $\{x\}$ in addition to the elementary operators and relators $\cap$, $\cup$, $\setminus$, $\supseteq$, and '$=$'. Given a collection $C$ of statements in this language, we begin as usual by applying decomposition at the propositional level, and then secondary decomposition. This allows us to assume for decidability purposes that $C$ consists of statements each having one of the forms

$$x = y \cup y',\ x = y \cap y',\ x = y \setminus y',\ x = y,\ \neg(x = y),\ y \in x,\ \neg(y \in x),\ x = \{y\}.$$

We then eliminate all the statements '$x = y$' by selecting a representative of any group of set variables known to be equal, and replacing each occurrence of a variable in the group by its selected representative.

Next we prepare $C$ for the analysis given below by enlarging it, but in a manner preserving satisfiability. This is done by collecting all the variables $y$ which appear in statements of the form '$y \in x$', '$\neg(y \in x)$', or '$x = \{y\}$'. We will call these $y$ the *left-hand* variables. Then, for each pair $y_1$, $y_2$ of such variables we add the statement

$$y_1 = y_2 \vee \neg(y_1 = y_2).$$

Since the indicated statements are universally valid, these additions evidently preserve satisfiability. Subsequently, we apply decomposition at the propositional level once more, and again eliminate all statements $x = y$ by selecting representatives in the manner described above. This leaves us with a modified collection $C$ of statements, each having one of the forms

$$x = y \cup y', \; x = y \cap y', \; x = y \setminus y', \; \neg(x = y), \; y \in x, \; \neg(y \in x), \; x = \{y\}. \quad (3.16)$$

But now, after the steps of preparation we have described, we can be sure that for any two distinct left-hand variables $y_1$ and $y_2$, an explicit inequality '$\neg(y_1 = y_2)$' is present in $C$. We denote by *Lvars* the collection of left-variables of $C$.

Now suppose our collection $C$ of statements has a model $\mathcal{M}$ with universe $\mathcal{U}$. As in our previous discussion of the elementary Boolean case, the set $A$ of places $p_u$ defined by

$$p_u(x) \leftrightarrow u \in \mathcal{M}(x),$$

where $u$ ranges over the points of $\mathcal{U}$, must be ample for the subcollection of elementary Boolean statements in $C$, namely those not of the form $y \in x$, $\neg(y \in x)$, or $x = \{y\}$. The points $\mathcal{M}(y) \in \mathcal{U}$ corresponding to left-hand variables $y$ appearing in $C$ define places $p_y$ (via our standard formula $p_y(x) \leftrightarrow \mathcal{M}(y) \in \mathcal{M}(x)$),[2] which plainly must have the following properties:

$p_y(x)$ is true if a statement '$y \in x$' appears in $C$;
$p_y(x)$ is false if a statement '$\neg(y \in x)$' appears in $C$;
$p_y(x)$ is true if a statement '$x = \{y\}$' appears in $C$.

We call a place $p_y$ having these three properties a *place at* $y$. Some of the places corresponding to points in the model $\mathcal{M}$ will be places at $y$ for some variable $y$ in the set $C$ of statements, others will not.

We now look a bit more closely at the structure of the model $\mathcal{M}$, with an eye toward accumulating enough properties of its places to guarantee the existence of at least one model. Note first of all that since set theory forbids all cycles

$$s_1 \in s_2 \in \cdots \in s_n \in s_1$$

of membership, it must be possible to arrange the sets $\mathcal{M}(x)$ of our model into an order for which the variable $x$ comes before $y$ whenever $\mathcal{M}(x)$ is a member of

[2] Strictly speaking, places $p_y$ should be denoted by $p_{\mathcal{M}(y)}$.

$\mathscr{M}(y)$. We will call any such order an *acceptable ordering* of the variables of $C$. Note that for any acceptable ordering, and any variables $y$ and $x$, $p_y(x)$ can only be true if $y$ precedes $x$ in this ordering.

For each place $p$ of the model we can let $M_p$ be the collection of all points $u$ of $\mathscr{U}$ such that $(u \in \mathscr{M}(x)) \leftrightarrow (p(x) = \text{true})$ for every variable $x$ appearing in a statement of $C$, minus all points having the form $\mathscr{M}(z)$ for some left-hand variable $z$. This allows us to write each set $\mathscr{M}(x)$ of the model in the following way for each variable $y$ appearing in $C$:

$$\mathscr{M}(x) = \{\mathscr{M}(z) : z \in Lvars \mid p_z(x)\} \cup \bigcup \{M_p : p \in A \mid p(x)\}. \tag{3.17}$$

The sets $M_p$ are clearly disjoint for distinct $p$, i.e. $M_p \cap M_q = \emptyset$ if $p \neq q$. If a statement '$x = \{y\}$' appears in $C$, then $\mathscr{M}(x)$ must be a singleton, so that

- $p_y$ must be the only place $p$ of the model $\mathscr{M}$ for which $p(x)$ is true,
- there is no left-hand variable $z$ distinct from $y$ such that $p_z = p_y$, and also
- $M_{p_y}$ must be null.

The following theorem shows that the conditions on the collection of places of $\mathscr{M}$ that we have just enumerated are sufficient to guarantee the existence of a model of $C$, and so gives us a procedure for determining the satisfiability of $C$.

**Theorem 3.3** *Let $C$ be a collection of statements of the form* (3.16), *and suppose that if $y_1$, $y_2$ are two distinct left-hand variables of $C$, an inequality '$\neg(y_1 = y_2)$' or '$\neg(y_2 = y_1)$' is present in $C$.*

*Then the following conditions are necessary and sufficient for $C$ to be satisfiable, i.e. to have a model $\mathscr{M}$:*

(i) *There exists an ample set $A$ of places $p$ for the subcollection of elementary Boolean statements in $C$.*
(ii) *For each left-hand variable $y$ appearing in a statement of $C$, there is a place $p_y$ at $y$ in $A$. Moreover, the variables appearing in the statements of $C$ can be arranged in an order $\prec$ such that $p_y(x)$ is false unless $y \prec x$.*
(iii) *If a statement '$x = \{y\}$' appears in $C$, then $p_y$ is the only place $p$ in $A$ for which $p(x)$ is true, and $y$ is the only left-hand variable $z$ such that $p_z = p_y$.*

*Proof* We saw above that the conditions (i–iii) are necessary.

Suppose conversely that they are satisfied. For each place $p$ in $A$ choose a set $M_p$ in such a way that all these sets are disjoint and non-null; however, if a statement '$x = \{y\}$' appears in $C$ (so that $y$ is a left-hand variable) we take $M_{p_y}$ to be null. We also suppose that each member of any set $M_p$ has larger cardinality than the total number $m$ of variables appearing in $C$, plus $K \cdot \#A$, where $K$ is the largest cardinality of any set $M_p$. (One way of doing this is to let the non-null sets $M_p$ be distinct singletons $\{u\}$, where each $u$ has a number of members exceeding $m + \#A$.) Then use formula (3.17) to define $\mathscr{M}(x)$ for each variable $x$ appearing in $C$. This is possible since by condition (ii) the variables appearing in the statements of $C$ can be arranged in an order for which all the $\mathscr{M}(z)$ appearing in the definition (3.17) of $\mathscr{M}(x)$ have been defined before (3.17) is used to define $\mathscr{M}(x)$. Note that the cardinality condition we have imposed ensures that every one of the sets

$$\{\, \mathscr{M}(z) : z \in Lvars \mid p_z(x) \,\}$$

appearing first on the right of any formula (3.17) is disjoint from every one of the sets

$$\bigcup\{\, M_p : p \in A \mid p(x) \,\},$$

appearing second on the right of any formula (3.17), every set $\mathscr{M}(x)$ has cardinality at most $m + K \cdot \#A$, while all the members of a set $\bigcup\{Mp : p \in A \mid p(x)\}$ must be members of some $M_p$, and hence must have cardinality greater than $m + K \cdot \#A$.

We now show that all the statements '$\neg(x = y)$' in $C$ are correctly modelled by the function $\mathscr{M}$ defined by (3.17). This is clear if there exists any $M_p \neq \emptyset$ for which $p(x)$ and $p(y)$ are different, say $p(x) = \mathsf{true}$ and $p(y) = \mathsf{false}$, since in this case it follows from (3.17) that $M_p$ will be a subset of $\mathscr{M}(x)$ and will be disjoint from $\mathscr{M}(y)$ (since the first and second terms of (3.17) are always disjoint and the $M_q$'s are pairwise disjoint). But we must prove it in general.

Suppose that our claim is false, and let $x$ be the first variable, in the ordering $\prec$ mentioned in condition (ii), for which there exists some statement '$\neg(x = y)$' or '$\neg(y = x)$' in $C$ such that $\mathscr{M}(x) = \mathscr{M}(y)$. Since the set $A$ of places is ample, there must exist a place $p$ in $A$ such that one of $p(x)$, $p(y)$ is true and the other is false. Suppose for definiteness that $p(x)$ is true, so $p(y)$ is false. We have already observed that if $M_p$ were nonempty, $\mathscr{M}(x) \neq \mathscr{M}(y)$, contrary to assumption. Hence $M_p = \emptyset$, so that $p$ must be of the form $p = p_w$, for some left-hand variable $w$. Then $p_w(x)$ is true, $w \prec x$ by condition (ii), and $\mathscr{M}(w)$ belongs to $\mathscr{M}(x)$ by (3.17). Hence $\mathscr{M}(w)$ belongs to $\mathscr{M}(y)$ also. But $\mathscr{M}(w)$ cannot belong to the second term of

$$\mathscr{M}(y) = \{\, \mathscr{M}(z) : z \in Lvars \mid p_z(y) \,\} \cup \bigcup\{\, M_p : p \in A \mid p(y) \,\},$$

since if it did it would belong to some $M_p$ such that $p(w)$ is true, whereas all the members of all $M_p$ have cardinality larger than $\mathscr{M}(w)$. Therefore $\mathscr{M}(w)$ must belong to the first term of $\mathscr{M}(y)$, i.e. must be identical with some $\mathscr{M}(z)$ for a left-hand variable $z$ for which $p_z(y)$ is true, therefore distinct from $w$. Since $w$ and $z$ are distinct left-hand variables, by hypothesis $C$ must contain a clause '$\neg(w = z)$' or '$\neg(z = w)$'. But now $\mathscr{M}(w) = \mathscr{M}(z)$ contradicts our assumption that $x$ is the first variable in the order $\prec$ for which there exists some statement '$\neg(x = y)$' or '$\neg(y = x)$' in $C$ such that $\mathscr{M}(x) = \mathscr{M}(y)$. This contradiction proves our claim that $\mathscr{M}(x) \neq \mathscr{M}(y)$ whenever a clause '$\neg(x = y)$' is present in $C$, and so shows that all such clauses are correctly modelled by $\mathscr{M}$.

Next we show that all other statements of $C$ are correctly modelled also. For statements $x = \{y\}$ this follows immediately from condition (iii) of our theorem and the fact that $M_{p_y} = \emptyset$. Statements '$y \in x$' are correctly modelled since the presence of such a statement implies that $\mathscr{M}(y)$ must belong to the first term of (3.17). Statements '$\neg(y \in x)$' are correctly modelled, since by its cardinality a set of the form $\mathscr{M}(z)$ can only belong to the first term of (3.17); but since all the $\mathscr{M}(z)$ are distinct for distinct left-hand variables, $\mathcal{M}(y)$ will only belong to the first term of (3.17) if $p_y(z)$ is true, which is impossible if '$\neg(y \in x)$' appears in $C$.

Statements $x = y \cup y'$ are correctly modelled since

$$\begin{aligned}
\mathcal{M}(x) &= \{\mathcal{M}(z) : z \in Lvars \mid p_z(x)\} \cup \bigcup \{\mathcal{M}(p) : p \in A \mid p(x)\} \\
&= \{\mathcal{M}(z) : z \in Lvars \mid p_z(y) \vee p_z(y')\} \\
&\quad \cup \bigcup \{\mathcal{M}(p) : p \in A \mid p(y) \vee p(y')\} \\
&= (\{\mathcal{M}(z) : z \in Lvars \mid p_z(y)\} \cup \bigcup \{\mathcal{M}(p) : p \in A \mid p(y)\}) \\
&\quad \cup (\{\mathcal{M}(z) : z \in Lvars \mid p_z(y')\} \cup \bigcup \{\mathcal{M}(p) : p \in A \mid p(y')\}) \\
&= \mathcal{M}(y) \cup \mathcal{M}(y').
\end{aligned}$$

Similarly, for statements $x = y \cap y'$ we have

$$\begin{aligned}
\mathcal{M}(x) &= \{\mathcal{M}(z) : z \in Lvars \mid p_z(x)\} \cup \bigcup \{\mathcal{M}(p) : p \in A \mid p(x)\} \\
&= \{\mathcal{M}(z) : z \in Lvars \mid p_z(y) \,\&\, p_z(y')\} \\
&\quad \cup \bigcup \{\mathcal{M}(p) : p \in A \mid p(y) \,\&\, p(y')\} \\
&= (\{\mathcal{M}(z) : z \in Lvars \mid p_z(y)\} \cup \bigcup \{\mathcal{M}(p) : p \in A \mid p(y)\}) \\
&\quad \cap (\{\mathcal{M}(z) : z \in Lvars \mid p_z(y')\} \cup \bigcup \{\mathcal{M}(p) : p \in A \mid p(y')\}) \\
&= \mathcal{M}(y) \cap \mathcal{M}(y')
\end{aligned}$$

since all the sets $M_p$ are disjoint, no $\mathcal{M}(x)$ belongs to any of them, and all the sets $\mathcal{M}(x)$ for $x \in Lvars$ are distinct. The same argument handles the case of statements '$s = t \setminus u$', completing the proof of our theorem. □

## 3.4 MLSS Plus the Predicates 'Finite' and 'Countable'

We can easily generalize MLSS by allowing the two additional set predicates 'Finite($s$)' and 'Countable($s$)' studied above.

Given a collection $C$ of statements each of which has one of the following forms

$$x = y \cup y',\ x = y \cap y',\ x = y \setminus y',\ x = y,\ \neg(x = y),\ y \in x,\ \neg(y \in x),\ x = \{y\},$$
$$\mathsf{Finite}(x),\ \mathsf{Countable}(x),\ \neg\mathsf{Finite}(x),\ \neg\mathsf{Countable}(x),$$

much as before, we can introduce two new variables Fi and Co, and for these variables introduce the following statements:

$$
\begin{aligned}
&\mathsf{Co} \supseteq \mathsf{Fi};\\
&\text{for each } x \text{ for which a statement } \mathsf{Finite}(x) \text{ is present in } C,\\
&\qquad \text{a statement } \mathsf{Fi} \supseteq x;\\
&\text{for each } x \text{ for which a statement } \mathsf{Countable}(x) \text{ is present in } C,\\
&\qquad \text{a statement } \mathsf{Co} \supseteq x;\\
&\text{for each } x \text{ for which a statement } \neg\mathsf{Finite}(x) \text{ is present in } C,\\
&\qquad \text{a statement } \neg(\mathsf{Fi} \supseteq x);\\
&\text{for each } x \text{ for which a statement } \neg\mathsf{Countable}(x) \text{ is present in } C,\\
&\qquad \text{a statement } \neg(\mathsf{Co} \supseteq x);\\
&\text{for each statement } x = \{y\} \text{ which is present in } C,\\
&\qquad \text{a statement } \mathsf{Fi} \supseteq x.
\end{aligned}
\tag{3.18}
$$

Then drop from $C$ all statements of the form

$$\mathsf{Finite}(x),\ \mathsf{Countable}(x),\ \neg\mathsf{Finite}(x),\ \neg\mathsf{Countable}(x),$$

and let $C'$ be the resulting modified collection of statements. Arguing much as in Sect. 3.2.1, it follows easily that if our original collection $C$ of statements has a model, so does our modified collection $C'$. Conversely, if $C'$ has a model, then as above there must exist an ample set of places for $C'$ and to these places we can assign disjoint sets $M_p$ according to the following rule:

if $p$ is of the form $p_y$ for some variable $y$ appearing in a statement $x = \{y\}$,
    let $M_p$ be null;
otherwise, if $p(\mathsf{Fi}) = \mathsf{true}$, then let $M_p$ be some single element;
otherwise, if $p(\mathsf{Co}) = \mathsf{true}$, then let $M_p$ be some countably infinite set;
otherwise, let $M_p$ be some uncountable set.

We also suppose, as in the preceding discussion of MLSS, that each member of $M_p$ has larger cardinality than $m + K \cdot \#A$, where $m$, $A$, and $K$ are as in that discussion, and then use (3.17) to define a model $\mathcal{M}$. The analysis given in the preceding section shows that this $\mathcal{M}$ correctly models all statements not involving the predicates 'Finite' and 'Countable'. It is plain that $\mathcal{M}(\mathsf{Fi})$ is finite and $\mathcal{M}(\mathsf{Co})$ is countable; hence all statements '$\mathsf{Finite}(x)$' and '$\mathsf{Countable}(x)$' originally present are correctly modelled also.

If any statement '$\neg\mathsf{Finite}(x)$' is present in $C$, then there exists a place $p$ such that $p(x)$ is true and $p(\mathsf{Fi})$ is false. $p$ cannot have the form $p_y$ for any variable $y$ appearing in any statement $z = \{y\}$ appearing in C, since if it did then the fact that $p_y(z)$ must be true and the statement $\mathsf{Fi} \supseteq z$ present in $C'$ would imply that $p_y(\mathsf{Fi})$ is true. Hence $M_p$ is infinite and so by (3.17) $\mathcal{M}(x)$ is infinite also. This shows that all statements '$\neg\mathsf{Finite}(x)$' are correctly modelled. The case of statements '$\neg\mathsf{Countable}(x)$' can be handled in much the same way, showing that our original and modified sets of statements are equisatisfiable.

## 3.5 The Tableau Method

The Davis–Putnam method for testing propositional satisfiability, which we discussed in Sect. 3.1, attains efficiency by making all possible 'deterministic' inferences (using clauses containing just one propositional symbol) before making any 'nondeterministic' inference (by exploring both possible truth values of some propositional symbol, when no more clauses containing just one propositional symbol remain. The *tableau method* to be described in this section generalizes this approach, first to statements in the unquantified language MLSS discussed earlier, and then to various extensions of MLSS.

Given an initial set of clauses, the tableau method finds their consequences transitively. The strategy used resembles that which we have already seen in the Davis–Putnam case. The deduction rules used for this are segregated into two classes: those which act 'deterministically' (like the use of a singleton clause in the Davis–Putnam algorithm), and those which act 'nondeterministically' (like the choice of a singleton to be given an arbitrary truth-value when there exists no singleton clause in the Davis–Putnam algorithm). This implicitly assumes that completion of a set of clauses using only the first class of rules will, in polynomial time, generate a relatively small clause set, so that exponentially growing costs will result only from nondeterministic application of the second, smaller, nondeterministic class of rules. This makes it reasonable to apply the deterministic rules as long as possible, checking for contradictions which might terminate many paths of expansion before more than a few nondeterministic rules need to be applied. In this strategy, we only apply a nondeterministic rule when no deterministic rule remains applicable. This strategy is also basic to the Davis–Putnam algorithm.

In the case of MLSS, which for convenience we now consider in a version allowing the operators '$\cup$', '$\cap$', '$\setminus$', $\{x\}$, and the relators '$\in$', '$\supseteq$', and '$=$', we work with two sets of propositions, one of which collects all currently available propositions of the forms

$$x = y,\ x \supseteq y,\ x \in y,\ \neg(x = y),\ \neg(x \supseteq y),\ \neg(x \in y),$$

and the other of which collects all propositions of the forms

$$x = y \cup z,\ x = y \cap z,\ x = y \setminus z,\ x = \{y\}.$$

Initially these two collections contain propositions representing the set of statements to be tested for satisfiability. A statement '$y \in x$' is added for each statement '$x = \{y\}$' initially present.

The initial collections of statements defined in this way are progressively modified as deductions are made. The deduction process will sometimes proceed deterministically, but sometimes branch nondeterministically, i.e. open a path of exploration which may need to be abandoned if it ends in a contradiction. Only statements of the form '$x \in y$', '$\neg(x \in y)$', and '$x = y$' are added in the course of deduction. However, the variables appearing in some of the other statements may change as equalities are deduced. Exploration of a branch fails immediately whenever two directly opposed statements such as '$x \in y$' and '$\neg(x \in y)$' are detected.

The working of the algorithm can be clarified by considering the way in which it will build a model of the set of statements with which it is working if one exists. This is done by examining the collection of all membership relationships '$x \in y$' deduced, first making sure that this contains no cycles (which are impossible if a model exists). If this check is passed we assign distinct sets of sufficiently large cardinality to all the variables which do not appear on the right of any deduced relationship '$x \in y$', and then process all the other variables in topologically sorted order of the membership relation '$x \in y$', modelling each $y$ as the collection of all $\mathcal{M}(x)$ for which a statement relationship '$x \in y$' has been deduced.

Equality is handled in a special way, which ensures that all statements '$x = y$' are modelled properly, and that all the operations '$y \cup z$', '$y \cap z$', '$y \setminus z$' are defined uniquely by their arguments. Specifically, whenever '$x = y$' has been deduced we choose one of $x$ and $y$ as a representative of the other, all of whose occurrences are then replaced by occurrences of the representative. This process may identify the right-hand sides of some statements of the form '$x = y \cup z$', '$x = y \cap z$', '$x = y \setminus z$', '$x = \{y\}$'; whenever this happens we immediately deduce that the left-hand sides are also equal. If a model is subsequently found we give each variable replaced in this way the same value as its representative.

The rules stated below will sometimes introduce new variables. These variables can only appear in statements of the form '$x \in y$' and '$\neg(x \in y)$', and only on the left of such statements. It will follow that whenever an equality '$x = y$' is deduced, one of $x$ and $y$ must be a variable initially present; in choosing representatives we always choose such a variable.

For the model-building procedure described above to work, we must be sure that every statement '$x \supseteq y$', '$\neg(x \supseteq y)$', '$\neg(x = y)$', '$x = y \cup z$', '$x = y \cap z$', '$x = y \setminus z$', and '$x = \{y\}$' is properly modelled. To this end, we make the following deductions:

- '$x \in z$' is deduced whenever '$x \in y$' and '$z \supseteq y$' are present.
- A new variable $x$ and statements '$x \in y$', '$\neg(x \in z)$' are set up whenever '$\neg(z \supseteq y)$' is present.
- '$x \in z$' is deduced whenever '$x \in y_1$' and '$z = y_1 \cup y_2$' are present. Likewise, '$x \in z$' is deduced whenever '$x \in y_2$' and '$z = y_1 \cup y_2$' are present. These two rules ensure that in the model eventually constructed, $\mathcal{M}(z)$ is no smaller than $\mathcal{M}(y_1) \cup \mathcal{M}(y_2)$.
- '$x \in y_1$' and '$x \in y_2$' are deduced whenever '$x \in z$' and '$z = y_1 \cap y_2$' are present. This ensures that in the model eventually constructed, $\mathcal{M}(z)$ is no larger than $\mathcal{M}(y_1) \cap \mathcal{M}(y_2)$.
- Whenever the statement '$x \in y$' has been deduced, and a statement '$y = \{z\}$' is present, the statement '$x = z$' is deduced. This ensures that the model of $y$ can contain at most one element.
- '$x \in y_1$' and '$\neg(x \in y_2)$' are deduced whenever '$x \in z$' and '$z = y_1 \setminus y_2$' are present. This ensures that in the model eventually constructed, $\mathcal{M}(z)$ is no larger than $\mathcal{M}(y_1) \setminus \mathcal{M}(y_2)$.

The set of rules stated above are all deterministic, but a few nondeterministic rules are required also. These are as follows.

- If '$x \in z$' and '$\neg(y \in z)$' have both been deduced, we deduce an inequality '$x \neq y$', setting this up as an alternation '$(x \not\supseteq y) \vee (y \not\supseteq x)$'. This ensures that $x$ and $y$ will have different models, implying that all statements '$\neg(y \in z)$' are correctly modelled. It is only necessary to do this when both $x$ and $y$ belong to the collection of variables initially present, since, as previously explained, variables not in this collection will always be assigned distinct sets as models.
- An alternation '$x \in y_1 \vee x \in y_2$', both of whose branches may need to be explored, is set up whenever '$x \in z$' and '$z = y_1 \cup y_2$' are present. This ensures that in the model eventually constructed, $\mathcal{M}(z)$ is no larger than $\mathcal{M}(y_1) \cup \mathcal{M}(y_2)$.
- Similarly, an alternation '$x \in z \vee x \notin y_2$' is set up whenever '$x \in y_1$' and '$z = y_1 \cap y_2$' are present. Likewise an alternation '$x \in z \vee x \notin y_1$' is set up whenever '$x \in y_2$' and '$z = y_1 \cap y_2$' are present. This ensures that in the model eventually constructed, $\mathcal{M}(z)$ is no smaller than $\mathcal{M}(y_1) \cap \mathcal{M}(y_2)$.
- Similarly, an alternation '$x \in z \vee x \in y_2$' is set up whenever '$x \in y_1$' and '$z = y_1 \setminus y_2$' are present. This ensures that in the model eventually constructed, $\mathcal{M}(z)$ is no smaller than $\mathcal{M}(y_1) \setminus \mathcal{M}(y_2)$.

These rules are sufficient, but to accelerate discovery of contradictions (which can cut off a branch of exploration before multiple alternations need to be resolved, an exponentially expensive matter when necessary) all possible deterministic deductions are made. These are:

- '$x \notin y$' is deduced whenever '$x \notin z$' and '$z \supseteq y$' are present.
- '$x \notin y_1$' is deduced whenever '$x \notin z$' and '$z = y_1 \cup y_2$' are present.
- '$x \notin y_2$' is deduced whenever '$x \notin z$' and '$z = y_1 \cup y_2$' are present.
- '$x \notin z$' is deduced whenever '$x \notin y_1$' and '$z = y_1 \cap y_2$' are present.
- '$x \notin z$' is deduced whenever '$x \notin y_2$' and '$z = y_1 \cap y_2$' are present.
- '$x \notin z$' is deduced whenever '$x \notin y_1$' and '$z = y_1 \setminus y_2$' are present.
- '$x \notin z$' is deduced whenever '$x \in y_2$' and '$z = y_1 \setminus y_2$' are present.

To further clarify the style of proof discussed above, we consider its application to the example

$$\neg\big((\{x\} = x \cup y) \rightarrow (x = \emptyset \,\&\, y = \{x\})\big)$$

which, decomposed propositionally and then initialized in the manner described above, breaks down into the two cases

$$z = \{x\},\ x \in z,\ z = x \cup y,\ \neg(x = \emptyset)$$

and

$$z = \{x\},\ x \in z,\ z = x \cup y,\ \neg\big(y = \{x\}\big).$$

In the first of these two cases we progressively deduce

$$y' \in x,\ y' \in z,\ y' = x,\ x \in x,$$

leading to a contradiction. The second case splits nondeterministically into the two cases

$$\neg(y \supseteq \{x\}) \quad \text{and} \quad \neg(\{x\} \supseteq y).$$

In the first of these cases we deduce

$$y' \in \{x\},\ \neg(y' \in y),\ y' \in z,\ y' \in x,\ y' = x\,,\ x \in x,$$

leading to a contradiction as before. In the second case we deduce

$$y' \in y,\ \neg(y' \in \{x\}),\ \neg(y' \in z),\ y' \in z,$$

leading again to a contradiction and so eliminating the last possible case.

The preceding discussion assumes that the collection of statements with which we deal has been resolved at the propositional level before the analysis described begins. However, it may often be better to integrate the propositional and the set-theoretic levels of exploration, so as to allow the impossibility of a set-theoretic exploration to rule out a whole family of propositional branches which otherwise might need to be explored individually before their (predictable) failure became apparent. This can be done as follows. By introducing additional intermediate variables we can suppose that all the atomic subformulae of our formulae have simple forms like $x \supseteq y$, $x = y$, $x \in y$ (and their negatives), along with statements like $x = y \cup z$, $x = y \cap z$, $x = y \setminus z$, $x = \{y\}$. Propositional calculus rules can be used in the standard way to write all the top-level propositions in our set as disjunctions like

$$x \supseteq y \vee x = y \vee x \in y \vee \cdots \tag{3.19}$$

in which some of the atoms present may be negated. We now arrange all the propositions (3.19) in order of increasing number of their atomic parts and work through them in the following way. Starting with the first proposition $F$, we select its atomic parts $A$ in order for processing. Each such $A$ is, when selected, added to our collection $\mathscr{AP}$ of atomic propositions, where it will remain unless/until the branch of exploration opened by this addition fails. If such a branch of exploration fails, the atomic formula $A$ that opened the branch is removed and its negative (which will now remain permanently) is added to $\mathscr{AP}$. At the same time the next atomic formula $A'$ after $A$ is selected and added to $\mathscr{AP}$. If there is no such $A'$, then the branch of exploration opened by the selection of $A$ fails; if $A$ belongs to the first formula $F$, then all possibilities have failed and the given set of propositions is unsatisfiable.

Once a branch of exploration is opened we make all possible deterministic and nondeterministic deductions from it, in the manner described above. Eventually either the branch will fail, or run out of deductions to make. In the latter case we examine all the formulae (3.19) following the $F$ containing the $A$ that opened the current branch of exploration. Formulae containing atoms $B$ present in our deduced collection of atoms are bypassed (since they must be satisfied already, and so tell us nothing new). The negatives of all such $B$ are removed from the formulae still to be processed (since these propositions are known to be false; note that this duplicates a deterministic deduction step of the Davis–Putnam algorithm). If any one of these formulae is thereby made null, the branch of exploration opened by $A$ fails. Otherwise the formulae following $F$ are rearranged in order of increasing number of their remaining atomic parts, and we move on to select an atomic subformula of the next formula $F'$ following $F$.

We illustrate this integrated style of proof, again using the example

$$\neg\big((\{x\} = x \cup y) \rightarrow \big(x = \emptyset \;\&\; y = \{x\}\big)\big)$$

whose negative is now expressed as the following set of three clauses

$$z = \{x\},\ x \in z,\ z = x \cup y,\ \big(\neg(x = \emptyset) \vee \neg(y = z)\big).$$

A branch of exploration is opened by adding '$\neg(c = \emptyset)$' to the first three clauses, giving the deductions

$$z = \{x\},\ x \in z,\ z = x \cup y,\ \neg(y = \emptyset),\ y' \in x,\ y' \in z,\ y' = x,\ x \in x$$

which fails. The alternate path then begins with

$$z = \{x\},\ x \in z,\ z = x \cup y,\ x = \emptyset,\ \big(\neg(y \supseteq z)\big) \vee \big(\neg(z \supseteq y)\big),$$

from which we deduce

$$z = \{x\},\ x \in z,\ z = x \cup y,\ x = \emptyset,\ \big(\neg(y \supseteq z)\big) \vee \big(\neg(z \supseteq y)\big),\ z = y,$$

and so

$$z = \{x\},\ x \in z,\ x = \emptyset,\ \neg(z \supseteq z),\ y' \in z,\ \neg(y' \in z),$$

which fails, confirming the validity of our original formula.

Tableau-based proof approaches have the interesting property that if they are sound, and even if they are not complete (so that there can exist contradictory sets of clauses which they are not able to extend to an obvious contradiction), any family of statements found to be contradictory because all branches of exploration fail really is unsatisfiable. This is because the tableau method implicitly makes and then discharges a sequence of suppositions, every one of which has led to a contradiction. So systems of tableau rules can be used even if they are incomplete as long as they converge, and, as a matter of fact, can be used in any individual case whose exploration does terminate, even if the system does not terminate for every possible input. All that is necessary is that such systems should be sound. Therefore if we use a fixed, table-driven tableau code, we can be certain of the rigor of its deductions as long as we know that all rules entered into each driving table are sound. This will necessarily be the case if all such rules are instances of universally quantified, previously proved theorems. For example, once cons, car, and cdr have been given their set-theoretic definitions and it has been proved that

$$\big(\forall x, y, u, v \,|\, [x,\, y]^{[1]} = x \;\&\; [x,\, y]^{[2]} = y \;\&\; \big(([x,\, y] = [u,\, v]) \rightarrow (x = u \;\&\; y = v)\big)\big)$$

we can be sure that the tableau rules derived from this statement are sound, and so we can add them to the table driving a generic tableau code.

A tableau-based proof approach which is sound but not complete can be regarded as a mechanism for searching, not all, but only certain possible lines of argument, namely those defined by its set of saturation and fulfilling rules. If we believe that a proof can result along these lines, this is a good way of searching for it.

## 3.6 Elementary Booleans Plus Map Primitives

Next we consider another unquantified generalization of the elementary Boolean language of sets with which we started in Sect. 3.2. This introduces variables designating maps between sets, which to ensure decidability we treat here as objects of a kind different from sets, designated by variables of a syntactically different, recognizable kind. (For convenience we will write set variables as letters $x, y, z$, etc., taken from the initial part of the alphabet, and designate maps by letters like $f, g$.) In addition to the elementary Booleans operators and comparators, the unquantified language we now wish to consider allows the map primitives

$f = g$, $\mathsf{range}(f) = x$, $\mathsf{domain}(f) = x$, $f_{|x} = g$ (map restriction),
$\mathsf{Svm}(f)$ ($f$ is a single-valued map), and
$\mathsf{Singinv}(f)$ ($f$ is the inverse of a single-valued map).

We will show that this language is decidable by reducing collections of statements in it to equisatisfiable collections of statements in which all variables designating maps, and all map-related operations, have been removed. As usual, we begin by applying decomposition at the propositional level, and then secondary decomposition, to the collection of statements originally given us. This means that we have only to deal with collections $C$ of statements each having one of the allowed elementary forms

$$x = y \cup z,\ x = y,\ \neg(x = y),\ \mathsf{range}(f) = x,\ \mathsf{domain}(f) = x,\ f_{|x} = g,\ f = g,\ \neg(f = g),\ \mathsf{Svm}(f),\ \neg\mathsf{Svm}(f),\ \mathsf{Singinv}(f),\ \neg\mathsf{Singinv}(f).$$

Now we proceed as follows.

(i) All equalities between sets or between maps are removed by selecting a representative of any group of set or map variables known to be equal, and replacing each occurrence of a variable in the group by its selected representative.

(ii) We replace each statement $\neg(f = g)$ by a statement of the form

$$\neg\big(\mathsf{range}(f_{|x_{\mathrm{new}}}) = \mathsf{range}(g_{|x_{\mathrm{new}}})\big).$$

This reflects the fact that if two maps are different, there must exist a set $s$ on which their ranges are different. (For example, this can be a singleton whose one member either belongs to the domain of one of the maps but not the other, or to both domains, but at which the functions have different values.)

(iii) All the map-related statements which remain at the end of step (ii) have one of the forms

$$\mathsf{range}(f) = x,\ \mathsf{domain}(f) = x,\ f_{|x} = g,$$
$$\mathsf{Svm}(f),\ \neg\mathsf{Svm}(f),\ \mathsf{Singinv}(f),\ \neg\mathsf{Singinv}(f).$$

We now proceed in the following way to eliminate all statements of the form $f_{|x} = g$. We enumerate all the set variables $x_1, \ldots, x_k$ which appear in statements of the form $f_{|x} = g$, and form the collection of all their 'Venn pieces'. These 'Venn pieces' are newly introduced symbols $V_{i_1,\ldots,i_k}$ for all intersections of the sets $x_j$ or their complements, with the obvious relationships defining the $V_{i_1,\ldots,i_k}$ in terms of the sets $x_j$ and vice versa. More specifically, the subscripts $i_1, \ldots, i_k$ of the Venn pieces are all possible sequences of 0's and 1's of length $k$ (which we also denote by $I$, to enhance readability), distinct Venn pieces are disjoint, and each $x_j$ is the union of all the Venn pieces

$$V_{i_1,\ldots,i_{j-1},1,i_{j+1},\ldots,i_k},$$

for $i_1, \ldots, i_{j-1}, i_{j+1}, \ldots, i_k$ ranging over $\{0, 1\}$.

Next we introduce the 'Venn pieces' of the maps $f$. These are symbols $f_I$ for all restrictions $f_{|V_I}$, for $I$ ranging over the collection $\{0, 1\}^k$ of binary $k$-tuples. We also introduce symbols $r_I^f$ and $d_I^f$ for their ranges and domains, respectively, and statements expressing each $f_{|x_j}$ in terms of these $r_I^f$ and $d_I^f$.

More specifically, for each symbol $f_I$, with $I \in \{0, 1\}^k$, we add the statements

$$r_I^f \neq \emptyset \leftrightarrow d_I^f \neq \emptyset \quad \text{and} \quad d_I^f \subseteq V_I.$$

Additionally, for each relationship $f_{|x_j} = g$ we add the statements

$$r_I^f = r_I^g, \quad d_I^f = d_I^g, \quad \text{and} \quad f_I = g_I,$$

for all binary $k$-tuples $I$ whose $j$th component is equal to 1, and the statements

$$r_J^g = \emptyset \text{ and } d_J^g = \emptyset,$$

for all binary $k$-tuples $J$ whose $j$th component is equal to 0.

Then we drop all statements of the form $f_{|x} = g$ and eliminate all simple equalities $f_I = g_I$ by closing them transitively and choosing a representative of each class.

(iv) Statements of the forms $\mathsf{range}(f) = x$ and $\mathsf{domain}(f) = x$ can be eliminated as follows. For each statement $\mathsf{range}(f) = x$, we add the statement

$$r_{I_1}^f \cup \cdots \cup r_{I_N}^f = x,$$

where $I_1, \ldots, I_N$ are all binary $k$-tuples. Likewise, for each statement $\mathsf{domain}(f) = x$ we add the statement

$$d_{I_1}^f \cup \cdots \cup d_{I_N}^f = x.$$

Then we drop all statements of type $\mathsf{range}(f) = x$ and $\mathsf{domain}(f) = x$.

(v) Let $C'$ be the resulting collection of statements. If $C'$ has a model $\mathcal{M}$ so does the original $C$ (ignoring statements $\mathsf{Svm}(f)$ and $\mathsf{Singinv}(f)$, and their negations) since we can construct the $\mathcal{M}(f_I)$ as either single-valued or non-single-valued maps (having single-valued or non-single-valued inverse) of each non-null $\mathcal{M}(d_I^f)$ onto the corresponding $\mathcal{M}(r_I^f)$, making all these sets countable.

To model a collection of statements $\mathsf{Svm}(f)$ and $\neg\mathsf{Svm}(f)$ we need only assign a truth value to each condition $\mathsf{Svm}(f_I)$, insisting that $\mathsf{Svm}(f)$ be equivalent to the conjunction of all the statements $\mathsf{Svm}(f_I)$, extended over all the Venn pieces of $f$.

To model a collection of statements $\mathsf{Singinv}(f)$ and $\neg\mathsf{Singinv}(f)$ we must add conditions $r_I^f \cap r_J^f = \emptyset$ for each clause $\mathsf{Singinv}(f)$ and for all the distinct pieces $r_I^f$ into which each original $\mathsf{range}(f)$ is decomposed, since then the union map of the Venn pieces $f_I$ of $f$ can have a single-valued inverse or not, as desired. We must also assign a truth value to each condition $\mathsf{Singinv}(f_I)$, and insist that $\mathsf{Singinv}(f)$ be equivalent to the conjunction of all the statements $\mathsf{Singinv}(f_I)$, extended over all the Venn pieces of $f$.

## 3.7 Various Commonly Occurring Decidable Extensions of MLSS

The decision algorithm for MLSS presented in Sect. 3.3 can be extended in useful ways by allowing otherwise uninterpreted function symbols subject to certain universally quantified statements to be intermixed with the other operators of MLSS. Note, however, that the statements decided by the method to be described remain unquantified; the quantified statements to which we refer appear only as implicit 'side conditions'.

The 'pairing' operator 'cons' and the two associated component extraction operators 'car' and 'cdr' exemplify the operator families to which our extension technique is applicable. As noted earlier, these operators can be given formal set-theoretic definitions:

$$\begin{aligned} [x, y] &:= \big\{\{x\}, \big\{\{x\}, \big\{\{y\}, y\big\}\big\}\big\}, \\ p^{[1]} &:= \mathsf{arb}\big(\mathsf{arb}(p)\big), \\ p^{[2]} &:= \mathsf{arb}\Big(\mathsf{arb}\Big(\mathsf{arb}\big(p \setminus \{\mathsf{arb}(p)\}\big) \setminus \{\mathsf{arb}(p)\}\Big)\Big). \end{aligned}$$

However, in most settings, the details of these definitions are irrelevant. Only the following properties of these operators matter:

- The object $[x, y]$ can be formed for any two sets $x, y$.
- Both of the sets $x, y$ from which $[x, y]$ is formed can be recovered uniquely from the single object $[x, y]$, since $[x, y]^{[1]} = x$ and $[x, y]^{[2]} = y$.

Almost all proofs in which the operators 'cons', 'car', and 'cdr' appear use only these facts about this triple of operators. That is, they implicitly treat these operators as a family of three otherwise uninterpreted operators, subject only to the conditions

$$\big(\forall x, y \,|\, [x, y]^{[1]} = x\big) \;\&\; \big(\forall x, y \,|\, [x, y]^{[2]} = y\big).$$

The treatment of 'cons', 'car', and 'cdr' throws away information about these operators (e.g. $[x, y]$ has cardinality 2 and $x^{[1]}$ is always a member of a member of $x$) that may become relevant in unusual situations, but this very rarely makes any difference.

Even though the underlying definitions are not always so strongly irrelevant as in the case of 'cons', 'car', and 'cdr', similar remarks apply to many other important families of operators. We list some of these, along with the universally quantified statements associated with them:

(i) arb:

$$\big(\forall x \,|\, \big(x = \emptyset \;\&\; \mathsf{arb}(x) = \emptyset\big) \vee \big(\mathsf{arb}(x) \in x \;\&\; \mathsf{arb}(x) \cap x = \emptyset\big)\big);$$

(ii) pairs of *mutually inverse functions* on a set $w$:

$$\big(\forall x \in w \mid f(x) \in w \;\&\; g(x) \in w \;\&\; f\big(g(x)\big) = x \;\&\; g\big(f(x)\big) = x\big);$$

(iii) *monotone functions*:

$$\big(\forall x, y \mid (x \supseteq y) \rightarrow \big(f(x) \supseteq f(y)\big)\big);$$

(iv) monotone functions having a known order relationship:

$$\begin{aligned}&\big(\forall x, y \mid (x \supseteq y) \rightarrow \big(f(x) \supseteq f(y)\big)\big) \;\&\; \big(\forall x, y \mid (x \supseteq y) \rightarrow \big(g(x) \supseteq g(y)\big)\big)\\ &\quad \& \;\big(\forall x \mid f(x) \supseteq g(x)\big);\end{aligned}$$

(v) monotone functions of several variables:

$$\big(\forall x, y, u, v \mid (x \supseteq y \;\&\; u \supseteq v) \rightarrow \big(f(x, u) \supseteq f(y, v)\big)\big);$$

(vi) *idempotent* functions on a set $w$:

$$\big(\forall x \in w \mid f(x) \in w \;\&\; f\big(f(x)\big) = f(x)\big);$$

(vii) *self-inverse* functions on a set:

$$\big(\forall x \in w \mid f(x) \in w \;\&\; f\big(f(x)\big) = x\big);$$

(viii) *total ordering relationships* on a set:

$$\begin{aligned}&\big(\forall x \in w,\; y \in w \,\big|\, \big(R(x, y) \vee R(y, x)\big) \;\&\; R(x, x)\big)\\ &\quad \& \;\big(\forall x \in w,\; y \in w,\; z \in w \,\big|\, \big(R(x, y) \;\&\; R(y, z)\big) \rightarrow R(x, z)\big);\end{aligned}$$

(ix) (multiple) functions with *known ranges* $w_j$ *and domains* $v_j$:

$$(\forall x \in v_j \mid f_j(x) \in w_j),$$

for multiple indices $j$ and $k$.

These are all mathematically significant relationships, as the existence of names associated with them attests.

These cases can all be handled by a common method under the following conditions. Suppose that we are given an unquantified collection $C$ of statements involving the operators of MLSS plus certain other function symbols $f$, $g$ of various numbers of arguments. After decomposing compound terms in the manner described earlier, we can suppose that all occurrences of these additional symbols are in simple statements of forms like

$$y = f(x), \quad y = g(x, z), \quad \text{etc.}$$

From these initially given statements we must be able to draw a 'complete' collection $S$ of consequences, involving the variables which appear in them, along with some finite number of additional variables that it may be necessary to introduce. The resulting collection of formulae, comprising $S$ and some 'residue' of the original $C$, will be entirely within the language of MLSS. 'Completeness' means that any model of the translated formula can be extended to include the original function symbols $f$, $g$, etc. in such a way that their interpretation $\mathcal{M}(f)$, $\mathcal{M}(g)$, etc. actually satisfies the desired properties (monotonicity, etc.).

In all cases listed above, $S$ will include at least *single-valuedness conditions*

$$x = u \rightarrow y = v$$

for all pairs $y = f(x)$, $v = f(u)$ originally present in $C$, so $S$ will consist of these statements plus others appropriate to the case being considered, as detailed below. Call these added statements $S$ the *extension conditions* for the given set of functions. We must find extension conditions comprising $S$ which encapsulate everything which the appearance of the functions in question tells us about the set variables which also appear.

If extension conditions can be found, satisfiability can be determined by replacing all the statements $y = f(x)$, $y = g(x, z)$ in our original collection by the extension conditions derived from them.

This gives us a systematic way of reducing various languages extending MLSS to pure MLSS. As we will see, this approach can be exploited, to some extent, with predicates too, thanks to the fact that certain properties of predicates can be represented using associated functions.

Note that this 'extension conditions' technique can be applied even if the recipe for removing universal quantifiers by adding compensating extension clauses is not complete, as long as it is sound, i.e. all the clauses added do follow from known properties of the functions or predicates removed.

Take Case (iii) above (the 'monotone functions' case) as an example. Here the extension conditions can be derived as follows. Let the function symbols known to designate monotone functions be $f$, etc. Replace all the statements $y = f(x)$, $v = f(u)$ originally present by statements

$$x \supseteq u \rightarrow y \supseteq v. \tag{3.20}$$

(Note that this implies the single-valuedness condition for $f$.) The added clauses ensure that if a model $\mathcal{M}$ exists, the set of pairs $[\mathcal{M}(x), \mathcal{M}(y)]$, formed for all the $x$ and $y$ initially appearing in clauses $y = f(x)$, defines a function $F$ which is monotone on its domain. This can be extended to a function $F'$ defined everywhere by defining $F'(s)$ as the union of all the $F(t)$, extended over all the elements $t$ of the domain of $F$ for which $s \supseteq t$. It is clear that the $F'$ defined in this way is also monotone and extends $F$. This proves that the clauses (3.20) express the proper extension condition in Case (iii). Note that the number of clauses (3.20) required is roughly as large as the square of the number of clauses $y = f(x)$ originally present.

To make this method of proof entirely clear we give an example. Suppose that we need to prove the implication

$$f\big(f(x \cup y)\big) \supseteq f\big(f(x)\big) \tag{3.21}$$

under the assumption that the function $f$ is monotone. By decomposing the compound terms which appear in this statement, we get the collection

$$\begin{array}{lll} z = x \cup y, & u = f(z), & w = f(u), \\ u' = f(x), & v' = f(u'), & \neg(w \supseteq v'), \end{array}$$

which we must prove to be unsatisfiable. The four statements

$$u = f(z), \qquad w = f(u), \qquad u' = f(x), \qquad v' = f(u')$$

in this collection give rise to the 12 extension conditions

$$\begin{array}{ll} (z \supseteq u) \rightarrow (u \supseteq w), & (u \supseteq z) \rightarrow (w \supseteq u), \\ (z \supseteq x) \rightarrow (u \supseteq u'), & (x \supseteq z) \rightarrow (u' \supseteq u), \\ (z \supseteq u') \rightarrow (u \supseteq v'), & (u' \supseteq z) \rightarrow (v' \supseteq u), \\ (u \supseteq x) \rightarrow (w \supseteq u'), & (x \supseteq u) \rightarrow (u' \supseteq w), \\ (u \supseteq u') \rightarrow (w \supseteq v'), & (u' \supseteq u) \rightarrow (v' \supseteq w), \\ (x \supseteq u') \rightarrow (u' \supseteq v'), & (u' \supseteq x) \rightarrow (v' \supseteq u'), \end{array}$$

which replace the four initial statements. It now becomes possible to see that

$$z = x \cup y, \qquad (z \supseteq x) \rightarrow (u \supseteq u'), \qquad (u \supseteq u') \rightarrow (w \supseteq v'), \qquad \neg(w \supseteq v')$$

is an unsatisfiable conjunction, proving the validity of (3.21).

### 3.7.1 Extension Conditions in the Other Cases Listed Above

We shall now describe the extension conditions applicable in the remaining cases listed above. In Case (i) (the arb case) the extension conditions are simply

$$\big((x = \emptyset \,\&\, \mathsf{arb}(x) = \emptyset) \vee (\mathsf{arb}(x) \in x \,\&\, \mathsf{arb}(x) \cap x = \emptyset)\big) \\ \& \big(x = u \to \mathsf{arb}(x) = \mathsf{arb}(u)\big). \quad (3.22)$$

(This last clause is the condition of 'single-valued functional dependence'.) Suppose now that $\mathcal{M}$ is a model of a collection of MLSS clauses, plus statements of the form $x = \mathsf{arb}(y)$, after first replacing all the $y = \mathsf{arb}(x)$, $v = \mathsf{arb}(u)$ originally given by the derived clauses

$$(x = \emptyset \,\&\, y = \emptyset) \vee (y \in x \,\&\, y \cap x = \emptyset) \,\&\, (x = u \to y = v).$$

Then plainly the set of pairs $[\mathcal{M}(x), \mathcal{M}(y)]$, formed for all the $x$ and $y$ appearing in the statements '$y = \mathsf{arb}(x)$' originally present, defines a single-valued function $A$ on its finite domain which satisfies

$$\big(s = \emptyset \,\&\, A(s) = \emptyset\big) \vee \big(A(s) \in s \,\&\, A(s) \cap s = \emptyset\big),$$

for all the elements of its domain. We can extend this to a function $A'$ defined everywhere by writing

$$A'(s) = \textbf{if } s \in \mathsf{domain}(A) \textbf{ then } A(s) \textbf{ else } \mathsf{arb}(s) \textbf{ end if},$$

where arb is the built-in choice operator of our version of set theory. $A'$ then satisfies the originally universally quantified condition for arb, verifying our claim that the clauses (3.22) are the proper extension conditions.

Case (iv) (monotone functions having a known order relationship) can be treated in much the same way as the somewhat simpler case (iii) discussed above. Given two such functions $f$, $g$, where it is known that $f(x) \supseteq g(x)$ is universally true, first force the known part of their domains to be equal by introducing a $u$ satisfying $g(x) = u$ for each initially given clause $f(x) = y$ and vice versa. Then proceed as in case (iii), but now add inclusions

$$x = v \to y \supseteq u$$

for every pair $g(v) = u$, $f(x) = y$ of clauses present. It is clear that the extensions of $g$ and $f$ defined in our discussion of the simpler case (iii) stand in the proper ordering relationship.

Case (v) (monotone functions of several variables) is also easy. We can proceed as follows. Given a function $f(x, y)$ which is to be monotone in both its variables, and also a set of clauses like $z = f(x, y)$, $w = f(u, v)$, introduce clauses

$$(x \supseteq u \,\&\, y \supseteq v) \to (z \supseteq w).$$

As above, let $\mathcal{M}$ be a model for our set of clauses. Then plainly the set of pairs $[[\mathcal{M}(x), \mathcal{M}(y)], \mathcal{M}(z)]$, formed for all the $x, y, z$ initially appearing in clauses $z = f(x, y)$, defines a function $F$ of two arguments which is monotone on its domain. This can be extended to a function $F'$ defined everywhere by defining $F'(s,t)$ as the union of all the $F(p,q)$, extended over all the pairs $p, q$ of the domain of $F$ for which $s \supseteq p$ and $t \supseteq q$.

The related case of *additive functions* of a set variable can also be treated in the way which we will now explain (but the very many clauses which this technique introduces hints that 'additivity' is a significantly harder case than 'monotonicity'). A set-valued function $f$ of sets is called 'additive' if

$$f(x \cup y) = f(x) \cup f(y)$$

for all $x$ and $y$. Given an otherwise uninterpreted function $f$ which is supposed to be additive, and clauses $y = f(x)$, introduce all the 'atomic parts' of all the variables $x$ which appear in such clauses. These are variables representing all the intersections of some of these sets $x$ with the complements of the other sets $x$. In terms of these intersections, which clearly are all disjoint, express each $x$ in terms of its atomic parts, namely as

$$x = a_{j_1} \cup \cdots \cup a_{j_k}.$$

Likewise, after introducing clauses $b_j = f(a_j)$ giving names to the range elements $f(a_j)$, write out all the relationships

$$y = b_{j_1} \cup \cdots \cup b_{j_k}$$

that derive from clauses $y = f(x)$. Finally, writing $\emptyset$ and $f(\emptyset)$ for uniformity as $a_0$ and $b_0$, add statements

$$a_j = a_0 \rightarrow b_j = b_0 \quad \text{and} \quad b_0 \subseteq b_j,$$

along with statements

$$a_j \cap a_i = \emptyset \quad (\text{with } i \neq j)$$

which express the disjointness of distinct sets $a_j$. Now suppose that the set of clauses we have written has a model $\mathcal{M}$ in which the $a_j, b_j, x, y$, etc. appearing above are represented by sets $\overline{a}_j, \overline{b}_j, \overline{x}, \overline{y}$, etc. and for each $s$, define the set-valued function $F(s)$ to be the union of all the sets $\overline{b}_j$ for which $s$ intersects $\overline{a}_j$. The function $F$ defined in this way is clearly additive. It is also clear that if a clause $y = f(x)$ is present in our initial collection, and the variables $x$ and $y$ are represented by sets $\overline{x}$ and $\overline{y}$, then $\overline{y} = F(\overline{x})$. Hence $F$ can represent $f$ in the model we have constructed, so $f$ can be represented by an additive function, proving that the clauses we have added to our original collection are the appropriate extension conditions.

Cases (vi) (idempotent functions on a set) and (vii) (self-inverse functions on a set) are also easy. In the case of idempotent function we can proceed as before, but adding a clause $y = f(y)$ whenever a clause $y = f(x)$ is present. Then we add implications

$$w = x \rightarrow z = y$$

whenever two clauses $y = f(x)$, $z = f(w)$ are present, and remove all the clauses $y = f(x)$. The added clauses ensure that if a model $\mathcal{M}$ exists, the mapping $F$ which sends $\mathcal{M}(x)$ to $\mathcal{M}(y)$ for each clause $y = f(y)$ initially present is single-valued, and since a clause

$$y = f(y)$$

has been added whenever a clause $y = f(x)$ is present this mapping is clearly idempotent where defined. It can be extended by mapping all elements not in the domain of $F$ to any selected element of the range of $F$.

The self-inverse function case (vii) can be handled in much the same way. Here one adds a clause

$$x = f(y)$$

whenever the clause $y = f(x)$ is present, and then adds all the implications needed to force a model of the pairs $[x, y]$ deriving from clauses $y = f(x)$ initially present to define a single-valued map which can model the original $f$. If a model $\mathcal{M}$ exists for the resulting set of clauses, the model $F$ of $f$ is self-inverse on its domain, which is the same as its range. $F$ can then be extended to a mapping defined for all $s$ by writing $f(s) = s$ for all elements not in its domain/range.

*Predicates representable by functions* in one of the classes analyzed above can be removed automatically by first replacing them by the functions that represent them, and then removing these functions by writing the appropriate extension conditions. For example, equivalence relationships $R(x, y)$ can be written as $f(x) = f(y)$ using a representing function $f$; $f$ only needs to be single-valued. Partial ordering relationships can be written as $f(x) \supseteq f(y)$ where $f$ only needs to be single-valued. $f$ is monotone iff the ordering relationship $R(x, y)$ is compatible with inclusion, in the sense that

$$\big(\forall x, y \mid (x \supseteq y) \rightarrow R(x, y)\big).$$

Monadic predicates $P(x)$ satisfying the condition

$$\big(\forall x, y \,\big|\, \big(P(x) \,\&\, P(y)\big) \rightarrow P(x \cup y)\big) \,\&\, \big(\forall x, y \,\big|\, \big(P(x) \,\&\, x \supseteq y\big) \rightarrow P(y)\big)$$

can be written in the form $P(x) \leftrightarrow (p \supseteq x)$. The predicates $\mathsf{Finite}(x)$, $\mathsf{Countable}(x)$, and $\mathsf{Is\_map}(x)$ illustrate this remark.

Case (viii) (total ordering relationships on a set) can be handled in the following way, which derives from the preceding remarks. Let $R$ be such a relationship. Introduce a representing function $f$ for it, i.e. $f(x) \supseteq f(y) \leftrightarrow R(x, y)$. Then $R$ is a total ordering iff the range elements $f(x)$ all belong to a collection of sets totally ordered by inclusion. So write a clause

$$y \supseteq v \vee v \supseteq y$$

for each pair of clauses $y = f(x)$, $v = f(u)$, and also write the conditions needed to ensure that $f$ is single-valued. If a model $\mathscr{M}$ exists for the resulting set of clauses, the model $F$ of $f$ plainly maps its domain into a collection of sets totally ordered by inclusion, and then $F$ can be extended to all other sets by sending them to $\emptyset$.

Case (ix) (multiple functions with known ranges and domains) is also very easy. For clarity, we will consider the special subcase of this in which two functions $f$, $g$ are given, along with two domain sets $d_1$, $d_2$, and two range sets $r_1$, $r_2$. The universally quantified conditions which must be satisfied are

$$(\forall x \in d_1 \mid f(x) \in r_1), \tag{3.23}$$

$$(\forall x \in d_2 \mid g(x) \in r_2), \tag{3.24}$$

along with some collection of unquantified clauses of MLSS.

We proceed as follows. For any two clauses $y = f(x)$, $y' = f(x')$ present in our set $C$ of clauses write a condition

$$x = x' \rightarrow y' = y', \tag{3.25}$$

and similarly for $g$. As usual, these reflect the single-valuedness of $f$ and $g$. For any clause $y = f(x)$ in $C$, write a condition

$$x \in d_1 \rightarrow y \in r_1, \tag{3.26}$$

and similarly for $g$, $d_2$, and $r_2$. Finally, write the conditions

$$\begin{aligned} d_1 \neq \emptyset &\rightarrow r_1 \neq \emptyset, \\ d_2 \neq \emptyset &\rightarrow r_2 \neq \emptyset. \end{aligned} \tag{3.27}$$

Then seek a model of the resulting set $S$ of clauses, which must plainly exist if our original set $C$ of clauses is consistent.

Conversely, suppose that the clauses $S$ have a model $\mathscr{M}$. Define a preliminary function $F$ (resp. $G$) as the set of all pairs $[\mathscr{M}(x), \mathscr{M}(y)]$ for which a clause $y = f(x)$ (resp. $y = g(x)$) is present in $C$. The clauses (3.25) plainly imply that $F$ is single-valued on its domain, and the clauses (3.26) ensure that $F$ maps the intersection of its domain with $d_1$ into $r_1$. If $\mathscr{M}(d_1) = \emptyset$, the quantified condition (3.23) is automatically satisfied. If $\mathscr{M}(d_1) \neq \emptyset$, the clause (3.27) ensures that $Mr_1 \neq \emptyset$, so we can extend $F$ to map all elements of $d_1$ not in its initial domain to any element of $r_1$ we choose. Repeating this construction for $g$, $d_2$, and $r_2$ plainly gives us a model of all our clauses in which $f$ and $g$ are represented by single-valued functions satisfying (3.23) and (3.24). Hence the clauses (3.25), (3.26), and (3.27) we have added are the extension conditions we require.

### 3.7.2 The Case of Mutually Inverse Functions

Extension conditions for Case (ii) (pairs of mutually inverse functions $f$, $g$ on a set $w$) can be formulated as follows. Write the clauses, described above, that force $f$

and $g$ to be single-valued. To these, add clauses

$$y = v \rightarrow x = u$$

derived from all the given statements $y = f(x)$, $v = f(u)$. These force $f$ to be 1-1 on the collection of elements $x$ known to be in its domain. (Note that this much also handles the case of functions known to be 1-1.) Do the same thing for $g$. Then add clauses

$$y = u \leftrightarrow x = v$$

derived from all the statement pairs $y = f(x)$, $v = g(u)$. Then, in the resulting model $\mathcal{M}$, the model functions $F$ and $G$ of $f$ and $g$ must both be 1-1 on their domains (e.g. for $F$ this is the collection of sets $\mathcal{M}(x)$ modelling points $x$ for which some clause $y = f(x)$ appears in our original set of statements), and $G$ must be the inverse of $F$ on $\mathsf{domain}(G) \cap \mathsf{range}(F)$. Since $G$ is 1-1 on its domain, it follows that the range of $G$ on $\mathsf{domain}(G) \setminus \mathsf{range}(F)$ must be disjoint from $\mathsf{domain}(F)$. Indeed, if a set $s$ is in $\mathsf{domain}(F) \cap \mathsf{range}(G)$ it must have the form $s = \mathcal{M}(x)$ where clauses $y = f(x)$ and $v = g(u)$ both appear in our original set of statements. But then $\mathcal{M}(u) = \mathcal{M}(y)$ is implied by an added clause, and hence $\mathcal{M}(u)$ is in the range of $F$. Similarly the range of $F$ on $\mathsf{domain}(F) \setminus \mathsf{range}(G)$ must be disjoint from $\mathsf{domain}(G)$. $F$ can therefore be extended to

$$\mathsf{range}(G_{|\mathsf{domain}(G) \setminus \mathsf{range}(F)})$$

(the range on the restriction) as the inverse of $G$, and similarly $G$ extended to

$$\mathsf{range}(F_{|\mathsf{domain}(F) \setminus \mathsf{range}(G)})$$

as the inverse of $F$. Let $F'$ and $G'$ be these extensions. Then plainly $\mathsf{domain}(F') = \mathsf{domain}(F) \cup \mathsf{range}(G)$, and so $\mathsf{range}(G') = \mathsf{range}(G) \cup \mathsf{domain}(F) = \mathsf{domain}(F')$ and vice versa. Hence the extensions $F'$ and $G'$ are mutually inverse with $\mathsf{domain}(F') = \mathsf{range}(G')$ and vice versa. $F'$ and $G'$ can now be extended to mutually inverse maps defined everywhere by using any 1-1 map of the complement of $\mathsf{domain}(F')$ onto the complement of $\mathsf{range}(F')$. This shows that the clauses listed above are the correct extension conditions for case (ii).

The extension conditions for the important car, cdr, and cons case can be worked out in similar fashion as follows. Regard $[x, y]$ as a family of one-parameter functions $\mathsf{cons}_x(y)$ dependent on the subsidiary parameter $x$. The ranges of all the functions $\mathsf{cons}_x$ in the family are disjoint (since $[x, y]$ can never equal $[u, v]$ if $x \neq u$). For the same reason, each $\mathsf{cons}_x$ is 1-1, and cdr is its (left) inverse, i.e. $\mathsf{cons}_x(y)^{[2]} = y$. Also, $\mathsf{cons}_x(y)^{[1]} = x$ everywhere. The extension conditions needed can then be stated as follows:

(i) 'cons' must be 'doubly 1-1' and well defined: add clauses

$$\big((x = u) \;\&\; (y = v)\big) \leftrightarrow (z = w)$$

derived from all pairs of initial clauses $z = [x, y]$, $w = [u, v]$.

(ii) ‘car’ and ‘cdr’ must stand in the proper inverse relationship to ‘cons’: add clauses

$$u = z \rightarrow x = v$$

derived from all pairs $z = [x, y]$, $v = u^{[1]}$, and all clauses

$$u = z \rightarrow y = v$$

derived from all pairs $z = [x, y]$, $v = u^{[2]}$ of initial statements.

Various other cases which can be handled by the ‘extension conditions’ technique, e.g. uninterpreted commutative functions of two variables, having the property

$$\big(\forall x, y \mid f(x, y) = f(y, x)\big),$$

can readily be handled by this technique. It might be possible to treat associativity also, possibly based on a prior MLSS-like theory of the concatenation operator.

Quite a number of decidable extensions of multilevel syllogistic have been treated in [CFO89, COP01].

## 3.8 More Examples of Decidable Sublanguages

### 3.8.1 Presburger's Decidable Quantified Language of Additive Arithmetic

In [Pre30], Mojżesz Presburger showed that the language of quantified statements whose variables all represent integers, and in which the only operations allowed are arithmetic addition and subtraction and the comparators $n > m$ and $n \geqslant m$, has a decidable satisfiability problem. (We will see in Chap. 6 that if the multiplication operator is added to this mix, the class of formulae that results admits of no algorithm for testing satisfiability.)

The technique used by Presburger is progressive elimination of quantifiers by replacement of existentially quantified set expressions by equivalent unquantified expressions of the same kind. This method of ‘quantifier elimination’ applies to a language $L$ if, given any formula

$$\big(\exists x \mid P(x)\big) \tag{3.28}$$

formed using just one quantifier, together with the operators allowed by the language, also the bound variable $x$ and various free variables $a_1, \ldots, a_n$, we can find an equivalent unquantified formula of the language, involving only the free variables $a_1, \ldots, a_n$, which is equivalent to (3.28). Note that universally quantified subformulae can always be reduced to existentially quantified form by use of the de Morgan rule

$$\big(\forall x \mid P(x)\big) \leftrightarrow \big(\neg\big(\exists x \mid \neg P(x)\big)\big).$$

If an unquantified formula equivalent to (3.28) always exists, we can work systematically through the syntax tree of any formula, from bottom to top, replacing all quantified subformulae with equivalent unquantified formulae, until no quantifiers remain. For (3.28) to be equivalent to an unquantified formula of the language $L$, it may be necessary to enlarge $L$ by adding some finite collection of supplementary operators and predicates. If quantification *à la* (3.28) of formulae written using every such operator collection requires the introduction of still more operators, quantifier elimination will fail; otherwise it can be applied.

A typical means of re-expressing (3.28) in unquantified form is to show that if (3.28) has a solution at all, some one of a finite collection of unquantified expressions $e_1, \ldots, e_k$ ('canonical solutions') written in terms of the free variables of (3.28) must be a solution. This allows (3.28) to be rewritten as the disjunction

$$P(e_1) \vee \cdots \vee P(e_k),$$

in which the quantified variable $x$ has been eliminated.

To apply these ideas to the Presburger language of additive arithmetic formulae described above, we need to introduce one additional operator into the language. This is the divisibility operator, which we will write in the next few paragraphs as $c \mid n$. In such expressions $c$ will always be a *positive* integer constant, and $n$ an integer-valued variable or expression.

In considering 'innermost' existentially quantified Presburger-formulae

$$(\exists n \mid P(n))$$

(that is, quantified formulae not containing any quantified subformulae) we can expand the (unquantified) 'body' $P(x)$ into a disjunction of conjunctions, and then use the predicate rule

$$(\exists x \mid P(x) \vee Q(x)) \leftrightarrow ((\exists x \mid P(x)) \vee (\exists x \mid Q(x)))$$

to move the existential quantifier in over the '$\vee$' operators. In the resulting formulae each $P$ is a conjunction of literals. These, in view of the equivalences

$$(a_k \cdot n > A_k) \leftrightarrow (a_k \cdot n \geqslant A_k + 1)$$

$$\neg(c_k \mid (d_k \cdot n + C_k)) \leftrightarrow \bigvee_{j=1}^{c_k - 1} (c_k \mid (d_k \cdot n + C_k + j)),$$

can therefore be written as

$$\left(\exists n \,\middle|\, \mathop{\&}_{k=1}^{I} (a_k \cdot n \geqslant A_k) \;\&\; \mathop{\&}_{k=1}^{J} (b_k \cdot n \leqslant B_k) \;\&\; \mathop{\&}_{k=1}^{L} (c_k \mid (d_k \cdot n + C_k))\right), \qquad (3.29)$$

where the $a_k$, $b_k$, $c_k$, and $d_k$ are positive integer constants, '$\cdot$' and '$+$' designate integer multiplication and addition, respectively,[3] and $A_k$, $B_k$, and $C_k$ are well-formed Presburger terms not containing $n$.

Suppose for the sake of definiteness that $I > 0$ in (3.29), and that (3.29) admits a solution $m$. Then among these solutions, all of which exceed the largest among the quotients $A_k/a_k$, there must exist a smallest $m_0$. This $m_0$ will have the form $(A_i + j)/a_i$, for some $i$ and some non-negative integer $j$. Let $c'_k$ denote the quotient $c_k/\mathsf{GCD}(c_k, d_k)$, for $k = 1, \dots, L$. Since $m_0$ is smallest, it must be impossible to subtract any multiple of $\ell_i = a_i \cdot \mathsf{lcm}(c'_1, \dots, c'_L)$ from $j$ and still have a non-negative integer. Hence

$$0 \leqslant j < \ell_i,$$

so that

$$m_0 \in \{(A_i + j)/a_i : 1 \leqslant i \leqslant I,\ 0 \leqslant j < \ell_i\}.$$

Thus (3.29) is equivalent to the following finite disjunction:

$$\bigvee_{i=1}^{I} \bigvee_{j=0}^{\ell_i - 1} \Bigg( \mathop{\&}_{k=1}^{I} \big(a_k \cdot (A_i + j) \geqslant a_i \cdot A_k\big) \ \&\ \mathop{\&}_{k=1}^{J} \big(b_k \cdot (A_i + j) \leqslant a_i \cdot B_k\big)$$
$$\&\ \mathop{\&}_{k=1}^{L} \big(a_i \cdot c_k \mid d_k \cdot (A_i + j) + a_i \cdot C_k\big) \ \&\ (a_i \mid A_i + j) \ \&\ (A_i + j \geqslant 0) \Bigg). \quad (3.30)$$

Note that (3.30) has substantially the same form as (3.29), but has one less existential quantifier. In passing from (3.29) to (3.30) we have essentially 'solved' for $n$:

"$n$ is $(a_i + j)/a_i$, where (3.30) serves to locate $i$ and $j$ within the finite set

$$\{[i, j] : 1 \leqslant i \leqslant I, 0 \leqslant j < L_i\}."$$

The case $I = 0$ can be reduced to the previous one, by pretending that the trivially true conjunct $n \geqslant 0$ is present. This corresponds to letting $I = 1$, $a_1 = 1$, $A_1 = 0$, and $\ell_1 = \mathsf{lcm}(c'_1, \dots, c'_L)$, so that (3.30) simplifies to

$$\bigvee_{j=0}^{\ell_1 - 1} \Bigg( \mathop{\&}_{k=1}^{J} (b_k \cdot j \leqslant B_k) \ \&\ \mathop{\&}_{k=1}^{L} \big(c_k \mid d_k \cdot j + C_k\big) \Bigg).$$

Decidability of the satisfiability problem for Presburger's language of quantified purely additive arithmetic now follows in the manner explained above.

[3]Notice that in the context of additive arithmetic, integer multiplication is admitted only in terms of the form $c \cdot A$, where $c$ is a positive integer constant and $A$ is a well-formed Presburger term; thus $c \cdot A$ can be considered as a short for $\underbrace{A + \cdots + A}_{c \text{ times}}$.

### 3.8.2 A Decidable Quantified Theory Involving Ordinals

Various interesting algebraic operations can be defined on the collection of all ordinals, in the following way. A set $s$ is said to be *well-ordered* if it is ordered by some ordering relationship $x > y$ for which $x > y$ is incompatible both with $x = y$ and $y > x$, and which is such that every nonempty subset $t$ of $s$ contains a smallest element $x$, which we can write as $\mathsf{Smallest}(t)$. Given a well-ordered set $s$, if we make the recursive definition

$$\begin{aligned}\mathsf{Enu}(x) =_{\mathrm{Def}} &\ \textbf{if}\ s \subseteq \{\,\mathsf{Enu}(y) : y \in x\,\}\ \textbf{then}\ s\\ &\ \textbf{else}\ \mathsf{Smallest}\big(s \setminus \{\,\mathsf{Enu}(y) : y \in x\,\}\big)\ \textbf{end if}\,,\end{aligned}$$

it is not hard to see that for any two ordinals $x$ and $y$ we have

$$(x \supsetneq y) \rightarrow \mathsf{Enu}(x) > \mathsf{Enu}(y) \vee s \cup \{s\} = \{\,\mathsf{Enu}(z) : z \in x\,\},$$

and from this then $\mathsf{Enu}$, restricted to the inverse image of $s$, is a one-to-one, order-preserving mapping of some unique ordinal $\alpha$ onto $s$ (where, as usual, ordinals are ordered by inclusion, or, equivalently, membership). The ordinal $\alpha$ derived from $s$ in this way is called the *order type* of $s$, and it can easily be seen that

$$\alpha = \mathsf{Min}\{\,\beta \in \mathsf{Ord} \mid s \subseteq \{\,\mathsf{Enu}(y) : y \in \beta\,\}\}.$$

The algebraic operations alluded to above are then defined by forming various well-ordered sets from pairs of ordinals and taking the order types of these sets.

Perhaps the easiest case is that of the Cartesian product $\{\,[x,\ y] : x \in \alpha_1,\ y \in \alpha_2\,\}$, with $\alpha_1$ and $\alpha_2$ ordinal numbers, which can be ordered lexicographically. The order type of this product is the so-called *ordinal product*, which we will write as $\alpha_1 *_o \alpha_2$. In much the same way we can order the set

$$\{\,[x_1,\ x_2,\ldots,x_k] : x_1 \in \alpha_1,\ x_2 \in \alpha_2,\ \ldots,\ x_k \in \alpha_k\,\}$$

of $k$-tuples lexicographically, thereby defining the $k$-fold ordinal product

$$\alpha_1 *_o \alpha_2 *_o \cdots *_o \alpha_k,$$

where $\alpha_1, \alpha_2, \ldots, \alpha_k$ are ordinal numbers. Since there is an evident order isomorphism (i.e. 1-1, order-preserving map) between $\alpha_1 *_o \alpha_2 *_o \alpha_3$ and each of the ordered sets

$$\{\,[y, x_3] : y \in \alpha_1 *_o \alpha_2,\ x_3 \in \alpha_3\,\}$$

and

$$\{\,[x_1,\ z] : x_1 \in \alpha_1,\ z \in \alpha_2 *_o \alpha_3\,\},$$

it follows that ordinal multiplication satisfies the associative law

$$(\alpha_1 *_o \alpha_2) *_o \alpha_3 = \alpha_1 *_o (\alpha_2 *_o \alpha_3).$$

Given any two ordinals $\alpha_1$ and $\alpha_2$, we can form a well-ordered set by ordering the collection

$$\{[0, x] : x \in \alpha_1\} \cup \{[1, y] : y \in \alpha_2\}$$

of pairs lexicographically. The order type of this set is called the *ordinal sum* of $\alpha_1$ and $\alpha_2$, which we will write as $\alpha_1 +_o \alpha_2$. The $k$-fold ordinal sum $\alpha_1 +_o \alpha_2 +_o \cdots +_o \alpha_k$ of $k$ ordinal numbers $\alpha_1, \alpha_2, \ldots, \alpha_k$ can be defined as the order type of the set of pairs

$$\{[0, x] : x \in \alpha_1\} \cup \{[1, x] : x \in \alpha_2\} \cup \cdots \cup \{[k-1, x] : x \in \alpha_k\},$$

ordered lexicographically. It is not hard to see that if $\alpha_1, \alpha_2, \alpha_3$ are ordinals, then both $(\alpha_1 +_o \alpha_2) +_o \alpha_3$ and $\alpha_1 +_o (\alpha_2 +_o \alpha_3)$ have the order type of the set

$$\{[0, x] : x \in \alpha_1\} \cup \{[1, y] : y \in \alpha_2\} \cup \{[2, y] : y \in \alpha_3\},$$

ordered lexicographically. Hence ordinal addition is also associative, i.e.

$$(\alpha_1 +_o \alpha_2) +_o \alpha_3 = \alpha_1 +_o (\alpha_2 +_o \alpha_3).$$

Note, however, that ordinal addition is not commutative. Indeed, if we denote by $\omega$ the set of all integers as is customary in the theory of ordinal numbers, we find that $\omega +_o 1$ is larger than $\omega$, but $1 +_o \omega$ is easily seen to be $\omega$. Note also that $\alpha +_o 1$ is easily seen to be the successor ordinal of $\alpha$ for each ordinal $\alpha$, and so is always strictly larger than $\alpha$.

The smallest ordinals are the finite integers $0, 1, 2, \ldots$ followed by the set $\omega$ of all integers, which is the smallest infinite ordinal. From these, we can form other ordinals using the operations just introduced:

$$\omega +_o 1,\ \omega +_o 2, \ldots, \omega +_o \omega = 2 *_o \omega,\ 3 *_o \omega, \ldots, \omega *_o \omega,\ \omega *_o \omega *_o \omega, \ldots.$$

We shall now have a look at the ordering and ordinal arithmetic relationships between these and related ordinals.

Suppose that we indicate the dependence of the $\mathsf{Enu}(x)$ function described above on the well-ordered set $s$ appearing in its definition by writing $\mathsf{Enu}(x)$ as $\mathsf{Enu}_s(x)$. Then it is easily proved by (transfinite) induction that if $t$ is a well-ordered set and $t \supseteq s$ we have $\mathsf{Enu}_s(\alpha) \geqslant \mathsf{Enu}_t(\alpha)$ for any ordinal $\alpha$ such that $\mathsf{Enu}_s(\alpha) \in s$. (Hint: first prove by induction that

$$t \setminus \{\mathsf{Enu}_t(y) : y \in \beta\} \supseteq s \setminus \{\mathsf{Enu}_s(y) : y \in \beta\}$$

for every ordinal $\beta$.) It follows that the order type of any subset $s$ of an ordinal $\alpha$ is the image under the Enu function of an ordinal no larger than $\alpha$. Since, as seen above, any well-ordered set is order-isomorphic to some ordinal, it follows at once that the order type of a subset of a well-ordered set $s$ can be no larger than the order type of $s$.

Using this last result it is easy to see that both addition and multiplication are non-decreasing functions of both their arguments. For example, if $\alpha_1$, $\alpha_2$, $\beta_1$, and $\beta_2$ are all ordinals, with $\alpha_1 \supseteq \beta_1$ and $\alpha_2 \supseteq \beta_2$, then $\alpha_1 *_o \alpha_2$ is the order type of the lexicographically ordered Cartesian product $C$ of $\alpha_1$ and $\alpha_2$, and $\beta_1 *_o \beta_2$ is the order type of the Cartesian product of $\beta_1$ and $\beta_2$, which is a subset of $C$ and has the same lexicographic order. Hence $\alpha_1 *_o \alpha_2$ is an ordinal no smaller than $\beta_1 *_o \beta_2$, showing that the operation of ordinal multiplication is monotone in both its arguments. The proof of the corresponding statement for ordinal addition, which is similar, is left to the reader.

Ordinal multiplication is right-distributive over ordinal addition. That is, we have

$$(\alpha_1 +_o \alpha_2) *_o \beta = (\alpha_1 *_o \beta) +_o (\alpha_2 *_o \beta),$$

whenever $\alpha_1$, $\alpha_2$, and $\beta$ are ordinals. To see this, note that $(\alpha_1 +_o \alpha_2) *_o \beta$ is easily seen to be the order type of the set

$$\{[0, x, y] : x \in \alpha_1,\ y \in \beta\} \cup \{[1, x, y] : x \in \alpha_2,\ y \in \beta\}$$

and $(\alpha_1 *_o \beta) +_o (\alpha_2 *_o \beta)$ can be identified with equal ease with the same set. This implies that the ordinal sum $\alpha +_o \alpha +_o \cdots +_o \alpha$ of $k$ copies of an ordinal $\alpha$ is the same as $k *_o \alpha$. On the other hand, the corresponding left distributive law fails for infinite ordinals: although $2 *_o \omega$ is $\omega +_o \omega$ (the order type of two copies of the integers, the second positioned after the whole of the first), $\omega *_o 2$ is the order type of the lexicographically ordered set of pairs

$$\{[x, 0] : x \in \omega\} \cup \{[x, 1] : x \in \omega\},$$

which is order-isomorphic to $\omega$ by the (integer arithmetic) mapping $[x, i] \mapsto 2 * x + i$.

A kind of subtraction can be defined for ordinals. More specifically, if $\alpha_1$ and $\alpha_2$ are ordinals and $\alpha_1 \supseteq \alpha_2$, then we can write $\alpha_1$ as an ordinal sum $\alpha_1 = \alpha_2 +_o \alpha_3$. (Conversely, by the result proved in the preceding paragraph, $\alpha_2 +_o \alpha_3$ can never be less than $\alpha_2$, since $\alpha_2$ can be written as $\alpha_2 +_o 0$.) Indeed, $\alpha_1$ is the union of $\alpha_2$ and $\alpha_1 \setminus \alpha_2$, whose elements are all larger than all elements in $\alpha_2$, from which it is easily seen that the order type of $\alpha_1$ is the ordinal sum of the order types of $\alpha_2$ and $\alpha_1 \setminus \alpha_2$.

Using the ordinal subtraction operation just described we can now show that the ordinal addition operation $\alpha +_o \beta$ is strictly monotone in its second (though not in its first) argument. Indeed, if $\beta' > \beta$, then $\beta'$ can be written as $\beta +_o \gamma$ for some non-zero ordinal $\gamma$, and so $\alpha +_o \beta' = \alpha +_o \beta +_o \gamma$ is larger than $\alpha +_o \beta$. On the other hand we have $2 +_o \omega = 1 +_o \omega = \omega$, showing that ordinal addition is not strictly monotone on its first argument.

For any two ordinals $\alpha_1$ and $\alpha_2$, of which the first is at least 2 and the second is non-zero, the ordinal product $\alpha_1 *_o \alpha_2$ is strictly larger than $\alpha_2$. Indeed we have $(\alpha_1 *_o \alpha_2) \supseteq (2 *_o \alpha_2) = (\alpha_2 +_o \alpha_2) \geqslant (\alpha_2 +_o 1) > \alpha_2$.

The equation $\alpha +_o \beta = \beta$, of which $1 +_o \omega = \omega$ is a special solution, is worth studying more closely. Note first of all that if $\beta \geqslant \omega *_o \alpha$, then using ordinal subtraction we can write $\beta$ as $\omega *_o \alpha +_o \gamma$ for some ordinal $\gamma$, so that

$$\alpha +_o \beta = \alpha +_o \omega *_o \alpha +_o \gamma = (1 +_o \omega) *_o \alpha +_o \gamma = \omega *_o \alpha +_o \gamma = \beta.$$

That is, we must have $\alpha +_o \beta = \beta$ whenever $\beta \geqslant \omega *_o \alpha$. Conversely, if $\alpha +_o \beta = \beta$, then

$$2 *_o \alpha +_o \beta = (\alpha +_o \alpha) +_o \beta = \alpha +_o (\alpha +_o \beta) = \alpha +_o \beta = \beta,$$

and so inductively $(k *_o \alpha) +_o \beta = \beta$ for every finite integer $k$, and so $k *_o \alpha \leqslant \beta$ for every finite integer $k$. It follows from this that $\omega *_o \alpha \leqslant \beta$. For if not, then we must have $\beta < \omega *_o \alpha$, so $\beta$ is isomorphic to a proper initial segment $s$ of the Cartesian product $C$ of $\omega$ and $\alpha$. Let $[m, x] = \mathsf{Smallest}(C - s)$ with $m \in \omega$ and $x \in \alpha$. Then $s$ is a proper initial segment of the Cartesian product of $m$ and $\alpha$, whose order type is $m *_o \alpha$. Thus $\beta < m *_o \alpha$, which contradicts the inequality $m *_o \alpha \leqslant \beta$ derived above. Therefore $\omega *_o \alpha \leqslant \beta$, as stated. Together all this proves that $\alpha +_o \beta = \beta$ if and only if $\beta \geqslant \omega *_o \alpha$, i.e. if and only if $\beta$ is 'substantially' larger than $\alpha$, in this sense. Note that our argument also proves that if $n$ and $m$ are ordinals, and $m \geqslant k *_o m$ for every finite integer $k$, then $m \geqslant \omega *_o m$.

Write the $k$-fold product of any ordinal $\alpha$ with itself as $\alpha^k$. The associative law for ordinal multiplication implies that $\alpha^j *_o \alpha^k = \alpha^{j+k}$ (where $j + k$ denotes the integer sum of $j$ and $k$.) If $\alpha$ is greater than 1, and in particular if $\alpha = \omega$, then the sequence of powers $\alpha, \alpha^2, \alpha^3, \ldots$ is strictly increasing. Indeed we have

$$\begin{aligned} \alpha^{i+1} &= \alpha *_o \alpha^i \geqslant 2 *_o \alpha^i = \alpha^i +_o \alpha^i \\ &\geqslant \alpha^i +_o 1 > \alpha^i. \end{aligned}$$

We will call an ordinal $\alpha$ a *polynomial ordinal* if it has the form

$$c_k *_o \omega^k +_o c_{k-1} *_o \omega^{k-1} +_o c_{k-2} *_o \omega^{k-2} +_o \cdots +_o c_1 *_o \omega +_o c_0,$$

where all the coefficients $c_i$ are finite integers. These ordinals, which we shall write as $\mathsf{Pord}(c_k, c_{k-1}, \ldots, c_0)$, have the following properties:

(i) Two polynomial ordinals

$$p = \mathsf{Pord}(c_k, c_{k-1}, \ldots, c_0) \quad \text{and} \quad p' = \mathsf{Pord}(c'_{k'}, c'_{k'-1}, \ldots, c'_0)$$

are distinct if their coefficient sequences $c_k, c_{k-1}, \ldots, c_0$ and $c'_{k'}, c'_{k'-1}, \ldots, c'_0$ are distinct, up to leading zeroes.

(ii) Two polynomial ordinals compare in the lexicographic order of their coefficients. (If one of the sequences of coefficients is shorter, it should be prefixed with zeroes to give it the length of the other sequence of coefficients.)

(iii) The ordinal sum of two polynomial ordinals $p = \mathsf{Pord}(c_k, c_{k-1}, \ldots, c_0)$ and $p' = \mathsf{Pord}(c'_{k'}, c'_{k'-1}, \ldots, c'_0)$ with $k \geqslant k'$ is given by the following rule:

If $p' = 0$, i.e. all its coefficients are zeroes, then the ordinal sum of $p$ and $p'$ is $\mathsf{Pord}(c'_{k'}, c'_{k'-1}, \ldots, c'_0)$. Otherwise, locate the leftmost position $i$ in which the second argument has a non-zero coefficient; take the coefficients of the first argument to the left of this position; in the $i$th position, add $c_i$ and $c'_i$; in later positions take the coefficients of the second argument. This rule is expressed by the formula

$$\begin{aligned}&\mathsf{Pord}(c_k, c_{k-1}, \ldots, c_0) +_o \mathsf{Pord}(c'_{k'}, c'_{k'-1}, \ldots, c'_0)\\&\qquad = \mathsf{Pord}(c_k, c_{k-1}, \ldots, c_{i+1}, c_i + c'_i, c'_{i-1}, \ldots, c'_0)\end{aligned}$$

for the sum of these two polynomial ordinals, where

$$c'_{k'} = c'_{k'-1} = \cdots = c'_{i+1} = 0 \quad \text{and} \quad c'_i \neq 0.$$

To prove (i–iii), note that (ii) implies (i), so that only (ii) and (iii) need be proved. (ii) can be proved as follows. Consider two polynomial ordinals $p$ and $p'$, having the general forms

$$p = \mathsf{Pord}(c_k, c_{k-1}, \ldots, c_0) \quad \text{and} \quad p' = \mathsf{Pord}\big(c'_k, c'_{k-1}, \ldots, c'_0\big) \tag{3.31}$$

and suppose that the first difference between their coefficients occurs at the position $i$. Since it is obvious from the definition of (3.31) and by associativity that

$$\begin{aligned}&\mathsf{Pord}(c_k, c_{k-1}, \ldots, c_0)\\&\qquad = \mathsf{Pord}(c_k, c_{k-1}, \ldots, c_{i+1}, 0, \ldots, 0) +_o \mathsf{Pord}(c_i, c_{i-1}, \ldots, c_0),\end{aligned}$$

and since the ordinal addition operator is strictly monotone in its second argument, we can suppose without loss of generality that $i = k$, and therefore need only prove that if two polynomial ordinals (3.31) differ in their first coefficient, the one with the larger first coefficient is larger. This is simply a matter of proving that $\mathsf{Pord}(c_k, c_{k-1}, \ldots, c_0) < (c_k + 1) *_o \omega^k$, i.e. that $\mathsf{Pord}(c_{k-1}, \ldots, c_0) < \omega^k$. But it is easily seen that $\mathsf{Pord}(c_{k-1}, \ldots, c_j) +_o \omega^k = \mathsf{Pord}(c_{k-1}, \ldots, c_{j+1}) +_o \omega^k$ for every $j \leqslant k$, from which it follows inductively that $\mathsf{Pord}(c_{k-1}, \ldots, c_0) +_o \omega^k = \omega^k$. It is easily seen from this that $\mathsf{Pord}(c_{k-1}, \ldots, c_0) < \omega^k$, as claimed, thus proving (ii).

To calculate the sum of two non-zero polynomial ordinals $\mathsf{Pord}(c_k, c_{k-1}, \ldots, c_0)$ and $\mathsf{Pord}(c'_i, c'_{i-1}, \ldots, c'_0)$ (both written with non-zero leading coefficients) we can note first of all that if $k < i$ then we can show, as at the end of the preceding paragraph, that $\mathsf{Pord}(c_k, c_{k-1}, \ldots, c_0) +_o c'_i *_o \omega^i = c'_i *_o \omega^i$. From this, (iii) follows immediately by associativity of ordinal addition in the special case in which $k < i$. Now suppose that $k \geqslant i$. Then by associativity of ordinal addition we have

$$\begin{aligned}&\mathsf{Pord}(c_k, c_{k-1}, \ldots, c_0) +_o \mathsf{Pord}\big(c'_i, c'_{i-1}, \ldots, c_0\big)\\&\quad = \big(\mathsf{Pord}(c_k, c_{k-1}, \ldots, c_{i+1}) +_o c_i *_o \omega^i +_o \mathsf{Pord}(c_{i-1}, \ldots, c_0)\big)\\&\qquad\qquad +_o \big(c'_i *_o \omega^i +_o \mathsf{Pord}\big(c'_{i-1}, \ldots, c'_0\big)\big)\end{aligned}$$

$$= \mathsf{Pord}(c_k, c_{k-1}, \ldots, c_{i+1}) +_o \left(c_i + c_i'\right) *_o \omega^i +_o \mathsf{Pord}\left(c_{i-1}', \ldots, c_0'\right)$$
$$= \mathsf{Pord}\left(c_k, c_{k-1}, \ldots, c_{i+1}, c_i + c_i', c_{i-1}', \ldots, c_0'\right),$$

proving (iii).

By the rule (ii) stated above, $\mathsf{Pord}(c_k, c_{k-1}, \ldots, c_0) < \omega^{k+1}$. Conversely, we will show that if $\alpha$ is any ordinal such that $\alpha < \omega^{k+1}$, then $\alpha$ is a polynomial ordinal of the form $\mathsf{Pord}(c_k, c_{k-1}, \ldots, c_0)$. To see this, argue inductively on $k$, and so suppose that our statement is true for all $k' < k$. Then find the largest integer $c$ such that $\alpha \geqslant c *_o \omega^k$; this must exist since we have seen above that if $\alpha \geqslant c *_o \omega^k$ for all integers $c$, it would follow that $\alpha \geqslant \omega^{k+1}$, which is impossible. By the subtraction principle stated above, we can write $\alpha = c *_o \omega^k +_o \beta$ for some ordinal $\beta$. If $\beta \geqslant \omega^k$, then

$$\alpha \geqslant c *_o \omega^k +_o \omega^k = (c+1) *_o \omega^k,$$

contradicting the definition of $c$. It follows by induction that $\beta$ is a polynomial ordinal and can be written as $\mathsf{Pord}(c_{k-1}, \ldots, c_0)$, from which it follows immediately that $\alpha = \mathsf{Pord}(c, c_{k-1}, \ldots, c_0)$, as asserted.

It follows that the smallest ordinals are precisely the polynomial ordinals, and that the first positive ordinal larger than all the polynomial ordinals is the union of all the powers $\omega^k$ for integer $k$. This is the order type of the collection of all infinite sequences $[\ldots, n_i, n_{i-1}, \ldots, n_0]$ of integers which contain all but finitely many non-zeroes, lexicographically ordered.

We will say that an ordinal $\alpha$ is *post-polynomial* if, whenever $\beta < \alpha$ and $p$ is a polynomial ordinal, $\beta +_o p < \alpha$ also. The first post-polynomial ordinal is the zero ordinal $\emptyset$; this is the only post-polynomial ordinal which is also polynomial. Moreover the sum $\alpha_1 +_o \alpha_2$ of any two post-polynomial ordinals is itself post-polynomial. For if $\beta$ is an ordinal such that $\beta < \alpha_1 +_o \alpha_2$ and $p$ is a polynomial ordinal, then if $\beta < \alpha_1$ we have $\beta +_o p < \alpha_1$ also, and therefore $\beta +_o p < \alpha_1 +_o \alpha_2$. On the other hand, if $\beta \geqslant \alpha_1$, we can write $\beta = \alpha_1 +_o \gamma$ for some ordinal $\gamma$, and by the strict monotonicity of ordinal addition in its second argument we must have $\gamma < \alpha_2$, so $\gamma +_o p < \alpha_2$, and therefore

$$\beta +_o p = \alpha_1 +_o \gamma +_o p < \alpha_1 +_o \alpha_2,$$

proving that $\beta +_o p < \alpha_1 +_o \alpha_2$ in all cases.

We shall now show that any ordinal $\alpha$ can be decomposed uniquely as an ordinal sum $\alpha = \mu +_o p$, where $\mu$ is post-polynomial and $p$ is a polynomial ordinal ($\mu$ and $p$ will be referred to as the post-polynomial and the polynomial parts of $\alpha$, respectively). Moreover, in this decomposition, ordinals $\alpha$ have exactly the lexicographic ordering of the corresponding pairs $[\mu, p]$. To show this, note first of all that the union $U$ of all the elements of any set $s$ of post-polynomial ordinals must itself be post-polynomial. Indeed, if $\gamma < u$, then $\gamma$ is a member of $U$ and hence of some $\delta$ in $u$, so that $\gamma +_o p < \delta$ for all polynomial ordinals $p$, and hence $\gamma +_o p < U$. It follows that the union $\nu$ of all the post-polynomial ordinals not greater than $\alpha$ is itself post-polynomial. Clearly $\mu$ is the largest post-polynomial ordinal not greater than $\alpha$. By the subtraction principle for ordinals stated above, there exists an ordinal

$\xi$ such that $\alpha = \nu +_o \xi$. The ordinal $\xi$ cannot be greater or equal to the first non-zero post-polynomial ordinal $\lambda$, since if it were, then we would have $\alpha \geqslant \nu +_o \lambda$, but we have seen above that $\nu +_o \lambda$ is post-polynomial, and since it is clearly greater than $\nu$ we have a contradiction. Hence $\xi$ is less than $\lambda$, and so is polynomial, proving that $\alpha$ can be decomposed as an ordinal sum $\alpha = \mu +_o p$ of the type stated above. Uniqueness is proved in the next paragraph.

The decomposition $\alpha = \mu +_o p$ of an ordinal $\alpha$ into the sum of a post-polynomial and a polynomial ordinal is unique, since if $\mu +_o p = \mu' +_o p'$ for distinct post-polynomial $\mu, \mu'$, then one of these two, say $\mu$, must be larger than the other. But then $\mu + p \geqslant \mu > \mu' +_o p'$, a contradiction. Similarly, if $\mu +_o p > \mu' +_o p'$, with $\mu, \mu'$ post-polynomial ordinals and $p, p'$ polynomial ordinals, we must have $\mu \geqslant \mu'$, and if $\mu = \mu'$, then $p > p'$ by the monotonicity of ordinal addition. This shows that the lexicographic ordering of the pairs $[\mu, p]$ corresponds exactly to the standard ordering of the corresponding ordinals $\alpha = \mu +_o p$.

In what follows we shall say that a polynomial ordinal is of *degree* $k$ if it has the form $\mathsf{Pord}(c_k, c_{k-1}, \ldots, c_0)$ with either $c_k \neq 0$ or $k = 0$. The function $\mathsf{Cf}_j(p)$ is defined to return the $j$th coefficient of the polynomial ordinal $p$, or, if $j$ exceeds the degree of $p$, to return 0. We extend this function to all ordinals by writing $\mathsf{Cf}_j(\beta +_o p) = \mathsf{Cf}_j(p)$ if $p$ is a polynomial ordinal and $\beta$ is post-polynomial. If $p = \mathsf{Pord}(c_k, c_{k-1}, \ldots, c_0)$ is a polynomial ordinal of degree $k$ and $j$ an integer, we let

$$\mathsf{Hi}_j(p) = \begin{cases} \mathsf{Pord}(c_k, c_{k-1}, \ldots, c_{j+1}) & \text{if } j < k \\ 0 & \text{otherwise} \end{cases}$$

and

$$\mathsf{Low}_j(p) = \begin{cases} \mathsf{Pord}(c_j, c_{j-1}, \ldots, c_0) & \text{if } j < k \\ p & \text{otherwise.} \end{cases}$$

These operations are extended to general ordinals in the same way we extended $\mathsf{Cf}_j$. Using these functions, we define three auxiliary functions $\alpha \mathbin{\mathring{-}} p$, $\alpha \frown p$, and $\alpha \backsim p$ for use below. These are defined for any ordinal $\alpha$ and polynomial ordinal $p$: If $p$ is of degree $d$ and $c$ is its leading coefficient and if $\mu$ is the post-polynomial part of $\alpha$, then we have

$$\begin{aligned} \alpha \mathbin{\mathring{-}} p &= \mu +_o \mathsf{Hi}_d(\alpha) *_o \omega^{d+1} +_o c' *_o \omega^d +_o \mathsf{Low}_{d-1}(p) \\ \alpha \frown p &= \mu +_o \mathsf{Hi}_d(\alpha) *_o \omega^{d+1} +_o \mathsf{Low}_{d-1}(p) \\ \alpha \backsim p &= \mu +_o \mathsf{Hi}_d(\alpha) *_o \omega^{d+1} +_o p \end{aligned}$$

(where $c'$ is $\mathsf{Cf}_d(\alpha) - c$, if this is positive, otherwise 0). Then we have $\mathsf{Hi}_d(\alpha \mathbin{\mathring{-}} p) = \mathsf{Hi}_d(\alpha)$; $\mathsf{Cf}_d(\alpha \mathbin{\mathring{-}} p)$ is $\mathsf{Cf}_d(\alpha) - c$ if this is positive, otherwise 0; and $\mathsf{Low}_{d-1}(\alpha \mathbin{\mathring{-}} p) = \mathsf{Low}_{d-1}(p)$. Similarly $\mathsf{Hi}_d(\alpha \frown p) = \mathsf{Hi}_d(\alpha)$; $\mathsf{Cf}_j(\alpha \frown p)$ is 0; and $\mathsf{Low}_{d-1}(\alpha \frown p) = \mathsf{Low}_{d-1}(p)$. Finally $\mathsf{Hi}_d(\alpha \backsim p) = \mathsf{Hi}_d(\alpha)$ and $\mathsf{Low}_d(\alpha \backsim p) = \mathsf{Low}_d(p)$.

We will also need to use various properties of these operators, as used in combination with each other and in combination with the comparator '>' and the equality

'='. These are as follows (where $y, z$ are arbitrary ordinals, and $p, q$ are polynomial ordinals of degrees $d$ and $d'$ and leading coefficients $c$ and $c'$, respectively):

$$
\begin{array}{rrl}
\text{(i)} & (\alpha +_o p) +_o q = & \alpha +_o (p +_o q) \\
\text{(ii)} & (\alpha +_o p) \mathbin{\stackrel{\circ}{-}} q = & \textbf{if } d > d' \textbf{ then } \alpha +_o (p \mathbin{\stackrel{\circ}{-}} q) \\
 & & \textbf{elseif } d' > d \textbf{ then } \alpha \mathbin{\stackrel{\circ}{-}} q \\
 & & \textbf{elseif } c \geqslant c' \textbf{ then } \alpha +_o (p \mathbin{\stackrel{\circ}{-}} q) \\
 & & \textbf{else } \alpha \mathbin{\stackrel{\circ}{-}} ((q \mathbin{\stackrel{\circ}{-}} p) \smile (q \frown q)) \textbf{ end if} \\
\text{(iii)} & (\alpha +_o p) \frown q = & \textbf{if } d > d' \textbf{ then } \alpha +_o (p \frown q) \\
 & & \textbf{else } \alpha \frown q \textbf{ end if} \\
\text{(iv)} & (\alpha +_o p) \smile q = & \textbf{if } d > d' \textbf{ then } \alpha +_o (p \smile q) \\
 & & \textbf{else } \alpha \smile q \textbf{ end if} \\
\text{(v)} & (\alpha \mathbin{\stackrel{\circ}{-}} p) +_o q = & \textbf{if } d > d' \textbf{ then } \alpha \mathbin{\stackrel{\circ}{-}} (p +_o q) \\
 & & \textbf{elseif } d' > d \textbf{ then } \alpha +_o q \\
 & & \textbf{elseif } \mathsf{Cf}_d(\alpha) < c \textbf{ then } \alpha \smile q \\
 & & \textbf{elseif } c \geqslant c' \textbf{ then } \alpha \mathbin{\stackrel{\circ}{-}} (p \mathbin{\stackrel{\circ}{-}} q) \\
 & & \textbf{else } \alpha +_o (q \mathbin{\stackrel{\circ}{-}} p) \textbf{ end if} \\
\text{(vi)} & (\alpha \mathbin{\stackrel{\circ}{-}} p) \mathbin{\stackrel{\circ}{-}} q = & \textbf{if } d > d' \textbf{ then } \alpha \mathbin{\stackrel{\circ}{-}} (p \mathbin{\stackrel{\circ}{-}} q) \\
 & & \textbf{elseif } d' > d \textbf{ then } \alpha \mathbin{\stackrel{\circ}{-}} q \\
 & & \textbf{else } \alpha \mathbin{\stackrel{\circ}{-}} (p +_o q) \textbf{ end if} \\
\text{(vii)} & (\alpha \mathbin{\stackrel{\circ}{-}} p) \frown q = & \textbf{if } d > d' \textbf{ then } \alpha \mathbin{\stackrel{\circ}{-}} (p \frown q) \\
 & & \textbf{else } \alpha \frown q \textbf{ end if} \\
\text{(viii)} & (\alpha \mathbin{\stackrel{\circ}{-}} p) \smile q = & \textbf{if } d > d' \textbf{ then } \alpha \mathbin{\stackrel{\circ}{-}} (p \smile q) \\
 & & \textbf{else } \alpha \smile q \textbf{ end if} \\
\text{(ix)} & (\alpha \frown p) +_o q = & \textbf{if } d > d' \textbf{ then } \alpha \frown (p +_o q) \\
 & & \textbf{elseif } d' > d \textbf{ then } \alpha +_o q \\
 & & \textbf{elseif } d' = d \textbf{ then } \alpha \smile q \textbf{ end if} \\
\text{(x)} & (\alpha \frown p) \mathbin{\stackrel{\circ}{-}} q = & \textbf{if } d > d' \textbf{ then } \alpha \frown (p \mathbin{\stackrel{\circ}{-}} q) \\
 & & \textbf{elseif } d' > d \textbf{ then } \alpha \mathbin{\stackrel{\circ}{-}} q \\
 & & \textbf{else } \alpha \frown q \textbf{ end if} \\
\text{(xi)} & (\alpha \frown p) \frown q = & \textbf{if } d \geqslant d' \textbf{ then } \alpha \frown (p \frown q) \\
 & & \textbf{else } \alpha \frown q \textbf{ end if} \\
\text{(xii)} & (\alpha \frown p) \smile q = & \textbf{if } d \geqslant d' \textbf{ then } \alpha \frown (p \smile q) \\
 & & \textbf{else } \alpha \smile q \textbf{ end if} \\
\text{(xiii)} & (\alpha \smile p) +_o q = & \textbf{if } d > d' \textbf{ then } \alpha \smile (p +_o q) \\
 & & \textbf{elseif } d' > d \textbf{ then } \alpha +_o q \\
 & & \textbf{elseif } d' = d \textbf{ then } \alpha \smile (p +_o q) \textbf{ end if} \\
\text{(xiv)} & (\alpha \smile p) \mathbin{\stackrel{\circ}{-}} q = & \textbf{if } d > d' \textbf{ then } \alpha \smile (p \mathbin{\stackrel{\circ}{-}} q) \\
 & & \textbf{elseif } d' > d \textbf{ then } \alpha \mathbin{\stackrel{\circ}{-}} q \\
 & & \textbf{elseif } d' = d \textbf{ then } \alpha \smile (p \mathbin{\stackrel{\circ}{-}} q) \textbf{ end if} \\
\text{(xv)} & (\alpha \smile p) \frown q = & \textbf{if } d \geqslant d' \textbf{ then } \alpha \smile (p \frown q) \\
 & & \textbf{else } \alpha \frown q \textbf{ end if} \\
\text{(xvi)} & (\alpha \smile p) \smile q = & \textbf{if } d \geqslant d' \textbf{ then } \alpha \smile (p \smile q) \\
 & & \textbf{else } \alpha \smile q \textbf{ end if}
\end{array}
$$

(xvii) $(\alpha +_o p > z) \leftrightarrow (\alpha \geqslant z +_o r'$
$\vee (\alpha \geqslant z \frown r \,\&\, (\mathsf{Cf}_d(z) < c$
$\vee (\alpha \geqslant \omega \mathbin{\dot{-}} r^* \,\&\, p \frown p > \mathsf{Low}_{d-1}(z))))$

(Here $r$ and $r'$ are, respectively the polynomial ordinals $\omega^d$ and $\omega^{d+1}$, and $r^*$ is the polynomial ordinal of degree $d$ whose leading coefficient is $\mathsf{Cf}_d(p)$ and whose remaining coefficients are 0.)

(xviii) $((\alpha \mathbin{\dot{-}} p) > z) \leftrightarrow (\alpha \geqslant (z +_o r')\vee$
$(\alpha \geqslant (z \frown r) \,\&$
$((\mathsf{Cf}_d(\alpha) \leqslant c \,\&\, p \frown p > \mathsf{Low}_d(z))$
$\vee (\mathsf{Cf}_d(\alpha) > c \,\&\, (\alpha > \omega + r^*$
$\vee (\alpha \geqslant \omega + r^* \,\&\, p \frown p > \mathsf{Low}_{d-1}(z)))))))$

(Here $r$, $r'$, and $r^*$ are as in (xvii).)

(xix) $((\alpha \frown p) > z) \leftrightarrow$ **if** $(p \frown p) > \mathsf{Low}_d(z)$ **then** $\alpha \geqslant \omega \frown r$
**else** $\alpha \geqslant \omega +_o r'$ **end if**

(Here $r$ and $r'$ are as in (xvii).)

(xx) $((\alpha \smile p) > z) \leftrightarrow \omega \leftrightarrow$ **if** $p > \mathsf{Low}_d(z)$ **then** $\alpha \geqslant \omega \frown r$
**else** $\alpha \geqslant \omega +_o r'$ **end if**

(Here $r$ and $r'$ are as in (xvii).)

(xxi) $((\alpha +_o p) > z) \leftrightarrow (\alpha \geqslant (z +_o r')$
$\vee (\alpha \geqslant (z \frown r) \,\&\, ((\mathsf{Cf}_d(z) < c)$
$\vee (\alpha \geqslant \omega \mathbin{\dot{-}} r^* \,\&\, p \frown p \geqslant \mathsf{Low}_{d-1}(z))))$

(Here $r$ and $r^*$ are as in (xvii).)

(xxii) $((\alpha \mathbin{\dot{-}} p) \geqslant z) \leftrightarrow (\alpha \geqslant (z +_o r')\vee$
$(\alpha \geqslant (z \frown r) \,\&$
$((\mathsf{Cf}_d(\alpha) \leqslant c \,\&\, p \frown p \geqslant \mathsf{Low}_d(z))$
$\vee (\mathsf{Cf}_d(\alpha) > c \,\&\, (\alpha > \omega + r^*$
$\vee (\alpha \geqslant \omega + r^* \,\&\, p \frown p \geqslant \mathsf{Low}_{d-1}(z)))))))$

(Here $r$ and $r^*$ are as in (xvii).)

(xxiii) $((\alpha \frown p) \geqslant z) \leftrightarrow$ **if** $(p \frown p) \geqslant \mathsf{Low}_d(z)$ **then** $\alpha \geqslant \omega \frown r$
**else** $\alpha \geqslant \omega +_o r'$ **end if**

(Here $r$ and $r'$ are as in (xvii).)

(xxiv) $((\alpha \smile p) \geqslant z) \leftrightarrow$ **if** $p \geqslant \mathsf{Low}_d(z)$ **then** $\alpha \geqslant \omega \frown r$
**else** $\alpha \geqslant \omega +_o r'$ **end if**

(Here $r$ and $r'$ are as in (xvii).)

(xxv) $\mathsf{Cf}_j(\alpha +_o p) =$ **if** $j > d$ **then** $\mathsf{Cf}_j(\alpha)$ **else** $\mathsf{Cf}_j(\alpha) + \mathsf{Cf}_j(p)$ **end if**

(xxvi) $\mathsf{Cf}_j(\alpha \mathbin{\dot{-}} p) =$ **if** $j > d$ **then** $\mathsf{Cf}_j(\alpha)$
**elseif** $\mathsf{Cf}_j(\alpha) \geqslant \mathsf{Cf}_j(p)$ **then** $\mathsf{Cf}_j(\alpha) - \mathsf{Cf}_j(p)$ **else** 0 **end if**

(xxvii) $\mathsf{Cf}_j(\alpha \frown p) =$ **if** $j > d$ **then** $\mathsf{Cf}_j(\alpha)$ **else** $\mathsf{Cf}_j(p')$ **end if**,
where $p'$ is the polynomial ordinal having the same coefficients as $p$, except that $\mathsf{Cf}_d(p')$ is zero.

(xxviii) $\mathsf{Cf}_j(\alpha \smile p) =$ **if** $j > d$ **then** $\mathsf{Cf}_j(\alpha)$ **else** $\mathsf{Cf}_j(p)$ **end if**.

These rules have the following proofs. (i) is a consequence of the associative law for ordinal addition. For (ii), note that if $d > d'$ then in the range of coefficients relevant to the formation of $(y +_o p) \mathbin{\dot{-}} q$ the coefficients of $y$ will have been replaced, in $y +_o p$, by those of $p$, from which the first case of (ii) follows immediately. On the other hand, if $d' > d$, then the difference between $y$ and $y +_o p$ is irrelevant to the formation of $(y +_o p) \mathbin{\mathring{-}} q$, and thus the second case of (ii) follows. Finally, if $d' = d$, then the coefficient $\mathsf{Cf}_d((y +_o p) \mathbin{\mathring{-}} q)$ is $\mathsf{Cf}_d(y) + (\mathsf{Cf}_d(p) - \mathsf{Cf}_d(q))$ if $p$ has a larger leading coefficient than $q$. However, if $q$ has a larger leading coefficient than $p$, then $\mathsf{Cf}_d((y +_o p) \mathbin{\mathring{-}} q)$ is $\mathsf{Cf}_d(y) - (\mathsf{Cf}_d(q) - \mathsf{Cf}_d(p))$, or 0 if this difference is negative. In both these cases, all lower coefficients are those of $q$, proving rule (ii) in the remaining cases.

In regard to rule (iii), note that if $d \geqslant d'$ then in the range of coefficients relevant to the formation of $(y +_o p) \frown q$ the coefficients of $y$ will have been replaced (in $y +_o p$) by those of $p$, from which the first case of (iii) follows immediately. On the other hand, if $d' > d$, then the difference between $y$ and $y +_o p$ is irrelevant to the formation of $(y +_o p) \mathbin{\mathring{-}} q$, and thus the second case of (iii) follows. The proofs of (iv), (vii), (viii), (xi), (xii), (xv), and (xvi) are essentially the same, so we leave details to the reader.

The proofs of the first two cases of rules (v), (vi), (ix), (x), (xiii), and (xiv) are much the same as that of the corresponding cases of rule (ii) and are also left to the reader. In the remaining cases of these rules, $p$ and $q$ have the same degree $d$. In all these cases, the coefficients $\mathsf{Cf}_j$ of the result being formed are always those of $q$ for $j < d$; only the coefficients $\mathsf{Cf}_d$ requires closer consideration. In regard to the $d = d'$ case of rule (v), note that in this case if the leading coefficient c of $p$ is larger than the corresponding coefficient of $y$, $y \mathbin{\mathring{-}} p$ will have a zero $d$th coefficient, so $(y \mathbin{\mathring{-}} p) +_o q$ will simply be $y \backsim q$. But if $c$ is not larger than the corresponding coefficient of $y$, then the $d$th coefficient of $(y \mathbin{\mathring{-}} p) +_o q$ will be $\mathsf{Cf}_d(y) + c - c'$, i.e. is that of $y \mathbin{\mathring{-}} (p \mathbin{\mathring{-}} q)$ if $c \geqslant c'$, but that of $y +_o (p \mathbin{\mathring{-}} q)$ otherwise. Since the remaining coefficients of $(y \mathbin{\mathring{-}} p) +_o q$ are those of $q$ in any case, Rule (v) follows.

The $d = d'$ case of rule (vi) follows in the same way since the $d$th coefficient of $(y \mathbin{\mathring{-}} p) \mathbin{\mathring{-}} q$ is always that of $y \mathbin{\mathring{-}} (p +_o q)$, and the remaining coefficients of $(y \mathbin{\mathring{-}} p) \mathbin{\mathring{-}} q$ are those of $q$. In the $d = d'$ case of rule (ix), the $d$th coefficient of $y \frown p$ is zero, hence the $d$th coefficient $(y \frown p) \mathbin{\mathring{-}} q$ is that of $q$, while the remaining coefficients are those of $q$, proving rule (ix) in this case. The $d = d'$ cases of rules (x), (xiii), and (xiv) follow by similar elementary observations, whose details are left to the reader.

Rules (xxv–xxvii) follow directly from the definitions of the operators $+_o$, $\mathring{-}$, $\frown$, and $\backsim$ and the coefficient functions $\mathsf{Cf}_j$. Their proofs are left to the reader.

To prove rule (xvii), note first of all that $(y +_o p) > \omega$ will hold either if $\mathsf{Hi}_d(y) > z$, in which case the values of $\mathsf{Low}_d(y +_o p)$ and $\mathsf{Low}_d(z)$ are all irrelevant, or otherwise if $\mathsf{Hi}_d(y) = \mathsf{Hi}_d(z)$ (which in this case we can write as $\mathsf{Hi}_d(y) \geqslant \mathsf{Hi}_d(z)$), in which case we must have $\mathsf{Low}_d(y +_o p) > \mathsf{Low}_d(z)$. But $\mathsf{Hi}_d(y) > \omega$ is equivalent to $y > \omega +_o r'$, and $\mathsf{Hi}_d(y) \geqslant \omega$ is equivalent to $y \geqslant \omega \frown r$, where $r$ and $r'$ are as in (xvii). (This last remark applies in the proofs of all the rules (xvii–xxv).) In the $y \geqslant \omega \frown r$ case of (xvii), if $c > \mathsf{Cf}_d(z)$ then $(y +_o p) > \omega$ is certainly true, while if $c <= \mathsf{Cf}_d(z)$ then we must have both $\mathsf{Hi}_{d-1}(y) \geqslant \mathsf{Hi}_d(z \mathbin{\mathring{-}} p)$ and $\mathsf{Low}_{d-1}(p) \geqslant \mathsf{Low}_{d-1}(z)$. The final clauses in (xvii) merely restate these conditions, by rewriting $\mathsf{Hi}_{d-1}(y) \geqslant \mathsf{Hi}_d(z \mathbin{\mathring{-}} p)$ as $\omega \mathbin{\mathring{-}} r^d$ and $\mathsf{Low}_{d-1}(p) \geqslant \mathsf{Low}_{d-1}(z)$ as $p \frown p > \mathsf{Low}_{d-1}(z)$.

The proofs of rules (xviii–xxiv) generally resemble that just given for rule (xvii), and in some cases are distinctly simpler. To prove rule (xviii), we note as above that $(y \mathbin{\dot{\overset{\circ}{-}}} p) > \omega$ will hold either if $\mathsf{Hi}_d(y) > z$, or otherwise if $(y \mathbin{\overset{\circ}{-}} p) \geqslant \omega$ & $\mathsf{Low}_d(y \mathbin{\overset{\circ}{-}} p) > \mathsf{Low}_d(z)$. If $\mathsf{Cf}_d(y) \leqslant c$ then $\mathsf{Low}_d(y \mathbin{\overset{\circ}{-}} p) = p \mathbin{\overset{\circ}{-}} p$; otherwise $\mathsf{Low}_d(y \mathbin{\overset{\circ}{-}} p) > \mathsf{Low}_d(z)$ is equivalent to

$$\mathsf{Cf}_d(y) > c \vee \big(\mathsf{Cf}_d(y) = c \,\&\, \mathsf{Low}_{d-1}(p) > \mathsf{Low}_{d-1}(z)\big),$$

which rule (xviii) merely restates.

The proofs of rules (xix), (xx), (xxiii), and (xxiv) are similar but simpler, and are left to the reader. The proof of rule (xxi) is almost the same as that of (xvii), merely involving a change from $p \frown p > \mathsf{Low}_{d-1}(z)$ to $p \frown p \geqslant \mathsf{Low}_{d-1}(z)$. The proof of rule (xxii) is like that of (xviii), merely involving the change of $p \frown p > \mathsf{Low}_{d-1}(z)$ and $p \frown p > \mathsf{Low}_d(z)$ to $p \frown p \geqslant \mathsf{Low}_{d-1}(z)$ and $p \frown p \geqslant \mathsf{Low}_d(z)$, respectively.

These observations complete our proofs of all the rules (i–xxvii) stated above.

Let LO be the language of quantified formulae whose variables designate ordinals and whose only allowed operation is that which forms the maximum of two ordinals $x$ and $y$, which for convenience we will write as $x \sqcup y$. In addition to the operator '$\sqcup$', we also assume that the language LO allows one to compare ordinal terms by means of the relators '$>$' and '$=$'. We say that a subexpression

$$\big(\exists x \mid P(x)\big)$$

of a formula of LO is *of level k* if it contains level $k-1$ subexpressions, but none of any higher level; quantifiers not containing any quantified subexpression will be said to be of level 0. Using this notion, we will show that the satisfiability problem for the language LO is decidable. The following result implies this, and gives a convenient form to the necessary decision procedure.

**Theorem 3.4** *Let S be a statement, in the language* LO, *containing no free variables, and suppose that L is the maximum level, in the sense defined above, of any quantified subexpression of S. Then the truth value of S, quantified over the collection of all ordinals, is the same as the truth value obtained if all the quantifiers in S are restricted to range over polynomial ordinals of degree at most L.*

Since every polynomial ordinal of degree at most $L$ is described by a set of $L+1$ integer coefficients, and comparisons between two such ordinals and the maximum of two such ordinals can be written as expressions involving only integer comparisons and sums, it follows from this theorem that the satisfiability problem for the language LO reduces to a special decision problem for Presburger's language of additive arithmetic, and so, by the result presented in the previous section, is decidable.

As an example illustrating the use of the theorem just stated, we consider the formula

$$\big(\exists x \mid \big(\forall x' \mid (x' < x) \rightarrow (\exists x^* \mid x^* > x' \,\&\, x^* < x)\big) \,\&\, (\exists y \mid y < x)\big). \qquad (3.32)$$

The universal clause in (3.32) states that $x$ is a limit ordinal, and the following existential clause states that $x$ is non-null. Thus the smallest possible $x$ satisfying the condition displayed in (3.32) is $\omega$. This example makes it plain that the predicate $\mathsf{Is\_limit}(x)$ stating that $x$ is a limit ordinal can be defined in the language LO. Therefore so can the predicates

$$\mathsf{Is\_limit\_2}(x) \leftrightarrow_{\mathrm{Def}} \big(\exists x \,\big|\, \big(\forall x' \mid (x' < x) \rightarrow \big(\exists x^* \mid x^* > x' \,\&\, x^* < x \\ \& \,\mathsf{Is\_limit}(x^*)\big)\big)\big)$$

$$\mathsf{Is\_limit\_3}(x) \leftrightarrow_{\mathrm{Def}} \big(\exists x \,\big|\, \big(\forall x' \mid (x' < x) \rightarrow \big(\exists x^* \mid x^* > x' \,\&\, x^* < x \\ \& \,\mathsf{Is\_limit\_2}(x^*)\big)\big)\big)$$

and so forth. From this, it is easy to see that one can write formulae in LO whose smallest solutions are the ordinals $\omega^2$, $\omega^3$, …, and indeed any polynomial ordinal. The theorem stated above tells us that ordinals larger than every polynomial ordinal cannot be described by formulae of LO, and bound the size of the ordinals that can be described by formulae of any specified quantifier nesting level.

To prove Theorem 3.4 stated above, we first note that any quantified formula $S$ of LO can be replaced by an equivalent formula of LO containing no occurrences of the binary operator '$\sqcup$' which returns the maximum of its arguments. To see this, we note that every atomic formula appearing in $S$ must be a comparison having either the form $t_1 > t_2$ or $t_1 = t_2$, where $t_1$ and $t_2$ are either simple variables or literals formed using the '$\sqcup$' operator. But if $t_1$ has the form $x \sqcup t$, where $x$ is some variable chosen for processing, we can rewrite $t_1 > t_2$ as

$$(x = t \,\&\, x > t_2) \vee (x > t \,\&\, x > t_2) \vee (t > x \,\&\, t > t_2),$$

and similarly rewrite $t_1 = t_2$ as

$$(x = t \,\&\, x = t_2) \vee (x > t \,\&\, x = t_2) \vee (t > x \,\&\, t = t_2).$$

Similar remarks apply if $t_2$ has the form $t_2 = x \sqcup t$. Applying these transformations repeatedly, as often as necessary, we eventually remove all occurrences of '$\sqcup$' from $S$, replacing it by a formula written only with quantifiers and the comparisons '$>$' and '$=$'. Note that the transformation we have described leaves the level of each quantifier in $S$ unchanged.

But now, having removed all occurrences of '$\sqcup$', we re-complicate our language LO by introducing the four additional operators $+_o$, $\mathring{-}$, $\frown$, and $\backsim$ described above, plus the family of auxiliary predicates $\mathsf{Cf}_j$, into it. Note once more that in occurrences $t +_o p$, $t \mathring{-} p$, $t \frown p$, and $t \backsim p$ of the operators $+_o$, $\mathring{-}$, $\frown$, and $\backsim$ the second argument $p$ is required to be some polynomial ordinal with coefficients known explicitly. Let LO$'$ designate the language LO, extended in this way, but with occurrences of '$\sqcup$' forbidden.

With this understanding, we process the existentially quantified subexpressions

$$\big(\exists x \mid P(x)\big) \tag{3.33}$$

of our given formula of LO′ in bottom-to-top syntax tree order. As processing proceeds, we continually apply rules (i–xvi) and (xxv–xxviii). This reduces all the literals appearing in $P(x)$ to forms like $y +_o p$, $y \mathbin{\mathring{-}} p$, $y \frown p$, and $y \backsim p$, where $y$ is a simple variable and $p$ an explicitly known polynomial ordinal, and every occurrence of a predicate $\mathsf{Cf}_j$ to the form $\mathsf{Cf}_j(y) = c$, where $y$ is a simple variable and both $j$ and $c$ are explicitly known integers. Note in this conditions that inequalities like $\mathsf{Cf}_j(y) \leqslant c$, where $c$ is some explicit integer constant, can be written as a disjunction of the equalities $\mathsf{Cf}_j(y) = e$, over all $e \leqslant c$, and so do not violate our requirement that all occurrences of $\mathsf{Cf}_j$ must be in contexts $\mathsf{Cf}_j(y) = c$. Likewise, inequalities $\mathsf{Cf}_j(y) > c$ are disjunctions of negated equalities $\mathsf{Cf}_j(y) = e$, over all $e \leqslant c$. $p$ conditions like $p \frown p > \mathsf{Low}_{d-1}(z)$, which appear in rules like (xvii) and (xviii), can be rewritten, if we use the fact that the order of polynomial ordinals is the lexical order of their coefficients, in terms of inequalities between the coefficients $\mathsf{Low}_j(z)$ and known integer constants, and then also as Boolean combinations of equalities $\mathsf{Cf}_j(y) = c$.

As the processing described in the preceding paragraph goes on, we always push conditionals introduced by applications of rules (i–xxviii) using relationships like

$$\textbf{if } C_1 \textbf{ then } A_1 \textbf{ elseif } C_2 \textbf{ then } A_2 \textbf{ elseif } \cdots \textbf{ else } C_k \textbf{ end if } +_o p$$
$$= \textbf{if } C_1 \textbf{ then } A_1 +_o p \textbf{ elseif } C_2 \textbf{ then } A_2 +_o p \textbf{ elseif } \cdots \textbf{ else } A_k +_o p \textbf{ end if}.$$

When the predicate level is reached we use rules (xvii–xxviii), plus rules like

$$\textbf{if } C_1' \textbf{ then } A_1' \textbf{ elseif } C_2' \textbf{ then } A_2' \textbf{ elseif } \cdots \textbf{ else } C_k' \textbf{ end if} \leftrightarrow$$
$$(C_1' \,\&\, A_1') \vee \big((\neg C_1') \,\&\, C_2' \,\&\, A_2'\big) \vee \cdots \vee \big((\neg C_1') \,\&\, (\neg C_2') \,\&\, \cdots \,\&\, (\neg C_{k-1}') \,\&\, A_k'\big)$$

to eliminate any conditional expressions that may have accumulated. The final Boolean combination that results is then reduced to a disjunction of conjunctions. We will prove recursively that this process can be used to reduce any level $k$ existential (in the sense defined above) to an equivalent disjunction of conjunctions, each involving only variables free in the existential, together with expressions of the form $y +_o p$, $y \mathbin{\mathring{-}} p$, $y \frown p$, and $y \backsim p$, where $p$ is a polynomial ordinal of degree at most $k$ with explicitly known constant integer coefficients, also the comparators '$>$', '$\geqslant$', and conditions of the form $\mathsf{Cf}_j(y) = c$, where $c$ is a known integer constant no greater than $k$.

To prove this by induction on $k$, suppose that it is already known for all existentials of level lower than $k$, and consider an existential (3.33) of level $k$ involving only the operators listed above. Then $P(x)$ begins (before application of the rules (i–xvi) and (xxv–xxviii)) as an expression involving combinations $t +_o p$, $t \mathbin{\mathring{-}} p$, $t \frown p$, and $t \backsim p$ with $p$ of degree at most $k - 1$, plus $\mathsf{Cf}_j$ with $j$ no larger than $k - 1$, and comparisons involving '$>$' and '$\geqslant$'. Application of the rules (i–xvi) and (xxv–xxviii) does not introduce any polynomial ordinals of higher degree, or any $\mathsf{Cf}_j$ with $j$ larger than $k - 1$. Call a subexpression of $P(x)$ *$x$-free* if it does not involve the bound variable $x$. When the predicate level is reached, comparisons of the form $y > \omega$ and $y \geqslant \omega$ are reduced using rules (xvii–xxiv), unless they are $x$-free, in which case they are left as they stand. Non $x$-free comparisons can have either one or two arguments in which $x$ appears. If $x$ appears only in the first of these two arguments, we use rules (xvii–xxiv) to rewrite the comparison as a conjunction of comparisons of the form $x > t$ and $x \geqslant t$, where $t$ is $x$-free, but where now polynomial ordinals of degree $k$ can appear in $t$ (e.g. as the polynomial $r'$ seen in rules (xvii–xx)). Conditions of the form $\mathsf{Cf}_j$ with $j$ no larger than $k-1$ can also appear. Cases in which $x$ appears only in the second of the two arguments of a comparison can be handled by rewriting $a > b$ as $\neg(b \geqslant a)$ and $a \geqslant b$ as $\neg(b > a)$. Cases in which $x$ appears in both arguments of a comparison will have forms like $x +_o p > x \overset{\circ}{-} q$ and $x \frown p \geqslant x \overset{\circ}{-} q$. To handle these, we observe that all such comparisons can be expressed as Boolean combinations of comparisons between known integers and coefficients $\mathsf{Cf}_j(x)$ with $j < k$, and so are in accord with the inductive condition we require.

Once the $P(x)$ of (3.33) has been rewritten in the manner described in the preceding paragraph, it can be further rewritten as a disjunction of conjunctions. Then we can use predicate relationships like

$$(\exists x \mid Q(x) \vee R(x)) \leftrightarrow ((\exists x \mid Q(x)) \vee (\exists x \mid R(x)))$$

to replace existentials of disjunctions by disjunctions of existentials. We can also move all $x$-free conjuncts out of the existential, at which point it only remains to consider existentially quantified subexpressions of the form (3.33) in which $P(x)$ is a conjunct $W$ of conditions of the following forms:

(a) $x > t$, where $t$ is $x$-free, and involves no polynomial ordinal of degree greater than $k$;
(b) $x \geqslant t$, where $t$ is $x$-free, and involves no polynomial ordinal of degree greater than $k$;
(c) negations of comparisons of the forms (a) and (b);
(d) conditions $\mathsf{Cf}_j(x) = c$, where $j \leqslant k$, and $j$ and $c$ are both known integers;
(e) conditions $\mathsf{Cf}_j(x) \neq c$, where $j$ and $c$ are as in (d).

If such a conjunction $W$ can be satisfied (i.e. if the existential (3.33) can have the value 'true'), then for each $j$ it can contain at most one conjunct $\mathsf{Cf}_j(x) = c$, since a second conjunct $\mathsf{Cf}_j(x) = c'$ with $x \neq c'$ would be inconsistent with this. Moreover, if there is such a conjunct, then any other conjunct $\mathsf{Cf}_j(x) \neq c'$ must either be inconsistent with or implied by this, and hence could be dropped. Also, conjuncts $x > t$ can be written as $x \geqslant t +_o 1$. Hence we can suppose without loss of generality that we have

(a′) no conjuncts of the form (a) and no negations of such conjuncts;
(b′) for each $j$, at most one conjunct of the form (d), and if so no conjuncts (e);
(c′) some finite collection of conjuncts of the form (e).

If, for particular values of the free variables which appear in it, such a $W$ is satisfied by some ordinal value of the bound variable $x$, it is satisfied by a smallest such $x$, which we shall call $x_0$. Of all the $t$ that appear in conditions of the form (b), let $t_0$ be the largest (for the same particular values of the free variables which appear in (3.33)). Then (by the subtraction principle stated earlier) $x_0$ can be written as $x_0 = t_0 +_o u$ for some ordinal $u$. Write $u = u' +_o p$, where $u'$ is a post-polynomial ordinal and $p$ is a polynomial ordinal. Then $t_0 +_o p$ is no larger than $t_0 +_o u' +_o p$, but satisfies all the conjuncts (b–e) present in $W$. Hence $x_0$ must have the form $t_0 +_o p$, where $p$ is a polynomial ordinal. We can show in much the same way that the degree of $p$ can be no larger than $k$. If, for a given $j$, $W$ contains a conjunct of kind (c), it specifies the corresponding coefficient of $t_0 +_o p$ uniquely, and in particular gives us an explicit upper limit for the corresponding coefficient of $p$. Moreover, if conjuncts (e) occur for a given $j$, and we let $c_0$ be the maximum of all the $c$ that occur in these conditions, then if there is a polynomial ordinal $p$ with $\mathsf{Cf}_j f(p) > c_0 + 1$ for which $t_0 +_o p$ satisfies all the conjuncts in $W$, then the same is true for $t_0 +_o p'$, where $p'$ is the same as $p$ except that its coefficient $\mathsf{Cf}_j f(p)$ is reduced to $c_0 + 1$. We see in much the same way that if, for a given $j$, $W$ contains neither a conjunct of form (d) nor of form (e), then the $p$ corresponding to the smallest $t_0 +_o p$ satisfying $W$ must have $\mathsf{Cf}_j f(p) = 0$. Overall we see that explicit upper limits are available for each of the $\mathsf{Cf}_j f(p)$ coefficients of the polynomial ordinal corresponding to the smallest $t_0 +_o p$ satisfying $W$. Hence, if we let $p_1, \ldots, p_n$ be an enumeration of all these polynomial ordinals, let $t$ vary over all the $x$-free expressions $t_1, \ldots, t_m$ appearing in conjuncts (b) of $W$, and let $x$ vary over all the corresponding sums $t_i +_o p_j$ (doing this for all the disjuncts into which (3.33) has been decomposed), then one of these $x$ will satisfy the quantified condition (3.33) if there exists any $x$ which satisfies it. It follows that (3.33) is equivalent to a disjunction of finitely many alternatives of the form $P(t_i +_o p_j)$, completing our inductive step and thereby completing our proof of the theorem stated above.

### *3.8.3 A Language of Additive Infinite Cardinal Arithmetic*

The decision algorithm just described carries over easily to the following quantified language LC. Variables in LC designate infinite cardinal numbers, and the only operation allowed is cardinal addition. Moreover, the language LC allows one to compare cardinal terms by means of the relators '>' and '='. As was shown by A. Tarski in [Tar56], the additive theory LC of infinite cardinals is decidable. To show this, let $\alpha$ be any ordinal, and let $\aleph_\alpha$ designate the $\alpha$th member, in increasing order, of the collection of all infinite cardinals. Since the sum (or product) of any two infinite cardinals is the larger of the two, the function $\aleph$ is an order isomorphism of the collection of all infinite cardinals, taken with the operation of cardinal addition, onto the collection of all ordinals, taken with the operation which forms the maximum of two ordinals. This operation evidently maps the satisfiability problem for LC to the satisfiability problem for the language LO studied above, and so is solved using the algorithm we have just given for determining the satisfiability of statements in LO.

More specifically, given a statement $S$ in the language LC, containing no free variables, for each cardinal variable $\nu$ occurring in $S$ we introduce a fresh ordinal variable $\alpha_\nu$ and substitute each subexpression in $S$ of the form

$$(\exists \nu \mid P(\nu))$$

by the equivalent expression

$$(\exists \alpha_\nu \mid P(\aleph_{\alpha_\nu})).$$

Then, we substitute each cardinal term of the form

$$\aleph_\beta + \aleph_\gamma$$

in the resulting statement by the equivalent term

$$\aleph_{\beta \sqcup \gamma},$$

until no term of the form $\aleph_\beta + \aleph_\gamma$ is left (we recall that the binary operator '$\sqcup$' returns the maximum of its arguments). Finally, we substitute each cardinal term $\aleph_\beta$ in the resulting statement by the corresponding ordinal term $\beta$. Let $S'$ be the statement so obtained. Plainly $S'$ is a statement in LO which is equisatisfiable with our initial statement $S$, as the reader can readily check, so that satisfiability of $S$ can be determined by applying to $S'$ the decision method outlined in the previous section.

By combining the above decidability result with the Presburger decision algorithm given in Sect. 3.8.1, we can obtain an algorithm for deciding the satisfiability of the quantified language LC* obtained from LC by letting variables denote cardinals which are allowed to be both finite and infinite.

To be more specific, it is convenient to extend the language LC* with an infinite endowment of *integer variables*, which are allowed to range over finite cardinals only, and *infinite cardinal variables*, which are allowed to range over infinite cardinals only. Then, given a statement $S$ in the language LC*, containing no free variables, for each cardinal variable $\nu$ occurring in $S$ we introduce a fresh integer variable $n_\nu$ and a fresh infinite cardinal variable $\kappa_\nu$, and substitute each subexpression in $S$ of the form

$$(\exists \nu \mid P(\nu))$$

by the equivalent expression

$$(\exists n_\nu \mid P(n_\nu)) \vee (\exists \kappa_\nu \mid P(\kappa_\nu)).$$

Let $S'$ be the statement resulting after the above substitutions. Plainly $S$ and $S'$ are equivalent. We call a term of the form $n_1 + \cdots + n_\ell$ of the extended language LC*, with $n_1, \ldots, n_\ell$ integer variables, a *finite term*. Likewise, a term of the form $\kappa_1 + \cdots + \kappa_g$, with $\kappa_1, \ldots, \kappa_g$ infinite cardinal variables, is called an *infinite term*. Finally, a term $t$ of the form $t_1 + t_2$ or $t_2 + t_1$, with $t_1$ a finite term and $t_2$ an infinite term, is called a *mixed-type term*, and in this case $t_1$ is referred to as the *finite part* of $t$ and $t_2$ as its *infinite part*. We perform the following simplification steps on $S'$:

(i) we substitute each mixed-type term in $S'$ with its infinite part, until no mixed-type term is left in $S'$;
(ii) we substitute each atomic subformula in $S'$ of the form $t_1 < t_2$, where $t_1$ is a finite term and $t_2$ is an infinite term, with the Boolean constant true;
(iii) we substitute each atomic subformula in $S'$ having one of the following types

$$t_1 = t_2, \qquad t_2 = t_1, \qquad t_2 < t_1,$$

where $t_1$ is a finite term and $t_2$ is an infinite term, with the Boolean constant false;
(iv) proceeding in bottom-to-top syntax tree order, we eliminate all occurrences of the Boolean constants true and false introduced by step (iii), following the elementary laws of propositional and first-order logics (for instance, $P \vee \mathsf{false}$ is simplified to $P$ and $(\exists x|\mathsf{true})$ is simplified to true);
(v) proceeding in bottom-to-top syntax tree order, for any formula $Q$ which does not contain any free occurrence of the variable $x$, we replace
   - each subformula of the form $(\exists x \mid Q)$ by $Q$,
   - each subformula of the form $(\exists x \mid P \,\&\, Q)$ by $(\exists x \mid P) \,\&\, Q$,
   - each subformula of the form $(\exists x \mid P \vee Q)$ by $(\exists x \mid P) \vee Q$,
   - etc.

Let $S''$ be the resulting statement after simplification steps (i-v). Plainly, $S''$ and $S$ are equivalent. Since by steps (i–iii) no atomic subformula of $S''$ can contain both integer and infinite cardinal variables, after the execution of step (v) no existential quantifier over an integer variable can fall within the scope of an existential quantifier over an infinite cardinal variable, and conversely. It follows that $S''$ is a propositional combination of statements (containing no free variables) of Presburger's quantified language of additive arithmetic and of the language LC. Therefore its truth value is a propositional function of the truth values of its components, which can be calculated algorithmically by the decision tests for Presburger's arithmetic and for the language LC, thus proving the decidability of the language LC*.

As an example, let us consider the formula

$$\big(\forall\lambda \,\big|\, (\exists\mu \mid (\exists\nu \mid \mu < \lambda \,\&\, \nu < \lambda \,\&\, \lambda = \mu + \nu))\big) \tag{3.34}$$

which is equivalent to

$$\neg\big(\exists\lambda \,\big|\, \neg(\exists\mu \mid (\exists\nu \mid \mu < \lambda \,\&\, \nu < \lambda \,\&\, \lambda = \mu + \nu))\big). \tag{3.35}$$

Plainly (3.34) is false, both for $\lambda$ finite (when $\lambda = 0, 1$) and for $\lambda$ infinite. After the substitution in (3.35) of the variables $\lambda$, $\mu$, and $\nu$ with $n_\lambda$, $\kappa_\lambda$, $n_\mu$, $\kappa_\mu$, $n_\nu$, and $\kappa_\nu$, formula (3.35) becomes

$$\begin{aligned}
\neg\Big(\big(\exists n_\lambda \,\big|\, \neg\big((\exists n_\mu \mid (\exists n_\nu \mid n_\mu < n_\lambda \,\&\, n_\nu < n_\lambda \,\&\, n_\lambda = n_\mu + n_\nu) \\
\vee (\exists \kappa_\nu \mid n_\mu < n_\lambda \,\&\, \kappa_\nu < n_\lambda \,\&\, n_\lambda = n_\mu + \kappa_\nu)) \\
\vee (\exists \kappa_\mu \mid (\exists n_\nu \mid \kappa_\mu < n_\lambda \,\&\, n_\nu < n_\lambda \,\&\, n_\lambda = \kappa_\mu + n_\nu) \\
\vee (\exists \kappa_\nu \mid \kappa_\mu < n_\lambda \,\&\, \kappa_\nu < n_\lambda \,\&\, n_\lambda = \kappa_\mu + \kappa_\nu))\big)\big) \\
\vee \big(\exists \kappa_\lambda \,\big|\, \neg\big((\exists n_\mu \mid (\exists n_\nu \mid n_\mu < \kappa_\lambda \,\&\, n_\nu < \kappa_\lambda \,\&\, \kappa_\lambda = n_\mu + n_\nu) \\
\vee (\exists \kappa_\nu \mid n_\mu < \kappa_\lambda \,\&\, \kappa_\nu < \kappa_\lambda \,\&\, \kappa_\lambda = n_\mu + \kappa_\nu)) \\
\vee (\exists \kappa_\mu \mid (\exists n_\nu \mid \kappa_\mu < \kappa_\lambda \,\&\, n_\nu < \kappa_\lambda \,\&\, \kappa_\lambda = \kappa_\mu + n_\nu) \\
\vee (\exists \kappa_\nu \mid \kappa_\mu < \kappa_\lambda \,\&\, \kappa_\nu < \kappa_\lambda \,\&\, n_\lambda = \kappa_\mu + \kappa_\nu))\big)\big)\Big).
\end{aligned}$$

After simplification steps (i–v), the latter becomes

$$\begin{aligned}
\neg\Big(\big(\exists n_\lambda \,\big|\, \neg(\exists n_\mu \mid (\exists n_\nu \mid n_\mu < n_\lambda \,\&\, n_\nu < n_\lambda \,\&\, n_\lambda = n_\mu + n_\nu))\big) \\
\vee \big(\exists \kappa_\lambda \,\big|\, \neg((\exists \kappa_\nu \mid \kappa_\nu < \kappa_\lambda \,\&\, \kappa_\lambda = \kappa_\nu) \vee (\exists \kappa_\mu \mid \kappa_\mu < \kappa_\lambda \,\&\, \kappa_\lambda = \kappa_\mu))\big)\Big),
\end{aligned}$$

which is unsatisfiable since

$$\big(\exists n_\lambda \,\big|\, \neg(\exists n_\mu \mid (\exists n_\nu \mid n_\mu < n_\lambda \,\&\, n_\nu < n_\lambda \,\&\, n_\lambda = n_\mu + n_\nu))\big)$$

is true (as can be computed by Presburger's decision test). Therefore our initial formula (3.34) is unsatisfiable too. The same undecidability result could have been established by observing that

$$\big(\exists n_\lambda \,\big|\, \neg(\exists n_\mu \mid (\exists n_\nu \mid n_\mu < n_\lambda \,\&\, n_\nu < n_\lambda \,\&\, n_\lambda = n_\mu + n_\nu))\big)$$

is true (as can be computed by a decision test for the language LC).

### 3.8.4 *Behmann's Quantified Language of Elementary Set-Theoretic Formulae*

We now turn our attention to the class of formulae studied by Heinrich Behmann in [Beh22], namely quantified formulae in which the unquantified expressions and predicates which appear are set-theoretic expressions formed from set-valued variables by use of the elementary set operators $a \cap b$, $a \cup b$, $a \setminus b$ and the set inclusion operators $a \supseteq b$ and $a \subseteq b$ (but excluding the membership operator $a \in b$, with $a$ and $b$ set-valued variables, which if allowed in the quantified setting we consider would at once make our formulae too general to be decidable by any algorithm).

We shall call the class of quantified set-theoretic formulae limited in this way the *Behmann formulae*.

It is easy to see that these formulae are powerful enough to restrict the cardinality of the sets which appear within them. For example, the condition

$$s \neq \emptyset \,\&\, \big(\neg(\exists x \mid s \supseteq x \,\&\, s \neq x \,\&\, x \neq \emptyset)\big)$$

is readily seen to express the condition $\mathsf{Is\_singleton}(s)$ that $s$ should be a singleton. Then, using this formula as a component we can write the formula

$$\big(\exists x, y \mid x \cap y = \emptyset \,\&\, x \cup y = s \,\&\, \mathsf{Is\_singleton}(x) \,\&\, \mathsf{Is\_singleton}(y)\big)$$

which is easily seen to express the condition $\#s = 2$. It should be plain that the condition $\#s = n$ can be expressed in much the same way for any given integer $n$. Thus Behmann's class of formulae is strong enough to express theorems like

$$\#s = 10 \rightarrow \big(\#(s \setminus t) > 4 \vee \#(s \cap t) > 4\big),$$

i.e. to express elementary facts about the cardinality of sets. Hence any algorithm able to decide the satisfiability of all Behmann formulae must be strong enough to decide certain elementary arithmetic statements. Behmann gave such an algorithm, which we will generalize in Sect. 3.8.4.1. We shall see that the decision procedure to be presented there uses as subprocedures the Presburger algorithm described in Sect. 3.8.1 and the decision algorithm for additive infinite cardinal arithmetic discussed in Sect. 3.8.3.

We begin our examination of Behmann's class of quantified formulae by confining ourselves to the case of formulae of type

$$\big(\exists x \mid P(x)\big) \tag{3.36}$$

in which the predicate $P$ is a conjunction of Boolean set-theoretic expressions formed from set-valued variables by use of the set operators $a \cap b$, $a \cup b$, $a \setminus b$, and the set inclusion operator $a \supseteq b$. If we allow ourselves to write set union as a sum, set intersection as an ordinary product, and the complement of the set $x$ as $\overline{x}$, then any formula (3.36) can be written as (a disjunction of formulae of the form)

$$\left(\exists x \;\middle|\; \mathop{\&}_{k=1}^{n} (a_k\, x + b_k\, \overline{x} = \emptyset) \,\&\, \mathop{\&}_{k=1}^{m} (c_k\, x + d_k\, \overline{x} \neq \emptyset)\right). \tag{3.37}$$

To see this, note that the only operators allowed in Behmann's language are union, intersection, and complementation, and the only comparators are $a \supseteq b$ and $a \subseteq b$. Inclusions of the form $a \supseteq b$ can be written as $b\overline{a} = \emptyset$, and similarly for $a \subseteq b$. Thus we can drop the '$\supseteq$' and '$\subseteq$' comparators and use equality with the nullset as our only comparator. Let $x$ be the variable which is quantified in the Behmann formula or subformula $(\exists x \mid B)$ that concerns us. Using the equivalence

$$(\exists x \mid P \vee Q) \leftrightarrow (\exists x \mid P) \vee (\exists x \mid Q)$$

as often as necessary, we can suppose without loss of generality that $B$ is a conjunction of comparisons, some negated, and so all having the form $t = \emptyset$ or $t \neq \emptyset$, where the term $t$ that appears is formed using the union, intersection, and complementation operators. Using De Morgan's rules for the complement, the distributivity of union over intersection, and the fact that $y\,y = y$ for any set $y$, we can rewrite $t$ as the union of three terms $t = t_1\,x + t_2\,\overline{x} + t_3$, where $t_1$, $t_2$, and $t_3$ are all set terms not containing the variable $x$. Then, making use of the fact that

$$t_1\,x + t_2\,\overline{x} + t_3 = \emptyset$$

is equivalent to

$$t_1\,x + t_2\,\overline{x} = \emptyset \;\&\; t_3 = \emptyset,$$

we can move the $x$-independent clause $t_3 = \emptyset$ out from under the quantifier, leaving us with an existentially quantified conjunction of equalities and inequalities of just the form seen in (3.37), as asserted.

In addition, since $(a = \emptyset \;\&\; b = \emptyset) \leftrightarrow (a + b = \emptyset)$, we can always assume $n = 1$ in (3.37). The detailed treatment of (3.37) rapidly grows complicated as $m$ increases; its general treatment, due to Behmann, will be reviewed below. However, since this treatment is hyperexponentially inefficient, we first examine the two simplest cases $m = 0$ and $m = 1$, in which easy and efficient techniques are available.

In the case $m = 0$ we must consider

$$\big(\exists x \mid (a\,x + b\,\overline{x}) = \emptyset\big), \tag{3.38}$$

which is to say $(\exists x \mid b \subseteq x \;\&\; x\,a = \emptyset)$. Here a (minimal) solution is $x = b$, so (3.38) is equivalent to $a\,b = \emptyset$.

Recursive use of this observation allows some multivariable cases resembling (3.38) to be solved easily, e.g. to solve

$$(\exists x, y \mid a_{11}\,x\,y + a_{10}\,x\,\overline{y} + a_{01}\,y\,\overline{x} + a_{00}\,\overline{x}\,\overline{y} = \emptyset) \tag{3.39}$$

we use (3.38) to rewrite it as

$$\big(\exists x \mid (a_{11}\,x + a_{01}\,\overline{x})\,(a_{10}\,x + a_{00}\,\overline{x}) = \emptyset\big). \tag{3.40}$$

'Multiplying out', we see that this is equivalent to

$$(\exists x \mid a_{11}\,a_{10}\,x + a_{01}\,a_{00}\,\overline{x} = \emptyset),$$

and so to $a_{11}\,a_{10}\,a_{01}\,a_{00} = \emptyset$.

We see in the same way that (3.40) has the solution $x = a_{01}\,a_{00}$, from which we obtain the solution

$$\begin{aligned} y &= a_{10}\,a_{01}\,a_{00} + a_{00}\,\overline{a_{01}\,a_{00}} \\ &= a_{10}\,a_{01}\,a_{00} + a_{00}\,\overline{a_{01}} \end{aligned}$$

for $y$.

Proceeding to the next level of recursion we can now treat

$$(\exists x, y, z \mid a_{111}\, x\, y\, z + a_{110}\, x\, y\, \overline{z} + a_{101}\, x\, \overline{y}\, z + a_{100}\, x\, \overline{y}\, \overline{z} + a_{011}\, \overline{x}\, y\, z + a_{010}\, \overline{x}\, y\, \overline{z} + a_{001}\, \overline{x}\, \overline{y}\, z + a_{000}\, \overline{x}\, \overline{y}\, \overline{z} = \emptyset).$$

Using our solution of (3.39) we can rewrite this as

$$\big(\exists x \mid (a_{111}\, x + a_{011}\, \overline{x})\, (a_{110}\, x + a_{011}\, \overline{x})\, (a_{101}\, x + a_{001}\, \overline{x})\, (a_{100}\, x + a_{000}\, \overline{x}) = \emptyset\big).$$

'Multiplying out', it follows as above that a solution exists if and only if

$$a_{111}\, a_{110}\, a_{101}\, a_{100}\, a_{011}\, a_{010}\, a_{001}\, a_{000} = \emptyset.$$

The reader will readily infer the condition for solvability of the corresponding $k$-variable case.

Next let $m = 1$ and consider

$$\big(\exists x \mid (a\, x + b\, \overline{x} = \emptyset)\, \&\, (c\, x + d\, \overline{x} \neq \emptyset)\big) \leftrightarrow \big(\exists x \mid (b \subseteq x)\, \&\, (x\, a = \emptyset)\, \&\, (c\, x + d\, \overline{x} \neq \emptyset)\big). \quad (3.41)$$

By adding a point $z \in c\, \overline{a}$ to a solution $x$ of (3.41) we never spoil the solution, and hence if (3.41) has a solution it has one of the form

$$b + c\, \overline{a} + y,$$

where $y$ must neither be included in $a$ nor in $c\, \overline{a}$. Since the choice of $y$ will only affect the term $d\, \overline{x}$ of (3.41), which we want to be as large as possible to maximize our chance of having $d\, \overline{x} \neq \emptyset$, it is best to take $y = \emptyset$. Thus, if (3.41) has a solution, it has the solution $b + c\, \overline{a}$. Therefore a solution will exist if and only if

$$a\, b = \emptyset\, \&\, c\, \overline{a} + d\, \overline{b} \neq \emptyset.$$

These conditions, like (3.41), involve one set equality and one inequality, so that inductive treatment of the $n$ variable case corresponding to (3.41) is possible. For example, we can consider

$$\big(\exists x, y \mid (a_{11}\, x\, y + a_{10}\, x\, \overline{y} + a_{01}\, \overline{x}\, y + a_{00}\, \overline{x}\, \overline{y} = \emptyset) \;\&\; (b_{11}\, x\, y + b_{10}\, x\, \overline{y} + b_{01}\, \overline{x}\, y + b_{00}\, \overline{x}\, \overline{y}) \neq \emptyset\big). \quad (3.42)$$

The inner existential of this can be written as the case of (3.41) in which

$$a = a_{11}\, x + a_{01}\, \overline{x}, \qquad b = a_{10}\, x + a_{00}\, \overline{x},$$
$$c = b_{11}\, x + b_{01}\, \overline{x}, \qquad d = b_{10}\, x + b_{00}\, \overline{x}$$

and so has a solution if and only if

$$(a_{11}\, x + a_{01}\, \overline{x}) \cdot (a_{10}\, x + a_{00}\, \overline{x}) = \emptyset$$

and

$$(b_{11}\,\overline{a_{11}}\,x + b_{01}\,\overline{a_{01}}\,\overline{x}) \cdot (b_{10}\,\overline{a_{10}}\,x + b_{00}\,\overline{a_{00}}\,\overline{x}) \neq \emptyset.$$

It follows that (3.42) is equivalent to

$$(\exists x \mid a_{11}\,a_{10}\,x + a_{01}\,a_{00}\,\overline{x} = \emptyset\ \&\ b_{11}\,\overline{a_{11}}\,b_{10}\,\overline{a_{10}}\,x + b_{01}\,\overline{a_{01}}\,b_{00}\,\overline{a_{00}}\,\overline{x} \neq \emptyset)$$

and hence, applying the solution of (3.41) once more, has a solution if and only if

$$a_{11}\,a_{10}\,a_{01}\,a_{00} = \emptyset$$

and

$$\left(b_{11}\,\overline{a_{11}}\,b_{10}\,\overline{a_{10}}(\overline{a_{11}\,a_{10}})\right) \cdot \left(b_{01}\,\overline{a_{01}}\,b_{00}\,\overline{a_{00}}(\overline{a_{01}\,a_{00}})\right) \neq \emptyset.$$

Moreover, if (3.42) has a solution at all, it has the solution

$$x_0 = a_{01}\,a_{00} + b_{11}\,\overline{a_{11}}\,b_{10}\,\overline{a_{10}}(\overline{a_{11}\,a_{10}}),$$

from which a value for $y$ can be calculated as follows. Substitute $x_0$ into (3.42), getting

$$(a_{11}\,x_0\,y + a_{10}\,x_0\,\overline{y} + a_{01}\,\overline{x_0}\,y + a_{00}\,\overline{x_0}\,\overline{y} = \emptyset)$$
$$\&\ (b_{11}\,x_0\,y + b_{10}\,x_0\,\overline{y} + b_{01}\,\overline{x_0}\,y + b_{00}\,\overline{x_0}\,\overline{y} \neq \emptyset)$$

as the condition that $y$ must satisfy. This is a case of (3.41), and therefore using the solution $b + c\,\overline{a}$ of (3.41) derived above we have

$$y = a_{10}\,x_0 + a_{00}\,\overline{x_0} + (b_{11}\,x_0 + b_{01}\,\overline{x_0}) \cdot \left(\overline{a_{11}\,x_0 + a_{01}\,\overline{x_0}}\right).$$

The common theme of these elementary examples is the progressive elimination of quantifiers. This same method will be generalized below to give a procedure for testing the satisfiability of any (extended) Behmann formula.

As another interesting elementary case we can consider quantified formulae built around a single set-theoretic equation $e(x_1, \ldots, x_n) = \emptyset$ but involving no set inequalities. Here we can allow arbitrary sequences of existential and universal quantifiers, and do not always insist that $e(x_1, \ldots, x_n)$ only involve Boolean operators, but suppose that existentially quantified variables only appear as arguments of Boolean operators. The simplest case is

$$(\exists x \mid \forall y \mid a_y\,x + b_y\,\overline{x} = \emptyset) \leftrightarrow \left(\exists x \,\middle|\, \left(\bigcup_y a_y\right) x + \left(\bigcup_y b_y\right) \overline{x} = \emptyset\right), \qquad (3.43)$$

where $\bigcup_y a_y$ designates the union of all the set values $a_y$, etc. Hence, by the above discussion of formula (3.38), (3.43) is equivalent to $(\forall y, z \mid a_y b_z = \emptyset)$, and has the solution $\bigcup_y b_y$ if the truth-value of (3.43) is 'true'. Similar elementary cases involving more complex sequences of existential and universal quantifiers can be treated in much the same way.

#### 3.8.4.1 The Extended Behmann Case

[Beh22] describes an algorithm for calculating the truth value of any formula quantified over sets and involving only Boolean operators, set inclusion and inequality. This can be generalized to a decision procedure for formulae quantified over both sets and cardinals involving besides the operators just mentioned, also integer constants, the set cardinality operator $\#S$, cardinal addition, and inequalities. Such formulae will be called TPB-*formulae* (after the initials of Tarski, Presburger, and Behmann). As noted previously, in considering any existentially quantified TPB-formula $(\exists \nu \mid P(\nu))$ or $(\exists x \mid P(x))$ (where, here and below, $\nu$ designates a cardinal and $x$ a set) we can assume that $P$ is a conjunction of literals. In fact, existentially quantified TPB-formulae over cardinals of the form $(\exists \nu \mid P(\nu))$ can be rewritten as

$$\big(\exists x_\nu \mid P(\#x_\nu)\big),$$

where $x_\nu$ stands for a fresh set-valued variable denoting a set having cardinality $\nu$. Hence, we only need to consider set-theoretic TPB-formulae of the form

$$\big(\exists x \mid P(x)\big), \tag{3.44}$$

with $x$ a set-valued variable and $P$ a conjunction of literals. Arguing much as in the preceding section, these can be written as

$$\left(\exists x \,\middle|\, \mathop{\&}_{k=1}^{N}\left(\sum_{j=1}^{P_k} \#(C_{kj}\,x + D_{kj}\,\overline{x}) + A_k \geqslant \sum_{j=P_k+1}^{R_k} \#(C_{kj}\,x + D_{kj}\,\overline{x}) + B_k\right)\right) \,\&\, Q, \tag{3.45}$$

where the $P_k$, $R_k$ and $N$ are integer constants, the $A_k$ and $B_k$ are valid cardinal-valued TPB-terms, the $C_{kj}$ and $D_{kj}$ are valid set-valued TPB-terms, and $Q$ is a valid TPB-formula, none of which involving the variable $x$.

To handle (3.45), we form all possible intersections $H_i$ of the sets $C_{kj}$, $D_{kj}$, and their complements. This gives us a collection $H_1, \ldots, H_R$ of sets. Each of the sets $C_{kj}$, $D_{kj}$ can then be written as a disjoint union of these $H_i$:

$$C_{kj} = \bigcup_{i \in G_{kj}} H_i,$$

$$D_{kj} = \bigcup_{i \in E_{kj}} H_i,$$

for $k = 1, \ldots, n$ and $j = 1, \ldots, Q_k$, and where $G_{kj}$ and $E_{kj}$ are subsets of $\{1, \ldots, R\}$.

Thus we have

$$C_{kj}\,x = \left(\bigcup_{i \in G_{kj}} H_i\right) x$$

and

$$D_{kj}\,\overline{x} = \Big(\bigcup_{i \in E_{kj}} H_i\Big)\overline{x},$$

for $k = 1, \ldots, n$ and $j = 1, \ldots, Q_k$, from which we see that (3.45) constrains only the cardinality of the sets $H_i\,x$ and $H_i\,\overline{x}$, for $i = 1, \ldots, R$. This observation allows (3.45) to be rewritten as

$$\Bigg(\exists \nu_1, \ldots, \nu_R, \mu_1, \ldots, \mu_R \;\Bigg|\; \Bigg(\mathop{\&}_{k=1}^{R} (\nu_k + \mu_k = \# H_k)$$

$$\& \mathop{\&}_{k=1}^{N} \Bigg( \sum_{j=1}^{P_k} \sum_{i \in G_{kj}} (\nu_i + \mu_i) + A_k \geqslant \sum_{j=P_k+1}^{R_k} \sum_{i \in G_{kj}} (\nu_i + \mu_i) + B_k \Bigg)\Bigg)\Bigg). \quad (3.46)$$

Once having put (3.45) into the form (3.46), we can apply the technique described in Sect. 3.8.3, using this repeatedly to eliminate the cardinal quantifiers

$$(\exists \nu_1, \ldots, \nu_R, \mu_1, \ldots, \mu_R \mid \cdots).$$

This will ultimately yield a valid TPB-formula equivalent to (3.45) but containing one less quantifier.

## 3.9 A Decision Algorithm for the Theory of Totally Ordered Sets

The (unquantified) theory of totally ordered sets allows variables designating elements of such a set, and un-negated or negated comparisons '>' and '=' between such elements. The comparison operator is assumed to satisfy all the assumptions standard for such comparators, i.e.

$$(\forall x, y, z \mid (x > y \;\&\; y > z) \rightarrow (x > z)),$$
$$(\forall x, y \mid (x > y) \rightarrow (\neg(y > x \vee y = x))),$$
$$(\forall x, y, z \mid x > y \vee y > x \vee x = y).$$

Since for the elements of such a set $\neg(x > y)$ is equivalent to $(y > x \vee y = x)$ and $x \neq y$ is equivalent to $(x > y \vee y > x)$, we can eliminate all the negated comparisons and thus have only to decide the satisfiability of a conjunction of comparisons, some of the form $x > y$ and others of the form $x = y$. By identifying all pairs of variables $x, y$ for which a conjunct $x = y$ is present, we can eliminate all occurrences of the '=' operator, and so have only to consider conjunctions of inequalities $x > y$. Such a conjunct is satisfiable if and only if it contains no cycle of relationships $x > y$. Indeed, if there is such a cycle it is clear that the given set of statements admits of no model by the elements of a totally ordered set. Conversely, if there is no such cycle, our variables can be topologically sorted into an order in which $x$ comes later than $y$ whenever $x > y$, and this very ordering gives us the desired model.

A related and equally easy decision problem is that for the (unquantified) ELEMENTARY THEORY OF SUBSETS OF TOTALLY ORDERED SETS. This is the language whose variables $s, t$ designate subsets of some totally ordered set $\mathcal{U}$, whose operators are the elementary set union, intersection, and difference operators $\cup$, $\cap$, and $\setminus$, whose comparators are '$\supseteq$' and '$=$', but where we also allow the comparator $s > t$ (and also $s \geqslant t$) which states that every element of $s$ is greater (in the given ordering of $\mathcal{U}$) than every element of $t$. We want this language to describe subsets of some universe of totally ordered sets, so we define models of any collection $S'$ of statements in the language to be a mapping of the variables which appear in $S'$ into subsets of some totally ordered set $\mathcal{U}$ with ordering '$>$', such that $s > t$ and $s \geqslant t$ are, respectively, equivalent to

$$(\forall x \in s,\ y \in t \mid x > y) \quad \text{and} \quad (\forall x \in s,\ y \in t \mid x \geqslant y).$$

To handle this language, it is convenient to make use of the notion of '*place*' introduced in our earlier discussion of decision algorithms for the language of elementary set operators and of the properties of that notion defined in Sect. 3.2. As usual, we reduce the satisfiability problem that confronts us to the satisfiability problem for a collection of conjuncts, each having one of the following forms:

$$\begin{array}{llll} s = t \cup u; & s = t \setminus u; & s = t \cap u; & \\ s = \emptyset; & s \neq \emptyset; & & \\ s > t; & s \geqslant t; & \neg(s > t); & \neg(s \geqslant t). \end{array} \tag{3.47}$$

Let $S'$ be the set of all conjuncts listed above, and let $S$ be the subset consisting of all those conjuncts listed in the first line of (3.47). We saw in Sect. 3.2 that, given any model $\mathcal{M}$ of $S$, and any point $p$ in the universe $\mathcal{U}$ of such a model, the function $f_P(s) \leftrightarrow (p \in \mathcal{M}s)$ defines a *place* for $S$, i.e. a Boolean-valued mapping of the variables and elementary expressions appearing in $S$, such that

$$\begin{array}{ll} f_P(s \cup t) = f_P(s) \vee f_P(t), & f_P(s \cap t) = f_P(s) \;\&\; f_P(t), \\ f_P(s \setminus t) = f_P(s) \;\&\; \left(\neg f_P(t)\right), & f_P(\emptyset) \quad = \mathsf{false}. \end{array}$$

We also saw in Sect. 3.2 that the set of all points $p$ in $\mathcal{U}$ defined an *ample* set of places, in the sense that for any conjunct of the form $s \neq \emptyset$ there must exist a place $f_p$ such that $f_p(s) = \mathsf{true}$. Conversely, given any ample set $P$ of places, the formula $\mathcal{M}s = \{f \in P \mid f(s) = \mathsf{true}\}$ defines a model of the set $S$ of conjuncts.

For our present purposes we need a slight reformulation of this result which allows individual places $f$ to be used more than once in a model. In this reformulation we use not simply a set $P$ of places, but a finite sequence $P'$ of places. We call such a sequence of places *ample* if the set of places $f_i$ that occur in it is ample. In this case, it is easily seen that the modified formula

$$\mathcal{M}s = \left\{i \mid f_i(s) = \mathsf{true}\right\} \tag{3.48}$$

also defines a model of the subset $S$ of conjuncts. Suppose now that the full set $S$ of conjuncts has a model with some universe $\mathcal{U}$, where as said above $\mathcal{U}$ must be ordered and its ordering '$>$' must model the operator $s > t$ of our language in the manner indicated above. For every conjunct $\neg(s > t)$ (resp. $\neg(s \geqslant t)$) in $S'$ choose a pair of points $p, q$ in $\mathcal{U}$ such that $p \in \mathcal{M}s$, $q \in \mathcal{M}t$, and $q \geqslant p$ (resp. $q > p$). To these points, add a point $p$ in $\mathcal{M}s$ for every conjunct $s \neq \emptyset$ in the set $S'$ of conjuncts. It is then clear that if we restrict our universe to this collection $\mathcal{U}'$ of points, i.e. take $\mathcal{M}'s = \mathcal{M}s \cap \mathcal{U}'$ for every variable $s$ of $S'$, we still have a model of the full set $S'$ of conjuncts. If these points $p_j$ are arranged in their '$<$' order, we will have $p_j > p_k$ if $j > k$. Now consider the sequence of places $f_j$ corresponding to these points, i.e. $f_j = f_{p_j}$. These have the property that if $f_j(s) = \mathsf{true}$ (equivalent to $p_j \in \mathcal{M}s$), and also $f_k(t) = \mathsf{true}$, then the presence in $S'$ of a conjunct $s > t$ (resp. $s \geqslant t$) implies $j > k$ (resp. $j \geqslant k$). Moreover, the presence in $S'$ of a conjunct $\neg(s > t)$ (resp. $\neg(s \geqslant t)$) implies the existence of indices $j, k$ satisfying $k \geqslant j$ (resp. $k > j$) and such that $f_j(s) = \mathsf{true}$ and $f_k(t) = \mathsf{true}$. Hence, if we take the $\mathcal{M}$ defined by formula (3.48), whose universe $\mathcal{U}$ is simply the set of integer indices of the finite sequence $P'$ of places, and give these points their ordinary integer ordering, $\mathcal{M}$ is a model of our full set $S'$ of conjuncts. This establishes the following conclusion, which clearly implies that the language presently under consideration has a solvable satisfiability problem:

A collection $S'$ of conjuncts of the form (3.47) is satisfiable if and only if it admits an ample sequence $f_j$ of places, in which no place occurs more than $n + 1$ times, where $n$ is the total number of conjuncts having either the form $\neg(s > t)$, or the form $\neg(s \geqslant t)$.

## 3.10 A Decision Algorithm for Ordered Abelian Groups

Ordered Abelian groups $G$ are characterized by the presence of an associative-commutative addition operator '$+$', with identity '0' and inverse '$-$', and also a comparison operator $x > y$ satisfying

$$\big(\forall x \in G,\ y \in G \mid \neg(x > x) \,\&\, (x > y \vee x = y \vee x < y)\big),$$

$$\big(\forall x \in G,\ y \in G,\ z \in G \mid (x > y \,\&\, y > z) \rightarrow (x > z)\big),$$

$$\big(\forall x \in G,\ y \in G,\ z \in G \mid (x > y) \rightarrow (z - y > z - x)\big)$$

(where $x - y$ abbreviates $x + -y$). The last axiom plainly implies that

$$\big(\forall x \in G,\ y \in G,\ z \in G \mid (x > y) \rightarrow (x + z > y + z)\big).$$

Familiar structures satisfying the above axioms are the standard additive groups based on $\mathbb{Z}$, $\mathbb{Q}$, and $\mathbb{R}$, to mention a few.

The decision problem for the *fully quantified* theory of ordered Abelian groups was solved by Yu. Gurevič in [Gur65]; here we will only show that the satisfiability of any finite collection $C$ of *unquantified* statements in this theory is decidable (more detail about this specialized decision algorithm is provided in [COSU03, Sect. 3]). Assume hence that $C$ is the conjunction, subject to the above axioms, of unquantified statements written using the operators '+', '−', '>', the constant 0, and variables. Note that if such a conjunction $C$ is satisfiable, i.e. has some model which is an ordered Abelian group $G'$, it can plainly be modelled in the subgroup $G$ of $G'$ generated by the elements of $G'$ which correspond to the variables appearing in $C$. Hence $C$ has a model which is an ordered Abelian group with *finitely many* generators. Conversely, if there exists such a model, then $C$ is satisfiable. Thus we can base our analysis on an understanding of the structure of finitely generated ordered Abelian groups $G$.

The additive group of reals contains many such ordered subgroups with finitely many generators, as does the additive group of real vectors of dimension $d$ for any $d$, if we order these vectors lexicographically. We will see in what follows that these examples are generic, in the sense that any ordered Abelian group endowed with a finite number $m$ of generators can be embedded into the additive group of real vectors of dimension (at most) $m$ by an order-preserving isomorphism (we will call such isomorphisms 'order isomorphisms' hereinafter).

This can be done as follows: By a well-known result (cf., e.g., [Fuc70]), Abelian groups with finitely many generators are decomposable, in an essentially unique way, as direct sums of finitely many copies of the group $\mathbb{Z}$ and of finitely many finite cyclic groups. The order axiom plainly rules out any finite cyclic components, so $G$ must be the direct sum of finitely many copies of the signed integers. We denote by $\mathsf{rank}(G)$ the number of these copies that appear in the direct sum representing $G$. A standard result, whose proof we will repeat below, tells us that this number depends only on $G$, not on the way in which $G$ is represented.

To see how the order in $G$ must be represented (cf. [KK74]), we will consider two cases separately: that in which $G$ has '*infinitesimals*', and that in which it does not. To this end, we define the subgroup $\mathsf{Inf}(G)$ of infinitesimals of $G$ (inclusive of 0, although this shall *not* be regarded as an infinitesimal) as follows:

$$\mathsf{Inf}(G) =_{\mathrm{Def}} \{ x \in G \mid \text{there exists a } y \text{ in } G \text{ such that } mx \leqslant y \text{ holds for all signed integers } m \},$$

where for $m > 0$, $mx$ designates the sum of $m$ copies of $x$; $mx$ is the zero element of $G$ if $m = 0$, and $mx = -(-m)x$ if $m < 0$. It is easy to show that $\mathsf{Inf}(G)$ is indeed a subgroup of $G$, and we leave this to the reader.

First suppose that $G$ contains no infinitesimals, i.e. $\mathsf{Inf}(G) = \{0\}$; then for each $x > 0$ and $y > 0$ there exists a positive integer $m$ such that $mx > y$. In this case we can show that the group must be order-isomorphic to an ordered subgroup of the additive group of reals. In the easy case in which there is just one generator, $G$ is plainly isomorphic to the ordered group of integers.

More generally, choose some $y > 0$ and then, for each $x$, consider the set $S(x)$ of all rationals $m/n$ with positive denominator $n$ such that $nx > my$:

$$S(x) =_{\mathrm{Def}} \{ m/n : m \in \mathbb{N},\ m \in \mathbb{N} \mid n > 0 \,\&\, nx > my \}.$$

This is defined independently of the way that $m/n$ is represented by a fraction, since the order axioms imply that if $nx > my$ then $knx > kmy$ for each positive $k$, and conversely if $knx > kmy$ then $nx \leqslant my$ is impossible. Also, for every $x \in G$, there is a positive integer $n$ such that $(\neg(n \in S(x)))$ & $(-n \in S(x))$, so $S(x)$ is neither empty nor all the rationals; moreover $S(x)$ is bounded above, because if $\neg(m/n \in S(x))$ (i.e., $my \geqslant nx$) and $m'/n' > m/n$ (i.e., $nm' > mn'$), then $\neg(m'/n' \in S(x))$ (i.e., $m'y \geqslant n'x$); finally, if $m/n \in S(x)$ then there are $m'$, $n'$ such that $m'/n' \in S(x)$ & $m'/n' > m/n$. Together these facts imply that, for each $x \in G$, $S(x)$ is a *cut* in the set of rationals, i.e. that there is a unique smallest real $r(x)$ such that $S(x) = \{a \in \mathbb{Q} \mid a < r(x)\}$.

We will now see that this mapping $x \mapsto r(x)$ is an injective order-preserving homomorphism of $G$ into the reals. Suppose in fact that $m/n < r(x)$ and $m'/n' < r(x')$ hold, both denominators $n$ and $n'$ being positive. Then $nx > my$ and $n'x > m'y$, so $nn'x > mn'y$ and $nn'x > m'ny$, and therefore

$$nn'(x+x') > (mn'+m'n)y,$$

from which it follows that $m/n + m'/n'$ belongs to $S(x+x')$. This proves that $(x+x') \geqslant r(x) + r(x')$. Now suppose that $r(x+x') > r(x) + r(x')$, and let $m/n$ and $m'/n'$, respectively, be rationals which approximate $r(x)$ (resp. $r(x')$) well enough from above so that we have $m/n + m'/n' < S(x+x')$, while $m/n > r(x)$ and $m'/n' > r(x')$. This implies that $nx \leqslant my$, $n'x \leqslant m'y$, and $nn'(x+x') > (mn'+m'n)y$. This is impossible since our first two inequalities imply that $nn'(x+x') \leqslant (mn'+m'n)y$. It follows that $r(x+x') > r(x) + r(x')$ is impossible, so $r(x+x') = r(x) + r(x')$, i.e. $r$ is a homomorphism of $G$ into the additive group of reals. Suppose next that $r(x) = 0$. Then we cannot have $x > 0$, since if we did then $nx > y$ would be true for some positive $n$, so $1/n$ would be a member of $S(x)$, implying that $r(x) \geqslant 1/n$, which is impossible. Similarly if $x < 0$ it would follow that $r(-x) \geqslant 1/n$ for some positive $n$, also impossible. Since $r$ has been seen to be additive, $r(-x) = -r(x)$, and it follows that $x$ must be 0, proving the injectivity of $r$. To see that $r$ is order preserving, consider $x, x' \in G$ such that $x' > x$, and let the rational number $m/n$ (with positive denominator) belong to $S(x)$; then $nx > my$, and so $nx' > my$ also, proving that $m/n$ belongs to $S(x')$. That is, $x' > x$ implies that $S(x') \supseteq S(x)$, and thus plainly implies that $r(x') \geqslant r(x)$; but we must exclude the possibility $r(x') = r(x)$, which by what we have seen above would imply $r(x'-x) = 0$, hence $x'-x = 0$, and hence $x' = x$. This completes our treatment of the case in which $G$ has no infinitesimals.

Next we will show that in the presence of infinitesimals, namely when $\mathsf{Inf}(G)$ is non-trivial, $G$ can be embedded into the lexicographically ordered additive group of real vectors of dimension $K$, for some $K$ not exceeding $\mathsf{rank}(G)$. To handle this case, we need to use a few more standard results about finitely generated Abelian groups, which we pause to derive. The first of these is the fact that $\mathsf{rank}(G)$ is independent of the way in which we represent $G$ as the sum of a finite collection of cyclic groups, i.e. as an additive group $N_k$ of integer vectors of length $k$. To see this, suppose that two such groups $N_k$ and $N_{k'}$ are isomorphic, and that $k > k'$. Let $f$ be an isomorphism of $N_k$ onto $N_{k'}$. If we embed $N_k$ and $N_{k'}$ into the corresponding spaces $N_k^*$ and $N_{k'}^*$ of vectors with rational coefficients, and extend $f$ to a linear mapping of $N_k^*$ into $N_{k'}^*$, then, since the dimension $k$ of $N_k^*$ exceeds that of $N_{k'}^*$, there exists a non-zero rational vector, and hence a non-zero integer vector in $N_k^*$ which $f$ maps to zero. This contradicts the fact that $f$ is an isomorphism, and so proves our assertion concerning $\mathsf{rank}(G)$.

Next we will show that any subgroup $S$ of a finitely generated ordered group $G$ is also finitely generated, and has rank no greater than the rank of $S$, again a standard result. By what has been proved above, we can suppose without loss of generality that $G$ is the additive group of integer vectors of dimension $d$. If there is no vector $v$ in $S$ whose first component is non-zero, then $S$ is a subgroup of the group of integer vectors of dimension $d-1$, and so (by our inductive hypothesis) there is nothing to prove. Otherwise let $v$ be such a vector with smallest possible first component $c_1$. Then any other $v'$ in $S$ must have a first component $c_1'$ which is divisible by $c_1$, since otherwise the greatest common divisor of $c_1'$ and $c_1$, which is the first component of some vector of the form $k*v+k'*v'$, where $k$ and $k'$ are integers, would be positive and smaller. It follows that every $v$ in $S$ can be written in the form $k*v+u$, where $u$ is a vector in $S$ whose first component is 0. Therefore, if we let $S'$ be the subgroup of $S$ consisting of all vectors whose first component is 0, $S'$ is a subgroup of the additive group of integer vectors of dimension $d-1$. By inductive hypothesis, $S'$ is a finitely generated group with at most $d-1$ generators. If we add $v$ to this set of generators, we clearly have a set of generators for $S$, proving our assertion.

In what follows we will also need to use the following facts.

**Lemma 3.1** *Let $(G,<)$ be a finitely generated ordered Abelian group, and let $B$ be a subgroup of $G$ such that*

$$x < y \text{ for each } x \text{ in } B \text{ and each positive } y \text{ in } G \setminus B. \tag{3.49}$$

*Then:*

(1) *If given the ordering '$<$' defined by*

$$(g+B) < (g'+B) \quad \text{iff} \quad g < g' \;\&\; (g+B) \neq (g'+B),$$

*the quotient group $G/B$ becomes an ordered Abelian group.*

(2) *The Cartesian product $H$ of $G/B$ and $B$, given the lexicographic order '$<$' defined by*

$$[x,y] < [x',y'] \quad \text{iff} \quad x < x' \lor (x = x' \;\&\; y < y')$$
$$\text{(in the ordering of } G/B \text{ described just above)}$$

*is an ordered Abelian group.*

(3) *$(G,<)$ and $H$ are order-isomorphic and* $\mathsf{rank}(G) = \mathsf{rank}(G/B) + \mathsf{rank}(B)$.

*Proof* To prove (1), note first of all that the relationship $(g+B) < (g'+B)$, i.e. $g < g'$, is independent of the elements $g$ and $g'$ chosen to represent $(g+B)$ and

$(g' + B)$. For if other $g$ and $g'$ were chosen, the difference $g' - g$ will change to $g' - g + b$, where $b$ is some element of $B$. But since $g' - g$ is positive, we must have $-b < g' - g$ by assumption (3.49), so $g' - g + b$ is positive also. Knowing this, we see at once that the relationship $(g + B) < (g' + B)$ is transitive, and that if $(g + B) < (g' + B)$ and $(h + B) < (h' + B)$, then $((g + h) + B) < ((g' + h') + B)$, proving (1).

(2) follows immediately from (1), since the Cartesian product of any two groups, lexicographically ordered, is always an ordered group. To prove (3), note that

(a) $B$ is a subgroup of a finitely generated Abelian group, and so (as proved above) is finitely generated.
(b) If $g_1, \ldots, g_n$ is a system of generators of $G$, then $(g_1 + B), \ldots, (g_n + B)$ is a system of generators of $G/B$ (not necessarily a minimal set of generators), so that $G/B$ is finitely generated.

Let $\{h_1 + B, \ldots, h_p + B\}$ be a minimal set of generators of $G/B$. Let $T$ be the map from $G$ onto $G/B$ defined as follows:

For each $g$ in $G$ there exist unique integers $k_1, \ldots, k_p$ such that

$$g + B = k_1(h_1 + B) + \cdots + k_p(h_p + B).$$

Using these $k_j$, put

$$T(g) = \big[g + B, g - (k_1 h_1 + \cdots + k_p h_p)\big].$$

It is not difficult to verify that for any two $g$, $g'$ in $G$ we have $T(g - g') = T(g) - T(g')$. Moreover, if $T(g) = 0$, we must have $g + B = 0$, so $k_1, \ldots, k_p$ must all be zero, and therefore $g = 0$. This shows that $T$ is an isomorphism of $G$ onto the Cartesian product group $H$ of $G/B$ and $B$. Since the rank of a finite group is independent of its representation, we also have $\mathsf{rank}(G) = \mathsf{rank}(G/B) + \mathsf{rank}(B)$. To show that $T$ is also an order isomorphism from $(G, <)$ onto the lexicographically ordered Cartesian product $H$ of $G/B$ and $B$, suppose that $g' > g$, and write $g' + B$ as

$$g' + B = k'_1(h_1 + B) + \cdots + k'_p(h_p + B).$$

Then if $g' + B \neq g + B$ we have $g' + B > g + B$ by (1) above, so

$$\big[g + B,\ g - (k_1 h_1 + \cdots + k_p h_p)\big] > \big[g' + B,\ g' - (k'_1 h_1 + \cdots + k'_p h_p)\big].$$

On the other hand, if $g' + B = g + B$ we have $k_j = k'_j$ for all $j$, and so

$$\big[g + B,\ g - (k_1 h_1 + \cdots + k_p h_p)\big] > \big[g' + B,\ g' - (k_1 h_1 + \cdots + k_p h_p)\big]$$

in this case also. Hence this inequality holds in any case, i.e. $T$ is both an isomorphism and an order isomorphism. □

Assume as above that $\mathsf{Inf}(G)$ is non-trivial. Then the condition (3.49) of the previous lemma holds for the proper subgroup $\mathsf{Inf}(G)$ of $G$. Indeed, if $x$ is infinitesimal and $y$ is positive and not infinitesimal, and $x < y$ is false, then $y < x$. Since $x$ is infinitesimal there exists some positive $z$ such that $mx < z$ for all integers $m$. Then plainly $my < z$ for all positive integers $m$, and since $y$ is positive this holds for all negative integers $m$ also. It follows that $y$ is infinitesimal, a contradiction proving our assertion.

It follows from (2) and (3) above that $(G, <)$ is isomorphic to the lexicographically ordered Cartesian product $H$ of $G/\mathsf{Inf}(G)$ and $\mathsf{Inf}(G)$, and that $\mathsf{rank}(G) = \mathsf{rank}(G/\mathsf{Inf}(G)) + \mathsf{rank}(\mathsf{Inf}(G))$. Moreover

(i) $G/\mathsf{Inf}(G)$ is non-trivial, i.e. $\mathsf{rank}(G/\mathsf{Inf}(G)) > 0$;
(ii) $G/\mathsf{Inf}(G)$ has no infinitesimals, i.e. $\mathsf{Inf}(G/\mathsf{Inf}(G)) = \{0\}$.

To prove (i), note that if $G/\mathsf{Inf}(G)$ were trivial, i.e. $\mathsf{Inf}(G) = G$, all elements, and in particular all generators, of $G$ would be infinitesimals. Thus for each generator $g_j$ there would exist a $y_j$ in $G$ such that $mg_j < y_j$ for every signed integer $m$. Let $y = y_1 + \cdots + y_p$ be the sum of all these $y_j$. Then $y$ is itself a sum $y = k_1 g_1 + \cdots + k_p g_p$ and therefore we have

$$y_1 + \cdots + y_p = k_1 g_1 + \cdots + k_p g_p < y_1 + \cdots + y_p,$$

a contradiction which shows that $G/\mathsf{Inf}(G)$ is non-trivial.

To prove (ii) we argue as follows. Suppose that $g + \mathsf{Inf}(G)$ is infinitesimal in $G/\mathsf{Inf}(G)$, i.e. that there exists a positive $y + \mathsf{Inf}(G)$ in $G/\mathsf{Inf}(G)$ such that $m(g + \mathsf{Inf}(G)) < y + \mathsf{Inf}(G)$ for all integers $m$. This gives $mg < y$ for all integer $m$, and then $g$ is plainly infinitesimal in $G$, so it must belong to $\mathsf{Inf}(G)$, i.e. $g + \mathsf{Inf}(G)$ must be the zero element of $G/\mathsf{Inf}(G)$, proving (ii).

Since $G/\mathsf{Inf}(G)$ is non-trivial by (i), we must have $\mathsf{rank}(\mathsf{Inf}(G)) < \mathsf{rank}(G)$. Now applying (3) inductively, it follows that $G$ is isomorphic to the lexicographically ordered Cartesian product of the sequence

$$G/\mathsf{Inf}(G),\ \mathsf{Inf}(G)/\mathsf{Inf}^2(G),\ \ldots,\ \mathsf{Inf}^{k-1}(G)/\mathsf{Inf}^k(G),\ \mathsf{Inf}^k(G)$$

of groups for each $k < \mathsf{rank}(G)$, where by definition $\mathsf{Inf}^i(G) = \mathsf{Inf}(\mathsf{Inf}^{i-1}(G))$. By (ii), each group in this sequence is a finitely generated Abelian group with no non-trivial infinitesimals. Since, as was shown above, each such group can be embedded into the additive group of reals, it follows that $G$ can be embedded into the additive group of real vectors of dimension $\mathsf{rank}(G)$, ordered lexicographically. This is the key conclusion at which the preceding arguments aimed.

It follows from what has now been established that, given any quantifier-free conjunction $C$ of statements in the theory of ordered Abelian groups which contains $n$ distinct variables, $C$ is satisfiable in some ordered Abelian group if and only if it is satisfied in the additive group of real vectors of dimension $n$, ordered lexicographically. But it is easy to reduce the satisfiability problem for the lexicographically ordered additive group of real vectors of dimension $n$ to the satisfiability problem for the additive group of reals. Indeed, a real vector of dimension $n$ simply consists of $n$ real numbers $x_1, \ldots, x_n$, addition of two such vectors is just addition of their individual components, and the condition $x < y$ for two vectors $x$ and $y$ can be written as the disjunction

$$x_1 < y_1 \vee (x_1 = y_1 \,\&\, x_2 < y_2) \vee \cdots \vee (x_1 = y_1 \,\&\, \cdots \,\&\, x_{n-1} = y_{n-1} \,\&\, x_n < y_n).$$

This observation shows that the satisfiability problem for any collection of unquantified statements in the theory of ordered Abelian groups reduces without difficulty to the problem of satisfying a corresponding collection of real linear equations and inequalities. This is the standard problem of linear programming, which can be tested for solvability using any convenient linear programming algorithm (cf., e.g., [IC94]). In conclusion, we have the following.

**Corollary 3.1** *The collection of unquantified statements of the theory of ordered Abelian groups has a decidable satisfiability problem.*

## 3.11 A Fragment of Analysis: Theory of Reals and Single-Valued Continuous Functions with Predicates 'Monotone', 'Convex', 'Concave', Real Addition, and Comparison

In this section we study the decision problem for a fragment of real analysis, which, besides the real operators '+', '−', '·', and '/', also provides predicates expressing strict and non-strict monotonicity, concavity, and convexity of continuous real functions over bounded or unbounded intervals, as well as strict and non-strict comparisons '>' and '⩾' between real numbers and functions. Decidability of the decision problem for this unquantified language, which is called $\mathsf{RMCF}^+$, is demonstrated by proving that if a formula in it is satisfiable, then it has a model in which its function-designating variables are mapped into piecewise combinations of parametrized quadratic polynomial and/or exponential functions, where the parameters are constrained only by conditions expressible in the decidable language of real numbers. We recall that the decision problem for $\mathsf{RMCF}^+$ has been solved in [CCG06].

### 3.11.1 Syntax of $\mathsf{RMCF}^+$

The language $\mathsf{RMCF}^+$ has two types of variables, namely *numerical* variables, denoted by $x, y, \ldots$, and *function* variables, denoted by $f, g, \ldots$. Numerical and function variables are supposed to range, respectively, over the set $\mathbb{R}$ of real numbers and the set of one-parameter continuous real functions over $\mathbb{R}$. $\mathsf{RMCF}^+$ also provides the numerical constants 0 and 1 and the function constants $\mathbf{0}$ and $\mathbf{1}$.

The language also includes two distinguished symbols, $-\infty$ and $+\infty$, which are restricted to occur only as 'range defining' parameters, as explained in the following definitions.

*Numerical terms* of RMCF$^+$ are defined recursively as follows:[4]

- every numerical variable $x, y, \ldots$ or constant 0, 1 is a numerical term;
- if $t_1, t_2$ are numerical terms, then so are $(t_1 + t_2)$, $(t_1 - t_2)$, $(t_1 \cdot t_2)$, and $(t_1/t_2)$;
- if $t$ is a numerical term and $f$ is a function variable or constant, then $f(t)$ is a numerical term.

An *extended* numerical variable (resp. term) is a numerical variable (resp. term) or one of the symbols $-\infty$ and $+\infty$.

*Function terms* of RMCF$^+$ are defined recursively as follows:

- every unary function variable $f, g, \ldots$ or constant $\mathbf{0}$ and $\mathbf{1}$ is a function term;
- if $F_1, F_2$ are function terms, then so are $(F_1 + F_2)$ and $(F_1 - F_2)$.

An *atomic formula* of RMCF$^+$ is an expression having one of the following forms:

$$\begin{array}{ll} t_1 = t_2, & t_1 > t_2, \\ (F_1 = F_2)_{[E_1,E_2]}, & (F_1 > F_2)_{[t_1,t_2]}, \\ \mathsf{Up}(F)_{[E_1,E_2]}, & \mathsf{Strict\_Up}(F)_{[E_1,E_2]}, \\ \mathsf{Down}(F)_{[E_1,E_2]}, & \mathsf{Strict\_Down}(F)_{[E_1,E_2]}, \\ \mathsf{Convex}(F)_{[E_1,E_2]}, & \mathsf{Strict\_Convex}(F)_{[E_1,E_2]}, \\ \mathsf{Concave}(F)_{[E_1,E_2]}, & \mathsf{Strict\_Concave}(F)_{[E_1,E_2]}, \end{array}$$

where $t_1, t_2$ stand for numerical terms, $F_1, F_2$ stand for function terms, and $E_1, E_2$ stand for extended numerical terms such that $E_1 \neq +\infty$ and $E_2 \neq -\infty$.

A *formula* of RMCF$^+$ is any propositional combination of atomic formulae, constructed using the logical connectives &, $\vee$, $\neg$, $\rightarrow$, etc.

### *3.11.2 Semantics of* RMCF$^+$

Next we define the intended semantics of RMCF$^+$.

A (real) *assignment* $\mathcal{M}$ for the language RMCF$^+$ is a map defined over terms and formulae of RMCF$^+$ in the following way:

***Definition of $\mathcal{M}$ for* RMCF$^+$*-terms***

- $\mathcal{M}x \in \mathbb{R}$ for every numerical variable $x$.
- $\mathcal{M}0 = 0$, $\mathcal{M}1 = 1$, $\mathcal{M}(+\infty) = +\infty$, and $\mathcal{M}(-\infty) = -\infty$.
- For every function variable $f$, $\mathcal{M}f$ is a continuous real function over $\mathbb{R}$.
- $\mathcal{M}\mathbf{0}$ and $\mathcal{M}\mathbf{1}$ are, respectively, the zero function and the constant function of value 1, i.e. $(\mathcal{M}\mathbf{0})(r) = 0$ and $(\mathcal{M}\mathbf{1})(r) = 1$ for every $r \in \mathbb{R}$.

[4] Throughout this section, '$\cdot$' denotes multiplication, often designated by '$*$' in the rest of the book.

- $\mathcal{M}(t_1 \odot t_2) = \mathcal{M}(t_1) \odot \mathcal{M}(t_2)$, for every numerical term $t_1 \odot t_2$, where $\odot$ is any of $+$, $-$, $\cdot$, and $/$.
- $\mathcal{M}(f(t)) = (\mathcal{M}f)(\mathcal{M}t)$, for every function variable $f$ and numerical term $t$.
- $\mathcal{M}(F_1 \odot F_2)$ is the real function $(\mathcal{M}F_1) \odot (\mathcal{M}F_2)$, where $\odot$ is either of the allowed functional operators $+$ and $-$ and $(\mathcal{M}F_1) \odot (\mathcal{M}F_2)$ is defined by the condition that $(\mathcal{M}(F_1 \odot F_2))(r) = (\mathcal{M}F_1)(r) \odot (\mathcal{M}F_2)(r)$ for every $r \in \mathbb{R}$.

***Definition of $\mathcal{M}$ for* RMCF$^+$*-formulae***

In the following $t_1, t_2$ will stand for numerical terms, $E_1, E_2$ for extended numerical terms, and $F_1, F_2$ for function terms.

- $\mathcal{M}(t_1 = t_2) = \mathsf{true}$ iff $\mathcal{M}t_1 = \mathcal{M}t_2$.
- $\mathcal{M}(t_1 > t_2) = \mathsf{true}$ iff $\mathcal{M}t_1 > \mathcal{M}t_2$.
- $\mathcal{M}((F_1 > F_2)_{[t_1,t_2]}) = \mathsf{true}$ iff either $\mathcal{M}t_1 > \mathcal{M}t_2$, or $\mathcal{M}t_1 \leqslant \mathcal{M}t_2$ and $(\mathcal{M}F_1)(r) > (\mathcal{M}F_2)(r)$ for every $r$ in $[\mathcal{M}t_1, \mathcal{M}t_2]$. (Observe that for decidability purposes literals of type $(F_1 > F_2)_{[t_1,t_2]}$ have been restricted to finite intervals $[t_1, t_2]$ only.)
- $\mathcal{M}((F_1 = F_2)_{[E_1,E_2]}) = \mathsf{true}$ iff either $\mathcal{M}E_1 > \mathcal{M}E_2$, or $\mathcal{M}E_1 \leqslant \mathcal{M}E_2$ and $(\mathcal{M}F_1)(r) = (\mathcal{M}F_2)(r)$ for every $r$ in $[\mathcal{M}E_1, \mathcal{M}E_2]$. (Here and below we use the interval notation $[x, y]$ even if $x = -\infty$ and/or $y = +\infty$.)
- $\mathcal{M}(\mathsf{Up}(F)_{[E_1,E_2]}) = \mathsf{true}$ (resp. $\mathcal{M}(\mathsf{Strict\_Up}(F)_{[E_1,E_2]}) = \mathsf{true}$) iff either $\mathcal{M}E_1 \geqslant \mathcal{M}E_2$, or $\mathcal{M}E_1 < \mathcal{M}E_2$ and the function $\mathcal{M}F_1$ is monotone non-decreasing (resp. strictly increasing) in the interval $[\mathcal{M}E_1, \mathcal{M}E_2]$.
- $\mathcal{M}(\mathsf{Down}(F)_{[E_1,E_2]}) = \mathsf{true}$ (resp. $\mathcal{M}(\mathsf{Strict\_Down}(F)_{[E_1,E_2]}) = \mathsf{true}$) iff either $\mathcal{M}E_1 \geqslant \mathcal{M}E_2$, or $\mathcal{M}E_1 < \mathcal{M}E_2$ and the function $\mathcal{M}F_1$ is monotone non-increasing (resp. strictly decreasing) in the interval $[\mathcal{M}E_1, \mathcal{M}E_2]$.
- $\mathcal{M}(\mathsf{Convex}(F)_{[E_1,E_2]}) = \mathsf{true}$ (resp. $\mathcal{M}(\mathsf{Strict\_Convex}(F)_{[E_1,E_2]}) = \mathsf{true}$) iff either $\mathcal{M}E_1 \geqslant \mathcal{M}E_2$, or $\mathcal{M}E_1 < \mathcal{M}E_2$ and the function $\mathcal{M}F_1$ is convex (resp. strictly convex) in the interval $[\mathcal{M}E_1, \mathcal{M}E_2]$.
- $\mathcal{M}(\mathsf{Concave}(F)_{[E_1,E_2]}) = \mathsf{true}$ (resp. $\mathcal{M}(\mathsf{Strict\_Concave}(F)_{[E_1,E_2]}) = \mathsf{true}$) iff either $\mathcal{M}E_1 \geqslant \mathcal{M}E_2$, or $\mathcal{M}E_1 < \mathcal{M}E_2$ and the function $\mathcal{M}F_1$ is concave (resp. strictly concave) in the interval $[\mathcal{M}E_1, \mathcal{M}E_2]$.

Logical connectives are interpreted in the standard way; thus, for instance, $\mathcal{M}(P_1 \,\&\, P_2) = (\mathcal{M}P_1) \,\&\, (\mathcal{M}P_2)$.

Let $P$ be an RMCF$^+$-formula and let $\mathcal{M}$ be an assignment for the language RMCF$^+$. Note once more that we say that $\mathcal{M}$ is a *model* for $P$ iff $\mathcal{M}(P) = \mathsf{true}$. If $P$ has a model, then it is *satisfiable*, otherwise it is *unsatisfiable*. If $P$ is true in every RMCF$^+$-assignment, then $P$ is a *theorem* of RMCF$^+$.[5] As usual, two formulae are *equisatisfiable* if either both of them are unsatisfiable, or both of them are satisfiable, and the *satisfiability problem* for RMCF$^+$ is the problem of finding an algorithm which can determine whether or not a given RMCF$^+$-formula is satisfiable. Such an algorithm is given below.

[5] Thus to show that a given formula of RMCF$^+$ is a theorem, one can prove that its negation is unsatisfiable by any RMCF$^+$-assignment.

Here are a few examples of statements which can be proved automatically using this decision algorithm.

*A strictly convex curve and a concave curve defined over the same interval can meet in at most two points.*

This statement can be formalized in $\mathsf{RMCF}^+$ as follows:

$$\begin{pmatrix} \mathsf{Strict\_Convex}(f)_{[E_1,E_2]} \\ \& \ \mathsf{Concave}(g)_{[E_1,E_2]} \\ \& \ \mathop{\&}_{i=1}^{3}(f(x_i) = g(x_i)) \\ \& \ \mathop{\&}_{i=1}^{3}(E_1 \leqslant x_i \ \& \ x_i \leqslant E_2) \end{pmatrix} \rightarrow (x_1 = x_2 \vee x_1 = x_3 \vee x_2 = x_3).$$

A second example is as follows:

*Let $g$ be a linear function. Then a function $f$, defined over the same domain as $g$, is strictly convex if and only if $f + g$ is strictly convex.*

Introduce a predicate symbol $\mathsf{Linear}(f)_{[E_1,E_2]}$ standing for

$$\mathsf{Convex}(f)_{[E_1,E_2]} \ \& \ \mathsf{Concave}(f)_{[E_1,E_2]}.$$

Note that if $\mathscr{M}$ is a real assignment for $\mathsf{RMCF}^+$, then $\mathscr{M}(\mathsf{Linear}(f)_{[E_1,E_2]}) = \mathsf{true}$ if and only if the function $\mathscr{M}f$ is linear in the interval $[\mathscr{M}E_1, \mathscr{M}E_2]$.

It is plain that the proposition shown above is equivalent to the following formula:

$$\mathsf{Linear}(g)_{[E_1,E_2]} \rightarrow \big(\mathsf{Strict\_Convex}(f)_{[E_1,E_2]} \leftrightarrow \mathsf{Strict\_Convex}(f+g)_{[E_1,E_2]}\big).$$

The following is a somewhat more interesting example.

*Let $f$ and $g$ be two real functions which take the same values at the endpoints of a closed interval $[a,b]$. Assume also that $f$ is strictly convex in $[a,b]$ and that $g$ is linear in $[a,b]$. Then $f(c) < g(c)$ holds at each point $c$ interior to the interval $[a,b]$.*

This proposition can be formalized in the following way in the language $\mathsf{RMCF}^+$.

$$\big(\mathsf{Strict\_Convex}(f)_{[x_1,x_2]} \ \& \ \mathsf{Linear}(g)_{[x_1,x_2]} \ \& \ f(x_1) = g(x_1) \\ \& \ f(x_2) = g(x_2) \ \& \ x_2 > x \ \& \ x > x_1\big) \rightarrow \big(g(x) > f(x)\big).$$

### 3.11.3 Preparing a Set of RMCF$^+$ Statements for Satisfiability Testing

We shall prove the decidability of formulae of RMCF$^+$ using a series of satisfiability-preserving steps which reduce the satisfiability problem for RMCF$^+$ to a more easily decidable satisfiability problem for an unquantified set of statements involving real numbers only.

We begin by noting that the decidability problem for RMCF$^+$ can be reduced in the usual way to that for statements which are conjunctions of basic literals, where each conjunct must have one of the following forms:

$$\begin{array}{ll}
x = y + w, & x = y \cdot w, \\
x > y, & y = f(x), \\
(f = g + h)_{[z_1, z_2]}, & (f > g)_{[x, y]}, \\
(\neg)\mathsf{Up}(f)_{[z_1, z_2]}, & (\neg)\mathsf{Strict_Up}(f)_{[z_1, z_2]}, \\
(\neg)\mathsf{Down}(f)_{[z_1, z_2]}, & (\neg)\mathsf{Strict_Down}(f)_{[z_1, z_2]}, \\
(\neg)\mathsf{Convex}(f)_{[z_1, z_2]}, & (\neg)\mathsf{Strict_Convex}(f)_{[z_1, z_2]}, \\
(\neg)\mathsf{Concave}(f)_{[z_1, z_2]}, & (\neg)\mathsf{Strict_Concave}(f)_{[z_1, z_2]}.
\end{array}$$

Here $x, y, w$ stand for numerical variables or constants, $z_1, z_2$ for extended numerical variables (where $z_1$ is not equal to $+\infty$ nor $z_2$ to $-\infty$), $f, g, h$ for function variables or constants, and the expression $(\neg)A$ denotes both the un-negated and negated literals $A$ and $(\neg A)$. Note that reduction of the full set of constructs allowed in RMCF$^+$ to the somewhat more limited set seen above requires application of the following equivalences to eliminate subtraction, division, and various negated cases:

$$\begin{aligned}
(f_1 = f_2 - f_3)_{[z_1, z_2]} &\leftrightarrow (f_2 = f_1 + f_3)_{[z_1, z_2]}, \\
(f_1 = f_2)_{[z_1, z_2]} &\leftrightarrow (f_1 = f_2 + \mathbf{0})_{[z_1, z_2]}, \\
t_1 = t_2 - t_3 &\leftrightarrow t_2 = t_1 + t_3, \\
t_1 = t_2 &\leftrightarrow t_1 = t_2 + 0, \\
t_1 = t_2 / t_3 &\leftrightarrow (t_3 \neq 0) \,\&\, (t_2 = t_1 \cdot t_3), \\
t_1 \neq t_2 &\leftrightarrow (t_2 > t_1) \vee (t_1 > t_2), \\
\big(\neg(t_1 > t_2)\big) &\leftrightarrow (t_1 = t_2) \vee (t_2 > t_1).
\end{aligned}$$

It is also easy to eliminate the negated forms of the predicates Up, Down, Convex, and Concave and the negated forms of the strict versions of these predicates. For example, to re-express the assertion $(\neg \mathsf{Up}(f)_{[z_1, z_2]})$, we can simply introduce two new variables $x$ and $y$ representing real numbers, and replace $(\neg \mathsf{Up}(f)_{[z_1, z_2]})$ by

$$x > y \,\&\, z_2 \geqslant x \,\&\, y \geqslant z_1 \,\&\, f(y) > f(x).$$

We leave it to the reader to verify that something quite similar to this can be done for the negations of all the relevant predicates.

In further preparation for what follows, we define a variable $x$ appearing in one of our formulae to be a *domain variable* if it appears either in a term $y = f(x)$ or as one of the $z_1$ or $z_2$ in a term like $(f = g + h)_{[z_1,z_2]}$, $\mathsf{Up}(f)_{[z_1,z_2]}$, or $\mathsf{Strict\_Concave}(f)_{[z_1,z_2]}$, etc. We can assume without loss of generality that for each such domain variable and for every function variable $f$ there exists a variable $y$ for which a conjunct $y = f(x)$ appears in our collection. (This $y$ simply represents the value of $f$ on the real value of $x$.) Indeed, if there is no such clause for $f$ and $x$, we can simply introduce a new variable $y$ and add $y = f(x)$ to our collection of conjuncts. It should be obvious to the reader that this addition preserves satisfiability.

Next we make the following observation. Let $x_1, \ldots, x_r$ be the domain variables which appear in our set of conjuncts. If a model $\mathcal{M}$ of these conjuncts exists, then $\mathcal{M}x_1, \ldots, \mathcal{M}x_r$ will be real numbers, of which some may be equal, and where the distinct values on this list will appear in some order along the real axis, and so divide it into subintervals. Each possible ordering of $\mathcal{M}x_1, \ldots, \mathcal{M}x_r$ will correspond to some permutation of $x_1, \ldots, x_r$ which puts $\mathcal{M}x_1, \ldots, \mathcal{M}x_r$ into increasing order, and so to some collection of conditions $x_i < x_{i+1}$ or $x_i = x_{i+1}$, which need to be written for all $i = 1, \ldots, r-1$. Where conditions $x_i = x_{i+1}$ appear, implying that two or more domain variables are equal, we identify all these variables with the first of them, and then also add statements $y = z + 0$ for any variables $y, z$ appearing in conjuncts $y = f(x_i)$, $z = f(x_j)$ involving domain variables that have been identified. It is understood that all possible orders of $\mathcal{M}x_1, \ldots, \mathcal{M}x_r$, and all possible choices of inequalities $x_i < x_{i+1}$ or equalities $x_i = x_{i+1}$ must be considered. If any of these alternatives leads to a set of conjuncts which can be satisfied, then our original set of conjuncts can be satisfied, otherwise not. This observation allows us to focus on each of these orderings separately, and so to consider sets of conjuncts supplied with clauses $x > y$ which determine the relative order of all the domain variables that appear.

Note that this last preparatory step can be expensive, so special care must be taken in implementing it. Nevertheless it clearly can be implemented, and after it is applied we are left with a set of conjuncts satisfying the two following conditions:

(i) Each conjunct in the set must have one of the following forms:

$$\begin{array}{ll} x = y + w, & x = y \cdot w, \\ x > y, & y = f(x), \\ (f = g + h)_{[z_1,z_2]}, & (f > g)_{[x,y]} \\ \mathsf{Up}(f)_{[z_1,z_2]}, & \mathsf{Strict\_Up}(f)_{[z_1,z_2]}, \\ \mathsf{Down}(f)_{[z_1,z_2]}, & \mathsf{Strict\_Down}(f)_{[z_1,z_2]}, \\ \mathsf{Convex}(f)_{[z_1,z_2]}, & \mathsf{Strict\_Convex}(f)_{[z_1,z_2]}, \\ \mathsf{Concave}(f)_{[z_1,z_2]}, & \mathsf{Strict\_Concave}(f)_{[z_1,z_2]}, \end{array} \tag{3.50}$$

where $x, y, w$ stand for numerical variables or constants, $z_1, z_2$ for extended numerical variables (but with $z_1$ not equal to $+\infty$ nor $z_2$ to $-\infty$), and $f, g, h$ for function variables.

(ii) The collection $x_1, \ldots, x_r$ of domain variables present in this set is arranged in a sequence for which a conjunct $x_i < x_{i+1}$ is present for all $i = 1, \ldots, r-1$.

***Removal of function literals***

Having simplified the satisfiability problem for $\mathsf{RMCF}^+$ in the manner just described, we will now show how to reduce it to a solvable satisfiability problem involving real numbers only. We use the following idea. If a set of conjuncts of the form (3.50) has a model $\mathscr{M}$, the domain variables $x_1, \ldots, x_r$ which appear in it will be represented by real numbers $\mathscr{M}x_1, \ldots, \mathscr{M}x_r$ which occur in strictly increasing order. Consider a conjunct like $\mathsf{Up}(f)_{[x,y]}$ or $\mathsf{Convex}(f)_{[x,y]}$ or $(f > g)_{[x,y]}$. For simplicity, at least in the case of the first two conjuncts, we first suppose that neither of $x$ and $y$ is infinite and that the interval $[x, y]$ is nonempty. Then we must have $x = x_j$ and $y = x_k$ for some $j$ and $k$ such that $j < k$. For $f$ to be non-decreasing in the range $[x_j, x_k]$, it is necessary and sufficient that it should be non-decreasing in each of the subranges $[x_i, x_{i+1}]$ for each $i$ from $j$ to $k-1$. For $f$ to be convex in the range $[x_j, x_k]$, it is necessary and sufficient that it should be convex in the overlapping set of ranges $[x_i, x_{i+2}]$ for each $i$ from $j$ to $k-2$ or, if $k = j+1$, convex in $[x_j, x_{j+1}]$. (The proof of this elementary fact is left to the reader.) For $f$ to dominate $g$ (pointwise) in $[x_j, x_k]$, i.e. $f(x) > g(x)$ for each $x$ in $[x_j, x_k]$, it is necessary and sufficient that $f$ dominates $g$ in each of the subintervals $[x_i, x_{i+1}]$, for each $i$ from $j$ to $k-1$. For $f$ to be non-decreasing in $[x_i, x_{i+1}]$ it is necessary that we should have $f(x_i) \leqslant f(x_{i+1})$, and if $f$ is piecewise linear with corners only at the points $x_i$ this is also sufficient. Hence the necessary and sufficient condition for such a non-decreasing function to exist in $[x_j, x_k]$ is

$$f(x_j) \leqslant f(x_{j+1}) \,\&\, \cdots \,\&\, f(x_{k-1}) \leqslant f(x_k).$$

For $f$ to be convex in $[x_i, x_{i+2}]$ it is necessary that the slope of the line connecting the points $(x_i, f(x_i))$ and $(x_{i+1}, f(x_{i+1}))$ be no larger than that of the line connecting the points $(x_i, f(x_i))$ and $(x_{i+2}, f(x_{i+2}))$. This condition can be written algebraically as

$$\frac{f(x_{i+1}) - f(x_i)}{x_{i+1} - x_i} \leqslant \frac{f(x_{i+2}) - f(x_i)}{x_{i+2} - x_i}$$

or, equivalently, as

$$\big(f(x_{i+1}) - f(x_i)\big) \cdot (x_{i+2} - x_i) \leqslant \big(f(x_{i+2}) - f(x_i)\big) \cdot (x_{i+1} - x_i).$$

Conjoining all these conditions gives (when $k > j+1$)

$$\begin{gathered}\big(f(x_{j+1}) - f(x_j)\big) \cdot (x_{j+2} - x_j) \leqslant \big(f(x_{j+2}) - f(x_j)\big) \cdot (x_{j+1} - x_j) \,\& \\ \cdots \\ \&\, \big(f(x_{k-1}) - f(x_{k-2})\big) \cdot (x_k - x_{k-2}) \leqslant \big(f(x_k) - f(x_{k-2})\big) \cdot (x_{k-1} - x_{k-2}).\end{gathered}$$

If $f$ is piecewise linear with corners only at the points $x_i$ this is also sufficient. Hence the conjunction just shown is necessary and sufficient for such a convex function to exist. Plainly the same remarks carry over to the non-increasing and concave cases if we simply reverse the inequalities appearing in the last few conditions displayed.

For $f$ to dominate $g$ in $[x_i, x_{i+1}]$ it is necessary that we should have $f(x_i) > g(x_i)$ and $f(x_{i+1}) > g(x_{i+1})$ and if both $f$ and $g$ are piecewise linear with corners only at the points $x_i$ this is also sufficient. Therefore the necessary and sufficient condition for $f$ to dominate $g$ in the interval $[x_j, x_k]$ is

$$f(x_j) > g(x_j) \,\&\cdots\&\, f(x_k) > g(x_k).$$

In the strictly increasing case the necessary conditions become

$$f(x_j) < f(x_{j+1}) \,\&\cdots\&\, f(x_{k-1}) < f(x_k).$$

A piecewise linear function satisfying these conditions is also strictly increasing, so these conditions are those necessary and sufficient for a function with the given values, and strictly increasing over the range $[x_j, x_k]$, to exist. For there to exist a strictly convex function in this range, the conditions

$$\begin{gathered}\big(f(x_{j+1}) - f(x_j)\big) \cdot (x_{j+2} - x_j) < \big(f(x_{j+2}) - f(x_j)\big) \cdot (x_{j+1} - x_j) \,\& \\ \cdots \\ \&\, \big(f(x_{k-1}) - f(x_{k-2})\big) \cdot (x_k - x_{k-2}) < \big(f(x_k) - f(x_{k-2})\big) \cdot (x_{k-1} - x_{k-2})\end{gathered}$$

are necessary. However, a piecewise linear function satisfying these conditions is not yet strictly convex, as the slope of such a function is constant, rather than increasing, in each of its intervals of linearity. But it is easy to correct this, simply by passing to functions which are piecewise quadratic (still with corners only at the points $x_i$), rather than linear. Such functions are determined by their end values $f(x_i)$ and $f(x_{i+1})$ and by one auxiliary value $f(x)$ at any point $x$ interior to $[x_i, x_{i+1}]$. It is convenient to let $x$ be the midpoint $x_i'$ of the interval $[x_i, x_{i+1}]$. Then for $f$ to be convex it is necessary that

$$2 \cdot f\big(x_i'\big) \leqslant f(x_i) + f(x_{i+1}),$$

and for $f$ to be strictly convex it is necessary that

$$2 \cdot f\big(x_i'\big) < f(x_i) + f(x_{i+1}).$$

(Here and below, the same remarks apply, with appropriate changes of sign, to the concave and strictly concave cases also.) If the function $f$ is known to be non-decreasing in the interval $[x_i, x_{i+1}]$ (because $[x_i, x_{i+1}]$ is included in some interval $[x_j, x_k]$ for which a statement $\mathsf{Up}(f)_{[x_j, x_k]}$ appears among our conjuncts), we must also write the conditions

$$f(x_i) \leqslant f\big(x_i'\big) \,\&\, f\big(x_i'\big) \leqslant f(x_{i+1}).$$

Similarly, if $f$ is known to be non-increasing we must write the conditions

$$f(x_i) \geqslant f(x_i') \,\&\, f(x_i') \geqslant f(x_{i+1}).$$

Likewise, if $f$ is known to dominate $g$ in $[x_i, x_{i+1}]$ we must add the condition

$$f(x_i') > g(x_i').$$

Note that if $f$ is known to be non-decreasing and strictly convex (resp. strictly concave) in an interval $[x_i, x_{i+1}]$, the strict inequality

$$f(x_i) < f(x_{i+1})$$

follows, since this is implied by the three known conditions

- $f(x_i) \leqslant f(x_i')$,
- $f(x_i') \leqslant f(x_{i+1})$, and
- $2 \cdot f(x_i') < f(x_i) + f(x_{i+1})$ (resp., $2 \cdot f(x_i') > f(x_i) + f(x_{i+1})$).

Plainly, the strict inequalities

$$f(x_i) > f(x_i') \quad \text{and} \quad f(x_i') > f(x_{i+1})$$

must hold as well. In all such cases we will therefore replace

$$f(x_i) \leqslant f(x_{i+1}), \;\; f(x_i) \leqslant f(x_i'), \;\; f(x_i') \leqslant f(x_{i+1})$$

by

$$f(x_i) < f(x_{i+1}), \; f(x_i) < f(x_i'), \;\; f(x_i') < f(x_{i+1}),$$

respectively, in our set of conjuncts, and similarly for intervals in which $f$ is known to be monotone non-increasing and strictly convex or concave. After these supplementary replacements, we can be sure that $f$ must be strictly monotone in every interval $[x_i, x_{i+1}]$ in which it needs to be both monotone and strictly convex or concave.

As already remarked, to model correctly conjuncts of the types Strict_Convex and Strict_Concave in the whole finite range $[x_1, x_r]$, we add a very small quadratic polynomial of the form

$$c_i \cdot (x - x_i) \cdot (x_{i+1} - x)$$

vanishing at the two endpoints of the interval $[x_i, x_{i+1}]$ to the linear function we initially have in each such interval at which strict concavity or convexity is required. The small constant $c_i$ should be chosen to be negative if strict convexity is required, but positive if strict concavity is required. Since this sign will always be the same as that of the difference

$$d_i = 2 \cdot f(x_i') - f(x_i) - f(x_{i+1}),$$

we can always take $c_i = \epsilon \cdot d_i$, where $\epsilon$ is any sufficiently small positive constant. Note that this will never spoil either the monotonicity or strict monotonicity of $f$ in the interval affected, since if $\epsilon$ is small enough strict monotonicity will never be affected, while the adjustments described in the preceding paragraph ensure that strict monotonicity rather than simple monotonicity will be known in every interval in which strict convexity or concavity is also required. Likewise, domination of $g$ by $f$ is not spoiled either, since $\epsilon$ can be taken small enough to maintain $g$ and $f$ separated in the interval affected.

It follows that the simple, purely algebraic inequalities on the points $x_1, \ldots, x_r$, the intermediate midpoints $x'_1, \ldots, x'_{r-1}$, and the corresponding function values $f(x_1), \ldots, f(x_r)$ and $f(x'_1), \ldots, f(x'_{r-1})$ derived in the two preceding paragraphs are both necessary and sufficient for the existence of a continuous function satisfying all the monotonicity and convexity conditions from which they were derived, at least in the finite interval $[x_1, x_r]$. We shall now extend this result to the two infinite end-intervals $[-\infty, x_1]$ and $[x_r, +\infty]$, thereby deriving a set of purely algebraic conditions fully equivalent to the initially given monotonicity and convexity conditions. It will then follow immediately that replacing the monotonicity and convexity conditions by the algebraic conditions derived from them replaces our initial set of conjuncts by an equisatisfiable set.

Of the two infinite end-intervals, first consider $[x_r, +\infty]$. Choose the two auxiliary points $x_{r+1}$ and $x_{r+2}$ in this interval, satisfying the inequalities

$$x_r < x_{r+1} \quad \text{and} \quad x_{r+1} < x_{r+2}.$$

Then we can write monotonicity and convexity conditions as above for the values $f(x_{r-1})$, $f(x_r)$, $f(x_{r+1})$, and $f(x_{r+2})$. As previously, if $f$ is both monotone non-decreasing and strictly concave or convex in $[x_r, +\infty]$, it follows that $f(x_r) < f(x_{r+1})$ and $f(x_{r+1}) < f(x_{r+2})$, so we replace the monotonicity inequalities $f(x_r) \leqslant f(x_{r+1})$ and $f(x_{r+1}) \leqslant f(x_{r+2})$ by their strict versions in this case. Then we can take $f$ to be piecewise linear with corners at the points $x_r$, $x_{r+1}$, and $x_{r+2}$, extending $f$ to the infinite range $[x_{r+2}, +\infty]$ with the same slope that it has on the interval $[x_{r+1}, x_{r+2}]$. This definition satisfies all the monotonicity and convexity conditions already present, except for that of strict convexity (or concavity) in the intervals $[x_r, x_{r+1}]$, $[x_{r+1}, x_{r+2}]$, and $[x_{r+2}, +\infty]$, if this is required. But, as in the cases considered above, these strict conditions can be forced in $[x_r, x_{r+1}]$ and $[x_{r+1}, x_{r+2}]$ by adding a sufficiently small quadratic term, whereas in the interval $[x_{r+2}, +\infty]$ we add the decaying exponential

$$\epsilon d_r \cdot \big(\mathsf{exp}(-x_{r+2}) - \mathsf{exp}(-x)\big)$$

instead, where $d_r = 2 \cdot f(x_{r+1}) - f(x_r) - f(x_{r+2})$ and, as before, $\epsilon$ is an extremely small positive number. This has the same convexity properties as the quadratic term seen above, and, for $\epsilon$ sufficiently small, is also without effect on the monotonicity properties of every strictly monotone linear function.

We leave it to the reader to verify that the same argument applies to the second infinite end-interval $[-\infty, x_1]$, but by introducing two auxiliary points $x_{-1}, x_0$ in this interval, which satisfy the inequalities $x_{-1} < x_0$ and $x_0 < x_1$. It follows that the conditions on the points $x_{-1}, x_0, x_1, \ldots, x_r, x_{r+1}, x_{r+2}$, the intermediate midpoints $x'_1, \ldots, x'_{r-1}$, and function values $f(x_j)$ and $f(x'_i)$, for $j = -1, 0, \ldots, r+1, r+2$ and $i = 1, \ldots, r-1$, that we have stated are necessary and sufficient for the existence of a continuous function having these values at the stated points and all the monotonicity and convexity properties from which these conditions were derived.

Since all the piecewise quadratic and exponential functions $f$ of which we make use are determined linearly by their values $y = f(x)$ at points $x$ which appear explicitly in our algorithm, any condition of the form $(f = g + h)_{[z_1, z_2]}$ which appears in our initial collection of conjuncts can be replaced by writing the corresponding conditions $f(x) = g(x) + h(x)$ for all of the domain variables appearing in these conjuncts.

We now summarize the results obtained in the last few paragraphs, putting them into an obviously programmable form.

Let a collection of conjuncts of the form (3.50) with domain variables $x_1, \ldots, x_r$ be given, and suppose that these satisfy the conditions (i) and (ii) found in the paragraph containing (3.50). Introduce additional variables $x'_i$ satisfying $x'_i = (x_i + x_{i+1})/2$, for each $i = 1, \ldots, r-1$, and also $x'_r, x'_{r+1}, x'_0$ and $x'_{-1}$ satisfying

$$x'_r = x_r + 1, \qquad x'_{r+1} = x_r + 2, \qquad x'_0 = x_1 - 1, \qquad x'_{-1} = x_1 - 2.$$

For each variable $x_j$ and $x'_j$ in this extended set, and each function symbol $f$ appearing in the set (3.50) of conjuncts for which there exists no conjunct of the form $y^f_j = f(x_j)$ or $y'^f_j = f(x'_j)$, introduce a new variable to play the role of $y^f_j$ or $y'^f_j$, along with the missing conjunct. Then replace all the conjuncts appearing in lines 3 through 7 of (3.50) in the following ways:

(a) Replace each conjunct $(f = g + h)_{[z_1, z_2]}$ by the conditions $y^f_j = y^g_j + y^h_j$ and $y'^f_j = y'^g_j + y'^h_j$, for all $x_j$ and $x'_j$ belonging to the finite interval $[z_1, z_2]$. (A slight adaptation of this formulation, which we leave to the reader to work out, is needed in the case of the two infinite end-intervals $[-\infty, x_1]$ and $[x_r, +\infty]$.)

(b) Replace each conjunct $(f > g)_{[x,y]}$ by the conditions $y^f_j > y^g_j$ and $y'^f_j > y'^g_j$, for all $x_j$ and $x'_j$ belonging to the interval $[x, y]$. (We recall that in this case the interval $[x, y]$ is restricted to be finite.)

(c) Replace each conjunct $\mathsf{Up}(f)_{[z_1,z_2]}$ (resp. $\mathsf{Strict\_Up}(f)_{[z_1,z_2]}$) by the conditions $y^f_j \leqslant y'^f_j$ and $y'^f_j \leqslant y^f_{j+1}$ (resp. $y_j{}^f < y'^f_j$ and $y'^f_j < y^f_{j+1}$), for all subintervals $[x_j, x_{j+1}]$ of the finite interval $[z_1, z_2]$. (A slight adaptation of this formulation, which we leave to the reader to work out, is needed in the case of the two infinite end-intervals $[-\infty, x_1]$ and $[x_r, +\infty]$.)

(d) Replace each conjunct $\mathsf{Down}(f)_{[z_1,z_2]}$ (resp. $\mathsf{Strict\_Down}(f)_{[z_1,z_2]}$) by the conditions $y^f_j \geqslant y'^f_j$ and $y'^f_j \geqslant y^f_{j+1}$ (resp. $y^f_j > y'^f_j$ and $y'^f_j > y^f_{j+1}$), for all subintervals $[x_j, x_{j+1}]$ of the finite interval $[z_1, z_2]$. (A slight adaptation of this formulation, which we leave to the reader to work out, is needed in the case of the two infinite end-intervals $[-\infty, x_1]$ and $[x_r, +\infty]$.)

(e) Replace each conjunct $\mathsf{Convex}(f)_{[z_1,z_2]}$ (resp. $\mathsf{Strict\_Convex}(f)_{[z_1,z_2]}$) by the conditions

$$\left(y^f_{i+1} - y^f_i\right) \cdot (x_{i+2} - x_i) \leqslant \left(y^f_{i+2} - y^f_i\right) \cdot (x_{i+1} - x_i)$$

and

$$2 \cdot y'^f_i \leqslant y^f_i + y^f_{i+1}$$

(resp. the same conditions, but with the inequality signs $\leqslant$ changed to strict inequality signs '<'), the first replacement being made for each subinterval $[x_i, x_{i+2}]$ of the finite interval $[z_1, z_2]$, and the second for each subinterval $[x_i, x_{i+1}]$ of the interval $[z_1, z_2]$. (This formulation must be adapted in the manner sketched previously to the cases of the two infinite end-intervals $[-\infty, x_1]$ and $[x_r, +\infty]$. We leave to the reader to formulate the required details.) Moreover, if a subinterval $[x_i, x_{i+1}]$ of a $[z_1, z_2]$ for which strict convexity is asserted is also one to which the predicate $\mathsf{Up}(f)_{[x_i,x_{i+1}]}$ or $\mathsf{Down}(f)_{[x_i,x_{i+1}]}$ applies in virtue of a replacement (c) or (d), change the unstrict inequalities replacing these latter predicates to strict inequalities.

(f) Replace each conjunct $\mathsf{Concave}(f)_{[z_1,z_2]}$ (resp. $\mathsf{Strict\_Concave}(f)_{[z_1,z_2]}$) by the conditions

$$\left(y^f_{i+1} - y^f_i\right) \cdot (x_{i+2} - x_i) \geqslant \left(y^f_{i+2} - y^f_i\right) \cdot (x_{i+1} - x_i)$$

and

$$2 \cdot y'^f_i \geqslant y^f_i + y^f_{i+1}$$

(resp. the same conditions, but with the inequality signs $\geqslant$ changed to strict inequality signs '>'), the first replacement being made for each subinterval $[x_i, x_{i+2}]$ of the interval $[z_1, z_2]$, and the second for each subinterval $[x_i, x_{i+1}]$ of the interval $[z_1, z_2]$. (This formulation must be adapted in the manner sketched previously to the cases of the two infinite end-intervals $[-\infty, x_1]$ and $[x_r, +\infty]$. We leave to the reader to formulate the required details.) Moreover, if a subinterval $[x_j, x_{j+1}]$ of a $[z_1, z_2]$ for which strict convexity is asserted is also one to which the predicate $\mathsf{Up}(f)_{[x_i,x_{i+1}]}$ or $\mathsf{Down}(f)_{[x_i,x_{i+1}]}$ applies in virtue of a replacement (c) or (d), change the unstrict inequalities replacing these latter predicates to strict inequalities.

These replacements convert our original set (3.50) of conjuncts into an equisatisfiable set of purely algebraic conditions.

To conclude our work we need an algorithm capable of determining whether the set of algebraic conditions (all of which are either linear or quadratic) to which the foregoing algorithm reduces our original set of conjuncts is satisfiable or unsatisfiable. Since this problem is a special case of the decision algorithm for Tarski's quantified algebraic language of real numbers [Tar51], such an algorithm certainly exists. This observation completes our proof that the language $\mathsf{RMCF}^+$ has a decidable satisfiability problem.

**A Final Example** To make the foregoing considerations somewhat more vivid, consider the way in which the proof of the third sample proposition listed above results from our algorithm, which can just as easily be used to prove it in the following generalized form.

*Let $f$ and $g$ be two real functions which take the same values at the endpoints of a closed interval $[a,b]$. Assume also that $f$ is strictly convex in $[a,b]$ and that $g$ is concave in $[a,b]$. Then $f(c) < g(c)$ holds at each point $c$ interior to the interval $[a,b]$.*

This can be formalized as follows:

$$\big(\mathsf{Strict\_Convex}(f)_{[x_1,x_2]} \;\&\; \mathsf{Concave}(g)_{[x_1,x_2]} \;\&\; f(x_1) = g(x_1)$$
$$\& \; f(x_2) = g(x_2) \;\&\; x_2 > x \;\&\; x > x_1\big) \rightarrow \big(g(x) > f(x)\big).$$

In this case the domain variables are $x_1, x_2$, and $x$, and it is clear that the only order in which they need to be considered is $x_1, x, x_2$. The negation of our theorem is then the conjunction of

$$\mathsf{Strict\_Convex}(f)_{[x_1,x_2]} \;\&\; \mathsf{Concave}(g)_{[x_1,x_2]}$$
$$\& \; f(x_1) = g(x_1) \;\&\; f(x_2) = g(x_2) \;\&\; f(x) \geqslant g(x).$$

The rules stated above replace the first two conjuncts by the algebraic conditions

$$\big(f(x) - f(x_1)\big) \cdot (x_2 - x_1) < \big(f(x_2) - f(x_1)\big) \cdot (x - x_1)$$

and

$$\big(g(x) - g(x_1)\big) \cdot (x_2 - x_1) \geqslant \big(g(x_2) - g(x_1)\big) \cdot (x - x_1).$$

The other algebraic conditions generated are not needed; these two conditions, together with the facts $f(x_1) = g(x_1)$ and $f(x_2) = g(x_2)$ plainly imply that $f(x) < g(x)$, which is inconsistent with $f(x) \geqslant g(x)$, an inconsistency which the Tarski algorithm alluded to above will detect.

## 3.12 The Resolution Method for Pure Predicate-Calculus Proving

Since all the set-theoretic concepts which we use can be expressed within the predicate calculus by adding predicate symbols and axioms, without any new rules of inference being needed, all the proofs in which we are interested can in principle be given without leaving this calculus. This observation has focussed attention on techniques for automatic discovery of predicate proofs. A very extensive literature concerning this built up over the past four decades. This section will explain some of the principal techniques used for this, even though (for reasons that will be set forth at the end of the section) the authors believe that the size of the collections of formulae which such techniques need to explore prevents them from contributing more than marginally to a verifier of the kind in which we are interested.

The standard predicate-calculus proof-search technique begins by putting all of the formulae of a collection $C$ of predicate statements to be tested for satisfiability first into prenex, and then into Skolem, normal form. All of the formulae in $C$ then have the form

$$(\forall x_1, x_2, \ldots, x_n \mid P),$$

where $P$ contains no quantifiers. Propositional calculus rules can then be used to rewrite the 'matrix' $P$ of this formula as a conjunction of disjunctions, each disjunction containing only atomic formulae, some of them possibly negated. We can then use the predicate rule

$$(\forall x_1, x_2, \ldots, x_n \mid P \,\&\, Q) \leftrightarrow \big((\forall x_1, x_2, \ldots, x_n \mid P) \,\&\, (\forall x_1, x_2, \ldots, x_n \mid Q)\big)$$

to break up the conjunctions, thereby reducing $C$ to an equisatisfiable set consisting only of formulae of the form

$$(\forall x_1, x_2, \ldots, x_n \mid A_1 \vee \cdots \vee A_k),$$

where each $A_j$ is an atomic formula built from the predicate and function symbols (including constants) which appear in $C$, or possibly the negative of such an atomic formula. It is this standardized *conjunctive normal form* input on which predicate-proof searches then concentrate.

Herbrand's theorem tells us that such a collection $C$ is unsatisfiable if and only if a propositional contradiction can be derived by substituting elements $e$ of the Herbrand universe for the variables of the resulting formulae in all possible ways. These elements are all the terms that can be formed using the constants and function symbols which appear in the formulae of $C$ (one initial constant being added if no such constant is initially present in $C$). But if one tries to base a search technique directly on this observation, the problem of the exponential growth of the Herbrand universe with the length of the terms allowed arises immediately. For example, even if $C$ contains only one constant d and two monadic function symbols $f$ and $g$, the collection of possible Herbrand terms includes all the combinations

$$f(f(g(f(g(g(\cdots(\mathsf{d})\cdots)))))),$$

whose number clearly grows exponentially with their allowed length.

Some more efficient way of searching the Herbrand universe is therefore vital. The input formulae themselves must somehow be made to guide the search. A general technique for accomplishing this, the so-called *resolution method*, was introduced by J. Alan Robinson in 1965 in his well-known paper [Rob65]. We can best explain how this works by stepping back for a moment from the predicate to the simpler propositional calculus.

### 3.12.1 Resolution in the Propositional Calculus

Suppose then that we are given a collection $C$ of formulae $F$ of the propositional calculus, each such $F$ being a disjunction of propositional symbols, some possibly negated. The resolution algorithm works on such sets by repeatedly finding pairs of formulae $F_1$, $F_2$ which have not yet been examined and which both contain some common atom $A$, but with opposite sign, and so have forms like

$$A \vee G_1 \quad \text{and} \quad (\neg A) \vee G_2$$

where $G_1$ and $G_2$ are subdisjunctions, and deducing the formula

$$G_1 \vee G_2$$

from them (this is an instance of the tautology $((A \rightarrow B) \& (\neg A \rightarrow D)) \rightarrow (B \vee D)$).

If an empty proposition can be deduced in this way, then the original collection $C$ of propositions is clearly unsatisfiable, since the last resolution step must involve two directly opposed propositions $A$, $\neg A$. We will show that, conversely, if the original collection $C$ of propositions is unsatisfiable, then an empty proposition can be deduced by resolution. Thus the ability to deduce an empty proposition via some sequence of resolution steps is necessary and sufficient for our original collection $C$ of propositions to be unsatisfiable.

To establish this claim, we proceed by induction on the total length, in characters, of all the propositions in $C$. So suppose that $C$ is unsatisfiable and that no empty proposition can be deduced from $C$ by resolution, but that for every unsatisfiable collection $C'$ of propositions of smaller total length there must exist a sequence of resolution steps which produces an empty proposition from $C'$.

Choose some propositional variable $A$ that occurs in $C$. Clearly $C$ has no model in which $A$ has the truth value true, so if we drop all the statements of $C$ in which $A$ occurs non-negated (since these are already satisfied by the choice of true for the truth-value of $A$), and use the tautology $((\neg\text{true}) \vee B) \leftrightarrow B$ to remove $A$ from all the remaining statements of $C$, we get a collection $C'$ of statements, clearly of smaller total length than $C$, which is unsatisfiable. Hence, by inductive assumption, there must exist some sequence of resolution steps which, applied to $C'$, yield the empty proposition. But then the very same sequence $s_1$ of resolutions, applied to the statements of $C'$ but before occurrences of $\neg A$ are removed, will succeed in deducing $\neg A$ by resolution.

In just the same way we can form a collection $C''$ of statements by dropping all the statements of $C$ in which A occurs negated and drop $A$ from the remaining statements. Since $C''$ must also be unsatisfiable, we can argue just as in the preceding paragraph to show that there must exist a deduction-by-resolution sequence $s_2$ from $C$ which produces the single-atom conclusion $A$. Putting $s_1$ and $s_2$ one after another, followed by a resolution step involving the formulae $\neg A$ and $A$, clearly gives a deduction by resolution from $C$ which produces the empty proposition from $C$, verifying our claim.

Suppose that we write the result of a resolution step acting on two formulae $F_1$ and $F_2$ and involving the propositional symbol $A$ as $F_1[A]F_2$. Then our overall sequence of resolution steps can be written as

$$\ldots(F_1[A]F_2)[B](F_3[D]F_4)\ldots,$$

the final result being an empty formula. Since each initial formula $F$ of $C$ occurs in this display only some finite number of times, we can give our sequence of resolutions the following form:

(i) Each of the formulae of $C$ is copied some number of times.
(ii) The resulting formulae, and the results produced from them by resolution steps, are used only once as inputs to further resolution steps.
(iii) An empty proposition results.

## *3.12.2 Resolution and Syntactic Unification in the Predicate Calculus*

In the predicate case, handled in the manner characterized by Herbrand's theorem, each of the resolution steps described above will involve an atomic formula $A$ and its negative $\neg A$. Both of these will be obtained by substituting elements of the Herbrand universe for variables appearing in atomic formulae $A_1$ and $A_2$ that are parts of formulae

$$F_1 = A_1 \vee B_1 \vee \cdots$$

and

$$F_2 = (\neg A_2) \vee B_2 \vee \cdots$$

of $C$. The substitutions applied must clearly make $A_1$ and $A_2$ identical. Robinson's predicate resolution method results from a close inspection of conditions necessary for there to exist a substitution

$$x_1 \hookrightarrow t_1, \ldots, x_n \hookrightarrow t_n$$

of Herbrand $t_j$ terms for the variables $x_1, \ldots, x_n$ appearing in $A_1$ and $A_2$ which does this, i.e. makes the two substituted forms identical.

To see what is involved, note that since such substitutions can never change the predicate symbols $P_1$ and $P_2$ with which the atomic formulae $A_1$ and $A_2$ begin, identity can never be produced if these two predicate symbols differ. More generally, if we walk the syntax trees of $A_1$ and $A_2$ in parallel down from their roots, identity can never result by substitution if we ever encounter a pair of corresponding nodes at which different function symbols or constants $f_1$ and $f_2$ appear. In this case we say that our parallel tree-walks *reveal a conflict*. If this never happens, then, when we reach an end-branch in one or another of these trees, we must find either

(a) a variable $x$ of the first tree matched to a compound term $t$ of the second tree (momentarily, in this section, we call 'compound' any term which is not a variable, even if it is just a constant);
(b) a variable $y$ of the second tree matched to a compound term $t'$ of the first tree;
(c) a variable $x$ of the first tree matched to a variable $y$ of the second tree.

Only in these cases can there exist a substitution for the variables of $A_1$ and $A_2$ which makes the two substituted forms identical. It also follows that (a), (b), and (c) together give us an explicit representation of the most general substitution $S$ (called the *Most General Unifier* of $A_1$ and $A_2$ and written $\mathsf{Mgu}(A_1, A_2)$) for the variables of $A_1$ and $A_2$ which makes the two substituted forms identical. This is obtained simply by collecting all the substitutions

$$x \hookrightarrow t, \dots, y \hookrightarrow t', \dots, x \hookrightarrow y, \dots \tag{3.51}$$

which appear in (a), (b), and (c), respectively, and whose role is to convert each of the pairs $[x, t]$ into an identity $x = t$ after the indicated substitutions have been performed for all variables.

As shown by the pair of formulae

$$P(x, x) \quad \text{and} \quad P\big(f(y), g(y)\big),$$

it is entirely possible that the collection (3.51) should contain multiple substitutions $x \hookrightarrow t_1$, $x \hookrightarrow t_2$ with the same left-hand sides. In this case, we must find further substitutions which make $t_1$ and $t_2$ identical. This is done by walking the syntax trees of $t_1$ and $t_2$ in parallel, and applying the collection process just described, following which we can drop $x \hookrightarrow t_2$ from our collection since the additional substitutions collected make it equivalent to $x \hookrightarrow t_1$. Since this process replaces substitutions $x \hookrightarrow t_2$ with substitutions having smaller right-hand sides it can be continued to completion, eventually either revealing a conflict or giving us a collection (3.51) of substitutions in which each left-hand variable $x$ appears in just one substitution.

However, as the following example shows, one more condition must be satisfied for the presumptive substitution (3.51) to be legal, i.e. to define a pattern of substitutions which allows all the substitutions (3.51) into equalities. Consider the two formulae

$$P\big(x, f(x)\big) \quad \text{and} \quad P\big(f(y), y\big).$$

Applying the procedure just described to these two formulae yields the substitutions

$$x \hookrightarrow f(y), \qquad y \hookrightarrow f(x).$$

The problem here is that there exists a cycle of variables $x, y, x$ such that each appears in the term to be substituted for the previous variable, i.e. $y$ appears in the term to be substituted for $x$ and $x$ in the term to be substituted for $y$. Any such substitution of compound terms $x'$ and $y'$ for $x$ and $y$, respectively, would give rise to identities

$$x' = f(y') \quad \text{and} \quad y' = f(x'),$$

and hence to $x' = f(f(x'))$, which is impossible.

The same argument applies in any case in which the collected substitutions (3.51) allow any cycle of variables such that each appears in the term to be substituted for the previous variable. On the other hand, if there is no such cycle of variables, then we can arrange the collection of all variables appearing in (3.51) in an order such that each variable on the left comes later in order than all the variables appearing on the right, and then progressive application of all these substitutions to the variables appearing on the right clearly reduces all of them to identities. In this case we say that a most general unifier $\mathsf{Mgu}(A_1, A_2)$ exists for the two atomic formulae $A_1, A_2$; otherwise we say that *unification fails*, either *by conflict* or *by a cycle*.

We can just as easily find the most general substitution which reduces multiple pairs $A_1, A_2,\ B_1, B_2$ to equality simultaneously. An easy way to do this is to introduce an otherwise unused artificial symbol $Y$, and then apply the unification technique just described to the pair of formulae

$$Y(A_1, B_1, \ldots) \quad \text{and} \quad Y(A_2, B_2, \ldots).$$

Clearly a substitution makes these two formulae identical if and only if it reduces all the pairs $A_1, A_2,\ B_1, B_2$ to equality simultaneously.

For use in the next section we will need a somewhat more precise statement concerning the relationship between the most general unifier of two sets of atoms or compound terms, and the other substitutions which unify these same atoms/terms. In deriving this statement it will be convenient to write

$$\mathsf{Mgu}\big([t_1, \ldots, t_n], [t_1', \ldots, t_n']\big) \tag{3.52}$$

for the most general simultaneous unifier of all the atoms/terms $t_j$ with the corresponding $t_j'$, and

$$\mathsf{All\_u}\big([t_1, \ldots, t_n], [t_1', \ldots, t_n']\big) \tag{3.53}$$

for the collection of all substitutions which unify all the atoms/terms $t_j$ simultaneously with the corresponding $t_j'$. Using these notations, take any $t_j$, $t_j'$ in the sequences shown. If these are atomic formulae or terms and have distinct initial symbols, unification is impossible. Otherwise if they are atoms/terms and have identical initial symbols, they will unify if and only if their arguments unify; hence we can replace $t_j$ and $t_j'$ by their argument sequences in (3.52) without changing its value. The same argument gives the same conclusion for (3.53).

If no further replacements of the kind just described are possible, then for each pair $t_j, t_j'$ either $t_j$ and $t_j'$ must be identical constants, or at least one of $t_j, t_j'$ must be a variable. We collect all pairs in which both are variables, which the substitutions in which we are interested must convert to identical terms, choose a representative for each of the groups of equivalent variables thereby defined, and, in all other terms/atoms, replace all occurrences of variables having such representative by their representative. Again it is obvious that this transformation of the $t_j$ and $t_j'$ changes neither (3.52) nor (3.53). Once this standardization of variables has been accomplished, we collect all cases in which a given variable $v$ appears as a $t_j$ or $t_j'$ and is mapped to a non-trivial $t'_j$ or $t_j$. All but one of these pairs are removed from the argument sequences of (3.52) and (3.53), and replaced with other pairs implying that each of the remaining terms must be equal to the term retained. Again this is a transformation that changes neither (3.52) nor (3.53).

The step just described may allow the whole sequence of steps that we have described to restart, so we keep iterating till none of the steps we have described are possible. At this point each $t_j$ in (3.52) will be matched either to an identical constant $t'_j$, or one of $t_j$ and $t'_j$ will be a variable that appears only once, while the other is a variable or term. Neither (3.52) nor (3.53) will have changed.

Whenever we have a corresponding pair $t_j, t'_j$ in which one member is a variable, we say that the term *expands* the variable. We shall call variables $x$ which appear somewhere in $t_1, \ldots, t_n, t'_1, \ldots, t'_n$, but do not have representatives and are not matched to non-trivial terms in pairs $t_j, t'_j$ *base variables.* We complete our calculation of Mgu by repeatedly replacing all variables that expand into non-trivial terms $t$ by these terms $t$. Again this transformation changes neither (3.52) nor (3.53). Since we have seen that unification is only possible if there is no cycle of expansions, this process must converge, at which point every remaining variable will either be a base variable, have a base variable as its representative, or be expanded into a term in which only base variables appear. Now let $S$ be a member of the set (3.53) of substitutions, i.e. a substitution which makes each $t_j$ equivalent to its corresponding $t'_j$. If $t_j$ and $t'_j$ are both variables then it is clear that $S$ must substitute the same term for both of them. If one of them, say $t_j$, is a variable and the other $t'_j$ is a term, then it is clear that the term which $S$ substitutes for $t_j$ must be the same as that which results by first substituting $t'_j$ for $t_j$, and then substituting $Sx$ for each base variable $x$ remaining in $t'_j$. Thus, if we let $S_0$ designate the restriction of $S$ to the base variables, it follows that the substitution $S$ (regarded as a mapping of variables into terms) factors as the product $M \circ S_0$, where $M$ is the most general unifier (3.52). We state this observation as a lemma.

**Lemma 3.2** *If two sequences $t_1, \ldots, t_n$ and $t'_1, \ldots, t'_n$ consisting of atomic formulae and/or terms can be unified by a substitution $S$ which makes each $t_j$ identical to its corresponding $t'_j$, then each substitution $S$ having this effect can be written as a product $S = M \circ S_0$, where $M$ is the most general unifier*

$$\mathsf{Mgu}([t_1, \ldots, t_n], [t'_1, \ldots, t'_n]),$$

*and the substitution $S_0$ replaces some of the base variables of $M$ by other variables or non-trivial terms. Conversely, by applying any substitution $S$ of the form $M \circ S_0$ to all of the $t_j$ and $t'_j$ we make each $t_j$ identical to its corresponding $t'_j$.*

The preceding discussion of resolution and unification gives us the following general way of handling the problem of finding a Herbrand contradiction which will show that a collection $C$ of predicate formulae given in our normal form

$$(\forall x_1, x_2, \ldots, x_n \mid A_1 \vee \cdots \vee A_k) \tag{3.54}$$

is unsatisfiable.

(Res-i) Guess, or search for, the pattern in which resolution steps can (or will) occur in a sequence of such steps (for substituted instances of our collection $C$ of formulae) leading to a propositional contradiction.

(Res-ii) The guess (or search) (i) implies that designated atomic formulae $A$ occurring in $C$, perhaps in multiple copies of formulae like (3.54) (but with the quantifiers in (3.54) removed), must unify in the pattern determined by the sequence of resolution steps. Check that this unification is actually possible. If so, the substitutions forced by the required unifications identify a collection of elements in the Herbrand universe which allow the pattern of resolutions found in step (i) to be executed, and thereby show that the set $C$ of predicate statements is unsatisfiable.

We can use the formula

$$(\exists x \mid (\forall y \mid P(x,y))) \to (\forall y \mid (\exists x \mid P(x,y)))$$

as a particularly simple example of the proof method just described. The negative of this implication, rewritten as a pair of clauses in Skolem normal form, is

$$\begin{aligned}&(\forall y \mid P(\mathsf{d}_1, y)),\\ &(\forall x \mid (\neg P(x, \mathsf{d}_2))).\end{aligned} \tag{3.55}$$

The substitutions $x \hookrightarrow \mathsf{d}_1$ and $y \hookrightarrow \mathsf{d}_2$ unify $P(\mathsf{d}_1, y)$ with $\neg P(x, \mathsf{d}_2)$, giving $P(\mathsf{d}_1, \mathsf{d}_2)$ and $\neg P(\mathsf{d}_1, \mathsf{d}_2)$, a clear contradiction which proves the unsatisfiability of (3.55), and so the universal validity of our original formula. Note that if we started with the reverse implication

$$(\forall y \mid (\exists x \mid P(x,y))) \to (\exists x \mid (\forall y \mid P(x,y)))$$

whose Skolemized inverse is

$$\begin{aligned}&(\forall y \mid P(f_1(y), y)),\\ &(\forall x \mid (\neg P(x, f_2(x)))),\end{aligned}$$

we would need to unify $P(f_1(y), y))$ and $P(x, f_2(x)))$, which leads to the (cyclic) impossibility

$$x \hookrightarrow f_1(y), \qquad y \hookrightarrow f_2(x).$$

This shows that the reverse implication is not universally valid.

A great variety of methods which aim to reduce the cost of the combinatorial search implicit in (Res-i) and (Res-ii) above have been published. Some are deterministic pruning schemes, which aim to eliminate whole subtrees of the search tree by showing that none of their descendant searches can succeed. Others are standardization techniques, which eliminate redundant work by performing the necessary searches in an order and manner allowing many redundancies to be eliminated, perhaps by detecting and bypassing them. Still others are heuristics guided by guesses concerning favourable unifications and sets of statements. These may involve some implicit or explicit notion of the distance separating an intermediate set of resolution steps from the full set needed to demonstrate unsatisfiability.

A short summary of some of these methods will be given below. The commonly encountered Horn case, in which each quantifier-stripped formula of the input contains at most one non-negated predicate atom, serves to illustrate some of the issues involved. Since every substituted instance of a Horn formula is also Horn, we can use the observation made in our earlier discussion of Horn sets in the propositional case to establish that only resolutions involving at least one positive unit formula need be considered, and that if the null clause can be deduced it can be deduced using just one of the negative unit formulae, and that only once.

We will use the set of (quantifier-stripped) formulae seen below as an example. Their unsatisfiability expresses the following theorem of elementary group theory: in a group with left inverse and a left identity, each element also has a right inverse. In these formulae, the normal group-theoretic operation $x * y$ is recast in pure predicate form by introducing a predicate $P(x, y, z)$ representing the relationship $z = x * y$. Inspection of the formulae displayed below shows that only this predicate is needed. The first two statements, respectively, express the hypotheses 'there is a left inverse' and 'there is a left identity'. The next two statements allow reassociation of products to the left and to the right. The final statement is the negative of the desired conclusion: 'there is an element a with no right inverse'.

$$P\big(i(x), x, \mathsf{e}\big)$$

$$P(\mathsf{e}, x, x)$$

$$\big(\neg P(x, y, u)\big) \vee \big(\neg P(y, z, v)\big) \vee \big(\neg P(u, z, w)\big) \vee P(x, v, w)$$

$$\big(\neg P(x, y, u)\big) \vee \big(\neg P(y, z, v)\big) \vee \big(\neg P(x, v, w)\big) \vee P(u, z, x)$$

$$\neg P(\mathsf{a}, x, \mathsf{e})$$

Since the set $C$ of formulae shown is evidently Horn, we can (in accordance with our earlier discussion of Horn sets) regard the two first formulae as 'inputs', the last formula as a 'goal', and the two remaining formulae as 'multiplication rules' which allow triples of inputs to be combined (if the simultaneous unifications required for this are possible) to produce new unit-formula inputs. We must then aim to find a sequence of such multiplications which reaches the negative of our 'goal' formula. This is a path-finding problem resembling others studied in the artificial intelligence literature. It is easily organized for efficiency in the following way. At any given moment a collection $Uc$ of positive unit formulae will be available. We form all triples of these formulae which can be combined using the two available 'multiplication rules' and generate new positive unit formulae. This step is repeated until either our goal formula is reached or the resulting computation becomes infeasible.

This way of looking at things reveals a (deep) pitfall that can affect resolution searches, even in particularly favourable Horn cases like the one under consideration. Since each of our two 'multiplication rules' allows the available inputs to be combined in up to three possible ways, each cycle of 'multiplication' can in the worst conceivable case increase the number $n$ of available atomic formulae to as much as $2n^3 + n$. Even starting from $n = 2$ this iteration increases very rapidly: 2; 18; 11,682; 3,188,464,624,818; ... Unless this exponential increase in the size of our search space is strongly limited by the failure of most of the unifications required by the 'multiplication' operations considered, we could hardly expect to search more than four levels deep without using some other idea to prune our search very drastically.

Deduction succeeds in the example shown above, in part because a quite 'shallow' proof is possible. This is a proof involving only two successive multiplications. Even without additional search optimizations, the proof is found after 75 unification attempts, of which seven successfully generate new atomic formulae. Two, rather than 16, formulae are added to the list of available atoms at the end of the first cycle of multiplication, so the branching factor is not nearly as bad as is indicated by the worst-case estimate given above, making it reasonable to estimate that proofs as much as six levels deep may be within reach of the resolution method in the pure Horn-clause case. The proof found is

$$
\begin{aligned}
P(i(i(X)), \mathsf{e}, X) \ &\text{from: } [P(i(X), X, \mathsf{e}), P(i(X), X, \mathsf{e}), P(\mathsf{e}, X, X)] \\
&\text{using: } [P(X, Y, U), P(Y, Z, V), P(U, Z, W), P(X, V, W)] \\
P(X, i(X), \mathsf{e}) \ &\text{from: } [P(i(i(X)), \mathsf{e}, X), P(\mathsf{e}, X, X), P(i(X), X, \mathsf{e})] \\
&\text{using: } [P(X, Y, U), P(Y, Z, V), P(X, V, W), P(U, Z, W)]
\end{aligned}
$$

The following formulae are generated but not used in the proof found:

$$
\begin{aligned}
&P(\mathsf{e}, \mathsf{e}, \mathsf{e}), \quad P(i(\mathsf{e}), X, X), \quad P(i(\mathsf{e}), \mathsf{e}, \mathsf{e}), \quad P(i(i(i(X))), X, \mathsf{e}), \\
&P(i(i(i(\mathsf{e}))), \mathsf{e}, \mathsf{e}), \quad P(i(i(\mathsf{e})), X, X), \quad P(i(i(\mathsf{e})), \mathsf{e}, \mathsf{e}), \\
&P(i(i(i(i(X)))), \mathsf{e}, X), \ P(i(i(i(\mathsf{e}))), X, X).
\end{aligned}
$$

Note that a few of these formulae are special cases of others or of input formulae, and so could be omitted. For example, $P(\mathsf{e}, \mathsf{e}, \mathsf{e})$ is a special case of $P(\mathsf{e}, X, X)$, and $P(i(\mathsf{e}), \mathsf{e}, \mathsf{e})$ is a special case of $P(i(\mathsf{e}), X, X)$.

Examination of the above list of useless atomic formulae reveals that some of them are *subsumed* by, i.e. are special cases of others, and hence visibly unnecessary. For example, $P(\mathsf{e}, \mathsf{e}, \mathsf{e})$ is a special case of $P(\mathsf{e}, X, X)$, and $P(i(i(\mathsf{e})), \mathsf{e}, \mathsf{e})$ is a special case of $P(i(i(\mathsf{e})), X, X)$. The unification procedure can be used to test for and eliminate these redundancies. If this is done, the number of unifications attempted in the preceding example falls to 87, and only the following four unneeded atomic formulae are generated:

$$
\begin{aligned}
&P(i(\mathsf{e}), X, X), \quad P(i(i(i(X))), X, \mathsf{e}), \ P(i(i(\mathsf{e})), X, X), \\
&P(i(i(i(i(X)))), \mathsf{e}, X), \ P(i(i(i(\mathsf{e}))), X, X).
\end{aligned}
$$

The following is a second Horn example (taken, like the example above, from [CL73, p. 160]).

$$D(x, x)$$
$$L(\mathsf{m}, \mathsf{a})$$
$$(\neg P(x)) \vee D(g(x), x)$$
$$(\neg P(x)) \vee L(\mathsf{m}, g(x))$$
$$(\neg P(x)) \vee L(g(x), x)$$
$$(\neg D(x, \mathsf{a})) \vee P(x)$$
$$(\neg D(x, y)) \vee (\neg D(y, z)) \vee D(x, z)$$
$$(\neg L(\mathsf{m}, x)) \vee (\neg L(x, \mathsf{a})) \vee D(f(x), x)$$
$$(\neg L(\mathsf{m}, x)) \vee (\neg L(x, \mathsf{a})) \vee (\neg P(f(x))) \vee Q$$
$$\neg Q$$

Here we have two inputs, seven multiplication rules (of these, four involve just one input, two involve two inputs each, and one involves three inputs), and one target, which in this case is a disjunction of three atoms rather than a single atom.

Deduction succeeds in this case after five levels of multiplication, involving 123 unification attempts of which 17 generate new atomic formulae, eight being used in the proof found, which is

| | | |
|---|---|---|
| $P(\mathsf{a})$ | from: | $[D(X, X)]$ |
| | using: | $[D(X, \mathsf{a}), P(X)]$ |
| $D(g(\mathsf{a}), \mathsf{a})$ | from: | $[P(\mathsf{a})]$ |
| | using: | $[P(X), D(g(X), X)]$ |
| $L(\mathsf{m}, g(\mathsf{a}))$ | from: | $[P(\mathsf{a})]$ |
| | using: | $[P(X), L(\mathsf{m}, g(X))]$ |
| $L(g(\mathsf{a}), \mathsf{a})$ | from: | $[P(\mathsf{a})]$ |
| | using: | $[P(X), L(g(X), X)]$ |
| $D(f(g(\mathsf{a})), g(\mathsf{a}))$ | from: | $[L(\mathsf{m}, g(\mathsf{a})), L(g(\mathsf{a}), \mathsf{a})]$ |
| | using: | $[L(\mathsf{m}, X), L(X, \mathsf{a}), D(f(X), X)]$ |
| $D(f(g(\mathsf{a})), \mathsf{a})$ | from: | $[D(f(g(\mathsf{a})), g(\mathsf{a})), D(g(\mathsf{a}), \mathsf{a})]$ |
| | using: | $[D(X, Y), D(Y, Z), D(X, Z)]$ |
| $P(f(g(\mathsf{a})))$ | from: | $[D(f(g(\mathsf{a})), \mathsf{a})]$ |
| | using: | $[D(X, \mathsf{a}), P(X)]$ |
| $Q$ | from: | $[L(\mathsf{m}, g(\mathsf{a})), L(g(\mathsf{a}), \mathsf{a}), P(f(g(\mathsf{a})))]$ |
| | using: | $[L(\mathsf{m}, X), L(X, \mathsf{a}), P(f(X)), Q]$ |

No subsumption cases occur during the processing of this example. Here the branching factor is seen to be quite small. The following atomic formulae are generated but not used in the final proof.

$$P(g(\mathsf{a})),\quad D(f(g(\mathsf{a})),g(\mathsf{a})),\quad D(g(g(\mathsf{a})),g(\mathsf{a})),\quad L(\mathsf{m},g(g(\mathsf{a}))),$$
$$L(g(g(\mathsf{a})),g(\mathsf{a})),\quad D(g(g(\mathsf{a})),\mathsf{a}),\quad D(g(f(g(\mathsf{a}))),f(g(\mathsf{a}))),$$
$$L(\mathsf{m},g(f(g(\mathsf{a})))),\ L(g(f(g(\mathsf{a}))),f(g(\mathsf{a}))),\ P(g(g(\mathsf{a}))).$$

In this case the search efficiency can be improved by using a simple heuristic, which attempts to find 'easy' proofs (those involving relatively short formulae) before trying harder ones. As new atomic formulae are generated, we prefer the shorter of the new formulae over the longer by sorting the newly generated formulae into order of increasing string length and adding just one new formula, the shortest, to the collection of inputs used during each cycle of multiplication. With this improvement we find the same proof after 48 unification attempts of which 12 generate new atomic formulae.

Another small group-theoretic example from Chang and Lee shows some of the difficulties that slow or block resolution proofs in more general cases. This states the axioms of group theory in the same ternary form as above, but also introduces a predicate $S(x)$ which asserts that $x$ is an element of a particular subgroup of the group implicit in the axioms. An axiom states that this subgroup is closed under the operation $x * I(y)$, and we are simply required to prove that the inverse of an element $b$ of the subgroup belongs to the subgroup. The input axioms are

$$P(i(x),x,\mathsf{e})$$
$$P(x,i(x),\mathsf{e})$$
$$P(\mathsf{e},x,x)$$
$$P(x,\mathsf{e},x)$$
$$S(\mathsf{b})$$
$$\neg S(i(\mathsf{b}))$$
$$(\neg P(x,y,u)) \vee (\neg P(y,z,v)) \vee (\neg P(u,z,w)) \vee P(x,v,w)$$
$$(\neg P(x,y,u)) \vee (\neg P(y,z,v)) \vee (\neg P(x,v,w)) \vee P(u,z,w)$$
$$(\neg S(x)) \vee (\neg S(y)) \vee (\neg P(x,i(y),z)) \vee S(z).$$

The proof found involves just two steps:

$$S(\mathsf{e}) \quad \text{from: } [S(\mathsf{b}), S(\mathsf{b}), P(X,i(X),\mathsf{e})]$$
$$\text{using: } [S(X), S(Y), P(X,i(Y),Z), S(Z)]$$
$$S(I(\mathsf{b})) \quad \text{from: } [S(\mathsf{e}), S(\mathsf{b}), P(\mathsf{e},X,X)]$$
$$\text{using: } [S(X), S(Y), P(X,i(Y),Z), S(Z)].$$

However, the search required makes many unification attempts and generates many useless formulae having forms like

$$P(\mathsf{e}, X, i(i(i(i(i(i(X)))))))$$
$$P(i(X), X, i(i(i(\mathsf{e}))))$$
$$P(i(i(i(i(\mathsf{e})))), \mathsf{e}, i(\mathsf{e})) \text{ etc.}$$

In this case the 'easy proofs' heuristic considered above greatly improves search efficiency, finding a proof after 139 unification attempts and the generation of 12 atomic formulae.

Next we present a technique that realizes the ideas of (Res-i) and (Res-ii) very directly in non-Horn cases. Before giving the details of this scheme, we need to take notice of a technical point overlooked in the preceding discussion. For resolution to work as claimed, even at the propositional level, duplicate occurrences of propositional symbols must be eliminated. For example, the two statements

$$A \vee A, \qquad (\neg A) \vee (\neg A) \tag{3.56}$$

are clearly contradictory and a null proposition follows immediately by resolution if these are simplified to $A$, $\neg A$. But if we resolve without eliminating duplicates, resolution leads only to $A \vee (\neg A)$ and thence back to the original statements (3.56), and so we can never reach an empty proposition. Both in the purely propositional and the predicate cases, we must remember to eliminate duplicate atomic formulae whenever resolution produces them.

Here is one way in which the steps (Res-i) and (Res-ii) above can be organized.

(a) We begin by guessing the number of times each of our input formulae (3.54) need to be used to generate distinct substituted instances in the refutation by resolution for which we are searching. This creates an initial collection $C$ of formulae $F$ which we strip of quantifiers. Distinct variables are used in each of these formulae, and the set Initial_atoms of all atomic formulae $A$ which they contain is formed. Each such $A$ is associated with the $F$ in $C$ in which it appears, and with the sign (negated or non-negated) with which it appears. The $F$ in $C$ are given some order, which is then extended to a compatible ordering of all the atomic formulae $A$ in these $F$.

(b) A preliminary survey is made of all the pairs $A_1, A_2$ in Initial_atoms, to determine the cases in which $A_1$ and $A_2$ can be unified. These are collected into two maps: can_rev($A_1$) holds all the $A_2$ of sign opposite to $A_1$ with which $A_1$ can unify, and can_same($A_1$) holds all the $A_2$ of the same sign as $A_1$ with which $A_1$ can unify.

(c) Once these maps have been collected we search for a combinatorial pattern representing a successful refutation by resolution. These must have the following properties:

    (c.i) Each atomic formula $A_1$ must be mapped into an element either of can_rev($A_1$) or can_same($A_1$) by a single-valued mapping match($A_1$).

(c.ii) If $A_2 = \mathsf{match}(A_1)$ belongs to $\mathsf{can\_rev}(A_1)$, then we must have $A_1 = \mathsf{match}(A_2)$.

(c.iii) It must be possible to unify all the atomic formulae $A_1$ with the corresponding $\mathsf{match}(A_1)$ simultaneously.

(c.iv) No two formulae $F_1$, $F_2$ in $C$ containing atomic formulae $A_1$, $\mathsf{match}(A_1)$ of opposite sign can be connected by a prior chain of links between matching atomic formulae of opposite signs.

(c.v) The collection of propositions generated from the $F$ in $C$ by identifying $A_1$ and $A_2$ whenever $A_2 = \mathsf{match}(A_1)$ is unsatisfiable.

Review of the conditions (c.i–c.v) shows them to be equivalent to the condition that corresponding substitutions into the formulae of $C$ define a group of resolution steps leading to an empty statement. The matches for which $\mathsf{match}(A_1)$ and $A_1$ have opposite signs correspond to resolution steps involving the atomic formulae $A_1$ and $\mathsf{match}(A_1)$; the matches for which $\mathsf{match}(A_1)$ and $A_1$ are of identical sign correspond to eliminations of duplicate atomic formulae. Condition (c.ii) states that the pairs of atomic formulae $A_1$, $\mathsf{match}(A_1)$ entering into resolution steps are symmetrically related. Condition (c.i) states that all the necessary unifications must be individually possible; (c.iii) states that all must be simultaneously possible. Condition (c.iv) excludes tautologous intermediate formulae containing two identical atoms of opposite sign. Condition (c.v) ensures that the pattern of resolutions chosen can lead to a null formula.

The unifiability check required in step (c.iii) above can be organized in the following way.

(c.iii.i) All the formulae $F$ in $C$ are parsed, and each node in the resulting syntax trees is marked with its associated predicate symbol, function symbol, or variable, and with all its descendant variables.

(c.iii.ii) When two groups of atomic formulae $A_1, A_2, \ldots, A_n$ and $B_1, B_2, \ldots, B_n$ are to be checked for simultaneous unifiability, we collect all the top-level terms $t_1, \ldots, t_m$ and $t'_1, \ldots, t'_m$ from them in order, form two corresponding atomic formulae $Z(t_1, \ldots, t_m)$ and $Z(t'_1, \ldots, t'_m)$ using an auxiliary predicate symbol $Z$, and test these two formulae for unifiability. All of the necessary operations can be managed efficiently using lists and sets of pointers to syntax tree nodes. Topological sorting can be used to check that a purported collection of substitutions leads to no cycles among variables.

To eliminate the repeated examination of failed unification patterns, some of the optimization heuristics that have been used in the many other resolution approaches described in the literature can be worked into the scheme presented above.

## 3.13 Universally Quantified Predicate Sentences Involving Function Symbols of One Argument Only

We shall now use some of the ideas developed in the preceding section to derive an algorithm for determining the satisfiability of sets of pure predicate sentences of the restricted form

$$(\forall x \mid P), \tag{3.57}$$

whose 'matrix' $P$ is a Boolean combination of atomic formulae $A(t_1, t_2, \ldots, t_k)$, where the argument terms $t_j$ must be built from constants and from the universally quantified variable using monadic function symbols only.

$$A(x, f(x), \ldots, f(g(f(h(f(f(x)))))))$$

is an example of such an atomic formula. Note that Skolemization of formulae

$$(\forall y \mid (\exists x_1, x_2, \ldots, x_n \mid Q)), \tag{3.58}$$

where the matrix $Q$ is subject to the same restriction, always leads to formulae of this kind, so that the algorithm we present will also decide the validity of formulae (3.58).

We begin our analysis by transforming $P$ propositionally into a conjunction of disjunctions of atomic formulae, each of which is either negated or non-negated. Since the predicate identity

$$(\forall y \mid R \,\&\, R') \leftrightarrow ((\forall y \mid R) \,\&\, (\forall y \mid R'))$$

can be used to decompose the conjunctions, we can suppose that each of the matrices $P$ in (3.57) is a disjunction of negated and non-negated atomic formulae.

Herbrand's theorem ensures us that (3.57) is satisfiable if and only if no propositional contradiction arises among any of the instances of (3.57) formed by substituting elements of the Herbrand universe $\mathscr{H}$ for the $x$ in (3.57). The appearance of such a contradiction will reflect the pattern in which substituted instances of atomic formulae $A$ and $B$ appearing in the matrices $P$ of such formulae become equal. For two such $A$ and $B$ to be made equal by any substitution they must unify. The discussion of unification developed in the preceding Sect. 3.12.2 tells us that two such atoms $A$ and $B$ (initially transformed to have different variables $x$ and $y$) will only unify in one of the following cases:

(i) They are made equal by replacing one of $x$ and $y$ by the other.
(ii) They are made equal by replacing the variable $x$ by some constant term $t$ and the variable $y$ by some other constant term $t'$.
(iii) They are made equal by replacing the variable $x$ by some term formed from the variable $y$ using the available monadic function symbols, for example replacing $x$ by $f(g(f(h(f(f(y))))))$.
(iv) They are made equal by replacing the variable $y$ by some term formed from the variable $x$ using the available function symbols.

In case (i) the two atomic formulae are equal if written using the same variable $x$. In case (ii) we have $A(t) = B(t')$ for the two constant terms $t$ and $t'$. In case (iii) we have the identity $A(t(y)) = B(y)$ for some term $t(y)$ formed using the available function symbols, and similarly in case (iv) we have $A(x) = B(t(x))$. In the first of these two cases we say that $B$ is *expressible in terms of A*. in the second that $A$ is expressible in terms of $B$. Note that expressibility in this sense is transitive. Moreover, if any $B$ is expressible in terms of two distinct $A_1$ and $A_2$, then there is clearly a substitution which makes $A_1$ and $A_2$ identical, so one of $A_1$ and $A_2$ must be expressible in terms of the other. Thus in each group of atomic formulae related by a chain of expressibility relationships there must be one, which we shall call $A$, in terms of which all the others are expressible, and which is such that $A$ is not expressible in terms of any other atomic formula $B$. We call such $A$ *basic* atomic formulae. Note that given two different basic atomic formulae $A$ and $B$, there can be no substitutions for the variables $x$ and $y$ they contain which makes $A$ and $B$ identical.

We now take the matrices $P$ of all the formulae of our collection, and introduce a new monadic predicate symbol $Q(x)$ for each basic atomic formula $A$ which appears in them. All the other atomic formulae $B$ can then be expressed uniquely in terms of these $Q$, as $Q(t)$, where $t$ is a term formed by applying the available function symbols to the variable $x$ appearing in $B$, or possibly $t$ is a constant term formed by applying these function symbols to a constant. Let $P'$ by the matrix formed by replacing each of the atomic formulae in $P$ by its corresponding $Q$, or, if $A$ is not basic, by the appropriate $Q(t)$. Since each basic atom $A(x)$ in $P$ has a unique corresponding $Q$, it is clear that if the set of formulae (3.57) has a model, so does the set of formulae

$$(\forall x \mid P') \tag{3.59}$$

derived from it in the manner just explained. Suppose conversely that (3.59) has a model $\mathcal{M}$, whose universe we may, by Herbrand's theorem, take to be the Herbrand universe $\mathcal{H}$. For each predicate symbol $Q$ appearing in one of the formulae (3.59), let $Q^{\mathcal{M}}$ be the Boolean function corresponding to it in the model $\mathcal{M}$. If $Q(x)$ has been used to represent a basic atomic formula $A(t_1(x), \ldots, t_k(x))$, define $A^{\mathcal{M}}(x_1, \ldots, x_k)$ to be $Q(x)$ for all tuples $x_1, \ldots, x_k$ of arguments in the Herbrand universe $\mathcal{H}$ which have the form $[t_1(x), \ldots, t_k(x)]$ for some $x$ in $\mathcal{H}$, but to be false for all other argument tuples. Since the tuples $[t_1(x), \ldots, t_k(x)]$ which appear as arguments of different basic atomic formulae in (3.57) must always be different if the predicate symbols $A$ appearing in these formulae are the same (since otherwise some substitution would unify the distinct basic atomic formulae, which is impossible), it follows that this definition of Boolean values is unique. Since no other argument tuples appear in (3.57), it follows that this assignment of Boolean mappings to the predicate symbols appearing in (3.57) gives a model of (3.57). Thus the sets (3.57) and (3.59) of formulae are equisatisfiable. But all of the predicate symbols which appear in (3.59) are monadic, so the satisfiability of (3.59) can be decided by a classical procedure described, e.g., in [Ack54]. It follows at once that the reduction which we have just described, used together with this procedure, decides the satisfiability of sets (3.57) of formulae.

## 3.14 The Knuth–Bendix Equational Method

### 3.14.1 Overview of the Method

The equational method introduced by Donald E. Knuth and Peter B. Bendix in their well-known paper [KB70] offers a general and systematic treatment of the algebraic process of 'simplification'.

It assumes that all the hypotheses to be dealt with are universally quantified equations of the form

$$(\forall x_1, x_2, \ldots, x_n \mid t = t'),$$

and determines whether these entail another such identity $t_0 = t_0'$.

Given a set $C$ of identities $t = t'$ whose implications are to be analyzed, one begins by arranging them in a 'downhill' direction $t \rightsquigarrow t'$, with the 'simpler' side of each identity on the right. The identities will always be used in this direction. One then determines whether these simplifications always lead to a unique ultimate reduction of every term $t$.

For this approach to be possible, some systematic notion of 'expression complexity' is required. Knuth and Bendix define such a complexity measure by adding up the total number of symbols in each expression, possibly with auxiliary assigned 'weights'. Expressions having the same total weight are ordered in a suitable lexicographic way. For this easy notion of complexity to be stable in the presence of substitution for variables, in a manner which guarantees that if *exp* is 'simpler' than *exp*′ then every substituted form of *exp* is 'simpler' than the corresponding substituted form of *exp*′, we also require that the number of occurrences of every variable in $t$ be at least as large as the corresponding number in $t'$. (Thus, systems including identities like $f(x, y, y) = f(x, x, y)$ are out of reach of the Knuth–Bendix method.)

When a clear direction of simplification can be defined in the way explained, we can reduce any expression *exp* to (a possibly non-unique) 'canonical' or 'irreducible' form by repeatedly (and nondeterministically) finding some subexpression $e$ of *exp* which is identical with a substituted version of the left-hand side of some simplification $t \rightsquigarrow t'$, and then replacing $e$ within *exp* by the corresponding substituted version $e'$ of the right-hand side $t'$ of this same simplification. If the irreducible form of each expression turns out to be unique, we will have an easy test for determining whether the equality of two expressions *exp*, *exp*′ is entailed by a collection of identities: reduce both *exp* and *exp*′ to their irreducible forms, and see if these are equal. Thus the essential point is to be able to determine when the irreducible form of every expression *exp* is unique.

Given an expression $e$ which contains another expression $e'$ as a subexpression, we can write $e$ as $a \ldots e' \ldots b$, where $a \ldots$ (resp. $\ldots b$) is the part of $e$ that precedes (resp. follows) its subexpression $e'$. If $\mathbf{s}$ denotes a substitution $x_j \hookrightarrow e_j$ which replaces each of a collection of variables by some expression and $e$ denotes an expression in which these variables appear, we will write '$(e\mathbf{s})$' for the result of replacing all occurrences of each of the variables $x_j$ by the corresponding $e_j$. We temporarily reserve the letter **s** (possibly subscripted) for substitutions of this kind.

We will see that the irreducible form of an expression $e$, i.e. a simplification of $e$ which cannot be simplified further, can only be non-unique when $e$ contains some subexpression *se*, which in turn has a sub-sub-expression *sse*, having the following property:

(i) *se* must have the form $(t\mathbf{s}_1)$, where $t$ is the left-hand side of some simplification $t \rightsquigarrow t'$ and $\mathbf{s}_1$ is a substitution (as above).
(ii) *sse* must have the form $(T\mathbf{s}_2)$, where $T$ is the left-hand side of some simplification $T \rightsquigarrow T'$ and $\mathbf{s}_2$ is also a substitution (as above).
(iii) In this situation we can write $e$ in either of two ways, namely either as $a\ldots(t\mathbf{s}_1)\ldots b$ or as $a\ldots a'\ldots(T\mathbf{s}_2)\ldots b'\ldots b$, and accordingly can simplify it in either of two ways, namely either to

$$a\ldots(t'\mathbf{s}_1)\ldots b \quad \text{or to} \quad a\ldots a'\ldots(T'\mathbf{s}_2)\ldots b'\ldots b.$$

These can only fail to have the same irreducible form if $a'\ldots(T'\mathbf{s}_2)\ldots b'$ and $(t'\mathbf{s}_1)$ can have different irreducible forms.

Now we can note that $(t\mathbf{s}_1)$ (resp. $(T\mathbf{s}_2)$) is a substituted form of the entire left-hand side of the simplification $t \rightsquigarrow t'$ (resp. $T \rightsquigarrow T'$). Hence there can exist an expression $e$ having two different ultimate simplifications only if there are a pair of simplifications $t \rightsquigarrow t'$ and $T \rightsquigarrow T'$ such that

(a) Some subexpression $s$ of $t$ can be 'unified' with $T$ by a pair $\mathbf{s}_1, \mathbf{s}_2$ of substitutions **s** which make $s\mathbf{s}_1$ and $T\mathbf{s}_2$ syntactically identical.
(b) The two simplifications $(t'\mathbf{s}_1)$ and $a'\ldots(T'\mathbf{s}_2)\ldots b'$ of $t$ thereby generated (where $t \equiv a''\ldots s\ldots b''$) have distinct irreducible forms $r_1$ and $r_2$.

In this case the identity $r_1 = r_2$ is plainly a consequence of our initial set of identities since it is obtained by simplifying $(t'\mathbf{s}_1)$ in two different ways. It may be possible to arrange this 'new' identity as a simplification $r_1 \rightsquigarrow r_2$ and add it to our initial set of simplifications, thereby getting an expanded set $E$ of simplifications, in which plainly $r_1$ and $r_2$ have the same simplified form $r_2$. If we are lucky, this expanded set of simplifications will give every expression a unique irreducible form, in which case we say that $E$ has '*attained completion*'. If this is not the case, we can repeat the procedure just described to find a further expansion of $E$, and hope that $E$ attains completion after some finite number of expansion steps.

As this process goes along we must always arrange the equalities $t = t'$ with which we are working as reductions $t \rightsquigarrow t'$, which means that some appropriate way of ordering the terms $e$ appearing in these clauses must always be kept available. In many cases the new equations $r = r'$ generated will fit immediately into the ordering of terms used previously. In such situations the term-ordering used need not be changed. If this is not the case, a new ordering can be adopted at any time (since the role of the ordering is merely subsidiary, i.e. serves only to define the direction of reduction). But when a new ordering is adopted one may well want to examine the existing equations to see if any can be dropped.

## *3.14.2 Details*

### 3.14.2.1 Ordering of Ground Terms

We suppose that a collection $C$ of (implicitly universal) identities $t = t'$ is given, and form the Herbrand universe $\mathscr{H}$ of all terms that can be built from the constants of $C$ using the function symbols which appear in $C$. (As usual, we add one 'priming' constant if none is available in $C$.) Assume that a non-negative integer weight $w(f)$ is associated with each constant $c$ and function symbol $f$, and that all the constants and function symbols have been arranged in some order, so that we can write $f > g$ if $f$ comes later than $g$ in this order. Function symbols of more than one argument can have 0 weight, but we assume that at most one monadic function symbol $f$ can have 0 weight and that all constants have positive weight.

Given this assumption we can define the weight $w(t)$ of a *ground* term (i.e. a term containing no variables, only constants and function symbols) to be the sum of the weights of all its constants and function symbols.

Note that each argument $a$ of a term $t$ of the form $f(a_1, \ldots, a_n)$ must have weight smaller than $w(t)$ unless $f$ is the unique monadic operator $L$ with weight 0, in which case $a$ and $L(a)$ have the same weight.

Using these weights we order the Herbrand universe $\mathscr{H}$ of ground terms $t$ as follows:

**if** $w(t_1) > w(t_2)$ **then** $t_1 > t_2$ (i.e., lighter terms come first)
**elseif** $w(t_1) = w(t_2)$, $t_1 \equiv f(a_1, \ldots, a_n)$, $t_2 \equiv g(b_1, \ldots, b_m)$ and $f > g$ **then** $t_1 > t_2$ (i.e. terms of the same weight are ordered by their principal operator; note that either $n$ or $m$ can be zero, i.e. either $f$ or $g$ can be a constant rather than a function symbol);
**elseif** $w(t_1) = w(t_2)$, $t_1 \equiv f(a_1, \ldots, a_n)$ and $t_2 \equiv f(b_1, \ldots, b_n)$, **then** $t_1 > t_2$ if $(a_1, \ldots, a_n) > (b_1, \ldots, b_n)$ in lexicographic order (i.e. terms of the same weight and principal operator are given the lexicographic order of their argument strings).

This recursive definition assigns a position in order to all ground terms. It is legitimate since in its recursive third case each of the arguments of a term like $t_1 \equiv f(a_1, \ldots, a_n)$ is either of smaller weight than $t_1$, or shorter than $t_1$.

**Lemma 3.3** *The ordering of ground terms just defined is a well-ordering, i.e. there can exist no infinite descending sequence $t_1 > t_2 > t_3 > \cdots$ of ground terms.*

*Proof* Suppose that such an infinite descending chain did exist. Then the weights $w(t_j)$ are also non-increasing, and so would necessarily reach their lower limit at some point. Hence we can assume without loss of generality that all the $t_j$ have the same weight and can assume inductively that this is the smallest weight for which an infinite descending sequence

$$t_1 > t_2 > \cdots$$

can exist. Consider the sequence $f_j$ of leading operators of the terms $t_j$. These must be non-increasing (in our assumed ordering of all function symbols of ground terms), and so must also reach their lower limit, so we can assume without loss of generality that all the $f_j$ are identical. Then the $f_j$ cannot be constants (i.e. parameterless function symbols) since if they were we would have $f_j = t_j$, contradicting $t_1 > t_2 > \cdots$. If they are all function symbols of positive weight, then their argument sequences $(a_1, a_2, \ldots, a_n)$ are sequences of elements of smaller weight descending in lexicographic order, and so by our inductive assumption there cannot be infinitely many of them. It remains to consider the case in which all the $f_j$ are monadic operators $f$ of weight 0, in which case $f$ must be the last operator in the assigned order of operators. In this case, we can write the $t_j$ as $f^{n_j}(b_j)$, where $n_j$ designates the number of successive occurrences of $f$ as the principal operator of $t_j$. Since all the $b_j$ are of equal weight, and $f$ is the last operator in the assigned order of operators, $f^{n_j}(b_j) > f^{n_k}(b_k)$ if $n_j > n_k$. Hence the integers $n_j$ must form a non-increasing sequence, which will therefore reach its lower limit $n$ at some point. In this case, we can assume without loss of generality that all the $n_j$ are equal, so that our sequence of terms has the form $f^n(b_j)$ for some fixed $n$, where all $b_j$ have lead operator different from $f$. Since the $b_j$ must form a decreasing sequence of terms, it follows by what we have already shown that the sequence $b_j$ cannot be infinite, so that we have a contradiction in all cases. □

#### 3.14.2.2 A Substitution-Invariant Partial Ordering of Non-ground Terms

To extend the ordering described above to *non-ground* terms, we give each variable the smallest weight of any constant, and order non-ground terms as follows:

**if** $w(t_1) > w(t_2)$ and each variable occurs at least as often in $t_1$ as it does in $t_2$, then $t_1 > t_2$;

**elseif** $w(t_1) = w(t_2)$ and each variable occurs at least as often in $t_1$ as it does in $t_2$, while $t_1 \equiv f(\ldots)$ and $t_2 \equiv g(\ldots)$ with $f > g$ (in the ordering of operators), then $t_1 > t_2$

**elseif** $t_1 \equiv f(a_1, \ldots, a_n)$ and $t_2 \equiv f(b_1, \ldots, b_n)$, then we order $t_1$ and $t_2$ in the lexicographic order of their argument strings.

**Otherwise** $t_2 > t_1$ (symmetrically), or $t_1$ and $t_2$ are unrelated (which we shall write as $t_1 ? t_2$).

$g(x, y, y)$ and $f(x, y, y)$ give us an example of unrelated terms.

Plainly, if $t_1 > t_2$ and we make a common substitution **s** for the variables that they contain, writing the substituted results as $(t_1\mathbf{s})$ and $(t_2\mathbf{s})$, then $(t_1\mathbf{s}) > (t_2\mathbf{s})$.

**Corollary 3.2** *There can be no infinite descending sequence* $t_1 > t_2 > \cdots$ *of non-ground terms.*

*Proof* Let **s** replace all variables by some constant $c$ of smallest possible weight. Then $(t_1\mathbf{s}) > (t_2\mathbf{s}) > \cdots$ will be an infinite descending chain of ground terms, which is impossible. □

**Lemma 3.4** *If $t_1 > t_2$ and $t$ is obtained from a term $t'$ by replacing one occurrence of $t_1$ by an occurrence of $t_2$, then $t' > t$.*

*Proof* Plainly $w(t') \geqslant w(t)$, and every variable occurs at least as often in $t'$ as in $t$. Also, at every level in its syntax tree, $t'$ has function arguments which are at least as large as those of $t$. □

### 3.14.2.3 Sets of Reductions

A set of identities $t = t'$ is called a *set of reductions* (relative to an ordering of all ground and non-ground terms) if, for each of its members, we have either $t > t'$ or $t' > t$. In this case we order the identities so that the left side is larger, and write the identity $t = t'$ as $t \rightsquigarrow t'$.

We can use the elementary identities of group theory as an example of this notion. These involve just two operators, multiplication and inversion, which for ease of reading we write in their usual infix and postfix forms as $x \star y$ and $x^-$, respectively. The standard elementary identities can be written as simplifications, and then

$$e \star x \rightsquigarrow x; \qquad x^- \star x \rightsquigarrow e; \qquad (x \star y) \star z \rightsquigarrow x \star (y \star z).$$

To order terms formed using these operators, we can use weights $w(e) = 1, w(-) = 0, w(\star) = 0$, and let '$-$' be the last operator. Note that in this ordering of terms $(x \star y) \star z > x \star (y \star z)$ since the leading operators are the same, but $x \star y > x$. That is, 'right-associations are smaller'.

Given a general set of reductions, any term $t$ can be fully reduced (in a non-unique way) by the following procedure;

> *Repeatedly find a subterm of $t$ having the form $(\ell\mathbf{s})$, where $\mathbf{s}$ is a substitution and $\ell \rightsquigarrow r$ is some reduction, and replace this subterm by $(r\mathbf{s})$.*

This process must terminate, since it steadily reduces $t$, in the ordering of terms we have defined.

**Definition 3.3** If every $t$ reduces to a *unique* final form $t^*$, the set of reductions is said to be *complete.*

We write $t \Rrightarrow t'$ if $t$ has a subterm of the form $(\ell\mathbf{s})$ where $\ell \rightsquigarrow r$ is some member of our set of reductions, and $t'$ is obtained by replacing this subterm by $(r\mathbf{s})$.

We write $t \Rrightarrow^* t'$ if some such sequence of subterm reductions leads from $t$ to $t'$.

**Lemma 3.5** (The 'PPW'—'Permanent parting of the ways' Lemma) *A set of reductions is complete iff, given any $t$ and two reductions $t \rightsquigarrow t'$ and $t \rightsquigarrow t''$ of it, there exists some $t^*$ such that $t' \Rrightarrow^* t^*$, $t'' \Rrightarrow^* t^*$.*

*Proof* If a set of reductions is complete, and $t^*$ is the unique full reduction of $t$, where $t \rightsquigarrow t'$ and $t \rightsquigarrow t''$, then clearly $t' \Rrightarrow^* t^*$ and $t'' \Rrightarrow^* t^*$. Conversely, suppose that $t$ can be fully reduced to two different irreducibles $t^*$ and $t^{**}$, so $t \Rrightarrow^* t^*$ and $t \Rrightarrow^* t^{**}$. Let $t$ be a minimal element for which this can happen. Then the first steps of these two different reductions must be different. Hence we must have $t \rightsquigarrow t_1 \Rrightarrow^* t^*$ and $t \rightsquigarrow t_2 \Rrightarrow^* t^{**}$, where $t_1$ and $t_2$ are different. By assumption, $t_1$ and $t_2$ can be reduced to a common element $t_3$, which can then be reduced fully to some $t^{***}$. Thus we have $t_1 \rightsquigarrow t_3 \Rrightarrow^* t^{***}$ and $t_2 \rightsquigarrow t_3 \Rrightarrow^* t^{***}$. One of $t^*$ and $t^{**}$ must be different from $t^{***}$; suppose by symmetry that this is $t^*$. Then $t_1 \Rrightarrow^* t^{***}$, but also $t_1 \Rrightarrow^* t^*$. That is, $t_1$ can be reduced to two different irreducible elements. Since $t_1$ is less than $t$, this must be impossible. □

**Definition 3.4** We write $t \sim t'$ if there is a chain of subterm substitutions $t \equiv t_1 \leftrightsquigarrow t_2 \leftrightsquigarrow t_3 \leftrightsquigarrow \cdots \leftrightsquigarrow t_n \equiv t'$, where each $t_{j+1}$ is obtained from the preceding $t_j$ by replacing some subterm of $t_j$ having the form $(\ell \mathbf{s})$, where $\mathbf{s}$ is a substitution and $\ell \rightsquigarrow r$ is some reduction, by the corresponding $(r\mathbf{s})$, or possibly $t_j$ is obtained from $t_{j+1}$ in this way.

**Lemma 3.6** *A set of reductions is complete iff any two $t \sim t'$ have the same full reduction $t^*$.*

*Proof* If $t$ has two different full reductions $t^*$, $t^{**}$, then plainly $t^* \sim t \sim t^{**}$, while both $t^*$ and $t^{**}$ are their own full reductions. Hence if any two equivalent irreducibles are identical, the set $R$ of reductions is complete. Conversely, let $R$ be complete. Suppose that $n$ is the smallest integer for which there exists a chain $t_1 \leftrightsquigarrow t_2 \leftrightsquigarrow t_3 \leftrightsquigarrow \cdots \leftrightsquigarrow t_n$ for which $t_1$ and $t_n$ have different final reductions. Then irrespective of whether $t_1 \rightsquigarrow t_2$ or $t_2 \rightsquigarrow t_1$ both have the same final reductions. Hence the two ends $t_2$ and $t_n$ of the smaller chain $t_2 \leftrightsquigarrow t_3 \leftrightsquigarrow \cdots \leftrightsquigarrow t_n$ would also have different final reductions, a contradiction which proves our lemma. □

The first lemma stated above implies that if a set of productions is not complete, there exists a 'parting of the ways' $t \rightsquigarrow t_1 \Rrightarrow^* t_1^*$ and $t \rightsquigarrow t_2 \Rrightarrow^* t_2^*$ where $t_1^*$ and $t_2^*$ are fully reduced and different, and where $t_1$ and $t_2$ have no common reduction. We call this a '*permanent parting of the ways*'. In this case the reduction $t \rightsquigarrow t_1$ replaces a subterm $w_1 \equiv (\ell_1 \mathbf{s}_1)$ of $t$ by $(r_1 \mathbf{s}_1)$. The reduction $t \rightsquigarrow t_2$ replaces a subterm $w_2 \equiv (\ell_2 \mathbf{s}_2)$ of $t$ by $(r_2 \mathbf{s}_2)$. The two subterms $w_1$ and $w_2$ cannot be disjoint (or the paths of reduction would be rejoinable). Hence one replaced part, say $w_2 \equiv (\ell_2 \mathbf{s}_2)$, must be a subterm of the other, i.e. of $w_1 \equiv (\ell_1 \mathbf{s}_1)$.

Let $(\ell_1' \mathbf{s}_1)$ be the subterm of $(\ell_1 \mathbf{s}_1)$ that is actually matched by $w_2$, i.e. $(\ell_1' \mathbf{s}_1) \equiv (\ell_2 \mathbf{s}_2)$. We can of course write the two identities $\ell_1 \rightsquigarrow r_1$ and $\ell_2 \rightsquigarrow r_2$ that we are using with disjoint sets of variables. If this is done, then the substitution $\mathbf{s}_1$ on the variables of $\ell_1'$ and the substitution $\mathbf{s}_2$ on the variables of $\ell_2$ can be seen as a common substitution $\mathbf{s}$ on all the variables together, and we have $(\ell_1' \mathbf{s}) \equiv (\ell_2 \mathbf{s})$. That is, $\mathbf{s}$ is a *unification* of $\ell_1'$ and $\ell_2$. Hence, by the analysis of unification given in the preceding Sect. 3.12.2, there is a most general unifier $\mathbf{m}$ such that $(\ell_1' \mathbf{m}) \equiv (\ell_2 \mathbf{m})$, and we can write $\mathbf{s}$ as the product $\mathbf{s} \equiv \mathbf{m} \circ \mathbf{t}$ of $\mathbf{m}$ and some other substitution $\mathbf{t}$.

Let $\ell_1''$ be the result of replacing the subterm $(\ell_1'\mathbf{m})$ of $(\ell_1\mathbf{m})$ by $(\ell_2\mathbf{m})$. Then $(r_1\mathbf{m})$ and $\ell_1''$ are two direct reductions of $(\ell_1\mathbf{m})$, i.e. $(\ell_1\mathbf{m}) \rightsquigarrow (r_1\mathbf{m})$ and $(\ell_1\mathbf{m}) \rightsquigarrow \ell_1''$. These two reductions must themselves be a 'permanent parting of the ways', since if there were further reductions

$$(\ell_1\mathbf{m}) \rightsquigarrow (r_1\mathbf{m}) \Rrightarrow^* s \quad \text{and} \quad (\ell_1\mathbf{m}) \rightsquigarrow \ell_1'' \Rrightarrow^* s,$$

we would also have

$$\big((\ell_1\mathbf{m})\mathbf{t}\big) \rightsquigarrow \big((r_1\mathbf{m})\mathbf{t}\big) \Rrightarrow^* (s\mathbf{t}) \quad \text{and} \quad \big((\ell_1\mathbf{m})\mathbf{t}\big) \rightsquigarrow (\ell_1''\mathbf{t}) \Rrightarrow^* (s\mathbf{t}),$$

implying the existence of reductions $t \rightsquigarrow t_1 \Rrightarrow^*$ (some $t^*$) and $t \rightsquigarrow t_2 \Rrightarrow^*$ (the same $t^*$), and so the two reductions $t \rightsquigarrow t_1$ and $t \rightsquigarrow t_2$ would not be a 'permanent parting of the ways', contrary to assumption. Therefore, if a set $R$ of reductions is not complete, we can find a 'parting of the ways' by unifying the left-hand side of one reduction $\ell_2 \rightsquigarrow r_2$ with a subword of the left-hand side of some other reduction $\ell_1 \rightsquigarrow r_1$, and then converting the resulting identity to an identity of the form $t = t'$, where both $t$ and $t'$ are irreducible. If the new identity $t = t'$ is not simply $t = t$, we call it a *superposition* of the two reductions $\ell_1 \rightsquigarrow r_1$ and $\ell_2 \rightsquigarrow r_2$. As we shall now see, this gives us the key to the Knuth–Bendix procedure.

### *3.14.3 Testing Completeness by Superposition of Reductions: The Knuth–Bendix Completion Process*

We saw in the preceding discussion that if a set of reductions is not complete, there exists a pair of reductions $\ell_1 \rightsquigarrow r_1$, $\ell_2 \rightsquigarrow r_2$, such that we can unify the left-hand side of the second reduction with a subterm of the left-hand side of the first, i.e. find substituted versions of both which allows the left-hand side of the first to be reduced either as a whole or by replacement of a subterm. This yields a pair of versions $t$, $t'$ of the substituted left-hand side known to be equal. We now reduce both $t$ and $t'$ to their irreducible forms $t^*$, $t^{**}$. If these are identical, then nothing new results. But if $t^*$ and $t^{**}$ are not identical (in spite of the fact that their equality is entailed by the other equalities in our set of reductions) and we can arrange them as a reduction $t^* \rightsquigarrow t^{**}$, then we can extend our set of reductions by adding $t^* \rightsquigarrow t^{**}$ to it. Adding $t^* \rightsquigarrow t^{**}$ to our original set of reductions clearly refines our notion of reduction, i.e. a term $t$ which was previously irreducible may now admit of further reductions. The Knuth–Bendix method consists in repeatedly adding all non-trivial superpositions of an existing set $R$ of reductions to $R$, in the hope of eventually reaching a complete set, for which all terms then have a unique canonical form. As we have seen, this would allow us to test two terms to determine whether or not their identity is entailed by our set of reductions just by reducing both of them to the irreducible form and checking these irreducible forms for identity.

### 3.14.4 More Details

When no reorderings of terms become necessary during its operation, the Knuth–Bendix completion process just described is a 'semi-decision algorithm' for determining whether the identity of two terms is entailed by a set of identities. That is, it searches for a completion of the given set of identities, either continuing to search indefinitely and endlessly finding new reductions, or eventually attaining completion. The overall procedure is that implied by the preceding discussion. In more detail, it is as follows.

Suppose that a set $\ell_i \rightsquigarrow r_i$ of reductions is given.

- Repeatedly resolve the left-hand sides of these reductions with subterms of the right-hand sides of these reductions in all possible ways, generating new pairs of irreducible terms $t^*, t^{**}$ known to be equal, in the manner described in the preceding section. Arrange $t^*$ and $t^{**}$ as a reduction $\ell^* \rightsquigarrow r^*$. Add these reductions $\ell^* \rightsquigarrow r^*$ to the set of reductions, using the same weights and operator ordering if possible.
- Change the weights and operator ordering if necessary. (These play only an auxiliary role.)
- Each time a new reduction $\ell^* \rightsquigarrow r^*$ is added, retest every other to see if it is now *subsumed*, and if so drop it from the set of reductions.

**Definition 3.5** A reduction $\ell \rightsquigarrow r$ belonging to a set $C$ of reductions is *subsumed* by the other members of $C$ iff $\ell$ and $r$ are both reducible to a common element by the set $C \setminus \{\ell \rightsquigarrow r\}$ obtained from $C$ by dropping the reduction $\ell \rightsquigarrow r$.

We continue adding new reductions until the resulting set becomes complete, or until whatever conclusion $t = t'$ we wish to test reduces to $t = t$. If this process runs unduly long we stop it.

### 3.14.5 Examples of the Knuth–Bendix Procedure

#### 3.14.5.1 Simple Associativity

First we consider what is almost the simplest possible system, that involving just a single dyadic operation (which we will write in infix form), and just one identity, namely the associative law

$$(x \star y) \star z = x \star (y \star z).$$

All weights, including $w(\star)$, are taken to be 1. The Knuth–Bendix ordering rule then gives

$$(x \star y) \star z > x \star (y \star z)$$

since $(x \star y) > x$, and so our system is seen to consist of the one reduction

$$(x \star y) \star z \rightsquigarrow x \star (y \star z).$$

This makes it clear that, in this system, term reduction consists in using the associative law to move parentheses to the right, so that the irreducible form of a term is its fully right-parenthesized form. This makes it clear that irreducible forms are unique in this simple system, so that our single reduction $R$ is already complete. To verify this using the formal Knuth–Bendix criterion, note that the only way of unifying the left side of $R$ with a subterm of the left side of $R$ (first rewritten using different variables) is to unite $(x \star y) \star z$ with the subword $(u \star v)$ of $(u \star v) \star w$. The unifying substitution converts this second term to $((x \star y) \star z) \star w$, which as we have seen in our general discussion can be reduced in two ways to produce $(x \star (y \star z)) \star w$ and $(x \star y) \star (z \star w)$. But in this case nothing new results since both of these terms have the same right-parenthesized form.

### 3.14.5.2 Minimal Axioms for the Theory of Free Groups

We now examine a more elaborate and interesting example, that of the elementary identities of group theory touched on earlier. These involve just two operators, multiplication and inversion, which for ease of reading we write in their usual infix and postfix forms as $x \star y$ and $x^-$, respectively. As before, we use weights $w(\mathsf{e}) = 1$, $w(-) = 0$, $w(\star) = 0$, and let '−' be the last operator. We begin with identities which state the existence of a left identity and left inverses, along with associativity. These are:

$$\begin{array}{lll} [\text{P1}] & \mathsf{e} \star x & \rightsquigarrow x; \\ [\text{P2}] & x^- \star x & \rightsquigarrow \mathsf{e}; \\ [\text{P3}] & (x \star y) \star z & \rightsquigarrow x \star (y \star z). \end{array}$$

Knuth–Bendix analysis of these identities will show that these initial identities imply that the left identity is also a right identity and that the left inverse is also a right inverse. (The reader may want to improve his/her appreciation of the Knuth–Bendix procedure by working out direct proofs of these facts.) We begin as follows. Superpose [P2] on [P3], getting:

$$[\text{P4}] \qquad x^- \star (x \star z) \rightsquigarrow z.$$

Now superpose [P1] on [P4], getting:

$$[\text{P5}] \qquad \mathsf{e}^- \star z \rightsquigarrow z.$$

Superpose [P2] on [P4], getting $x^{--} \star (x^- \star x) \rightsquigarrow x$, or

$$[\text{P6}] \qquad x^{--} \star \mathsf{e} \rightsquigarrow x.$$

Superpose [P6] on [P3], getting $(x^{--} \star \mathsf{e}) \star z \rightsquigarrow x^{--} \star\star(\mathsf{e} \star z)$, or

$$\text{[P7]} \qquad x^{--} \star z \rightsquigarrow x \star z.$$

Now replace [P6] by

$$\text{[P8]} \qquad x \star \mathsf{e} \rightsquigarrow x.$$

Thus the left identity is a right identity, and [P6] reduces to

$$\text{[P9]} \qquad x^{--} \rightsquigarrow x.$$

Now [P8], [P5] superpose to give

$$\text{[P10]} \qquad \mathsf{e}^{-} \rightsquigarrow \mathsf{e}.$$

Now [P2] and [P9] superpose to $x^{--} \star x^{-} \rightsquigarrow \mathsf{e}$, or

$$\text{[P11]} \qquad x \star x^{-} \rightsquigarrow \mathsf{e}.$$

Thus the left inverse is also a right inverse. Two more derived identities complete the set:

$$\mathsf{e} \star x \rightsquigarrow x; \qquad x \star \mathsf{e} \rightsquigarrow x; \qquad x^{-} \star x \rightsquigarrow \mathsf{e}; \qquad x \star x^{-} \rightsquigarrow \mathsf{e};$$
$$\mathsf{e}^{-} \rightsquigarrow \mathsf{e}; \qquad x^{--} \rightsquigarrow x; \qquad (x \star y) \star z \rightsquigarrow x \star (y \star z);$$
$$x^{-} \star (x \star z) \rightsquigarrow z; \qquad x \star (x^{-} \star z) \rightsquigarrow z;$$
$$(x \star y)^{-} \rightsquigarrow y^{-} \star x^{-}.$$

The normal form of any term in this theory is obtained by expanding it out using $(x \star y)^{-} \rightsquigarrow y^{-} \star x^{-}$ as often as possible, associating to the right, performing as many cancellations $x \star x^{-} \rightsquigarrow \mathsf{e}$, $x^{-} \star x \rightsquigarrow \mathsf{e}$, $x^{--} \rightsquigarrow x$ as possible, and removing $\mathsf{e}$ from all products. This is of course a standard normal form for the elements of free groups.

## References


[Ack54] Ackermann, W.: Solvable Cases of the Decision Problem. North-Holland, Amsterdam (1954)

[Beh22] Behmann, H.: Beiträge zur Algebra der Logik insbesondere zum Entscheidungsproblem. Math. Ann. **86**, 163–220 (1922)

[CCG06] Cantone, D., Cincotti, G., Gallo, G.: Decision algorithms for fragments of real analysis. I. Continuous functions with strict convexity and concavity predicates. J. Symb. Comput. **41**(7), 763–789 (2006)

[CFO89] Cantone, D., Ferro, A., Omodeo, E.G.: Computable Set Theory. International Series of Monographs on Computer Science, vol. 6, p. 347. Clarendon, Oxford (1989)

[CL73] Chang, C.-L., Lee, R.C.-T.: Symbolic Logic and Mechanical Theorem Proving. Computer Science and Applied Mathematics. Academic Press, New York (1973)

[COP01] Cantone, D., Omodeo, E.G., Policriti, A.: Set Theory for Computing. From Decision Procedures to Declarative Programming with Sets. Monographs in Computer Science. Springer, Berlin (2001)

[COSU03] Cantone, D., Omodeo, E.G., Schwartz, J.T., Ursino, P.: Notes from the logbook of a proof-checker's project. In: Dershowitz, N. (ed.) Verification: Theory and Practice (Essays Dedicated to Zohar Manna on the Occasion of His 64th Birthday). LNCS, vol. 2772, pp. 182–207. Springer, Berlin (2003)

[DP60] Davis, M., Putnam, H.: A computational procedure for quantification theory. J. ACM **3**(7), 201–215 (1960)

[Fuc70] Fuchs, L.: Abelian Groups. Academic Press, New York (1970)

[Gur65] Gurevič, Y.: Elementary properties of ordered Abelian groups. Transl. AMS **46**, 165–192 (1965)

[IC94] Ignizio, J.P., Cavalier, T.M.: Linear Programming. International Series in Industrial and Systems Engineering. Prentice Hall, New York (1994)

[KB70] Knuth, D.E., Bendix, P.B.: Simple word problems in universal algebras. In: Leech, J. (ed.) Computational Problems in Abstract Algebra, pp. 263–297. Pergamon, Oxford (1970)

[KK74] Kokorin, A.I., Kopytov, V.M.: Fully Ordered Groups. Wiley, New York (1974)

[Pre30] Presburger, M.: Über die Völlständigkeit eines gewissen Systems der Arithmetik ganzer Zahlen, in welchem die Addition als einzige Operation hervortritt. In: Comptes-rendus du premier Congrès des mathematiciens des Pays Slaves, Warsaw, pp. 92–101 (1930)

[Rob65] Robinson, J.A.: A machine-oriented logic based on the resolution principle. J. ACM **12**(1), 23–41 (1965). Reprinted in Siekmann, J., Wrightson, G.: Automation of Reasoning I and II. Springer (1983)

[Tar51] Tarski, A.: A Decision Method for Elementary Algebra and Geometry. Berkeley University Press, Berkeley (1951)

[Tar56] Tarski, A.: Ordinal Algebras. North-Holland, Amsterdam (1956)

# Chapter 4
# More on the Structure of the Verifier System

In this chapter we describe our verifier and its underlying design in more detail. The chapter falls into two parts: (i) An account of the general syntax and overall structure of proofs acceptable to the verifier. (ii) A listing of the mechanisms actually chosen from the list of candidate inference mechanisms surveyed in the preceding chapter for inclusion in the verifier's initial endowment. We explain the syntax used to invoke each of the verifier's built-in inference mechanisms.[1]

## 4.1 Introduction to the General Syntax and Overall Structure of Proofs

### *4.1.1 The Syntax of Proofs*

The Ref verifier (also known as Referee or as ÆtnaNova), accessible on the Web,[2] is fed script files, called *scenarios*, consisting of successive definitions, theorems, and auxiliary commands, which Ref either certifies as constituting a valid sequence or rejects as defective. In the case of rejection, the verifier attempts to pinpoint the troublesome locations within a scenario, so that errors can be located and repaired. Step timings are produced for all correct proofs, to help the user in spotting places where appropriate modifications could speed up proof processing.

The bulk of the text normally submitted to the verifier consists of theorems and proofs. Some theorems (and their proofs) are enclosed within so-called *theories*, whose external conclusions these internal theorems serve to justify. This lets scenarios be subdivided into modules, which increases readability and supports proof reuse (cf. Sects. 1.4.2.6 and 4.1.4).

[1]For additional information and more detailed information, cf. http://setl.dyndns.org/EtnaNova/login/Ref_user_manual.html.

[2]Cf. http://setl.dyndns.org/EtnaNova/login/.

J.T. Schwartz et al., *Computational Logic and Set Theory*,
DOI 10.1007/978-0-85729-808-9_4, © Springer-Verlag London Limited 2011

The verifier allows input and checking of the text to be verified to be divided into multiple *sessions* (cf. Sect. 4.4).

The following example, which appears early in Ref's main proof scenario to be surveyed in the next chapter (cf. Sect. 5.1), illustrates the syntactic form of Ref proofs:[3]

THEOREM 8*a*: [Members of ordinals are ordinals] $\mathsf{Ord(S)} \,\&\, \mathsf{T} \in \mathsf{S} \to \mathsf{Ord(T)}$.
PROOF:

$\mathsf{Suppose\_not(s,\ t)} \Longrightarrow$ AUTO

-- We proceed by contradiction. If our theorem is false, there is an ordinal s having a member t which is not an ordinal.

$\mathsf{Use\_def(Ord)} \Longrightarrow \mathsf{Stat1} : \neg(\langle\forall x \in t \mid x \subseteq t\rangle \,\&\, \langle\forall x \in t,\ y \in t \mid x \in y \vee y \in x \vee x = y\rangle)$

-- Hence, by definition of ordinal, t must either have a member a not included in t, or a pair b, c of distinct members not related by membership.

$\langle a,\ b,\ c\rangle \hookrightarrow \mathsf{Stat1} \Longrightarrow$ AUTO

-- But since s is an ordinal, it must include its member t, so that the second case is impossible.

$\mathsf{Use\_def(Ord)} \Longrightarrow \mathsf{Stat2} : \langle\forall x \in s \mid x \subseteq s\rangle \,\&$
$\mathsf{Stat3} : \langle\forall x \in s,\ y \in s \mid x \in y \vee y \in x \vee x = y\rangle$
$\langle t\rangle \hookrightarrow \mathsf{Stat2} \Longrightarrow$ AUTO
$\mathsf{Suppose} \Longrightarrow b,\ c \in t \,\&\, \neg(b \in c \vee c \in b \vee b = c)$
$\langle b,\ c\rangle \hookrightarrow \mathsf{Stat3} \Longrightarrow$ AUTO
$\mathsf{Discharge} \Longrightarrow \mathsf{Stat4} : a \not\subseteq t \,\&\, a \in t$

-- Thus we need only consider the first case, in which a is a member but not a subset of t. In this case there plainly exists a d in a but not in t. Plainly a is a member of s, and thus a subset of s; so d is also a member of s.

$\langle d\rangle \hookrightarrow \mathsf{Stat4} \Longrightarrow d \in a \,\&\, d \notin t$
$\langle a\rangle \hookrightarrow \mathsf{Stat2} \Longrightarrow a \subseteq s$
$\mathsf{ELEM} \Longrightarrow d \in s$

-- By definition of ordinal, it follows that d either equals t, is a member of t, or that t is a member of d. But all three of these cases are impossible, since any would imply the existence of a membership cycle. This contradiction proves our theorem.

$\langle d,\ t\rangle \hookrightarrow \mathsf{Stat3} \Longrightarrow d \in t \vee t \in d \vee t = d$
$\langle \mathsf{Stat4}\rangle\, \mathsf{Discharge} \Longrightarrow$ QED

[3] As seen here, we often enclose quantified formulae within '⟨' and '⟩'—instead of within '(' and ')'—to make matching parentheses more visible.

As seen in this example, each theorem owns a label (in the case at hand: '8a'). This label (optionally followed by a comment, as shown above) is followed by a syntactically valid logical formula: the *conclusion* or 'claim' of the theorem. This claim should be terminated by a final period (i.e. '.') and be followed by the theorem's *proof*, which must be introduced by the keyword 'Proof :', and terminated by the reserved symbol 'QED'.

As the above example illustrates, a theorem's proof consists of a sequence of *statements* (also called *inference steps*), each of which consists of a *hint* portion (e.g.: Use_def(Ord), $\langle a, b, c \rangle \hookrightarrow$Stat1, Discharge, ELEM) separated by the sign $\Longrightarrow$ from the *assertion* of the statement. Each assertion must be a syntactically well-formed formula in Ref's set-theoretic language; each hint must reference one of the basic inference mechanisms that Ref provides (see list below), and may also supply this inference mechanism with auxiliary parameters (e.g.: Use_def(Ord), Suppose_not(s, t)), including the context of preceding statements in which it should operate (e.g., $\langle$Stat4$\rangle$Discharge draws a contradiction from the conjunction of all assertions following the label Stat4). When no ambiguity or obscurity ensues from this, an assertion can be represented laconically by the keyword AUTO. Thus, in the above proof: when AUTO occurs in the initial Suppose_not-statement, it obviously stands for the assertion $\mathsf{Ord}(s)\ \&\ t \in s\ \&\ \neg\mathsf{Ord}(t)$, contrary to the sought conclusion; when it occurs in the $\langle a, b, c \rangle \hookrightarrow$Stat1-statement, it stands for the formula

$$(a \in t\ \&\ a \not\subseteq t) \vee \big(b \in t\ \&\ c \in t\ \&\ \neg(b \in c \vee c \in b \vee b = c)\big),$$

because this is what results from the assertion bearing the label Stat1 when its bound occurrences of variables get replaced by the new constants a, b, c; dually, in the $\langle t \rangle \hookrightarrow$Stat2 and in the $\langle b, c \rangle \hookrightarrow$Stat3 statement AUTO stands for $t \in s \rightarrow t \subseteq s$ and for $(b \in s\ \&\ c \in s) \rightarrow (b \in c \vee c \in b \vee b = c)$, respectively.

The following table lists the main inference mechanisms which currently constitute the inferential armory of Ref:

1. ELEM $\Longrightarrow \cdots$ Proof by extended elementary set-theoretic reasoning. (Cf. Sect. 4.1.2.)
   TELEM $\Longrightarrow \cdots$ Variant of ELEM (see below).
2. Suppose $\Longrightarrow \cdots$ Introduces hypothesis, available in a local range of the proof, to be 'discharged' subsequently. (Cf. Sect. 4.1.3.)
3. Discharge $\Longrightarrow \cdots$ Closes the proof range opened by the last previous 'Suppose' statement, and makes negation of prior supposition available. (Cf. Sect. 4.1.3.)
4. Suppose_not $\Longrightarrow \cdots$ Specialized form of 'Suppose', used to open proof-by-contradiction arguments. (Cf. Sect. 4.1.3.)
5. $\langle e_1, \ldots, e_n \rangle \hookrightarrow$Stat_*label* $\Longrightarrow \cdots$ Substitutes given expressions or newly generated constants into a prior labelled statement. (Cf. Sect. 4.3.9.)
6. $\langle e_1, \ldots, e_n \rangle \hookrightarrow$*Theorem_name* $\Longrightarrow \cdots$ Substitutes given expressions into a prior universally quantified theorem. (Cf. Sect. 4.3.9.)
7. Use_def(*symbol*) $\Longrightarrow \cdots$ Expands a defined symbol into its definition. (Cf. Sect. 4.2.)

8. Loc_def $\Longrightarrow$ *symbol_name(params)* $= \cdots$ Defines a new function symbol, constant, or predicate symbol for use within a single proof.
9. EQUAL $\Longrightarrow \cdots$ Makes deduction by substitution of equals for equals, possibly in a universally quantified formula. (Cf. Sect. 4.3.3.)
10. SIMPLF $\Longrightarrow \cdots$ Makes deduction by removal of set-former expressions nested within other set formers or quantifiers.
11. ALGEBRA $\Longrightarrow \cdots$ Deduces an algebraic consequence using statements proved or assumed previously. (Cf. Sect. 4.3.5.)
12. Set_monot $\Longrightarrow \cdots$ Handles set formers and exploits set-theoretic monotonicity relationships. (Cf. Sect. 4.3.4.)
    Pred_monot $\Longrightarrow \cdots$ Handles quantifiers and the finiteness predicate and exploits set-theoretic monotonicity relationships. (Cf. Sect. 4.3.4.)
13. Assump $\Longrightarrow \cdots$ Cites an available theory assumption during a proof being conducted within a theory.
14. APPLY$\cdots$ $\Longrightarrow \cdots$ Draws conclusions from theorems previously proved in a theory. Note that 'Skolemization' is handled as a special case of APPLY. (Cf. Sect. 4.1.4.)

In the five sections which follow, after outlining the inference mechanisms give our verifier most of its special flavour, we explain its notion of *inference step context* and describe how contexts can be restricted by means of statement labels.

### *4.1.2 The* ELEM *Primitive and 'Blobbing'*

Among Ref's inference primitives, ELEM is the most central (its use being, often, tacitly combined with other forms of inference). ELEM implements *multilevel syllogistic*, a decision algorithm which determines whether a given unquantified set-theoretic formula involving individual variables (which designate sets) and a restricted collection of set operators is satisfiable. (A tableau-fashioned account of a decision procedure for this fragment of set theory is given in Sect. 3.5.) Using the ELEM algorithm, the Ref verifier can identify many cases in which a conjunction constructed by negating one statement of a proof and conjoining a selection of earlier statements is unsatisfiable, so that the statement follows from the preceding context. When not all the constructs appearing in this context (e.g. quantifiers and set formers) are part of Ref's built-in syllogistic, a preprocessing step, called *blobbing*, replaces all parts of the current context whose principal operators are not recognized by the decision algorithm by 'blobs', i.e. by new variables designating either sets (when they occur as terms) or propositions (when they occur as subformulae). This blobbing operation replaces syntactically identical (or recognizably equal) parts of a conjunction by the same variable. It is also able to treat as equal well-formed parts which only differ by the renaming of bound variables in quantifiers or set formers, and also treats existential quantifiers as negated universal quantifiers.

The primary function of blobbing is to reduce all the constructs that appear in proof statements submitted to ELEM to the ones which multilevel syllogistic can handle. Blobbing is also used to introduce other simplifications which extend the power of ELEM beyond that of simple multilevel syllogistic and improve system performance.

Blobbing consists of three subphases: (1) *pre-blobbing*, which makes reductions such as the reduction of any part of the form Finite(#$X$) to Finite($X$) (justified by the remark that the cardinality of a set $X$ is finite if and only if $X$ is finite); (2) *blobbing proper*, during which subterms whose lead constructs are not known to the multilevel syllogistic algorithm are replaced by set names and quantified subformulae are replaced by propositional variables; (3) *post-blobbing*, which drops parts of a purported contradiction when it is clear that they can play no role in establishing its contradictory nature.

In some cases the verifier provides a few efficiency-oriented variants of the ELEM deduction primitive. These are invoked by prefixing the keyword ELEM with a parenthesized label (as we will see again in Sect. 4.1.5) which may include various special characters. Including the character "*" just before the closing parenthesis of the prefix suppresses the normal internal examination of special functions like cons, car, and cdr (the ordered pair constructor $x, y \mapsto [x, y]$ and its associated projections $p \mapsto p^{[1]}$, $p \mapsto p^{[2]}$, normally treated by the method discussed in Sect. 3.7.2), i.e. it treats these as unknown functions whose occurrences must be 'blobbed'. This treats statements like

$$[x,[y,z]] = [x_2,[y_2,z_2]] \,\&\, [x,[y,z]] = [x_3,[y_3,z_3]] \,\&\, [x,[y,z]] = [x_4,[y_4,z_4]]$$

as if they read

$$xyz = xyz_2 \,\&\, xyz = xyz_3 \,\&\, xyz = xyz_4,$$

and so makes deduction of

$$[x_2,[y_2,z_2]] = [x_3,[y_3,z_3]]$$

from the conjunction shown above easy. Without modification of the ELEM primitive's operation this same deduction would require many seconds. This coarse treatment is of course incapable of deducing the implication

$$[x,[y,z]] = [x_2,[y_2,z_2]] \rightarrow (x = x_2 \,\&\, y = y_2 \,\&\, z = z_2)$$

which it sees as

$$xyz = xyz_2 \rightarrow (x = x_2 \,\&\, y = y_2 \,\&\, z = z_2)\,.$$

In such cases we must simply allow a more extensive search than is generally used. (The verifier normally cuts off ELEM deduction searches after about 10 seconds.) Including the character "+" instead of "*" in a prefix attached to ELEM raises this limit to 40 seconds. Note that an empty prefix, i.e. "$\langle\,\rangle$", can be used to indicate that a statement is to be derived without additional context, i.e. that it is universally valid as it stands. Therefore the right way of obtaining the implication just displayed by ELEM deduction is to write it as

$$\langle + \rangle \text{ELEM} \Longrightarrow ([x, [y, z]] = [x_2, [y_2, z_2]]) \to ((x = x_2) \ \& \ (y = y_2) \ \& \ (z = z_2)).$$

### 4.1.3 *The* Suppose_not, QED, Suppose, Discharge *Primitives*

Suppose_not statements occur, exclusively and always, as the first inference step in Ref proofs. They have the form

$$\text{Suppose\_not}(c_1, \ldots, c_n) \Longrightarrow \cdots,$$

where $c_1, \ldots, c_n$ are distinct constants local to a proof, which correspond in number and in positions to the distinct unquantified variables appearing in the statement $T$ of the corresponding theorem. Such theorem variables (whose first letters are always capitalized for emphasis) are in fact understood to be universally quantified; and in a proof by contradiction the constants $c_i$ replace them during deduction of a contradiction. Accordingly, the statement which follows $\Longrightarrow$ in the Suppose_not step must be logically equivalent to the negation of an instantiated version of $T$. At the end of the proof there must appear a statement of the form

$$\text{Discharge} \Longrightarrow \text{QED}$$

which matches the Suppose_not and indicates that a contradiction was derived by assuming the existence of a counterexample to $T$.

A Suppose statement has the form

$$\text{Suppose} \Longrightarrow B \cdots,$$

where the formula $B$ that follows $\Longrightarrow$ can involve no constants save those already available in the part of the proof preceding it (including globally defined constants, constants of the form $c_\Theta$ local to the current theory, constants generated within the proof by substitution of an existentially bound variable, and constants generated by application of a THEORY—cf. Sect. 4.1.4).

Every step $C$ coming after a Suppose $\Longrightarrow B$ can exploit the temporary assumption $B$ as part of its context, until the following Discharge statement which matches this Suppose statement and so eliminates this assumption, along with all the intermediate steps $C$ which were derived from it.

As already said, Discharge statements always match Suppose and Suppose_not statements within a proof, in the same balanced way in which closed parentheses match open parentheses within an arithmetic expression. A matching Suppose/Discharge pair of statements is often used to encapsulate parts of the proof which constitute a digression from the main stream of the proof.

To see how this inference primitive works, let us consider the following proof fragment:

$$\begin{array}{c} C \\ \textsf{Suppose} \Longrightarrow B \\ D \\ \textsf{Discharge} \Longrightarrow A. \end{array}$$

Here the Suppose and Discharge are taken to match each other, so that $C$ represents the overall context available before the Suppose, $D$ represents the context portion derived from the temporary assumption $B$, and $A$ is the assertion which the Discharge yields. Ref will only regard this derivation as legitimate if it can find an intermediate formula $D'$ implied by $C\&B\&D$ and such that $A$ 'trivially' follows from the formula $C\&(B \rightarrow D')$.

Our verifier's 'Suppose' and 'Discharge' capabilities make a convenient form of 'natural deduction' available. Any syntactically well-formed formula can be the assertion of a 'Suppose' statement, i.e. you can suppose what you like. For example,

$$\textsf{Suppose} \Longrightarrow 2+2=4$$

and

$$\textsf{Suppose} \Longrightarrow 2+2=5$$

are both perfectly legal. However, all the assumptions made in the course of a theorem's proof must be Discharged before the end of the proof. A Discharge statement of the form

$$\textsf{Discharge} \Longrightarrow \mathit{some\_conclusion}$$

constructs its conclusion as $p \rightarrow q$, where $p$ is the assertion of the matching Suppose statement and $q$ is the assertion of the last inference preceding the Discharge. For example, the following sequence of 'Suppose' and 'Discharge' statements proves the propositional tautology $P \rightarrow ((P \rightarrow Q) \rightarrow Q)$:

$$\begin{array}{l} \textsf{Suppose} \Longrightarrow P \\ \quad \textsf{Suppose} \Longrightarrow P \rightarrow Q \\ \quad\quad \textsf{ELEM} \Longrightarrow Q \\ \quad \textsf{Discharge} \Longrightarrow (P \rightarrow Q) \rightarrow Q \\ \textsf{Discharge} \Longrightarrow P \rightarrow \big((P \rightarrow Q) \rightarrow Q\big). \end{array}$$

### *4.1.4* **THEORY** *Application*

Ref incorporates a technical notion of 'theory' designed, for large-scale proof-development, to play a role similar to the notion of object class in large-scale programming. As discussed in [OS02], such a mechanism can be very useful for 'proof-engineering'.

The theories we allow, like procedures in a programming language, have lists of formal parameters. Each 'theory' requires its parameters to meet a set of assumptions. When 'applied' to a list of actual parameters that have been shown to meet the assumptions, a theory will instantiate several additional 'output' set, predicate, and function symbols, and then supply a list of theorems initially proved explicitly (relative to the formal parameters) by the user inside the theory itself. These theorems will generally involve the new symbols.

As an illustration of the usefulness of the THEORY construct, let us now exploit the familiar theory of equivalence relations seen in Sect. 1.4.2.6 in order to define the set $\mathbb{R}$ of all real numbers. Since the apparent simplicity of the reals as Dedekind cuts is marred by problems concerning the treatment of negative reals, we opted for Cantor's approach based on rational Cauchy sequences. Thus our construction of the reals runs as follows:

-- The set of rational sequences

DEF 46. $\mathsf{Seq}_{\mathbb{Q}} =_{\mathrm{Def}} \{\mathsf{f} : \mathsf{f} \subseteq \mathbb{N} \times \mathbb{Q} \mid \mathsf{domain(f)} = \mathbb{N} \;\&\; \mathsf{Svm(f)}\}$

-- The constant 0 rational sequence

DEF 47. $\mathbf{0}_{\mathbb{QS}} =_{\mathrm{Def}} \mathbb{N} \times \{\mathbf{0}_{\mathbb{Q}}\}$

-- The constant 1 rational sequence

DEF 48. $\mathbf{1}_{\mathbb{QS}} =_{\mathrm{Def}} \mathbb{N} \times \{\mathbf{1}_{\mathbb{Q}}\}$

-- Pointwise sum of rational sequences

DEF 49. $\mathsf{F} +_{\mathbb{QS}} \mathsf{G} =_{\mathrm{Def}} \{[\mathsf{p}^{[1]}, \mathsf{p}^{[2]} +_{\mathbb{Q}} \mathsf{G}[\mathsf{p}^{[1]}]] : \mathsf{p} \in \mathsf{F}\}$

-- Pointwise additive inverse of rational sequence

DEF 50. $\mathsf{Rev}_{\mathbb{QS}}(\mathsf{F}) =_{\mathrm{Def}} \{[\mathsf{p}^{[1]}, \mathsf{Rev}_{\mathbb{Q}}(\mathsf{p}^{[2]})] : \mathsf{p} \in \mathsf{F}\}$

-- Pointwise absolute value of rational sequence

DEF 51. $|\mathsf{F}|_{\mathbb{QS}} =_{\mathrm{Def}} \{[\mathsf{p}^{[1]}, |\mathsf{p}^{[2]}|_{\mathbb{Q}}] : \mathsf{p} \in \mathsf{F}\}$

-- Pointwise difference of rational sequences

DEF 52. $\mathsf{F} -_{\mathbb{QS}} \mathsf{G} =_{\mathrm{Def}} \mathsf{F} +_{\mathbb{QS}} \mathsf{Rev}_{\mathbb{QS}}(\mathsf{G})$

-- Product of rational sequences

DEF 53. $\mathsf{F} *_{\mathbb{QS}} \mathsf{G} =_{\mathrm{Def}} \{[\mathsf{p}^{[1]}, \mathsf{p}^{[2]} *_{\mathbb{Q}} \mathsf{G}[\mathsf{p}^{[1]}]] : \mathsf{p} \in \mathsf{F}\}$

-- Pointwise reciprocal of rational sequence

DEF 54. $\mathsf{Recip}_{\mathbb{QS}}(\mathsf{F}) =_{\mathrm{Def}} \mathsf{Shifted\_seq}(\{[\mathsf{i}, \mathsf{Recip}_{\mathbb{Q}}(\mathsf{F[i]})] : \mathsf{i} \in \mathbb{N}\},$
$\mathsf{arb}(\{\mathsf{h} \in \mathbb{N} \mid \langle \forall \mathsf{i} \in \mathbb{N} \backslash \mathsf{h} \mid \mathsf{F[i]} \neq \mathbf{0}_{\mathbb{Q}} \rangle\}))$

-- Pointwise quotient of rational sequences

DEF 55. $\mathsf{F} /_{\mathbb{QS}} \mathsf{G} =_{\mathrm{Def}} \mathsf{F} *_{\mathbb{QS}} \mathsf{Recip}_{\mathbb{QS}}(\mathsf{G})$

-- Rational Cauchy sequences

DEF 56. $\mathsf{Cau}_{\mathbb{Q}} =_{\mathrm{Def}} \{\mathsf{f} : \mathsf{f} \in \mathsf{Seq}_{\mathbb{Q}} \mid \langle \forall \varepsilon \in \mathbb{Q} \mid \varepsilon >_{\mathbb{Q}} \mathbf{0}_{\mathbb{Q}} \rightarrow$
$\mathsf{Finite}(\{\mathsf{i} \cap \mathsf{j} : \mathsf{i} \in \mathbb{N}, \mathsf{j} \in \mathbb{N} \mid |\mathsf{f[i]} -_{\mathbb{Q}} \mathsf{f[j]}|_{\mathbb{Q}} >_{\mathbb{Q}} \varepsilon\})\rangle\}$

-- Equivalence of rational sequences

DEF 57. $\mathsf{F} \approx_{\mathbb{QS}} \mathsf{G} \leftrightarrow_{\mathrm{Def}} \langle \forall \varepsilon \in \mathbb{Q} \mid \varepsilon >_{\mathbb{Q}} \mathbf{0}_{\mathbb{Q}} \rightarrow$
$\mathsf{Finite}(\{\mathsf{x} : \mathsf{x} \in \mathsf{domain(F)} \mid |\mathsf{F[x]} -_{\mathbb{Q}} \mathsf{G[x]}|_{\mathbb{Q}} >_{\mathbb{Q}} \varepsilon\})\rangle$

THEOREM 465: $\mathsf{F} \in \mathsf{Cau}_{\mathbb{Q}} \rightarrow \mathsf{F} \approx_{\mathsf{QS}} \mathsf{F}$. PROOF: ···

THEOREM 466: $\mathsf{F}, \mathsf{G}, \mathsf{H} \in \mathsf{Cau}_{\mathbb{Q}} \rightarrow \big(\mathsf{F} \approx_{\mathsf{QS}} \mathsf{G} \rightarrow (\mathsf{G} \approx_{\mathsf{QS}} \mathsf{H} \leftrightarrow \mathsf{H} \approx_{\mathsf{QS}} \mathsf{F})\big)$. PROOF: ···

-- Now that we know that $\approx_{\mathsf{QS}}$ is an equivalence relationship,
we can apply the equiv_classes theory to it, to derive

APPLY $\langle \mathsf{Eqc}_\Theta : \mathbb{R},\ f_\Theta : \mathsf{Cau\_to\_}\mathbb{R} \rangle$ equiv_classes$\big(\mathsf{E(f, g)} \mapsto \mathsf{f} \approx_{\mathsf{QS}} \mathsf{g},\ \mathsf{s} \mapsto \mathsf{Cau}_{\mathbb{Q}}\big)$
$\Longrightarrow$

THEOREM 467: $\langle \forall \mathsf{f} \in \mathsf{Cau}_{\mathbb{Q}}, \mathsf{g} \in \mathsf{Cau}_{\mathbb{Q}} \mid \mathsf{f} \approx_{\mathsf{QS}} \mathsf{g} \leftrightarrow \mathsf{Cau\_to\_}\mathbb{R}(\mathsf{f}) = \mathsf{Cau\_to\_}\mathbb{R}(\mathsf{g}) \rangle$
$\& \langle \forall \mathsf{r} \in \mathbb{R} \mid \mathsf{arb(r)} \in \mathsf{Cau}_{\mathbb{Q}} \ \&\ \mathsf{Cau\_to\_}\mathbb{R}(\mathsf{arb(r)}) = \mathsf{r} \rangle$
$\& \langle \forall \mathsf{f} \in \mathsf{Cau}_{\mathbb{Q}} \mid \mathsf{Cau\_to\_}\mathbb{R}(\mathsf{f}) \in \mathbb{R} \rangle \ \&\ \langle \forall \mathsf{f} \in \mathsf{Cau}_{\mathbb{Q}} \mid \mathsf{f} \approx_{\mathsf{QS}} \mathsf{arb}(\mathsf{Cau\_to\_}\mathbb{R}(\mathsf{f})) \rangle$.

Let us observe, as an incidental remark, that in spite of its relative length this list of statements works better than Dedekind's approach, because it allows us to 'lift' laws already proved for rational numbers into corresponding laws for rational Cauchy sequences, and thereby into laws concerning the reals (which are viewed here as the $\approx_{\mathsf{QS}}$-classes of such sequences).

**Use of External Provers** In order to provide the Ref proof verifier with the ability to accept proofs generated by various external provers, as explained and exemplified in [FO10, pp. 44–47]), one can resort to a syntactic extension of the normal Ref APPLY directive. I.e., external provers shall be regarded as sources of variant Ref THEORYs. When such a prover is being used, the normal keyword APPLY used to invoke a THEORY must be changed to "APPLY_provername", where "provername" names the external prover in question. In this case, the normal Ref THEORY declaration is expanded to list Ref-syntax translations of all the theorems being drawn from the external prover, and of all the external symbol definitions on which these depend. An external file, also named in the modified Ref APPLY directive, must be provided as certification of each such THEORY. Ref will then examine this file to establish that it is a valid proof, by the external prover named, of all the theorems which the THEORY claims.

### *4.1.5 Context of an Inference Step*

Until a proof is complete and acceptable to the Ref verifier, it is undesirable to let efficiency concerns interfere with one's focus on the logic of the proof. Once an initial version of the proof has been accepted by Ref, one can speed up its processing by supplying *contexts* (see above) for the most time-consuming proof steps. Ref allows one to optimize proof steps by automated context discovery.

Statement assertions and parts of compounds connected by the conjunction sign "&" can be labelled for explicit subsequent reference within a proof by appending a reserved notation of the form 'Stat*nnn* :' to them, where *nnn* designates any integer. These are the labels used in hints of statements of the form

$$\langle e_1, \ldots, e_m \rangle \hookrightarrow \mathsf{Stat}nnn \Longrightarrow \cdots$$

The context of a hint defines the collection of preceding statements, within the proof in which the hint appears, which the inference mechanism invoked by the hint should use in deducing the assertion to which the hint is attached. Since the efficiency of an inference mechanism often degrades very rapidly (e.g. exponentially or worse) with the size of the context with which it is working, appropriate restriction of context can be crucial to successful completion of an inference. Inferences which the verifier cannot complete within a reasonable amount of time are abandoned with a diagnostic message "Abandoned...", or with the more specific message "Failure..." if the inference method is able to certify that the inference finally attempted is impossible. Hint keywords like ELEM, EQUAL, SIMPLF, and ALGEBRA can be supplied with context indications by prefixing them (in the cases of ELEM and Discharge) or suffixing them (in all other cases) with a statement label, or a comma-separated list of such labels, as in the examples

$$\langle \mathsf{Stat3} \rangle \mathrm{ELEM} \Longrightarrow s \notin \{x \subseteq o \mid \mathsf{Ord}(x) \& P(x)\}$$

and

$$\langle \mathsf{Stat3}, \mathsf{Stat4}, \mathsf{Stat9} \rangle \mathrm{ELEM} \Longrightarrow s \notin \{x \subseteq o \mid \mathsf{Ord}(x) \& P(x)\}.$$

The first form of prefix defines the context of an inference to be the collection of all statements in the proof, back to the point of last previous occurrence of the statement label in the proof (but not within ranges of the proof that are already closed in virtue of the fact that they are included between a preceding Discharge statement and its matching Suppose statement—see below). The second form of prefix defines the context of an inference to be the collection of statements explicitly named in the prefix. If no context is specified for an inference, then its context is understood to be the collection of all preceding statements in the same proof (not including statements enclosed within previously closed Suppose/Discharge ranges). This unrestricted default context is workable for simple enough inferences in short enough proofs.

**The Ref Proof Step Optimizer** Ref's automated proof optimizer attempts to determine, for each line $L$ in a proof, a close-to-minimal subset of the set of all prior lines in the proof which is large enough to serve as a context for the proof of $L$, i.e. large enough to be inconsistent with the negation $\neg L$ of $L$. To this end, it collects a list of prior statements, called 'critical', which it believes to be necessary for the desired inconsistency. Initially this list of critical statements consists of all the statements preceding $L$. A first binary search over ranges of statements shortens this to the smallest range $R$ of statements preceding $L$ which is large enough to be inconsistent with $\neg L$. The first statement $F$ in this range is added to an (initially empty) list $C$. This reflects the fact that if $F$ is removed from $R$, the set $R \cup \{\neg L\}$ of statements is no longer inconsistent.

Let $R'$ be $R$ after $F$ is removed. Plainly $C \cup R' \cup \{\neg L\}$ is inconsistent. But $R'$ may be larger than it need be to guarantee this property. So a second binary search is made, to shorten $R'$ to the smallest range $R''$ of statements which is large enough for $C \cup R'' \cup \{\neg L\}$ to be inconsistent. The first statement of $R''$ is then moved from $R''$ to $C$. This operation is repeated as often as needed to produce a final list $C$ of critical statements such that $C \cup \{\neg L\}$ is inconsistent. This list $C$ of statements is returned by the proof optimizer as the context to be used in proving $L$.

The code described in the preceding paragraphs is organized using a

**procedure** `test_range(critical_list,range_tup,statement)`

which sets up the inconsistency tests described and then calls Ref's underlying ELEM procedure.

To mark a proof for invocation of the automated analysis just described, one simply changes the normal "$\Longrightarrow$" mark of its initial Suppose_not to "$\Rrightarrow$". To mark a single step of a proof for application of this analysis, one changes its "$\Longrightarrow$" mark to "$\Rrightarrow$". The first such mark encountered in a proof (if any) turns off the 'analyze by default' option if this has been set by marking the initial Suppose_not.

Here are a few illustrative examples of the output produced by Ref's automated proof optimizer:

> The lines of context needed to prove citation of theorem T116 in line 9, namely:
> (domain($f$) $\subseteq \mathbb{N}$) & (range($f$) $\subseteq \mathbb{Q}$) are T116 plus [1, 5]
> The lines of context needed to prove citation of theorem T220 in line 10, namely:
> $g \subseteq (\mathbb{N} \times \mathbb{Q})$ are T220 plus [1, 7, 9]
> The lines of context needed to prove citation of theorem T85 in line 12, namely:
> domain($f \circ h$) = domain($h$) are T85 plus [1, 7]

## 4.2 The Syntax and Semantics of Definitions

Definitions introduce new predicate and function symbols into the ken of our verifier. Predicate definitions have the syntactic form

$$P(x_1, x_2, \ldots, x_n) \leftrightarrow_{\mathrm{Def}} pexp.$$

Function definitions have the form

$$f(x_1, x_2, \ldots, x_n) =_{\mathrm{Def}} fexp.$$

In both these cases, $x_1, x_2, \ldots, x_n$ must be a list of distinct variables; only these variables can occur unbound on the right of the definition, and $P$ (resp. $f$) must be a predicate (resp. function) symbol that has never been defined previously. In the first (resp. second) case *pexp* (resp. *fexp*) must be a syntactically well-formed predicate expression (resp. function expression).[4] Two cases of each form of definition, the non-recursive and the recursive, arise. In non-recursive predicate (resp. function) definitions, *pexp* (resp. *fexp*) can only contain previously defined predicate and function symbols, plus the free variables $x_1, x_2, \dots, x_n$ (and, of course, any other bound variables). In recursive definitions the predicate (resp. function) symbol being defined is allowed to appear on the right-hand side of the definition, but then other syntactic conditions must be imposed to guarantee the legality of the definition. More specifically, in the function case, we allow recursive definitions of the general form

$$\begin{aligned} f(s, x_2, \dots, x_n) =_{\mathrm{Def}} d\big(\{&g\big(f(x, h_2(s, x, x_2, \dots, x_n), h_3(s, x, x_2, \dots, x_n), \dots, \\ &\quad h_n(s, x, x_2, \dots, x_n)\big), s, x, x_2, \dots, x_n\big) : x \in s \mid \\ &P\big(f(x, h_2(s, x, x_2, \dots, x_n), h_3(s, x, x_2, \dots, x_n), \dots, \\ &\quad h_n(s, x, x_2, \dots, x_n)\big), s, x, x_2, \dots, x_n\big)\}, s, x_2, \dots, x_n\big). \end{aligned}$$

Here $g$, $d$, and $h_2, \dots, h_n$ must be previously defined functions of the indicated number of arguments, and $P$ must be a previously defined predicate of the indicated number of arguments.

The following informal argument indicates why it is reasonable to expect definitions of the general form displayed above to specify a function that is well defined for each possible argument list $s, x_2, \dots, x_n$. If the initial argument $s$ is the null set $\emptyset$, the definition reduces to

$$f(\emptyset, x_2, \dots, x_n) =_{\mathrm{Def}} d(\emptyset, \emptyset, x_2, \dots, x_n),$$

i.e. to an ordinary set-theoretic definition in which the function being defined does not appear on the right. Since, in intuitive terms, we can think of the collection of all sets as being arranged in a members-first order, we can suppose that $f(x, y_2, \dots, y_n)$ is known for each $x \in s$ and for all $y_2, \dots, y_n$ before the value $f(s, x_2, \dots, x_n)$ is required. But then the definition shown above clearly specifies $f(s, x_2, \dots, x_n)$ in terms of (i) values of $f$ which are already known, (ii) known functions and predicates, along with (iii) a single set-former operation.

Although it is not hard to convert this informal line of reasoning into a more formal argument involving transfinite induction, we shall not do so, but will simply allow free use of inductive definitions of the form shown above.

In the predicate case, the same line of reasoning shows that we can allow recursive definitions of the form

$$\begin{aligned} &P(s, x_2, \dots, x_n) \leftrightarrow_{\mathrm{Def}} \\ &\qquad d\big(\{g(s, x, x_2, \dots, x_n) : x \in s \mid P(x, x_2, \dots, x_n)\}, s, x_2, \dots, x_n\big) = \emptyset, \end{aligned}$$

---

[4] We keep the sign $\leftrightarrow_{\mathrm{Def}}$ distinct from $=_{\mathrm{Def}}$ for clarity, but this distinction is not very important.

where again $g$ and $d$ must be previously defined functions of the indicated number of arguments. In the special case in which the function $d$ has the form

$$d(t, s, x_2, \ldots, x_n) = \{x : x \in t \mid \neg Q(s, x, x_2, \ldots, x_n)\},$$

where $Q$ is some previously defined predicate, the recursive predicate definition seen above can be recast in the form

$$P(s, x_2, \ldots, x_n) \leftrightarrow_{\text{Def}}$$
$$(\forall x \in s \mid P(x, x_2, \ldots, x_n) \rightarrow Q(s, g(s, x, x_2, \ldots, x_n), x_2, \ldots, x_n)).$$

Accordingly, we allow recursive predicate definitions of this latter form also.

To illustrate the use of recursive definitions, we show how one can define functions on sets which, when they are restricted to natural numbers in the von Neumann representation, become the usual operations of unitary incrementation and decrementation, addition, multiplication, subtraction, quotient, remainder, and greatest common divisor (for this, we use an auxiliary operation '$\mathsf{coRem}(X, Y)$', which finds the maximum multiple of $Y$ less than or equal to $X$):

$$\begin{aligned}
\mathsf{next}(W) &=_{\text{Def}} W \cup \{W\},\\
\mathsf{prec}(V) &=_{\text{Def}} \mathsf{arb}(\{w : w \in V \mid \mathsf{next}(w) = V\}),\\
\mathsf{plus}(X, Y) &=_{\text{Def}} X \cup \bigcup \{\mathsf{next}(\mathsf{plus}(X, v)) : v \in Y\},\\
\mathsf{times}(X, Y) &=_{\text{Def}} \bigcup \{\mathsf{plus}(\mathsf{times}(X, v), X) : v \in Y\},\\
\mathsf{minus}(X, Y) &=_{\text{Def}} \mathsf{arb}(\{v : v \in \mathsf{next}(X) \mid \mathsf{plus}(v, Y) = X\}),\\
\mathsf{coRem}(X, Y) &=_{\text{Def}} \bigcup (\mathsf{next}(X) \cap \{\mathsf{plus}(\mathsf{coRem}(v, Y), Y) : v \in X\}),\\
\mathsf{Divides}(X, Y) &\leftrightarrow_{\text{Def}} \mathsf{coRem}(X, Y) = X,\\
\mathsf{quot}(X, Y) &=_{\text{Def}} \bigcup \{\mathsf{next}(\mathsf{quot}(v, Y)) : v \in X \mid\\
&\qquad \mathsf{plus}(\mathsf{coRem}(v, Y), Y) \in \mathsf{next}(X)\},\\
\mathsf{rem}(X, Y) &=_{\text{Def}} \mathsf{arb}(\{w : w \in Y \mid \mathsf{plus}(\mathsf{coRem}(X, Y), w) = X\}),\\
\mathsf{gcd}(X, Y) &=_{\text{Def}} \textbf{if } X = \emptyset \textbf{ then } Y \textbf{ else}\\
&\bigcup \{\mathsf{next}(w) : w \in X \mid \mathsf{Divides}(\mathsf{next}(w), X) \,\&\, \mathsf{Divides}(\mathsf{next}(w), Y)\} \textbf{ end if}.
\end{aligned}$$

An alternative characterization of the greatest common divisor, equally convenient but more procedural in flavour (indeed, inspired by the classical Euclid algorithm) can be given by

$$\mathsf{gcd}(X, Y) = \textbf{if } Y = 0 \textbf{ then } X \textbf{ else } \mathsf{gcd}(Y, \mathsf{rem}(X, Y)) \textbf{ end if}.$$

This cannot be proposed as a definition, though, because the form of recursion seen here does not have the same syntactic evidence of legitimacy as the forms of recursions used in the definitions above.

## 4.3 Other Techniques Used in the Verifier as Implemented

### *4.3.1 Supplementary Proof Mechanisms for the* ELEM *Rule*

Because of their special importance, the treatment of arb and of the 'cons-car-cdr' group is built into ELEM. The use of supplementary proof mechanisms for handling other extended ELEM deductions like those described in Sect. 3.7 is switched on in the following way. Each of the cases listed there is given a name, specifically[5]

(ii) INVERSE_PAIR,
(iii) MONOTONE_FCN,
(iv) MONOTONE_GROUP,
(v) MONOTONE_MULTIVAR,
(vi) IDEMPOTENT,
(vii) SELF_INVERSE,
(viii) TOTAL_ORDERING,
(ix) RANGE_AND_DOMAIN.

To enable the use of supplementary inferencing for a particular operator belonging to one of these named classes, one writes a verifier command of a form like

ENABLE_ELEM(*class_name*; *operator_list*),

where *class_name* is one of the names in the preceding list, and *operator_list* lists the operator symbols for which the designated style of inferencing is to be applied. An example is

ENABLE_ELEM(MONOTONE_FCN; Un)

which states that during ELEM inferencing the 'union of elements' operator Un is to be treated as an otherwise uninterpreted symbol for a monotone increasing set operator. The *operator_list* parameter of an 'ENABLE_ELEM' command must consist of the number of operators appropriate to the *class_name* used, e.g. IDEMPOTENT calls for a single operator as its operator list but MONOTONE_GROUP and INVERSE_PAIR each call for a list of two operators $f, g$.

The ENABLE_ELEM command scans the list of all currently available theorems for theorems of form suitable to the type of inference defined by the *class_name* parameter. For example, MONOTONE_FCN calls for a theorem of the form

$$\big(\forall x, y \mid (x \supseteq y) \rightarrow \big(f(x) \supseteq f(y)\big)\big),$$

where $f$ is the function symbol that appears as *operator_list* in this case; IDEMPOTENT calls for a theorem of the form

$$\big(\forall x, y \mid f\big(f(x)\big) = f(x)\big).$$

[5]Case (i) in Sect. 3.7 referred to the operator arb, which, as remarked above, is built into ELEM. Treatment of the other cases is unimplemented as yet in the Ref verifier.

Thus, for example, the command ENABLE_ELEM(MONOTONE_FCN; Un) calls for the theorem

$$(\forall x, y \mid (x \supseteq y) \to (\mathsf{Un}(x) \supseteq \mathsf{Un}(y))).$$

Cardinality is another example; the command ENABLE_ELEM(MONOTONE_FCN; #) calls for the theorem

$$(\forall x, y \mid (x \supseteq y) \to (\#x \supseteq \#y)).$$

If the required theorem is not found an error message is issued; otherwise the declared style of inferencing becomes available for the operator or operators listed.

Since extension of ELEM inferencing is not without its efficiency costs, one may wish to switch it on and off selectively. To switch off extended ELEM inferencing of a specified kind for specified operators one uses a command

DISABLE_ELEM(*class_name*, *operator_list*)

whose *class_name* parameter must reference one of the names which could occur in an ENABLE_ELEM(*class_name*; ···) directive. This disables use of the ELEM extensions described above for the indicated operators. Of course, a subsequent ENABLE_ELEM command can switch this back on.

## 4.3.2 *Limited Predicate Proof*

In some situations, we can combine the ELEM style of unquantified proof described in the preceding pages with predicate reasoning, provided that we hold down the computational cost of proof searches by imposing artificial limitations on the information used. An example of such a situation is that in which a deduction is to be made by combining a collection of statements in the unquantified language of MLSS with one or more universally quantified statements like

$$(\forall s, t \mid (\mathsf{Ord}(s) \,\&\, \mathsf{Ord}(t)) \to (s \in t \lor t \in s \lor s = t)),$$

where $\mathsf{Ord}(s)$ is the predicate stating that $s$ is an ordinal. Although in the full context of set theory use of such statements opens a path to very many subsequent deductions, and so has consequences that are quite undecidable, the special case of universally quantified statements which contain no symbols designating operators and only uninterpreted predicates is more tractable. This limited case can be handled in the following way. Suppose that we deal with a collection $C$ of unquantified statements of the language MLSS, together with a collection $U$ of universally quantified statements of the form

$$(\forall x_1, \dots, x_n \mid P), \tag{4.1}$$

where $P$ is built from some collection of uninterpreted predicates $Q(x_1, \ldots, x_n)$ and contains no function symbols. Gather all the variables $s$ that appear in the statements of $C$, substitute them in all possible ways for the bound variables of (4.1), and decompose the resulting collection of statements at the propositional level. To the original collection $C$ this would add a finite number of statements of the form

$$Q(s_1, \ldots, s_n),$$

some of which may be negated. But instead of adding these statements, which involve predicate constructions, proceed as follows. For each such $Q(s_1, \ldots, s_n)$ introduce a unique propositional symbol $Q^{s_1,\ldots,s_n}$ and add $Q^{s_1,\ldots,s_n}$, negated in the pattern inherited from the $Q(s_1, \ldots, s_n)$, instead of the $Q(s_1, \ldots, s_n)$ to $C$. Then, for all pairs of argument tuples $s_1, \ldots, s_n$ and $t_1, \ldots, t_n$ which appear in such statements (with the same $Q$) add an implication

$$(s_1 = t_1 \,\&\, \cdots \,\&\, s_n = t_n) \rightarrow \big(Q^{s_1,\ldots,s_n} = Q^{t_1,\ldots,t_n}\big). \tag{4.2}$$

This gives a collection $C'$ of statements, all of which are in MLSS. It is clear that $C'$ is satisfiable if $C$ and $U$ are simultaneously satisfiable. Conversely, let $C'$ have a model $\mathcal{M}$. The conditions (4.2) that we have added to $C$ imply that the Boolean values $Q^{s_1,\ldots,s_n}$ derive from a single-valued predicate function via the relationship

$$Q^{s_1,\ldots,s_n} = Q(s_1, \ldots, s_n).$$

Let $D$ be the collection of all the elements of the model $\mathcal{M}$ that correspond to symbols which appear in statements belonging to $C$.

Then plainly

$$(\forall x_1 \in D, \ldots, x_n \in D \mid P). \tag{4.3}$$

Choose some $s_0$ in $D$ and let $r$ be the idempotent map of the entire universe of sets onto $D$ defined by

$$r(x) =_{\text{Def}} \textbf{if } x \in D \textbf{ then } x \textbf{ else } s_0 \textbf{ end if}.$$

If we show the dependence of the predicate $P$ on its free variables $x_1, \ldots, x_n$ by writing it as $P(x_1, \ldots, x_n)$, then (4.3) is clearly equivalent to

$$\big(\forall x_1, \ldots, x_n \mid P\big(r(x_1), \ldots, r(x_n)\big)\big). \tag{4.4}$$

Extend each of the predicates $Q^{\mathcal{M}}$ from its restriction to the Cartesian product $D \times D \times \cdots \times D$ to a universally defined predicate $Q_+^{\mathcal{M}}$ by taking

$$Q_+^{\mathcal{M}}(x_1, \ldots, x_n) = Q\big(r(x_1), \ldots, r(x_n)\big).$$

Then it is clear that the predicates $Q_+^{\mathcal{M}}$ model both the statements of $C$ and the universally quantified statement (4.1). This shows that the collection $C'$ has a model if and only if the union of $C$ and $U$ has a model, proving that the satisfiability of $C \cup U$ is decidable.

Given any collection of universally quantified statements $U$ and collection $C$ of unquantified statements of MLSS, we can treat them as if the predicates appearing in the statements of $U$ were uninterpreted, i.e. had no known properties except those given explicitly by the statements in $U$. Even though this throws away a great deal of information that can be quite useful, there are many situations in which it achieves an inference step needed for a particular argument. Note that the inference mechanism described need not treat predicates like $x \in y$ and $x \supseteq y$ present in a universally quantified statement as uninterpreted predicates if they contain no operator signs not available in MLSS, even though the preceding argument fails if this is not done: the inference method used remains sound nevertheless. However, compounds like $\#t \subseteq \#s$ must be treated as uninterpreted multiparameter predicates, just as if they read $Q_{\#}(s,t)$. Similarly a compound like $\mathsf{Finite}(\mathsf{domain}(f))$ must be treated as if it involved a special predicate $F_d(f)$. Any information that this loses lies out of reach of the elementary extension of MLSS described in the preceding paragraphs.

Our verifier provides an inference mechanism, designated by the keyword 'THUS',[6] which extends ELEM deduction in the manner just explained. To make a universally quantified statement available to this mechanism, one writes

$$\text{ENABLE\_THUS}(\textit{statement\_of\_theorem}),$$

for example

$$\text{ENABLE\_THUS}\big((\mathsf{Ord}(S) \;\&\; T \in S) \rightarrow \mathsf{Ord}(T)\big).$$

To disable use of a theorem by 'THUS' inferencing, one can write

$$\text{DISABLE\_THUS}(\textit{statement\_of\_theorem}).$$

The following list shows some of the commonly occurring theorems suitable for use with the 'THUS' inferencing mechanism.

$$\text{ENABLE\_THUS}\big((\forall s,t \mid \\ \big(\mathsf{Ord}(s) \;\&\; \mathsf{Ord}(t)\big) \rightarrow (s \subseteq t \vee t \subseteq s)\big)\big)$$

$$\text{ENABLE\_THUS}\big((\forall s,t \mid \\ \big(\mathsf{Ord}(s) \;\&\; \mathsf{Ord}(t)\big) \rightarrow (s \in t \vee t \in s \vee s = t)\big)\big)$$

$$\text{ENABLE\_THUS}\big((\forall s,t \mid \\ \big(\mathsf{Ord}(s) \;\&\; t \in s\big) \rightarrow \mathsf{Ord}(t)\big)\big)$$

$$\text{ENABLE\_THUS}\big((\forall s,t \mid \\ \big(\mathsf{Ord}(s) \;\&\; \mathsf{Ord}(t)\big) \rightarrow \big(t \subseteq s \leftrightarrow (t \in s \vee t = s)\big)\big)\big)$$

[6] The mechanisms described in the ongoing of this section are unimplemented as yet in Ref.

$$\text{ENABLE\_THUS}\big((\forall s \mid \text{Is\_cardinal}(s) \rightarrow \text{Ord}(s))\big)$$

$$\text{ENABLE\_THUS}\big((\forall f, g \mid (g \subseteq f)\ \&\ \text{Is\_map}(f) \rightarrow \text{Is\_map}(g))\big)$$

$$\text{ENABLE\_THUS}\big((\forall f, g \mid (g \subseteq f)\ \&\ \text{Svm}(f) \rightarrow \text{Svm}(g))\big)$$

$$\text{ENABLE\_THUS}\big((\forall f, g \mid (g \subseteq f)\ \&\ 1\_1(f) \rightarrow 1\_1(g))\big)$$

$$\text{ENABLE\_THUS}\big((\forall f, g \mid \big(\text{Is\_map}(f)\ \&\ \text{Is\_map}(g)\big) \rightarrow \text{Is\_map}(f \cup g))\big)$$

$$\text{ENABLE\_THUS}\big((\forall f, s \mid \text{Is\_map}(f) \rightarrow \text{Is\_map}(f_{|s}))\big)$$

$$\text{ENABLE\_THUS}\big((\forall f, s \mid \text{Svm}(f) \rightarrow \text{Svm}(f_{|s}))\big)$$

$$\text{ENABLE\_THUS}\big((\forall f, s \mid 1\_1(f) \rightarrow 1\_1(f_{|s}))\big)$$

$$\text{ENABLE\_THUS}\big((\forall f, g \mid \big(\text{Svm}(f)\ \&\ \text{Svm}(g)\big) \rightarrow \text{Svm}(f \circ g))\big)$$

$$\text{ENABLE\_THUS}\big((\forall f, g \mid \big(1\_1(f)\ \&\ 1\_1(g)\big) \rightarrow 1\_1(f \circ g))\big)$$

$$\text{ENABLE\_THUS}\big((\forall s, t \mid (t \subseteq s) \rightarrow (\#t \subseteq \#s))\big)$$

$$\text{ENABLE\_THUS}\big((\forall s \mid \text{Is\_cardinal}(\#s))\big)$$

$$\text{ENABLE\_THUS}\big((\forall f \mid 1\_1(f) \rightarrow \big(\#\text{range}(f) = \#\text{domain}(f)\big))\big)$$

$$\text{ENABLE\_THUS}\big((\forall f \mid \text{Svm}(f) \rightarrow \big(\#\text{range}(f) = \#\text{domain}(f)\big))\big)$$

$$\text{ENABLE\_THUS}\big((\forall f \mid \text{Svm}(f) \rightarrow \big(\#\text{domain}(f) = \#f\big))\big)$$

$$\text{ENABLE\_THUS}\big((\forall s \mid \mathsf{Is\_cardinal}(s) \leftrightarrow (s = \#s))\big)$$

$$\text{ENABLE\_THUS}\big((\forall s, t \mid \big(\mathsf{Finite}(s) \;\&\; s \supseteq t\big) \rightarrow \mathsf{Finite}(t))\big)$$

$$\text{ENABLE\_THUS}\big((\forall f \mid 1\_1(f) \rightarrow \big(\mathsf{Finite}(\mathsf{domain}(f)) \leftrightarrow \mathsf{Finite}\big(\mathsf{range}(f)\big)\big))\big)$$

$$\text{ENABLE\_THUS}\big((\forall f \mid \big(\mathsf{Svm}(f) \;\&\; \mathsf{Finite}\big(\mathsf{domain}(f)\big)\big) \rightarrow \mathsf{Finite}\big(\mathsf{range}(f)\big))\big)$$

$$\text{ENABLE\_THUS}\big((\forall s \mid \mathsf{Finite}(s) \leftrightarrow \mathsf{Finite}(\#s))\big)$$

$$\text{ENABLE\_THUS}\big((\forall s, t \mid \big(\mathsf{Finite}(s) \;\&\; t \subseteq s \;\&\; t \neq s\big) \rightarrow (\#t \in \#s))\big)$$

$$\text{ENABLE\_THUS}\big((\forall x \mid \big(\mathsf{Ord}(\mathbb{N}) \;\&\; \neg\mathsf{Finite}(\mathbb{N})\big) \;\&\; \big(\big(\mathsf{Is\_cardinal}(X) \;\&\; \mathsf{Finite}(X)\big) \leftrightarrow (X \in \mathbb{N})\big))\big)$$

$$\text{ENABLE\_THUS}\big((\forall n, m \mid \big(\mathsf{Finite}(n) \;\&\; \mathsf{Finite}(m)\big) \leftrightarrow \mathsf{Finite}(n \cup m))\big)$$

$$\text{ENABLE\_THUS}\big((\forall n, m \mid \mathsf{Finite}(n + m) \leftrightarrow \mathsf{Finite}(n \cup m))\big)$$

$$\text{ENABLE\_THUS}\big((\forall n, m \mid \big(\mathsf{Finite}(n) \;\&\; \mathsf{Finite}(m)\big) \leftrightarrow \mathsf{Finite}(n + m))\big)$$

Besides using all the MLSS statements available in the context in which it is invoked, the inference mechanism invoked by the keyword 'THUS' makes use of all the explicit and implicit universally quantified statements found in that context, including non-membership statements like

$$b \notin \big\{e(x) : x \in s \mid P(x)\big\},$$

which are equivalent to

$$\big(\forall x \mid \neg\big(b = e(x) \;\&\; x \in s \;\&\; P(x)\big)\big).$$

This extends the reach of the automatic substitution mechanism invoked by 'THUS'.

### 4.3.3 Proof by Equality

Proof by equality tests two expressions for equality or two atomic formulae for equivalence, by standardizing their bound variables and then descending their syntax trees in parallel until differing nodes are found. These differing nodes are then examined to determine if the context of the equality proof step contains theorems which imply that the syntactically different constructs seen are in fact equal or equivalent. Suppose, for example, that an assertion

$$\{g(e(x), f(y)) : x \in s,\ y \in t \mid P(x, y)\} = a$$

has been proved, and that

$$\{g(e'(x), f'(y)) : x \in s,\ y \in t \mid P'(x, y)\} = a$$

is to be deduced from it. Syntactic comparison reveals the differences between $e$ and $e'$, $f$ and $f'$, $P$ and $P'$. Our verifier's proof by equality procedure will then generate the three statements

$$(\forall x \in s \mid e(x) = e'(x)),$$
$$(\forall y \in t \mid f(y) = f'(y)),$$
$$(\forall x \in s, y \in t \mid P(x, y) \leftrightarrow P'(x, y))$$

and attempt to find all of them in the available context. If this succeeds, the proof by equality inference will be accepted. If not, the equality procedure will go one step higher in the syntax tree of these two formulae, generate the pair of statements

$$(\forall x \in s,\ y \in t \mid g(e(x), f(y)) = g(e'(x), f'(y))),$$
$$(\forall x \in s,\ y \in t \mid P(x, y) \leftrightarrow P'(x, y))$$

and search for them in the available context. This gives a second way in which proof by equality can succeed.

Proof by equality uses the equalities available in its context transitively. Since the inner suboperations of the proof by equality routine are either purely syntactic or are simple searches, this kind of inference is quite efficient.

### 4.3.4 Proof by Monotonicity

Our verifier includes a 'proof-by-monotonicity' feature which keeps track of all operators and predicates for which monotonicity properties have been proved, and also of all relationships of domination between monadic operators and predicates. This mode of inference uses an efficient, syntactic mechanism and so works quite rapidly when it applies. Proof by monotonicity allows statements like

$$(n \supseteq k \;\&\; m \supseteq j) \rightarrow \#\big(\{[x, 0] : x \in n\} \cup \{[x, 1] : x \in m\}\big) \supseteq \#\big(\{[x, 0] : x \in k\} \cup \{[x, 1] : x \in j\}\big) \quad (4.5)$$

and

$$(n \supseteq k \;\&\; m \supseteq j) \rightarrow \#\{[x, y] : x \in n,\ y \in m\} \supseteq \#\{[x, y] : x \in k,\ y \in j\}$$

to be derived immediately. Since the formulae appearing on the right are essentially the definitions of the cardinal addition and multiplication operators, respectively, this easily gives us the formulae

$$(n \supseteq k \;\&\; m \supseteq j) \rightarrow (n + m \supseteq k + j)$$

and

$$(n \supseteq k \;\&\; m \supseteq j) \rightarrow (n * m \supseteq k * j),$$

which can then be used as the basis for further inferences by monotonicity.

Proof by monotonicity works in the following way. The monotonicity properties of all of the verifier's built-in predicates and operators are known *a priori*. For example, $x \in s$ is monotone increasing in its second parameter, whereas $s \supseteq t$ is monotone increasing in its first parameter and monotone decreasing in its second parameter. $s \cup t$ and $s \cap t$ are monotone increasing in both their parameters; $s \setminus t$ is monotone increasing in its first parameter and monotone decreasing in its second. Quantifiers and set formers like

$$(\forall x, y \in s \mid P) \quad \text{and} \quad (\exists x, y \in s \mid P)$$

and

$$\{x, y \in s \mid P\}$$

depend in known monotone fashion on the sets which restrict their bound variables, and preserve the monotonicity properties of their qualifying clauses $P$. The same remark applies to set formers like

$$\{e(x, y) : x \in s,\ y \subseteq t \mid P\}.$$

The propositional operators &, $\vee$, $\neg$, $\rightarrow$ transform the monotonicity properties of their predicate arguments in known ways. $a \;\&\; b$ and $a \vee b$ are monotone increasing in both their parameters; $\neg a$ is monotone decreasing. $a \rightarrow b$ is monotone increasing in its second parameter and monotone decreasing in its first parameter.

These rules allow the monotonicity properties of compound expressions like

$$\{e(x, y) : x \in s,\ y \subseteq t \mid (\forall z, w \mid ([[z, x], [w, y]] \in u \rightarrow z \in v))\} \quad (4.6)$$

to be calculated directly by a procedure which processes its syntax tree bottom up and assigns a dependency characteristic to each node encountered. For example, the expression just displayed is monotone increasing in $s$, $t$, and $v$, but monotone decreasing in $u$.

Besides the properties 'monotone increasing' and 'monotone decreasing', there is one other property which it is easy and profitable to track in this way. As previously explained, an operator $f(x,\ldots)$ of one or more parameters is said to be *additive* in a parameter $x$ if

$$f(x \cup y,\ldots) = f(x,\ldots) \cup f(y,\ldots)$$

for all $x$ and $y$, and a predicate $P(x,\ldots)$ is said to be additive if

$$P(x \cup y,\ldots) \leftrightarrow \big(P(x,\ldots) \,\&\, P(y,\ldots)\big).$$

Using this notion we can easily see that an example like (4.6) is additive in $s$, but not necessarily in its other parameters.

Many of the operators and predicates which appear repeatedly in the sequence of theorems and proofs to which Chap. 5 and Chap. 7 are devoted have useful monotonicity properties. These include

| | |
|---|---|
| Is_map, domain, range | additive |
| Is_map, Svm, 1_1 | decreasing |
| $\bigcup, \mathscr{P}, \#$ | increasing |
| $f\vert_a$ | additive in both parameters |
| $\bigcup$, Finite | additive |
| $\cup, +, \cap, *$ | increasing in both parameters |
| $\in, \subseteq$ | increasing in second parameter |
| $\supseteq, \setminus, -, /$ | increasing in first parameter, decreasing in second. |

The three commands[7]

ENABLE_ELEM(MONOTONE_FCN; *operator_and_predicate_list*)

ENABLE_ELEM(MONOTONE_GROUP; *operator_and_predicate_list*)

ENABLE_ELEM(MONOTONE_MULTIVAR; *operator_and_predicate_list*)

discussed in the previous Sect. 4.3.1 can be used to make the monotonicity properties of other operators available for use in proof-by-monotonicity deductions once these properties have been proved. This enlarges the class of expressions which can be handled automatically. For example, it follows immediately that

$$\#\mathscr{P}\Big(\bigcup\big(\text{domain}(f) \cup \text{range}(f)\big)\Big)$$

is monotone increasing in $f$.

[7] Primitives Set_monot and Pred_monot supporting proof by monotonicity are available in the Ref system as implemented, but the ENABLE_ELEM directive is not implemented yet.

Many of the monotonicity properties which appear in the table shown above follow readily using proof by monotonicity. For example, from the definition of the predicate Is_map, namely

$$\mathsf{Is\_map}(f) \leftrightarrow_{\mathrm{Def}} f = \big\{ \big[x^{[1]}, x^{[2]}\big] : x \in f \big\}$$

it is not hard to show that

$$\mathsf{Is\_map}(f) \leftrightarrow \big(\forall x \in f \mid x = \big[x^{[1]}, x^{[2]}\big]\big).$$

But the predicate on the right is obviously monotone decreasing in $f$, and so it follows that $\mathsf{Is\_map}(f)$ has this same property. The facts that the predicates $\mathsf{Svm}(f)$ ($f$ is a single-valued function) and $\mathsf{1\_1}(f)$ are also monotone decreasing then follow immediately from the definitions of these predicates, which are

$$\mathsf{Svm}(f) \leftrightarrow_{\mathrm{Def}} \mathsf{Is\_map}(f) \;\&\; \big(\forall x \in f,\ y \in f \,\big|\, \big(x^{[1]} = y^{[1]}\big) \to (x = y)\big)$$

and

$$\mathsf{1\_1}(f) \leftrightarrow_{\mathrm{Def}} \mathsf{Svm}(f) \;\&\; \big(\forall x \in f,\ y \in f \,\big|\, \big(x^{[2]} = y^{[2]}\big) \to (x = y)\big).$$

Similarly the fact that $f_{|a}$ is additive in both its parameters follows immediately from its definition, which is

$$f_{|a} =_{\mathrm{Def}} \big\{ p \in f \mid p^{[1]} \in a \big\}.$$

Many small theorems used later in this book follow more or less immediately using proof by monotonicity. Some of these are

Theorem: $\big((G \subseteq F) \;\&\; \mathsf{Is\_map}(F)\big) \to \mathsf{Is\_map}(G)$,
Theorem: $\big((G \subseteq F) \;\&\; \mathsf{Svm}(F)\big) \to \mathsf{Svm}(G)$,
Theorem: $\big((G \subseteq F) \;\&\; \mathsf{1\_1}(F)\big) \to \mathsf{1\_1}(G)$,
Theorem: $\big(\mathsf{Is\_map}(F) \;\&\; \mathsf{Is\_map}(G)\big) \to \mathsf{Is\_map}(F \cup G)$,
Theorem: $F_{|A \cup B} = F_{|A} \cup F_{|B}$,
Theorem: $(F \cup G)_{|A} = F_{|A} \cup G_{|A}$.

The verifier's proof-by-monotonicity mechanism can examine statements whose topmost operator (after explicit or implicit universal quantifiers have been stripped off) is '→' to see if the conclusion of the implication found is an inclusion derivable from the implication's hypotheses via proof by monotonicity. This allows a one-step derivation of statements like (4.5) considered above.

### *4.3.5 Algebraic Deduction*

Once the sequence of set-theoretic proofs with which we will be concerned in Chap. 5 has moved along to the point at which the integers, rationals, and reals have been defined and their main properties established, the normal apparatus of algebraic proof becomes important. One relies on this to establish useful elementary identities on algebraic expressions, and also to show that algebraic combinations of elements belonging to particular sets (e.g. integers, reals, real functions and sequences, etc.) belong to these same sets. Inferences of this latter sort follow readily by syntactic transitivity arguments of the kind discussed already. Algebraic identities follow readily by expansion of multivariate polynomials to normal form, or by systematic or randomized testing of the values of polynomials and rational functions. Expansion to normal form can be used even for non-commutative multiplication operators.

To enable 'proof by algebra' for particular addition, subtraction, and multiplication operators, one issues a verifier command of a form like[8]

$$\text{ENABLE\_ALGEBRA}(s; \oplus; \otimes)$$

or

$$\text{ENABLE\_ALGEBRA}\big(s; \oplus(\mathsf{zero\_constant}); \ominus; \otimes\big)$$

or

$$\text{ENABLE\_ALGEBRA}\big(s; \oplus(\mathsf{zero\_constant}); \ominus; \otimes(\mathsf{unit\_constant})\big)$$

etc. An example is

$$\text{ENABLE\_ALGEBRA}\big(\mathbb{N}; +(\emptyset); \cdot(\{\emptyset\})\big)$$

where $\mathbb{N}$ denotes the set of integers. In these commands '$s$' should designate the set in which the algebraic operators work and on which they are closed. If a 'zero_constant' is supplied with the $\oplus$, it should designate the additive identity for the system. Similarly, if a 'unit_constant' is supplied with the $\otimes$, it should designate the multiplicative identity for the system.

The ENABLE_ALGEBRA command scans the list of all currently available theorems for theorems which reference the operators and object $s$ appearing as ENABLE-_ALGEBRA parameters, collecting all those which state required algebraic rules like

$$\big(\forall x \in s, y \in s \mid (x \oplus y) \in s \;\&\; (x \oplus \mathsf{zero\_constant}) = x\big)$$

and similar commutative, associative, and distributive rules. Automatic algebraic reasoning is turned on if proofs of all the basic axioms of polynomial arithmetic are found. To suspend the use of algebraic reasoning for a given collection of operators one writes a command like

$$\text{DISABLE\_ALGEBRA}(\oplus),$$

where $\oplus$ designates the addition operator that must be present in the group of operators whose automated treatment is being disabled.

[8]A primitive, ALGEBRA, supporting algebraic deduction is available in the Ref system as implemented, but the ENABLE_ALGEBRA directive is not implemented yet.

### 4.3.6 Proof by Closure

Proof by closure is an important special case of the more general 'proof by structure' technique explained in the next section. It works in those common cases in which certain small theorems of the general form

$$\big(P_1(x) \;\&\; P_2(y) \;\&\; \cdots \;\&\; P_k(y)\big) \rightarrow Q\big(f(x,y)\big)$$

will be applied repeatedly. The three statements

$$(x \in \mathbb{N} \;\&\; y \in \mathbb{N}) \rightarrow (x+y) \in \mathbb{N},$$
$$\big(x \in \mathbb{Z} \;\&\; y \in \mathbb{Z} \;\&\; \mathsf{Is\_nonneg}_{\mathbb{Z}}(x) \;\&\; \mathsf{Is\_nonneg}_{\mathbb{Z}}(y)\big) \rightarrow \mathsf{Is\_nonneg}_{\mathbb{Z}}(x *_{\mathbb{Z}} y),$$
$$\big(x \in \mathbb{Z} \;\&\; y \in \mathbb{Z} \;\&\; \mathsf{Is\_nonzero}_{\mathbb{Z}}(x) \;\&\; \mathsf{Is\_nonzero}_{\mathbb{Z}}(y)\big) \rightarrow \mathsf{Is\_nonzero}_{\mathbb{Z}}(x *_{\mathbb{Z}} y),$$

where $\mathbb{N}$ denotes the set of integers and $\mathbb{Z}$ the set of all signed integers are examples.

Common arguments involving obvious uses of such results can be handled by examining the syntax tree of functional expressions $e$ mentioned in the course of a proof, and marking each with all of the monadic attributes the verifier has been instructed to track. All the nodes in the syntax tree of such $e$ are then marked with the attributes which visibly apply, by a 'workpile' algorithm which works by transitive closure, examining each parent node one of whose children has just acquired a new attribute, until no additional attributes result. The propositions generated by this technique are then made available in the current proof context without explicit mention, for use in other proof steps.

To enable this kind of automatic treatment of particular predicates, one issues a verifier command of forms like[9]

$$\text{WATCH}\big(x : x \in \mathbb{Z};\; x : \mathsf{Is\_nonneg}_{\mathbb{Z}}(x);\; x : \mathsf{Is\_nonzero}_{\mathbb{Z}}(x)\big).$$

The verifier then scans the list of all currently available theorems for theorems whose hypotheses are all conjunctions of statements involving the currently enabled predicates with a single variable as argument, and whose conclusions are clauses asserting that some combination of these variables also has a property defined by a predicate being watched. To drop one or more predicates from watched status, one issues a verifier command of a form like

$$\text{DONT\_WATCH}\big(x : x \in \mathbb{Z};\; x : \mathsf{Is\_nonneg}_{\mathbb{Z}}();\; x : \mathsf{Is\_nonzero}_{\mathbb{Z}}()\big).$$

The conclusions produced by the WATCH mechanism automatically become available to the verifier's other proof mechanisms, but can also be captured explicitly by an inference introduced by the special keyword THUS, which also has access to the conclusions produced by the algebraic inference mechanisms described above.

---

[9] As of today, the directives WATCH and DONT_WATCH have not been implemented in Ref.

This makes accelerated inferences like the following possible. Suppose that a statement '$x \in \mathbb{Z}$' has been established. Then the inference

$$\text{THUS} \Longrightarrow ((x *_{\mathbb{Z}} x) +_{\mathbb{Z}} ((x *_{\mathbb{Z}} x) *_{\mathbb{Z}} (x *_{\mathbb{Z}} x))) \in \mathbb{Z}$$
$$\& \ \mathsf{Is\_nonneg}_{\mathbb{Z}}((x *_{\mathbb{Z}} x) +_{\mathbb{Z}} ((x *_{\mathbb{Z}} x) *_{\mathbb{Z}} (x *_{\mathbb{Z}} x)))$$

is immediate.

### *4.3.7 The Behind-the-Scenes Activity of Proof by Structure*

Ref's typelessness contrasts with the more elaborate type systems common in some other automated proof systems. Setting efficiency considerations aside (Ref typically verifies roughly 200 proofs per minute, so these are not of central interest), the advantage of a type system from the point of view of a proof system's user is that numerous small statements concerning the membership of variables in sets key to mathematical discourse (such as the reals, the integers, the real sequences, etc.) are handled implicitly. Once an appropriate type system has been set up, this implicit treatment makes such statements available without further user effort. But a familiar disadvantage of static typing is that, once introduced into a system's foundations, it tends to become over-rigid. This inspires efforts to generalize type systems, and tends to generate baroque intellectual structures unfamiliar to the working mathematician.

For this reason Ref prefers the 'lean and mean' typeless approach of Zermelo–Fraenkel–von Neumann set theory. But then, to recapture the main advantages of a typed approach, it provides the internal, dynamic, type-like mechanism called '*proof by structure*' described in the following paragraphs.

Proof by structure uses a simple internal language of *structure descriptors* ("types", in a weak sense) to keep track of the top structural levels of sets appearing in scenario proofs. Any special set defined in a scenario, for example $\mathbb{N}$, the set of all integers, or $\mathbb{R}$, the set of all reals, can be used as a primary *structure symbol* in this language. This descriptor attaches to all members of the set, for instance any integer has the descriptor $\mathbb{N}$. A significant but less basic example is $\mathbb{Z}_+$, the set of all non-negative signed integers, which does not occur in our present scenarios but could easily be defined. Structure descriptors need not be confined to sets, but can also designate classes, like the classes Ord and Card of all ordinals and of all cardinals, the classes Finite and Infinite of all finite and of all infinite sets, the class NonVoid of all nonnull sets and the class $\mathscr{V}$ of all sets.

Given any symbols $S, S_1, S_2, \ldots$ representing structures, we can then form new structure descriptors:

1. $\{S\}$ describes a set all of whose elements have the descriptor $S$. For example, the set $\mathbb{N}$ has the descriptor $\{\mathbb{N}\}$; the set $\mathscr{P}(\mathbb{N})$ of all sets of integers has the descriptor $\{\{\mathbb{N}\}\}$.

2. $[S_1, S_2]$ describes a pair whose components have, respectively, the descriptors $S_1$ and $S_2$.

These constructions can be compounded. For example

1. $\{[\mathbb{N},\mathbb{N}]\}$ describes a set of integer pairs (and so applies to $\mathbb{Z}$, the set $\{[i, j] : i \in \mathbb{N}, j \in \mathbb{N} \mid i = 0 \vee j = 0\}$ of *signed* integers);
2. $\{[\mathbb{N},\mathscr{V}]\}$ describes a map from integers to elements of any kind, e.g. it describes any finite or infinite(ly denumerable) sequence.

A given set can have several descriptors. For example, a finite sequence of signed integers has the descriptors $\{[\mathbb{N},\mathbb{Z}]\}$ and Finite. Since $\mathbb{Z}$ itself has the descriptor $\{[\mathbb{N},\mathbb{N}]\}$, a sequence of signed integers also has the descriptor $\{[\mathbb{N},[\mathbb{N},\mathbb{N}]]\}$, which in any given situation we may wish either to use or ignore. Infinite sequences of rationals have the descriptors $\{[\mathbb{N},\mathbb{Q}]\}$ and Infinite. Real numbers in Cantor's representation are equivalence classes of such sequences, and accordingly have the descriptors $\{\{[\mathbb{N},\mathbb{Q}]\}\}$ and {Infinite}.

The verifier's internal proof-by-structure mechanism tracks the descriptors of variables and expressions appearing in proofs as precisely as it can. For example, a variable $x$ known to satisfy a clause $x \in \mathbb{N}$ has the descriptor $\mathbb{N}$, while if $x$ is known to satisfy $x \in \mathbb{Z}$ it gets the descriptors $\mathbb{Z}$ and $[\mathbb{N},\mathbb{N}]$.

Setformers and other basic constructors operate in a known way on structure descriptors. Suppose, for example, that $s$ is a set known to have some descriptor $\{D\}$, and that $e(x)$ is an expression having the free variable $x$. Suppose that $e(x)$ can be seen to map elements having the descriptor $D$ into elements having the descriptor $D'$. Then

$$\{e(x) : x \in s \mid P\}$$

has the descriptor $\{D'\}$, while

$$\{[x, e(y)] : x \in s,\ y \in s \mid P\}$$

has the descriptor $\{[D, D']\}$.

When a set $s$ is known to have a descriptor $\{D\}$, any element $x$ for which $x \in s$ has been proved is known to have the descriptor $D$. If $D$ is a primitive descriptor representing a special set, this gives us the assertion $x \in D$, for example $x \in \mathbb{N}$, which may be needed as an auxiliary hypothesis for the application of some theorem. Similarly any set $s$ having the descriptor $\{[\mathbb{N},\mathbb{N}]\}$ is known to satisfy Is_map($s$), and also

$$(\forall x \in s \mid x^{[1]} \in \mathbb{N} \,\&\, x^{[2]} \in \mathbb{N}).$$

Deriving conclusions of this kind automatically is the principal function of the system of structure descriptors.

Many other basic set-theoretic operations have known effects on descriptors. These often follow from the definitions of the operators in question. For example:

(1) If $s$ has the descriptor $\{D\}$, then so does every one of its subsets, and $\mathscr{P}(s)$ has the descriptor $\{\{D\}\}$.

(2) If $s$ has the descriptor $\{\{D\}\}$, then $\bigcup s$ has the descriptor $\{D\}$. Note hat this follows automatically from the definition

$$\{x : y \in s,\ x \in y\}$$

of $\bigcup s$, since the bound variable $y$ in the iterator has the descriptor $\{D\}$, so each of the $x$ has the descriptor $D$, and the set as a whole has the descriptor $\{D\}$.

(3) If $s_1$ and $s_2$ both have a descriptor $\{D\}$, then so does $s_1 \cup s_2$.

(4) If $s_1$ and $s_2$ both have the descriptor Finite, then so does $s_1 \cup s_2$.

(5) If $s_1$ and $s_2$ have descriptors $\{D_1\}$ and $\{D_2\}$, respectively, then $s_1 \cap s_2$ has both descriptors $\{D_1\}$ and $\{D_2\}$. Even if $s_2$ has no descriptor, $s_1 \cap s_2$ and $s_1 \setminus s_2$ have the descriptor $\{D_1\}$, as does any set $s$ for which an assertion $s \subseteq s_1$ has been proved.

(6) If $s_1$ has the descriptor Finite, so do $s_1 \cap s_2$ and $s_1 \setminus s_2$, as does any set $s$ for which an assertion $s \subseteq s_1$ has been proved.

(7) If $s_1$ and $s_2$ have the descriptor Finite, so does any set former

$$\{e : x \in s_1,\ y \in s_2 \mid P\},$$

or any set former $\{e : x \in s_1 \mid P\}$.

(8) $\#s$ always has the descriptor Card. Since the class of cardinals has the descriptor {Ord}, $\#s$ also has the descriptor Ord, as does any $x$ known to be a cardinal. If $s$ has the descriptor Finite, then $\#s$ has the descriptor $\mathbb{N}$. Since $\mathbb{N}$ itself has the descriptor {Finite}, $\#s$ also has the descriptor Finite.

(9) If $s$ has the descriptor $\{D\}$, then any set former like $\{x : x \subseteq s \mid P\}$ is known to have the descriptor $\{\{D\}\}$; this result obviously generalizes.

(10) If sets $s$ and $t$ have the descriptors $\{D\}$ and $\{D'\}$, respectively, then their Cartesian product $s \times t$ has the descriptor $\{[D, D']\}$. If $s$ and $t$ both have the descriptor Finite, so does $s \times t$.

(11) If $s$ and $t$ have descriptors $\{[D, D']\}$ and $\{[D', D'']\}$, respectively, then $t \circ s$ has the descriptor $\{[D, D'']\}$. If $s$ and $t$ both have the descriptor Finite, so does $t \circ s$.

(12) If $s$ and $t$ have descriptors $D, D'$, respectively, then $[s, t]$ has the descriptor $[D, D']$. If $u$ has the descriptor $[D, D']$, then $u^{[1]}$ has the descriptor $D$ and $u^{[2]}$ has the descriptor $D'$.

(13) If $F$ has the descriptor $\{[D, D']\}$, then its inverse $(F)^{-1}$ has the descriptor $\{[D', D]\}$, and any of its domain restrictions $F_{|s}$ has the descriptor $\{[D, D']\}$. If $F$ has the descriptor Finite, then $(F)^{-1}$ and $F_{|s}$ both have the descriptor Finite also.

There may be useful extensions of these ideas to single-valued and one-one maps; also to topological situations, spaces of continuous functions, etc.

Some important conclusions result immediately by use of structure descriptors. For example, the cardinal sum of $s_1$ with $s_2$ is defined as

$$\#\big(\{[x, 0] : x \in s_1\} \cup \{[x, 1] : x \in s_2\}\big),$$

making it obvious that the sum of two integers is an integer. Similarly, the definition of cardinal product, namely

$$\#\{[x, y] : x \in s_1,\ y \in s_2\}$$

makes it obvious that the product of two integers is an integer. Since the difference of integers $n, m$ is defined by $\#(n \setminus m)$, it also follows immediately that the difference of integers is an integer.

Ordinals also have the descriptor {Ord}, since any element of an ordinal is an ordinal. Any $\bigcup s$ of a set having the descriptor {Ord} has the descriptor Ord. It may be worth carrying the set next($\mathbb{N}$) as an additional descriptor. If this is done, $\bigcup s$ will be known to have the descriptor next($\mathbb{N}$) if $s$ has the descriptor {$\mathbb{N}$}, and so to have the descriptor $\mathbb{N}$ (i.e. to be an integer) if there is another $s'$ having the descriptor next($\mathbb{N}$) for which a statement $s \in s'$ is available.

In many cases a definition or theorem appearing in a scenario will characterize the action on structure descriptors of one or more of the function symbols appearing in it. The examples given just above illustrate this. Such facts, combined with the other rules given above, extend the verifier's ability to track the structures of objects appearing in proofs. For example, if $s$, $t$, and $u$ are sets known to have the descriptor {$\mathbb{N}$}, then

$$\{(x * y) + z : x \in s,\ y \in t,\ z \in u \mid P\}$$

is also known to have the descriptor {$\mathbb{N}$}.

The theory of summation yields the fact that $\sum f$ has the descriptor $D$ if $f$ has the descriptors {[$d$, $D$]} and Finite, and if the $\oplus$ operator appearing in the summation can be shown to map pairs of objects having the descriptor $D$ into objects having this same descriptor. Thus, for example, the sum or product of any set former like

$$\{[[x, y, z], (x * y) + z] : x \in s,\ y \in t,\ z \in u \mid P\}$$

is also known to be an integer if $s$, $t$, and $u$ are sets known to have the descriptors {$\mathbb{N}$} and Finite.

The structure definition mechanism explained above carries over in a useful way to recursively defined functions (in our set-theoretic context, these can be functions defined by transfinite induction). To see why such extension is possible, we first note that the system of descriptors extends readily to function symbols, since these are very close semantically to sets of pairs. For example, the descriptor {[$D_1$, $D_2$]} can be ascribed to any one-parameter function symbol which maps each object having the descriptor $D_1$ into an object having the descriptor $D_2$. Similarly, the descriptor {[[$D_1$, $D_2$], $D_3$]} can be ascribed to any two-parameter function symbol which yields an object having the descriptor $D_3$ whenever its two parameters have the respective descriptors $D_1$ and $D_2$. (For example, the integer addition operator + has the descriptor {[[$\mathbb{N}$, $\mathbb{N}$], $\mathbb{N}$]}, but also the descriptors {[[$\mathcal{V}$, $\mathcal{V}$], Ord]}, since it always produces an ordinal, and the descriptor {[[Finite, Finite], $\mathbb{N}$]}, since it produces an integer for any two finite inputs.) In the three-parameter case, {[[[$D_1$, $D_2$], $D_3$], $D_4$]}

can be ascribed to any three-parameter function symbol which yields an object having the descriptor $D_4$ whenever its three parameters have the respective descriptors $D_1$, $D_2$, and $D_3$.

Using these descriptors, we can state the rule for function application as follows: If a one-parameter function symbol $f$ has the descriptor $\{[D_1, D_2]\}$, and $x$ has the descriptor $D_1$, then $f(x)$ has the descriptor $D_2$. Similarly, if a two-parameter function symbol $f$ has the descriptor $\{[[D_1, D_2], D_3]\}$, and its two arguments $x_1, x_2$ have the descriptors $D_1, D_2$, then $f(x_1, x_2)$ has the descriptor $D_3$. We leave it to the reader to formulate the rules for more than two arguments.

Function compounding acts in an obvious way on descriptors, for example if $f$ has the descriptor $\{[D_1, D_2]\}$ and $g$ has the descriptor $\{[D_2, D_3]\}$, then $g(f(\cdot))$ has the descriptor $\{[D_1, D_3]\}$. Rules like this make it obvious why

$$\#\big(\big\{[x,0] : x \in s_1\big\} \cup \big\{[x,1] : x \in s_2\big\}\big),$$

yields an integer for every pair of integer arguments: the functional expression $\{[x,0] : x \in s_1\}$ has the descriptor $\{[\mathsf{Finite}, \mathsf{Finite}]\}$ simply because it is a set former with $s_1$ as its only free variable, and likewise for $\{[x,1] : x \in s_2\}$. Since the union operator $\cup$ has the descriptor $\{[[\mathsf{Finite}, \mathsf{Finite}], \mathsf{Finite}]\}$, it follows immediately that $\{[x,0] : x \in s_1\} \cup \{[x,1] : x \in s_2\}$ has the descriptor $\{[[\mathsf{Finite}, \mathsf{Finite}], \mathsf{Finite}]\}$ also. Since $\#$ has the descriptors $\{[\mathsf{Finite}, \mathsf{Finite}]\}$ and $\{[\mathcal{V}, \mathsf{Ord}]\}$, $\#(\{[x,0] : x \in s_1\} \cup \{[x,1] : x \in s_2\})$ has the descriptors $\{[[\mathbb{N}, \mathbb{N}], \mathsf{Finite}]\}$ and $\{[[\mathbb{N}, \mathbb{N}], \mathsf{Ord}]\}$, and therefore $\{[[\mathbb{N}, \mathbb{N}], \mathbb{N}]\}$. Much the same argument applies to the integer product.

Next consider a transfinite recursive definition of one of the general types we allow, namely

$$f(s,t) =_{\mathrm{Def}} d\big(\big\{g\big(f\big(x, h(s,t)\big), s, t\big) : x \in s \,\big|\, P\big(x, f\big(x, h(s,t)\big), s, t\big)\big\}, s, t\big),$$

where we assume that the functions $d$, $g$, and $h$ have been defined prior to the occurrence of the recursive definition shown. In working with this definition one needs to establish that $f$ has some descriptor $\{[[D_1, D_2], D_3]\}$, i.e. that it yields an element having descriptor $D_3$ for any input arguments with descriptors $D_1$, $D_2$, respectively.

This conclusion is valid under the following circumstances: we need to know that the null set has descriptor $D_1$, that one can ascribe the descriptor $\{D_1\}$ to any set which has the descriptor $D_1$, and that there exists a descriptor $D'$ such that

(a) $h$ has the descriptor $\{[[D_1, D_2], D_2]\}$;
(b) $g$ has the descriptor $\{[[[D_3, D_1], D_2], D']\}$;
(c) $d$ has the descriptor $\{[[[\{D'\}, D_1], D_2], D_3]\}$.

Then in the ground case of the transfinite recursive definition $f(\emptyset, t)$ has the value $d(\emptyset, s, t)$, and so must produce an element with the descriptor $D_3$. In the remaining case it follows inductively (given that $s$ and $t$ have the respective descriptors $D_1$, $D_2$) that $f(x, h(s,t))$ has the descriptor $D_3$ for every $x \in s$, so that $g(f(x, h(s,t)), s, t)$ has the descriptor $D'$, and so

$$\big\{g\big(f\big(x, h(s,t)\big), s, t\big) : x \in s \,\big|\, P\big(x, f\big(x, h(s,t)\big), s, t\big)\big\} \tag{4.7}$$

has the descriptor $\{D'\}$. Therefore the right side of the recursive definition seen above has the descriptor $D_3$, and it follows inductively that $f$ has the descriptor $\{[[D_1, D_2], D_3]\}$.

If $s$ has the descriptor Finite, then the set (4.7) will have this descriptor also, and so if $d$ has the descriptor $\{[[[\mathsf{Finite}, \mathsf{Finite}], D_2], \mathsf{Finite}]\}$, $f$ will have the descriptor $\{[[\mathsf{Finite}, D_2], \mathsf{Finite}]\}$. On the other hand, if $d$ is a monadic operator like the selector arb (which is postulated to satisfy $\mathsf{arb}(\emptyset) = \emptyset \,\&\, (X \neq \emptyset \rightarrow \mathsf{arb}(X) \in X)$), and so has the descriptor $\{[\{D_3\}, D_3]\}$ (where the null set must have the descriptor $D_3$), then $g$ must have the descriptor $\{[[[\mathsf{Finite}, \mathsf{Finite}], D_2], \mathsf{Finite}]\}$, and $s$ the descriptors $\{\mathsf{Finite}\}$ and Finite, for $f(s,t)$ to have the descriptor Finite. In this case $f$ has once again the descriptor $\{[[\mathsf{Finite}, D_2], \mathsf{Finite}]\}$.

### *4.3.8 'Blobbing' More General Formulae Down to a Specified Decidable or Semi-decidable Sublanguage of Set Theory*

'BLOBBING' captures Aristotle's insight that statements true in logic are true because their form can be matched to some template known to generate true statements only. The basic syntactic technique which it involves can be explained as follows: Suppose that we are given a language $L$ for which a full or partial decision algorithm is available. Then any formula $F$ can be 'reduced' or 'blobbed down' to a formula in the language $L$, in the following way. Work top-down through the syntax tree of $F$, until some operator not belonging to the language $L$ is encountered. Replace the whole subexpression $G$ below this level by a 'blob', i.e. by a freshly generated variable (either individual or propositional, as appropriate).

'Blobs' generated in this way from separate subformulae of $F$ should be made identical wherever possible; this can be done whenever they are structurally identical up to renaming of bound variables, or where part of the structure belongs to an equational theory for which a decision or quasi-decision algorithm is available. The 'blobbed' variant of $F$ is the formula that results from this replacement. If the blobbed version of $F$ is a consequence of the blobbed versions of the union of all our previous assumptions and conclusions, then $F$ follows from these assumptions and conclusions, and can therefore be added to the set of available conclusions. 'Default' or 'ELEM' deduction is the special case of this general observation which results when we blob down to an extended multilevel syllogistic, of the kind described above.

The following is an example of 'blobbing'. Given the input formula

$$\begin{aligned}\big(\{m(x) : x \in s \mid x \subseteq t\} \subseteq \{m(x) : x \in s \mid x \in t\}\\ \&\, \{m(x) : x \in s \mid x \in t\} \subseteq \{m(x) : x \in s \mid x \subseteq t \vee r\}\big)\\ \rightarrow \{m(y) : y \in s \mid y \subseteq t\} \subseteq \{m(x) : x \in s \mid x \subseteq t \vee r\},\end{aligned}$$

its blobbed version (blobbed down to the elementary theory of sets and inclusion relationships) is

$$(1\_ \subseteq 2\_ \ \& \ 2\_ \subseteq 3\_) \rightarrow 1\_ \subseteq 3\_$$

which makes the truth of our original, rather enigmatic formula obvious.

## 4.3.9 Accelerated Instantiation of Quantifiers and Set Formers

Steps which simply generate instances of quantified formulae and implicitly quantified formulae involving set formers are common in the proofs in which we will be interested. For example, we may need to deduce the contradiction

$$\neg\big(e(c) = e(a) \ \& \ a \in s\big),$$

for some fresh symbol $a$, from the set-theoretic statement

$$e(c) \notin \big\{e(x) : x \in s\big\},$$

or to deduce

$$\big(\big(a \in s \ \& \ c = e(a) \ \& \ P(a)\big) \ \& \ \neg\big(a \in s \ \& \ c = e'(a) \ \& \ P'(a)\big)\big)$$
$$\vee \ \big(\big(\neg\big(b \in s \ \& \ c = e(b) \ \& \ P(b)\big)\big) \ \& \ \big(b \in s \ \& \ c = e'(b) \ \& \ P'(b)\big)\big),$$

where $a$ and $b$ are two newly generated symbols, from a previously proved set-theoretic statement

$$\big(c \in \big\{e(x) : x \in s \mid P(x)\big\} \ \& \ \neg\big(c \in \big\{e'(x) : x \in s \mid P'(x)\big\}\big)\big)$$
$$\vee \ \big(\big(\neg\big(c \in \big\{e(x) : x \in s \mid P(x)\big\}\big)\big) \ \& \ c \in \big\{e'(x) : x \in s \mid P'(x)\big\}\big).$$

Our verifier handles steps of this common kind in the following friendly way. All variable names which are not explicitly bound by quantifiers (or bound in set formers) are temporarily regarded as 'constants', i.e. substitutions for them are temporarily forbidden. We first search for quantifiers, which may be nested several levels deep within propositional structures like

$$\big(\big(\forall x \mid P(x)\big) \ \& \cdots \big(\exists y \mid Q(y)\big) \cdots\big)$$
$$\vee \cdots \rightarrow \cdots \neg\big(\forall z \mid R(z)\big) \cdots$$

but not nested within other quantifiers. We generate unique bound variables for each of these quantifiers, also making sure that they are distinct from any free variables that appear.

Each quantifier in such a propositional structure has an implicit 'sign', determined by the following simple rules:

(i) Un-nested universals are positive, while un-nested existentials are negative.
(ii) The nesting of a quantifier within a construction $a \,\&\, b$ or $a \vee b$ does not affect its sign.
(iii) Each level of nesting of a quantifier within a negation $\neg a$ reverses its sign, e.g. $\neg \cdots \neg \cdots \neg \cdots (\exists y \mid Q(y))$ is positive.
(iv) $a \to b$ is simply $(\neg b) \vee a$.

In nested propositional constructs like those shown above, we could if we wanted move any quantifier out to the front by using the standard rules

$$(\forall x \mid (P(x) \,\&\, A)) \leftrightarrow ((\forall x \mid P(x)) \,\&\, A)$$

$$(\forall x \mid (P(x) \vee A)) \leftrightarrow ((\forall x \mid P(x)) \vee A)$$

$$(\exists x \mid (P(x) \,\&\, A)) \leftrightarrow ((\exists x \mid P(x)) \,\&\, A)$$

$$(\exists x \mid (P(x) \vee A)) \leftrightarrow ((\exists x \mid P(x)) \vee A),$$

where we assume that the variable $x$ is not free in $A$. Once moved out these quantifiers could be instantiated, subject to the normal rules:

(a) Only a previously unused constant symbol can be substituted for a negatively (existentially) quantified bound variable.
(b) Any constant expression at all can be substituted for a positively (universally) quantified bound variable.

It is clear that the instantiations allowed by these rules can be performed without the preliminary step of moving the quantifier to the front. Any number of negative quantifiers can be replaced, one after another, by hitherto unused constant symbols. Then any number of positive quantifiers can be replaced by any desired expressions. It is clear that these rules apply also to nested quantifiers, which can be subjected to sequences of instantiations moving inward. Note, however, that an existential nested within a universal can never be instantiated unless the universal is first instantiated in accordance with the rule we have stated.

Given a formula $F$ and a second $F'$, it is easy to determine, by comparing their syntax trees, whether $F'$ arises from $F$ by such a set of instantiations. If it does, then $F'$ is valid deduction from $F$. Our verifier allows steps of this kind to be indicated simply by writing the keyword INSTANCE.[10]

Here are a few examples showing that this works well for various familiar pure-predicate cases:

To prove

$$(\forall x \mid P(x)) \to (\exists x \mid P(x))$$

we form its negative

$$(\forall x \mid P(x)) \,\&\, \neg(\exists x \mid P(x))$$

[10] While the accelerated instantiation mechanism is implemented in the current Ref system, the INSTANCE facility is not available yet: the instantiating substitution must be indicated explicitly.

and then the instance

$$P(c) \mathbin{\&} \neg P(c)$$

which is clearly impossible, proving the validity of our first statement. Similarly we can prove the validity of

$$(\exists y \mid (\forall x \mid P(x,y))) \to (\forall x \mid (\exists y \mid P(x,y)))$$

by forming its negative, which is

$$(\exists y \mid (\forall x \mid P(x,y))) \mathbin{\&} (\neg(\forall x \mid (\exists y \mid P(x,y)))),$$

and then instantiating this to the impossible $P(d,c) \mathbin{\&} \neg P(d,c)$.

Statements involving membership in set formers can be treated in much the same way, since

$$a \in \{e(x) : x \in s \mid P(x)\}$$

is a synonym for

$$(\exists x \mid a = e(x) \mathbin{\&} x \in s \mathbin{\&} P(x)).$$

Thus every membership (resp. non-membership) statement counts initially as negative (resp. positive) and instantiates to $a = e(c) \mathbin{\&} c \in s \mathbin{\&} P(c)$ (resp. $a \neq e(c) \vee c \notin s \vee \neg P(c)$), where $c$ must be a new constant if the context of the set former makes it negative, but can be any expression if the context of the set former makes it positive. This observation makes it possible to recognize the deduction shown at the very start of this section as an instantiation, which can be written as

$$\text{INSTANCE}(\mathsf{Stat1}) \Longrightarrow \neg(e(c) = e(c) \mathbin{\&} c \in s)$$

in our verifier. Similarly, the deduction in the second example at the start of this section is a combination of positive and negative instantiations which can be written as

$$\begin{aligned}&\text{INSTANCE}(\mathsf{Stat2}) \Longrightarrow\\ &\quad((a \in s \mathbin{\&} c = e(a) \mathbin{\&} P(a)) \mathbin{\&} \neg(a \in s \mathbin{\&} c = e'(a) \mathbin{\&} P'(a)))\\ &\quad\vee((\neg(b \in s \mathbin{\&} c = e(b) \mathbin{\&} P(b))) \mathbin{\&} (b \in s \mathbin{\&} c = e'(b) \mathbin{\&} P'(b))).\end{aligned}$$

Note finally that the Boolean equivalence operator '$\leftrightarrow$' must be decomposed into its two parts $a \mathbin{\&} b \vee (\neg b) \mathbin{\&} (\neg a)$, since these give different signs to quantifiers or set formers nested within them.

### *4.3.10 Computation with Hereditarily Finite Sets*

Set theory, as we will work with it later in this book, is a family of sentences concerning objects, some of which lie far beyond the finite realm within which conventional computational mechanisms can operate. But the hereditarily finite sets considered earlier are accessible to computation and can model all standard computational processes in quite a satisfactory way. These are the sets which can be constructed starting from the null set $\{\}$ by repeatedly forming sets of the form $\{s_1, s_2, \ldots, s_n\}$ using elements $s_1, s_2, \ldots, s_n$ previously defined. Five examples are

$$\{\}, \{\{\}\}, \{\{\}, \{\{\}\}\}, \{\{\{\}, \{\{\}\}\}\}, \{\{\{\}\}, \{\{\{\}, \{\{\}\}\}\}\}, \text{etc.}$$

We can readily define the standardized representation $\mathsf{rep}(s)$ of each such set $s$ recursively as

$$\mathsf{rep}(s) = \{\mathsf{rep}(s_1), \mathsf{rep}(s_2), \ldots, \mathsf{rep}(s_n)\},$$

where we assume that (after duplicates have been removed) the elements on the right are arranged in *lexicographic order*. This is the particular ordering which places a set $d$ before another set $t$ (where both $d$ and $t$ are hereditarily finite and $d \neq t$) when the following holds: if the elements of the 'symmetric difference' $(d \setminus t) \cup (t \setminus d)$ are recursively arranged in lexicographic order, then the largest of them happens to belong to $t$.

Any suitable computer encoding of the system of strings defined in this way can be used as the basis of a system for programmed computation with (entirely general) hereditarily finite sets.

Hereditarily finite sets satisfy several general induction principles. If there exists a hereditarily finite set (resp. finite) $t$ satisfying $P(t)$, where $P$ is any predicate, then there also exists a hereditarily finite (resp. finite) set $t'$ satisfying

$$P(t') \,\&\, (\forall t \subseteq t' \mid (t \neq t') \rightarrow \neg P(t)).$$

A second induction principle that is sometimes easier to apply is as follows. If there exists a hereditarily finite set $t$ satisfying $P(t)$, where $P$ is any predicate, then there also exists a hereditarily finite set $t'$ satisfying

$$P(t') \,\&\, (\forall t \in t' \mid \neg P(t)).$$

This second induction principle remains valid for infinite sets.

An adequate computational system based on hereditarily finite sets needs only the following modest collection of primitives.

(i) Given a set $s$, we can form the singleton set $\{s\}$. (This primitive function maps sets to sets.)
(ii) Any two sets can be tested for equality (they are equal if and only if their standard representations are the same). (The primitive $s_1 = s_2$ maps pairs of sets to Boolean values.)
(iii) Any set $s$ can be tested for membership in any other. $s_1$ is a member of $s_2$ if and only if $s_1$ is equal to one of the items in the list of members defining $s_2$. (The primitive $s_1 \in s_2$ maps pairs of sets to Boolean values.)

(iv) We can find an element arbb($s$) of any set $s$ other than the null set. (This primitive function maps sets to sets.) It is convenient to let $x = $ arbb($s$) be the first element of $s$ in the lexicographic order described above. This ensures that arbb($s$) and $s$ have no element in common, since if there were any such element $y$, then $y$ would come before $x$ in the standard order of elements of $x$ (indeed, an easy inductive argument shows that $v$ lexicographically precedes $u$ whenever $v \in u$), contradicting our assumption that $x$ is the first of these elements. (To complete the definition of the function arbb, it is convenient to put arbb($\{\}$) $= \{\}$.)

(v) Given two sets $s_1$, $s_2$ we can form the set $s_1$ with $s_2$ obtained by adding $s_2$ to the list of elements of $s_1$. If $s_2$ is already on this list, then $s_1$ with $s_2$ is just $s_1$. (This primitive maps sets to sets.)

(vi) Given two sets $s_1$, $s_2$ we can form the set $s_1$ less $s_2$ obtained by removing $s_2$ from the list of elements of $s_1$. If $s_2$ is not on this list, then $s_1$ with $s_2$ is just $s_1$. (This primitive also maps sets to sets.)

(vii) New set-valued and new Boolean-valued functions of hereditarily finite sets can be introduced by writing (direct or recursive) definitions

> **function** *name*($s_1, s_2, \ldots, s_n$);
>     **return if** *cond*$_1$ **then** *expn*$_1$
>     **elseif** *cond*$_2$ **then** *expn*$_2$
>        . . .
>     **elseif** *cond*$_m$ **then** *expn*$_m$
>     **else** *expn*$_{m+1}$ **end if** ;
> **end** *name*.

Here all the *cond*$_1, \ldots,$ *cond*$_m$ must be nested, Boolean-valued expressions built using primitive or previously defined function names, plus the elementary Boolean operations &, $\vee$, $\neg$, etc., the constant $\emptyset$ representing $\{\}$, and the variables $s_1, s_2, \ldots, s_n$. Either all the *expn*$_1$, *expn*$_2, \ldots,$ *expn*$_{m+1}$ must be set-valued, in which case the defined function 'name' is also set-valued, or all the *expn*$_1$, *expn*$_2, \ldots,$ *expn*$_{m+1}$ must be Boolean-valued, in which case the defined function 'name' is also Boolean-valued.

Function definitions of this type can be used to program many other basic and advanced set-theoretic functions. For example, we can write

> **function** union($s_1, s_2$);
>     **return if** $s_1 = \emptyset$ **then** $s_2$
>         **else** union$\big(s_1$ less arbb($s_1$), $s_2\big)$ with arbb($s_1$) **end if** ;
> **end** union;

> **function** difference($s_1, s_2$);
>     **return if** $s_2 = \emptyset$ **then** $s_1$
>         **else** difference$\big(s_1$ less arbb($s_2$), $s_2$ less arbb($s_2$)$\big)$ **end if** ;
> **end** difference;

```
function incs(s1, s2);
    return difference(s2, s1) = ∅;
end incs;

function intersection(s1, s2);
    return difference(s1, difference(s1, s2));
end intersection;

function next(s); return s with s; end next;

function last(s);
    return if s = ∅ then ∅ elseif s = {arbb(s)} then arbb(s)
        else last(s less arbb(s)) end if ;
end last;

function prev(s); return s less last(s); end prev;

function is_integer(s);
    return if s = ∅ then true
        else s = next(prev(s)) & is_integer(prev(s)) end if ;
end is_integer.
```

Note that the hereditarily finite sets $s$ for which is_integer($s$) is true are precisely those of the recursive form

$$\{\{\}, \{\{\}\}, \{\{\}, \{\{\}\}\}, \ldots, \mathsf{prev}(s)\},$$

which represent integers in their von Neumann encoding. For such integers $n$ we have $\mathsf{last}(n) = n - 1$, $\mathsf{last}(n - 1) = n - 2$, etc.

From here we can easily go on to define the cardinality operator and all the standard arithmetic operations, e.g.

```
function #s;
    return if s = ∅ then ∅
        else next(#(s less arbb(s))) end if ;
end #;

function sum(s1, s2);
    return if s1 = ∅ then #s2
        else next(sum(prev(s1), s2)) end if ;
end sum;

function product(s1, s2);
    return if s1 = ∅ then ∅
        else sum(s2, product(prev(s1), s2)) end if ;
end product;
```

```
function exp(s1, s2);
    return if s2 = ∅ then {∅}
        else product(s1, exp(s1, prev(s2))) end if;
end exp;

function minus(s1, s2);  return #difference(s1, s2);  end minus.
```

Our next group of procedures lets us work with maps:

```
function ordered_pair(s1, s2);
    return {{s1}, {{s1}, {s2, {s2}}}};
end ordered_pair;

function s^[1];  return arbb(arbb(s));  end _^[1];

function s^[2];
    return arbb(s less arbb(s)) less arbb(s)^[1];
end _^[2];

function is_pair(s);
    return s = ordered_pair(s^[1], s^[2]);
end is_pair;

function is_map(s);
    return if s = ∅ then true
        else is_pair(arbb(s)) & is_map(s less arbb(s)) end if;
end is_map;

function domain(s);
    return if s = ∅ then ∅
        elseif is_pair(arbb(s)) then
            domain(s less arbb(s)) with arbb(s)^[1]
        else domain(s less arbb(s))
        end if;
end domain;

function range(s);
    return if s = ∅ then ∅
        elseif is_pair(arbb(s)) then
            range(s less arbb(s)) with arbb(s)^[2]
        else range(s less arbb(s))
        end if;
end range;

function is_single_valued(s);
    return #s = #domain(s);
end is_single_valued;
```

```
function restriction(s1, s2);
    return if s1 = ∅ then ∅
        elseif is_pair(arbb(s1)) & arbb(s1)[1] ∈ s2 then
            restriction(s1 less arbb(s1), s2) with arbb(s1)
        else restriction(s1 less arbb(s1), s2)
end restriction;

function values_at(s1, s2);
    return range(restriction(s2, {s1}));
end values_at;

function value_at(s1, s2);
    return arbb(values_at(s1, s2));
end value_at;

function last_of(s);  return value_at(prev(#s), s);  end last_of.
```

Another useful notion is '$s_1$ *is a sequence of elements of* $s_2$':

```
function is_sequence(s);
    return is_map(s) & is_single_valued(s)
        & is_integer(domain(s));
end is_sequence;

function is_sequence_of(s1, s2);
    return is_sequence(s1)
        & incs(s2, range(s1)) = ∅;
end is_sequence_of.
```

Function definitions like those seen above are said to be '*mirrored in logic*' if for each function definition

```
function name(s1, s2, ..., sn);
    return if cond1 then expn1
        elseif cond2 then expn2
            ...
        elseif condm then expnm
        else expnm+1 end if ;
end name
```

we have defined a corresponding logical symbol '*Name*' for which the statement

$$
\begin{aligned}
(\forall s_1 \in \mathsf{HF},\ s_2 \in \mathsf{HF}, \ldots,\ s_n \in \mathsf{HF} \mid \\
\mathit{Name}(s_1, s_2, \ldots, s_n) = {} & \textbf{if } \mathit{cond}_1 \textbf{ then } \mathit{expn}_1 \\
& \textbf{elseif } \mathit{cond}_2 \textbf{ then } \mathit{expn}_2 \\
& \ldots \\
& \textbf{elseif } \mathit{cond}_m \textbf{ then } \mathit{expn}_m \\
& \textbf{else } \mathit{expn}_{m+1} \textbf{ end if} )
\end{aligned}
$$

is available as a theorem. (In case 'name' is Boolean-valued, '$\leftrightarrow$' must supersede '$=$' in the above statement.) It will now be shown that every one of the function definitions given above and all others like them can be mirrored in logic. This lets us use the following general lemma as one of our mechanisms of deduction.

#### 4.3.10.1 Mirroring Lemma

**Lemma 4.1** (Mirroring) *Let $name(s_1, s_2, \ldots, s_n)$ be a set-valued function appearing in a sequence of functions defined in the manner described above, and let $c_1, c_2, \ldots, c_{n+1}$ be hereditarily finite sets represented by logical terms $e_1, e_2, \ldots, e_{n+1}$ as described above. Suppose that the calculated value of $name(c_1, c_2, \ldots, c_n)$ is $c_{n+1}$. Suppose that 'Name' is the logical function symbol which mirrors 'name'. Then the formula*

$$Name(e_1, e_2, \ldots, e_n) = e_{n+1}$$

*is a theorem. Similarly, if 'name' is a Boolean-valued function, then*

$$Name(e_1, e_2, \ldots, e_n) \leftrightarrow e_{n+1}$$

*is a theorem.*

*Proof* Our proof will proceed by induction on the number $h$ of steps involved in an evaluation of a function having a definition like

$$
\begin{aligned}
&\textbf{function } \mathit{name}(s_1, s_2, \ldots, s_n); \\
&\quad \textbf{return if } \mathit{cond}_1(s_1, s_2, \ldots, s_n) \textbf{ then } \mathit{expn}_1(s_1, s_2, \ldots, s_n) \\
&\qquad \textbf{elseif } \mathit{cond}_2(s_1, s_2, \ldots, s_n) \textbf{ then } \mathit{expn}_2(s_1, s_2, \ldots, s_n) \\
&\qquad \ldots \\
&\qquad \textbf{elseif } \mathit{cond}_m \textbf{ then } \mathit{expn}_m(s_1, s_2, \ldots, s_n) \\
&\qquad \textbf{else } \mathit{expn}_{m+1}(s_1, s_2, \ldots, s_n) \textbf{ end if}; \\
&\textbf{end } \mathit{name}
\end{aligned}
$$

on the actual parameters $c_1, \ldots, c_n$.

To get started, we must check that each primitive of our programming language (singleton formation, equality, etc.) is properly mirrored by a suitable construct of our basic system of logic, which is trivial save for the case of arbb, which cannot simply be mirrored by the choice operator arb. To see where the difficulty lies, consider e.g. the doubleton set $s = \{\{\}, \{\{\{\}\}\}\}$; it is then plain that whereas the programming operation arbb must give the result $\mathsf{arbb}(s) = \{\}$, the logical operator arb is not committed to do the same. However, we can introduce in logic a correspondent 'Arbb' of arbb in the following fashion. We recursively define the lexicographic strict ordering as

$$\mathsf{Smaller}(x, y) \leftrightarrow_{\mathrm{Def}} \big\{v \in y \,\big|\, \big\{w \in (x \cup y) \mid \mathsf{Smaller}(v, w)\big\} \subseteq (x \cap y)\big\} \setminus x \neq \emptyset,$$

and then state that 'Arbb' must pick the smallest element out of any set $x$:

$$\mathsf{Arbb}(x) =_{\mathrm{Def}} \mathsf{arb}\big(\big\{v \in x \,\big|\, \big\{w \in x \mid \mathsf{Smaller}(w, v)\big\} = \emptyset\big\}\big).$$

Suppose now that the assertion of the mirroring lemma is true for all evaluations having fewer steps than $h$. The final step in an evaluation of the recursive function displayed above will end at some branch, say the $k$th branch, of the conditional expression following the keyword **'return'**, and will be preceded by evaluation of all the conditions

$$cond_1(c_1, c_2, \ldots, c_n),\ cond_2(c_1, c_2, \ldots, c_n), \ldots, cond_k(c_1, c_2, \ldots, c_n)$$

which appear before this branch, and of the expression

$$expn_k(c_1, c_2, \ldots, c_n)$$

occurring in the $k$th branch. This last expression will return some value '*val*', which then becomes the value $c_{n+1}$ returned by the function '*name*'. In the situation considered, the first $k-1$ Boolean conditions must have the value 'false' and the $k$th must have the value 'true'. Since all of these subevaluations must involve fewer steps than $h$, there must exist proofs of the theorems

$$\neg Cond_1(e_1, e_2, \ldots, e_n),\ \neg Cond_2(e_1, e_2, \ldots, e_n), \ldots,$$
$$\neg Cond_{k-1}(e_1, e_2, \ldots, e_n),\ Cond_k(e_1, e_2, \ldots, e_n),$$

and there must also exist a proof of the statement

$$Expn_k(e_1, e_2, \ldots, e_n) = e_{n+1},$$

where $e_i$ designates $c_i$ for $i = 1, \ldots, n$ and $e_{n+1}$ designates *val*.

It follows from these results that we can prove

$$\begin{array}{l}\textbf{if } Cond_1(e_1, e_2, \ldots, e_n) \textbf{ then } Expn_1(e_1, e_2, \ldots, e_n)\\ \quad \textbf{elseif } Cond_2(e_1, e_2, \ldots, e_n) \textbf{ then } Expn_2(e_1, e_2, \ldots, e_n)\\ \quad \ldots\\ \quad \textbf{elseif } Cond_m \textbf{ then } Expn_m(e_1, e_2, \ldots, e_n)\\ \quad \textbf{else } Expn_{m+1}(e_1, e_2, \ldots, e_n) \textbf{ end if } = e_{n+1}.\end{array}$$

Since

$$\big(\forall s_1 \in \mathsf{HF},\ s_2 \in \mathsf{HF}, \ldots, s_n \in \mathsf{HF} \mid \mathit{Name}(s_1, s_2, \ldots, s_n) = \\ \textbf{if } \mathit{Cond}_1(s_1, s_2, \ldots, s_n) \textbf{ then } \mathit{Expn}_1(s_1, s_2, \ldots, s_n) \\ \textbf{elseif } \mathit{Cond}_2(s_1, s_2, \ldots, s_n) \textbf{ then } \mathit{Expn}_2(s_1, s_2, \ldots, s_n) \\ \ldots \\ \textbf{elseif } \mathit{Cond}_m(s_1, s_2, \ldots, s_n) \textbf{ then } \mathit{Expn}_m(s_1, s_2, \ldots, s_n) \\ \textbf{else } \mathit{Expn}_{m+1}(s_1, s_2, \ldots, s_n) \textbf{ end if}\big),$$

this proves that $\mathit{Name}(e_1, e_2, \ldots, e_n) = e_{n+1}$. □

Note that the mirroring lemma only provides us with a way of proving statements giving particular constant values of recursively defined functions and predicates, but not a way of proving any universally quantified statement. For example,

$$\mathsf{Domain}\big(\mathsf{With}\big(\{\mathsf{Ordered\_pair}(0,0)\}, \mathsf{Ordered\_pair}(1,1)\big)\big) = \mathsf{With}\big(\{0\}, 1\big)$$

follows by mirroring, but no universally quantified statement like

$$\big(\forall x \mid \mathsf{Is\_integer}(x) \rightarrow \big(x = \emptyset \vee \big(x = \mathsf{Next}\big(\mathsf{Prev}(x)\big) \;\&\; \mathsf{Is\_integer}\big(\mathsf{Prev}(x)\big)\big)\big)\big)$$

can be proved simply by mirroring. In fact, even a statement like

$$\mathsf{Domain}\big(\mathsf{With}\big(\{\mathsf{Ordered\_pair}(0,x)\}, \mathsf{Ordered\_pair}(1,y)\big)\big) = \mathsf{With}(0,1)$$

lies beyond the reach of the mirroring lemma, since it involves the symbolic variables $x$ and $y$.

#### 4.3.10.2 Deduction by Semi-symbolic Computation

A useful and much more general 'Deduction by semi-symbolic computation' primitive is included in our verifier. This operation lets us use recursive relationships as means of easy computational deduction within the completely controlled environment in which a verifier must operate. The idea is to evaluate certain elementary operations on hereditarily finite sets explicitly, while leaving all other expressions unchanged. Recursive relationships are used as long as they apply, allowing complex identities and logical equivalences to be derived by single deduction steps. We shall see that this makes a wide variety of 'Mathematica'-like (cf. [Wol03]) conclusions directly available within the verifier.

A prototypical example is furnished by the recursive identity

$$\big(\mathsf{Is\_seq}(B) \;\&\; m \in \mathsf{domain}(B) \;\&\; \mathsf{range}(B) \subseteq \mathbb{N}\big) \rightarrow \\ \sum(B_{|m}) = \textbf{if } m = 0 \textbf{ then } 0 \textbf{ else } \sum(B_{|m}) = \Big(\sum B_{|(m-1)}\Big) + B[m] \textbf{ end if}$$

(where $\mathbb{N}$ denotes the set of integers, and the predicate $\mathsf{Is\_seq}(t)$ is true if $t$ is a sequence, i.e. a mapping whose domain is either a finite integer or the set $\mathbb{N}$ of all integers). This simple general theorem is easily proved using the definition of the summation operator $\sum$ that we shall see in Sect. 5.8. Deduction by semi-symbolic computation lets us apply this in the case $m = 100$ to get the theorem

$$\big(\mathsf{Is\_seq}(B)\ \&\ 100 \in \mathsf{domain}(B)\ \&\ \mathsf{range}(B) \subseteq \mathbb{N}\big) \rightarrow$$
$$\sum(B_{|100}) = 0 + B[0] + B[1] + \cdots + B[100],$$

as an immediate conclusion. Clearly derivations of statements like this would otherwise require tediously lengthy and repetitive sequences of steps. Another common case is the evaluation of expressions like

$$\mathsf{Value\_at}\big(j,\ \{\mathsf{Ordered\_pair}(0, x_0), \mathsf{Ordered\_pair}(1, x_1), \ldots, \mathsf{Ordered\_pair}(k, x_k)\}\big),$$

which it would otherwise be tedious to deal with but which are easily handled by semi-symbolic computation.

But in fact the method of deduction by semi-symbolic computation is much more general. To explain this assertion, we must first define an appropriate relationship between the language of computation with hereditarily finite sets and the purely set-theoretic language of the verifier. This can be done as follows. We first define the relator $x \in^+ s$ ("$x$ is an eventual member of $s$") by the following formula:

$$(x \in^+ s) \leftrightarrow_{\mathrm{Def}} (x \in s \vee (\exists y \in s \mid x \in^+ y)).$$

As highlighted above, operations on hereditarily finite sets which can be defined and evaluated recursively include all the propositional connectives, $s_1 \cup s_2$, $s_1 \cap s_2$, $s_1 \setminus s_2$, all elementary set comparisons, all quantifiers over hereditarily finite ranges, all set formers over hereditarily finite ranges, $\#s$, all elementary arithmetic operations, the pair-former $[x, y]$, the operations $s^{[1]}$ and $s^{[2]}$ for pairs (note, however, that the choice operator $\mathsf{arb}(s)$ cannot be calculated in this way), the set operators $\mathsf{range}(s)$, $\mathsf{domain}(s)$, $\bigcup s$, $\mathscr{P}(s)$, the predicate $\mathsf{is\_single\_valued}(s)$, set and tuple formers by enumeration, the operator which evaluates the range of the restriction $f_{|s}$ of a hereditarily finite map $f$ to an hereditarily finite set $s$, the Cartesian product operator $s_1 \times s_2$, the inverse-map operator $f^{-1}$, the map-restriction operator $f_{|s}$, the concatenation operator $s_1$ $\mathsf{cat}$ $s_2$, if-expressions, case-expressions, and various others. By the mirroring lemma proved above, the value produced when one evaluates such an expression is always logically equal to the original expression, provided of course that the operator signs appearing in the expression have their standard meanings.

Next suppose that an implication of the form

$$\big(P(B)\ \&\ s \in \mathsf{HF}\big) \rightarrow F(s,B) = \textbf{if}\ C_1(s)\ \textbf{then}\ e_1(s,B)$$
$$\textbf{elseif}\ C_2(s)\ \textbf{then}\ e_2(s,B)$$
$$\ldots$$
$$\textbf{elseif}\ C_n(s)\ \textbf{then}\ e_n(s,B)$$
$$\textbf{else}\ F(s,B)\ \textbf{end if}$$

has been shown to hold for all hereditarily finite sets $s$. We assume here that the conditions $C_j(s)$ involve only the elementary operations listed above. However, the expressions $e_j(s,B)$ on the other hand can be more general, and involve:

(i) subexpressions $e_j^{(1)}(s)$ in which only elementary operations appear;
(ii) recursive appearances $F(e_j^{(2)}(s),B)$ of the function $F$, in which the parts $e_j^{(2)}(s)$ contain only elementary operations;
(iii) other subexpressions;
(iv) other recursive appearances $F(e_j^{(3)}(s,B), e_j^{(4)}(s,B))$ of $F$.

This implication can be used as a recursive procedure in the following way: suppose that $P(B)$ is true and that $s$ is a hereditarily finite set given explicitly. Calculate all the conditions $C_j(s)$ one after another, until one evaluating to 'true' is found. (If none such is found, stop the computation; $F(s,B)$ simply evaluates to itself.) If some first $C_j(s)$ evaluates to 'true', calculate the corresponding $e_j(s,B)$ recursively. This is done by going through the syntax tree of $e_j(s,B)$ in bottom-to-top order, evaluating all elementary subexpressions of the form $\mathsf{exp}(s)$ directly, expanding each recursive occurrence of $F$ having the form $F(e(s),B)$, where $e(s)$ is elementary, recursively, and leaving all other subexpressions untouched. If this process fails to terminate it can simply be stopped after a while, but if it terminates it will yield an identity $F(s,B) = expn(s,B)$. Deduction by semi-symbolic computation makes this identity available as a theorem, in the form

$$\big(P(B)\ \&\ s \in \mathsf{HF}\big) \rightarrow F(s,B) = expn(s,B).$$

A typical, relatively elaborate application of this general form of deduction by semi-symbolic computation makes it possible to obtain 'Mathematica'-like conclusions by syntactic means in a very direct way. Many of the 'formula-driven' parts of elementary and intermediate-level mathematics are covered by this technique.

Derivative manipulations in calculus furnish a characteristic example. Suppose, e.g., that one has defined the derivative '$\mathsf{Deriv}$' as a map from smooth functions of a real variable to their derivative functions, and that the specific real functions '$\mathsf{sin}$', '$\mathsf{cos}$', '$\mathsf{exp}$', along with the basic rules for differentiation and the derivatives of these specific functions, have also been defined. This basic information can then be built up in the following way into general symbolic-manipulation mechanisms allowing direct derivation of composite relationships like

$$\mathsf{Deriv}\big(\{[x, \mathsf{cos}(\mathsf{cos}(x))] : x \in \mathbb{R}\}\big) = \{[x, \mathsf{sin}(\mathsf{cos}(x)) *_{\mathbb{R}} \mathsf{sin}(x)] : x \in \mathbb{R}\}, \quad (4.8)$$

where $\mathbb{R}$ designates the set of real numbers. For this, we first define an appropriate class of (hereditarily finite) syntax trees as follows:

$$\begin{aligned}\mathsf{wf}(t) \leftrightarrow_{\mathrm{Def}} & \big(\mathsf{is\_tuple}(t) \,\&\, \#t = 3 \,\&\, t[0] \in \{\text{``}+\text{''}, \text{``}*\text{''}, \text{``}-\text{''}\} \,\&\, \mathsf{wf}(t[1]) \,\&\, \mathsf{wf}(t[2])\big) \\ & \vee \big(\mathsf{is\_tuple}(t) \,\&\, \#t = 2 \,\&\, t[0] \in \{\text{``sin''}, \text{``cos''}, \text{``exp''}\} \,\&\, \mathsf{wf}(t[1])\big) \\ & \vee \big(\mathsf{is\_string}(t) \,\&\, t = \text{``}x\text{''}\big) \vee \mathsf{is\_integer}(t).\end{aligned}$$

Next we write a definition for the intended semantic meaning of a well-formed tree, which for the example at hand is an elementary function of reals to reals:

$$\begin{aligned}\mathsf{tree\_value}(t) =_{\mathrm{Def}} & \ \mathbf{if}\ \mathsf{is\_tuple}(t) \,\&\, \#t = 3 \,\&\, t[0] = \text{``}+\text{''}\ \mathbf{then} \\ & \quad \mathsf{tree\_value}(t[1]) +' \mathsf{tree\_value}(t[2]) \\ & \mathbf{elseif}\ \mathsf{is\_tuple}(t) \,\&\, \#t = 3 \,\&\, t[0] = \text{``}*\text{''}\ \mathbf{then} \\ & \quad \mathsf{tree\_value}(t[1]) *' \mathsf{tree\_value}(t[2]) \\ & \mathbf{elseif}\ \mathsf{is\_tuple}(t) \,\&\, \#t = 3 \,\&\, t[0] = \text{``}-\text{''}\ \mathbf{then} \\ & \quad \mathsf{tree\_value}(t[1]) -' \mathsf{tree\_value}(t[2]) \\ & \mathbf{elseif}\ \mathsf{is\_tuple}(t) \,\&\, \#t = 2 \,\&\, t[0] = \text{``cos''}\ \mathbf{then} \\ & \quad \mathsf{cos} \circ \mathsf{tree\_value}(t[1]) \\ & \mathbf{elseif}\ \mathsf{is\_tuple}(t) \,\&\, \#t = 2 \,\&\, t[0] = \text{``sin''}\ \mathbf{then} \\ & \quad \mathsf{sin} \circ \mathsf{tree\_value}(t[1]) \\ & \mathbf{elseif}\ \mathsf{is\_tuple}(t) \,\&\, \#t = 2 \,\&\, t[0] = \text{``exp''}\ \mathbf{then} \\ & \quad \mathsf{exp} \circ \mathsf{tree\_value}(t[1]) \\ & \mathbf{elseif}\ \mathsf{is\_string}(t) \,\&\, t = \text{``}x\text{''}\ \mathbf{then} \\ & \quad \{[x, x] : x \in \mathbb{R}\} \\ & \mathbf{else}\ \{[x, \mathsf{float}(t)] : x \in \mathbb{R}\}\ \mathbf{end\ if}.\end{aligned} \quad (4.9)$$

Here the predicate is_tuple($t$) states that $t$ is a finite sequence (i.e. a mapping whose domain is an integer). The operator $+'$ designates the pointwise sum of two functions, namely

$$f +' g = \{[x, f[x] + g[x]] : x \in \mathsf{domain}(f) \cap \mathsf{domain}(g)\},$$

and similarly for $*'$ and $-'$; note that "$+$" symbolizes real rather than integer summation here, and similarly for "$*$" and "$-$". Also $f \circ g$ will designate the composition of the two functions $f$ and $g$. 'float' is the function which embeds the integers into the reals.

The next step is to define the operation on trees which builds their formal derivatives. This is

$$\begin{aligned}\mathsf{formal\_deriv}(t) =_{\mathrm{Def}} \textbf{if } & \mathsf{wf}(t) \,\&\, \#t = 3 \,\&\, t[0] = \text{``}+\text{''} \textbf{ then}\\ & \quad [\text{``}+\text{''}, \mathsf{formal\_deriv}(t[1]), \mathsf{formal\_deriv}(t[2])]\\ \textbf{elseif } & \mathsf{wf}(t) \,\&\, \#t = 3 \,\&\, t[0] = \text{``}*\text{''} \textbf{ then}\\ & \quad [\text{``}+\text{''}, [\text{``}*\text{''}, \mathsf{formal\_deriv}(t[1]), t[2]],\\ & \qquad [\text{``}*\text{''}, t[1], \mathsf{formal\_deriv}(t[2])]]\\ \textbf{elseif } & \mathsf{wf}(t) \,\&\, \#t = 3 \,\&\, t[0] = \text{``}-\text{''} \textbf{ then}\\ & \quad [\text{``}-\text{''}, \mathsf{formal\_deriv}(t[1]), \mathsf{formal\_deriv}(t[2])]\\ \textbf{elseif } & \mathsf{wf}(t) \,\&\, \#t = 2 \,\&\, t[0] = \text{``cos''} \textbf{ then}\\ & \quad [\text{``}-\text{''}, 0, [\text{``}*\text{''}, [\text{``sin''}, t[1]], \mathsf{formal\_deriv}(t[1])]]\\ \textbf{elseif } & \mathsf{wf}(t) \,\&\, \#t = 2 \,\&\, t[0] = \text{``sin''} \textbf{ then}\\ & \quad [\text{``}*\text{''}, [\text{``cos''}, t[1]], \mathsf{formal\_deriv}(t[1])]\\ \textbf{elseif } & \mathsf{wf}(t) \,\&\, \#t = 2 \,\&\, t[0] = \text{``exp''} \textbf{ then}\\ & \quad [\text{``}*\text{''}, [\text{``exp''}, t[1]], \mathsf{formal\_deriv}(t[1])]\\ \textbf{elseif } & \mathsf{wf}(t) \,\&\, t = \text{``}x\text{''} \textbf{ then } 1\\ \textbf{else } & 0 \textbf{ end if}.\end{aligned}$$

Given these definitions, it is not hard to prove the following recursive relationship:

$$\big(t \in \mathsf{HF} \,\&\, \mathsf{wf}(t)\big) \rightarrow \mathsf{Deriv}\big(\mathsf{tree\_value}(t)\big) = \mathsf{tree\_value}\big(\mathsf{formal\_deriv}(t)\big).$$

In sketch, the proof is as follows: suppose not, i.e. suppose that there exists a $t$ such that

$$t \in \mathsf{HF} \,\&\, \mathsf{wf}(t) \,\&\, \mathsf{Deriv}\big(\mathsf{tree\_value}(t)\big) \neq \mathsf{tree\_value}\big(\mathsf{formal\_deriv}(t)\big) \\ \& \, \mathsf{wf}\big(t[1]\big) \,\&\, \mathsf{wf}\big(t[2]\big).$$

Choose a smallest such $t$, in the ordering defined by the relationship $\in^+$. For this, we must have

$$(j \in \mathbb{N} \,\&\, 0 < j \,\&\, j < \#t) \rightarrow \\ \Big(\mathsf{Deriv}\big(\mathsf{tree\_value}(t[j])\big) = \mathsf{tree\_value}\big(\mathsf{formal\_deriv}(t[j])\big)\Big). \quad (4.10)$$

From this, we can derive a series of conclusions which collectively contradict our supposition. For example, if

$$\mathsf{is\_tuple}(t) \,\&\, \#t = 3 \,\&\, t[0] = \text{``}+\text{''} \,\&\, \mathsf{wf}\big(t[1]\big) \,\&\, \mathsf{wf}\big(t[2]\big),$$

then we have

$$\mathsf{Deriv}(\mathsf{tree\_value}(t[1])) = \mathsf{tree\_value}(\mathsf{formal\_deriv}(t[1])) \;\&$$
$$\mathsf{Deriv}(\mathsf{tree\_value}(t[2])) = \mathsf{tree\_value}(\mathsf{formal\_deriv}(t[2])),$$

since $t[1] \in^{+} t \;\&\; t[2] \in^{+} t$. Thus if

$$\mathsf{wf}(t) \;\&\; \#t = 3 \;\&\; t[0] = \text{“}+\text{”} \;\&\; \mathsf{wf}(t[1]) \;\&\; \mathsf{wf}(t[2]),$$

so that $\mathsf{tree\_value}(t) = \mathsf{tree\_value}(t[1]) +' \mathsf{tree\_value}(t[2])$ by (4.9), we must also have

$$\mathsf{Deriv}(\mathsf{tree\_value}(t)) = \mathsf{Deriv}(\mathsf{tree\_value}(t[1])) +' \mathsf{Deriv}(\mathsf{tree\_value}(t[2]))$$

by the standard theorem on the derivative of the sum of two real functions, which we assume to have been proved separately, along with the corresponding elementary results for products, quotients, sin and cos, exp, etc. Hence in this case the conjunct (4.10) seen above cannot hold.

To apply this in the most convenient manner, we will sometimes require one more inductive relationship for use as a computational rule, namely

$$
\begin{aligned}
\mathsf{tree\_value}(t)[x] = \;& \textbf{if } \mathsf{wf}(t) \;\&\; \#t = 3 \;\&\; t[0] = \text{“}+\text{”} \textbf{ then} \\
& \quad \mathsf{tree\_value}(t[1])[x] + \mathsf{tree\_value}(t[2])[x] \\
& \textbf{elseif } \mathsf{wf}(t) \;\&\; \#t = 3 \;\&\; t[0] = \text{“}*\text{”} \textbf{ then} \\
& \quad \mathsf{tree\_value}(t[1])[x] * \mathsf{tree\_value}(t[2])[x] \\
& \textbf{elseif } \mathsf{wf}(t) \;\&\; \#t = 3 \;\&\; t[0] = \text{“}-\text{”} \textbf{ then} \\
& \quad \mathsf{tree\_value}(t[1])[x] - \mathsf{tree\_value}(t[2])[x] \\
& \textbf{elseif } \mathsf{wf}(t) \;\&\; \#t = 2 \;\&\; t[0] = \text{“cos”} \textbf{ then} \\
& \quad \mathsf{cos}(\mathsf{tree\_value}(t[1])[\mathsf{x}]) \\
& \textbf{elseif } \mathsf{wf}(t) \;\&\; \#t = 2 \;\&\; t[0] = \text{“sin”} \textbf{ then} \\
& \quad \mathsf{cos}(\mathsf{tree\_value}(t[1])[\mathsf{x}]) \\
& \textbf{else } \mathsf{wf}(t) \;\&\; \#t = 2 \;\&\; t[0] = \text{“exp”} \textbf{ then} \\
& \quad \mathsf{exp}(\mathsf{tree\_value}(t[1])[\mathsf{x}]) \\
& \textbf{elseif } \mathsf{wf}(t) \;\&\; t = \text{“}x\text{”} \textbf{ then } x \\
& \textbf{else } \mathsf{float}(t) \textbf{ end if}.
\end{aligned}
$$

We also need to show that

$$(t \in \mathsf{HF} \;\&\; \mathsf{wf}(t)) \rightarrow \mathsf{Is\_single\_valued}(\mathsf{tree\_value}(t)),$$

which follows readily by an induction like that sketched above.

Putting all this together, it follows that we can:

(i) Deduce a general theorem, like that outlined above, which relates the syntax trees of a class of formulae of interest to the semantic (set-theoretic) values of these trees;
(ii) Supply the well-formed tree $t$ of the formula we want;
(iii) Then Deriv(tree_value($t$)) and tree_value(formal_deriv($t$)) can be evaluated automatically, and the identity

$$\mathsf{Deriv}\big(\mathsf{tree\_value}(t)\big) = \mathsf{tree\_value}\big(\mathsf{formal\_deriv}(t)\big)$$

can be made available as a theorem directly.

This allows derivative calculations like (4.8) to become theorems without further proof, if we simply supply an appropriate syntax tree to a deduction by semi-symbolic computation.

Since the tree $t$ required for this little procedure is available directly from the formula of interest (e.g. cos(cos($x$))), we can even package very useful theorem-generators of this form as Mathematica-like computational tools, i.e. introduce auxiliary system commands having forms like

$$\mathsf{DIFFERENTIATE} : \mathsf{cos}\big(\mathsf{cos}(x)\big).$$

This command can simply parse its input formula to obtain the tree of interest, generate the additional boilerplate seen in (4.8), and make this available as a theorem.

Simple system-extension tools for doing just this are described below.

In addition to the specific use just sketched, deduction by semi-symbolic computation is applicable in a wide variety of other circumstances. These include:

- computations with partial derivatives;
- symbolic integration and differentiation;
- manipulation of series and of combinatorial coefficients;
- other Mathematica-like symbolic computations;
- elementary arguments concerning continuity and smoothness;
- elementary reasoning concerning object types;
- polynomial computations in one and several variables;
- use of trigonometric identities;
- matrix computations and linear algebra;
- some asymptotic estimates;
- some numerical computation, e.g. approximate evaluation of integrals;
- Boolean computations;
- computations with finite groups, sets of permutations, and computations in modular arithmetic.

Deduction by semi-symbolic computation is also available for Boolean equivalences of the form

$$\big(P(B)\ \&\ s \in \mathsf{HF}\big) \rightarrow \big(Q(s,B) \leftrightarrow \begin{array}{l}\textbf{if } C_1(s) \textbf{ then } e_1(s,B)\\ \textbf{elseif } C_2(s) \textbf{ then } e_2(s,B)\\ \dots\\ \textbf{elseif } C_n(s) \textbf{ then } e_n(s,B)\\ \textbf{else } F(s,B) \textbf{ end if}\big)\end{array}$$

and yields implications of the form

$$\big(P(B)\ \&\ s \in \mathsf{HF}\big) \rightarrow \big(Q(s,B) \leftrightarrow expn(s,B)\big).$$

Deduction by semi-symbolic computation can also be given nondeterministic and/or interactive form. To make it nondeterministic, we can supply a set of identities,

$$\big(P(B)\ \&\ s \in \mathsf{HF}\big) \rightarrow F(s,B) = \begin{array}{l}\textbf{if } C_{1j}(s) \textbf{ then } e_{1j}(s,B)\\ \textbf{elseif } C_{2j}(s) \textbf{ then } e_{2j}(s,B)\\ \dots\\ \textbf{elseif } C_{nj}(s) \textbf{ then } e_{nj}(s,B)\\ \textbf{else } F(s,B) \textbf{ end if},\end{array}$$

$j = 1, \dots, k$, rather than a single such identity. In the presence of such a set $\mathsf{SI}$ of initial identities and of the assumption $P(B)$ we can supply a target identity, and then explore the set of substitutions generated by $\mathsf{SI}$ nondeterministically in all possible patterns, until either the target identity is generated or all possible substitutions have been examined.

## 4.4 Dividing Long Proof Verifications into Multiple Separate 'Sessions'

Several seconds of computer time may be required to certify conclusions dependent on contexts that are at all complex. For this reason, it is often appropriate to divide the verification of lengthy sequences of proofs into multiple successive verifier sessions. The following verifier mechanism makes this possible.[11] Two special verifier directives 'SAVE(*file_name*)' and 'RESTART(*file_name*$_1$, *file_name*$_2$)' are provided. In both of these commands, '*file_name*' should name some file available in the file system of the computer on which the verifier is running. When encountered, SAVE(*file_name*) writes all the theorems, definitions, and theories established prior to the point at which it is encountered. These are written to the named file along with one half $H_1$ of a cryptographically secure checksum for the file. The other half $H_2$ of the checksum is retained by the verifier in a hidden data structure that allows

[11] The feature described in this section is as yet unimplemented in the Ref system.

$H_2$ to be retrieved if $H_1$ is given. The file names of any session record written in this way can be passed to the RESTART(*file_name*1, *file_name*2) command as its first parameter. The second parameter '$file\_name_2$' should be the name of a text file of purported proofs of additional theorems which are to be verified. The verifier then reads all the definitions, theorem statements, and theory descriptors previously written to $file\_name_1$, which it can accept as valid without additional verification once the fact that the text in the file conforms to the two available checksum halves is verified. These definitions, theorem statements, and theories then become available for use in the session opened by the RESTART($file\_name_1$, $file\_name_2$) statement. Once some or all of the new text supplied in $file\_name_2$ has been brought to the point at which it will verify, a new 'SAVE(*file_name*)' statement can be executed to store the newly certified definitions, theorem statements, and theory descriptors. In this way large libraries of theorems can be accumulated through multiple verifier sessions. Note that proof files written by the SAVE(*file_name*) operation can be copied without losing their validity, and so can be made available over the Web as community resources.

A few supplementary commands are provided to increase the flexibility of the verifier's multisession capability. The commands

$$\mathsf{DELETE\_THEOREM}(theorem\_label_1, \ldots, theorem\_label_n)$$

and

$$\mathsf{DELETE\_THEORY}(theory\_label_1, \ldots, theory\_label_n)$$

delete comma-separated lists of labelled theorems and theories, respectively. The command

$$\mathsf{DELETE\_DEFINITION}(symbol_1, \ldots, symbol_n)$$

deletes the definition of all labelled symbols, along with all theorems and further definitions in which any symbol with a deleted definition appears. The parameter of the command

$$\mathsf{RENAME}(old\_symbol_1, new\_symbol_1; \ldots; old\_symbol_n, new\_symbol_n)$$

must be a semicolon-separated list of symbol pairs delimited by commas. The *new_symbols* which appear must be predicate and function symbols never used before. This command replaces each occurrence of every $old\_symbol_j$ in every theorem, definition, and theory known at the point of the RENAME command by the corresponding $new\_symbol_j$.

The RESTART command is available in the generalized form

$$\mathsf{RESTART}(file\_name_1, \ldots, file\_name_n, file\_name_{n+1}).$$

Here $file\_name_1, \ldots, file\_name_n$ must be a list of files, each written by some preceding SAVE(*file_name*) command, and $file\_name_{n+1}$ should be the name of a text file of purported proofs of additional theorems which are to be verified. After examining the checksums of $file\_name_1, \ldots, file\_name_n$ to ensure their validity, the contents of these files are scrutinized to verify that all symbols defined in more than one of these files have identical definitions in all the files in which they are defined, and that all theorems and theories with identical labels are completely identical. If the files pass this test, their contents are combined and the new-text file $\mathit{file\_name}_{n+1}$ is then processed in the normal way.

## References

[FO10] Formisano, A., Omodeo, E.: Theory-specific automated reasoning. In: Dovier, A., Pontelli, E. (eds.) A 25-Year Perspective on Logic Programming—Achievements of the Italian Association for Logic Programming, GULP. LNCS, vol. 6125, pp. 37–63. Springer, Berlin (2010). Chap. 3

[OS02] Omodeo, E.G., Schwartz, J.T.: A 'Theory' mechanism for a proof-verifier based on first-order set theory. In: Kakas, A., Sadri, F. (eds.) Computational Logic: Logic Programming and beyond—Essays in honour of Bob Kowalski, Part II, vol. 2408, pp. 214–230. Springer, Berlin (2002)

[Wol03] Wolfram, S.: The Mathematica Book, 5th edn., p. 1464. Wolfram Media, Champaign (2003)

# Chapter 5
# A Closer Examination of the Sequence of Definitions and Theorems Presented in this Book

As recalled in the preface, before undertaking the writing of this book J. Schwartz began to develop a large-scale proof scenario which was meant to serve as "an essential part of the feasibility study that must precede the development of any ambitious proof-checker" [OS02, p. 229].

Ideally, this proof scenario should have culminated in the proof of the celebrated *Cauchy integral theorem* on analytic functions shown at the end of this chapter; but then we, the authors, decided to rush into the implementation of the verifier ÆtnaNova presented in Chap. 4. This absorbed much of our energies; moreover, as soon as the proof-checker became available, we tended to explore into diverging directions (the Stone representation theorem for Boolean algebra, finite state automata, correctness of the Davis–Putnam–Logemann–Loveland procedure, etc.). As a consequence, our work on the foundations of analysis became slower, and we have developed perhaps a half—take this as a rough estimate—of the proofs necessary for the achievement of our initial goal.

This chapter shows the salient steps leading towards that (as yet) unachieved goal. We expand a broad survey of main definitions and theorems. Proof-checked proofs are available for virtually all of the theorems listed in the following Sects. 5.1 through 5.11 (albeit, occasionally, these were cast in slightly different terms), and for many other theorems not shown here;[1] but the more advanced material surveyed in Sect. 5.12 still awaits formalized proofs.

[1]The largest proof scenario ever submitted to our verifier is available at http://setl.dyndns.org/EtnaNova/login/common_scenario.txt as raw text, and at http://setl.dyndns.org/EtnaNova/login/search_folder/scenario.pdf as a pretty-printed pdf-file.

J.T. Schwartz et al., *Computational Logic and Set Theory*,
DOI 10.1007/978-0-85729-808-9_5, 

## 5.1 Basic Operations of Set Theory and the Theory of Ordinals

### 5.1.1 Pairs, Set Formers, and Maps

Our first step is to give the following definition of the notion of ordered pair. Its details are unimportant; all that matters is that the first and second components of an ordered pair can be reconstructed uniquely from the pair itself. The five theorems which follow Definition 1 ensure us that this is the case, and give explicit (but subsequently irrelevant) formulae for extracting the first and second components of an ordered pair.

$$\text{Def 1 : [Ordered pair] } [x,\ y] =_{\text{Def}} \big\{\{x\},\ \big\{\{x\},\ \big\{\{y\},\ y\big\}\big\}\big\}$$

$$\text{Theorem 1 :}\quad \mathsf{arb}\big(\{X\}\big) = X$$

$$\text{Theorem 1a :}\quad X \in Y \to \mathsf{arb}\big(\{Y,\ X\}\big) = X$$

$$\text{Theorem 2 :}\quad \mathsf{arb}\big([X,\ Y]\big) = \{X\}$$

$$\text{Theorem 3 :}\quad \mathsf{arb}\big(\mathsf{arb}\big([X,\ Y]\big)\big) = X$$

$$\text{Theorem 4 :}\quad \mathsf{arb}\Big(\mathsf{arb}\Big(\mathsf{arb}\big([X,\ Y] \setminus \big\{\mathsf{arb}\big([X,\ Y]\big)\big\}\big) \setminus \big\{\mathsf{arb}\big([X,\ Y]\big)\big\}\Big)\Big) = Y$$

The two following definitions simply capture the two formulae which extract the first and second components of an ordered pair.

$$\text{Def 2 : } p^{[1]} =_{\text{Def}} \mathsf{arb}\big(\mathsf{arb}(p)\big)$$

$$\text{Def 3 : } p^{[2]} =_{\text{Def}} \mathsf{arb}\Big(\mathsf{arb}\Big(\mathsf{arb}\big(p \setminus \big\{\mathsf{arb}(p)\big\}\big) \setminus \big\{\mathsf{arb}(p)\big\}\Big)\Big)$$

All our subsequent work with ordered pairs uses only the properties stated in Theorems 5, 6, and 7, which now follow immediately. These are the properties which are built into our verifier's ELEM deduction mechanism.

$$\text{Theorem 5 :}\quad [X,\ Y]^{[1]} = X$$

$$\text{Theorem 6 :}\quad [X,\ Y]^{[2]} = Y$$

$$\text{Theorem 7 :}\quad [X,\ Y] = \big[[X,\ Y]^{[1]},\ [X,\ Y]^{[2]}\big]$$

Next we give a few small theories which make elementary properties of set formers available in a convenient form. These are

THEORY setformer$\big(e(x),\ e'(x),\ \mathsf{s},\ P(x),\ P'(x)\big)$

$$\big(\forall x \in \mathsf{s} \mid e(x) = e'(x)\big) \,\&\, \big(\forall x \in \mathsf{s} \mid P(x) \leftrightarrow P'(x)\big)$$

$\Longrightarrow$

$$\big\{e(x) : x \in \mathsf{s} \mid P(x)\big\} = \big\{e'(x) : x \in \mathsf{s} \mid P'(x)\big\}$$

END setformer;

THEORY setformer$_0\big(e(x),\ \mathsf{s},\ P(x)\big)$

$\Longrightarrow$

$$(\mathsf{s} \neq \emptyset) \to \big(\{e(x) : x \in \mathsf{s}\} \neq \emptyset\big)$$
$$\big(\{x \in \mathsf{s} \mid P(x)\} \neq \emptyset\big) \to \big(\{e(x) : x \in \mathsf{s} \mid P(x)\} \neq \emptyset\big)$$

END setformer$_0$;

THEORY setformer$_2\big(e(x),\ e'(x),\ f(x,y),\ f'(x,y),\ \mathsf{s},\ P(x,y),\ P'(x,y)\big)$

[Elementary properties of setformers]

$$\big(\forall x \in \mathsf{s} \mid e(x) = e'(x)\big) \,\&$$
$$\big(\forall x \in \mathsf{s} \,\big|\, \big(\forall y \in e(x) \mid f(x,y) = f'(x,y)\big)\big) \,\&$$
$$\big(\forall x \in \mathsf{s} \,\big|\, \big(\forall y \in e(x) \mid P(x,y) \leftrightarrow P'(x,y)\big)\big)$$

$\Longrightarrow$

$$\big\{f(x,y) : x \in \mathsf{s},\ y \in e(x) \mid P(x,y)\big\}$$
$$= \big\{f'(x,y) : x \in \mathsf{s},\ y \in e'(x) \mid P'(x,y)\big\}$$

END setformer$_2$;

The first and third of the above theories simply allow equals-by-equals replacement in set formers involving single and double iterations, respectively. The second ensures us that set formers involving non-empty iterations must define non-empty sets. All the required proofs involve tedious elementary detail which the availability of these theories allows us to elide subsequently.

We go on to define the basic notions of mapping (a mapping is simply a set all of whose elements are ordered pairs), the domain and range of a mapping, and the notions of single-valued and one-to-one mappings. This is done by the five following definitions.

$$\text{Def 4} : \mathsf{Is\_map}(f) \leftrightarrow_{\mathrm{Def}} f = \big\{\big[x^{[1]},\ x^{[2]}\big] : x \in f\big\}$$

$$\text{Def 5} : \mathsf{domain}(f) =_{\mathrm{Def}} \big\{x^{[1]} : x \in f\big\}$$

$$\text{Def 6} : \mathsf{range}(f) =_{\mathrm{Def}} \big\{x^{[2]} : x \in f\big\}$$

$$\text{Def 7} : \mathsf{Svm}(f) =_{\mathrm{Def}} \mathsf{Is\_map}(f) \,\&\, \big(\forall x \in f \,\big|\, \big(\forall y \in f \,\big|\, (x^{[1]} = y^{[1]}) \to (x = y)\big)\big)$$

$$\text{Def 8} : \mathsf{1\_1}(f) \leftrightarrow_{\mathrm{Def}} \mathsf{Svm}(f) \,\&\, \big(\forall x \in f \,\big|\, \big(\forall y \in f \,\big|\, (x^{[2]} = y^{[2]}) \to (x = y)\big)\big)$$

### 5.1.2 Transfinite Induction

Next we state, and subsequently prove, a general principle of transfinite induction. For ease of use, this is captured as a theory called 'transfinite_induction'. It states that, given any predicate $P(\cdot)$ which is true for some set, there must exist a set $m$ for which $P$ is true, but for all whose members $P$ is false. This principle, which follows very directly from our strong form of the axiom of choice, is encapsulated in the following theory.

$$\begin{array}{l}\text{THEORY transfinite\_induction}\big(\mathsf{n}, P(x)\big)\\ \quad P(\mathsf{n})\\ \Longrightarrow (\mathsf{m}_\Theta)\\ \quad P(\mathsf{m}_\Theta)\ \&\ \big(\forall k \in \mathsf{m}_\Theta \mid \neg P(k)\big)\\ \text{END transfinite\_induction;}\end{array}$$

### 5.1.3 Ordinals

Our next strategic aim is to define the notion of 'ordinal number', and to prove the basic properties of ordinals. We follow von Neumann in defining an ordinal as a set properly ordered by membership, and for which members of members are also members. This ties the ordinal concept very directly to the most basic concepts of set theory, allowing the properties of ordinals to be established by using only elementary properties of sets and set formers, with occasional use of transfinite induction. The key results proved are: (a) the collection of all ordinals is itself properly ordered by membership, and members of ordinals are ordinals, but (b) this collection is not a set; (c) any set can be put into 1-1 correspondence with an ordinal.

The formal statement of the property '$s$ in an ordinal' is as follows.

$$\begin{array}{l}\text{Def 10}: \mathsf{Ord}(s) \leftrightarrow_{\text{Def}} (\forall x \in s \mid x \subseteq s)\ \& \\ \big(\forall x \in s \,\big|\, \big(\forall y \in s \mid (x \in y \vee y \in x \vee x = y)\big)\big)\end{array}$$

Since we have defined ordinals in a directly set-theoretic way, the notion of 'successor ordinal' (the next ordinal after a given ordinal) also has an elementary set-theoretic definition: the set obtained from $s$ by adding $s$ itself as a (necessarily new) member. Formally, this is as follows.

$$\text{Def 11}: \mathsf{next}(s) =_{\text{Def}} s \cup \{s\}$$

Next we prove the basic properties of ordinals. Theorem 9, which serves as an auxiliary lemma, states that each proper sub-ordinal $T$ of an ordinal $S$ is the smallest element of the complement $(S \setminus T)$. We then prove that the intersection of any two ordinals is an ordinal, and that, given any two ordinals, one is a subset of the other (so that their intersection is simply the smaller of the two and their union is the larger). Somewhat more precisely, given any two distinct ordinals one is a member of the other (which tells us that comparison between ordinals can be expressed either by inclusion or by membership). Every element of an ordinal is also an ordinal, and if $s$ is an ordinal then next($s$) is a larger, and indeed the next larger, ordinal.

The class of sets cannot be a set (i.e. there can be no set of which all sets are members, since if there were this would have to be a member of itself). Similarly, there can be no ordinal of which all ordinals are members (since if there were, the union of all elements of this set would have to be the largest ordinal, and hence would be a member of itself). These two facts, which tell us that 'all sets' and 'all ordinals' are both too large to be sets, are Theorems 12 and 13 in the following group.

$$\text{Theorem 8}: \ \big(\mathsf{Ord}(S)\ \&\ T \in S\big) \to \big(\mathsf{Ord}(T)\ \&\ T \subseteq S\big)$$

$$\text{Theorem 9}: \ \big(\mathsf{Ord}(S)\ \&\ \mathsf{Ord}(T)\ \&\ T \subseteq S\big) \to \big(T = S \vee \big(T = \mathsf{arb}(S \setminus T)\ \&\ T \in S \setminus T\big)\big)$$

$$\text{Theorem 10}: \ \mathsf{Ord}(\emptyset)\ \&\ \big(\big(\mathsf{Ord}(S)\ \&\ \mathsf{Ord}(T)\big) \to \big((S \subseteq T \vee T \subseteq S)\ \&\ \mathsf{Ord}(S \cap T)\ \&\ \mathsf{Ord}(S \cup T)\big)\big)$$

$$\text{Theorem 11}: \ \big(\mathsf{Ord}(S)\ \&\ \mathsf{Ord}(T)\big) \to (S \in T \vee T \in S \vee S = T)$$

$$\text{Theorem 12}: \ [\text{The class of all sets is not a set}]\ \neg(\forall y \mid y \in X))$$

$$\text{Theorem 13}: \ [\text{The class of ordinals is not a set}]\ \neg\big(\forall x \mid \big(x \in Os \leftrightarrow \mathsf{Ord}(x)\big)\big)$$

$$\text{Theorem 14}: \ \big(\mathsf{Ord}(S)\ \&\ \mathsf{Ord}(T)\big) \to (T \subseteq S \leftrightarrow T \in S \vee T = S)$$

$$\text{Theorem 15}: \ \big(\mathsf{Ord}(S)\ \&\ \mathsf{Ord}(T)\big) \to (T \notin S \leftrightarrow S \subseteq T)$$

$$\text{Theorem 16}: \ \mathsf{Ord}(S) \to \big(\mathsf{Ord}\big(\mathsf{next}(S)\big)\ \&\ \big(T \in \mathsf{next}(S) \leftrightarrow \big(T \subseteq S\ \&\ \mathsf{Ord}(T)\big)\big)\big)$$

### 5.1.4 The Ordinal Enumerability Theorem

Next we prove that every set $s$ can be put into one-to-one correspondence with an ordinal. This is done by defining a correspondence between ordinals and elements of $s$ recursively: the element corresponding to any ordinal $o$ is the first element, if any, not corresponding to any smaller ordinal. Since we have already proved that the collection of all ordinals is too large to be a set, this enumeration must ultimately cover the whole of $s$. This is the '*enumeration theorem*' fundamental to our subsequent work with cardinal numbers.

The following definition formalizes the enumeration technique just described.

Def 9 : [The enumeration of a set] $\mathsf{enum}(X, S) =_{\mathrm{Def}}$ **if** $S \subseteq \{\mathsf{enum}(y, S) : y \in X\}$ **then** $S$ **else** $\mathsf{arb}(S \setminus \{\mathsf{enum}(y, S) : y \in X\})$ **end if**

The following six theorems do the work necessary to prove the Enumeration theorem, which is the last of them. Theorem 17 is a lemma for Theorems 18 and 19, which state that $\mathsf{enum}(X, S)$ is always either a member of $S$, or, past a certain point, the whole of $S$. Theorem 20 states that if an ordinal is large enough to enumerate $S$, so is every larger ordinal. Theorem 20 states that $\mathsf{enum}(X, S)$ defines a 1-1 correspondence up to the point at which the whole of $S$ has been enumerated, and Theorem 21 states that the whole of $S$ must eventually be enumerated (since otherwise we would have a 1-1 correspondence of all ordinals with a subset of $S$, contradicting the fact that there are too many ordinals to constitute a set).

Theorem 17 : $(\mathsf{Ord}(X) \,\&\, S \in \{\mathsf{enum}(y, S) : y \in X\}) \rightarrow (S \subseteq \{\mathsf{enum}(y, S) : y \in X\})$

Theorem 18 : $\mathsf{enum}(X, S) = S \vee \mathsf{enum}(X, S) \in S$

Theorem 19 : $(\mathsf{enum}(X, S) = S \,\&\, Y \supseteq X) \rightarrow (\mathsf{enum}(Y, S) = S)$

Theorem 20 : [The enumeration of a set is 1-1] $(\mathsf{Ord}(X) \,\&\, \mathsf{Ord}(W) \,\&\, X \neq W) \rightarrow (S \in \{\mathsf{enum}(y, S) : y \in X\} \vee S \in \{\mathsf{enum}(y, S) : y \in W\} \vee \mathsf{enum}(X, S) \neq \mathsf{enum}(W, S))$

Theorem 21 : [Enumeration lemma] $(\exists x \mid \mathsf{Ord}(x) \,\&\, S \in \{\mathsf{enum}(y, S) : y \in x\})$

Theorem 22 : [Enumeration theorem] $(\exists x \mid \mathsf{Ord}(x) \,\&\, S = \{\mathsf{enum}(y, S) : y \in x\} \,\&\, (\forall y \in x \mid (\forall z \in x \mid (y \neq z) \rightarrow (\mathsf{enum}(y, S) \neq \mathsf{enum}(z, S)))))$

## 5.2 Elementary Laws on Map Constructs

Our next goal is to define the notion of the cardinality of a set $s$, i.e. the number, finite or infinite, of its elements. As appears in definition 15 below, this is simply the smallest ordinal which can be put into 1-1 correspondence with $s$. But in preparation for this definition we first define a few more elementary set-theoretic notions and prove a few more elementary properties of maps. The notions defined are: the restriction of a map to a set, the inverse map of a map, the identity map on a set, and map composition. The image of a point $x$ under a map[2] is defined as the unique element (or, if not unique, the element chosen by 'arb') of the range of the restriction

[2] To distinguish the image resulting from application of a map $f$ to an element $x$ from the image of the same $x$ under a global function $g$, we will denote the former as $f[x]$ and the latter as $g(x)$.

of the map to the singleton $\{x\}$. The following block of definitions formalize these ideas.

Def 12 : [Map restriction] $f_{|a} =_{\text{Def}} \{ p \in f \mid p^{[1]} \in a \}$

Def 13 : [Value of single-valued function] $f[x] =_{\text{Def}} \mathsf{arb}(f_{|\{x\}})^{[2]}$

Def 14 : [Map product] $f \circ g =_{\text{Def}} \{ [x^{[1]}, y^{[2]}] : x \in g,\ y \in f \mid x^{[2]} = y^{[1]} \}$

Def 14*a* : [Inverse map] $f^{-1} =_{\text{Def}} \{ [x^{[2]}, x^{[1]}] : x \in f \}$

Def 14*b* : [Identity map] $\mathsf{id}_s =_{\text{Def}} \{ [x, x] : x \in s \}$

Def 14*c* : [Inverse image] $f \upharpoonleft \{s\} =_{\text{Def}} \mathsf{range}(f^{-1}{}_{|s})$

A collection of elementary theorems expressing familiar set-theoretic facts is proved next: the restriction of a map to a set is a submap of the original map; a set is a map if and only if all its elements are ordered pairs; a subset of a map is a map. A subset of a single-valued map is a map. A subset of a one-to-one map is a one-to-one map. Theorems 24 and 25 just express the intersection and difference of two sets as set formers.

Theorem 23 : $F_{|A} \subseteq F$

Theorem 24 : $S \cap T = \{x \in S \mid x \in T\}$

Theorem 25 : $S \setminus T = \{x \in S \mid x \notin T\}$

Theorem 26 : $\mathsf{Is\_map}(F) \leftrightarrow (\forall x \in f \mid x = [x^{[1]}, x^{[2]}])$

Theorem 27 : $(G \subseteq F\ \&\ \mathsf{Is\_map}(F)) \rightarrow \mathsf{Is\_map}(G)$

Theorem 28 : $(G \subseteq F\ \&\ \mathsf{Svm}(F)) \rightarrow \mathsf{Svm}(G)$

Theorem 29 : $(G \subseteq F\ \&\ \mathsf{1\_1}(F)) \rightarrow \mathsf{1\_1}(G)$

Continuing this series of elementary set-theoretic propositions, we have the following results: The first and second components of any element of a map belong to the map's domain and range, respectively. The union of two maps is a map. The restriction of a map to a union set is the union of the separate restrictions. The restriction of the union of two maps to a set is the union of their separate restrictions. A map is its restriction to its own domain. Map products are associative.

Theorem 30 : $(X \in F) \rightarrow (X^{[1]} \in \mathsf{domain}(F))$

Theorem 31 : $(X \in F) \rightarrow \big(X^{[2]} \in \mathsf{range}(F)\big)$

Theorem 33 : $\big(\mathsf{Is\_map}(F)\ \&\ \mathsf{Is\_map}(G)\big) \rightarrow \mathsf{Is\_map}(F \cup G)$

Theorem 34 : $F_{|(A \cup B)} = (F_{|A}) \cup (F_{|B})$

Theorem 35 : [Associativity of map multiplication] $F \circ (G \circ H) = (F \circ G) \circ H$

Theorem 36 : $(F \cup G)_{|A} = (F_{|A}) \cup (G_{|A})$

Theorem 37 : $F_{|\mathsf{domain}(F)} = F$

Three additional theorems in this elementary group state that (i) the image under a map of any element of its domain belongs to its range; (ii) A single-valued map can be written as the set of all pairs built from images of its domain elements; (iii) The range of a single-valued map is the collection of all image elements of its domain.

Theorem 38 : $\big(X \in \mathsf{domain}(F)\big) \rightarrow \big(F[X] \in \mathsf{range}(F)\big)$

Theorem 39 : $\mathsf{Svm}(F) \leftrightarrow F = \big\{ \big[x,\ F[x]\big] : x \in \mathsf{domain}(F) \big\}$

Theorem 39*a* : $\mathsf{Svm}(F) \rightarrow \big(F = \big\{ \big[x,\ F[x]\big] : x \in \mathsf{domain}(F) \big\}\ \&$
$\mathsf{range}(F) = \big\{ F[x] : x \in \mathsf{domain}(F) \big\}\big)$

It is convenient to repackage the elementary results just stated as a theory which puts every one-parameter function symbol $f$ onto correspondence with a single-valued map $g$ which sends each element $x$ of the map's domain into $g(x)$ as image element. The theory shown below does this, and also expresses the range of $g$ and the condition that $g$ should be one-to-one in terms of $f$.

THEORY $\mathsf{fcn\_symbol}\big(f(x),\ \mathsf{g},\ \mathsf{s}\big)$
$\quad \mathsf{g} = \big\{ \big[x,\ f(x)\big] : x \in \mathsf{s} \big\}$
$\Longrightarrow$
$\quad \mathsf{domain(g)} = \mathsf{s}$
$\quad \big(\forall x \in \mathsf{s} \mid \mathsf{g}[x] = f(x)\big)$
$\quad (X \notin \mathsf{s}) \rightarrow \big(\mathsf{g}[X] = \emptyset\big)$
$\quad \mathsf{range(g)} = \big\{ f(x) : x \in \mathsf{s} \big\}$
$\quad \mathsf{Svm(g)}$
$\quad \big(\forall x \in \mathsf{s} \big| \big(\forall y \in \mathsf{s} \big| \big(f(x) = f(y)\big) \rightarrow (x = y)\big)\big) \rightarrow \mathsf{1\_1(g)}$
END fcn_symbol;

In working with maps we often need to use elementary properties of ordered pairs. The following theorems are two such: Any ordered pair can be written in standard fashion in terms of its formal first and second component. Any element of a map is an ordered pair. The small utility theory which follows states that every set former involving only ordered pairs defines a map.

Theorem 40 : $(U = [A, B]) \rightarrow (U = [U^{[1]}, U^{[2]}])$

Theorem 41 : $(\mathsf{Is\_map}(F) \,\&\, U \in F) \rightarrow (U = [U^{[1]}, U^{[2]}])$

THEORY Iz_map$(a(x), b(x), \mathsf{s})$
$\Longrightarrow$
$\mathsf{Is\_map}(\{[a(x), b(x)] : x \in \mathsf{s}\})$ &
$\mathsf{domain}(\{[a(x), b(x)] : x \in \mathsf{s}\}) = \{a(x) : x \in \mathsf{s}\}$ &
$\mathsf{range}(\{[a(x), b(x)] : x \in \mathsf{s}\}) = \{b(x) : x \in \mathsf{s}\}$
END Iz_map

More elementary utility results on maps and their ranges and domains now follow. The domain and range operators are both additive, and if one is null so is the other. A single-valued map sends the first component of any pair in it to the second component of the same pair. The union of two single-valued maps with disjoint domains is a single-valued map. The union of two one-to-one maps with disjoint domains and ranges is a one-to-one map. Any restriction of a map is a map; any restriction of a single-valued map is a single-valued map; any restriction of a one-to-one map is a one-to-one map. The range of any restriction of a map is a subset of the map's range, and the domain of a map's restriction to a set $s$ is the intersection of $s$ and the map's domain. If the range of a map $g$ is included in the domain of a map $f$, the domain of the composite map $f \circ g$ is the domain of $g$, and its range is the range of the restriction of $f$ to the range of $g$. Hence if the range of $g$ equals the domain of $f$, the range of the composite map equals the range of $f$.

Theorem 42 : $\mathsf{domain}(F \cup G) = \mathsf{domain}(F) \cup \mathsf{domain}(G)$

Theorem 43 : $\mathsf{range}(F \cup G) = \mathsf{range}(F) \cup \mathsf{range}(G)$

Theorem 44 : $\mathsf{domain}(F) = \emptyset \leftrightarrow \mathsf{range}(F) = \emptyset$

Theorem 45 : $(\mathsf{Svm}(F) \,\&\, x \in F) \rightarrow (F[X^{[1]}] = X^{[2]})$

Theorem 46 : [Union of single-valued maps] $(\mathsf{Svm}(F) \,\&\, \mathsf{Svm}(G) \,\&\, \mathsf{domain}(F) \cap \mathsf{domain}(G) = \emptyset) \rightarrow \mathsf{Svm}(F \cup G)$

Theorem 47 : $\mathsf{Is\_map}(F) \rightarrow \mathsf{Is\_map}(F_{|S})$

Theorem 48 : $\mathsf{Svm}(F) \to \mathsf{Svm}(F_{|S})$

Theorem 49 : $\mathsf{1\_1}(F) \to \mathsf{1\_1}(F_{|S})$

Theorem 50 : $\mathsf{range}(F_{|S}) \subseteq \mathsf{range}(F)$

Theorem 50$a$ : $\mathsf{domain}(F_{|S}) = \mathsf{domain}(F) \cap S$

Theorem 51 : $\big(\mathsf{range}(G) \subseteq \mathsf{domain}(F)\big) \to$
$\big(\mathsf{range}(F \circ G) = \mathsf{range}(F_{|\mathsf{range}(G)})\ \&\ \mathsf{domain}(F \circ G) = \mathsf{domain}(G)\big)$

Theorem 51$a$ : $\big(\mathsf{range}(G) = \mathsf{domain}(F)\big) \to$
$\big(\mathsf{range}(F \circ G) = \mathsf{range}(F)\ \&\ \mathsf{domain}(F \circ G) = \mathsf{domain}(G)\big)$

Theorem 52 : [Union of 1-1 maps] $(\mathsf{1\_1}(F)\ \&\ \mathsf{1\_1}(G)\ \&$
$\mathsf{range}(F) \cap \mathsf{range}(G) = \emptyset\ \&\ \mathsf{domain}(F) \cap \mathsf{domain}(G) = \emptyset) \to \mathsf{1\_1}(F \cup G)$

Next we have a block of elementary results on map inverses. The inverse of a map $f$ is a map, whose domain is the range of $f$ and vice versa. The inverse of the inverse of a map is the map itself. If a map is one-to-one, so is its inverse. The inverse of a one-to-one map $f$ sends the image under $f$ of each element $x$ of the domain of $f$ into $x$, and vice versa. The composite of a map and its inverse sends every element $x$ of the map's domain into $x$, and symmetrically the composite of the inverse of $f$ and $f$ sends each element $y$ of the range of $f$ into $y$.

Theorem 53 : $\mathsf{Is\_map}(F^{-1})\ \&\ \mathsf{range}(F^{-1}) = \mathsf{domain}(F)\ \&$
$\mathsf{domain}(F^{-1}) = \mathsf{range}(F)$

Theorem 54 : $\mathsf{Is\_map}(F) \to \big(F = (F^{-1})^{-1}\big)$

Theorem 55 : $\mathsf{1\_1}(F) \to \big(\mathsf{1\_1}(F^{-1})\ \&\ F = (F^{-1})^{-1}\ \&$
$\mathsf{range}(F^{-1}) = \mathsf{domain}(F)\ \&\ \mathsf{domain}(F^{-1}) = \mathsf{range}(F)\big)$

Theorem 56 : $\mathsf{1\_1}(F) \to \big(\forall x \in \mathsf{domain}(F) \mid F^{-1}[F[x]] = x\big)$

Theorem 57 : $\mathsf{1\_1}(F) \to \big(\forall x \in \mathsf{range}(F) \mid F[F^{-1}[x]] = x\big)$

Next we give a few elementary results on identity maps, i.e. maps which send every element of some set $s$ into itself. Every such map is one-to-one, inverse to itself, and has $s$ as its range and domain. The composite of any single-valued map $f$ with its inverse is the identity map on the range of $f$, and, if $f$ is one-to-one, the composite in the reverse order is the identity map on the domain of $f$.

Theorem 58 : [Elementary Properties of identity maps] $\text{1\_1}(\text{id}_S)$ &
$\text{domain}(\text{id}_S) = S$ & $\text{range}(\text{id}_S) = S$ &
$(\text{id}_S)^{-1} = \text{id}_S$ &
$(\forall x \in S \mid \text{id}_S[x] = x)$ &
$\big(\text{Is\_map}(F) \rightarrow (((\text{domain}(F) \subseteq S) \rightarrow (F \circ \text{id}_S = F))$
$\& \, ((\text{range}(F) \subseteq S) \rightarrow (\text{id}_S \circ F = F)))\big)$

Theorem 59 : $\text{Svm}(F) \rightarrow \big(F \circ F^{-1} = \text{id}_{\text{range}(F)}\big)$

Theorem 60 : $\text{1\_1}(F) \rightarrow \big(F \circ F^{-1} = \text{id}_{\text{range}(F)} \,\&\, F^{-1} \circ F = \text{id}_{\text{domain}(F)}\big)$

The final theorems in our collection of elementary results focus on composite maps. If two maps are one-to-one and inverse to each other, their composite is the identity map on the domain of one of them, and the composite in the opposite order is the identity map on the corresponding range. The composite of two maps is a map, the composite of two single-valued maps is a single-valued map, and the composite of two one-to-one maps is a one-to-one map. If $f$ and $g$ are two single-valued maps with the range of $g$ included in the domain of $f$, then their composite sends each $x$ in the domain of $f$ into the $g$-image of the $f$-image of $x$, and both the composite map and its range can be written as set former expressions. Map composition is distributive over map union.

Theorem 61 : [An inverse pair of maps must be 1-1 and must be each others inverses]
$\big(\text{Is\_map}(F)$ & $\text{Is\_map}(G)$ &
$\text{domain}(F) = \text{range}(G)$ &
$\text{range}(F) = \text{domain}(G)$ &
$F \circ G = \text{id}_{\text{range}(F)}$ &
$G \circ F = \text{id}_{\text{domain}(F)}\big) \rightarrow \;\; (\text{1\_1}(F) \,\&\, G = F^{-1})$

Theorem 62 : $\text{Is\_map}(F \circ G)$

Theorem 63 : $\big(\text{Svm}(F) \,\&\, \text{Svm}(G)\big) \rightarrow \text{Svm}(F \circ G)$

Theorem 64 : $\big(\text{Svm}(F) \,\&\, \text{Svm}(G) \,\&\, x \in \text{domain}(G)$ &
$\text{range}(G) \subseteq \text{domain}(F)\big) \rightarrow \big((F \circ G)[X] = F\big[G[X]\big]\big)$

Theorem : [Map product formula] $\big(\text{Svm}(F)$ & $\text{Svm}(G)$ &
$\text{range}(G) \subseteq \text{domain}(F)\big) \rightarrow \big(F \circ G = \big\{\big[x,\, F\big[G[x]\big]\big] : x \in \text{domain}(G)\big\}$ &
$\big(X \in \text{domain}(G) \rightarrow (F \circ G)[X] = F\big[G[X]\big]\big)$ &
$\text{domain}(F \circ G) = \text{domain}(G)$ &
$\text{range}(F \circ G) = \big\{F\big[G[x]\big] : x \in \text{domain}(G)\big\}$ &
$\text{range}(F \circ G) \subseteq \text{range}(F)\big)$

Theorem 65 : $\big(\text{1\_1}(F) \,\&\, \text{1\_1}(G)\big) \rightarrow \text{1\_1}(F \circ G)$

Theorem 66 : $(F \cup H) \circ G = (F \circ G) \cup (H \circ G)$

Theorem 67 : $G \circ (F \cup H) = (G \circ F) \cup (G \circ H)$

## 5.3 Cardinality of a Set; Cardinal Numbers

Now we are ready to go on to the theory of cardinal numbers, in preparation for which we Skolemize the theorem which states that any set has a standard enumeration, to get the following definition, which gives a name to the ordinal which enumerates each set in the standard way.

Def_by_app 14d :
$\mathsf{Ord}\big(\mathsf{enum\_Ord}(S)\big)$ & $S = \big\{\mathsf{enum}(y, S) : y \in \mathsf{enum\_Ord}(S)\big\}$ &
$\big(\forall y \in \mathsf{enum\_Ord}(S) \,\big|\, \big(\forall z \in \mathsf{enum\_Ord}(S) \,|\,$
$(y \neq z) \rightarrow \big(\mathsf{enum}(y, S) \neq \mathsf{enum}(z, S)\big)\big)\big)$

We can now define the cardinal number of a set $s$ to be the least ordinal with which it can be put into one-to-one correspondence. Accordingly an ordinal is a cardinal if it can not be put into one-to-one correspondence with any smaller ordinal. The two following definitions capture these ideas.

Def 15 : [Cardinality] $\#s =_{\mathrm{Def}} \mathsf{arb}\big($
$\{x : x \in \mathsf{next}\big(\mathsf{enum\_Ord}(s)\big) \,|$
$\big(\exists f \,|\, \big(\mathsf{1\_1}(f)$ & $\mathsf{domain}(f) = x$ & $\mathsf{range}(f) = s\big)\big)\}\big)$

Def 16 : [Cardinal] $\mathsf{Is\_cardinal}(s) \leftrightarrow_{\mathrm{Def}} \mathsf{Ord}(s)$ &
$\big(\forall y \in s \,\big|\, \big(\forall f \,|\, \neg\big(\mathsf{domain}(f) = y\big) \vee \neg\big(\mathsf{range}(f) = s\big) \vee \neg\big(\mathsf{Svm}(f)\big)\big)\big)$

In working with cardinals (and in particular with products of cardinals) we will need various elementary facts about Cartesian products. The Cartesian product of two sets $s$ and $t$ is simply the set of all pairs whose first component belongs to $s$ and whose second component belongs to $t$. Formally this is

Def 17 : [Cartesian Product] $s \times t =_{\mathrm{Def}} \big\{[x, y] : x \in s,\ y \in t\big\}$

The two following theorems state associativity and commutativity properties of the Cartesian product: $(A\times B)\times C$ and $A\times(B\times C)$ are always in natural one-to-one correspondence, as are $(A\times B)$ and $(B\times A)$. These facts will subsequently imply the associativity and commutativity of cardinal multiplication.

Theorem 68 : $\big(F = \big\{\big[[[x, y], z], [x, [y, z]]\big] : x \in A,\ y \in B,\ z \in C\big\}\big) \rightarrow$
$\big(\mathsf{1\_1}(F)$ & $\mathsf{domain}(F) = \big((A\times B)\times C\big)$ & $\mathsf{range}(F) = \big(A\times(B\times C)\big)\big)$

Theorem 69 : $\big(F = \{[[x, y], [y, x]] : x \in A,\ y \in B\}\big) \rightarrow$
$\big(\mathsf{1\_1}(F)\ \&\ \mathsf{domain}(F) = (A \times B)\ \&\ \mathsf{range}(F) = (B \times A)\big)$

Now we go on to the study of cardinals, beginning with a few relevant facts about ordinals, stated in the next block of theorems. Theorem 70 states that the standard enumeration function $\mathsf{enum}(x, s) = \mathsf{enum\_s}(x)$ defined earlier is the identity (in $x$) if $s$ is an ordinal. Theorem 71 states that every set can be put into one-to-one correspondence with a certain smallest ordinal. Then we show that the enumerating ordinal of a set has the same cardinality as the set, and that if a set $s$ of ordinals includes a set $t$, then $\mathsf{arb}(s)$ is smaller than $\mathsf{arb}(t)$. These are both lemmas needed later. Theorem 74 states a related lemma, needed later to prove that the cardinal number of a set $s$ is at least as large as the cardinal number of any of its subsets.

Theorem 70 : $\big(\mathsf{Ord}(S)\ \&\ X \in S\big) \rightarrow \big(\mathsf{enum}(X, S) = X\big)$

Theorem 71 : [Cardinality Lemma] $\mathsf{Ord}(\#S)\ \&$
$\big(\exists f \mid \mathsf{1\_1}(f)\ \&\ \mathsf{range}(f) = S\ \&\ \mathsf{domain}(f) = \#S\big)\ \&$
$\big(\neg\big(\exists o \in \#S \,\big|\, \big(\exists g \mid \mathsf{1\_1}(g)\ \&\ \mathsf{range}(g) = S\ \&\ \mathsf{domain}(g) = o\big)\big)\big)$

Theorem 72 : [The enumerating ordinal of a set has the same cardinality as the set]
$\big(\exists o \,\big|\, \big(\mathsf{Ord}(o)\ \&\ S = \{\mathsf{enum}(x, S) : x \in o\}\ \&\ \#o = \#S\big)\big)$

Theorem 73 : ['arb' is monotone decreasing for non-empty sets of ordinals]
$\big(\mathsf{Ord}(R)\ \&\ R \supseteq S\ \&\ S \supseteq T\big) \rightarrow \big(\mathsf{arb}(S) \in \mathsf{arb}(T) \vee \mathsf{arb}(S) = \mathsf{arb}(T) \vee T = \emptyset\big)$

Theorem 74 : [Lemma for following theorem] $\big(\mathsf{Ord}(S)\ \&\ T \subseteq S\ \&\ X \in S\ \&\ Y \in X\big)$
$\rightarrow \big(\mathsf{enum}(Y, T) \in \mathsf{enum}(X, T) \vee \mathsf{enum}(X, T) \supseteq T\big)$

Theorem 75 : [Subsets enumerate at least as rapidly] $\big(\mathsf{Ord}(S)\ \&\ T \subseteq S\ \&\ X \in S\big) \rightarrow$
$\big(\mathsf{enum}(X, T) \supseteq X\big)$

Theorem 76 : $\big(\mathsf{Ord}(S)\ \&\ T \subseteq S\big) \rightarrow \big(\{\mathsf{enum}(x, T) : x \in S\} \supseteq T\big)$

Theorem 77 : $\big(\mathsf{Ord}(S)\ \&\ T \subseteq S\big) \rightarrow$
$\big(\exists x \subseteq S \,\big|\, \big(\mathsf{Ord}(x)\ \&\ T = \{\mathsf{enum}(y, T) : y \in x\}\big)$
$\&\ \big(\forall y \in x \,\big|\, \big(\forall z \in x \mid (y \neq z) \rightarrow \big(\mathsf{enum}(y, T) \neq \mathsf{enum}(z, T)\big)\big)\big)\big)$

The block of theorems which now follow encapsulate a few basic properties of the $\#s$ operator, e.g. its monotonicity.

Theorem 78 : [Single-valued maps have 1-1 partial inverses] $\mathsf{Svm}(F) \rightarrow$
$\big(\exists h \,\big|\, \big(\mathsf{domain}(h) = \mathsf{range}(F)\ \&\ \mathsf{range}(h) \subseteq \mathsf{domain}(F)\ \&$
$\mathsf{1\_1}(h)\ \&\ \big(\forall x \in \mathsf{range}(F) \mid F\big[h[x]\big] = x\big)\big)\big)$

Theorem 79 : [One-one maps are cardinality preserving]
$\mathsf{1\_1}(F) \rightarrow \big(\#\mathsf{range}(F) = \#\mathsf{domain}(F)\big)$

Theorem 80 : [Cardinality theorem] $\mathsf{Is\_cardinal}(\#S)$ & $\mathsf{Ord}(\#S)$
$\big(\exists f \mid \big(\mathsf{1\_1}(f)\ \&\ \mathsf{range}(f) = S\ \&\ \mathsf{domain}(f) = \#S\big)\big)$

Theorem 81 : $\#S = \emptyset \leftrightarrow S = \emptyset$

Theorem 82 : [Uniqueness of Cardinality] $\big(\mathsf{Is\_cardinal}(C)\ \&$
$\big(\exists f \mid \big(\mathsf{1\_1}(f)\ \&\ \mathsf{range}(f) = S\ \&\ \mathsf{domain}(f) = C\big)\big)\big) \rightarrow (C = \#S)$

Theorem 83 : [Subsets of an ordinal have a cardinality that is no larger than the ordinal]
$\big(\mathsf{Ord}(S)\ \&\ T \subseteq S\big) \rightarrow (\#T \subseteq S)$

Theorem 84 : [Subset cardinality theorem] $(T \subseteq S) \rightarrow (\#T \subseteq \#S)$

Theorem 85 : [Single-valued mapping cannot increase cardinality]
$\mathsf{Svm}(F) \rightarrow \big(\#\mathsf{range}(F) \subseteq \#\mathsf{domain}(F)\big)$

### *5.3.1 Finiteness*

All the preceding results are as true for infinite sets, ordinals, and cardinals as for finite objects. We now go on to introduce the important notion of finiteness and to prove its basic properties. The definition is as follows: a set $s$ is *finite* if it cannot be mapped into any proper subset of itself by a one-to-one mapping.[3]

Def 18 : [Finiteness] $\mathsf{Finite}(s) \leftrightarrow_{\mathrm{Def}}$
$\neg\big(\exists f \mid \mathsf{1\_1}(f)\ \&\ \mathsf{domain}(f) = s\ \&\ \mathsf{range}(f) \subseteq s\ \&\ s \neq \mathsf{range}(f)\big)$

An equivalent property is that $s$ should not be the single-valued image of any proper subset of itself. To begin work with the basic notion of finiteness, we prove that the null set is finite, that any subset of a finite set is finite, and that a set is finite if and only if its cardinality (with which it is in one-to-one correspondence) is finite. It is also proved (Theorems 102, 103, and 104) that two sets in one-to-one correspondence are both finite if either is, and that the image of a finite set under a single-valued map is always finite.

Along the way we prove a utility collection of results on the finiteness and cardinality of maps, and of their ranges and domains. These are as follows. Both the range and domain of a mapping have a cardinality no larger than that of the map

[3]Following Tarski [Tar24] we could have adopted the following alternative definition of finite sets, equivalent for any practical purpose to the definition given here:

$$\mathsf{Finite}(f) \leftrightarrow_{\mathrm{Def}} \big(\forall g \in \mathscr{P}\big(\mathscr{P}(f)\big) \setminus \{\emptyset\} \,\big|\, \big(\exists m \mid g \cap \mathscr{P}(m) = \{m\}\big)\big),$$

i.e., $f$ is finite if and only if every non-null set $g$ constituted by subsets of $f$ owns an inclusion-minimal element $m$. This will be shown in Sect. 7.5.

itself. If a map is single-valued, it has the same cardinality as its domain. If $t$ is a non-null subset of $s$, then there exists a single-valued mapping whose domain is $s$ and whose range is $t$; this map can be one-to-one if and only if $s$ and $t$ have the same cardinality. A set $s$ is a cardinal if and only if it is its own cardinality, i.e. $s = \#s$. The cardinality operator '#' is idempotent, and the membership operation for cardinals has the trichotomy and transitivity properties of a comparison operator.

We also prove the basic lemmas (Theorems 96 and 97) that we will use to show that cardinal multiplication is associative and commutative once this multiplication operation has been defined, and the lemma (Theorem 100) needed to show that the power operation $2^C$ is well-defined for cardinal numbers $C$.

Theorem 86 : [∅ is a finite cardinal] $\mathsf{Ord}(\emptyset)\ \&\ \mathsf{Finite}(\emptyset)\ \&\ \mathsf{Is\_cardinal}(\emptyset)$

Theorem 87 : $\#\mathsf{domain}(F) \subseteq \#F$

Theorem 88 : $\#\mathsf{range}(F) \subseteq \#F$

Theorem 89 : $\mathsf{Svm}(F) \rightarrow (\#\mathsf{domain}(F) = \#F)$

Theorem 90 : [Condition for existence of a single-valued map between two sets]
$\#S \supseteq \#T \leftrightarrow \big(T = \emptyset\ \vee$
$\big(\exists f \mid (\mathsf{Svm}(f)\ \&\ \mathsf{domain}(f) = S\ \&\ \mathsf{range}(f) = T)\big)\big)$

Theorem 91 : $\#S = \#T \leftrightarrow \big(\exists f \mid \big(\mathsf{1\_1}(f)\ \&\ \mathsf{domain}(f) = S\ \&\ \mathsf{range}(f) = T\big)\big)$

Theorem 92 : $\mathsf{Is\_cardinal}(S) \leftrightarrow S = \#S$

Theorem 93 : $\#S = \#\#S$

Theorem 94 : [All cardinals are comparable] $\#S \in \#T \vee \#S = \#T \vee \#T \in \#S$

Theorem 95 : [Cardinal comparison is transitive]
$(\#S \in \#T\ \&\ \#T \in \#R) \rightarrow (\#S \in \#R)$

Theorem 96 : [Associative law for cardinals] $\#\big((A \times B) \times C\big) = \#\big(A \times (B \times C)\big)$

Theorem 97 : [Commutative law for cardinals] $\#(A \times B) = \#(B \times A)$

Theorem 98 : [A subset of a finite set is finite] $\big(\mathsf{Finite}(S)\ \&\ S \supseteq T\big) \rightarrow \mathsf{Finite}(T)$

Theorem 100 : [A 1-1 map on a set induces a 1-1 map on the power set of its domain]
$\big(\mathsf{1\_1}(F)\ \&\ S \subseteq \mathsf{domain}(F)\ \&\ T \subseteq \mathsf{domain}(F)\ \&\ S \neq T\big) \rightarrow$
$\big(\mathsf{range}(F_{|S}) \neq \mathsf{range}(F_{|T})\big)$

Theorem 103 : [One-one maps preserve finiteness]
$\mathsf{1\_1}(F) \to \big(\mathsf{Finite}(\mathsf{domain}(F)) \leftrightarrow \mathsf{Finite}(\mathsf{range}(F))\big)$

Theorem 104 : [A single-valued map with finite domain has a finite range]
$\big(\mathsf{Svm}(F) \,\&\, \mathsf{Finite}(\mathsf{domain}(F))\big) \to \mathsf{Finite}(\mathsf{range}(F))$

Theorem 105 : $\mathsf{Finite}(S) \leftrightarrow \mathsf{Finite}(\#S)$

Our next block of theorems works further into the properties of finite sets. We show that any proper subset of a finite set $s$ has a smaller cardinality than $s$ (this condition is equivalent to finiteness), that any member of a finite ordinal is finite (so that any infinite ordinal is larger than any finite ordinal), that the addition of a singleton to a finite set gives a finite set. This implies that any singleton is finite, and that the successor set $\mathsf{next}(s)$ of a finite set is always finite. We prove the equivalence of a second possible definition of finiteness: $s$ is finite if and only if it cannot be the single-valued image of any of its proper subsets.

Theorem 110 is a simple utility lemma asserting that any two elements of a set can be interchanged by a one-to-one mapping of the set into itself. Theorem 111 collects various elementary properties of single-valued maps, their domains, and their restrictions.

Theorem 106 : [Proper subsets of a finite set have fewer elements]
$\big(\mathsf{Finite}(S) \,\&\, T \subseteq S \,\&\, T \neq S\big) \to (\#T \in \#S)$

Theorem 107 : $\mathsf{Finite}(S) \leftrightarrow \neg\big(\exists f \mid \big(\mathsf{Svm}(f) \,\&\, \mathsf{range}(f) = S$
$\&\, \mathsf{domain}(f) \subseteq S \,\&\, S \neq \mathsf{domain}(f)\big)\big)$

Theorem 108 : $\big(\mathsf{Ord}(S) \,\&\, \mathsf{Finite}(S) \,\&\, T \in S\big) \to \mathsf{Finite}(T)$

Theorem 109 : [Any infinite ordinal is larger than any finite ordinal]
$\big(\mathsf{Ord}(S) \,\&\, \mathsf{Ord}(T) \,\&\, \big(\neg\mathsf{Finite}(S)\big) \,\&\, \mathsf{Finite}(T)\big) \to (T \in S)$

Theorem 110 : [Interchange Lemma] $(X \in S \,\&\, Y \in S) \to \big(\exists f \mid \big(\mathsf{1\_1}(f) \,\&$
$\mathsf{range}(f) = S \,\&\, \mathsf{domain}(f) = S \,\&\, f[X] = Y \,\&\, f[Y] = X\big)\big)$

Theorem 111 : $\mathsf{Svm}(F) \to \big(F_{|S} = \big\{\big[x,\ F[x]\big] : x \in \mathsf{domain}(f) \mid x \in S \,\&$
$\mathsf{domain}(F_{|S})\big\} = \big\{x \in \mathsf{domain}(F) \mid x \in S\big\} \,\&$
$\mathsf{range}(F_{|S}) = \big\{F[x] : x \in \mathsf{domain}(f) \mid x \in S\big\}\big)$

Theorem 113 : $\mathsf{Finite}(S) \leftrightarrow \mathsf{Finite}\big(S \cup \{X\}\big)$

Theorem 114 : $\mathsf{Finite}(S) \to \mathsf{Finite}\big(\mathsf{next}(S)\big)$

## 5.4 The Set of All Integers, Basic Arithmetic of Integers and Cardinals

Our next main goal is to prove that the collection of all finite ordinals is a set (this set, which is also the set of all finite cardinals, is of course the set of integers, and hence the foundation stone of all traditional mathematics). This is done by using the infinite set $\mathsf{s}_\infty$ whose existence is assumed in the axiom of infinity to prove that there exists an infinite ordinal. The set $\mathbb{N}$ of integers can then be defined as the least infinite ordinal, which we show is also a cardinal. We also show that a cardinal is finite if and only if it is a member of $\mathbb{N}$, and define the standard integers $1, 2, 3$, etc. as $\mathsf{next}(\emptyset)$, $\mathsf{next}(1)$, $\mathsf{next}(2)$, etc., and prove that these are all distinct.

Theorem 115 : $\neg\mathsf{Finite}(\mathsf{s}_\infty)$

Theorem 116 : [Infinite cardinality theorem] $\neg\mathsf{Finite}(\#\mathsf{s}_\infty)$

Theorem 117 : [All finite ordinals are cardinals]
$\big(\mathsf{Ord}(X)\ \&\ \mathsf{Finite}(X)\big) \rightarrow \mathsf{Is\_cardinal}(X)$

Def 18a : [The set of integers] $\mathbb{N} =_{\mathrm{Def}} \mathsf{arb}\big(\{\, x \in \mathsf{next}(\#\mathsf{s}_\infty) \mid \neg\mathsf{Finite}(x)\,\}\big)$

Theorem 118 : [The set of integers is an infinite ordinal consisting of all finite ordinals]
$\mathsf{Ord}(\mathbb{N})\ \&\ \big(\neg\mathsf{Finite}(\mathbb{N})\big)\ \&\ \big(\big(\mathsf{Is\_cardinal}(X)\ \&\ \mathsf{Finite}(X)\big) \leftrightarrow X \in \mathbb{N}\big)$

Def 18b : [Standard definitions of the finite integers]
$1 = \mathsf{next}(\emptyset)\ \&\ 2 = \mathsf{next}(1)\ \&\ 3 = \mathsf{next}(2)\ \&\ \cdots$

Theorem 119 : $\mathsf{Ord}(\emptyset)\ \&\ \emptyset \in \mathbb{N}\ \&\ 1 \in \mathbb{N}\ \&\ 2 \in \mathbb{N}\ \&\ 3 \in \mathbb{N}$

Theorem 120 : [The set of integers is a cardinal] $\mathsf{Is\_cardinal}(\mathbb{N})$

Theorem 121 : $\{\emptyset, 1, 2, 3\} \subseteq \mathbb{N}\ \&$
$1 \neq \emptyset\ \&\ 2 \neq \emptyset\ \&\ 3 \neq \emptyset\ \&\ 1 \neq 2\ \&\ 1 \neq 3\ \&\ 2 \neq 3$

Our next block of theorems continues to develop the basic principles of arithmetic, and hence brings us into standard mathematics. The notions of addition, multiplication, (unsigned) subtraction, division, and remainder after division are first defined using simple set-theoretic constructions. (The sum of two cardinals $n$ and $m$ is the cardinality of the union of any two disjoint sets in 1-1 correspondence with $n$ and $m$, respectively; the product of $n$ and $m$ is the cardinality of the Cartesian product of the sets $m$ and $n$; their difference is the cardinality of the difference set $m \setminus n$.) The quotient of $m$ over $n$ is the largest $k$ whose product with $n$ is included in $m$, and the remainder is $m - ((m/n) * n)$ as usual. All this is formalized in the six following definitions, which also include the definition of the notion of powerset.

Def 19 : [Cardinal sum] $n + m =_{\text{Def}} \#\big(\{[x, \emptyset] : x \in n\} \cup \{[x, 1] : x \in m\}\big)$

Def 20 : [Cardinal product] $N * M =_{\text{Def}} \#(N \times M)$

Def 21 : $\mathscr{P}(s) =_{\text{Def}} \{x : x \subseteq s\}$

Def 22 : [Cardinal difference] $N - M =_{\text{Def}} \#(N \setminus M)$

Def 23 : [Integer quotient] $M/N =_{\text{Def}} \bigcup \{k \in \mathbb{N} \mid k * N \subseteq M\}$
[Note that $x/\emptyset = \mathbb{N}$ for $x \in \mathbb{N}$]

Def 24 : [Integer Remainder] $M \bmod N =_{\text{Def}} M - \big((M/N) * N\big)$

Next a few necessary lemmas are proved. The sets which appear in the definition of cardinal summation are disjoint and have the same cardinality as the sets from which they are formed; the null set is a one-to-one map with null range and domain; and a single ordered pair defines a one-to-one map. We also prove a simple utility formula for maps constructed out of just two ordered pairs.

Theorem 122 : $\{[x, \emptyset] : x \in N\} \cap \{[x, 1] : x \in M\} = \emptyset$

Theorem 123 : $\mathsf{Is\_map}(\emptyset)$ & $\mathsf{Svm}(\emptyset)$ & $\mathsf{1\_1}(\emptyset)$ & $\mathsf{range}(\emptyset) = \emptyset$ & $\mathsf{domain}(\emptyset) = \emptyset$

Theorem 124 : $\mathsf{Svm}(\{[X, Y]\})$ & $\mathsf{1\_1}(\{[X, Y]\})$ & $\{[X, Y]\}[X] = Y$

Theorem 125 : $(X \neq Z) \rightarrow \big(\{[X, Y], [Z, W]\}[X] = Y\big)$

Theorem 126 : $\#\{[x, \emptyset] : x \in M\} = \#M$ & $\#\{[x, 1] : x \in N\} = \#N$

In preparation for a closer examination of the rules of cardinal arithmetic, we prove next that the cardinal sum and product of two sets can be calculated either from the sets or from their cardinal numbers. We so show that any proper subset of a finite set has a smaller cardinal number.

Theorem 127 : $N + M = \#N + \#M$

Theorem 128 : $N + M = N + \#M$

Theorem 129 : $N * M = \#N * \#M$

Theorem 130 : $N * M = N * \#M$

Theorem 131 : $\big(\mathsf{Finite}(N)$ & $M \subseteq N$ & $M \neq N\big) \rightarrow (\#M \in \#N)$

Since the following discussion will occasionally use inductive arguments which refer to the subsets of a finite set, it is convenient to make these available in a theory. This states that, given any predicate $P(x)$ which is true for some finite set, there exists a finite set $s$ for which $P(s)$ is true, but $P(s')$ is false for all proper subsets of $s$.

$$\begin{array}{l} \text{THEORY finite\_induction}\big(\mathsf{n},\ P(x)\big) \\ \quad \mathsf{Finite(n)}\ \&\ P(\mathsf{n}) \\ \Longrightarrow (\mathsf{m}_\Theta) \\ \quad \mathsf{m}_\Theta \subseteq \mathsf{n}\ \&\ P(\mathsf{m}_\Theta)\ \& \\ \quad \big(\forall k \subseteq \mathsf{m}_\Theta \mid (k \neq \mathsf{m}_\Theta) \rightarrow \big(\neg P(k)\big)\big) \\ \text{END finite\_induction} \end{array}$$

Now we are ready to prove the main elementary properties of integer arithmetic. We show that the union of two finite sets is finite, and that a cardinal sum of two sets is finite if and only if the union of the two sets (i.e. both of the two sets) is finite. The statements '*zero times any n equals zero*', and '*one times any n equals n*' are proved in several convenient equivalent forms. We show that $n \cap m$ is at least as large as $m$ if $n$ is not zero, and show how to express the cardinal sum as the cardinality of two distinct Cartesian product sets, whose disjointness is then demonstrated. Then the distributive and commutative laws for cardinal (and hence integer) arithmetic are established by relating them to corresponding set-theoretic constructions. Finally we show that the Cartesian product of two finite sets is finite, and that the converse holds as long as neither of the sets is empty.

Theorem 132 : $\big(\mathsf{Finite}(N)\ \&\ \mathsf{Finite}(M)\big) \leftrightarrow \mathsf{Finite}(N \cup M)$

Theorem 133 : $\mathsf{Finite}(N + M) \leftrightarrow \mathsf{Finite}(N \cup M)$

Theorem 134 : $\big(\mathsf{Finite}(N)\ \&\ \mathsf{Finite}(M)\big) \leftrightarrow \mathsf{Finite}(N + M)$

Theorem 135 : $N \times \emptyset = \emptyset\ \&\ \emptyset \times N = \emptyset$

Theorem 136 : $N * \emptyset = \emptyset$

Theorem 137 : $\emptyset * N = \emptyset$

Theorem 138 : $\#N + \emptyset = \#N$

Theorem 139 : $\#\big(\{C\} \times N\big) = \#N$

Theorem 140 : $\#\big(N \times \{C\}\big) = \#N$

Theorem 141 : $1 * N = \#N$

Theorem 142 : $N * 1 = \#N$

Theorem 143 : $(M \neq \emptyset) \rightarrow \big(\#(N \times M) \supseteq \#N\big)$

Theorem 144 : $N + M = \#\big((N \times \{\emptyset\}) \cup (M \times \{1\})\big)$

Theorem 145 : $(A \cap B = \emptyset) \rightarrow \big((X \times A) \cap (Y \times B) = \emptyset\big)$

Theorem 146 : $N + M = M + N$

Theorem 147 : $N * M = M * N$

Theorem 148 : $\big((A \times X) \cap (B \times X)\big) = (A \cap B) \times X \; \& \; \big((A \times X) \cup (B \times X)\big) = (A \cup B) \times X \; \& \; \big((X \times A) \cap (X \times B)\big) = X \times (A \cap B) \; \& \; \big((X \times A) \cup (X \times B)\big) = X \times (A \cup B)$

Theorem 149 : $N + (M + K) = (N + M) + K$

Theorem 150 : $N * (M * K) = (N * M) * K$

Theorem 151 : $N * (M + K) = (N * M) + (N * K)$

Theorem 152 : $\big(\mathsf{Finite}(N) \;\&\; \mathsf{Finite}(M)\big) \rightarrow \mathsf{Finite}(N * M)$

Theorem 153 : $\big((\mathsf{Finite}(N) \;\&\; \mathsf{Finite}(M)) \vee (N = \emptyset \vee M = \emptyset)\big) \leftrightarrow \mathsf{Finite}(N * M)$

Next a few well-known results concerning power sets and their cardinalities are proved. The power set of the null set is the singleton $\{\emptyset\}$. The power set of a set $s$ is finite if and only if $s$ is finite, but (Cantor's theorem, the historical root of the whole theory of infinite cardinals) always has a larger cardinality than $s$.

Theorem 154 : $\mathscr{P}(\emptyset) = \{\emptyset\}$

Theorem 155 : $\mathsf{Finite}(N) \leftrightarrow \mathsf{Finite}\big(\mathscr{P}(N)\big)$

Theorem 156 : [Cantor's Theorem] $\#N \in \#\mathscr{P}(N)$

Next we prove some properties of cardinal subtraction, along with some auxiliary properties of the cardinal sum: $n - n$ is always $\emptyset$, $n - \emptyset$ is $n$, $(n - m) + m$ and $m + (n - m)$ are both $n$ if $m$ is no larger than $n$. The cardinality of the union set $s \cup t$ is the cardinal sum of $s$ and $t$ if the two sets are disjoint, and this value depends only on the cardinalities of the sets involved.

Theorem 157 : $N - N = \emptyset$

Theorem 158 : $N - \emptyset = \#N$

Theorem 159 : [Disjoint sum Lemma] $(N \cap M = \emptyset) \rightarrow \big(N + M = \#(N \cup M)\big)$

Theorem 160 : $(N \cap M = \emptyset \,\&\, N' \cap M' = \emptyset \,\&\, \#N = \#N' \,\&\, \#M = \#M') \rightarrow \big(\#(N + M) = \#(N' + M')\big)$

Theorem 161 : [Subtraction lemma] $(M \subseteq N) \rightarrow \big(\#N = \#M + (N - M)\big)$

Theorem 162 : [Subtraction lemma] $(\#M \in \#N \vee \#M = \#N) \rightarrow \big(\#N = \#M + (\#N - \#M)\big)$

Because of the set-theoretic way in which we have defined ordinals, the maximum of a set $s$ of ordinals is simply the union of all the ordinals. This fact is captured in our next block of theorems, which begins with the very simple definition of the concept 'union set'.

Def 25 : [Union set] $\bigcup S =_{\text{Def}} \{x : x \in y,\ y \in S\}$

Our next two theorems capture the fact stated just above: the union of a set $s$ of ordinals is always an ordinal, and is the least upper bound of $s$.

Theorem 163 : [Union set as an upper bound] $\big(\forall x \in S \mid x \subseteq \bigcup S\big) \,\&\, \big((\forall x \in S \mid x \subseteq T) \rightarrow \big(\bigcup S \subseteq T\big)\big)$

Theorem 164 : [The union of a set of ordinals is an ordinal] $\big(\forall x \in S \mid \mathsf{Ord}(x)\big) \rightarrow \mathsf{Ord}\big(\bigcup S\big)$

Now we prove two basic elementary properties of division: $n/m$ is no larger than $n$ unless $m$ is $\emptyset$, and is an integer if $n$ and $m$ are both integers. We also show that the sum, product, and difference of integers is an integer.

Theorem 165 : $(M \neq \emptyset) \rightarrow (N/M \subseteq N)$

Theorem 166 : $(M \neq \emptyset \,\&\, N \in \mathbb{N}) \rightarrow (N/M \in \mathbb{N} \,\&\, N/M \subseteq N)$

Theorem 167 : $(N \in \mathbb{N} \,\&\, M \in \mathbb{N}) \rightarrow (N + M \in \mathbb{N} \,\&\, N * M \in \mathbb{N} \,\&\, N - M \in \mathbb{N})$

Next several results on the monotonicity of addition, multiplication, and subtraction are given. Once we have extended the notion of 'integer' to that of 'signed integer' these will become the standard monotonicity properties for algebraic combinations of signed integers, and ultimately of rational numbers and of reals. We show that: integer addition is strictly monotone in both of its arguments (several variants of this result are given); integer multiplication is monotone in both of its arguments (but not strictly, unless $\emptyset$ is excluded as a factor). We also prove that subtraction is strictly monotone in its arguments, and establish the cancellation rule for unsigned addition needed later to justify the definition of signed addition and its relationship to signed subtraction.

Theorem 169 : [Strict monotonicity of addition] $(M \in \mathbb{N} \,\&\, N \in \mathbb{N} \,\&\, N \neq \emptyset) \rightarrow (M \in M + N)$

Theorem 170 : [Strict monotonicity of addition] $(M \in \mathbb{N} \,\&\, N \in \mathbb{N} \,\&\, K \in N) \rightarrow (M + K \in M + N)$

Theorem 171 : [Cancellation] $(M \in \mathbb{N} \,\&\, N \in \mathbb{N} \,\&\, K \in \mathbb{N} \,\&\, M + K = N + K) \rightarrow (M = N)$

Theorem 172 : [Monotonicity of addition] $(M \subseteq N) \rightarrow (M + K \subseteq N + K)$

Theorem 173 : [Monotonicity of multiplication] $(M \subseteq N) \rightarrow (M * K \subseteq N * K)$

Theorem 174 : [Monotonicity of addition] $(M \in \mathbb{N} \,\&\, N \in \mathbb{N} \,\&\, K \in \mathbb{N}) \rightarrow (M + K \subseteq N + K \leftrightarrow M \subseteq N)$

Theorem 175 : [Strict monotonicity of subtraction] $(N \in \mathbb{N} \,\&\, K \in N \,\&\, M \supseteq N) \rightarrow (M - N \in M - K)$

Our next, rather miscellaneous block of theorems show that subtraction stands in the correct relationship to addition, and prove some related facts on the monotonicity of addition. We also show that the cardinality of any singleton is 1, that only the empty set has cardinality zero, and that if a cardinal product is zero one of its two factors must be zero. This last statement is subsequently used in constructing rational numbers.

Theorem 176 : $(M \in \mathbb{N} \,\&\, N \in \mathbb{N} \,\&\, K \in \mathbb{N} \,\&\, N \supseteq M \,\&\, N - M \supseteq K) \rightarrow \big(N \supseteq M + K \,\&\, N - (M + K) = (N - M) - K\big)$

Theorem 177 : $(M \in \mathbb{N} \,\&\, N \in \mathbb{N}) \rightarrow \big((M + N) - N = M\big)$

Theorem 178 : [Integer division with remainder] $(M \in \mathbb{N} \,\&\, N \in \mathbb{N} \,\&\, N \neq \emptyset) \rightarrow \big(M/N \in \mathbb{N} \,\&\, M \supseteq \big((M/N) * N\big) \,\&\, M \bmod N \in N\big)$

Theorem 179 : $\#\{S\} = \{\emptyset\}$

Theorem 180 : $(\#N = \emptyset) \rightarrow (N = \emptyset)$

Theorem 181 : $\#N * \#M = \emptyset \leftrightarrow (N = \emptyset \vee M = \emptyset)$

Theorem 182 : $(N \supseteq M) \rightarrow \big((N - K) \supseteq (M - K)\big)$

Theorem 183 : $\big(\mathsf{Finite}(N) \,\&\, N \supseteq M\big) \rightarrow \big(\#(N \setminus M) = \#(\#N \setminus \#M)\big)$

Theorem 184 : $(N \in \mathbb{N} \,\&\, M \in \mathbb{N}) \rightarrow \big((N + M) - M = N\big)$

Theorem 185 : $(N \in \mathbb{N} \,\&\, M \in \mathbb{N} \,\&\, K \in \mathbb{N}) \rightarrow$
$\big((N \supseteq M) \leftrightarrow \big((N + K) \supseteq (M + K)\big)\big)$

Theorem 186 : $(N \supseteq M) \rightarrow \big(\#N = \#M + \#(N \setminus M)\big)$

Theorem 187 : $(N \in \mathbb{N} \,\&\, M \in \mathbb{N} \,\&\, K \in \mathbb{N} \,\&\, N \supseteq M) \rightarrow$
$\big((N + K) - (M + K) = N - M\big)$

Theorem 188 : $(N \in \mathbb{N} \,\&\, M \in \mathbb{N}) \rightarrow$
$\big(N = M + (N - M) \vee N = M - (M - N)\big)$

## 5.5 The Cardinal Product Theorem

Although our main goal is now to move on to the principal notions and theorems of analysis, we digress to prove that the sum and product of any two infinite cardinals degenerates to their maximum. The two following theories prepare for this. Given any ordinal-valued function f on a set s, the first theory constructs the subset '$\mathsf{rng}_\Theta$' of s on which f assumes its minimum. The second theory tells us that any well-ordering of a set s defines a one-to-one mapping of some ordinal $o$ onto s which realizes an isomorphism of the natural ordering of $o$ (by the '$\in$' relator) to the given ordering of s. It also asserts that the mapping sends all ordinals larger than $o$ onto s, and all smaller ordinals onto an initial slice of s, i.e. all elements of s up to some given $v$ in s.

THEORY ordval_fcn(s, f($x$)); [Elementary functions of ordinal-valued functions]
$\mathsf{s} \neq \emptyset \,\&\, \big(\forall x \in \mathsf{s} \mid \mathsf{Ord}(f(x))\big)$
$\Longrightarrow (\mathsf{rng}_\Theta)$
$\mathsf{rng}_\Theta = \big\{x : x \in \mathsf{s} \mid \mathsf{f}(x) = \mathsf{arb}(\{\mathsf{f}(y) : y \in \mathsf{s}\})\big\} \,\&$
$\mathsf{rng}_\Theta \neq \emptyset \,\&\, \big(\forall x \in \mathsf{rng}_\Theta \mid \big(\forall y \in \mathsf{s} \mid (\mathsf{f}(x) = \mathsf{f}(y)) \rightarrow y \in \mathsf{rng}_\Theta\big)\big) \,\&$
$\mathsf{rng}_\Theta \subseteq \mathsf{s} \,\&\, \big(\forall x \in \mathsf{rng}_\Theta \mid \big(\forall y \in \mathsf{s} \mid \mathsf{f}(x) \subseteq \mathsf{f}(y)\big)\big)$
END ordval_fcn;

THEORY well_ordered_set(s, $x \lhd y$);

$(\forall x \in \mathsf{s} \mid \neg x \lhd x)$ &
$\big(\forall x \in \mathsf{s} \big| \big(\forall y \in \mathsf{s} \big| \big(\forall z \in \mathsf{s} \mid (x \lhd y \,\&\, y \lhd z) \rightarrow x \lhd z\big)\big)\big)$ &
$\big(\forall t \subseteq \mathsf{s} \big| (t \neq \emptyset) \rightarrow \big(\exists x \in t \big| \big(\forall y \in t \mid (x \lhd y \vee x = y)\big)\big)\big)$

$\Longrightarrow$ (orden$_\Theta$)

$(X \in \mathsf{s} \,\&\, Y \in \mathsf{s}) \rightarrow (X \lhd Y \vee Y \lhd X \vee X = Y)$

$\mathsf{s} \subseteq \{\mathsf{orden}_\Theta(y) : y \in X\} \leftrightarrow \mathsf{orden}_\Theta(X) = \mathsf{s}$

$\big(\mathsf{orden}_\Theta(X) \neq \mathsf{s}\big) \rightarrow \big(\mathsf{orden}_\Theta(X) \in \mathsf{s}\big)$

[Well-ordering is isomorphic to ordinal enumeration]

$\big(\mathsf{Ord}(U) \,\&\, \mathsf{Ord}(V) \,\&\, \mathsf{orden}_\Theta(U) \neq \mathsf{s} \,\&\, \mathsf{orden}_\Theta(V) \neq \mathsf{s}\big) \rightarrow$
$\big(\mathsf{orden}_\Theta(U) \lhd \mathsf{orden}_\Theta(V) \leftrightarrow U \in V\big)$

$\big(\mathsf{Ord}(U) \,\&\, \mathsf{orden}_\Theta(U) \neq \mathsf{s}\big) \rightarrow \big(\mathsf{orden}_\Theta(U) = \{\mathsf{orden}_\Theta(x) : x \in U\}\big)$

$\big(\mathsf{Ord}(U) \,\&\, \mathsf{Ord}(V) \,\&\, \mathsf{orden}_\Theta(U) \neq \mathsf{s} \,\&\, \mathsf{orden}_\Theta(V) \neq \mathsf{s} \,\&\, U \neq V\big)$
$\rightarrow \big(\mathsf{orden}_\Theta(U) \neq \mathsf{orden}_\Theta(V)\big)$

$\big(\exists o \mid \mathsf{Ord}(o) \,\&\, \mathsf{s} = \{\mathsf{orden}_\Theta(x) : x \in o\}$ &
$\big(\forall x \in o \mid \mathsf{orden}_\Theta(x) \neq \mathsf{s}\big) \,\&\, \mathsf{1\_1}\big(\{[x, \mathsf{orden}_\Theta(x)] : x \in o\}\big)\big)$

$\big(\mathsf{Ord}(V) \,\&\, \mathsf{orden}_\Theta(V) \neq \mathsf{s}\big) \rightarrow$
$\big(\mathsf{1\_1}\big(\{[x, \mathsf{orden}_\Theta(x)] : x \in V\}\big)$ &
$\mathsf{domain}\big(\{[x, \mathsf{orden}_\Theta(x)] : x \in V\}\big) = V$ &
$\mathsf{range}\big(\{[x, \mathsf{orden}_\Theta(x)] : x \in V\}\big) = \{u \in \mathsf{s} : u \lhd \mathsf{orden}_\Theta(V)\}\big)$

END well_ordered_set;

Instrumental to the theory just seen, it is convenient to develop before it this one:

THEORY well_founded_set(s, $x \lhd y$);

$\big(\forall t \subseteq \mathsf{s} \mid t \neq \emptyset \rightarrow \big(\exists x \in t \mid (\forall y \in t \mid \neg y \lhd x)\big)\big)$

$\Longrightarrow$ (orden$_\Theta$, o$_\Theta$)

$(X \in \mathsf{s} \,\&\, Y \in \mathsf{s}) \rightarrow \big((X \lhd Y \rightarrow \neg Y \lhd X) \,\&\, \neg X \lhd X\big)$

$\mathsf{s} \subseteq \{\mathsf{orden}_\Theta(y) : y \in X\} \leftrightarrow \mathsf{orden}_\Theta(X) = \mathsf{s}$

$\big(\mathsf{orden}_\Theta(X) \neq \mathsf{s}\big) \rightarrow \big(\mathsf{orden}_\Theta(X) \in \mathsf{s}\big)$

$\big(\mathsf{Ord}(U) \,\&\, \mathsf{Ord}(V) \,\&\, \mathsf{orden}_\Theta(U) \neq \mathsf{s} \,\&\, \mathsf{orden}_\Theta(U) \lhd \mathsf{orden}_\Theta(V)\big)$
$\rightarrow U \in V$

$\{u : u \in \mathsf{s} \mid u \lhd \mathsf{orden}_\Theta(V)\} \subseteq \{\mathsf{orden}_\Theta(x) : x \in V\}$

...

$\big(\mathsf{o}_\Theta \in \mathsf{next}(\#\mathscr{P}(\mathsf{s})) \,\&\, \mathsf{Ord}(\mathsf{o}_\Theta) \,\&\, \mathsf{s} = \{\mathsf{orden}_\Theta(x) : x \in \mathsf{o}_\Theta\}$ &
$\big(\forall x \in \mathsf{o}_\Theta \mid \mathsf{orden}_\Theta(x) \neq \mathsf{s}\big) \,\&\, \mathsf{1\_1}\big(\{[x, \mathsf{orden}_\Theta(x)] : x \in \mathsf{o}_\Theta\}\big)\big)$

END well_founded_set;

The next seven theorems lead up to the Cardinal Square theorem which is the main result of our digression. The main theorems are 194 and 195, which state that the cardinal product of any infinite cardinal $n$ with itself, or with any smaller non-zero cardinal, is simply $n$, and 192, which states that the sum of two infinite cardinals is simply the larger of the two. The remaining theorems in the block displayed are preparatory. Theorem 189 states that addition of a single new element to an infinite set does not change its cardinality. Theorems 190 and 191 tell us that any infinite set $s$ can be divided into two parts, both of the same cardinality as $s$. Theorem 193 tells us that any infinite set is in 1-1 correspondence with the Cartesian product of some other set $t$ with itself.

Theorem 189 : [One-more lemma] $\big(\neg\mathsf{Finite}(S)\big) \rightarrow \big(\#S = \#\big(S \cup \{C\}\big)\big)$

Theorem 190 : [Division-by-2 lemma]
$\big(\neg\mathsf{Finite}(S)\big) \rightarrow \big(\exists T \mid \#\big(T \times \{\emptyset, 1\}\big) = \#S\big)$

Theorem 191 : [Cardinal doubling theorem] $\big(\mathsf{Is\_cardinal}(S)\ \&\ \big(\neg\mathsf{Finite}(S)\big)\big) \rightarrow$
$\big(\#\big(S \times \{\emptyset, 1\}\big) = \#S\big)$

Theorem 192 : $\big(\neg\mathsf{Finite}(S)\big) \rightarrow \big(S + T = \#S \cup \#T\ \&\ \#(S \cup T) = \#S \cup \#T\big)$

Theorem 193 : [Cardinal square-root lemma] $\big(\neg\mathsf{Finite}(S)\big) \rightarrow$
$\big(\exists T \mid \#(T \times T) = \#S\big)$

Theorem 194 : [Cardinal square theorem] $\big(\neg\mathsf{Finite}(S)\big) \rightarrow \big(\#(S \times S) = \#S\big)$

Theorem 195 : [Cardinal product theorem]
$\big(T \in S \setminus \{\emptyset\}\ \&\ \mathsf{Is\_cardinal}(S)\ \&\ \big(\neg\mathsf{Finite}(S)\big)\big) \rightarrow (S * T = S)$

## 5.6 The Signed Integers

Returning to our main line of development, we now introduce the set $\mathbb{Z}$ (from the German: '*Zahlen*') of signed integers as the set of pairs $[x, \emptyset]$ (representing the positive integers) and $[\emptyset, x]$ (representing the integers of negative sign). The formal definition is as follows.

Def 26 : [Signed Integers] $\mathbb{Z} =_{\mathrm{Def}} \big\{ [x, y] : x \in \mathbb{N}, y \in \mathbb{N} \mid x = \emptyset \vee y = \emptyset \big\}$

Any pair of integers can be reduced to a signed integer by subtracting the smaller of its two components from the larger. This operation, introduced by the following definition, appears repeatedly in our subsequent proofs of the properties of signed integers.

Def 27 : [Signed integer reduction to normal form] $\mathsf{Red}(p) =_{\mathrm{Def}}$
$\big[p^{[1]} - \big(p^{[1]} \cap p^{[2]}\big),\ p^{[2]} - \big(p^{[1]} \cap p^{[2]}\big)\big]$

Next we extend the notions of sum, product, and difference to signed integers, and also define three elementary operators, the absolute value, negative, and sign of a signed integer, that have no direct analog for unsigned integers. The sum of two signed integers $i$ and $j$ is simply the reduction of their componentwise sum. The absolute value of $i$ is the maximum of its two components (only one of which will be non-zero). The negative of $i$ is simply $i$ with its components reversed. The difference of two signed integers is then simply the sum of the first and the negative of the second. The product of signed integers is defined as the reduction of an algebraic combination of their components, formed in a way that reflects the standard 'law of signs'. A signed integer is positive if its second component is null; otherwise it is negative.

$[\emptyset, \emptyset]$ is the 'signed integer' $\emptyset$, and the 1-1 mapping $x \mapsto [x, \emptyset]$, whose inverse is simply $y \mapsto y^{[1]}$, embeds $\mathbb{N}$ into the set of signed integers, in a manner allowing easy extension of the addition, subtraction, multiplication, and division operators to signed integers.

The relevant formal definitions are as follows.

$$\text{Def 28}: \text{[Signed sum] } m +_{\mathbb{Z}} n =_{\text{Def}} \mathsf{Red}\big(\big[m^{[1]} + n^{[1]},\ m^{[2]} + n^{[2]}\big]\big)$$

$$\text{Def 28}a: \text{[Absolute value] } |m|_{\mathbb{Z}} =_{\text{Def}} \big[m^{[1]} + m^{[2]},\ \emptyset\big]$$

$$\text{Def 28}b: \text{[Negative] } -_{\mathbb{Z}}(m) =_{\text{Def}} \big[m^{[2]},\ m^{[1]}\big]$$

$$\text{Def 29}: \text{[Signed product] } m *_{\mathbb{Z}} n =_{\text{Def}} \mathsf{Red}\big(\big[\big(m^{[1]} * n^{[1]}\big) + \big(m^{[2]} * n^{[2]}\big),\ \big(m^{[1]} * n^{[2]}\big) + \big(n^{[1]} * m^{[2]}\big)\big]\big)$$

$$\text{Def 32}: \text{[Signed difference] } n -_{\mathbb{Z}} m =_{\text{Def}} \mathsf{Red}\big(\big[m^{[2]} + n^{[1]},\ m^{[1]} + n^{[2]}\big]\big)$$

$$\text{Def 33}: \text{[Sign of a signed integer] } \mathsf{Is\_nonneg}(x) \leftrightarrow_{\text{Def}} x^{[1]} \supseteq x^{[2]}$$

The sequence of about 30 theorems which follows establishes all the main properties of signed integers, deriving these from the properties of unsigned integers established previously. The proofs involved are all elementary, though sometimes a bit tedious. Theorem 196 is a lemma asserting that the reduction of any pair of unsigned integers is a signed integer. Theorem 197 merely restates the way in which signed integers are defined using integers. Theorem 199 begins our main work, by showing that the set of signed integers is closed under addition and multiplication.

$$\text{Theorem 196}: \quad (M \in \mathbb{N} \,\&\, N \in \mathbb{N}) \rightarrow \mathsf{Red}\big([M,\ N]\big) \in \mathbb{Z}$$

$$\text{Theorem 197}: \quad (N \in \mathbb{Z}) \rightarrow \big(N = \big[N^{[1]},\ N^{[2]}\big] \,\&\, \big(N^{[1]} = \emptyset \vee N^{[2]} = \emptyset\big) \,\&\, N^{[1]} \in \mathbb{N} \,\&\, N^{[2]} \in \mathbb{N} \,\&\, \mathsf{Red}(N) = N \,\&\, \big(N^{[1]} \cap N^{[2]}\big) = \emptyset\big)$$

$$\text{Theorem 199}: \quad (N \in \mathbb{Z} \,\&\, M \in \mathbb{Z}) \rightarrow (N +_{\mathbb{Z}} M \in \mathbb{Z} \,\&\, N *_{\mathbb{Z}} M \in \mathbb{Z})$$

To move toward our goal of establishing all the basic elementary properties of signed integers, we first prove some auxiliary properties of the reduction mapping 'Red' which normalizes pairs of integers by subtraction, sending them into equivalent signed integers. We show that Red($[n, m]$) remains invariant if a common integer is added to $n$ and $m$, that Red($[n, n]$) is always the signed zero element $[\emptyset, \emptyset]$, and that the signed addition and multiplication operations remain invariant if one of their arguments $[n, m]$ is replaced by Red($[n, m]$). The proofs are all elementary, but many involve examination of multiple cases.

Theorem 200 : $(N \in \mathbb{N}) \rightarrow \big(\mathsf{Red}([N, N]) = [\emptyset, \emptyset]\big)$

Theorem 201 : $(J \in \mathbb{N} \,\&\, K \in \mathbb{N} \,\&\, M \in \mathbb{N}) \rightarrow$
$\big(\mathsf{Red}([J +_{\mathbb{Z}} M, K +_{\mathbb{Z}} M]) = \mathsf{Red}([J, K])\big)$

Theorem 202 : $(J \in \mathbb{N} \,\&\, K \in \mathbb{N} \,\&\, N \in \mathbb{N} \,\&\, M \in \mathbb{N}) \rightarrow$
$\big([J, K] +_{\mathbb{Z}} [N, M] = [J, K] +_{\mathbb{Z}} \mathsf{Red}([N, M])\big)$

Theorem 203 : $(K \in \mathbb{Z} \,\&\, N \in \mathbb{N} \,\&\, M \in \mathbb{N}) \rightarrow$
$\big(K +_{\mathbb{Z}} [N, M] = K +_{\mathbb{Z}} \mathsf{Red}([N, M])\big)$

Theorem 204 : $(K \in \mathbb{Z} \,\&\, N \in \mathbb{N} \,\&\, M \in \mathbb{N}) \rightarrow$
$\big(K *_{\mathbb{Z}} [N, M] = K *_{\mathbb{Z}} \mathsf{Red}([N, M])\big)$

Moving on toward proof of the basic properties of signed integers, we first prove commutativity of signed integer addition via two preliminary lemmas which give commutativity for corresponding sums of ordered pairs of integers, and then commutativity, associativity, and distributivity of signed integer multiplication. Next, after a lemma which states that the reduction of a signed integer is the signed integer itself, we show that the mapping of $n$ into $[n, \emptyset]$ sends integers into signed integers in a manner which makes unsigned addition, multiplication, and subtraction correspond to signed addition, multiplication, and subtraction, respectively.

Theorem 205 : [Commutativity lemma, 1] $(K \in \mathbb{Z} \,\&\, N \in \mathbb{N} \,\&\, M \in \mathbb{N})$
$\rightarrow \big(K +_{\mathbb{Z}} [N, M] = [N, M] +_{\mathbb{Z}} K\big)$

Theorem 206 : [Commutativity lemma, 2] $(J \in \mathbb{N} \,\&\, K \in \mathbb{N} \,\&\, N \in \mathbb{N} \,\&\, M \in \mathbb{N})$
$\rightarrow \big([J, K] +_{\mathbb{Z}} [N, M] = [N, M] +_{\mathbb{Z}} [J, K]\big)$

Theorem 207 : [Commutative law for addition] $(N \in \mathbb{Z} \,\&\, M \in \mathbb{Z}) \rightarrow$
$(N +_{\mathbb{Z}} M = M +_{\mathbb{Z}} N)$

Theorem 208 : $(J \in \mathbb{N} \,\&\, K \in \mathbb{N} \,\&\, N \in \mathbb{N} \,\&\, M \in \mathbb{N}) \rightarrow$
$\big([J, K] +_{\mathbb{Z}} [N, M] = \mathsf{Red}([J, K]) +_{\mathbb{Z}} \mathsf{Red}([N, M])\big)$

Theorem 209 : [Commutative law for multiplication] $(N \in \mathbb{Z} \,\&\, M \in \mathbb{Z}) \rightarrow$
$(N *_{\mathbb{Z}} M = M *_{\mathbb{Z}} N)$

Theorem 210 : [Associative law] $(K \in \mathbb{Z} \,\&\, N \in \mathbb{Z} \,\&\, M \in \mathbb{Z})$
$\rightarrow \big(N +_{\mathbb{Z}} (M +_{\mathbb{Z}} K) = (N +_{\mathbb{Z}} M) +_{\mathbb{Z}} K\big)$

Theorem 211 : [Distributive law] $(K \in \mathbb{Z} \,\&\, N \in \mathbb{Z} \,\&\, M \in \mathbb{Z})$
$\rightarrow \big(N *_{\mathbb{Z}} (M +_{\mathbb{Z}} K) = (N *_{\mathbb{Z}} M) +_{\mathbb{Z}} (N *_{\mathbb{Z}} K)\big)$

Theorem 212 : $(N \in \mathbb{N}) \rightarrow \big(\mathsf{Red}([N, \emptyset]) = [N, \emptyset]\big)$

Theorem 213 : [Embedding of integers in signed integers] $(N \in \mathbb{N} \,\&\, M \in \mathbb{N})$
$\rightarrow \Big(\big([N + M, \emptyset] = [N, \emptyset] +_{\mathbb{Z}} [M, \emptyset]\big) \,\&$
$\big([N * M, \emptyset] = [N, \emptyset] *_{\mathbb{Z}} [M, \emptyset]\big) \,\&$
$\big(N \supseteq M \rightarrow \big([N, \emptyset] -_{\mathbb{Z}} [M, \emptyset] = [N - M, \emptyset]\big)\big)\Big)$

Next we give a few elementary theorems on the operation of sign reversal for signed integers: the law of signs for multiplication, the rule that $-(-n)$ is $n$, and the fact that $n + (-n)$ is $\emptyset$.

Theorem 214 : $(N \in \mathbb{N} \,\&\, M \in \mathbb{N}) \rightarrow \big(-_{\mathbb{Z}}(\mathsf{Red}([M, N])) = \mathsf{Red}([N, M])\big)$

Theorem 215 : $(N \in \mathbb{Z} \,\&\, M \in \mathbb{Z}) \rightarrow \big(N *_{\mathbb{Z}} -_{\mathbb{Z}}(M) = -_{\mathbb{Z}}(N *_{\mathbb{Z}} M)\big)$

Theorem 216 : [Inversion lemma] $(N \in \mathbb{Z} \,\&\, M \in \mathbb{Z})$
$\rightarrow \big(-_{\mathbb{Z}}(N *_{\mathbb{Z}} M) = -_{\mathbb{Z}}(N) *_{\mathbb{Z}} M \,\&\, -_{\mathbb{Z}}(N *_{\mathbb{Z}} M) = N *_{\mathbb{Z}} -_{\mathbb{Z}}(M)\big)$

Theorem 217 : [Double inversion] $(K \in \mathbb{Z}) \rightarrow \big(-_{\mathbb{Z}}\big(-_{\mathbb{Z}}(K)\big) = K\big)$

Theorem 218 : $(N \in \mathbb{Z}) \rightarrow$
$\big(-_{\mathbb{Z}}(N) \in \mathbb{Z} \,\&\, -_{\mathbb{Z}}(N) +_{\mathbb{Z}} N = [\emptyset, \emptyset] \,\&\, -_{\mathbb{Z}}\big(-_{\mathbb{Z}}(N)\big) = N\big)$

Our next four theorems lead up to the proof that signed integer multiplication is associative. The first three results state this in special cases. This stepwise approach is needed since a large number of cases need to be examined.

Theorem 219 : [Associativity lemma, 1] $(K \in \mathbb{N} \,\&\, N \in \mathbb{N} \,\&\, M \in \mathbb{N})$
$\rightarrow \big([N, \emptyset] *_{\mathbb{Z}} \big([M, \emptyset] *_{\mathbb{Z}} [K, \emptyset]\big) = \big([N, \emptyset] *_{\mathbb{Z}} [M, \emptyset]\big) *_{\mathbb{Z}} [K, \emptyset]\big)$

Theorem 220 : [Associativity lemma, 2] $(K \in \mathbb{Z} \,\&\, N \in \mathbb{N} \,\&\, M \in \mathbb{N})$
$\rightarrow \big([N, \emptyset] *_{\mathbb{Z}} \big([M, \emptyset] *_{\mathbb{Z}} K\big) = \big([N, \emptyset] *_{\mathbb{Z}} [M, \emptyset]\big) *_{\mathbb{Z}} K\big)$

Theorem 221 : [Associativity lemma, 3] $(K \in \mathbb{Z} \,\&\, N \in \mathbb{N} \,\&\, M \in \mathbb{Z})$
$\rightarrow \big([N, \emptyset] *_{\mathbb{Z}} (M *_{\mathbb{Z}} K) = \big([N, \emptyset] *_{\mathbb{Z}} M\big) *_{\mathbb{Z}} K\big)$

Theorem 222 : [Associativity law] $(K \in \mathbb{Z} \,\&\, N \in \mathbb{Z} \,\&\, M \in \mathbb{Z})$
$\rightarrow \big(N *_{\mathbb{Z}} (M *_{\mathbb{Z}} K) = (N *_{\mathbb{Z}} M) *_{\mathbb{Z}} K\big)$

The final block of theorems in this 'signed integer' group show that $n + (-m)$ is $n - m$, that $-(n + m)$ is $-n - m$, that $[1, \emptyset]$ is the multiplicative identity for signed integer multiplication, and that [∅, ∅] is the additive identity. All the proofs are elementary.

Theorem 223 : $(N \in \mathbb{Z} \,\&\, M \in \mathbb{Z}) \rightarrow \big(N -_{\mathbb{Z}} M = N +_{\mathbb{Z}} -_{\mathbb{Z}}(M)\big)$

Theorem 224 : $(N \in \mathbb{Z} \,\&\, M \in \mathbb{Z}) \rightarrow \big(N = M +_{\mathbb{Z}} (N -_{\mathbb{Z}} M)\big)$

Theorem 225 : $(N \in \mathbb{Z} \,\&\, M \in \mathbb{Z}) \rightarrow \big(-_{\mathbb{Z}}(N +_{\mathbb{Z}} M) = -_{\mathbb{Z}}(N) +_{\mathbb{Z}} -_{\mathbb{Z}}(M)\big)$

Theorem 226 : $[\emptyset,\ 1] *_{\mathbb{Z}} [\emptyset,\ 1] = [1,\ \emptyset]$

Theorem 227 : $(K \in \mathbb{Z}) \rightarrow \big(K *_{\mathbb{Z}} [1,\ \emptyset] = K\big)$

Theorem 228 : $(K \in \mathbb{Z} \,\&\, M \in \mathbb{Z}) \rightarrow \big(K -_{\mathbb{Z}} M = K +_{\mathbb{Z}} (M *_{\mathbb{Z}} [\emptyset,\ 1])\big)$

Theorem 229 : $(K \in \mathbb{Z}) \rightarrow \big(K -_{\mathbb{Z}} K = [\emptyset,\ \emptyset]\big)$

Theorem 230 : $(K \in \mathbb{Z}) \rightarrow \big(K +_{\mathbb{Z}} [\emptyset,\ \emptyset] = K\big)$

Theorem 231 : $(K \in \mathbb{Z}) \rightarrow \big([\emptyset,\ \emptyset] +_{\mathbb{Z}} K = K\big)$

Next, in direct preparation for the introduction of the set of rational numbers, we prove that the set of signed integers is an 'integral domain' in which multiplication has the standard algebraic cancellation property. This is done in Theorems 232 and 234. We also show that multiplication is distributive over subtraction, and that the negative of a signed integer can be expressed as its product with the signed integer −1, i.e. [∅, 1].

Theorem 232 : [$\mathbb{Z}$ is an integral domain] $(N \in \mathbb{Z} \,\&\, M \in \mathbb{Z})$
$\rightarrow \big((M *_{\mathbb{Z}} N = [\emptyset,\ \emptyset]) \rightarrow (M = [\emptyset,\ \emptyset] \vee N = [\emptyset,\ \emptyset])\big)$

Theorem 233 : [Distributivity of subtraction] $\big((N \in \mathbb{Z}) \,\&\, (M \in \mathbb{Z}) \,\&\, (K \in \mathbb{Z})\big)$
$\rightarrow \big((M *_{\mathbb{Z}} N) -_{\mathbb{Z}} (K *_{\mathbb{Z}} N) = (M -_{\mathbb{Z}} K) *_{\mathbb{Z}} N\big)$

Theorem 234 : [$\mathbb{Z}$ cancellation] $\big((N \in \mathbb{Z}) \,\&\, (M \in \mathbb{Z}) \,\&\, (K \in \mathbb{Z})\big)$
$\rightarrow \big((M *_{\mathbb{Z}} N = K *_{\mathbb{Z}} N) \,\&\, (N \neq [\emptyset,\ \emptyset])\big) \rightarrow (M = K)\big)$

Theorem 235 : [Multiplication by −1] $(N \in \mathbb{Z}) \rightarrow \big(-_{\mathbb{Z}}(N) = [\emptyset,\ 1] *_{\mathbb{Z}} N\big)$

This completes our work on the basic properties of signed integers.

## 5.7 Induction Principles for Ordinals

To prepare for what will come later we give various results stating principles of induction. Many of these are cast as theories, for convenience of use. We also prove various auxiliary results on the set of 'ultimate members' of a set $s$, i.e. all those $t$ which can be connected to $s$ via a finite chain of membership relations. These are used in some of the work with the principles of induction in which we are interested. The main result is simply that the collection of ultimate members of a set is also a set.

The first theory developed simply tells us that any predicate $P(\cdot)$ of an ordinal which is not always false admits some ordinal for which it is true, but for which the $P$ is false for all smaller ordinals. This tailored variant of the more general principle of transfinite induction stated earlier is sometimes the most convenient form in which to carry out a transfinite inductive proof.

THEORY ordinal_induction$\big(o,\ P(x)\big)$
  Ord$(o)$ & $P(o)$
$\Longrightarrow (t)$
  Ord$(t)$ & $P(t)$ & $t \subseteq o$ & $\big(\forall x \in t \,\big|\, (\neg P(x))\big)$
END ordinal_induction

Next we define the set Ult_membs$(s)$ of 'ultimate members' of a set $s$, which plays a role in some of our versions of transfinite induction, and prove its properties. The definition is as follows.

$$\text{Def 35a}: \text{Ult\_membs}(s) =_{\text{Def}} s \cup \big\{ y : u \in \big\{ \text{Ult\_membs}(x) : x \in s \big\},\ y \in u \big\}.$$

The eight elementary theorems which follow state various basic properties of Ult_membs$(s)$. Theorems 236, 239, and 242 state that Ult_membs$(s)$ always includes $s$, is increasing in $s$, but is identical to $s$ if $s$ is an ordinal. Theorem 240 states that Ult_membs$(\{s\})$ is almost the same as Ult_membs$(s)$, containing the set $s$ as its only additional member; Theorem 241 specializes this result to ordinals. Theorem 237 gives a convenient inductive definition of Ult_membs$(s)$, and Theorem 238 states that Ult_membs$(s)$ contains all members of members of $s$. Theorem 243 tells us that if $y \in s$, then Ult_membs$(y)$ is a subset of Ult_membs$(s)$.

$$\text{Theorem 236}: \quad S \subseteq \text{Ult\_membs}(S)$$

$$\text{Theorem 237}: \quad \text{Ult\_membs}(S) = S \cup \big\{ y : x \in S,\ y \in \text{Ult\_membs}(x) \big\}$$

$$\text{Theorem 238}: \quad (X \in S \,\&\, Y \in X) \rightarrow \big(Y \in \text{Ult\_membs}(S)\big)$$

$$\text{Theorem 239}: \quad \text{Ord}(S) \rightarrow \big(\text{Ult\_membs}(S) = S\big)$$

$$\text{Theorem 240}: \quad \text{Ult\_membs}\big(\{S\}\big) = \{S\} \cup \text{Ult\_membs}(S)$$

$$\text{Theorem 241}: \quad \text{Ord}(S) \rightarrow \big(\text{Ult\_membs}\big(\{S\}\big) = S \cup \{S\}\big)$$

$$\text{Theorem 242}: \quad \big(Y \in \text{Ult\_membs}(S)\big) \rightarrow \big(\text{Ult\_membs}(Y) \subseteq \text{Ult\_membs}(S)\big)$$

$$\text{Theorem 243}: \quad \big(Y \in \text{Ult\_membs}(S)\big) \rightarrow \big(Y \subseteq \text{Ult\_membs}(S)\big)$$

### 5.7.1 *Mathematical Induction for Integers*

Next we give four variants of the principle of mathematical induction, one based on the preceding work with 'Ult_membs', two others specialized to the set of integers. Two of these are designed to facilitate arguments by 'double induction' on a pair of indices.

THEORY transfinite_member_induction$\big(n, P(x)\big)$
$P(n)$
$\Longrightarrow (m)$
$m \in$ Ult_membs$(\{n\})$ $\& \ P(m) \ \& \ \big(\forall k \in m \mid (\neg P(k))\big)$
END transfinite_member_induction;

THEORY double_transfinite_induction$\big(n, k, R(x, y)\big)$
$R(n, k)$
$\Longrightarrow (m, j)$
$R(m, j) \ \& \ \big(\forall h \in m \,\big|\, \big(\forall i \,\big|\, (\neg R(h, i))\big)\big) \ \& \ \big(\forall i \in j \,\big|\, (\neg R(m, i))\big)$
END double_transfinite_induction;

THEORY mathematical_induction$\big(n, P(x)\big)$
$n \in \mathbb{N} \ \& \ P(n)$
$\Longrightarrow (m)$
$m \in \mathbb{N} \ \& \ P(m) \ \& \ \big(\forall k \in m \,\big|\, (\neg P(k))\big)$
END mathematical_induction;

THEORY double_induction$\big(n, k, R(n, k)\big)$
$\{n, k\} \subseteq \mathbb{N} \ \& \ R(n, k)$
$\Longrightarrow (m, j)$
$m \in \mathbb{N} \ \& \ j \in \mathbb{N} \ \& \ R(m, j) \ \&$
$\big(\forall h \in m \,\big|\, \big(\forall i \in \mathbb{N} \,\big|\, (\neg R(h, i))\big)\big) \ \& \ \big(\forall i \in j \,\big|\, (\neg R(m, i))\big)$
END double_induction.

## 5.8 Equivalence Relationships and Classes; the General Summation Operator; Recursion

This is where the two important 'theories' mentioned earlier, viz. the theory of equivalence classes and the theory of Sigma, enter into game. The former of these, given a set s and a dyadic relation which behaves as an equivalence relationship over it, splits s into maximal sets of mutually equivalent elements, also selecting arb$(\kappa)$ within each such equivalence class $\kappa$ as a convenient standard representative for the class. We do not enter into further detail on this issue, which has already been discussed.

As previously noted, the theory of Sigma is a formal substitute for the common but informal mathematical use of 'three dot' summation (and product) notations like

$a_1 + a_2 + \cdots + a_n$ and $a_1 * a_2 * \cdots * a_n$. In the following formulation (slightly more general than the one seen in Sect. 1.4.2.6), 'Sigma_theory' allows us to associate an overall sum of range values with any map having a finite domain and range included in a set for which a commutative and associative addition operator with a zero element is defined. It also tells us that summation is additive for pairs of such maps having disjoint domains.

$$
\begin{array}{l}
\textsc{Theory}\ \mathsf{Sigma\_theory}(\mathsf{s}, u \oplus v, \mathsf{e}) \\
\quad \mathsf{e} \in s \,\&\, \big(\forall x \in \mathsf{s} \mid (\forall y \in \mathsf{s} \mid x \oplus y \in \mathsf{s})\big) \\
\quad (\forall x \in \mathsf{s} \mid x \oplus \mathsf{e} = x) \,\&\, \big(\forall x \in \mathsf{s} \mid (\forall y \in \mathsf{s} \mid x \oplus y = y \oplus x)\big) \\
\quad \big(\forall x \in \mathsf{s} \big| \big(\forall y \in \mathsf{s} \big| \big(\forall z \in \mathsf{s} \mid (x \oplus y) \oplus z = x \oplus (y \oplus z)\big)\big)\big) \\
\Longrightarrow (\Sigma_\Theta) \text{ -- \textit{finite summation over a commutative monoid}} \\
\quad \Sigma_\Theta(\emptyset) = \mathsf{e} \,\&\, \big(Y \in \mathsf{s} \rightarrow \Sigma_\Theta\big(\{[X, Y]\}\big) = Y\big) \\
\quad \big(\mathsf{Finite}(F) \,\&\, \mathsf{range}(F) \subseteq \mathsf{s}\big) \rightarrow \\
\qquad \big(\Sigma_\Theta(F) \in \mathsf{s} \,\&\, \Sigma_\Theta(F) = \Sigma_\Theta(F \cap G) \oplus \Sigma_\Theta(F \setminus G)\big) \\
\quad \big(\mathsf{Finite}(F) \,\&\, \mathsf{range}(F) \subseteq \mathsf{s} \,\&\, \mathsf{Is\_map}(F)\big) \rightarrow \\
\qquad \big(\Sigma_\Theta(F) = \Sigma_\Theta(F_{|T}) \oplus \Sigma_\Theta(F_{|\mathsf{domain}(F) \setminus T})\big) \\
\quad \big(\mathsf{Finite}(F) \,\&\, \mathsf{range}(F) \subseteq \mathsf{s} \,\&\, \mathsf{Svm}(F) \,\&\, \mathsf{Svm}(G) \,\&\, \\
\qquad \mathsf{domain}(F) = \mathsf{domain}(G)\big) \rightarrow \\
\qquad\quad \Sigma_\Theta(F) = \Sigma_\Theta\big(\big\{\big[y,\ \Sigma_\Theta(F_{|G^{\dashv}\{y\}})\big] : y \in \mathsf{range}(G)\big\}\big) \\
\quad \big(\mathsf{Finite}(F) \,\&\, \mathsf{range}(F) \subseteq \mathsf{s} \,\&\, \mathsf{Svm}(F) \,\&\, \mathsf{1\_1}(G) \,\&\, \\
\qquad \mathsf{domain}(F) = \mathsf{domain}(G)\big) \rightarrow \\
\qquad\quad \Sigma_\Theta(F) = \Sigma_\Theta\big(\big\{\big[y,\ F\big[G^{-1}[y]\big]\big] : y \in \mathsf{range}(G)\big\}\big) \\
\textsc{End}\ \mathsf{Sigma\_theory}.
\end{array}
$$

Inside Sigma_theory, a recursive characterization of $\Sigma_\Theta$ is provided so as to enforce the equality

$$
\begin{array}{l}
\Sigma_\Theta(F) = \mathbf{if}\ F = \emptyset\ \mathbf{then}\ \mathsf{e} \\
\qquad\qquad \mathbf{elseif}\ \mathsf{arb}(F)^{[2]} \in \mathsf{s}\ \mathbf{then} \\
\qquad\qquad\quad \mathsf{arb}(F)^{[2]} \oplus \Sigma_\Theta\big(F \setminus \{\mathsf{arb}(F)\}\big) \\
\qquad\qquad \mathbf{else}\ \Sigma_\Theta\big(F \setminus \{\mathsf{arb}(F)\}\big)\ \mathbf{end\ if}
\end{array}
$$

for every finite set $F$.

Legitimizing such a recursive construction in our formal setting is in fact possible on the basis of the remark that the strict inclusion relation $\subsetneq$ is well-founded over the finite sets. To do this, we first develop a theory which allows construction of a function by recursion over a set endowed with a well-founded relationship:

$$
\begin{array}{l}
\textsc{Theory}\ \mathsf{wellfdd\_recursive\_fcn}\big(\mathsf{s},\ y \lhd x,\ \mathsf{f}(b, x, t),\ \mathsf{g}(r, y, x, t),\ \mathsf{P}(r, y, x, t)\big) \\
\quad \big(\forall t \subseteq \mathsf{s} \mid t \neq \emptyset \rightarrow \big(\exists x \in t \mid (\forall y \in t \mid \neg y \lhd x)\big)\big) \\
\qquad\qquad \text{-- } \lhd \text{ \textit{is thereby assumed to be irreflexive and well-founded on} } \mathsf{s}
\end{array}
$$

$\Longrightarrow$ ($\mathsf{rec}_\Theta$, $\mathsf{rk}_\Theta$)

$(\forall x, t \mid x \in \mathsf{s} \to \mathsf{rec}_\Theta(x, t) =$
$\mathsf{f}(\{\mathsf{g}(\mathsf{rec}_\Theta(y, t), y, x, t) : y \in \mathsf{s} \mid y \lhd x \;\&$
$\mathsf{P}(\mathsf{rec}_\Theta(y, t), y, x, t)\}, x, t))$

$\Big(\forall x, t \mid x \in \mathsf{s} \to \mathsf{rk}_\Theta(x, t) = \bigcup\{\mathsf{next}(\mathsf{rk}_\Theta(y, t)) : y \in \mathsf{s} \mid y \lhd x \;\&$
$[y, x] \in t\}\Big)$

END wellfdd_recursive_fcn.

This form of recursion cannot be exploited directly for the class of all finite sets ordered by $\subsetneq$, because finite sets form a proper class. But consider a pair of functions rec and rec′, both of which satisfy the same recursive relationship (based on $\subsetneq$) on their domains $d$, which are assumed to be such that every subset of a member of $d$ is finite and belongs to $d$. (For example, $d$ might be $\{x : x \subseteq s \mid \mathsf{Finite}(x)\}$.) One easily sees that rec and rec′ necessarily agree on the intersection of their domains, and so have a common single-valued extension. Thanks to this possibility of amalgamation, we make the following theory, through which we can carry out constructions of the kind needed inside the theory of Sigma:

THEORY finite_recursive_fcn($\mathsf{f}(b, x, t)$, $\mathsf{g}(r, y, x, t)$, $\mathsf{P}(r, y, x, t)$)
$\Longrightarrow$ ($\mathsf{rec}_\Theta$)
$(\forall x, t \mid \mathsf{Finite}(x) \to \mathsf{rec}_\Theta(x, t) =$
$\mathsf{f}(\{\mathsf{g}(\mathsf{rec}_\Theta(y, t), y, x, t) : y \subseteq x \mid y \neq x \;\&\; \mathsf{P}(\mathsf{rec}_\Theta(y, t), y, x, t)\}, x, t))$
END finite_recursive_fcn.

## 5.9 Formal Fractions and Rational Numbers

Returning again to our main line of development, we prepare for the intended introduction of rational numbers (which follows a bit later) by defining the set of formal *fractions* of signed integers and establishing the algebraic properties of these fractions. This will allow us to define *rational numbers* as equivalence classes of fractions under the usual ‘equality of cross-products’ equivalence relationship. Note that the path followed is that of the standard algebraic construction of a field from an integral domain.

The set of *fractions* is simply the set of ordered pairs of signed integers, of which the second (the ‘denominator’) must be non-zero.

Def 35 : $\mathsf{Fr} =_{\mathrm{Def}} \{[x, y] : x \in \mathbb{Z}, y \in \mathbb{Z} \mid y \neq [\emptyset, \emptyset]\}$

Two fractions are equivalent, i.e. stand in the relationship $\mathsf{Same\_frac}(p,q)$, if their cross-products are equal.

$$\text{Def 36}: \mathsf{Same\_frac}(p,q) \leftrightarrow_{\text{Def}} p^{[1]} *_{\mathbb{Z}} q^{[2]} = p^{[2]} *_{\mathbb{Z}} q^{[1]}$$

The 'Same_frac' relationship is an equivalence relationship.

$$\text{Theorem 245}: \ (X \in \mathsf{Fr} \,\&\, Y \in \mathsf{Fr}) \\ \rightarrow \big(\big(\mathsf{Same\_frac}(X,Y) \leftrightarrow \mathsf{Same\_frac}(Y,X)\big) \,\&\, \mathsf{Same\_frac}(X,X)\big)$$

$$\text{Theorem 246}: \ (X \in \mathsf{Fr} \,\&\, Y \in \mathsf{Fr} \,\&\, Z \in \mathsf{Fr}) \\ \rightarrow \big(\big(\mathsf{Same\_frac}(X,Y) \,\&\, \mathsf{Same\_frac}(Y,Z)\big) \rightarrow \mathsf{Same\_frac}(X,Z)\big)$$

At this point, the theory of equivalence classes can be used to introduce the set $\mathbb{Q}$ of rational numbers (i.e. the equivalence classes of fractions), and a map $\mathsf{Fr\_to\_}\mathbb{Q}$ of fractions into rationals such that $\mathsf{Same\_frac}(x,y)$ is equivalent to $\mathsf{Fr\_to\_}\mathbb{Q}(x) = \mathsf{Fr\_to\_}\mathbb{Q}(y)$.

$$\text{Theorem 247}: \ \big(\forall y \in \mathbb{Q} \mid \mathsf{arb}(y) \in \mathsf{Fr} \,\&\, \mathsf{Fr\_to\_}\mathbb{Q}\big(\mathsf{arb}(y)\big) = y\big) \,\& \\ \big(\forall x \in \mathsf{Fr} \mid \mathsf{Fr\_to\_}\mathbb{Q}(x) \in \mathbb{Q}\big) \,\& \\ \big(\forall x \in \mathsf{Fr} \big| \big(\forall y \in \mathsf{Fr} \mid \mathsf{Same\_frac}(x,y) \leftrightarrow \mathsf{Fr\_to\_}\mathbb{Q}(x) = \mathsf{Fr\_to\_}\mathbb{Q}(y)\big)\big) \,\& \\ \big(\forall x \in \mathsf{Fr} \mid \mathsf{Same\_frac}\big(x, \mathsf{arb}\big(\mathsf{Fr\_to\_}\mathbb{Q}(x)\big)\big)\big)$$

Having now introduced rationals as equivalence classes of fractions, we can define the zero and unit rationals, and the algebraic operations on rationals, from the corresponding notions for fractions. The reciprocal of a rational is obtained by simply inverting any of the fractions which represent it. These familiar ideas are captured by the following sequence of definitions. Note that multiplication of fractions is componentwise, but that to add one must first multiply their denominators to put the two fractions being added over a 'common denominator'. Division of rationals is defined as multiplication by the reciprocal, subtraction as addition of the negative. A rational is non-negative if any (hence all) of its representative fractions have numerator and denominator of the same sign; $x$ is greater than (or equal to) $y$ if $x - y$ is non-negative. These standard notions are formalized by the following group of definitions.

$$\text{Def 37}: [\text{The zero rational}]\ 0_{\mathbb{Q}} =_{\text{Def}} \mathsf{Fr\_to\_}\mathbb{Q}\big([[0,\,0],\,[1,\,0]]\big)$$

$$\text{Def 37}a: [\text{The unit rational}]\ 1_{\mathbb{Q}} =_{\text{Def}} \mathsf{Fr\_to\_}\mathbb{Q}\big([[1,\,0],\,[1,\,0]]\big)$$

$$\text{Def 38}: [\text{Rational sum}]\ x +_{\mathbb{Q}} y =_{\text{Def}} \\ \mathsf{Fr\_to\_}\mathbb{Q}\big(\big[\big(\mathsf{arb}(x)^{[1]} *_{\mathbb{Z}} \mathsf{arb}(y)^{[2]}\big) +_{\mathbb{Z}} \big(\mathsf{arb}(y)^{[1]} *_{\mathbb{Z}} \mathsf{arb}(x)^{[2]}\big), \\ \mathsf{arb}(x)^{[2]} *_{\mathbb{Z}} \mathsf{arb}(y)^{[2]}\big]\big)$$

$$\text{Def 39}: [\text{Rational product}]\ x *_{\mathbb{Q}} y =_{\text{Def}} \\ \mathsf{Fr\_to\_}\mathbb{Q}\big(\big[\mathsf{arb}(x)^{[1]} *_{\mathbb{Z}} \mathsf{arb}(y)^{[1]},\ \mathsf{arb}(x)^{[2]} *_{\mathbb{Z}} \mathsf{arb}(y)^{[2]}\big]\big)$$

Def 40 : [Reciprocal] $\mathsf{Recip}(x) =_{\text{Def}} \mathsf{Fr\_to\_}\mathbb{Q}([\mathsf{arb}(x)^{[2]}, \mathsf{arb}(x)^{[1]}])$

Def 41 : [Rational quotient] $x /_{\mathbb{Q}} y =_{\text{Def}} x *_{\mathbb{Q}} \mathsf{Recip}(y)$

Def 42 : [Rational negative] $-_{\mathbb{Q}}(x) =_{\text{Def}} \mathsf{Fr\_to\_}\mathbb{Q}([-_{\mathbb{Z}}(\mathsf{arb}(x)^{[1]}), \mathsf{arb}(x)^{[2]}])$

Def 43 : [Non-negative rational] $\mathsf{Is\_nonneg}_{\mathbb{Q}}(x) =_{\text{Def}}$
$\mathsf{Is\_nonneg}(\mathsf{arb}(x)^{[1]} *_{\mathbb{Z}} \mathsf{arb}(x)^{[2]})$

Def 44 : [Rational subtraction] $x -_{\mathbb{Q}} y =_{\text{Def}} x +_{\mathbb{Q}} -_{\mathbb{Q}}(y)$

Def_by_app 45 : [Rational comparison]
$x \geqslant_{\mathbb{Q}} y \leftrightarrow \mathsf{Is\_nonneg}_{\mathbb{Q}}(x -_{\mathbb{Q}} y)$

Our subsequent work with rationals and reals will involve a great deal of elementary work with inequalities between sums and differences, for which the following theory of addition in ordered sets (just now, though tacitly, referred to) prepares.

THEORY $\mathsf{Ordered\_add}(\mathsf{g}, \mathsf{e}, X \oplus Y, X \ominus Y, \mathsf{rvz}(X), \mathsf{nneg}(X))$
$\mathsf{e} \in \mathsf{g} \,\&\, (\forall x \in \mathsf{g} \mid x \oplus \mathsf{e} = x \,\&\, x \oplus \mathsf{rvz}(x) = \mathsf{e} \,\&\, \mathsf{rvz}(x) \in g)$
$(\forall x \in \mathsf{g} \mid (\forall y \in \mathsf{g} \mid x \oplus y \in \mathsf{g} \,\&\, x \oplus y = y \oplus x \,\&\, x \oplus \mathsf{rvz}(y) = x \ominus y))$
$(\forall x \in \mathsf{g} \mid (\forall y \in \mathsf{g} \mid (\forall z \in \mathsf{g} \mid (x \oplus y) \oplus z = x \oplus (y \oplus z))))$
$(\forall x \in \mathsf{g} \mid (\forall y \in \mathsf{g} \mid (\mathsf{nneg}(x) \,\&\, \mathsf{nneg}(y)) \to \mathsf{nneg}(x \oplus y)))$
$(\forall x \in \mathsf{g} \mid (\mathsf{nneg}(x) \vee \mathsf{nneg}(\mathsf{rvz}(x))) \,\&\, ((\mathsf{nneg}(x) \,\&\, \mathsf{nneg}(\mathsf{rvz}(x))) \to (x = \mathsf{e})))$
$\Longrightarrow (\geqslant_g, \leqslant_g, >_g, <_g)$
$X \geqslant_g Y \leftrightarrow \mathsf{nneg}(X \oplus \mathsf{rvz}(Y))$
$X \leqslant_g Y \leftrightarrow Y \geqslant_g X$
$X >_g Y \leftrightarrow X \geqslant_g Y \,\&\, X \neq Y$
$X <_g Y \leftrightarrow Y >_g X$
$(X \in \mathsf{g} \,\&\, Y \in \mathsf{g} \,\&\, (X = Y \vee \neg(X \geqslant_g Y))) \to Y \leqslant_g X$
END Ordered_add

The next four theorems give miscellaneous ordering properties of the signed integers used to prove corresponding properties of the rationals. If $n$ is a signed integer, either $n$ or $-n$ is non-negative, and if both are non-negative then $n$ is 0. The sum and product of two non-negative integers is non-negative, and the square of any signed integer is non-negative.

Theorem 248 : $(X \in \mathbb{Z}) \to$
$((\mathsf{Is\_nonneg}(X) \vee \mathsf{Is\_nonneg}(-_{\mathbb{Z}}(X))) \,\&$
$((\mathsf{Is\_nonneg}(X) \,\&\, \mathsf{Is\_nonneg}(-_{\mathbb{Z}}(X))) \to (X = [0, 0])))$

Theorem 249 : $(X \in \mathbb{Z} \,\&\, Y \in \mathbb{Z} \,\&\, \mathsf{Is\_nonneg}(X) \,\&\, \mathsf{Is\_nonneg}(Y))$
$\to (\mathsf{Is\_nonneg}(X +_{\mathbb{Z}} Y) \,\&\, \mathsf{Is\_nonneg}(X *_{\mathbb{Z}} Y))$

$$\text{Theorem 250}: \ (X \in \mathbb{Z}) \rightarrow \mathsf{Is\_nonneg}(X *_{\mathbb{Z}} X)$$

$$\text{Theorem 251}: \ \big(X \in \mathbb{Z} \,\&\, Y \in \mathbb{Z} \,\&\, X \neq [0,\, 0] \,\&\, \mathsf{Is\_nonneg}(X)\big) \rightarrow \big(\mathsf{Is\_nonneg}(\, X *_{\mathbb{Z}} Y\,) \leftrightarrow \mathsf{Is\_nonneg}(Y)\big)$$

Now we begin to work with rationals. Any fraction is a pair of signed integers with non-zero second component. Any member of a rational is a pair of signed integers, and, indeed, a fraction. If two pairs of fractions $x$, $y$ and $w$, $z$ are equivalent as rationals, then the sum of $x$ and $w$ is equivalent to the sum of $y$ and $z$, and similarly for the products. The rational sum of a rational $x$ with the class containing a fraction $[y,\, z]$ can be obtained by adding any fraction in $x$ to $[y,\, z]$, and then forming the equivalence class of the result. Much the same statement applies to products of rationals.

$$\text{Theorem 252}: \ X \in \mathsf{Fr} \leftrightarrow \big(X = \big[X^{[1]},\, X^{[2]}\big] \,\&\, X^{[1]} \in \mathbb{Z} \,\&\, X^{[2]} \in \mathbb{Z} \,\&\, X^{[2]} \neq [0,\, 0]\big)$$

$$\text{Theorem 253}: \ (N \in \mathbb{Q}) \rightarrow \big(\mathsf{arb}(N) \in \mathsf{Fr} \,\&\, \mathsf{arb}(N) = \big[\mathsf{arb}(N)^{[1]},\, \mathsf{arb}(N)^{[2]}\big] \,\&\, \mathsf{arb}(N)^{[1]} \in \mathbb{Z} \,\&\, \mathsf{arb}(N)^{[2]} \in \mathbb{Z} \,\&\, \mathsf{arb}(N)^{[2]} \neq [0,\, 0]\big)$$

$$\text{Theorem 254}: \ \big(X \in \mathsf{Fr} \,\&\, Y \in \mathsf{Fr} \,\&\, \mathsf{Same\_frac}(X, Y) \,\&\, W \in \mathsf{Fr} \,\&\, Z \in \mathsf{Fr} \,\&\, \mathsf{Same\_frac}(W, Z)\big) \rightarrow \mathsf{Same\_frac}\big(\big[\big(X^{[1]} *_{\mathbb{Z}} W^{[2]}\big) +_{\mathbb{Z}} \big(W^{[1]} *_{\mathbb{Z}} X^{[2]}\big),\, X^{[2]} *_{\mathbb{Z}} W^{[2]}\big],\, \big[\big(Y^{[1]} *_{\mathbb{Z}} Z^{[2]}\big) +_{\mathbb{Z}} \big(Z^{[1]} *_{\mathbb{Z}} Y^{[2]}\big),\, Y^{[2]} *_{\mathbb{Z}} Z^{[2]}\big]\big)$$

$$\text{Theorem 255}: \ \big(X \in \mathsf{Fr} \,\&\, Y \in \mathsf{Fr} \,\&\, \mathsf{Same\_frac}(X, Y) \,\&\, W \in \mathsf{Fr} \,\&\, Z \in \mathsf{Fr} \,\&\, \mathsf{Same\_frac}(W, Z)\big) \rightarrow \mathsf{Same\_frac}\big(\big[X^{[1]} *_{\mathbb{Z}} W^{[1]},\, X^{[2]} *_{\mathbb{Z}} W^{[2]}\big],\, \big[Y^{[1]} *_{\mathbb{Z}} Z^{[1]},\, Y^{[2]} *_{\mathbb{Z}} Z^{[2]}\big]\big)$$

$$\text{Theorem 256}: \ \big(X \in \mathbb{Q} \,\&\, Y \in \mathbb{Z} \,\&\, Z \in \mathbb{Z} \,\&\, Z \neq [0,\, 0]\big) \rightarrow \big(X +_{\mathbb{Q}} \mathsf{Fr\_to\_}\mathbb{Q}([Y,\, Z]) = \mathsf{Fr\_to\_}\mathbb{Q}\big(\big[\big(\mathsf{arb}(X)^{[1]} *_{\mathbb{Z}} Z\big) +_{\mathbb{Z}} \big(\mathsf{arb}(X)^{[2]} *_{\mathbb{Z}} Y\big),\, \big(\mathsf{arb}(X)^{[2]} *_{\mathbb{Z}} Z\big)\big]\big)\big)$$

$$\text{Theorem 257}: \ \big(X \in \mathbb{Q} \,\&\, Y \in \mathbb{Z} \,\&\, Z \in \mathbb{Z} \,\&\, Z \neq [0,\, 0]\big) \rightarrow \big(X *_{\mathbb{Q}} \mathsf{Fr\_to\_}\mathbb{Q}([Y,\, Z]) = \mathsf{Fr\_to\_}\mathbb{Q}\big(\big[\mathsf{arb}(X)^{[1]} *_{\mathbb{Z}} Y,\, \mathsf{arb}(X)^{[2]} *_{\mathbb{Z}} Z\big]\big)\big)$$

Continuing our work with rationals, we have: The fractions $[n,\, m]$ and $[-n,\, -m]$ are equivalent as rationals. If two equivalent fractions both have non-negative denominators, they both have non-negative numerators, and in this case so does their product. A fraction $[n,\, m]$ is non-negative if and only if $[-n,\, -m]$ is non-negative. If one of two equivalent fractions is non-negative, so is the other. Rational addition and multiplication are both commutative and associative. The rational sum of a rational $x$ with the class containing a fraction $[y,\, z]$ can be obtained by adding any fraction in $x$ to $[y,\, z]$ in the reverse order from that considered just above, and then forming the equivalence class of the result; similarly for products of rationals.

The sum of a rational with its negative is the zero rational. The zero rational is the additive identity for rationals. The standard laws of subtraction apply to rationals.

Theorem 258 : $(X \in \mathsf{Fr}) \rightarrow \mathsf{Same\_frac}\big(X, \big[-_{\mathbb{Z}}\big(X^{[1]}\big), -_{\mathbb{Z}}\big(X^{[2]}\big)\big]\big)$

Theorem 259 : $\big(X \in \mathsf{Fr} \;\&\; Y \in \mathsf{Fr} \;\&\; \mathsf{Same\_frac}(X, Y) \;\&\; \mathsf{Is\_nonneg}\big(X^{[2]}\big) \;\&$ $\mathsf{Is\_nonneg}\big(Y^{[2]}\big)\big) \rightarrow$ $\big(\big(\mathsf{Is\_nonneg}\big(X^{[1]}\big) \vee X^{[1]} = [0, 0]\big) \leftrightarrow \big(\mathsf{Is\_nonneg}\big(Y^{[1]}\big) \vee Y^{[1]} = [0, 0]\big)\big)$

Theorem 261 : $\big(X \in \mathsf{Fr} \;\&\; Y \in \mathsf{Fr} \;\&\; \mathsf{Same\_frac}(X, Y)\big) \rightarrow$ $\big(\mathsf{Is\_nonneg}\big(X^{[1]} *_{\mathbb{Z}} X^{[2]}\big) \leftrightarrow \mathsf{Is\_nonneg}\big(Y^{[1]} *_{\mathbb{Z}} Y^{[2]}\big)\big)$

Theorem 262 : $(X \in \mathsf{Fr}) \rightarrow$ $\big(\mathsf{Is\_nonneg}_{\mathbb{Q}}(X) \leftrightarrow \mathsf{Is\_nonneg}_{\mathbb{Q}}\big(\big[-_{\mathbb{Z}}\big(X^{[1]}\big), -_{\mathbb{Z}}\big(X^{[2]}\big)\big]\big)\big)$

Theorem 263 : $\big(X \in \mathsf{Fr} \;\&\; Y \in \mathsf{Fr} \;\&\; \mathsf{Same\_frac}(X, Y)\big) \rightarrow$ $\big(\mathsf{Is\_nonneg}_{\mathbb{Q}}(X) \leftrightarrow \mathsf{Is\_nonneg}_{\mathbb{Q}}(Y)\big)$

Theorem 264 : [Commutativity of Addition] $(N \in \mathbb{Q} \;\&\; M \in \mathbb{Q}) \rightarrow$ $(N +_{\mathbb{Q}} M = M +_{\mathbb{Q}} N)$

Theorem 265 : $\big(X \in \mathbb{Q} \;\&\; Y \in \mathbb{Z} \;\&\; Z \in \mathbb{Z} \;\&\; \mathrm{N} \neq [0, 0]\big) \rightarrow$ $\big(\mathsf{Fr\_to\_}\mathbb{Q}([Y, Z]) +_{\mathbb{Q}} X =$ $\mathsf{Fr\_to\_}\mathbb{Q}\big(\big[\big(\mathsf{arb}(X)^{[1]} *_{\mathbb{Z}} Z\big) +_{\mathbb{Z}} \big(\mathsf{arb}(X)^{[2]} *_{\mathbb{Z}} Y\big), \big(\mathsf{arb}(X)^{[2]} *_{\mathbb{Z}} Z\big)\big]\big)\big)$

Theorem 266 : $\big(X \in \mathbb{Z} \;\&\; Y \in \mathbb{Z} \;\&\; Z \in \mathbb{Z} \;\&\; W \in \mathbb{Z} \;\&\; Y \neq [0, 0] \;\&$ $W \neq [0, 0]\big) \rightarrow \big(\mathsf{Fr\_to\_}\mathbb{Q}([X, Y]) +_{\mathbb{Q}} \mathsf{Fr\_to\_}\mathbb{Q}([Z, W]) =$ $\mathsf{Fr\_to\_}\mathbb{Q}\big(\big[(X *_{\mathbb{Z}} W) +_{\mathbb{Z}} (Z *_{\mathbb{Z}} Y), Y *_{\mathbb{Z}} W\big]\big)\big)$

Theorem 267 : [Commutativity of Multiplication] $(N \in \mathbb{Q} \;\&\; M \in \mathbb{Q}) \rightarrow$ $(N *_{\mathbb{Q}} M = M *_{\mathbb{Q}} N)$

Theorem 268 : $\big(X \in \mathbb{Q} \;\&\; y \in \mathbb{Z} \;\&\; Z \in \mathbb{Z} \;\&\; Z \neq [0, 0]\big) \rightarrow$ $\big(\mathsf{Fr\_to\_}\mathbb{Q}([Y, Z]) *_{\mathbb{Q}} X = \mathsf{Fr\_to\_}\mathbb{Q}\big(\big[\mathsf{arb}(X)^{[1]} *_{\mathbb{Z}} Y, \mathsf{arb}(X)^{[2]} *_{\mathbb{Z}} Z\big]\big)\big)$

Theorem 269 : $(K \in \mathbb{Q} \;\&\; N \in \mathbb{Q} \;\&\; M \in \mathbb{Q}) \rightarrow$ $\big(N +_{\mathbb{Q}} (M +_{\mathbb{Q}} K) = (N +_{\mathbb{Q}} M) +_{\mathbb{Q}} K\big)$

Theorem 270 : $(M \in \mathbb{Q}) \rightarrow (M = M +_{\mathbb{Q}} 0_{\mathbb{Q}})$

Theorem 271 : $(M \in \mathbb{Q}) \rightarrow \big(M +_{\mathbb{Q}} -_{\mathbb{Q}}(M) = 0_{\mathbb{Q}}\big)$

Theorem 272 : $(N \in \mathbb{Q} \;\&\; M \in \mathbb{Q}) \rightarrow \big(N = M +_{\mathbb{Q}} (N -_{\mathbb{Q}} M)\big)$

Theorem 273 : $(K \in \mathbb{Q} \,\&\, N \in \mathbb{Q} \,\&\, M \in \mathbb{Q}) \rightarrow \big(N *_{\mathbb{Q}} (M *_{\mathbb{Q}} K) = (N *_{\mathbb{Q}} M) *_{\mathbb{Q}} K\big)$

The next fifteen theorems complete our collection of elementary results concerning rationals.

Theorem 274 : $\big(K \in \mathbb{Z} \,\&\, N \in \mathbb{Z} \,\&\, M \in \mathbb{Z} \,\&\, K \neq [0,\, 0] \,\&\, M \neq [0,\, 0]\big) \rightarrow \big(\mathsf{Fr\_to\_}\mathbb{Q}([N,\, M]) = \mathsf{Fr\_to\_}\mathbb{Q}([K *_{\mathbb{Z}} N,\, K *_{\mathbb{Z}} M])\big)$

Theorem 275 : $(K \in \mathbb{Q} \,\&\, N \in \mathbb{Q} \,\&\, M \in \mathbb{Q}) \rightarrow \big(N *_{\mathbb{Q}} (M +_{\mathbb{Q}} K) = (N *_{\mathbb{Q}} M) +_{\mathbb{Q}} (N *_{\mathbb{Q}} K)\big)$

Theorem 276 : $\big(X \in \mathbb{Z} \,\&\, y \in \mathbb{Z} \,\&\, Y \neq [0,\, 0]\big) \rightarrow \big(\mathsf{Is\_nonneg}_{\mathbb{Q}}\big(\mathsf{Fr\_to\_}\mathbb{Q}([X,\, Y])\big) \leftrightarrow \mathsf{Is\_nonneg}(X *_{\mathbb{Z}} Y)\big)$

Theorem 277 : $(M \in \mathbb{Q}) \rightarrow (M = M *_{\mathbb{Q}} 1_{\mathbb{Q}})$

Theorem 278 : $(M \in \mathbb{Q} \,\&\, M \neq 0_{\mathbb{Q}}) \rightarrow \big(\mathsf{Recip}(M) \in \mathbb{Q} \,\&\, M *_{\mathbb{Q}} \mathsf{Recip}(M) = 1_{\mathbb{Q}}\big)$

Theorem 279 : $(N \in \mathbb{Q} \,\&\, M \in \mathbb{Q} \,\&\, M \neq 0_{\mathbb{Q}}) \rightarrow \big(N = M *_{\mathbb{Q}} (N /_{\mathbb{Q}} M)\big)$

Theorem 280 : $\mathsf{Is\_nonneg}_{\mathbb{Q}}(0_{\mathbb{Q}}) \,\&\, \mathsf{Is\_nonneg}_{\mathbb{Q}}(1_{\mathbb{Q}})$

Theorem 281 : $(X \in \mathbb{Q}) \rightarrow \Big(\big(\mathsf{Is\_nonneg}_{\mathbb{Q}}(X) \vee \mathsf{Is\_nonneg}_{\mathbb{Q}}\big(-_{\mathbb{Q}}(X)\big)\big) \,\&\, \Big(\big(\mathsf{Is\_nonneg}_{\mathbb{Q}}(X) \,\&\, \mathsf{Is\_nonneg}_{\mathbb{Q}}\big(-_{\mathbb{Q}}(X)\big)\big) \rightarrow (X = 0_{\mathbb{Q}})\Big)\Big)$

Theorem 282 : $(X \in \mathbb{Q}) \rightarrow (X = X *_{\mathbb{Q}} 1_{\mathbb{Q}})$

Theorem 283 : $(X \in \mathbb{Q}) \rightarrow \big(X = 0_{\mathbb{Q}} \leftrightarrow \mathsf{arb}(x)^{[1]} = [0,\, 0]\big)$

Theorem 284 : $\big(X \in \mathbb{Q} \,\&\, Y \in \mathbb{Q} \,\&\, \mathsf{Is\_nonneg}_{\mathbb{Q}}(X) \,\&\, \mathsf{Is\_nonneg}_{\mathbb{Q}}(Y)\big) \rightarrow \big(\mathsf{Is\_nonneg}_{\mathbb{Q}}(X +_{\mathbb{Q}} Y) \,\&\, \mathsf{Is\_nonneg}_{\mathbb{Q}}(X *_{\mathbb{Q}} Y)\big)$

Theorem 291 : $(X \in \mathbb{Q} \,\&\, Y \in \mathbb{Q} \,\&\, X_1 \in \mathbb{Q} \,\&\, X >_{\mathbb{Q}} Y \,\&\, X_1 >_{\mathbb{Q}} 0_{\mathbb{Q}}) \rightarrow (X *_{\mathbb{Q}} X_1 >_{\mathbb{Q}} Y *_{\mathbb{Q}} X_1)$

Theorem 292 : $1_{\mathbb{Q}} >_{\mathbb{Q}} 0_{\mathbb{Q}}$

Theorem 293 : $(X \in \mathbb{Q} \,\&\, X >_{\mathbb{Q}} 0_{\mathbb{Q}}) \rightarrow \big(\mathsf{Recip}(X) >_{\mathbb{Q}} 0_{\mathbb{Q}}\big)$

Theorem 294 : $(X \in \mathbb{Q} \,\&\, Y \in \mathbb{Q} \,\&\, X >_{\mathbb{Q}} Y) \rightarrow \big(X >_{\mathbb{Q}} (X +_{\mathbb{Q}} Y)/_{\mathbb{Q}} (1_{\mathbb{Q}} + 1_{\mathbb{Q}}) \,\&\, (X +_{\mathbb{Q}} Y)/_{\mathbb{Q}} (1_{\mathbb{Q}} + 1_{\mathbb{Q}}) >_{\mathbb{Q}} Y\big)$

## 5.10 Real Numbers

We have now proved enough about the rational numbers to be able to go on to define the set of *real numbers* and prove their basic properties. Historically this has been done in several ways, which offer competing advantages when computer-based verification is intended. In Dedekind's approach, which is the most directly set-theoretic of all, a real number is defined simply as a set of rational numbers, bounded above, which contains no largest element and which contains each rational $y$ smaller than any of its members. Sums are easily defined for real numbers defined in this way, but it is only easy to define products for positive reals directly. This forces separate treatment of real products involving negative reals, causing the proof of statements like the associativity of multiplication to break up into an irritating number of separate cases. For this reason, we choose a different approach, originally developed by Cantor in 1872 (cf. [Can72]), in which real numbers are defined as follows. Call an infinite sequence $x_n$ of rational numbers a *Cauchy sequence* if, for every positive rational $r$, there exists an integer $N$ such that the absolute value $|x_n - x_m|$ is less than $r$ whenever $m$ and $n$ are both larger than $N$. Sequences of this kind can be added, subtracted, and multiplied componentwise and their sums, differences, and products are still Cauchy sequences. We can now introduce an equivalence relationship Same_real between pairs $x, y$ of such sequences: Same_real$(x, y)$ is true if and only if, for every positive rational $r$, there exists an integer $N$ such that the absolute value $|x_n - y_n|$ is less than $r$ whenever $n$ is larger than $N$. The set of equivalence classes of Cauchy sequences, formed using the equivalence relationship Same_real, is then the set of real numbers. If two pairs of Cauchy sequences $x, y$ and $w, z$ are equivalent, then the (componentwise) sum of $x$ and $w$ is equivalent to the sum of $y$ and $z$, and similarly for the products and differences. Hence these operations define corresponding operations on the real numbers, which are easily seen to have the same properties of associativity, commutativity, and distributivity, and the same relationship to comparison operators defined similarly.

Given any rational number $r$ we can form a sequence repeating $r$ infinitely often, and then map $r$ to the equivalence class (under Same_real) of this sequence. This construction is readily seen to embed the rationals into the reals, in a manner that preserves addition, multiplication, and subtraction. The zero rational maps in this way into an additive identity for real addition, and the unit rational into the multiplicative identity for reals. If a Cauchy sequence $y_n$ is not equivalent to the zero of reals, then it is easily seen that for all sufficiently large $n$ the absolute values $|y_n|$ are non-zero and have a common lower bound. Hence for any other Cauchy sequence $x_n$ we can form the rational quotients $x_n / y_n$ for all sufficiently large $n$, and it is easy to see that this gives a Cauchy sequence whose equivalence class depends only on that of $x$ and $y$. It follows that this construction defines a quotient operator $x/y$ for real numbers, and it is not hard to prove that this quotient operator relates to real multiplication in the appropriate inverse way.

This approach, based on rational Cauchy sequences, for introducing reals has been outlined in more formal terms in Sect. 4.1.4. We have opted for it, on the basis of pragmatic considerations; but we initially inclined towards the charming simplicity of the definition of the reals as Dedekind cuts over the rationals. The list below shows the most basic definitions and theorem streamlining this competing approach:

Def 46 : [The real numbers as the set of Dedekind cuts] $\mathbb{R} =_{\text{Def}} \big\{ s : s \subseteq \mathbb{Q} \,\big|\, (\forall x \in s \mid (\exists y \in s \mid y >_{\mathbb{Q}} x)) \,\&\, \big(\forall x \in s \,\big|\, \big(\forall y \in \mathbb{Q} \mid (x >_{\mathbb{Q}} y) \to (y \in s)\big)\big)\big\} \setminus \{\emptyset, \mathbb{Q}\}$

Def 47 : [Real 0 and 1] $0_{\mathbb{R}} =_{\text{Def}} \{x \in \mathbb{Q} \mid 0_{\mathbb{Q}} >_{\mathbb{Q}} x\}$ & $1_{\mathbb{R}} =_{\text{Def}} \{x \in \mathbb{Q} \mid 1_{\mathbb{Q}} >_{\mathbb{Q}} x\}$

Def 48 : [Real sum] $X +_{\mathbb{R}} Y =_{\text{Def}} \{u +_{\mathbb{Q}} v : u \in X,\ v \in Y\}$

Def 49 : [Real negative] $-_{\mathbb{R}}(X) =_{\text{Def}} \big\{ -_{\mathbb{Q}}(u) +_{\mathbb{Q}} v : u \in \mathbb{Q} \setminus X,\ v \in 0_{\mathbb{R}} \big\}$

Def 50 : [Real subtraction] $X -_{\mathbb{R}} Y =_{\text{Def}} X +_{\mathbb{R}} -_{\mathbb{R}}(Y)$

Def 51 : [Absolute value] $|X| =_{\text{Def}} X \cup -_{\mathbb{R}}(X)$
[i.e. the larger of $X$ and $-_{\mathbb{R}}(X)$]

Def 52 : [Real multiplication of absolute values] $X \,{}_{|}{*}_{|\mathbb{R}}\, Y =_{\text{Def}} \big\{ u *_{\mathbb{Q}} v : u \in |X| \,\&\, v \in |Y| \mid \neg(0_{\mathbb{Q}} >_{\mathbb{Q}} u \vee 0_{\mathbb{Q}} >_{\mathbb{Q}} v) \big\} \cup 0_{\mathbb{R}}$

Def 53 : [Real multiplication] $X *_{\mathbb{R}} Y =_{\text{Def}}$
**if** $X \supseteq 0_{\mathbb{R}} \leftrightarrow Y \supseteq 0_{\mathbb{R}}$ **then** $X \,{}_{|}{*}_{|\mathbb{R}}\, Y$ **else** $-_{\mathbb{R}} (X \,{}_{|}{*}_{|\mathbb{R}}\, Y)$ **end if**

Def 54 : [Real absolute reciprocal] $|\frac{1}{\cdot}|(X) =_{\text{Def}} \bigcup \big\{ y : y \in \mathbb{R} \mid |X| *_{\mathbb{R}} y \subseteq \big\{ r \in \mathbb{Q} \mid \text{Fr\_to\_}\mathbb{Q}([1,\ 1]) >_{\mathbb{Q}} r \big\}\big\}$

Def 55 : [Real reciprocal] $\text{Recip}_{\mathbb{R}}(X) =_{\text{Def}}$
**if** $X \supseteq 0_{\mathbb{R}}$ **then** $|\frac{1}{\cdot}|(X)$ **else** $-_{\mathbb{R}} \big(|\frac{1}{\cdot}|(X)\big)$ **end if**

Def 56 : [Real quotient] $X /_{\mathbb{R}} Y =_{\text{Def}} x *_{\mathbb{R}} \text{Recip}_{\mathbb{R}}(Y)$

Def 56*a* : [Non-negative real] $\text{Is\_nonneg}_{\mathbb{R}}(X) =_{\text{Def}} 0_{\mathbb{R}} \subseteq X$

Def 56*b* : [Real comparison, 1] $X >_{\mathbb{R}} Y \leftrightarrow_{\text{Def}} \text{Is\_nonneg}_{\mathbb{R}}(X -_{\mathbb{R}} Y) \,\&\, \big(\neg(X = Y)\big)$

Def 56*c* : [Real comparison, 2] $X \geqslant_{\mathbb{R}} Y \leftrightarrow_{\text{Def}} \text{Is\_nonneg}_{\mathbb{R}}(X -_{\mathbb{R}} Y)$

Def 57 : [Real square root] $\sqrt{X} =_{\text{Def}} \bigcup \{ y : y \in \mathbb{R} \mid (y *_{\mathbb{R}} y) \subseteq X \}$

Theorem 295 : $(X \in \mathbb{Q}) \to \big(\{y : y \in \mathbb{Q} \mid x >_{\mathbb{Q}} y\} \in \mathbb{R}\big)$

Theorem 297 : $(N \in \mathbb{R}) \to (N \subseteq \mathbb{Q})$

Theorem 298 : $(N \in \mathbb{R}) \to \big(\exists m \in \mathbb{Q} \mid (\forall x \in N \mid m >_{\mathbb{Q}} x)\big)$

Theorem : $\big(N \in \mathbb{Z} \,\&\, M \in \mathbb{Z} \,\&\, M \neq [0,0] \,\&\, \mathsf{Is\_nonneg}(M)\big) \to$
$\big(\exists k \in \mathbb{Z} \mid \mathsf{Is\_nonneg}\big(N -_{\mathbb{Z}} (k *_{\mathbb{Z}} M)\big) \,\&$
$\mathsf{Is\_nonneg}\big(((k +_{\mathbb{Z}} [1,0]) *_{\mathbb{Z}} M)\big) -_{\mathbb{Z}} N\big)$

Theorem : $(N \in \mathbb{R}) \to \big(N = N +_{\mathbb{R}} -_{\mathbb{R}}(N) = 0_{\mathbb{R}}\big)$

Theorem : $(N \in \mathbb{R} \,\&\, M \in \mathbb{R}) \to (N \,{}_{|}{*}_{|\mathbb{R}} M = M \,{}_{|}{*}_{|\mathbb{R}} N)$

Theorem : $\big(N \in \mathbb{R} \,\&\, M \in \mathbb{R} \,\&\, \mathsf{Is\_nonneg}_{\mathbb{R}}(-_{\mathbb{R}}(M))\big) \to$
$(N >_{\mathbb{R}} N +_{\mathbb{R}} M \vee N = N +_{\mathbb{R}} M)$

Theorem : $(N \in \mathbb{R} \,\&\, M \in \mathbb{R}) \to (N \cup M \in \mathbb{R})$

Theorem : [Least upper bound] $(S \neq \emptyset \,\&\, S \subseteq \mathbb{R}) \to (\bigcup S \in \mathbb{R} \vee \bigcup S = \mathbb{Q})$

After the foregoing series of definitions and preparatory theorems we now begin to prove the basic properties of the real numbers.[4] The sum, product, and quotient of two real numbers is a real number. The zero and unit reals are both non-negative, and the unit is larger. The zero real is the additive identity for reals. The sum and product of two reals and the negative of a real are both reals. The sum of any real and its negative is the zero real. Real addition and multiplication are commutative. The absolute value of a real $x$ is a real which is non-negative and at least as large as $x$. The absolute value of a real $x$ is $x$ if $x$ is non-negative, otherwise it is the negative of $x$. The absolute value of a real $x$ is also the absolute value of the negative of $x$.

Theorem 296 : $0_{\mathbb{R}} \in \mathbb{R} \,\&\, 1_{\mathbb{R}} \in \mathbb{R} \,\&$
$\mathsf{Is\_nonneg}_{\mathbb{R}}(0_{\mathbb{R}}) \,\&\, \mathsf{Is\_nonneg}_{\mathbb{R}}(1_{\mathbb{R}}) \,\&\, 1_{\mathbb{R}} >_{\mathbb{R}} 0_{\mathbb{R}}$

Theorem 299 : $(N \in \mathbb{R} \,\&\, M \in \mathbb{R}) \to (N +_{\mathbb{R}} M \in \mathbb{R})$

Theorem 300 : $(N \in \mathbb{R} \,\&\, M \in \mathbb{R}) \to (N +_{\mathbb{R}} M = M +_{\mathbb{R}} N)$

Theorem 301 : $(N \in \mathbb{R}) \to (N = N +_{\mathbb{R}} 0_{\mathbb{R}})$

Theorem 302 : $(N \in \mathbb{R}) \to \big(-_{\mathbb{R}}(N) \in \mathbb{R}\big)$

Theorem : $(N \in \mathbb{R} \,\&\, M \in \mathbb{R}) \to \big(N = M +_{\mathbb{R}} (N -_{\mathbb{R}} M)\big)$

[4]From this point on it is immaterial whether the reals have been introduced as Dedekind cuts or as equivalence classes of rational Cauchy sequences.

Theorem : $(N \in \mathbb{R} \,\&\, M \in \mathbb{R}) \rightarrow (N *_{\mathbb{R}} M \in \mathbb{R})$

Theorem : $(N \in \mathbb{R} \,\&\, M \in \mathbb{R}) \rightarrow (N *_{\mathbb{R}} M = M *_{\mathbb{R}} N)$

Theorem : [The reals are a linearly ordered set]
$(N \in \mathbb{R} \,\&\, M \in \mathbb{R}) \rightarrow$
$\big((N \geqslant_{\mathbb{R}} M \vee M \geqslant_{\mathbb{R}} N) \,\&\, \big((N \geqslant_{\mathbb{R}} M \,\&\, M \geqslant_{\mathbb{R}} N) \rightarrow N = M\big)\big)$

Theorem : $(N \in \mathbb{R}) \rightarrow \big(|N| \in \mathbb{R} \,\&\, |N| \geqslant_{\mathbb{R}} N\big)$

Theorem : $(N \in \mathbb{R}) \rightarrow$
$\big(|N| = \textbf{ if } \mathsf{Is\_nonneg}_{\mathbb{R}}(N) \textbf{ then } N \textbf{ else } -_{\mathbb{R}}(N) \textbf{ end if}\big)$

Theorem : $(N \in \mathbb{R}) \rightarrow \big(|N| = \big|-_{\mathbb{R}}(N)\big|\big)$

Continuing our series of theorems giving elementary properties of real numbers, we have the following. The absolute value of a real number $n$ is at least as large as $n$, and is non-negative. The sum of a non-negative real $n$ and a negative real $m$ has an absolute value which is less than or equal to either $n$ or the reverse of $m$. The sum of $n$ and the absolute value of $m$ is at least as large as $n$. The absolute value of $n + m$ is no larger than the sum of the absolute value of $m$ and the absolute value of $n$. The absolute value of the product of $n$ and $m$ equals the product of the two separate absolute values, and a similar result holds for the quotient. Real addition and multiplication are commutative and associative, and multiplication is distributive over addition. The sum of two non-negative reals is non-negative. The negative of the negative of a real $n$ is $n$. The unit real is the multiplicative identity, and the product of any non-zero real with its reciprocal is the unit real. Division of reals is the inverse of real multiplication. The only real number $n$ for which $n$ and $-n$ are both non-negative is the real zero. If the sum of two non-negative reals $m$ and $n$ is zero, then both $m$ and $n$ are zero. If $n$ is greater than $n$ and $k$ is positive, all being reals, then the product of $n$ and $k$ is greater than the product of $m$ and $k$. The reciprocal of a positive real is positive. The average of two reals $n$ and $m$ lies between $n$ and $m$. There is one and only one non-negative square root of a non-negative real. If both $m$ and $n$ are non-negative reals, the square root of their product is the product of their separate square roots.

Theorem : $(N \in \mathbb{R}) \rightarrow$
$\big(|N| \in \mathbb{R} \,\&\, \big(|N| >_{\mathbb{R}} N \vee |N| = N\big) \,\&\, \big(|N| >_{\mathbb{R}} 0_{\mathbb{R}} \vee |N| = 0_{\mathbb{R}}\big)\big)$

Theorem : $\big(N \in \mathbb{R} \,\&\, M \in \mathbb{R} \,\&\, \mathsf{Is\_nonneg}_{\mathbb{R}}(N) \,\&\, \big(\neg \mathsf{Is\_nonneg}_{\mathbb{R}}(M)\big)\big) \rightarrow$
$\big(N >_{\mathbb{R}} |N +_{\mathbb{R}} M| \vee N = |N +_{\mathbb{R}} M| \vee -_{\mathbb{R}}(M) >_{\mathbb{R}} |N +_{\mathbb{R}} M| \vee$
$-_{\mathbb{R}}(M) = |N +_{\mathbb{R}} M|\big)$

Theorem : $(N \in \mathbb{R} \,\&\, M \in \mathbb{R}) \rightarrow \big(N +_{\mathbb{R}} |M| >_{\mathbb{R}} N \vee N +_{\mathbb{R}} |M| = N\big)$

Theorem : $(N \in \mathbb{R} \,\&\, M \in \mathbb{R}) \rightarrow \big(|N| +_{\mathbb{R}} |M| >_{\mathbb{R}} |N +_{\mathbb{R}} M| \vee |N| +_{\mathbb{R}} |M| = |N +_{\mathbb{R}} M|\big)$

Theorem : $(N \in \mathbb{R} \,\&\, M \in \mathbb{R}) \rightarrow \big(|N| +_{\mathbb{R}} |M| >_{\mathbb{R}} |N -_{\mathbb{R}} M| \vee |N| +_{\mathbb{R}} |M| = |N -_{\mathbb{R}} M|\big)$

Theorem : $(N \in \mathbb{R} \,\&\, M \in \mathbb{R}) \rightarrow \big(|N| *_{\mathbb{R}} |M| = |N *_{\mathbb{R}} M|\big)$

Theorem : $(N \in \mathbb{R} \,\&\, M \in \mathbb{R} \,\&\, M \neq 0_{\mathbb{R}}) \rightarrow \big(|N| /_{\mathbb{R}} |M| = |N /_{\mathbb{R}} M|\big)$

Theorem : $(K \in \mathbb{R} \,\&\, N \in \mathbb{R} \,\&\, M \in \mathbb{R}) \rightarrow \big(N +_{\mathbb{R}} (M +_{\mathbb{R}} K) = (N +_{\mathbb{R}} M) +_{\mathbb{R}} K\big)$

Theorem : $(N \in \mathbb{R}) \rightarrow -_{\mathbb{R}}\big(-_{\mathbb{R}}(N)\big) = N$

Theorem : $(K \in \mathbb{R} \,\&\, N \in \mathbb{R} \,\&\, M \in \mathbb{R}) \rightarrow \big(N *_{\mathbb{R}} (M *_{\mathbb{R}} K) = (N *_{\mathbb{R}} M) *_{\mathbb{R}} K\big)$

Theorem : $(K \in \mathbb{R} \,\&\, N \in \mathbb{R} \,\&\, M \in \mathbb{R}) \rightarrow \big(N *_{\mathbb{R}} (M +_{\mathbb{R}} K) = (N *_{\mathbb{R}} M) +_{\mathbb{R}} (N *_{\mathbb{R}} K)\big)$

Theorem : $\big(X \in \mathbb{R} \,\&\, Y \in \mathbb{R} \,\&\, \mathsf{Is\_nonneg}_{\mathbb{R}}(X) \,\&\, \mathsf{Is\_nonneg}_{\mathbb{R}}(Y)\big) \rightarrow \big(\mathsf{Is\_nonneg}_{\mathbb{R}}(X +_{\mathbb{R}} Y) \,\&\, \mathsf{Is\_nonneg}_{\mathbb{R}}(X *_{\mathbb{R}} Y)\big)$

Theorem : $(M \in \mathbb{R}) \rightarrow (M = M *_{\mathbb{R}} 1_{\mathbb{R}})$

Theorem : $(M \in \mathbb{R} \,\&\, M \neq 0_{\mathbb{R}}) \rightarrow \big(\mathsf{Recip}_{\mathbb{R}}(M) \in \mathbb{R} \,\&\, M *_{\mathbb{R}} \mathsf{Recip}_{\mathbb{R}}(M) = 1_{\mathbb{R}}\big)$

Theorem : $(N \in \mathbb{R} \,\&\, M \in \mathbb{R} \,\&\, M \neq 0_{\mathbb{R}}) \rightarrow \big(N = M *_{\mathbb{R}} (N /_{\mathbb{R}} M)\big)$

Theorem : $(X \in \mathbb{R}) \rightarrow \Big(\big(\mathsf{Is\_nonneg}_{\mathbb{R}}(X) \vee \mathsf{Is\_nonneg}_{\mathbb{R}}\big(-_{\mathbb{R}}(X)\big)\big) \,\&\, \Big(\big(\mathsf{Is\_nonneg}_{\mathbb{R}}(X) \,\&\, \mathsf{Is\_nonneg}_{\mathbb{R}}\big(-_{\mathbb{R}}(X)\big)\big) \rightarrow (X = 0_{\mathbb{R}})\Big)\Big)$

Theorem : $(X \in \mathbb{R}) \rightarrow (X = X *_{\mathbb{R}} 1_{\mathbb{R}})$

Theorem : $\big(X \in \mathbb{R} \,\&\, Y \in \mathbb{R} \,\&\, \mathsf{Is\_nonneg}_{\mathbb{R}}(X) \,\&\, \mathsf{Is\_nonneg}_{\mathbb{R}}(Y) \,\&\, X +_{\mathbb{R}} Y = 0_{\mathbb{R}}\big) \rightarrow (X = 0_{\mathbb{R}} \,\&\, Y = 0_{\mathbb{R}})$

Theorem : $(X \in \mathbb{R} \,\&\, Y \in \mathbb{R} \,\&\, X' \in \mathbb{R} \,\&\, X >_{\mathbb{R}} Y \,\&\, X' >_{\mathbb{R}} 0_{\mathbb{R}}) \rightarrow (X *_{\mathbb{R}} X' >_{\mathbb{R}} Y *_{\mathbb{R}} X')$

Theorem : $(X \in \mathbb{R} \,\&\, X >_{\mathbb{R}} 0_{\mathbb{R}}) \rightarrow \big(\mathsf{Recip}(X) >_{\mathbb{R}} 0_{\mathbb{R}}\big)$

Theorem : [The average of two real numbers lies between them]
$(X \in \mathbb{R} \,\&\, Y \in \mathbb{R} \,\&\, X >_{\mathbb{R}} Y) \rightarrow$
$\big(X >_{\mathbb{R}} (X +_{\mathbb{R}} Y)/_{\mathbb{R}} (1_{\mathbb{R}} +_{\mathbb{R}} 1_{\mathbb{R}}) \,\&\, (X +_{\mathbb{R}} Y)/_{\mathbb{R}} (1_{\mathbb{R}} +_{\mathbb{R}} 1_{\mathbb{R}}) >_{\mathbb{R}} Y\big)$

Theorem : $\big(X \in \mathbb{R} \,\&\, \mathsf{Is\_nonneg}_{\mathbb{R}}(X)\big) \rightarrow$
$\big(\sqrt{X} \in \mathbb{R} \,\&\, \mathsf{Is\_nonneg}_{\mathbb{R}}\big(\sqrt{X}\big) \,\&\, \sqrt{X} *_{\mathbb{R}} \sqrt{X} = X\big)$

Theorem : $\big(X \in \mathbb{R} \,\&\, Y \in \mathbb{R} \,\&\, Y *_{\mathbb{R}} Y = X \,\&\, \mathsf{Is\_nonneg}_{\mathbb{R}}(Y)\big) \rightarrow$
$\big(Y = \sqrt{X}\big)$

Theorem : $\big(X \in \mathbb{R} \,\&\, \mathsf{Is\_nonneg}_{\mathbb{R}}(X) \,\&\, Y \in \mathbb{R} \,\&\, \mathsf{Is\_nonneg}_{\mathbb{R}}(Y)\big) \rightarrow$
$\big(\sqrt{X *_{\mathbb{R}} Y} = \sqrt{X} *_{\mathbb{R}} \sqrt{Y}\big)$

## 5.11 Complex Numbers

This completes the elementary part of our work with real numbers. Since one of our main goals is to state and prove the Cauchy integral theorem, we must also define the *complex numbers* and prove their basic properties. This is done in the entirely standard way, which traces back to Gauss. Complex numbers are defined as pairs of real numbers. They are added componentwise, and multiplied in a manner reflecting the desire to make [0, 1] a square root of −1. The norm of a complex number is its length as a two-dimensional vector. The reciprocal of a complex number is obtained by reversing its second component and then dividing both components of the result by the square of its norm. The quotient of two complex numbers is the first times the reciprocal of the second. The zero complex number is the pair whose components are both the zero real. The unit complex number has the unit real number as its first component.

Def 58 : [Complex numbers] $\mathbb{C} =_{\mathrm{Def}} \mathbb{R} \times \mathbb{R}$

Def 59 : [Complex sum] $x +_{\mathbb{C}} y =_{\mathrm{Def}} \big[x^{[1]} +_{\mathbb{R}} y^{[1]},\, x^{[2]} +_{\mathbb{R}} y^{[2]}\big]$

Def 60 : [Complex product] $x *_{\mathbb{C}} y =_{\mathrm{Def}}$
$\big[\big(x^{[1]} *_{\mathbb{R}} y^{[1]}\big) -_{\mathbb{R}} \big(x^{[2]} *_{\mathbb{R}} y^{[2]}\big),\, \big(x^{[1]} *_{\mathbb{R}} y^{[2]}\big) +_{\mathbb{R}} \big(x^{[2]} *_{\mathbb{R}} y^{[1]}\big)\big]$

Def 61 : [Complex norm] $|x|_{\mathbb{C}} =_{\mathrm{Def}} \sqrt{\big(x^{[1]} *_{\mathbb{R}} x^{[1]}\big) +_{\mathbb{R}} \big(x^{[2]} *_{\mathbb{R}} x^{[2]}\big)}$

Def 62 : [Complex reciprocal] $\mathsf{Recip}_{\mathbb{C}}(x) =_{\mathrm{Def}}$
$\big[x^{[1]}/_{\mathbb{R}} \big(|x|_{\mathbb{C}} *_{\mathbb{R}} |x|_{\mathbb{C}}\big),\, -_{\mathbb{R}}\big(x^{[2]}/_{\mathbb{R}} \big(|x|_{\mathbb{C}} *_{\mathbb{R}} |x|_{\mathbb{C}}\big)\big)\big]$

Def 63 : [Complex quotient] $x /_{\mathbb{C}} y =_{\mathrm{Def}} x *_{\mathbb{C}} \mathsf{Recip}_{\mathbb{C}}(y)$

Def 63$a$ : $-_{\mathbb{C}}(x) =_{\text{Def}} \left[-_{\mathbb{R}}(x^{[1]}),\ -_{\mathbb{R}}(x^{[2]})\right]$

Def 63$b$ : $n -_{\mathbb{C}} m =_{\text{Def}} n +_{\mathbb{C}} -_{\mathbb{C}}(m)$

Def 63$x$ : $0_{\mathbb{C}} =_{\text{Def}} [0_{\mathbb{R}},\ 0_{\mathbb{R}}]$

Def 63$y$ : $1_{\mathbb{C}} =_{\text{Def}} [1_{\mathbb{R}},\ 0_{\mathbb{R}}]$

The basic elementary properties of the complex numbers are now established by a series of elementary algebraic proofs. Any pair of reals is a complex number and vice versa. The complex sum and product of any two complex numbers is a complex number. The zero complex number is the additive identity, and the unit complex number is the multiplicative identity. The negative of a complex number is its additive inverse. Complex addition and multiplication are commutative and associative; multiplication is distributive over addition. The norm of any complex number is a non-negative real number. The negative of a complex number $z$ has the same norm as $z$. The norm of a complex product is the product of the separate norms. The norm of a complex quotient is the quotient of the separate norms. Any non-zero complex number has a multiplicative inverse, the inverse of multiplication being given by the complex division operator, which is easily defined using the complex reciprocal.

Theorem : $\big((X \in \mathbb{R} \,\&\, Y \in \mathbb{R}) \rightarrow ([X,\ Y] \in \mathbb{C})\big)\ \&$
$\big((M \in \mathbb{C}) \rightarrow \big(M = \left[M^{[1]},\ M^{[2]}\right] \,\&\, M^{[1]} \in \mathbb{R} \,\&\, M^{[2]} \in \mathbb{R}\big)\big)$

Theorem : $(N \in \mathbb{C} \,\&\, M \in \mathbb{C}) \rightarrow (N +_{\mathbb{C}} M \in \mathbb{C})$

Theorem : $(N \in \mathbb{C} \,\&\, M \in \mathbb{C}) \rightarrow (N +_{\mathbb{C}} M = M +_{\mathbb{C}} N)$

Theorem : $(N \in \mathbb{C}) \rightarrow (N = N +_{\mathbb{C}} 0_{\mathbb{C}})$

Theorem : $(N \in \mathbb{C}) \rightarrow \big(-_{\mathbb{C}}(N) \in \mathbb{C} \,\&\, -_{\mathbb{C}}(-_{\mathbb{C}}(N)) = N\big)$

Theorem : $(N \in \mathbb{C}) \rightarrow \big(N +_{\mathbb{C}} -_{\mathbb{C}}(N) = 0_{\mathbb{C}}\big)$

Theorem : $(N \in \mathbb{C} \,\&\, M \in \mathbb{C}) \rightarrow \big(N = M +_{\mathbb{C}} (N -_{\mathbb{C}} M)\big)$

Theorem : $(N \in \mathbb{C} \,\&\, M \in \mathbb{C}) \rightarrow (N *_{\mathbb{C}} M = M *_{\mathbb{C}} N)$

Theorem : $(N \in \mathbb{C}) \rightarrow \big(|N|_{\mathbb{C}} \in \mathbb{R} \,\&\, \mathsf{Is\_nonneg}_{\mathbb{R}}(|N|_{\mathbb{C}})\big)$

Theorem : $(N \in \mathbb{C}) \rightarrow \big(|N|_{\mathbb{C}} = |-_{\mathbb{C}}(N)|_{\mathbb{C}}\big)$

Theorem : $(N \in \mathbb{C} \,\&\, M \in \mathbb{C}) \rightarrow$
$\big((|N|_{\mathbb{C}} +_{\mathbb{C}} |M|_{\mathbb{C}}) >_{\mathbb{R}} |N +_{\mathbb{C}} M|_{\mathbb{C}} \vee \big(|N|_{\mathbb{C}} +_{\mathbb{C}} |M|_{\mathbb{C}} = |N +_{\mathbb{C}} M|_{\mathbb{C}}\big)\big)$

$$\text{Theorem}: \ (N \in \mathbb{C} \,\&\, M \in \mathbb{C}) \rightarrow \big(|N|_{\mathbb{C}} *_{\mathbb{C}} |M|_{\mathbb{C}} = |N *_{\mathbb{C}} M|_{\mathbb{C}}\big)$$

$$\text{Theorem}: \ (N \in \mathbb{C} \,\&\, M \in \mathbb{C} \,\&\, M \neq 0_{\mathbb{C}}) \rightarrow \big(|N|_{\mathbb{C}}/_{\mathbb{R}} |M|_{\mathbb{C}} = |N/_{\mathbb{C}} M|_{\mathbb{C}}\big)$$

$$\text{Theorem}: \ (N \in \mathbb{C} \,\&\, M \in \mathbb{C}) \rightarrow (N *_{\mathbb{C}} M \in \mathbb{C})$$

$$\text{Theorem}: \ (K \in \mathbb{C} \,\&\, N \in \mathbb{C} \,\&\, M \in \mathbb{C}) \rightarrow \big(N +_{\mathbb{C}} (M +_{\mathbb{C}} K) = (N +_{\mathbb{C}} M) +_{\mathbb{C}} K\big)$$

$$\text{Theorem}: \ (K \in \mathbb{C} \,\&\, N \in \mathbb{C} \,\&\, M \in \mathbb{C}) \rightarrow \big(N *_{\mathbb{C}} (M *_{\mathbb{C}} K) = (N *_{\mathbb{C}} M) *_{\mathbb{C}} K\big)$$

$$\text{Theorem}: \ (K \in \mathbb{C} \,\&\, N \in \mathbb{C} \,\&\, M \in \mathbb{C}) \rightarrow \big(N *_{\mathbb{C}} (M +_{\mathbb{C}} K) = (N *_{\mathbb{C}} M) +_{\mathbb{C}} (N *_{\mathbb{C}} K)\big)$$

$$\text{Theorem}: \ (M \in \mathbb{C}) \rightarrow (M = M *_{\mathbb{C}} 1_{\mathbb{C}})$$

$$\text{Theorem}: \ (M \in \mathbb{C} \,\&\, M \neq 0_{\mathbb{C}}) \rightarrow \big(\mathsf{Recip}_{\mathbb{C}}(M) \in \mathbb{C} \,\&\, M *_{\mathbb{C}} \mathsf{Recip}_{\mathbb{C}}(M) = 1_{\mathbb{C}}\big)$$

$$\text{Theorem}: \ (N \in \mathbb{C} \,\&\, M \in \mathbb{C} \,\&\, M \neq 0_{\mathbb{C}}) \rightarrow \big(N = M *_{\mathbb{C}} (N/_{\mathbb{C}} M)\big)$$

$$\text{Theorem}: \ 0_{\mathbb{C}} \in \mathbb{C} \,\&\, 1_{\mathbb{C}} \in \mathbb{C}$$

## 5.12 Functions of Real and Complex Variables

Now we take our first steps into analysis proper, i.e. take up the theory of functions of real and complex variables. The set $\mathbb{RF}$ of real functions is defined as the set of all single-valued functions whose domain is the set $\mathbb{R}$ of all real numbers and whose range is a subset of $\mathbb{R}$. The zero function is that element of $\mathbb{RF}$ all of whose values are zero. Functions in $\mathbb{RF}$ are added and multiplied pointwise, reversed pointwise, and compared pointwise. The least upper bound of any set of functions in $\mathbb{RF}$ is formed by taking the least upper bound of the function values at each point.[5] The positive part of a real function is formed by taking its pointwise maximum with the identically zero real function.

[5]Let the view of real numbers as Dedekind cuts momentarily surface again. To be consistent with the approach that sees reals as equivalence classes of rational Cauchy sequences, in the formal specification given below we should apply an *ad hoc* 'least upper bound' operation (rather than the union operation) to a set of reals. Sloppiness on this point gives us the opportunity to signal a little advantage of the approach based on Dedekind cuts, which can represent the l.u.b. operation, $-\infty$, and $+\infty$ by $\bigcup$, $\emptyset$, and $\mathbb{Q}$, respectively.

Def 64 : [Real functions of a real variable] $\mathbb{RF} =_{\text{Def}}$
$\{ f \subseteq (\mathbb{R}\times\mathbb{R}) \mid \mathsf{Svm}(f) \,\&\, \mathsf{domain}(f) = \mathbb{R} \}$

Def 66 : [Sum of real functions] $f +_{\mathbb{RF}} g =_{\text{Def}} \{ [x, f[x] +_{\mathbb{R}} g[x]] : x \in \mathbb{R} \}$

Def 67 : [Product of real functions] $f *_{\mathbb{RF}} g =_{\text{Def}} \{ [x, f[x] *_{\mathbb{R}} g[x]] : x \in \mathbb{R} \}$

Def 68 : [LUB of a set of real functions] $\mathsf{LUB}(s) =_{\text{Def}}$
$\{ [x, \bigcup \{ f[x] : f \in s \}] : x \in \mathbb{R} \}$

Def 69 : [Constant zero function] $0_{\mathbb{RF}} =_{\text{Def}} \{ [x, 0_{\mathbb{R}}] : x \in \mathbb{R} \}$

Def 70 : [Comparison of real functions] $f >_{\mathbb{RF}} g \leftrightarrow_{\text{Def}}$
$f \neq g \,\&\, (\forall x \in \mathbb{R} \mid f[x] \supseteq g[x])$

Def 71 : [Positive part of real function] $\mathsf{PosPart}(f) =_{\text{Def}}$
$\{ [x, \textbf{if } f[x] \geqslant_{\mathbb{R}} 0_{\mathbb{R}} \textbf{ then } f[x] \textbf{ else } 0_{\mathbb{R}} \textbf{ end if}] : x \in \mathbb{R} \}$

Def 72 : [Reverse of a real function] $-_{\mathbb{RF}}(f) =_{\text{Def}} \{ [x, -_{\mathbb{R}}(f[x])] : x \in \mathbb{R} \}$

The most elementary properties of real functions follow directly and trivially from these definitions. Addition and multiplication of real functions are commutative and associative; multiplication of such functions is distributive over addition.

Theorem : $(N \in \mathbb{RF} \,\&\, M \in \mathbb{RF}) \rightarrow (N +_{\mathbb{RF}} M = M +_{\mathbb{RF}} N)$

Theorem : $(N \in \mathbb{RF} \,\&\, M \in \mathbb{RF}) \rightarrow (N +_{\mathbb{RF}} M = M +_{\mathbb{RF}} N)$

Theorem : $(N \in \mathbb{RF} \,\&\, M \in \mathbb{RF}) \rightarrow (N *_{\mathbb{RF}} M = M *_{\mathbb{RF}} N)$

Theorem : $(K \in \mathbb{RF} \,\&\, N \in \mathbb{RF} \,\&\, M \in \mathbb{RF}) \rightarrow$
$(N +_{\mathbb{RF}} (M +_{\mathbb{RF}} K) = (N +_{\mathbb{RF}} M) +_{\mathbb{RF}} K)$

Theorem : $(K \in \mathbb{RF} \,\&\, N \in \mathbb{RF} \,\&\, M \in \mathbb{RF}) \rightarrow$
$(N *_{\mathbb{RF}} (M +_{\mathbb{RF}} K) = (N *_{\mathbb{RF}} M) +_{\mathbb{RF}} (N *_{\mathbb{RF}} K))$

Theorem : $(K \in \mathbb{RF} \,\&\, N \in \mathbb{RF} \,\&\, M \in \mathbb{RF}) \rightarrow$
$(N *_{\mathbb{RF}} (M *_{\mathbb{RF}} K) = (N *_{\mathbb{RF}} M) *_{\mathbb{RF}} K)$

Theorem : $(K \in \mathbb{RF} \,\&\, N \in \mathbb{RF} \,\&\, M \in \mathbb{RF}) \rightarrow$
$(N *_{\mathbb{RF}} (M +_{\mathbb{RF}} K) = (N *_{\mathbb{RF}} M) +_{\mathbb{RF}} (N *_{\mathbb{RF}} K))$

To progress to less trivial results in real analysis we need to define various basic notions of summation and convergence. In order to arrive at our target, the Cauchy integral theorem, with minimal delay, we ruthlessly omit all results not lying along the direct path to this target, even though inclusion of many of these results would usefully illuminate the lines of thought that enter into the definitions, theorems, and proofs we are compelled to include. This may lead the reader not previously familiar with analysis to feel that we are giving many bones with little meat. For a fuller account of the historical and technical background of the results from analysis presented in this book, any introductory account of real and complex function theory can be consulted. Among these we note [Bri97]; also the older classic [Lan66].

The sum of the values of any real-valued mapping having a finite domain is defined by specializing the general 'Theory of Sigma' described above to this general case. We can then define the sum of a convergent series of positive real values (on any domain) as the least upper bound of all its finite sub-sums. (Note, however, that it can easily be shown that this value will only be a finite real if no more than a countable number of the function values are non-zero.) By further specializing the 'Theory of Sigma' using real function addition rather than real addition we can define the notion of sum for finite series of real functions, and then by taking least upper bounds we can define the sum of a convergent series of positive real functions.

Def_by_app 73 : [Sums for real maps with finite domains]
$$\big(\mathsf{Svm}(F)\ \&\ \mathsf{range}(F) \subseteq \mathbb{R}\ \&\ \mathsf{Finite}(F)\big) \rightarrow$$
$$\Big(\big(\textstyle\sum(F) \in \mathbb{R}\big)\ \&\ \big((P \in F) \rightarrow \big(\textstyle\sum(\{P\}) = P^{[2]}\big)\big)\ \&$$
$$\big(\textstyle\sum(F) = \big(\textstyle\sum(F_{|A}) +_{\mathbb{R}} \textstyle\sum(F_{|\mathsf{domain}(F)\setminus A})\big)\big)\Big)$$

Def 73$b$ : [Sums of absolutely convergent infinite series of positive values]
$$\textstyle\sum^{\infty}(F) =_{\mathrm{Def}} \bigcup\big\{\textstyle\sum(F_{|s}) : s \subseteq \mathsf{domain}(F) \mid \mathsf{Finite}(s)\big\}$$

Def_by_app 74 : [Sums for series of real functions]
$$\big(\mathsf{Svm}(Ser)\ \&\ \mathsf{range}(Ser) \subseteq \mathbb{RF}\ \&\ \mathsf{Finite}(Ser)\big) \rightarrow$$
$$\Big(\big(\textstyle\sum_{\mathbb{F}}(Ser) \in \mathbb{RF}\big)\ \&\ \big((P \in Ser) \rightarrow \big(\textstyle\sum_{\mathbb{F}}(\{P\}) = P^{[2]}\big)\big)\ \&$$
$$\big(\textstyle\sum_{\mathbb{F}}(Ser) = \big(\textstyle\sum_{\mathbb{F}}(Ser_{|A}) +_{\mathbb{RF}} \textstyle\sum_{\mathbb{F}}(Ser_{|\mathsf{domain}(Ser)\setminus A})\big)\big)\Big)$$

Def 75 : [Sums of absolutely convergent infinite series of real functions]
$$\textstyle\sum_{\mathbb{F}}^{\infty}(Ser) =_{\mathrm{Def}} \mathsf{LUB}\big(\big\{\textstyle\sum_{\mathbb{F}}(Ser_{|s}) : s \subseteq \mathsf{domain}(Ser) \mid \mathsf{Finite}(s)\big\}\big)$$

It is now easy to give the basic definitions of the theory of integration of real functions. We first define the notion of a 'block function'. This is simply a function of a real variable which is zero everywhere outside a bounded interval of reals, and constant inside this interval. We introduce a name for the set of all such functions. The 'integral' of any such function is the length of the interval on which it is non-zero, times its value. The Lebesgue 'upper integral' of any positive real-valued function $f$ of a real number is the greatest lower bound of all sums of integrals of countable sequences $f_i$ of positive block functions for which the pointwise sum of the sequence of values $f_i[x]$ is at least as large as $f[x]$ for each real $x$. (It is easily seen that this value depends only on the positive part of $f$.) The (Lebesgue) integral of any real function $f$ is the upper integral of $f$ minus the upper integral of the negative of $f$. The key result at which these definitions hint (but, of course, do not prove) is that this integral is additive for a very wide class of functions, and that if a sequence $g_n$ of functions in this class converges (in an appropriate sense) to a limit function $g$, then the integrals of the $g_n$ converge to the integral of $g$.

Def 76 : [Block function] $\mathsf{Bl\_f}(A, B, C) =_{\text{Def}}$
$\{[x, \textbf{if } x \geqslant_{\mathbb{R}} A \,\&\, B \geqslant_{\mathbb{R}} x \textbf{ then } C \textbf{ else } 0_{\mathbb{R}} \textbf{ end if}] : x \in \mathbb{R}\}$

Def 77 : [Block function integral] $\mathsf{BFInt}(F) =_{\text{Def}}$
$\mathsf{arb}(\{c *_{\mathbb{R}} (b -_{\mathbb{R}} a) : a \in \mathbb{R},\ b \in \mathbb{R},\ c \in \mathbb{R} \mid \mathsf{Bl\_f}(a, b, c) = F\})$

Def 78 : [Block functions] $\mathsf{RBF} =_{\text{Def}} \{\mathsf{Bl\_f}(a, b, c) : a \in \mathbb{R},\ b \in \mathbb{R},\ c \in \mathbb{R}\}$

Def 79 : [Product of a non-empty family of sets] $\mathsf{GLB}(S) =_{\text{Def}}$
$\{x : x \in \mathsf{arb}(S) \mid (\forall y \in S \mid x \in y)\}$

Note that this last definition describes the product of an arbitrary collection $s$ of sets; this is the set of all members of any chosen member of $s$ which belong to all the other members of $s$.

Def 80 : [Lebesgue Upper Integral of a Positive Function] $\int^+(F) =_{\text{Def}}$
$\mathsf{GLB}(\{\{[n, \mathsf{BFInt}(ser[n])] : n \in \mathbb{N}\} : ser \subseteq \mathbb{N} \times \mathsf{RBF} \mid$
$\mathsf{Svm}(ser) \,\&\, (\sum_{\mathbb{F}}^{\infty}(ser) >_{\mathbb{RF}} F)\})$

Def 81 : [Lebesgue Integral] $\int(F) =_{\text{Def}}$
$\int^+(\mathsf{PosPart}(F)) -_{\mathbb{R}} \int^+(\mathsf{PosPart}(-_{\mathbb{RF}}(F)))$

We also need to develop some of the results concerning continuity and differentiability which lie at the traditional heart of analysis. We begin by giving the standard 'epsilon-delta' definition of continuity: a single-valued, real-valued function $f$ of a real variable is continuous if for each $x$ in its domain, and each positive real value $\varepsilon$, there exists some real value $\delta$ such that the absolute value of the real difference $f[x] - f[y]$ is less than $\varepsilon$ whenever $y$ belongs to the domain of $f$ and the absolute value of the real difference $x - y$ is less than $\delta$. Since for later use we will need to generalize notions like this to the multivariable case, we also define the notion of Euclidean $n$-space (namely as the collection of all real-valued sequences of length $n$, i.e. the set of all real-valued functions defined on the integer $n$), and the standard norm, i.e. vector length in this space, which is the square root of the sum of squares of the components of a vector (i.e. the values of the corresponding function). We also need the notion of the (componentwise) difference of two $n$-dimensional vectors, which we define as the pointwise difference of the functions corresponding to these vectors. This lets us extend the 'epsilon-delta' definition of continuity from real functions of real variables to vector-valued functions of vector-valued variables, and also real-valued functions of vector-valued variables. A vector-valued function $f$ of a vector-valued argument $x$ is continuous if for each $x$ in its domain, and each positive real value $\varepsilon$, there exists some real value $\delta$ such that the norm of the vector difference $f[x] - f[y]$ is less than $\varepsilon$ whenever $y$ belongs to the domain of $f$ and the norm of the vector difference $x - y$ is less than $\delta$. The definition of continuity for real-valued functions of vector-valued variables is similar.

Def 82 : [Continuous function of a real variable] $\mathsf{Is\_continuous\_RF}(F) \leftrightarrow_{\mathrm{Def}}$
$F \subseteq (\mathbb{R}\times\mathbb{R})$ & $\mathsf{Svm}(F)$ &
$(\forall x \in \mathsf{domain}(F) \,|\, (\forall \varepsilon \in \mathbb{R} \,|\, (\exists \delta \in \mathbb{R} \,|\, (\forall y \in \mathsf{domain}(F) \mid \delta >_{\mathbb{R}} 0_{\mathbb{R}}$ &
$((\varepsilon >_{\mathbb{R}} 0_{\mathbb{R}}$ & $\delta >_{\mathbb{R}} |x -_{\mathbb{R}} y|) \rightarrow (\varepsilon >_{\mathbb{R}} |F[x] -_{\mathbb{R}} F[y]|))))))$

Def 83 : [Euclidean $n$-space] $\mathbf{E}(N) =_{\mathrm{Def}}$
$\{ f \subseteq (N\times\mathbb{R}) \mid \mathsf{Svm}(f)$ & $\mathsf{domain}(f) = N \}$

Def 84 : [Euclidean norm] $\|F\| =_{\mathrm{Def}} \sqrt{\sum(F)}$

Def 85 : [Difference of real functions] $F -_{\mathbb{RF}} G =_{\mathrm{Def}}$
$\{ [x,\ F[x] -_{\mathbb{R}} G[x]] : x \in \mathsf{domain}(F) \}$

Def 86 : [Continuous vector-valued function on Euclidean $n$-space]
$\mathsf{Is\_continuous\_REnF}(F, M, N) \leftrightarrow_{\mathrm{Def}} F \subseteq (\mathbf{E}(M)\times\mathbf{E}(N))$ & $\mathsf{Svm}(F)$ &
$(\forall x \in \mathsf{domain}(F) \mid (\forall \varepsilon \in \mathbb{R} \mid$
$(\exists \delta \in \mathbb{R} \mid (\forall y \in \mathsf{domain}(F) \mid$
$\delta >_{\mathbb{R}} 0_{\mathbb{R}}$ & $((\varepsilon >_{\mathbb{R}} 0_{\mathbb{R}}$ & $\delta >_{\mathbb{R}} \|x -_{\mathbb{RF}} y\|)$
$\rightarrow (\varepsilon >_{\mathbb{R}} \|F[x] -_{\mathbb{RF}} F[y]\|))))))$

Def 86$a$ : [Continuous real-valued function on Euclidean $n$-space]
$\mathsf{Is\_continuous\_REnF}(F, N) \leftrightarrow_{\mathrm{Def}} F \subseteq (\mathbf{E}(N)\times\mathbb{R})$ & $\mathsf{Svm}(F)$ &
$(\forall x \in \mathsf{domain}(F) \,|\, (\forall \varepsilon \in \mathbb{R} \mid$
$(\exists \delta \in \mathbb{R} \,|\, (\forall y \in \mathsf{domain}(F) \mid$
$\delta >_{\mathbb{R}} 0_{\mathbb{R}}$ & $((\varepsilon >_{\mathbb{R}} 0_{\mathbb{R}}$ & $\delta >_{\mathbb{R}} \|x -_{\mathbb{RF}} y\|)$
$\rightarrow (\varepsilon >_{\mathbb{R}} |F[x] -_{\mathbb{R}} F[y]|))))))$

Our next aim is to define the notion of derivative in some convenient way. We do this by considering pairs of real-valued functions $f$, *df* of a real variable $x$, and forming the function $g$ of two real variables $x$ and $y$ which equals the difference-quotient $(f[x] - f[y])/(x - y)$ if $x$ and $y$ are different, but $df[x]$ if $x = y$. Then $f$ is said to be (continuously) *differentiable* in its domain $D$ if there exists some continuous function *df* having the same domain such that the function $g$, formed in this way, is continuous on the product set of $D$ with itself. It is easily seen that if $f$ is differentiable there can exist only one *df* which makes $g$ continuous, allowing us to speak of *the* derivative of $f$ if $f$ has a derivative. It is also easy to see that if two functions $f$ and $h$ of a real variable have derivatives *df* and *dh*, respectively, then so do their sum and product, and that the derivative of the sum is $df + dh$, while the derivative of the product is $df * h + f * dh$. (However, we do not give the proofs of these results.)

Def 87 : [Difference-and-diagonal trick] $\mathsf{DD}(F, Df) =_{\mathrm{Def}}$
$\{ \textbf{if } x[0] \neq x[1] \textbf{ then } (F[x[0]] -_{\mathbb{R}} F[x[1]])/_{\mathbb{R}} (x[0] -_{\mathbb{R}} x[1])$
$\textbf{else } Df[x[0]] \textbf{ end if } : x \in \mathbf{E}(2) \}$

Def 88 : [Derivative of function of a real variable] $\mathsf{Der}(F) =_{\text{Def}}$
$\mathsf{arb}\big(\{ df \in \mathbb{RF} \mid \mathsf{domain}(F) = \mathsf{domain}(df)\ \&$
$\mathsf{Is\_continuous\_REnF}\big(\mathsf{DD}(F, df)_{|\mathsf{domain}(F)\times\mathsf{domain}(F)}, 2\big) \}\big)$

Next we extend the preceding notions to complex functions of a complex variable (i.e. single-valued functions defined on the set of complex numbers whose range is included in the set of complex numbers), and to complex-valued functions on complex Euclidean $n$-space. This space is defined as the collection of all real-valued sequences of length $n$, i.e. the set of all complex-valued functions defined on the integer $n$, and the difference of vectors is defined as the pointwise difference of the corresponding functions. The norm for such vectors is defined as the sum of the squares of the absolute values of their (complex) components. Using this simple definition of norm, the standard 'epsilon-delta' definition of continuity extends readily to the complex case.

Def 89 : [Complex functions of a complex variable] $\mathbb{CF} =_{\text{Def}}$
$\{ f \subseteq (\mathbb{C}\times\mathbb{C}) \mid \mathsf{Svm}(f)\ \&\ \mathsf{domain}(f) = \mathbb{C} \}$

Def 90 : [Complex Euclidean $n$-space] $\mathbf{E}_{\mathbb{C}}(N) =_{\text{Def}}$
$\{ f \subseteq (N\times\mathbb{C}) \mid \mathsf{Svm}(f)\ \&\ \mathsf{domain}(f) = N \}$

Def 91 : [Complex Euclidean norm] $\| F \|_{\mathbb{C}} =_{\text{Def}}$
$\sqrt{\sum\big(\{ [m, |F[m]|_{\mathbb{C}} *_{\mathbb{R}} |F[m]|_{\mathbb{C}}] : m \in \mathsf{domain}(F) \}\big)}$

Def 92 : [Difference of complex functions] $F -_{\mathbb{CF}} G =_{\text{Def}}$
$\{ [x, F[x] -_{\mathbb{C}} G[x]] : x \in \mathbb{C} \}$

Def 93 : [Continuous function of a complex variable] $\mathsf{Is\_continuous\_CF}(F) \leftrightarrow_{\text{Def}}$
$F \subseteq (\mathbb{C}\times\mathbb{C})\ \&\ \mathsf{Svm}(F)\ \&$
$\big(\forall x \in \mathsf{domain}(F) \mid \big(\forall \varepsilon \in \mathbb{R} \mid \big(\exists \delta \in \mathbb{R} \mid \big(\forall y \in \mathsf{domain}(F) \mid$
$\delta >_{\mathbb{R}} 0_{\mathbb{R}}\ \&\ \big((\varepsilon >_{\mathbb{R}} 0_{\mathbb{R}}\ \&\ \delta >_{\mathbb{R}} |x -_{\mathbb{C}} y|_{\mathbb{C}})$
$\rightarrow (\varepsilon >_{\mathbb{R}} |F[x] -_{\mathbb{C}} F[y]|_{\mathbb{C}})\big)\big)\big)\big)\big)$

Def 94 : [Continuous complex-valued function on complex Euclidean $n$-space]
$\mathsf{Is\_continuous\_CEnF}(F, N) \leftrightarrow_{\text{Def}}$
$F \subseteq \big(\mathbf{E}_{\mathbb{C}}(N)\times\mathbb{C}\big)\ \&\ \mathsf{Svm}(F)\ \&$
$\big(\forall x \in \mathsf{domain}(F) \mid \big(\forall \varepsilon \in \mathbb{R} \mid \big(\exists \delta \in \mathbb{R} \mid \big(\forall y \in \mathsf{domain}(F) \mid$
$\delta >_{\mathbb{R}} 0_{\mathbb{R}}\ \&\ \big((\varepsilon >_{\mathbb{R}} 0_{\mathbb{R}}\ \&\ \delta >_{\mathbb{R}} \|x -_{\mathbb{CF}} y\|_{\mathbb{C}})$
$\rightarrow (\varepsilon >_{\mathbb{R}} |F[x] -_{\mathbb{C}} F[y]|_{\mathbb{C}})\big)\big)\big)\big)\big)$

It is now easy to extend the 'difference-and-diagonal trick' used to define the derivative of real-valued functions of a real variable to the complex case. Again we consider pairs of functions $f, df$, this time complex-valued functions of a complex variable $x$, and form the function $g$ of two complex variables $x$ and $y$ which equals the difference-quotient $(f[x] - f[y])/(x - y)$ if $x$ and $y$ are different, but

$df[x]$ if $x = y$. Then $f$ is said to be (continuously) differentiable in its domain $D$ if there exists some continuous function $df$ having the same domain as $f$ such that the function $g$, formed in this way, is continuous on the product set of $D$ with itself.

Def 95 : [Difference-and-diagonal trick, complex case] $\mathsf{CDD}(F, Df) =_{\mathrm{Def}}$
$\{$ **if** $x[0] \neq x[1]$ **then** $(F[x[0]] -_{\mathbb{C}} F[x[1]])/_{\mathbb{C}} (x[0] -_{\mathbb{C}} x[1])$
**else** $Df[x[0]]$ **end if** $: x \in \mathbf{E}_{\mathbb{C}}(2) \}$

Def 96 : [Derivative of function of a complex variable] $\mathsf{CDer}(F) =_{\mathrm{Def}}$
$\mathsf{arb}(\{ df \in \mathbb{CF} \mid \mathsf{domain}(F) = \mathsf{domain}(df)\ \&$
$\mathsf{Is\_continuous\_CEnF}(\mathsf{CDD}(F, df)_{|\mathsf{domain}(F) \times \mathsf{domain}(F)}, 2) \})$

It has been known since the 1821 work of Cauchy that the consequences of differentiability for complex functions of a complex variable (defined in an open subset of the complex plane) are much stronger than the corresponding assumption in the real case, a fact for which our target theorem, the Cauchy integral theorem, is central. Here a subset of the complex plane is said to be *open* if it contains some sufficiently small disk around each point of its domain. Functions of a complex variable differentiable in an open set are said to be *analytic* functions of the complex variable. One such function, of particular importance, is the complex exponential function, which can be defined as the unique analytic function exp having the entire complex plane as its domain which is equal to its own derivative and takes on the unit complex value at the zero point of the complex plane. The two mathematical constants e and $\pi$ can both be defined in terms of this function, in the following way: e is the value which exp takes on at the point $[1_{\mathbb{R}}, 0_{\mathbb{R}}]$ of the complex plane, and $\pi$ is the smallest real positive $x$ for which $\mathsf{exp}([0_{\mathbb{R}}, x])$ is $-_{\mathbb{R}}(1_{\mathbb{R}})$. That is, we define $\pi$ as the smallest positive root of Euler's famous, indeed ineffable, formula $\mathsf{e}^{\mathsf{i} * \pi} = -1$.

Def 97 : [Open set in the complex plane] $\mathsf{Is\_open\_C\_set}(S) \leftrightarrow_{\mathrm{Def}}$
$(\forall z \in S \mid (\exists \varepsilon \in \mathbb{R} \mid (\varepsilon >_{\mathbb{R}} 0_{\mathbb{R}}\ \&$
$(\forall w \in S \mid (\varepsilon >_{\mathbb{R}} |z -_{\mathbb{C}} w|_{\mathbb{C}}) \rightarrow (w \in S)))))$

Def 98 : [Analytic function of a complex variable] $\mathsf{Is\_analytic\_CF}(F) \leftrightarrow_{\mathrm{Def}}$
$\mathsf{Is\_continuous\_CF}(F)\ \&\ \mathsf{Is\_open\_C\_set}(\mathsf{domain}(F))\ \&\ \mathsf{CDer}(F) \neq 0$

Def 99 : [Complex exponential function] $\mathsf{C\_exp\_fcn} =_{\mathrm{Def}}$
$\mathsf{arb}(\{ F \subseteq \mathbb{C} \times \mathbb{C} : \mathsf{domain}(F) = \mathbb{C}\ \&\ \mathsf{Is\_analytic\_CF}(F)\ \&\ \mathsf{CDer}(F) = F\ \&$
$F[[0_{\mathbb{R}}, 0_{\mathbb{R}}]] = [1_{\mathbb{R}}, 0_{\mathbb{R}}] \})$

Def 100 : [The constant $\pi$] $\pi =_{\mathrm{Def}}$
$\mathsf{arb}(\{ x \in \mathbb{R} \mid x >_{\mathbb{R}} 0_{\mathbb{R}}\ \&\ \mathsf{C\_exp\_fcn}([0_{\mathbb{R}}, x]) = [-_{\mathbb{R}}(1_{\mathbb{R}}), 0_{\mathbb{R}}]\ \&$
$(\forall y \in \mathbb{R} \mid (\mathsf{C\_exp\_fcn}([0_{\mathbb{R}}, y]) = [-_{\mathbb{R}}(1_{\mathbb{R}}), 0_{\mathbb{R}}]) \rightarrow (0_{\mathbb{R}} >_{\mathbb{R}} y \vee y \geqslant_{\mathbb{R}} x)) \})$

To move on to the statement, and eventually the proof, of Cauchy's integral theorem we must define the notion of 'complex line integral' involved in that theorem. For this, we need various slight modifications of the foregoing material, and in particular the notions of continuity and differentiability for complex-valued functions of a real variable. These involve the following easy modifications of the 'epsilon-delta' definition and the difference-and-diagonal trick described above. A ('closed') real interval is the set of all points lying between two real values (including these values themselves). A *continuously differentiable curve* in the complex plane is a continuous complex-valued function defined on an interval of the real line which is continuously differentiable on its domain. The complex line integral of a complex-valued function $f$ defined on such a curve is defined by taking the complex product of $f$ by the derivative of the curve, integrating the real part (i.e. pointwise first component) and the imaginary part (pointwise second component) of the resulting product function, and rejoining these two values into a complex number.

Def 101 : [Continuous complex function on the reals] $\mathsf{Is\_continuous\_CoRF}(F)$
$\leftrightarrow_{\mathrm{Def}} F \subseteq (\mathbb{R}\times\mathbb{C})$ & $\mathsf{Svm}(F)$ &
$(\forall x \in \mathsf{domain}(F) \mid (\forall \varepsilon \in \mathbb{R} \mid (\exists \delta \in \mathbb{R} \mid (\forall y \in \mathsf{domain}(F) \mid$
$((\delta >_{\mathbb{R}} 0_{\mathbb{R}})\ \&\ (\varepsilon >_{\mathbb{R}} 0_{\mathbb{R}})\ \&\ \delta >_{\mathbb{R}} |x -_{\mathbb{R}} y|)$
$\rightarrow (\varepsilon >_{\mathbb{R}} \|F[x] -_{\mathbb{C}} F[y]\|_{\mathbb{C}})))))$

Def 102 : [Difference-and-diagonal trick, real-to-complex case] $\mathsf{CRDD}(F, Df) =_{\mathrm{Def}}$
$\{$ **if** $x[0] \neq x[1]$ **then**
$(F(x[0]) -_{\mathbb{C}} F(x[1]))/_{\mathbb{C}}(x[0] -_{\mathbb{C}} x[1])$
**else** $Df(x[0])$ **end if** $: x \in \mathbf{E}(2)\}$

Def 103 : [Continuous complex function on $\mathbf{E}(n)$] $\mathsf{Is\_continuous\_CREnF}(F, N)$
$\leftrightarrow_{\mathrm{Def}} F \subseteq (\mathbf{E}(N)\times\mathbb{C})$ & $\mathsf{Svm}(F)$ &
$(\forall x \in \mathsf{domain}(F) \mid (\forall \varepsilon \in \mathbb{R} \mid (\exists \delta \in \mathbb{R} \mid (\forall y \in \mathsf{domain}(F) \mid$
$((\delta >_{\mathbb{R}} 0_{\mathbb{R}})\ \&\ (\varepsilon >_{\mathbb{R}} 0_{\mathbb{R}})\ \&\ (\delta >_{\mathbb{R}} \|x -_{\mathbb{RF}} y\|))$
$\rightarrow (\varepsilon >_{\mathbb{R}} \|F[x] -_{\mathbb{CF}} F[y]\|_{\mathbb{C}})))))$

Def 104 : [Derivative of complex function of a real variable] $\mathsf{CRDer}(F) =_{\mathrm{Def}}$
$\mathsf{arb}(\{df \in \mathbb{CF} \mid \mathsf{domain}(F) = \mathsf{domain}(df)$ &
$\mathsf{Is\_continuous\_CREnF}(\mathsf{CRDD}(F, df)_{|\mathsf{domain}(F)\times\mathsf{domain}(F)}, 2)\})$

Def 105 : [Real Interval] $\mathsf{Interval}(A, B) =_{\mathrm{Def}} \{x \in \mathbb{R} \mid x \geqslant_{\mathbb{R}} A\ \&\ B >_{\mathbb{R}} x\}$

Def 106 : [Continuously differentiable curve in the complex plane]
$\mathsf{Is\_CD\_curv}(F, A, B)$
$\leftrightarrow_{\mathrm{Def}}$ $\mathsf{Is\_continuous\_CoRF}(F)$ & $\mathsf{domain}(F) = \mathsf{Interval}(A, B)$ &
$\mathsf{Is\_continuous\_CoRF}(\mathsf{CRDer}(F))$

Def 107 : [Complex line integral] $\oint_A^B(F, Crv) =_{\text{Def}}$

$$[\int(\{[x, \textbf{if } x \notin \mathsf{Interval}(A, B)] \textbf{ then } 0_{\mathbb{R}} \textbf{ else } (F[Crv[x]] *_{\mathbb{C}} \mathsf{CRDer}(Crv)[x])^{[1]} : x \in \mathbb{R}\}),$$
$$\int(\{[x, \textbf{if } x \notin \mathsf{Interval}(A, B)] \textbf{ then } 0_{\mathbb{R}} \textbf{ else } (F[Crv[x]] *_{\mathbb{C}} \mathsf{CRDer}(Crv)[x])^{[2]} : x \in \mathbb{R}\})]$$

Now finally we can state the Cauchy integral theorem and the Cauchy integral formula derived from it. The Cauchy integral formula states that if $f$ is an analytic function defined in some open subset of the complex plane, and if $c_1$ and $c_2$ are two continuously differentiable closed curves (i.e. curves which end where they start), both having ranges in $s$, and if each of the values of $c_1$ differs sufficiently little from the corresponding value of $c_2$, then the two line integrals of $f$ over the two curves must be equal. This is proved by deforming the first curve smoothly into the second, and proving that the derivative of the resulting line integral in the deformation parameter must be zero: a function of a real parameter whose derivative is zero in an interval must be constant in that interval.

To avoid topological complications we state the Cauchy integral formula, which follows from the Cauchy integral theorem, in a somewhat special case: If $f$ is a function analytic in an open set including the closed unit circle of the complex plane, and $z$ is any point interior to that circle, then the line integral of the quotient $f[w]/(2 * \pi) * (w - z)$ over the unit circle is always $f[z]$. Note that in the formal statement of this theorem given below, the unit circle is represented by the curve $w = \mathsf{C\_exp\_fcn}([0_{\mathbb{R}}, x])$, where the real parameter value $x$ varies between 0 and $2 * \pi$. Though we do not follow up on its possible generalizations, Cauchy integral formula can be stated much more generally: it is true whenever $f$ is analytic in a domain of any shape including the whole of any smooth closed complex curve in the complex plane and its interior, provided that $w$ is a point interior to the curve about which the curve winds just once. But to state and prove the Cauchy integral formula in this generalized form we would need to develop the theory of winding numbers, which would extend the present work beyond its appointed length.

Theorem : [Cauchy integral theorem]

$$\mathsf{Is\_analytic}_{\mathbb{CF}}(F) \rightarrow (\exists \varepsilon \in \mathbb{R} \mid \varepsilon >_{\mathbb{R}} 0_{\mathbb{R}} \,\&\, (\forall crv_1, crv_2 \mid \mathsf{Is\_CD\_curv}(crv_1, 0_{\mathbb{R}}, 1_{\mathbb{R}}) \,\&\, \mathsf{Is\_CD\_curv}(crv_2, 0_{\mathbb{R}}, 1_{\mathbb{R}}) \,\&\, crv_1[0_{\mathbb{R}}] = crv_1[1_{\mathbb{R}}] \,\&\, crv_2[0_{\mathbb{R}}] = crv_2[1_{\mathbb{R}}] \,\&\, (\forall \mathsf{x} \in \mathsf{Interval}(0_{\mathbb{R}}, 1_{\mathbb{R}}) \mid \varepsilon \geqslant_{\mathbb{R}} |crv_1[\mathsf{x}] -_{\mathbb{C}} crv_2[\mathsf{x}]|_{\mathbb{C}}) \rightarrow \oint_{0_{\mathbb{R}}}^{1_{\mathbb{R}}}(F, crv_1) = \oint_{0_{\mathbb{R}}}^{1_{\mathbb{R}}}(F, crv_2)))$$

Theorem : [Cauchy integral formula]

$$(\mathsf{Is\_analytic}_{\mathbb{CF}}(F) \,\&\, \mathsf{domain}(F) \supseteq \{z \in \mathbb{C} : 1_{\mathbb{R}} \geqslant_{\mathbb{R}} |z|_{\mathbb{C}}\}) \rightarrow (\forall z \in \mathbb{C} \mid (1_{\mathbb{R}} >_{\mathbb{R}} |z|_{\mathbb{C}}) \rightarrow F[z] = \oint_{0_{\mathbb{R}}}^{\pi +_{\mathbb{R}} \pi}(\{[x, F[x]/_{\mathbb{C}}(x -_{\mathbb{C}} z)] : x \in \mathbb{C} \setminus \{z\}\}, \{[x, \mathsf{C\_exp\_fcn}([0_{\mathbb{R}}, x])] : x \in \mathbb{R}\}))$$

# References

[Bri97] Bridges, D.S.: Foundations of Real and Abstract Analysis. Graduate Texts in Mathematics, vol. 174. Springer, Berlin (1997)

[Can72] Cantor, G.: Über die Ausdehnung eines Satzes aus der Theorie der trigonometrischen Reihen. Math. Ann. **5**, 123–132 (1872)

[Lan66] Landau, E.: Foundation of Analysis. The Arithmetic of Whole, Rational, Irrational and Complex Numbers, 3rd edn. Chelsea, New York (1966)

[OS02] Omodeo, E.G., Schwartz, J.T.: A 'Theory' mechanism for a proof-verifier based on first-order set theory. In: Kakas, A., Sadri, F. (eds.) Computational Logic: Logic Programming and Beyond—Essays in honour of Bob Kowalski, Part II, vol. 2408, pp. 214–230. Springer, Berlin (2002)

[Tar24] Tarski, A.: Sur les ensembles fini. Fundam. Math. **VI**, 45–95 (1924)

# Chapter 6
# Undecidability and Unsolvability

For completeness sake and to enjoy the intellectual insight that these results provide, we derive several of the main classical results on undecidability and unsolvability in this chapter.

## 6.1 Chaitin's Theorem

Some of the most famous results concerning undecidability and unsolvability are easy to prove using an elegant line of argument due to Gregory Chaitin. Define the *information content* $I(s)$ of a binary sequence $s$ as the length (measured, like $s$, in bits) of the shortest program $P$ which prints $s$ and then stops. $P$ should be written in some agreed-upon programming language $L$. We will see below that changing $L$ to some other language $L'$ leaves $I(s)$ unchanged except for addition of a quantity bounded by a constant $C(L, L')$ depending only on the languages $L$ and $L'$. Thus, asymptotically speaking, $I(s)$ is independent of $L$.

Let $|s|$ designate the length of the binary sequence $s$. Then, since $s$ can always be printed by the program '*print*($s$)' (in which $s$ appears as an explicit constant), it is clear that $I(s)$ must be bounded above by $|s| + C$, where $C$ depends only on the programming language $L$ being used. Of course, this upper bound is sometimes far too large, since there are sequences $s$ whose information content is much less than their length. For example, the information content of the decimal sequence consisting of the digit 1 followed by one trillion zeros is not much larger than that of its defining expression $10^{10^{24}}$, whose binary form is only a few dozen bits long. On the other hand, a simple counting argument shows that most sequences of length $n$ must have an information content close to $n$. Indeed, the number of programs representable by binary sequences of length at most $n - c$ is less than $2^{n-c+1}$, and not all of these programs print anything or stop, so the number of binary sequences of information content at most $n - c$ (i.e. the set of outputs of all these programs) is less than $2^{n-c+1}$. But, since the number of sequences of length $n$ is $2^n$, it follows immediately that the fraction of these sequences having information content no more

J.T. Schwartz et al., *Computational Logic and Set Theory*,
DOI 10.1007/978-0-85729-808-9_6, © Springer-Verlag London Limited 2011

than $n - c$ is at most $2^{-c+1}$. For $c$ large enough this fraction will be very small, so most binary sequences of length $n$ must have a larger information content.

Chaitin's theorem can now be stated as follows.

**Theorem 6.1** *If $A$ is any consistent set of axioms for mathematics, then there is a constant $c = c(A)$, depending only on $A$ (and, indeed, only on the information content of $A$), such that no statement of the form $I(s) > c$ can be proved using only the axioms $A$.*

*Proof* The proof is deliciously simple. For any constant $k$, let $P(k)$ be the program which

1. Generates all possible sequences of formulae, in order of increasing length.
2. Checks these sequences to verify that their component formulae are syntactically well-formed and that each formula in the sequence follows directly (in terms of the rules of logical inference available) from the formulae which precede it. Sequences not having this property should immediately be dropped, and $P$ should go on to examine the next sequence in turn.

   (As we have already emphasized, it is inherent in the very definition of formal logic that there must exist procedures for testing the well-formedness of formulae, and for determining whether one formula is an immediate consequence of others, since otherwise the logical system used would not meet Leibniz' fundamental criterion that arguments in it must be 'safe and really analytic'.)
3. Checks the final formula in each surviving sequence (this is the 'theorem proved') to determine whether it has the form '$I(s) > k$'. If so, it prints $s$ and stops. If not, it goes on to examine the next sequence in turn.

Observe that the length of the program $P(k)$ equals $L + \log k$, for a suitable constant $L$, if we assume that a binary encoding of $k$ occurs in $P(k)$. Let $c$ be any constant such that $c > L + \log c$.

If there exists any proof of a statement of the form '$I(s) > c$' then plainly the procedure $P(c)$ will eventually find a statement of this form, along with its proof. But then our program, whose length is less than $c$, prints a sequence $s$ whose information content is provably greater than $c$, so that $s$ cannot be printed by any program of length at most $c$. Our logical system is therefore inconsistent, contrary to assumption. □

The following variant of Chaitin's theorem can be proved in much the same way.

**Theorem 6.2** *There exists no program $R$ which can determine the information content $I(s)$ of an arbitrary binary sequence $s$.*

*Proof* Suppose that $R$ exists, and write the program $P$ which

1. generates all binary sequences $s$, in order of increasing length;
2. uses $R$ to determine their information content;

3. stops when this content is seen to be large, say one million, and prints the sequence $s$; otherwise continues.

Since there are sequences of information content at least one million, $P$ will eventually find one such and print it. But then this sequence is printed by the program $P$ that we have just described, whose length is clearly much less than one million bits. Hence we have a contradiction, proving that $R$ cannot exist. □

To see that the information content $I(s)$ of a binary sequence varies only slightly when the programming language $L$ used to define it is changed, we simply argue as follows. Programs written in any language $L$ can be compiled to run on any adequate hardware system $S$. The size of the compiler required depends only on $L$, and so can be written as $c(L)$. The instructions of $S$ can be simulated in any other reasonable programming language $L'$, and the size of the interpreter required for this depends only on $L'$ and can therefore be written as $c'(L')$. This gives us a way of transforming any program $P$ of length $k$ and written in the language $L$ into a program $P'$ of length $k + c(L) + c'(L')$ written in the language $L'$ which produces the same results. Note also that $P'$ eventually halts if and only if $P$ does. Hence the minimum-length program in $L'$ for producing $s$ is of length no greater than $k + c(L) + c'(L')$. Since this same argument applies in the reverse direction, it follows that $|I(s) - I'(s)|$ is bounded above by a constant.

### 6.1.1 Undecidability Results Derivable from Chaitin's Theorem

It is now easy to derive the following results, some directly from Chaitin's theorem and the variant of it which we have stated, others by adapting Chaitin's line of argument.

**Theorem 6.3** (Existence of undecidable statements) *Let $A$ be any consistent set of axioms for mathematics. Then there exists a mathematical formula $F$ which is such that neither $F$ nor its negation $\neg F$ can be proved using only the axioms $A$.*

*Proof* Consider the set of all binary sequences $s$ of length $c + k$ whose information content $I(s)$ exceeds $c$, where $c$ is the constant $c$ appearing in Chaitin's theorem and $k$ will be specified below. We know by Chaitin's theorem that none of the formulae $I(s) > c$ involving these sequences $s$ can be proved (even though all are true). Consider the set of such sequences $s$ for which '$\neg(I(s) > c)$' can be proved (several such proofs may be possible without inconsistency, even though all these statements are false). There can be at most $2^{c+1}$ such sequences, since we can prove (and indeed, have proved) that the total number of sequences of information content less than $c$ is at most $2^c$. For all the others, i.e. for all but a fraction $2^{-k}$ of statements of the form $I(s) > c$, neither the statement nor its negative is provable. So all these statements are undecidable in terms of the axioms $A$. □

**Theorem 6.4** (Turing: Unsolvability of the halting problem) *There exists no procedure $R$ which, given the text of a program $P$, determines whether $P$ eventually halts.*

*Proof* Let $s$ be a binary sequence. Set up the program $P$ which

1. generates all programs $Q$ of length up to the length $|s|$ of $s$;
2. uses $R$ to determine whether $Q$ eventually halts, and if not immediately eliminates $Q$;
3. progressively increments an integer number_of_steps, and then runs each of the remaining programs $Q$ (i.e., under simulation) for number_of_steps, determining whether it has stopped or not, and if so whether it has printed $s$;
4. stops immediately once a program which prints $s$ is found; otherwise continues;
5. stops once all the programs $Q$ to be examined have halted.

It is clear from the description of this program that it will eventually halt (since it simulates only a finite number of programs, each of which eventually halts). When $P$ halts it will have determined the information content of $s$ (possibly by showing that this is at least the length of $s$). But, by the variant of Chaitin's theorem proved above, this is impossible. □

**Theorem 6.5** (Nonexistence of a decision algorithm for elementary arithmetic) *There exists no procedure $R$ which, given a (quantified) formula of elementary arithmetic, determines whether or not $P$ is true.*

*Proof* Since programs written in any programming language can be compiled to run (in assembly language) on any adequate hardware system, it follows from Turing's theorem that there exists no procedure which, given some adequate computer system $S$, can determine whether an arbitrary assembly-language program for $S$ stops. We take $S$ to be a system easily modelled using arithmetic operations only. Specifically, we model the memory $M$ of $S$ as a large positive integer divided into $W$-bit 'words' (so that the $j$th word of $M$ is extracted by the operation

$$\left(M/2^{jW}\right) \bmod 2^W .$$

Each of the registers of $S$, including its 'instruction location counter' ILC, is then modelled by an additional $W$-bit integer, which we can store at fixed low addresses in the memory integer $M$. To simulate one cycle of $S$'s operation, we simply extract the instruction word addressed by ILC using the formula just displayed, use a similar formula to extract the memory words this instruction involves, and calculate the instruction result, which can always be expressed as a Boolean, and hence algebraic, combination of the registers it involves. The next value of ILC can be calculated in the same way for the same reason. To store a $W$-bit word $x$ into memory location $j$, we simply change the integer $M$ into

$$\left(M - \left(M \bmod 2^{jW}\right)\right) + X\,2^{(j-1)W} + \left(M \bmod 2^{(j-1)W}\right).$$

This makes it plain that the effect of any individual operation of $S$ can be expressed as an elementary operation on the integers used to represent the states of $S$.

Hence, if the state of $S$ on its $j$th cycle is $M$, then the state of $S$ on its $(j+1)$st cycle will be $F(M)$, where $F$ is some elementary arithmetic operation whose details reflect the architectural details of $S$.

Now suppose that the memory of $S$ is initialized to $M_0$, and start $S$ running. It will eventually halt iff there exists a sequence of $M_i$ integers satisfying the quantified but otherwise elementary arithmetic formula

$$(i = 0 \to M_i = M_0) \,\&\, \big(\forall i \mid M_{i+1} = F(M_i)\big) \,\&\, \big(\exists j \mid H(M_j)\big),$$

where $H(M)$ is the elementary arithmetic predicate which expresses the condition that the operation executed when $S$ is in state $M$ is the 'Halt' instruction. So, if there existed an algorithm which could decide the truth of all formulae of the kind just displayed, we could use it to determine whether an arbitrary program $P$ eventually halts, contradicting Turing's theorem. □

**Theorem 6.6** (Church: Nonexistence of a decision algorithm for predicate calculus) *There exists no procedure R which, given a (quantified) sentence of pure predicate calculus, determines whether or not P is valid, i.e. true irrespective of the meanings assigned to the constants and function symbols which appear in it.*

*Proof* We can encode the integers (in 'monadic' notation) as

$$0, \mathsf{Succ}(0), \mathsf{Succ}\big(\mathsf{Succ}(0)\big), \mathsf{Succ}\big(\mathsf{Succ}\big(\mathsf{Succ}(0)\big)\big), \ldots$$

In this universe of data objects, every integer except 0 has a predecessor $\mathsf{Pred}(n)$ such that $n = \mathsf{Succ}(\mathsf{Pred}(n))$. We can then express all other arithmetic functions recursively starting only with the constant '0' and the function symbols 'Succ' and 'Pred', e.g. as

**function** $\mathsf{plus}(n, m)$; **return if** $m = 0$ **then** $n$
  **else** $\mathsf{Succ}\big(\mathsf{plus}(n, \mathsf{Pred}(m))\big)$ **end if** ; **end** plus;

**function** $\mathsf{times}(n, m)$; **return if** $m = 0$ **then** 0
  **else** $\mathsf{plus}\big(\mathsf{times}(n, \mathsf{Pred}(m)), n\big)$ **end if** ; **end** times;

**function** $\mathsf{exp}(n, m)$; **return if** $m = 0$ **then** $\mathsf{Succ}(0)$
  **else** $\mathsf{times}\big(\mathsf{exp}(n, \mathsf{Pred}(m)), n\big)$ **end if** ; **end** exp;

**function** $\mathsf{minus}(n, m)$; **return if** $n = 0$ **then** 0 **elseif** $m = 0$ **then** $n$
  **else** $\mathsf{minus}\big(\mathsf{Pred}(n), \mathsf{Pred}(m)\big)$ **end if** ; **end** minus;

**function** $\mathsf{gt}(n, m)$; **return** $\mathsf{minus}(n, m) \neq 0$; **end** gt;

**function** len_le$(n, m)$; **return** $\mathsf{gt}\big(\mathsf{exp}\big(\mathsf{Succ}\big(\mathsf{Succ}(0)\big), m\big), n\big)$; **end** len_le;

**function** $\mathsf{div}(n, m)$; **return if** $m = 0 \vee \mathsf{gt}(m, n)$ **then** 0
  **else** $\mathsf{Succ}\big(\mathsf{div}\big(\mathsf{minus}(n, m), m\big)\big)$; **end** div;

**function** $\mathsf{rem}(n, m)$; **return** $\mathsf{minus}\big(n, \mathsf{times}\big(m, \mathsf{div}(n, m)\big)\big)$; **end** rem.

Continuing in the same way, we can build up a recursive function

$$\mathsf{stops\_and\_outputs}(P, m, s)$$

which is true iff the program $P$ (written in the assembly language of the abstract computer which appears in the proof of the immediately preceding theorem "Nonexistence of a decision algorithm for elementary arithmetic") halts after $m$ steps, having then produced the output $s$.

Such recursive functions can readily be mirrored in predicate calculus, e.g. by the quantified predicate statements

$$\begin{aligned}
&(\forall n \mid (n = 0 \vee \mathsf{Succ}(\mathsf{Pred}(n)) = n))\\
&(\forall n \mid \mathsf{Succ}(n) \neq 0) \;\&\; (\forall n, m \mid \mathsf{Succ}(n) = \mathsf{Succ}(m) \rightarrow n = m)\\
&(\forall n, m \mid \mathsf{Plus}(n, 0) = n \;\&\; \mathsf{Plus}(n, \mathsf{Succ}(m)) = \mathsf{Succ}(\mathsf{Plus}(n, m)))\\
&(\forall n, m \mid \mathsf{Times}(n, 0) = 0 \;\&\; \mathsf{Times}(n, \mathsf{Succ}(m)) = \mathsf{Plus}(\mathsf{Times}(n, m), n))\\
&(\forall n, m \mid \mathsf{Exp}(n, 0) = \mathsf{Succ}(0) \;\&\; \mathsf{Exp}(n, \mathsf{Succ}(m)) = \mathsf{Times}(\mathsf{Exp}(n, m), n))\\
&(\forall n, m \mid \mathsf{Minus}(0, m) = 0 \;\&\; \mathsf{Minus}(n, 0) = n \;\&\\
&\qquad\qquad\qquad \mathsf{Minus}(\mathsf{Succ}(n), \mathsf{Succ}(m)) = \mathsf{Minus}(n, m))\\
&(\forall n, m \mid \mathsf{Gt}(n, m) \leftrightarrow \mathsf{Minus}(n, m) \neq 0)\\
&(\forall n, m \mid \mathsf{Len_le}(n, m) \leftrightarrow \mathsf{Gt}(\mathsf{Exp}(\mathsf{Succ}(\mathsf{Succ}(0)), m), n))\\
&(\forall n, m \mid (\mathsf{Gt}(n, m) \rightarrow \mathsf{Div}(n, m) = 0) \;\&\; ((\neg \mathsf{Gt}(n, m)) \rightarrow\\
&\qquad\qquad\qquad \mathsf{Div}(n, m) = \mathsf{Succ}(\mathsf{Div}(\mathsf{Minus}(n, m), m))))\\
&(\forall n, m \mid \mathsf{Rem}(n, m) = \mathsf{Minus}(n, \mathsf{Times}(m, \mathsf{Div}(n, m))))
\end{aligned}$$

and so on, up to the point at which the function $\mathsf{stops\_and\_outputs}(P, m, s)$ is mirrored by a similar predicate formula. Since predicate substitution of formulae for variables, followed by simplification, generalizes the process of recursive evaluation of the procedures listed above, each recursive evaluation translates immediately into a predicate proof, so that whenever one of our functions, e.g. $\mathsf{stops\_and\_outputs}(P_0, m_0, s_0)$ evaluates to true for given constant values $P_0$, $m_0$, $s_0$ there will exist a predicate-calculus proof of the statement

$$\mathsf{stops\_and\_outputs}(P_0, m_0, s_0).$$

(This observation appears in Sect. 4.3.10.1 as the 'Mirroring Lemma'.)

Now choose any sufficiently large integer $k$, and consider the predicate statement

$$\begin{aligned}
&(\exists P, n \mid \mathsf{Stops_and_outputs}(P, n, s) \;\&\; \mathsf{Len_le}(P, k)\\
&\qquad \& \;(\neg \mathsf{Len_le}(s, \mathsf{Times}(\mathsf{Succ}(\mathsf{Succ}(0)), k)))).
\end{aligned}$$

Call this formula $F$. It simply states that the length of $s$ is at least $2k$ and that the information content of $s$ is no more than half its length $k = (2k)/2$. We have seen at the start of the present section that $F$ can only be true for a small minority $N$ of all sufficiently long sequences. This fact was established by an entirely elementary counting argument, readily translatable into predicate-calculus terms.

It follows that, given any sufficient large $k$, the formula $F$ can only be proved for a small minority of the sequences $s_0$ of length $k$. Indeed, if $F$ could be proved for too many individual sequences $s_0$, the count $N$ would be exceeded, and so the Peano axioms of elementary arithmetic would be self-contradictory within predicate calculus. Hence for any sufficiently large $k$ there will exist many $s$ for which $F = F(s)$ is not provable.

Now suppose that a procedure $R$ for deciding the provability of predicate-calculus formulae exists. Using $R$, construct the program which

1. examines all programs $P$, and sequences $s$ of length at least $k$, in order of increasing total length;
2. uses $R$ to determine whether $F(s)$ is provable;
3. stops as soon as it finds an $s$ such that $F(s)$ is not provable, and prints $s$.

Since we have seen that there must exist many $s$ such that $F(s)$ is not provable, this procedure must eventually stop and print some such $s$. The $s$ which is printed must have complexity at least $k$. Indeed, if this were false, there would exist a program $P_0$ of length less than $k$ which stopped after some finite number $n_0$ of steps and printed $s$. Hence the value of the recursive functions stops_and_outputs($P_0, n_0, s$), and len_le($P_0, k$) would be true, implying, as we have seen above, that

$$\text{Stops\_and\_outputs}(P_0, n_0, s)\ \&\ \text{Len\_le}(P_0, k)$$

is provable; but we have chosen an $s$ for which this is false.

Hence $s$ has complexity at least $k$. But it is the output of the short program listed above. This is a contradiction for all sufficiently large $k$. Hence $R$ cannot exist, and Church's theorem follows. □

## 6.2 The Two Gödel Theorems

Next we turn to the proof of Gödel's two famous theorems. These rest upon the construction of a trick proposition $G$ which asserts its own unprovability, and which therefore can be regarded as a technically precise rendering of the ancient paradoxical sentence 'This sentence is false'. Note that this sentence is troublesome for any system of formalized discourse in which it or anything like it can be given meaning, since it plainly can neither be true nor false.

Gödel's first theorem (in the improved form given to it by Rosser) asserts that (if we assume that the logical system in which $G$ is being considered is consistent) neither $G$ nor its negative can be proved; hence $G$ must be undecidable. (This is no longer as surprising as it was when first discovered by Gödel, since theorems like Chaitin's show the existence of large classes of undecidable statements.) Gödel's second theorem uses much the same statement $G$ as an auxiliary to prove that the logical theory containing $G$ cannot be used to prove its own consistency.

All of Gödel's reasonings will become easy once we have clarified the foundations on which they rest. Since the line of argument used is somewhat more delicate than those needed in the preceding sections of this chapter, we begin with a more careful discussion of technical foundations than was given above. This more detailed discussion continues to emphasize the basic role of set theory. Note that the preparatory considerations which follow fall naturally into two parts, a first 'programming part' which is followed by a short discussion of the relationship of 'programming' to 'proof'.

## *6.2.1 Programming Considerations*

The mechanism of computation with hereditarily finite sets discussed earlier (cf. Sect. 4.3.10) can easily be used to define strings and such basic operations on them as concatenation, slicing, and substring location. To this end, we use the definition of 'sequence of elements of a set $s$' given previously. We apply this to define the notion of 'a sequence of decimal digits', and of the integer value that such a sequence represents. This is done as follows:

```
function two(); return {∅, {∅}}; end two;

function four(); return sum(two(), two()); end four;

function ten(); return sum(sum(two(), four()), four()); end ten;

function is_decimal_sequence(s);
    return is_sequence_of(s, ten());
end is_decimal_sequence;

function decimal_value_of(s);
    return if (s = ∅) ∨ ¬is_decimal_sequence(s) then ∅
        else sum(last_of(s), product(ten(),
            decimal_value_of(s less ordered_pair(prev(#s), last_of(s)))))
        end if;
end decimal_value_of.
```

The standard abbreviations 0, 1, 2, 3, 4, 5, 6, 7, 8, 9 for the ten members of ten() can now be introduced:

$$0 = \emptyset,\ 1 = \text{next}(0),\ 2 = \text{next}(1),\ 3 = \text{next}(2),\ 4 = \text{next}(3),\ 5 = \text{next}(4), \ldots$$

along with the convention that a sequence $d_0 d_1 \ldots d_n$ of such digit characters designates the decimal_value_of the decimal sequence

$$\{\text{ordered\_pair}(0, d_0), \text{ordered\_pair}(1, d_1), \ldots, \text{ordered\_pair}(n, d_n)\}. \quad (6.1)$$

We also adopt the 'ASCII' convention that a character is simply an integer less than 256, and a string is simply a sequence of characters. That is,

**function** is_string($s$); **return** is_sequence_of($s$, 256); **end** is_string.

We also adopt the standard manner of writing strings within double quotes and the convention that a quoted sequence "$d_0d_1\dots d_n$" of characters designates the sequence (6.1). For example, "Abba" designates the sequence

$$\{\text{ordered\_pair}(0,65),\ \text{ordered\_pair}(1,98),\ \text{ordered\_pair}(2,98),\ \text{ordered\_pair}(3,97)\}.$$

The string concatenation, slicing, and substring location functions now have the following forms.

```
function shift(s, n);
    return if s = ∅ then ∅
        else shift( s less arb(s), n ) with
            ordered_pair( sum( arb(s)^[1], n), arb(s)^[2] ) end if ;
end shift;

function concatenate(s1, s2);
    return union( s1, shift(s2, #s1) );
end concatenate;

function slice_starting(s, n);
    return if ¬is_sequence(s) then ∅
        elseif n ∈ #s then
            slice_starting( restriction( s, prev(#s) ), n ) with
                ordered_pair( minus( prev(#s), n ), last_of(s) )
    else ∅ end if ;
end slice_starting

function slice(s, n, m);
    return slice_starting( restriction(s, m), n );
end slice;

function location_in(s1, s2);
    return if s1 = ∅ then 0
        elseif #s2 ∈ #s1 then next( #s2 )
        elseif slice( s2, 0, prev(#s1) ) = s1 then 0
        else next(location_in( s1, slice_starting(s2, 1))) end if ;
end location_in.
```

The next two functions, respectively, define the result of appending an additional component to each of the elements of a set $s$ of sequences, and the collection of all ordered subsequences of a sequence $s$.

```
function append_to_elements(s, x);
    return if s = ∅ then ∅
        else append_to_elements(s less arb(s), x) with
            concatenate(arb(s), {ordered_pair(0, x)}) end if ;
end append_to_elements;

function subsequences(s);
    return if ¬is_sequence(s) then ∅
        elseif s = {arb(s)} then {∅, s}
        else union(subsequences(restriction(s, prev(#s))),
            append_to_elements(restriction(s, prev(#s)), last_of(s)) end if ;
end subsequences.
```

It should be clear that, having arrived at this point, we can go on to define any of the more advanced string-manipulation functions familiar from the computer-science literature, including functions which test a string for well-formedness according to any reasonable grammar, functions which detect and list the free variables of predicate and set-theoretic formulae, and functions which substitute specified terms for these free variables.

One such function that is needed below is that which tests an arbitrary hereditarily finite set to determine whether it is a sequence of strings. This is

```
function is_string_sequence(s);
    return if s = ∅ then true
        elseif ¬is_string(last_of(s)) then false
        else is_string_sequence(s less ordered_pair(prev(#s), last_of(s)))
    end if ;
end is_string.
```

We will not carry all of this out in detail, but simply note that full programming details, very close to those alluded to here, form part of the code libraries which implement the verifier system discussed in Chap. 4. (These are written in the SETL language of [SDDS86], which is very close to the more restricted set-theoretic language considered above.)

One other simple but more specialized string-manipulation function, which we call $\mathsf{subst}(s_1, s_2)$, will be used below. This is defined in the following way. Unless $s_1$ is a syntactically well-formed string of our language, $\mathsf{subst}(s_1, s_2)$ is the empty string $\{\}$. Otherwise the '**subst**' operator finds the first free variable in $s_1$ and replaces every occurrence of this variable by an occurrence of the string $s_2$. For example,

$$\mathsf{subst}(\text{"}(\forall z \mid F(x, g(x,y), z))\text{"}, \text{"}Abba\text{"}) = \text{"}(\forall z \mid F(Abba, g(Abba, y), z))\text{"},$$

but

$$\mathsf{subst}(\text{"}(\forall z \mid F(x, g(x,y), z)\text{"}, \text{"}Abba\text{"}) = \{\}$$

since its first argument string is syntactically ill-formed.

Note finally that any other universal form of computation, for example computation with strings or computation with integers, can substitute for the style of set-theoretic computation we have outlined. This follows from the fact that our set-theoretic computations can be programmed to run on any standard computer, simply by encoding all hereditarily finite sets by bitstrings in any way that supports the primitive operations listed above and the simple style of recursion that we have assumed. It is even easier to program all the above set-theoretic operations in a string language. To program them in pure arithmetic, one can simply regard strings as integers written to base 256.

### 6.2.2 *Programming and Proof; 'Mirroring' Programmable Set-Theoretic Functions*

A sequence of strings, every one of which is a syntactically legal formula of the language of logic, is a *proof* if every string in it is either an axiom or is derived via some allowed rule of inference from some finite subcollection of strings, each of which appears earlier in the sequence.

This definition can be applied in very general settings. We need not insist that the axioms allowed form a finite collection, but only that it must be possible to program the function

$$\text{is\_axiom}(s)$$

which tests statements $s$ to see if they are axioms. Similarly, we need not insist on any particular form for the rules of inference, but must only demand that we can program the function

$$\text{last\_is\_consequence}(s)$$

which tests a finite sequence of statements to verify that the last component $s(\text{prev}(\#s))$ of the sequence is a valid immediate consequence of the formulae which precede it in $s$. We insist that 'last_is_consequence' (and 'is_axiom') must be programmable in order to prevent the acceptability of a proof from being a matter of debate. As a matter of convenience we assume that

$$\text{is\_axiom}(x) \leftrightarrow \text{last\_is\_consequence}\big(\{\,\text{ordered\_pair}(0, x)\,\}\big).$$

Note that, given a procedure for testing 'last_is_consequence', the condition that a sequence of statements should be a proof is unambiguous, since this condition can be tested by calculating the value of the second function shown below.

```
function follows_from_element(list_of_subsequences, conclusion);
    return if list_of_subsequences = ∅ then is_axiom(conclusion)
        else
            last_is_consequence( concatenate( arb(list_of_subsequences),
                    { ordered_pair(0, conclusion) } ) ) ∨
            follows_from_element( list_of_subsequences less
                    arb(list_of_subsequences), conclusion )
        end if ;
end follows_from_element;

function is_proof(s);
    return if s = ∅ ∨ ¬is_string_sequence(s) then false
        elseif s = { arb(s) } then is_axiom(s^[2]) else
            is_proof( s less ordered_pair( prev(#s), last_of(s) ) ) &
            follows_from_element( subsequences( s less last_of(s) ), last_of(s))
    end if ;
end is_proof.
```

A string is then a theorem if and only if it is the last element of some sequence of strings which is a proof.

The preceding definitions allow us to formulate the notion of '*logical system*' in very general ways. But to relate a logical system to a computational system in the most useful way it is appropriate to impose a few additional conditions. First of all, we want each of the objects with which we will compute to have a representation in our logical system. The techniques described in our earlier discussion of computation with hereditarily finite sets can be used for this.To be sure that all such sets can be represented in our language, we can simply agree that some standard string representation of each such set must count as a syntactically well-formed term of our language, and that there should be a predicate Is_HF($s$) which is true whenever $s$ is the standardized string representation of such a set. Note that the condition that a string $s$ is such a representation can easily be tested by a programmable function. Next, we agree that our system must include an equality predicate having all the customary properties, and must also include a collection of function symbols Singleton($s$), Arb($s$), With($s_1, s_2$), Less($s_1, s_2$) having the indicated number of parameters. Moreover, every statement of a form like

$$\text{Singleton}(s_1) = s_2,\ \text{Arb}(s_1) = s_2,\ \text{With}(s_1, s_2) = s_3,\ \ldots,$$

for which $s_1, s_2, s_3$, etc., are standard string representations of hereditarily finite sets and the corresponding Boolean values $\{s_1\} = s_2$, $\text{arb}(s_1) = s_2$, etc., are true, must be an axiom (or theorem). There must also exist a predicate symbol In($s_1, s_2$) of two variables for which the statement

$$\text{In}(s_1, s_2)$$

is an axiom or theorem whenever $s_1$ and $s_2$ are standard string representations of hereditarily finite sets and

$$s_1 \in s_2$$

is true. Similarly, we require that there must exist a predicate symbol $\mathsf{Incs}(s_1, s_2)$ for which the statement

$$\mathsf{Incs}(s_1, s_2)$$

is a theorem whenever $s_1$ and $s_2$ are standard string representations of hereditarily finite sets and

$$s_1 \supseteq s_2$$

is true.

We also assume that the function Arb satisfies

$$(s = \emptyset \,\&\, \mathsf{Arb}(s) = \emptyset) \vee$$
$$\big(\mathsf{In}\big(\mathsf{Arb}(s), s\big) \,\&\, \big(\forall x \mid \mathsf{Is\_HF}(x) \rightarrow \neg\big(\mathsf{In}\big(x, \mathsf{Arb}(s)\big) \,\&\, \mathsf{In}(x, s)\big)\big)\big),$$

whenever $s$ is the standard representation of a hereditarily finite set, and that axioms are at hand allowing us to deduce such elementary set-theoretic statements as

$$\mathsf{In}\big(x, \mathsf{Singleton}(y)\big) \leftrightarrow x = y, \qquad \mathsf{In}\big(x, \mathsf{With}(s, y)\big) \leftrightarrow \big(\mathsf{In}(x, s) \vee x = y\big),$$

etc., whenever the variables involved are standard string representations of hereditarily finite sets. Elementary set-theoretic facts of this kind will be used in what follows, where we will sometimes write predicates like $\mathsf{In}(x, s)$ in their more standard infix form.

We also wish to impose conditions that allow our logical system to imitate any function definition legal in the system for computation with hereditarily finite sets described earlier, and which ensure that any legal computation can be modelled by a corresponding proof. This can most conveniently be done as follows. We suppose our logical system to allow (1) variables, (2) predicate and function symbols of any number of arguments, which must be nestable to form expressions, (3) existential and universal quantifiers subject to the usual rules (so that our logical system must always include all the standard mechanisms of the ordinary predicate calculus), and (4) conditional expressions formed using the keywords '**if** $\cdots$ **then** $\cdots$ **elseif** $\cdots$ **else** $\cdots$ **end if**' in the usual way.

Recursive definition of new function and predicate symbols, for example in a style like

$$\begin{aligned}
&\textbf{define } \mathit{Name}(s_1, s_2, \ldots, s_n) =_{\mathrm{Def}} \textbf{ if } \mathit{cond}_1 \textbf{ then } \mathit{expn}_1\\
&\quad \textbf{elseif } \mathit{cond}_2 \textbf{ then } \mathit{expn}_2\\
&\quad\quad \ldots\\
&\quad \textbf{elseif } \mathit{cond}_m \textbf{ then } \mathit{expn}_m\\
&\quad \textbf{else } \mathit{expn}_{m+1} \textbf{ end if },
\end{aligned} \tag{6.2}$$

must also be possible under the same conditions in which the corresponding function definition would be allowed and would be certain to converge. (As for function definitions in a programming language, in such definitions the variables $s_1, s_2, \ldots, s_n$ must all be distinct and the symbol '*Name*' being defined must never have been used before.) For function symbols such a definition must imply the universally quantified equality

$$\begin{aligned}
\big(\forall s_1, s_2, \ldots, s_n \mid \quad & \big(\mathsf{Is_HF}(s_1) \,\&\cdots\&\, \mathsf{Is_HF}(s_1)\big) \rightarrow\\
\mathit{Name}(s_1, s_2, \ldots, s_n) = & \textbf{ if } \mathit{cond}_1 \textbf{ then } \mathit{expn}_1\\
& \textbf{elseif } \mathit{cond}_2 \textbf{ then } \mathit{expn}_2\\
& \quad \ldots\\
& \textbf{elseif } \mathit{cond}_m \textbf{ then } \mathit{expn}_m\\
& \textbf{else } \mathit{expn}_{m+1} \textbf{ end if } \big)
\end{aligned}$$

and for predicate symbols the corresponding universally quantified logical equivalence. (More is said later about the situations in which such recursive definitions are legitimate, i.e. situations in which we can be sure, on essentially syntactic grounds, that the corresponding recursive functions would be certain to converge.)

Provided that the conditions necessary for convergence discussed below are systematically respected, any sequence of set- and Boolean-valued function definitions in our set-theoretic programming language can be 'mirrored' simply by translating each function definition

```
function name(s1, s2, ..., sn);
   return if cond1 then expn1
      elseif cond2 then expn2
         ...
      elseif condm then expnm
      else expnm+1 end if ;
end name
```

into the above definition (6.2) of a similarly-named logical symbol. For example, the definition

```
function union(s1, s2);
    return if s1 = ∅ then s2
        else union(s1 less arb(s1), s2) with arb(s1) end if ;
end union
```

of the function 'union' translates into the logical definition

$$\textbf{define}\ \mathsf{Union}(s_1,\ s_2)\ =_{\text{Def}}\ \textbf{if}\ s_1 = \emptyset\ \textbf{then}\ s_2$$
$$\textbf{else}\ \mathsf{With}\big(\mathsf{Union}\big(\mathsf{Less}\big(s_1, \mathsf{Arb}(s_1)\big), s_2\big), \mathsf{Arb}(s_1)\big)\ \textbf{end if}\ .$$

We will use the term '*mirroring*', or more specifically 'mirroring in logic', for the systematic translation process just described. The 'mirrored' versions of the elementary set-theoretic functions appearing in our earlier discussion of computation with hereditarily finite sets will be written using the same names as the programmed functions, but the first letter of the name will be capitalized to indicate that it is a symbol of logic rather than a function name used in programming.

The elementary axioms and stipulations listed in the preceding paragraphs serve to ensure that all computations with hereditarily finite set described previously can be 'mirrored' by elementary logical proofs, in the manner described by our earlier 'Mirroring Lemma'. Note that the condition that a string should be any one of these required axioms (or theorems) can easily be tested by a programmable function. In addition to these required axioms (or some subset from which the rest of these required assertions can be proved), any number of other axioms are allowed.

We also want our logical system to include a principle of induction strong enough to subsume the ordinary principle of mathematical induction. Since integers are defined objects, rather than primitive objects, of our system, it is convenient to formulate our principle of induction in set-theoretic rather than integer-related terms. This can be done as follows. Since the sets spoken of in our logical system are all assumed to be finite (in fact, to be hereditarily finite), there can exist no indefinitely long descending sequence of subsets of any of our sets. Hence any predicate which is true for the null set and true for a set $s$ whenever it is true for all proper subsets of $s$ must be true for all sets $s$. In formal terms this is

$$\big(P(\emptyset)\ \&$$
$$\big(\forall x \mid \big(\mathsf{Is\_HF}(x)\ \&\ \big(\forall y \mid \big(\mathsf{Is\_HF}(y)\ \&\ \mathsf{Incs}(x, y)\ \&\ x \neq y\big) \rightarrow P(y)\big)\big) \rightarrow P(x)\big)\big)$$
$$\rightarrow \big(\forall z \mid \mathsf{Is\_HF}(z) \rightarrow P(z)\big).$$

Similarly, since the standard representation of any member of a set $s$ must be shorter than that of $s$, there can be no indefinitely long sequence of sets, each of which is a member of the preceding set in the sequence. Hence any predicate which is true for the null set and true for a set $s$ whenever it is true for all the members of $s$ must be true for all sets $s$. In formal terms this second principle of induction is

$$\big(P(\emptyset) \mathbin{\&} \big(\forall x \mid \big(\mathsf{Is\_HF}(x) \mathbin{\&} \big(\forall y \mid \big(\mathsf{Is\_HF}(y) \mathbin{\&} y \in x\big) \to P(y)\big)\big) \to P(x)\big)\big) \\ \to \big(\forall z \mid \mathsf{Is\_HF}(z) \to P(z)\big).$$

The first of these inductive principles (*subset induction*) is valid only for finite sets; the second (*membership induction*) carries over to the general set theory considered later in this book, which also allows infinite sets.

These statements are taken as axioms for every syntactically legal predicate formula $P$ of our theory. Note that the condition that a formula should arise in this way, i.e. by substitution of a predicate formula for the symbol $P$ appearing in the two preceding axiom templates, is computationally testable. Thus no incompatibility arises with our general demand that there must always exist a programmed function which tests formulae to determine whether they are legal axioms.

### 6.2.3 Additional Comments on the Legitimacy of Recursive Definitions

Recursive definitions are legitimate in situations in which the corresponding function definitions are certain to converge. Consider a definition of the form

**define** *Name*($s_1, s_2, \ldots, s_n$) $=_{\text{Def}}$ **if** $cond_1$ **then** $expn_1$
  **elseif** $cond_2$ **then** $expn_2$
  ...
  **elseif** $cond_m$ **then** $expn_m$
  **else** $expn_{m+1}$ **end if** .

If this definition is not recursive, i.e. if all the predicate and function symbols which appear in it have been defined previously, it is legitimate whenever it is syntactically legal. But if the defined function '*Name*' appears within the body of the definition, then conditions must be imposed on the arguments of each such appearance for its legitimacy to be guaranteed. More specifically, consider any such appearance of '*Name*', and suppose that it has the form $Name(e_1, e_2, \ldots, e_n)$. Then we must be able to prove that the sequence $e_1, e_2, \ldots, e_n$ is 'lexicographically smaller' than $s_1, s_2, \ldots, s_n$, in the sense that there exists an integer $k$ no larger than $n$ such that

$$s_1 \supseteq e_1,\ s_2 \supseteq e_2, \ldots, s_k \supseteq e_k$$

can be proved in the context in which $Name(e_1, e_2, \ldots, e_n)$ appears, and that $e_j \neq s_j$ can also be proved for some $j$ between 1 and $k$. These assertions must be proved under the hypothesis that all the conditions $cond_1, cond_2, \ldots, cond_{h-1}$ appearing on if-statement branches preceding the branch containing the occurrence $Name(e_1, e_2, \ldots, e_n)$ are false, while $cond_h$ is true if $Name(e_1, e_2, \ldots, e_n)$ appears within $expn_h$.

As an example, consider the previously cited definition

$$\textbf{define } \mathsf{Union}(s_1, s_2) =_{\mathsf{Def}} \textbf{if } s_1 = \emptyset \textbf{ then } s_2$$
$$\textbf{else } \mathsf{With}\big(\mathsf{Union}\big(\mathsf{Less}\big(s_1, \mathsf{Arb}(s_1)\big), s_2\big), \mathsf{Arb}(s_1)\big) \textbf{ end if};$$

Since the function 'Union' being defined also appears on the right of the definition, this definition is recursive. To be sure that it is legitimate, we must show that the one appearance of 'Union' on the right, which is as the expression

$$\mathsf{Union}\big(\mathsf{Less}\big(s_1, \mathsf{Arb}(s_1)\big), s_2\big),$$

has arguments certain to be lexicographically smaller than the initial arguments $s_1, s_2$, in the context in which $\mathsf{Union}(\mathsf{Less}(s_1, \mathsf{Arb}(s_1)))$ appears. This is so because we can show that its first argument $\mathsf{Less}(s_1, \mathsf{Arb}(s_1))$ is included in and not equal to $s_1$ in the context in which it appears. Indeed, in this context we can be certain that $s_1 \neq \emptyset$, so

$$s_1 \supseteq \mathsf{Less}\big(s_1, \mathsf{Arb}(s_1)\big)$$

by elementary set theory, and since $s_1 \neq \emptyset$, $\mathsf{Arb}(s_1)$ is in $s_1$ but not in $\mathsf{Less}(s_1, \mathsf{Arb}(s_1))$, so

$$\mathsf{Less}\big(s_1, \mathsf{Arb}(s_1)\big) \neq s_1.$$

Elementary arguments of this kind can be given in for each logical predicate and function-symbol definitions mirroring the programmed functions appearing in our earlier discussion of computation with hereditarily finite sets. We leave the work of verifying this to the reader. However, some of the arguments necessary appear in the following section on basic properties of integers.

### *6.2.4 Properties of Integers*

To show that the inductive principles formulated above subsume ordinary integer induction, we can prove the few needed basic properties of integers as given by the set-theoretic encodings and definitions given earlier. For convenience, we list the recursive definitions corresponding to the relevant function definitions appearing in our earlier discussion of computation with hereditarily finite sets. These are

$$\textbf{define } \mathsf{Next}(s) =_{\mathsf{Def}} \mathsf{With}(s, s);$$

$$\begin{aligned}&\textbf{define } \mathsf{Last}(s) =_{\mathsf{Def}} \textbf{if } s=\emptyset \textbf{ then } \emptyset\\ &\quad \textbf{elseif } s = \mathsf{Singleton}\big(\mathsf{Arb}(s)\big) \textbf{ then } \mathsf{Arb}(s)\\ &\quad \textbf{else } \mathsf{Last}\big(\mathsf{Less}\big(s, \mathsf{Arb}(s)\big)\big) \textbf{ end if};\end{aligned}$$

$$\textbf{define } \mathsf{Prev}(s) =_{\mathsf{Def}} \mathsf{Less}\big(s, \mathsf{Last}(s)\big);$$

$$\begin{aligned}&\textbf{define } \mathsf{Is\_integer}(s) \leftrightarrow_{\mathsf{Def}} \textbf{if } s=\emptyset \textbf{ then } \mathsf{true}\\ &\quad \textbf{else } s = \mathsf{Next}\big(\mathsf{Prev}(s)\big) \,\&\, \mathsf{Is\_integer}\big(\mathsf{Prev}(s)\big) \textbf{ end if}.\end{aligned}$$

We begin by showing that

$$\big(\forall x \mid \big(\mathsf{Is\_integer}(x) \to \big(x=\emptyset \vee \big(x = \mathsf{Next}\big(\mathsf{Prev}(x)\big) \,\&\, \mathsf{Is\_integer}\big(\mathsf{Prev}(x)\big)\big)\big)\big)\big),$$

a statement which we will call the 'Next_Prev' lemma. To prove this, suppose that it is false. Then there exists an $x$ such that

$$\mathsf{Is\_integer}(x) \,\&\, (x \neq \emptyset) \,\&\, \big(x \neq \mathsf{Next}\big(\mathsf{Prev}(x)\big) \vee \big(\neg \mathsf{Is\_integer}\big(\mathsf{Prev}(x)\big)\big)\big).$$

On the other hand, by definition of 'Is_integer' we have

$$\begin{aligned}&\mathsf{Is\_integer}(x) \leftrightarrow \textbf{if } x=\emptyset \textbf{ then } \mathsf{true}\\ &\qquad\qquad \textbf{else } \big(x = \mathsf{Next}\big(\mathsf{Prev}(x)\big) \,\&\, \mathsf{Is\_integer}\big(\mathsf{Prev}(x)\big)\big) \textbf{ end if}.\end{aligned}$$

It follows from the above that

$$\begin{aligned}&x = \mathsf{Next}\big(\mathsf{Prev}(x)\big) \,\&\, \mathsf{Is\_integer}\big(\mathsf{Prev}(x)\big) \,\&\\ &\big(x \neq \mathsf{Next}\big(\mathsf{Prev}(x)\big) \vee \big(\neg \mathsf{Is\_integer}(\mathsf{Prev}(x))\big)\big),\end{aligned}$$

a contradiction proving the 'Next_Prev' lemma.

Another simple lemma of this kind needed below is what might be called the 'Prev_Next' lemma:

$$\big(\forall x \mid \mathsf{Is\_HF}(x) \to x = \mathsf{Prev}\big(\mathsf{Next}(x)\big)\big).$$

By the definition of 'Next' this is equivalent to

$$\big(\forall x \mid \mathsf{Is\_HF}(x) \to x = \mathsf{Prev}\big(\mathsf{With}(x, x)\big)\big).$$

Suppose that this is false, so that there exists a $w$ such that

$$\mathsf{Is\_HF}(w) \,\&\, w \neq \mathsf{Prev}\big(\mathsf{With}(w, w)\big).$$

By definition of 'Prev', this means that

$$w \neq \mathsf{Less}\big(\mathsf{With}(w, w), \mathsf{Last}\big(\mathsf{With}(w, w)\big)\big),$$

so $\mathsf{Last}(\mathsf{With}(w,w)) \neq w$. Hence our assertion will follow if we can prove that

$$\big(\forall x \mid \mathsf{Is\_HF}(x) \rightarrow x = \mathsf{Last}\big(\mathsf{With}(x,x)\big)\big).$$

It is most convenient to prove this in the generalized form

$$\big(\forall x, y \,\big|\, \big(\mathsf{Is\_HF}(x)\ \&\ \mathsf{Is\_HF}(y)\big) \rightarrow \big(\mathsf{Incs}(x,y) \rightarrow \big(x = \mathsf{Last}\big(\mathsf{With}(y,x)\big)\big)\big)\big).$$

Suppose that this last statement is false. Then there exist $u$ and $v$ such that

$$\mathsf{Is\_HF}(u)\ \&\ \mathsf{Is\_HF}(v)\ \&\ \mathsf{Incs}(u,v)\ \&\ \big(u \neq \mathsf{Last}\big(\mathsf{With}(v,u)\big)\big).$$

Consider the predicate $Q(x)$ defined by

$$\mathsf{Incs}(u,x) \rightarrow \big(u = \mathsf{Last}(\mathsf{With}(x,u))\big).$$

Applying the above-discussed subset induction principle to $Q$, noting that $Q(v)$ is false, gives

$$\big(\neg Q(\emptyset)\big) \vee$$
$$\neg\big(\forall x \,\big|\, \big(\mathsf{Is\_HF}(x)\ \&\ \big(\forall y \,\big|\, \big(\mathsf{Is\_HF}(y)\ \&\ \mathsf{Incs}(x,y)\ \&\ x \neq y\big) \rightarrow Q(y)\big)\big) \rightarrow Q(x)\big)\big).$$

If $x = \emptyset$, then $\mathsf{With}(x,u) = \mathsf{Singleton}(u)$, and therefore $\mathsf{Last}(\mathsf{With}(x,u)) = u$. This shows that $Q(\emptyset)$ is true, so the formula just displayed simplifies to its second disjunct, implying the existence of an $x$ such that

$$\big(\forall y \,\big|\, \big(\mathsf{Is\_HF}(y)\ \&\ \mathsf{Incs}(x,y)\ \&\ x \neq y\ \&\ \mathsf{Incs}(u,y)\big) \rightarrow u = \mathsf{Last}\big(\mathsf{With}(y,u)\big)\big)\ \&$$
$$\mathsf{Is\_HF}(x)\ \&\ \mathsf{Incs}(u,x)\ \&\ u \neq \mathsf{Last}\big(\mathsf{With}(x,u)\big).$$

Using the definition of Last, and noting that $\mathsf{With}(x,u) \neq \emptyset$, we have

$$\begin{aligned}\mathsf{Last}\big(\mathsf{With}(x,u)\big) = \ &\textbf{if } \mathsf{With}(x,u) = \mathsf{Singleton}\big(\mathsf{Arb}\big(\mathsf{With}(x,u)\big)\big)\\ &\textbf{then } \mathsf{Arb}\big(\mathsf{With}(x,u)\big)\\ &\textbf{else } \mathsf{Last}\big(\mathsf{Less}\big(\mathsf{With}(x,u),\ \mathsf{Arb}(\mathsf{With}(x,u))\big)\big)\ \textbf{end if}.\end{aligned}$$

It follows that we cannot have $\mathsf{With}(x,u) = \mathsf{Singleton}(\mathsf{Arb}(\mathsf{With}(x,u)))$, since $u$ is in $\mathsf{With}(x,u)$, so this would imply that $\mathsf{With}(x,u) = \mathsf{Singleton}(u)$, and so $\mathsf{Last}(\mathsf{With}(x,u)) = u$, contradicting $u \neq \mathsf{Last}(\mathsf{With}(x,u))$. Hence $x \neq \emptyset$ and also

$$\mathsf{Last}\big(\mathsf{With}(x,u)\big) = \mathsf{Last}\big(\mathsf{Less}\big(\mathsf{With}(x,u),\ \mathsf{Arb}\big(\mathsf{With}(x,u)\big)\big)\big).$$

Since $\mathsf{With}(x,u) \neq \emptyset$, we must have

$$\mathsf{Arb}\big(\mathsf{With}(x,u)\big) \in \mathsf{With}(x,u),$$

so either $\mathsf{Arb}(\mathsf{With}(x,u)) = u$ or $\mathsf{Arb}(\mathsf{With}(x,u)) \in x$.

But $\mathsf{Arb}(\mathsf{With}(x,u)) = u$ is impossible, since if $y$ is any element of $x$, then, since $\mathsf{Incs}(u,x)$, $y$ would also be an element of $u$, contradicting

$$\mathsf{Intersection}\big(\mathsf{Arb}\big(\mathsf{With}(x,u)\big), \mathsf{With}(x,u)\big) = \emptyset.$$

It follows that we must have

$$\mathsf{Arb}\big(\mathsf{With}(x,u)\big) \in x,$$

from which it follows that

$$\mathsf{Less}\big(\mathsf{With}(x,u), \mathsf{Arb}\big(\mathsf{With}(x,u)\big)\big) = \mathsf{With}\big(\mathsf{Less}\big(x, \mathsf{Arb}\big(\mathsf{With}(x,u)\big)\big), u\big).$$

Then plainly

$$\mathsf{Incs}\big(x, \mathsf{Less}\big(x, \mathsf{Arb}\big(\mathsf{With}(x,u)\big)\big)\big) \,\&\, x \neq \mathsf{Less}\big(x, \mathsf{Arb}\big(\mathsf{With}(x,u)\big)\big),$$

so from

$$\big(\forall y \,|\, \big(\mathsf{Incs}(x,y) \,\&\, x \neq y \,\&\, \mathsf{Incs}(u,x)\big) \rightarrow \big(u = \mathsf{Last}\big(\mathsf{With}(y,u)\big)\big)\big)$$

we have

$$u = \mathsf{Last}\big(\mathsf{With}\big(\mathsf{Less}\big(x, \mathsf{Arb}\big(\mathsf{With}(x,u)\big)\big), u\big)\big),$$

and therefore $u = \mathsf{Last}(\mathsf{With}(x,u))$, a contradiction completing our proof of the 'Prev_Next' lemma.

For what follows we also need the lemma

$$\big(\forall x \mid \mathsf{Is\_HF}(x) \rightarrow \big(x = \emptyset \vee \mathsf{Last}(x) \in x\big)\big).$$

To prove this, suppose that it is false, so that there exists a $u$ such that

$$\mathsf{Is\_HF}(u) \,\&\, u \neq \emptyset \,\&\, \neg\big(\mathsf{Last}(u) \in u\big).$$

Consider the predicate $Q(x)$ defined by $x = \emptyset \vee (\mathsf{Last}(x) \in x)$. Applying the subset induction principle to $Q$, and noting that $Q(u)$ is false, gives

$$\begin{aligned}&(\neg Q(\emptyset)) \vee \\ &\neg\big(\forall x \,\big|\, \big(\mathsf{Is\_HF}(x) \,\&\, \big(\forall y \,\big|\, \big(\mathsf{Is\_HF}(y) \,\&\, \mathsf{Incs}(x,y) \,\&\, x \neq y\big) \rightarrow Q(y)\big)\big) \rightarrow Q(x)\big),\end{aligned}$$

so, since $Q(\emptyset)$ is true, there exists an $x$ for which

$$\big(\forall y \,\big|\, \big(\mathsf{Is\_HF}(y) \,\&\, \mathsf{Incs}(x,y) \,\&\, x \neq y\big) \rightarrow Q(y)\big) \,\&\, \mathsf{Is\_HF}(x) \,\&\, \neg Q(x),$$

where plainly $x \neq \emptyset$. That is,

$$\begin{aligned}&\big(\forall y \,\big|\, \big(\mathsf{Is\_HF}(y) \,\&\, \mathsf{Incs}(x,y) \,\&\, x \neq y\big) \rightarrow \big(y = \emptyset \vee \mathsf{Last}(y) \in y\big)\big) \\ &\qquad\qquad \&\, \mathsf{Is\_HF}(x) \,\&\, x \neq \emptyset \,\&\, \neg\big(\mathsf{Last}(x) \in x\big).\end{aligned}$$

Using the definition of 'Last' we have

$$\begin{aligned}\mathsf{Last}(x) = \textbf{if } x = \emptyset \textbf{ then } \emptyset \\ \textbf{elseif } x = \mathsf{Singleton}\big(\mathsf{Arb}(x)\big) \textbf{ then } \mathsf{Arb}(x) \\ \textbf{else } \mathsf{Last}\big(\mathsf{Less}\big(x, \mathsf{Arb}(x)\big)\big) \textbf{ end if}.\end{aligned}$$

Since $x \neq \emptyset$ the first of the cases appearing in this last formula is ruled out, and since it then follows that $\mathsf{Arb}(x) \in x$, the second of these cases is excluded also. Hence we have $\mathsf{Last}(x) = \mathsf{Last}(\mathsf{Less}(x, \mathsf{Arb}(x)))$. But then we also have

$$\mathsf{Incs}\big(x, \mathsf{Less}\big(x, \mathsf{Arb}(x)\big)\big) \,\&\, \mathsf{Less}\big(x, \mathsf{Arb}(x)\big) \neq x,$$

and so it follows from

$$\big(\forall y \,\big|\, \big(\mathsf{Is\_HF}(y) \,\&\, \mathsf{Incs}(x, y) \,\&\, x \neq y\big) \rightarrow \big(y = \emptyset \vee \mathsf{Last}(y) \in y\big)\big)$$

that

$$\mathsf{Last}\big(\mathsf{Less}\big(x, \mathsf{Arb}(x)\big)\big) \in \mathsf{Less}\big(x, \mathsf{Arb}(x)\big).$$

Since $\mathsf{Incs}(x, \mathsf{Less}(x, \mathsf{Arb}(x)))$ and $\mathsf{Last}(\mathsf{Less}(x, \mathsf{Arb}(x))) = \mathsf{Last}(x)$, we see that $\mathsf{Last}(x) \in x$, completing our proof of the statement

$$\big(\forall x \mid x = \emptyset \vee \mathsf{Last}(x) \in x\big).$$

#### 6.2.4.1 Peano's Principle of Mathematical Induction

Now we prove that Peano's standard principle of *mathematical induction* applies to integers as we have defined them. This is done by showing that for every formula $P$ of our theory with one free variable we have

$$\begin{aligned}P(0) \,\&\, \big(\forall y \,\big|\, \big(\mathsf{Is\_integer}(y) \,\&\, P(y)\big) \rightarrow P\big(\mathsf{Next}(y)\big)\big) \rightarrow \\ \big(\forall x \mid \mathsf{Is\_integer}(x) \rightarrow P(x)\big).\end{aligned}$$

To prove this statement, suppose that it is false, so that there exists an $x$ such that

$$P(0) \,\&\, \big(\forall y \,\big|\, \big(\mathsf{Is\_integer}(y) \,\&\, P(y)\big) \rightarrow P\big(\mathsf{Next}(y)\big)\big) \,\&\, \mathsf{Is\_integer}(x) \,\&\, \big(\neg P(x)\big).$$

Consider the predicate expression $Q(y)$ defined by '$\mathsf{Is\_integer}(y) \rightarrow P(y)$'. Since $(\forall z \mid Q(z))$ is false (for $z = x$ in particular), an application of the subset induction principle to $Q$ gives

$$\begin{aligned}&\big(\neg Q(0)\big) \vee \\ &\big(\neg\big(\forall x \,\big|\, \big(\mathsf{Is\_HF}(x) \,\&\, \big(\forall y \,\big|\, \big(\mathsf{Is\_HF}(y) \,\&\, \mathsf{Incs}(x, y) \,\&\, x \neq y\big) \rightarrow Q(y)\big)\big) \rightarrow Q(x)\big)\big),\end{aligned}$$

so that there exists an $x$ such that

$$(\neg Q(0)) \vee \big((\forall y \mid (\mathsf{Is\_HF}(y) \,\&\, \mathsf{Incs}(x,y) \,\&\, x \neq y) \rightarrow Q(y)) \,\&\, \mathsf{Is\_HF}(x) \,\&\, \neg Q(x)\big),$$

that is

$$\big(\mathsf{Is\_integer}(0) \,\&\, \neg P(0)\big) \vee \Big(\big(\forall y \mid (\mathsf{Is\_HF}(y) \,\&\, \mathsf{Incs}(x,y) \,\&\, x \neq y\big) \rightarrow \big(\mathsf{Is\_integer}(y) \rightarrow P(y)\big)\big) \,\&\, \mathsf{Is\_HF}(x) \,\&\, \mathsf{Is\_integer}(x) \,\&\, \neg P(x)\Big).$$

Since $P(0)$ must be true and $\mathsf{Is\_integer}(y)$ implies $\mathsf{Is\_HF}(y)$, this simplifies to

$$\big(\forall y \mid \big(\mathsf{Incs}(x,y) \,\&\, x \neq y \,\&\, \mathsf{Is\_integer}(y)\big) \rightarrow P(y)\big) \,\&\, \mathsf{Is\_integer}(x) \,\&\, \neg P(x).$$

Since $P(0)$ is true, we have $x \neq 0$, so by the Next_Prev lemma we have

$$\big(\forall y \mid \big(\mathsf{Incs}(x,y) \,\&\, x \neq y \,\&\, \mathsf{Is\_integer}(y)\big) \rightarrow P(y)\big) \,\&\, \mathsf{Is\_integer}(x) \,\&\, \mathsf{Is\_integer}\big(\mathsf{Prev}(x)\big) \,\&\, \neg P\big(\mathsf{Next}(\mathsf{Prev}(x))\big).$$

Thus, since $(\forall y \mid (\mathsf{Is\_integer}(y) \,\&\, P(y)) \rightarrow P(\mathsf{Next}(y)))$, we must have

$$\big(\forall y \mid \big(\mathsf{Incs}(x,y) \,\&\, x \neq y \,\&\, \mathsf{Is\_integer}(y)\big) \rightarrow P(y)\big) \,\&\, \mathsf{Is\_integer}\big(\mathsf{Prev}(x)\big) \,\&\, \big(\neg P\big(\mathsf{Prev}(x)\big)\big)\big).$$

Using the definition of 'Prev' we have

$$\mathsf{Prev}(x) = \mathsf{Less}\big(x, \mathsf{Last}(x)\big),$$

and so, since it was proved above that $\mathsf{Last}(x)$ is in $x$ whenever $x \neq 0$, it follows that

$$\mathsf{Incs}\big(x, \mathsf{Prev}(x)\big) \,\&\, x \neq \mathsf{Prev}(x) \,\&\, \mathsf{Is\_integer}\big(\mathsf{Prev}(x)\big).$$

But then

$$\big(\forall y \mid \big(\mathsf{Incs}(x,y) \,\&\, x \neq y \,\&\, \mathsf{Is\_integer}(y)\big) \rightarrow P(y)\big)$$

implies that $P(\mathsf{Prev}(x))$, contradicting $\neg P(\mathsf{Prev}(x))$, and so completing our proof of Peano's standard axiom of induction.

To complete our discussion it is worth proving the remaining Peano axioms for integers, which in our set-theoretic formulation are

(i) $\mathsf{Is\_integer}(0)$;
(ii) $(\forall x \mid \mathsf{Is\_integer}(x) \rightarrow \mathsf{Is\_integer}(\mathsf{Next}(x)))$;
(iii) $(\forall x \mid \mathsf{Next}(x) \neq 0)$;
(iv) $(\forall x, y \mid (\mathsf{Is\_integer}(x) \,\&\, \mathsf{Is\_integer}(y) \,\&\, \mathsf{Next}(x) = \mathsf{Next}(y)) \rightarrow x = y)$.

The first two statements follow from the definition

$$(\forall x \mid \mathsf{Is\_integer}(x) \leftrightarrow \textbf{if } x = \emptyset \textbf{ then } \mathsf{true}$$
$$\textbf{else } x = \mathsf{Next}\big(\mathsf{Prev}(x)\big) \,\&\, \mathsf{Is\_integer}(x) \textbf{ end if}\,\big).$$

Since by definition $\mathsf{Next}(x) = x$ with $x$, $\mathsf{Next}(x) \neq \emptyset$ follows by elementary set-theoretic reasoning.

Finally, since it has been shown above that $\mathsf{Is\_integer}(x)$ implies $x = \mathsf{Prev}(\mathsf{Next}(x))$, statement (iv) follows immediately.

This completes our discussion of the relationship between standard integer induction and the set-theoretic induction principles stated above.

The inductive proofs given in the preceding pages are intended to typify the large but generally straightforward family of proofs needed to show that the elementary functions of sequences, lists of sequences, strings, etc. defined above necessarily have their familiar properties. For example, it can be shown in this way that string concatenation is associative, i.e. that

$$(\forall x_1, x_2, x_3 \,\big|\, (\mathsf{Is\_string}(x_1) \,\&\, \mathsf{Is\_string}(x_2) \,\&\, \mathsf{Is\_string}(x_3)\big) \rightarrow$$
$$\big(\mathsf{Concatenate}\big(\mathsf{Concatenate}(x_1, x_2), x_3\big) =$$
$$\mathsf{Concatenate}\big(x_1, \mathsf{Concatenate}(x_2, x_3)\big)\big)\big).$$

Or, as another example, we can show that the same final string is obtained by first deleting the final character of a (non-empty) string $x_2$ and then appending the result to a string $x_1$ as would be obtained by first appending the two strings and then deleting the final character of what results. In formal terms this is

$$\big(\forall x_1, x_2 \,\big|\, \big(\mathsf{Is\_string}(x_1) \,\&\, \mathsf{Is\_string}(x_2)\big) \rightarrow$$
$$\mathsf{Concatenate}\big(x_1, \mathsf{Less}\big(x_2, \mathsf{Ordered\_pair}\big(\mathsf{Prev}(\#x_2), \mathsf{Last\_of}(x_2)\big)\big)\big)$$
$$= \mathsf{Less}\big(\mathsf{Concatenate}(x_1, x_2),$$
$$\mathsf{Ordered\_pair}\big(\mathsf{Prev}\big(\#\mathsf{Concatenate}(x_1, x_2)\big),$$
$$\mathsf{Last\_of}\big(\mathsf{Concatenate}(x_1, x_2)\big)\big)\big)\big)\big).$$

Since many such proofs will be given later in this book in full, computer-verified detail (albeit in a somewhat different setting, viz. general set theory rather than the more limited theory of hereditarily finite sets on which the present section concentrates), we prove no theorems of the kind illustrated by our two examples, other than those already proved above. Instead, we content ourselves with the broad claim that all the results of this elementary kind of whose correctness one could convince oneself after careful examination can also be proved formally. To attain conviction that this is so, the reader may wish to try his/her hand at a few such proofs, for example the proofs of the two examples just given. The line of reasoning found below depends on a few theorems of this kind, of which the statement

$$\big(\forall x_1, x_2 \,\big|\, \big(\mathsf{Is\_proof}(x_1) \,\&\, \mathsf{Is\_proof}(x_2)\big) \rightarrow \mathsf{Is\_proof}\big(\mathsf{Concatenate}(x_1, x_2)\big)\big),$$

where 'ls_proof' is the logical symbol mirroring the recursive function 'is_proof', is typical. Computer verification of the line of reasoning given below would require systematic, computer-verified proof of a finite collection of such statements.

### 6.2.5 A Final Remark on Proof and Computation

The mirroring lemma shows that our logical system 'envelops' the process of computation with hereditarily finite sets, in the sense that any value $name(c_1, c_2, \ldots, c_n)$ derivable by computation can also be derived in another way, namely by proving a theorem of the form $Name(e_1, e_2, \ldots, e_n) = e_{n+1}$. In cases favourable for proof, the length of the proof required may be considerably shorter than the computation it replaces, even allowing for the great difference in speed between human thought and electronic computation. For example, we can easily prove that

$$\mathsf{Exp}(10, 40) = 10000000000000000000000000000000000000000,$$

supplying the required proof in a time much shorter than that needed to verify this same fact by direct computation. Similarly, given two functions $f(s_1, s_2, \ldots, s_n)$ and $g(s_1, s_2, \ldots, s_n)$ and the symbols $F$ and $G$ which mirror them, we may be able to prove a theorem of the form

$$(\forall s_1, s_2, \ldots, s_n \mid F(s_1, s_2, \ldots, s_n) = G(s_1, s_2, \ldots, s_n)),$$

thus allowing replacement of $f$ by $g$, whose computation may be much faster.

More generally, the mirroring lemma gives us the following result. Suppose that some logical system in which we are able to embed our computational system is consistent, and let the logical symbol '*Fcn*' mirror some recursively defined function '*fcn*'. Then, given representations of two hereditarily finite sets $s_1$ and $s_2$, there exists a proof of the logical statement '$Fcn(s_1) = s_2$' if and only if $fcn(s_1)$ evaluates to $s_2$. Indeed, the mirroring lemma shows that '$Fcn(s_1) = s_2$' must be a theorem if $fcn(s_1)$ evaluates to $s_2$. Conversely, if our logical system is consistent, there can exist at most one $s_2$ for which '$Fcn(s_1) = s_2$' is provable, and so by the mirroring lemma the one $s_2$ for which this is provable must be the value of $fcn(s_1)$ derivable by computation.

### 6.2.6 A Technical Adjustment

To avoid a technical issue that would otherwise arise it is convenient to formulate the 'follows_from_element' function defined at the start of Sect. 6.2.2 in a slightly different way. To this end, we first define the auxiliary function

**function** ax($x$); **return if** is_axiom($x$) **then** $x$ **else** "true" **end if** ; **end** ax.

Then is_axiom(ax($x$)) is always true, and in fact the expressions is_axiom($x$) and $x =$ ax($x$) are always equal.

We also introduce the following function

```
function lic(x);
    return if is_sequence(x) & last_is_consequence(x) then x
        else ordered_pair(0, "true") end if;
end lic;
```

so that

$$\text{last\_is\_consequence}\big(\text{lic}(x)\big)$$

is true for every $x$.

This enables us to write the follows_from_element in the following modified way, which will be more convenient in what follows:

```
function follows_from_element(list_of_subsequences, conclusion);
  return if list_of_subsequences = ∅ then conclusion = ax(conclusion)
    else concatenate(arb(list_of_subsequences),
                {ordered_pair(0, conclusion)}) =
          lic(concatenate(arb(list_of_subsequences),
                {ordered_pair(0, conclusion)}))∨
          follows_from_element(list_of_subsequences less
                arb(list_of_subsequences), ordered_pair(0, conclusion))
    end if;
end follows_from_element.
```

It is convenient to assume that there exists some reasonably small integer $k_0$ such that every sequence $s$ for which last_is_consequence($s$) is true has length at most $k_0$. All common logic systems satisfy this condition (generally with $k_0$ not much larger than 4), which in any case is easily replaced if necessary. At any rate, assuming this condition, we may as well assume that every sequence $x$ for which last_is_consequence($x$) is true is of length exactly $k_0$, since shorter sequences of hypotheses can be left-padded with an appropriate number of copies of the trivial hypothesis 'true'.

### 6.2.7 The 'Provability' Predicate Pr($s$)

Given the availability of existential and universal quantifiers within a logic system, we can at once define a predicate which states that the string $s$ is provable. This is simply

$$\textbf{define}\ \text{Pr}(s) \leftrightarrow_{\text{Def}} \big(\exists p \mid \text{Is\_proof}(p)\ \&\ \text{Last\_of}(p) = s\big),$$

which we can also write as

$$\textbf{define}\ \mathsf{Pr}(s) \leftrightarrow_{\mathrm{Def}} \big(\exists p \mid \mathsf{Is\_proof\_of}(p,s)\big),$$

if we introduce the intermediate definition

$$\textbf{define}\ \mathsf{Is\_proof\_of}(p,s) \leftrightarrow_{\mathrm{Def}} \mathsf{Is\_proof}(p)\ \&\ \mathsf{Last\_of}(p) = s$$

which states that $p$ is a proof culminating in the statement $s$.

This predicate differs from those previously considered in one important respect. All of these others correspond to recursive functions which converge to some definite set-theoretic value whenever they are applied to the appropriate number of hereditarily finite arguments. Pr is a more abstract existential, which if programmed would correspond to a search loop not guaranteed to converge.

We shall now establish several important properties of this predicate, for subsequent use. Note first that the concatenation $\mathsf{Concatenate}(p_1, p_2)$ of any two proofs is also a proof, since each element of the first part of the concatenation is either an axiom or a consequence of preceding statements, and similarly for the second part of the concatenation. Moreover, if $p$ is a proof and we concatenate any formula which is a valid consequence of a subsequence of the formulae in $p$ to $p$, then the result is also a proof.

Next note that given $s_1, s_2$, and $s_3$ for which $s_3$ has the form $s_1 \to s_2$ (i.e., $s_3 = \mathsf{Concatenate}(\mathsf{Concatenate}(s_1, \text{“} \to \text{”}), s_2)$) then

$$\big(\mathsf{Pr}(s_1)\ \&\ \mathsf{Pr}(s_3)\big) \to \mathsf{Pr}(s_2).$$

For if not we would have $\mathsf{Pr}(s_1)\ \&\ \mathsf{Pr}(s_3)\ \&\ (\neg\mathsf{Pr}(s_2))$, and so using the definitions of $\mathsf{Pr}(s_1)$ and $\mathsf{Pr}(s_3)$ we could find $p_1$ and $p_3$ for which we have

$$\mathsf{Is\_proof}(p_1)\ \&\ \mathsf{Last\_of}(p_1) = s_1\ \&\ \mathsf{Is\_proof}(p_3)\ \&\ \mathsf{Last\_of}(p_3) = s_3.$$

But then the concatenation of $p_1$, $p_3$, and the single formula $s_2$ is a proof of $s_2$, since $s_2$ follows by propositional implication from the two formulae $s_1$ and $s_3$.

We can write this result as the implication

$$\mathsf{Pr}\big(\mathsf{Concatenate}\big(\mathsf{Concatenate}(s_1, \text{“} \to \text{”}), s_2\big)\big) \to \big(\mathsf{Pr}(s_1) \to \mathsf{Pr}(s_2)\big),$$

or, in a more drastically abbreviated notation,

$$\mathsf{Pr}(s_1 \to s_2) \to \big(\mathsf{Pr}(s_1) \to \mathsf{Pr}(s_2)\big).$$

We can show in much the same way that given $s_1$, $s_2$, and $s_3$, if $s_3$ has the form $s_1\ \&\ s_2$ (i.e., $s_3 = \mathsf{Concatenate}(\mathsf{Concatenate}(s_1, \text{“ \& ”}), s_2)$), then

$$\big(\mathsf{Pr}(s_1)\ \&\ \mathsf{Pr}(s_2)\big) \to \mathsf{Pr}(s_3).$$

This result can be written as the implication

$$\big(\mathsf{Pr}(s_1)\ \&\ \mathsf{Pr}(s_2)\big) \to \mathsf{Pr}\big(\mathsf{Concatenate}\big(\mathsf{Concatenate}(s_1, \text{“ \& ”}), s_2\big)\big),$$

or, again abbreviating more drastically, as

$$(\mathsf{Pr}(s_1) \mathbin{\&} \mathsf{Pr}(s_2)) \to \mathsf{Pr}(s_1 \mathbin{\&} s_2).$$

Next suppose that $Q(x)$ is any expression involving one free variable $x$ for which we have

$$\mathsf{Pr}((\forall y \mid Q(y))).$$

Then $\mathsf{Is\_proof\_of}(p, (\forall y \mid Q(y)))$ for some $p$. But then, for any $x$, the concatenation $p'$ of $p$ with the single statement $Q(x)$ is also a proof, so

$$\mathsf{Is\_proof\_of}(\mathsf{Concatenate}(p, \mathsf{Singleton}(\mathsf{Ordered\_pair}(0, Q(x)))), Q(x)),$$

where $x$ denotes the standard representation of any hereditarily finite set. This shows that

$$\mathsf{Pr}((\forall y \mid Q(y)) \to (\forall x \mid \mathsf{Pr}(Q(x))).$$

Finally, if $s$ is an axiom, i.e. if $\mathsf{Is\_axiom}(s)$ where 'Is_axiom' is the predicate symbol that mirrors the Boolean function 'is_axiom', then the one-element sequence $\{\mathsf{Ordered\_pair}(\emptyset, s)\}$ is easily shown to satisfy $\mathsf{Is\_proof}(\{\mathsf{Ordered\_pair}(\emptyset, s)\})$. Since we must also have $\mathsf{Cdr}(\mathsf{Arb}(\{\mathsf{Ordered\_pair}(\emptyset, s)\})) = \mathsf{Cdr}(\mathsf{Ordered\_pair}(\emptyset, s)) = s$, it follows that $\mathsf{Is\_proof\_of}(\{\mathsf{Ordered\_pair}(\emptyset, s)\}, s)$. Conversely any proof of length 1 must have the form $\{\mathsf{Ordered\_pair}(\emptyset, s)\}$ where $s$ is an axiom, i.e. satisfies $\mathsf{Is\_axiom}(s)$.

Our next goal is to prove the following.

### *6.2.8 Proof Visibility Lemma*

Let $s$ be any string representing a syntactically well-formed logical formula. Then

$$\mathsf{Pr}(s) \to \mathsf{Pr}(\mathsf{Pr}(s)).$$

In intuitive terms this simply states that any proof of $s$ can be turned (rather explicitly) into a proof that $s$ has a proof; i.e. the existence of a proof of $s$ is always 'visible' rather than 'cryptic'. We prove this as follows. Assuming that it is false, there is an $s$ such that $\mathsf{Pr}(s) \mathbin{\&} \neg\mathsf{Pr}(\mathsf{Pr}(s))$, and so there exists a sequence $p$ of strings such that

$$\mathsf{Is\_proof}(p) \mathbin{\&} s = \mathsf{Last\_of}(p) \mathbin{\&} \neg\mathsf{Pr}(\mathsf{Pr}(s)).$$

Hence, since $\mathsf{Last\_of}(p) = \mathsf{Value\_at}(p, \mathsf{Prev}(\#p))$, there exists an integer $n$ such that

$$\mathsf{Is\_proof}(p) \mathbin{\&} n \in \#p \mathbin{\&} \neg\mathsf{Pr}(\mathsf{Pr}(\mathsf{Value\_at}(p, n))).$$

Let $n$ be the smallest such integer. Then, by definition of Is_proof, either

$$\mathsf{Value\_at}(p,n) = \mathsf{Ax}\big(\mathsf{Value\_at}(p,n)\big),$$

or there exists a finite sequence $n_1, n_2, \ldots, n_k$ of integers, all smaller than $n$, such that

$$\begin{aligned}&\mathsf{Last\_is\_consequence}\big(\\ &\big[\mathsf{Value\_at}(p,n_1), \mathsf{Value\_at}(p,n_2), \ldots, \mathsf{Value\_at}(p,n_1), \mathsf{Value\_at}(p,n)\big]\big)\end{aligned}$$

which, as noted previously, means in more formal terms that there exists an $x$ such that

$$\begin{aligned}&\mathsf{Value\_at}(p,n_1) = \mathsf{Value\_at}\big(\mathsf{Lic}(x),0\big) \ \& \cdots \&\\ &\mathsf{Value\_at}(p,n_k) = \mathsf{Value\_at}\big(\mathsf{Lic}(x),k-1\big) \ \&\\ &\mathsf{Value\_at}(p,n) = \mathsf{Value\_at}\big(\mathsf{Lic}(x),k\big),\end{aligned}$$

where the function symbol 'Lic' mirrors the function 'lic' introduced above. In the first of these cases ($\mathsf{Value\_at}(p,n) = \mathsf{Ax}(\mathsf{Value\_at}(p,n))$) we reason as follows. For every $x$ the sequence of formulae

$$\begin{aligned}&\mathsf{Is\_proof}\big(\mathsf{Singleton}\big(\mathsf{Ordered\_pair}\big(0, \mathsf{Ax}(x)\big)\big)\big)\\ &\mathsf{Is\_proof\_of}\big(\mathsf{Singleton}\big(\mathsf{Ordered\_pair}\big(0, \mathsf{Ax}(x)\big), \mathsf{Ax}(x)\big)\big)\\ &\big(\exists p \mid \mathsf{Is\_proof\_of}\big(p, \mathsf{Ax}(x)\big)\big)\\ &\mathsf{Pr}\big(\mathsf{Ax}(x)\big)\end{aligned}$$

is the skeleton of a proof whose intermediate details the reader should easily be able to fill in. If we denote this completed proof

$$\ldots$$

$$\mathsf{Is\_proof}\big(\mathsf{Singleton}\big(\mathsf{Ordered\_pair}\big(0, \mathsf{Ax}(x)\big)\big)\big)$$

$$\ldots$$

$$\mathsf{Is\_proof\_of}\big(\mathsf{Singleton}\big(\mathsf{Ordered\_pair}\big(0, \mathsf{Ax}(x)\big), \mathsf{Ax}(x)\big)\big)$$

$$\ldots$$

$$\big(\exists p \mid \mathsf{Is\_proof\_of}\big(p, \mathsf{Ax}(x)\big)\big)$$

$$\ldots$$

$$\mathsf{Pr}\big(\mathsf{Ax}(x)\big)$$

by $cp$, then $cp$ is an explicit proof whose final statement is $\mathsf{Pr}(\mathsf{Ax}(x))$, allowing us to conclude that $\mathsf{Pr}(\mathsf{Pr}(\mathsf{Ax}(x)))$ for every $x$. Thus, if $\mathsf{Axiom}(s)$, so that $s = \mathsf{Ax}(s)$, we have $\mathsf{Pr}(\mathsf{Pr}(s))$. This proves that the implication

$$\mathsf{Axiom}(s) \rightarrow \mathsf{Pr}\big(\mathsf{Pr}(s)\big)$$

holds for all $s$, so that if Axiom(Value_at($p, n$)) we have Pr(Pr(Value_at($p, n$))), contradicting (¬Pr(Pr(Value_at($p, n$)))), and so ruling out the case Axiom(Value_at ($p, n$)).

Next suppose that there exists a finite sequence $n_1, n_2, \ldots, n_{k_0-1}$ of integers, all smaller than $n$, such that

$$\text{Last\_is\_consequence}\big(\\ \text{Value\_at}(p, n_1), \text{Value\_at}(p, n_2), \ldots, \text{Value\_at}(p, n_{k_0-1}), \text{Value\_at}(p, n)\big).$$

(Here and in what follows, $k_0$ is the common length of sequences $x$ for which Last_is_consequence($x$) is true.) Then by inductive hypothesis we have

$$\text{Pr}\big(\text{Pr}\big(\text{Value\_at}(p, n_j)\big)\big)$$

for each $j$ from 1 to $k_0 - 1$. Also the sequence of formulae

$$\begin{aligned}
&\text{Suppose}: \big(\exists y \mid \text{Pr}\big(\text{Value_at}\big(\text{Lic}(y), 0\big)\big) \,\&\cdots\&\\
&\quad \text{Pr}\big(\text{Value_at}\big(\text{Lic}(y), k_0 - 2\big)\big) \,\&\\
&\quad \big(\neg\text{Pr}\big(\text{Value_at}\big(\text{Lic}(y), k_0 - 1\big)\big)\big)\big)\\
&\text{Skolemize}: \text{Pr}\big(\text{Value_at}\big(\text{Lic}(x), 0\big)\big) \,\&\cdots\&\\
&\quad \text{Pr}\big(\text{Value_at}\big(\text{Lic}(x), k_0 - 2\big)\big) \,\&\\
&\quad \big(\neg\text{Pr}\big(\text{Value_at}\big(\text{Lic}(x), k_0 - 1\big)\big)\big)\\
&\text{Skolemize}: \text{Is_proof_of}\big(\text{Value_at}\big(\text{Lic}(x), 0\big)\big)\\
&\qquad\qquad\qquad\ldots\\
&\text{Skolemize}: \text{Is_proof_of}\big(\text{Value_at}\big(\text{Lic}(x), k_0 - 2\big)\big)\\
&\quad \text{Is_proof_of}\big(\text{Concatenate}\big(\text{Concatenate}\big(\cdots\\
&\quad \text{Concatenate}\big(\text{Concatenate}(p_1, p_2)\cdots, p_{k_0-2}\big),\\
&\qquad \text{Pr}\big(\text{Value_at}\big(\text{Lic}(y), k_0 - 1\big)\big)\big)\big)\big)\\
&\qquad \big(\exists p \mid \text{Is_proof_of}\big(p, \text{Value_at}\big(\text{Lic}(x), k_0 - 1\big)\big)\big)\\
&\text{Pr}\big(\text{Value_at}\big(\text{Lic}(x), k_0 - 1\big)\big)\\
&\text{false}\\
&\text{Discharge}: \big(\forall y \,\big|\, \big(\text{Pr}\big(\text{Value_at}\big(\text{Lic}(y), 0\big)\big) \,\&\cdots\&\\
&\quad \text{Pr}\big(\text{Value_at}\big(\text{Lic}(y), k_0 - 2\big)\big)\big) \rightarrow\\
&\qquad \text{Pr}\big(\text{Value_at}\big(\text{Lic}(y), k_0 - 1\big)\big)\big)
\end{aligned}$$

is the skeleton of a proof whose intermediate details the reader should again be able to fill in. This proof (when completed) shows explicitly that

$$(\forall y \mid (\mathsf{Pr}(\mathsf{Value\_at}(\mathsf{Lic}(y), 0)) \,\&\, \cdots \,\& \\ \mathsf{Pr}(\mathsf{Value\_at}(\mathsf{Lic}(y), k_0 - 2))) \rightarrow \\ \mathsf{Pr}(\mathsf{Value\_at}(\mathsf{Lic}(y), k_0 - 1)))$$

and so we have

$$\mathsf{Pr}((\forall y \mid (\mathsf{Pr}(\mathsf{Value\_at}(\mathsf{Lic}(y), 0)) \,\&\, \cdots \,\& \\ \mathsf{Pr}(\mathsf{Value\_at}(\mathsf{Lic}(y), k_0 - 2))) \rightarrow \\ \mathsf{Pr}(\mathsf{Value\_at}(\mathsf{Lic}(y), k_0 - 1)))).$$

From this it follows, as noted above, that

$$(\forall x \mid \mathsf{Pr}((\mathsf{Pr}(\mathsf{Value\_at}(\mathsf{Lic}(x), 0)) \,\&\, \cdots \,\& \\ \mathsf{Pr}(\mathsf{Value\_at}(\mathsf{Lic}(x), k_0 - 2))) \rightarrow \\ \mathsf{Pr}(\mathsf{Value\_at}(\mathsf{Lic}(x), k_0 - 1))))).$$

By definition of 'Last_is_consequence' we have

$$(\exists y \mid \mathsf{Value\_at}(p, n_1) = \\ \mathsf{Value\_at}(\mathsf{Lic}(y), 0) \,\&\, \cdots \,\&\, \mathsf{Value\_at}(p, n_{k_0}) = \\ \mathsf{Value\_at}(\mathsf{Lic}(y), k_0 - 2) \,\& \\ \mathsf{Value\_at}(p, n) = \mathsf{Value\_at}(\mathsf{Lic}(y), k_0 - 1))$$

so

$$\mathsf{Value\_at}(p, n_1) = \mathsf{Value\_at}(\mathsf{Lic}(x_0), 0) \,\&\, \cdots \\ \&\, \mathsf{Value\_at}(p, n_{k_0}) = \\ \mathsf{Value\_at}(\mathsf{Lic}(x_0), k_0 - 2) \,\& \\ \mathsf{Value\_at}(p, n) = \mathsf{Value\_at}(\mathsf{Lic}(x_0), k_0 - 1)$$

for some $x_0$. From this it follows, using the last universally quantified formula appearing above, that

$$\mathsf{Pr}((\mathsf{Pr}(\mathsf{Value\_at}(p, n_1)) \,\&\, \cdots \,\&\, \mathsf{Pr}(\mathsf{Value\_at}(p, n_k))) \\ \rightarrow \mathsf{Pr}(\mathsf{Value\_at}(p, n))).$$

Hence, using the previously established implication $(\mathsf{Pr}(a \rightarrow b) \rightarrow (\mathsf{Pr}(a) \rightarrow \mathsf{Pr}(b))$, we have

$$\mathsf{Pr}(\mathsf{Pr}(\mathsf{Value\_at}(p, n_1)) \,\&\, \cdots \,\&\, \mathsf{Pr}(\mathsf{Value\_at}(p, n_k))) \\ \rightarrow \mathsf{Pr}(\mathsf{Pr}(\mathsf{Value\_at}(p, n)))$$

and then by repeated use of the implication $\mathsf{Pr}(a)\ \&\ \mathsf{Pr}(b) \rightarrow \mathsf{Pr}(a\ \&\ b)$ established earlier it follows that

$$\big(\mathsf{Pr}\big(\mathsf{Pr}\big(\mathsf{Value\_at}(p, n_1)\big)\big)\ \&\ \cdots\ \&\ \mathsf{Pr}\big(\mathsf{Pr}\big(\mathsf{Value\_at}(p, n_{k_0})\big)\big)\big) \rightarrow \mathsf{Pr}\big(\mathsf{Pr}\big(\mathsf{Value\_at}(p, n)\big)\big).$$

Since $\mathsf{Pr}(\mathsf{Pr}(\mathsf{Value\_at}(p, n_j)))$ for all $j$ from 1 to $k_0$, it follows that $\mathsf{Pr}(\mathsf{Pr}(\mathsf{Value\_at}(p, n))$, completing our demonstration of the Proof Visibility Lemma.

### 6.2.9 Gödel's Trick Sentence

Gödel's trick sentence $G$ is now simply

$$\neg\mathsf{Pr}\big(\mathsf{Subst}\big(\text{“}\neg\mathsf{Pr}\big(\mathsf{Subst}(x, x)\text{”}, \text{“}\neg\mathsf{Pr}\big(\mathsf{Subst}(x, x)\big)\text{”}\big),$$

where '$\mathsf{Subst}$' is the logical symbol that mirrors the two-parameter string function '$\mathsf{subst}$' introduced above.

In this statement, and repeatedly in what follows, the quoted string "$\neg\mathsf{Pr}(\mathsf{Subst}(x, x))$" appears. It should be kept in mind that this is simply an abbreviation for the character sequence

$$10, 111, 116, 32, 80, 114, 40, 83, 117, 98, 115, 116, 40, 120, 44, 120, 41, 41,$$

that is, for the set constant

$$\big\{\ \mathsf{ordered\_pair}(0, 110), \mathsf{ordered\_pair}(1, 111), \mathsf{ordered\_pair}(2, 116), \mathsf{ordered\_pair}(3, 32), \mathsf{ordered\_pair}(4, 80), \mathsf{ordered\_pair}(5, 114), \mathsf{ordered\_pair}(6, 40), \mathsf{ordered\_pair}(7, 83), \mathsf{ordered\_pair}(8, 117), \mathsf{ordered\_pair}(9, 98), \mathsf{ordered\_pair}(10, 115), \mathsf{ordered\_pair}(11, 116), \mathsf{ordered\_pair}(12, 40), \mathsf{ordered\_pair}(13, 120), \mathsf{ordered\_pair}(14, 44), \mathsf{ordered\_pair}(15, 120), \mathsf{ordered\_pair}(16, 41), \mathsf{ordered\_pair}(17, 41)\big\}.$$

Note that since $x$ is the only free variable of the syntactically well-formed string "$\neg\mathsf{Pr}(\mathsf{Subst}(x, x))$", the functional expression

$$\mathsf{subst}\big(\text{“}\neg\mathsf{Pr}\big(\mathsf{Subst}(x, x)\text{”}, \text{“}\neg\mathsf{Pr}\big(\mathsf{Subst}(x, x)\text{”}\big)$$

evaluates to

$$\text{“}\neg\mathsf{Pr}\big(\mathsf{Subst}\big(\text{“}\neg\mathsf{Pr}\big(\mathsf{Subst}(x, x)\text{”}, \text{“}\neg\mathsf{Pr}\big(\mathsf{Subst}(x, x)\text{”}\big)\text{”}$$

and therefore the logical statement

$$\mathsf{Subst}(\text{``}\neg\mathsf{Pr}(\mathsf{Subst}(x,x)\text{''}, \text{``}\neg\mathsf{Pr}(\mathsf{Subst}(x,x)\text{''}) = \text{``}\neg\mathsf{Pr}\big(\mathsf{Subst}(\text{``}\neg\mathsf{Pr}(\mathsf{Subst}(x,x))\text{''}, \text{``}\neg\mathsf{Pr}(\mathsf{Subst}(x,x))\text{''})\big)\text{''}$$

which mirrors this evaluation is a theorem. Therefore so is

$$\mathsf{Pr}\big(\mathsf{Subst}(\text{``}\neg\mathsf{Pr}(\mathsf{Subst}(x,x))\text{''}, \text{``}\neg\mathsf{Pr}(\mathsf{Subst}(x,x))\text{''})\big) \leftrightarrow \mathsf{Pr}\big(\text{``}\neg\mathsf{Pr}(\mathsf{Subst}(\text{``}\neg\mathsf{Pr}(\mathsf{Subst}(x,x))\text{''}, \text{``}\neg\mathsf{Pr}(\mathsf{Subst}(x,x)))\text{''}\big).$$

Hence

$$\big(\neg\mathsf{Pr}(\mathsf{Subst}(\text{``}\neg\mathsf{Pr}(\mathsf{Subst}(x,x))\text{''}, \text{``}\neg\mathsf{Pr}(\mathsf{Subst}(x,x))\text{''}))\big) \leftrightarrow \big(\neg\mathsf{Pr}(\text{``}\neg\mathsf{Pr}(\mathsf{Subst}(\text{``}\neg\mathsf{Pr}(\mathsf{Subst}(x,x))\text{''}, \text{``}\neg\mathsf{Pr}(\mathsf{Subst}(x,x))\text{''}))\text{''})\big)$$

is a theorem. Defining $G$ as

$$\big(\neg\mathsf{Pr}(\mathsf{Subst}(\text{``}\neg\mathsf{Pr}(\mathsf{Subst}(x,x))\text{''}, \text{``}\neg\mathsf{Pr}(\mathsf{Subst}(x,x))\text{''}))\big),$$

we see that

$$G \leftrightarrow \big(\neg\mathsf{Pr}(\text{``}G\text{''})\big)$$

is also a theorem.

### 6.2.10 Rosser's Variant of Gödel's Trick Sentence

This variant is obtained by replacing the predicate '$\neg\mathsf{Pr}(s)$', i.e.

$$\big(\forall p \mid \neg\mathsf{Is\_proof\_of}(p,s)\big),$$

by the modified predicate $\mathsf{Prr}(s)$ defined by

$$\mathsf{Prr}(s) =_{\mathrm{Def}} \big(\forall p \,\big|\, (\neg\mathsf{Is\_proof\_of}(p,s)) \vee \big(\exists q \mid \mathsf{Shorter}(q,p)\ \&\ \mathsf{Is\_proof\_of}(q, \mathsf{Neg}(s))\big)\big).$$

Here '$\mathsf{Neg}$' is a function symbol which mirrors the operation which simply negates a string by prepending '$\neg$' to it, and $\mathsf{Shorter}$ is a predicate symbol which mirrors the function $\mathsf{shorter}(q,p)$ that tests one sequence of strings (its first parameter $q$) to verify that it is shorter than its second parameter.

Note that whereas '$\neg\mathsf{Pr}(s)$' states that $s$ has no proof, $\mathsf{Prr}(s)$ states that either $s$ has no proof or that, if it does, there exists a shorter proof of the negation of $s$. In a consistent logical system these two conditions are the same, since the added clause $(\exists q \mid \mathsf{Shorter}(q,p)\ \&\ \mathsf{Is\_proof\_of}(q, Neg(s)))$ implies that the negation of $s$ has a proof and hence implies that $s$ can have no proof. Nevertheless this technical reformulation of the condition '¬Pr($s$)' is advantageous for the argument given two paragraphs below.

Rosser's trick sentence is now

$$\neg\mathsf{Prr}(\mathsf{Subst}(\text{“}\mathsf{Prr}(\mathsf{Subst}(x,x)\text{”}, \text{“}\mathsf{Prr}(\mathsf{Subst}(x,x))\text{”}),$$

where 'Subst' is as before. Reasoning as above we find that since $x$ is the only free variable of the syntactically well-formed string "Prr(Subst($x, x$))", the functional expression

$$\mathsf{subst}(\text{“}\mathsf{Prr}(\mathsf{Subst}(x,x)\text{”}, \text{“}\mathsf{Prr}(\mathsf{Subst}(x,x)\text{”})$$

evaluates to

$$\text{“}\mathsf{Prr}(\mathsf{Subst}(\text{“}\mathsf{Prr}(\mathsf{Subst}(x,x)\text{”}, \text{“}\mathsf{Prr}(\mathsf{Subst}(x,x)\text{”})\text{”}$$

and so the logical statement

$$\begin{aligned}&\mathsf{Subst}(\text{“}\mathsf{Prr}(\mathsf{Subst}(x,x)\text{”},\text{“}\mathsf{Prr}(\mathsf{Subst}(x,x)\text{”}) =\\ &\quad\text{“}\mathsf{Prr}(\mathsf{Subst}(\text{“}\mathsf{Prr}(\mathsf{Subst}(x,x))\text{”}, \text{“}\mathsf{Prr}(\mathsf{Subst}(x,x))\text{”}))\text{”}\end{aligned}$$

which mirrors this evaluation is a theorem. Therefore so is

$$\begin{aligned}&\mathsf{Prr}(\mathsf{Subst}(\text{“}\mathsf{Prr}(\mathsf{Subst}(x,x))\text{”}, \text{“}\mathsf{Prr}(\mathsf{Subst}(x,x))\text{”})) \leftrightarrow\\ &\quad\mathsf{Prr}(\text{“}\mathsf{Prr}(\mathsf{Subst}(\text{“}\mathsf{Prr}(\mathsf{Subst}(x,x))\text{”}, \text{“}\mathsf{Prr}(\mathsf{Subst}(x,x)))\text{”}).\end{aligned}$$

Defining Gr as Prr(Subst("Prr(Subst($x, x$))", "Prr(Subst($x, x$))"))), we see that Gr ↔ Prr("Gr") is also a theorem.

### *6.2.11 Proof of Rosser's Variant of Gödel's First Theorem*

Given that we have just exhibited a proof of the statement Gr ↔ ¬Prr("Gr"), it is now easy to complete the proof that (if the proof system $T$ in which we reason is consistent) neither Gr nor (¬Gr) can be provable, showing that Gr is undecidable in $T$, which is Rosser's strengthened version of Gödel's first theorem.

For suppose first that Gr is provable. Then using Gr ↔ Prr("Gr"), we can conclude Prr("*Gr*"), i.e. that

$$(\forall p \mid (\neg\mathsf{Is\_proof\_of}(p, \text{“Gr”})) \vee (\exists q \mid \mathsf{Shorter}(q, p)\ \&\ \mathsf{Is\_proof\_of}(q, \mathsf{Neg}(\text{“Gr”})))).$$

So either Gr is not provable, or there exists a proof of the negation of Gr. But if our logical system is consistent, this last implies that Gr is not provable in either case.

Suppose next that '¬Gr' is provable, and let $q_0$ be a proof of '¬Gr'. Using Gr ↔ Prr("Gr") once more we can deduce that (¬Prr("*Gr*")), i.e. that

$$\begin{aligned}&(\exists p \mid \mathsf{Is\_proof\_of}(p, \text{“Gr”})\ \&\ (\forall q \mid (\neg\mathsf{Shorter}(q, p))\vee\\ &\quad(\neg\mathsf{Is\_proof\_of}(q, \mathsf{Neg}(\text{“Gr”}))))).\end{aligned}$$

Let $p_0$ be a proof satisfying this existential statement, so that

$$\text{Is\_proof\_of}(p_0, \text{Gr}) \;\&\; \left(\neg\text{Shorter}(q_0, p_0)\right).$$

It follows that the length of the proof $p_0$ is less than or equal to the length of $q_0$, so that we can find $p_0$ explicitly by searching the finite collection of proofs that are no longer than $q_0$. But then we have proofs of both Gr and the negation of Gr, and so a contradiction, which we have assumed to be impossible.

### *6.2.12 Proof of Gödel's Second Theorem*

This states that if our logical system is consistent it must be impossible to prove '$\neg$Pr(false)' in it. To show this, let $p_0$ denote the proof of the theorem $G \leftrightarrow (\neg\text{Pr}(\text{“}G\text{”}))$ derived above. The implication $G \rightarrow (\neg\text{Pr}(\text{“}G\text{”}))$ follows by one additional step. Hence, if $p$ is a proof of $G$, then the concatenation of $p$ and $p_0$, plus two additional steps, gives a proof of '$\neg\text{Pr}(\text{“}G\text{”})$', showing that $\text{Pr}(\text{“}G\text{”})$ implies $\text{Pr}(\text{“}\neg\text{Pr}(G)\text{”})$. Thus we have proved $\text{Pr}(\text{“}G\text{”}) \rightarrow \text{Pr}(\text{“}\neg\text{Pr}(G)\text{”})$.

Now, if a statement and its negative can both be proved, then by concatenating these two proofs and adding one more step we obtain a proof of Pr(false). Hence if our logical system is consistent and its consistency, i.e. the statement '$\neg$Pr(false)', can be proved within it, then the implication

$$\text{Pr}(\text{“}\neg\text{Pr}(G)\text{”}) \rightarrow (\neg\text{Pr}(\text{“Pr}(G)\text{”})),$$

and so $\text{Pr}(\text{“}G\text{”}) \rightarrow (\neg\text{Pr}(\text{“Pr}(G)\text{”}))$, follows from $\text{Pr}(\text{“}G\text{”}) \rightarrow (\neg\text{Pr}(\text{“Pr}(G)\text{”}))$. But the implication $\text{Pr}(\text{“}G\text{”}) \rightarrow \text{Pr}((\text{“Pr}(G)\text{”})$ was proved in the earlier Sect. 6.2.8 (Proof Visibility lemma). This proves that $(\neg\text{Pr}(\text{“}G\text{”}))$, and since $G \leftrightarrow (\neg\text{Pr}(\text{“}G\text{”}))$ we have a proof of $G$, whose existence immediately implies $\text{Pr}(\text{“}G\text{”})$, a contradiction. Thus it must be impossible to prove '$\neg$Pr(false)' within our logical system, as asserted.

## 6.3 Axioms of Reflection

The large-cardinal axioms discussed in Sect. 2.4.2.3 give one way of extending the axioms of set theory to increase their power, but as these stand they have been of little direct interest for our subsequent work, since their most immediate consequences are relatively specialized theorems in set theory which we do not need or prove. There is, however, a different (but, as we shall see, not entirely unrelated) class of axioms, the so called *axioms of reflection*, which can be added to the axioms of set theory and are of more direct practical interest. These are axioms of the form

$$\text{Pr}(\text{‘}F\text{’}) \rightarrow F,$$

that is, statements which assert that if a formula $F$ has a proof (a fact that we may, for example, be able to establish nonconstructively), then $F$ follows. The potential practical importance of statements of this type is that they make the collection of proof mechanisms available to us indefinitely extensible, since we may be able to establish general theorems of the form

$$(\forall s \mid A(s) \rightarrow \mathsf{Pr}(B(s))),$$

where $A$ and $B$ have recursive definitions that allow them to be calculated mechanically, or at least established easily, for hereditarily finite sets $s$. Then, whenever a formula $F$ is seen to satisfy '$F$' $= B(s)$ for some $s$ satisfying $A(s)$, we may be able to deduce $\mathsf{Pr}$('$F$') easily or automatically, and then $F$ immediately by an axiom of reflection.

However, Gödel's second theorem tells us that the additional axioms we desire must be set up carefully, since it is not immediately obvious that added axioms of reflection do not introduce contradictions. Let $T$ be a logical system to which Gödel's second theorem applies. That theorem implies that we cannot expect to prove all statements of the form

$$\mathsf{Pr}_T(\text{'}F\text{'}) \rightarrow F \tag{6.3}$$

in any consistent logical system, and indeed there is a strengthening of Gödel's theorem, known as Löb's theorem, which shows that (6.3) can only be proved in $T$ if $F$ itself can be proved in $T$. Nevertheless, one can ask whether the addition of all the statements (6.3) to a consistent system $T$ produces a more powerful but still consistent system $T'$, and in particular whether the collection $T$ of statements can be modelled in some more powerful system $T^*$ in which (6.3) can be proved. We shall show in the following pages that if $T^*$ is the collection ZFC of Zermelo–Fraenkel axioms of set theory extended by some assumption implying the existence of a large inaccessible cardinal $N$, so that $\mathscr{H}(N)$ is the universe for the model of ZFC considered in Sect. 2.4.2.3, and if $T$ is the weakening of $T^*$ which only asserts the existence of those inaccessible cardinals smaller than $N$, then (6.3) can be proved in $T^*$, and hence $T^*$ implies the consistency of the system obtained from $T$ by adding the desired axioms of reflection.

Several technical problems must be handled along the way to this goal. The first of these lies in the fact that the axioms we want to add involve the predicate $\mathsf{Pr}(s)$, which is substantially more composite than the ordinary axioms of set theory. To handle this we write a set of auxiliary axioms, whose consistency with the axioms of set theory is not at issue since with suitable definition of the symbols appearing in them they are all provable consequences of the ZFC axioms. These auxiliary axioms allow us to write a formula for the needed predicate $\mathsf{Pr}$. To avoid the addition of too much clutter to set-theory's streamlined basic axiom set, we will put these new axioms rather more succinctly than is done in our main series of definitions and proofs, but always in a provably equivalent way. The series of statements which we will now develop accomplishes this. We begin with

- $\big(x \in \{a, b\}\big) \leftrightarrow (x = a \vee x = b)$,
- $(x \in a \cup b) \leftrightarrow (x \in a \vee x \in b)$,
- $[x, y] = \big\{\{x\}, \big\{\{x\}, \big\{\{y\}, y\big\}\big\}\big\}$,
- $\mathsf{Is\_next}(s, t) \leftrightarrow \big(\forall x \mid (x \in t) \leftrightarrow (x \in s \vee x = s)\big)$,
- $\mathsf{Is\_integer}(n) \leftrightarrow \Big(\forall x \mid (x \in n \vee x = n) \rightarrow \big(x = \emptyset \vee \big(\exists y \in x \mid \mathsf{Is\_next}(y, x)\big)\big)\Big)$,
- $\mathsf{Svm}(f) \leftrightarrow \Big(\big(\forall x \in f \,\big|\, (\exists y, z \mid x = [y, z])\big)$
  $\quad\& \big(\forall x, y, z \,\big|\, \big([x, y] \in f \;\&\; [x, z] \in f\big) \rightarrow y = z\big)\Big)$,
- $\mathsf{Is\_seq}(f) \leftrightarrow \Big(\mathsf{Svm}(f)$
  $\quad\& \Big(\exists n \mid \mathsf{Is\_integer}(n) \;\&\; \Big(\forall x \mid (x \in f) \leftrightarrow \big(\exists y, m \in n \mid x = [m, y]\big)\Big)\Big)\Big)$.

The above statements define the notions of integers $n$ and sequences of length $n$. Our next aim is to define the notion of (ZFC) 'formula', which for succinctness we define as what would normally be called the syntax tree of a formula. We encode these trees as collections of nodes, each node being a sequence whose first component is an integer encoding the node type and whose remaining components are the syntactic subparts appropriate for the type of node. The allowed node types, and their distinguishing codes, are as follows:

0: variable or constant,
1: &-operator,
2: $\vee$-operator,
3: $\rightarrow$-operator,
4: $\leftrightarrow$-operator,
5: $\neg$-operator,
6: false,
7: true,
8: equality sign,
9: $\forall$,
10: $\exists$,
11: $\in$,
12: atomic formula involving predicate,
13: term involving function symbol.

Note that all of the 'encoded' forms of axioms which appear in the following discussion are written using only the elementary set-theoretic constructions

- $\{x\}$,
- $\{x, y\}$,
- $[x, y]$,
- $x \cup y$,
- $\mathsf{Seq2}(x, y)$, which is defined as $\{[0, x], [1, y]\}$,
- $\mathsf{Seq3}(x, y, z)$, which is defined as $\mathsf{Seq2}(x, y) \cup \{[2, z]\}$, and
- operators of propositional and predicate calculus.

These conventions for encoding formulae are captured in the following (necessarily case-ridden) definition of the predicate Is_formula, which the reader will want to analyze closely.

$$\begin{aligned}
&\mathsf{Is_formula}(f) \leftrightarrow \big(\mathsf{Is_seq}(f)\ \&\\
&\quad\big(\exists g, h \mid \mathsf{Is_formula}(g)\ \&\ \mathsf{Is_formula}(h)\ \&\\
&\quad\ \big((\exists v \mid \mathsf{Is_integer}(v)\ \&\ f = \mathsf{Seq2}(0, v)\big)\\
&\qquad \vee f = \mathsf{Seq3}(1, g, h) \vee f = \mathsf{Seq3}(2, g, h) \vee f = \mathsf{Seq3}(3, g, h)\\
&\qquad \vee f = \mathsf{Seq3}(4, g, h) \vee f = \mathsf{Seq2}(5, g) \vee f = \big\{[0, 6]\big\} \vee f = \big\{[0, 7]\big\}\\
&\qquad \vee \big(f = \mathsf{Seq3}(8, g, h)\ \&\ [0, 13] \in g\ \&\ [0, 13] \in h\big)\\
&\qquad \vee \big(f = \mathsf{Seq3}(11, g, h)\ \&\ [0, 13] \in g\ \&\ [0, 13] \in h\big)\\
&\qquad \vee \big([0, 9] \in f\ \&\ [1, g] \in f\ \&\ \big(\forall j \mid (1 \in j) \rightarrow \big(\exists v \,\big|\, \big[j, [0, v]\big] \in f\big)\big)\big)\\
&\qquad \vee \big([0, 10] \in f\ \&\ [1, g] \in f\ \&\ \big(\forall j \mid (1 \in j) \rightarrow \big(\exists v \,\big|\, \big[j, [0, v]\big] \in f\big)\big)\big)\\
&\qquad \vee \big([0, 12] \in f\ \&\ \big(\exists v \mid \mathsf{Is_integer}(v)\ \&\ \big[1, \mathsf{Seq2}(0, v)\big] \in f\big)\ \&\\
&\qquad\quad \big(\forall j \mid (1 \in j) \rightarrow \big(\exists sf \mid \mathsf{Is_formula}(sf)\ \&\ \big([0, 0] \in sf \vee [0, 13] \in sf\big)\big)\big)\big)\\
&\qquad \vee \big([0, 13] \in f\ \&\ \big(\exists v \mid \mathsf{Is_integer}(v)\ \&\ \big[1, \mathsf{Seq2}(0, v)\big] \in f\big)\ \&\\
&\qquad\quad \big(\forall j \mid (1 \in j) \rightarrow \big(\exists sf \mid \mathsf{Is_formula}(sf)\ \&\ \big([0, 0] \in sf \vee [0, 13] \in sf\big)\big)\big)\big)\big)\big)\big).
\end{aligned}$$

Note that the encoding of formulae defined by the above formula uses sequences Seq2(0, $v$), where $v$ can be any integer, to encode variables, function symbols, and predicate symbols, without explicitly stating that the integers $v$ appearing in these three different usages must be distinct. Thus in one setting Seq2(0, 1) may designate a particular variable, but in another this same pair may designate a predicate or function symbol, quite a different thing. Confusion is avoided by the fact that these usages are distinguished by the contexts in which these pairs appear. Specifically, predicate symbols (resp. function symbols) will only appear as the second component of a sequence whose first component is the code '12' (resp. '13'), where variables cannot appear. For example, in

$$\big\{ [0, 12], \big[1, \mathsf{Seq2}(0, 1)\big], \big[2, \mathsf{Seq2}(0, 1)\big] \big\}$$

the first occurrence of Seq2(0, 1) unambiguously designates a predicate symbol and the second occurrence of Seq2(0, 1) unambiguously designates a variable. Thus if we associate some predicate name like 'Foo' with appearances of Seq2(0, 1) in predicate contexts and choose to associate strings like '$v_n$' with appearances of Seq2(0, $n$) as variables, the sequence seen above will decode unambiguously as 'Foo($v_1$)'.

It is now easy to state a comprehensive set of rules for the operation 'Subst' which replaces every free occurrence of a variable $x$ in a formula $F$ with a designated subformula $G$. We also need the operation which calculates the set of all bound variables of a formula, and the operation which calculates all the free variables of a formula.

The following axiom defines the operation ‘Subst’.

$$
\begin{aligned}
&\big(f = \mathsf{Seq2}(0, x) \rightarrow \mathsf{Subst}(f, x, g) = g\big)\\
&\quad \& \, \big((\exists y \,|\, (f = \mathsf{Seq2}(0, y)) \,\&\, (\neg(y = x))\big) \rightarrow \mathsf{Subst}(f, x, g) = f\big)\\
&\quad \& \, \big(\big(([0, 9] \in f \vee [0, 10] \in f\big) \,\&\, \big(\exists j \mid 1 \in j \,\&\, [j, x] \in f\big)\big) \rightarrow\\
&\qquad \mathsf{Subst}(f, x, g) = f\big)\\
&\quad \& \, \big(\big(([0, 9] \in f \vee [0, 10] \in f\big) \,\&\, \big(\neg(\exists j \mid 1 \in j \,\&\, [j, x] \in f)\big)\big) \rightarrow\\
&\qquad \big(\exists j, h, tail \,\big|\, \big(f = \mathsf{Seq2}(j, h) \cup tail\big) \,\&\, \big(\forall k, h_2 \mid [k, h_2] \in tail \rightarrow 1 \in k\big)\\
&\qquad\quad \& \, \mathsf{Subst}(f, x, g) = \mathsf{Seq2}\big(j, \mathsf{Subst}(h, x, g)\big) \cup tail\big)\big)\\
&\quad \& \, \big([0, 1] \in f \vee [0, 2] \in f \vee [0, 3] \in f \vee [0, 4] \in f \vee [0, 8] \in f \vee [0, 11] \in f\big)\\
&\quad \& \, \big(\exists j, b, c \mid f = \mathsf{Seq3}(j, b, c)\\
&\qquad \& \, \mathsf{Subst}(f, x, g) = \mathsf{Seq3}\big(j, \mathsf{Subst}(b, x, g), \mathsf{Subst}(c, x, g)\big)\big)\\
&\quad \& \, \big([0, 5] \in f\big)\\
&\quad \& \, \big(\exists j, b \mid f = \mathsf{Seq2}(j, b) \,\&\, \mathsf{Subst}(f, x, g) = \mathsf{Seq2}\big(j, \mathsf{Subst}(b, x, g)\big)\big)\\
&\quad \& \, \big([0, 6] \in f \vee [0, 7] \in f\big) \,\&\, \mathsf{Subst}(f, x, g) = f\\
&\quad \& \, \big([0, 12] \in f \vee [0, 13] \in f\big)\\
&\quad \& \, \big(\forall y \,\big|\, (([0, y] \in f) \leftrightarrow ([0, y] \in \mathsf{Subst}(f, x, g)))\big)\\
&\quad \& \, \big(\forall y \,\big|\, (([1, y] \in f) \leftrightarrow ([1, y] \in \mathsf{Subst}(f, x, g)))\big)\\
&\quad \& \, \big(\forall y, j \,\big|\, \big(1 \in j \rightarrow \big(([j, y] \in f) \leftrightarrow \big([j, \mathsf{Subst}(y, x, g)\big] \in \mathsf{Subst}(f, x, g)\big)\big)\big)\big).
\end{aligned}
$$

The following axiom defines the set of all bound variables of a formula.

$$
\begin{aligned}
&\big(\big((\neg \mathsf{Is\_formula}(f)\big) \vee [0, 6] \in f \vee [0, 7] \in f\big) \rightarrow \mathsf{Bound\_vars}(f) = \emptyset\big)\\
&\quad \& \, \big(\big([0, 1] \in f \vee [0, 2] \in f \vee [0, 3] \in f \vee [0, 4] \in f \vee [0, 8] \in f \vee [0, 11] \in f\big)\\
&\qquad \rightarrow \big(\exists g, h \mid [1, g] \in f \,\&\, [2, h] \in f\\
&\qquad\qquad \& \, \mathsf{Bound\_vars}(f) = \mathsf{Bound\_vars}(g) \cup \mathsf{Bound\_vars}(h)\big)\big)\\
&\quad \& \, \big(\big([0, 5] \in f\big) \rightarrow \big(\exists g \mid [1, g] \in f \,\&\, \mathsf{Bound\_vars}(f) = \mathsf{Bound\_vars}(g)\big)\big)\\
&\quad \& \, \big(\big([0, 12] \in f \vee [0, 13] \in f\big) \rightarrow \mathsf{Bound\_vars}(f) = \emptyset\big)\\
&\quad \& \, \big(\big([0, 9] \in f \vee [0, 10] \in f\big)\\
&\qquad \rightarrow \big(\big(\exists s \,\big|\, \big(\forall x \mid (x \in s) \leftrightarrow \big(\exists j \,\big|\, \big([j, x] \in f \,\&\, 1 \in j\big)\big)\big) \,\&\\
&\qquad\qquad \big(\exists g \mid [1, g] \in f \,\&\, \mathsf{Bound\_vars}(f) = \mathsf{Bound\_vars}(g) \cup s\big)\big)\big)\big).
\end{aligned}
$$

The following axiom defines the set of all free variables of a formula.

$$((\neg \mathsf{Is\_formula}(f) \vee [0,6] \in f \vee [0,7] \in f) \rightarrow (\mathsf{Free\_vars}(f) = \emptyset))$$
$$\& (([0,12] \in f \vee [0,13] \in f) \rightarrow$$
$$(\forall x \mid (x \in \mathsf{Free\_vars}(f)) \leftrightarrow (\exists j, g \mid 1 \in j \,\&\, [j, g] \in f$$
$$\& \, x \in \mathsf{Free\_vars}(g))))$$
$$\& (([0,0] \in f) \rightarrow (\forall x \mid (x \in \mathsf{Free\_vars}(f)) \leftrightarrow ([1, x] \in f)))$$
$$\& (([0,1] \in f \vee [0,2] \in f \vee [0,3] \in f \vee [0,4] \in f \vee$$
$$[0,8] \in f \vee [0,11] \in f) \rightarrow$$
$$(\exists g, h \mid [1, g] \in f \,\&\, [2, h] \in f$$
$$\& \, \mathsf{Free\_vars}(f) = \mathsf{Free\_vars}(g) \cup \mathsf{Free\_vars}(h)))$$
$$\& (([0,5] \in f) \rightarrow (\exists g \mid [1, g] \in f \,\&\, \mathsf{Free\_vars}(f) = \mathsf{Free\_vars}(g)))$$
$$\& (([0,9] \in f \vee [0,10] \in f) \rightarrow$$
$$(\exists s \mid (\forall x \mid (x \in s) \leftrightarrow (\exists j \mid [j, x] \in f \,\&\, 1 \in j)) \,\&$$
$$(\exists g \mid [1, g] \in f \,\&$$
$$(\forall y \mid (y \in \mathsf{Free\_vars}(f)) \leftrightarrow (y \in \mathsf{Free\_vars}(g) \,\&\, (\neg (y \in s))))))).$$

Our next step is to define the notion of predicate axiom in coded form. This merely formalizes the statements made in our earlier discussion of the predicate calculus. We begin with encodings of the list of propositional axioms given earlier. Then encodings of predicate axioms (ii–v) follow, and finally encodings of the equality-related predicate axioms (vi–viii). Predicate axiom (v) is simplified slightly (but to an equivalent axiom) by insisting that a term substituted for a free variable in a formula $F$ must have no variables in common with the bound variables of $F$.

$$\mathsf{Is\_propositional\_axiom}(s) \leftrightarrow$$
$$(\exists p, q, r \mid \mathsf{Is\_formula}(p) \,\&\, \mathsf{Is\_formula}(q) \,\&\, \mathsf{Is\_formula}(r) \,\&$$
$$((s = \mathsf{Seq3}(4, \mathsf{Seq3}(1, p, q), \mathsf{Seq3}(1, q, p)))$$
$$\vee (s = \mathsf{Seq3}(4, \mathsf{Seq3}(1, p, \mathsf{Seq3}(1, q, r)), \mathsf{Seq3}(1, \mathsf{Seq3}(1, p, q), r)))$$
$$\vee (s = \mathsf{Seq3}(4, \mathsf{Seq3}(1, p, p), p))$$
$$\vee (s = \mathsf{Seq3}(4, \mathsf{Seq3}(2, p, q), \mathsf{Seq3}(2, q, p)))$$
$$\vee (s = \mathsf{Seq3}(4, \mathsf{Seq3}(2, p, \mathsf{Seq3}(2, q, r)), \mathsf{Seq3}(2, \mathsf{Seq3}(2, p, q), r)))$$
$$\vee (s = \mathsf{Seq3}(4, \mathsf{Seq3}(2, p, p), p))$$

$$
\begin{aligned}
&\vee \big(s = \mathsf{Seq3}\big(4, \mathsf{Seq2}\big(5, \mathsf{Seq3}(1, p, q)\big), \mathsf{Seq3}\big(2, \mathsf{Seq2}(5, p), \mathsf{Seq2}(5, q)\big)\big)\big) \\
&\vee \big(s = \mathsf{Seq3}\big(4, \mathsf{Seq2}\big(5, \mathsf{Seq3}(2, p, q)\big), \mathsf{Seq3}\big(1, \mathsf{Seq2}(5, p), \mathsf{Seq2}(5, q)\big)\big)\big) \\
&\vee \big(s = \mathsf{Seq3}\big(4, \mathsf{Seq3}\big(1, \mathsf{Seq3}(2, p, q), r\big), \\
&\quad \mathsf{Seq3}\big(2, \mathsf{Seq3}(1, p, r), \mathsf{Seq3}(1, q, r)\big)\big)\big) \\
&\vee \big(s = \mathsf{Seq3}\big(4, \mathsf{Seq3}\big(2, \mathsf{Seq3}(1, p, q), r\big), \\
&\quad \mathsf{Seq3}\big(1, \mathsf{Seq3}(2, p, r), \mathsf{Seq3}(2, q, r)\big)\big)\big) \\
&\vee \big(s = \mathsf{Seq3}\big(3, \mathsf{Seq3}(4, p, q), \mathsf{Seq3}\big(4, \mathsf{Seq3}(1, p, r), \mathsf{Seq3}(1, q, r)\big)\big)\big) \\
&\vee \big(s = \mathsf{Seq3}\big(3, \mathsf{Seq3}(4, p, q), \mathsf{Seq3}\big(4, \mathsf{Seq3}(2, p, r), \mathsf{Seq3}(2, q, r)\big)\big)\big) \\
&\vee \big(s = \mathsf{Seq3}\big(3, \mathsf{Seq3}(4, p, q), \mathsf{Seq3}\big(4, \mathsf{Seq2}(5, p), \mathsf{Seq2}(5, q)\big)\big)\big) \\
&\vee \big(s = \mathsf{Seq3}\big(4, \mathsf{Seq3}(3, p, q), \mathsf{Seq3}\big(2, \mathsf{Seq2}(5, p), q\big)\big)\big) \\
&\vee \big(s = \mathsf{Seq3}\big(4, \mathsf{Seq3}(4, p, q), \mathsf{Seq3}\big(1, \mathsf{Seq3}(3, p, q), \mathsf{Seq3}(3, q, p)\big)\big)\big) \\
&\vee \big(s = \mathsf{Seq3}\big(3, \mathsf{Seq3}(1, p, q), p\big)\big) \\
&\vee \big(s = \mathsf{Seq3}\big(3, \mathsf{Seq3}\big(1, \mathsf{Seq3}(4, p, q), \mathsf{Seq3}(4, q, r)\big), \mathsf{Seq3}(4, p, r)\big)\big) \\
&\vee \big(s = \mathsf{Seq3}\big(3, \mathsf{Seq3}(4, p, q), \mathsf{Seq3}(4, q, p)\big)\big) \\
&\vee \big(s = \mathsf{Seq3}(4, p, p)\big) \\
&\vee \big(s = \mathsf{Seq3}\big(4, \mathsf{Seq3}\big(1, p, \mathsf{Seq2}(5, p)\big), \mathsf{Seq2}(0, 6)\big)\big) \\
&\vee \big(s = \mathsf{Seq3}\big(4, \mathsf{Seq3}\big(2, p, \mathsf{Seq2}(5, p)\big), \mathsf{Seq2}(0, 7)\big)\big) \\
&\vee \big(s = \mathsf{Seq3}\big(4, \mathsf{Seq2}\big(5, \mathsf{Seq2}(5, p)\big), p\big)\big) \\
&\vee \big(s = \mathsf{Seq3}\big(4, \mathsf{Seq3}\big(1, p, \mathsf{Seq2}(0, 7)\big), p\big)\big) \\
&\vee \big(s = \mathsf{Seq3}\big(4, \mathsf{Seq3}\big(1, p, \mathsf{Seq2}(0, 6)\big), \mathsf{Seq2}(0, 6)\big)\big) \\
&\vee \big(s = \mathsf{Seq3}\big(4, \mathsf{Seq3}\big(2, p, \mathsf{Seq2}(0, 7)\big), \mathsf{Seq2}(0, 7)\big)\big) \\
&\vee \big(s = \mathsf{Seq3}\big(4, \mathsf{Seq3}\big(2, p, \mathsf{Seq2}(0, 6)\big), p\big)\big) \\
&\vee \big(s = \mathsf{Seq2}(0, 7)\big) \\
&\vee \big(s = \mathsf{Seq3}\big(4, \mathsf{Seq3}\big(1, \mathsf{Seq3}(3, p, q), \mathsf{Seq3}(3, q, p)\big)\big)\big)\big)\big).
\end{aligned}
$$

Having now defined the notion of 'propositional axiom', we go on to describe that of 'predicate axiom'. Note that the coded forms of the predicate axioms listed previously appear in the following formula in the order Axiom (ii), Axiom (iii), Axiom (iv), Axiom (v).

$$
\begin{aligned}
&\mathsf{Is\_predicate\_axiom}(s) \leftrightarrow \\
&\quad \big(\mathsf{Is\_propositional\_axiom}(s) \vee \\
&\quad\quad \big(\exists p, q, x, y, z, u, v, w, c, c1 \mid \\
&\quad\quad\quad \mathsf{Is\_formula}(p) \mathbin{\&} \mathsf{Is\_formula}(q) \mathbin{\&} x = [0, u] \\
&\quad\quad\quad\quad \mathbin{\&} y = [0, v] \mathbin{\&} z = [0, w] \mathbin{\&} c = [0, c1] \\
&\quad\quad\quad\quad \mathbin{\&} \big(\big(s = \mathsf{Seq3}\big(3, \mathsf{Seq3}\big(1, \mathsf{Seq3}\big(9, \mathsf{Seq3}(3, p, q), \mathsf{Seq2}(0, x)\big), \\
&\quad\quad\quad\quad\quad\quad \mathsf{Seq3}\big(9, p, \mathsf{Seq2}(0, x)\big)\big), \mathsf{Seq3}\big(9, q, \mathsf{Seq2}(0, x)\big)\big)\big) \\
&\quad\quad\quad\quad\quad \vee \big(s = \mathsf{Seq3}\big(4, \mathsf{Seq2}\big(5, \mathsf{Seq3}\big(9, \mathsf{Seq2}(5, p), \mathsf{Seq2}(0, x)\big)\big), \\
&\quad\quad\quad\quad\quad\quad \mathsf{Seq3}\big(10, p, \mathsf{Seq2}(0, x)\big)\big)\big) \\
&\quad\quad\quad\quad\quad \vee \big(\big(s = \mathsf{Seq3}\big(4, p, \mathsf{Seq3}(9, p, \mathsf{Seq2}(0, x))\big)\big) \mathbin{\&} \big(\neg\big(x \in \mathsf{Free\_vars}(p)\big)\big)\big) \\
&\quad\quad\quad\quad\quad \vee \big(\exists g \mid \mathsf{Is\_formula}(g) \mathbin{\&} [0, 13] \in g \\
&\quad\quad\quad\quad\quad\quad \mathbin{\&} \big(\neg\big(\exists v \mid v \in \mathsf{Free\_vars}(g) \mathbin{\&} v \in \mathsf{Bound\_vars}(p)\big)\big) \\
&\quad\quad\quad\quad\quad\quad \mathbin{\&} \big(s = \mathsf{Seq3}\big(3, \mathsf{Seq3}\big(9, p, \mathsf{Seq2}(0, x)\big), \mathsf{Subst}(p, x, g)\big)\big)\big)\big)\big)\big).
\end{aligned}
$$

The collection of axioms specific to set theory can now be defined in coded form. Of course, we need to define codes for the function and predicate symbols which appear in these axioms. We do this as follows:

20: unordered pair,
21: ordered pair,
22: union sign ∪,
23: Is_next,
24: Is_integer,
25: Svm,
26: Is_seq,
27: Seq2,
28: Seq3,
29: null set symbol ∅,
30: power set symbol $\mathscr{P}$.

Note that the axioms needed fall into two groups, a first 'specialized' group corresponding to the ten set-theoretic axioms displayed earlier in this section, and a remaining 'general' group corresponding to the standard ZFC axioms. The first group is needed to define various predicates and operators which appear along the path to our final definition of the provability predicate 'Pr', which we must define formally in order to state our desired axioms of reflection. The second serve to ensure that the set theory in which we are working behaves in the standard way.

With this understanding, we can encode the collection of ZFC axioms as follows. Note that the first two axioms encoded in what follows are the axiom of subsets and the axiom of replacement, the latter of these in the form

$$\big(\forall x, y, z \,\big|\, (f \;\&\; \mathsf{Subst}(f, y, z)) \rightarrow (y = z)\big) \\ \rightarrow \big(\forall z \,\big|\, \big(\exists c \,\big|\, \big(\forall y \mid (y \in c) \leftrightarrow (\exists x \mid x \in z \;\&\; f)\big)\big)\big).$$

The remaining encoded axioms occur in the following order: axiom of subsets, nullset axiom, power set axiom, union set axiom. axiom of infinity, of choice, definition of 'Is_integer', of 'Is_map', of 'Is_seq', axiom of extensionality, definition of unordered pair, axiom of union of two sets, definition of ordered pair, and of 'Is_ext'.

$$\mathsf{Is\_ZF\_axiom}(s) \leftrightarrow$$

$$\big(\exists a, b, f, m, n, n, s, t, u, w, x, y, z,$$
$$a1, b1, f1, m1, n1, n1, s1, t_1, u1, w1, x1, y1, z1 \mid$$
$$a = \mathsf{Seq2}(0, a1) \;\&\; b = \mathsf{Seq2}(0, b1) \;\&\; f = \mathsf{Seq2}(0, f1) \;\&\; m = \mathsf{Seq2}(0, m1)$$
$$\& \; n = \mathsf{Seq2}(0, n1) \;\&\; s = \mathsf{Seq2}(0, s1) \;\&\; t = \mathsf{Seq2}(0, t_1) \;\&\; u = \mathsf{Seq2}(0, u1)$$
$$\& \; x = \mathsf{Seq2}(0, x1) \;\&\; y = \mathsf{Seq2}(0, y1) \;\&\; z = \mathsf{Seq2}(0, z1)$$
$$\& \; \big(\big(\big(\mathsf{Is\_formula}(f) \;\&\; x \notin \mathsf{Free\_vars}(f) \;\&\; z \notin \mathsf{Free\_vars}(f)\big) \;\&$$
$$\big(s = \mathsf{Seq3}\big(9, \mathsf{Seq3}\big(10, \mathsf{Seq3}\big(9, \mathsf{Seq3}\big(4, \mathsf{Seq3}(11, y, z),$$
$$\mathsf{Seq3}\big(1, \mathsf{Seq3}(11, y, x), f\big)\big), y\big), z\big), x\big)\big)\big) \vee$$
$$\big(\big(\mathsf{Is\_formula}(f) \;\&\; c \notin \mathsf{Free\_vars}(f) \;\&\; z \notin \mathsf{Free\_vars}(f)\big) \;\&$$
$$\big(\big(s = \mathsf{Seq3}\big(3, \mathsf{Seq3}\big(9, \mathsf{Seq3}\big(3, \mathsf{Seq3}\big(1, f, \mathsf{Subst}(f, y, z)\big),$$
$$\mathsf{Seq3}(8, y, z)\big), x\big) \cup \big\{[3, y]\big\} \cup \big\{[4, z]\big\}, \mathsf{Seq3}\big(9, \mathsf{Seq3}\big(10, \mathsf{Seq3}\big(9, \mathsf{Seq3}\big(4,$$
$$\mathsf{Seq3}(11, y, c), \mathsf{Seq3}\big(10, \mathsf{Seq3}\big(1, \mathsf{Seq3}(11, x, z), f\big), x\big)\big), y\big), c\big), z\big)\big)\big)$$
$$\vee \big(s = \mathsf{Seq2}\big(9, \mathsf{Seq3}\big(5, \mathsf{Seq3}\big(11, x, \mathsf{Seq2}\big(13, \mathsf{Seq2}(0, 29)\big)\big)\big), x\big)\big)\big)$$
$$\vee \big(s = \mathsf{Seq3}\big(9, \mathsf{Seq3}\big(8, \mathsf{Seq3}\big(11, z, \mathsf{Seq3}\big(13, \mathsf{Seq2}(0, 30), t\big)\big),$$
$$\mathsf{Seq3}\big(9, \mathsf{Seq3}\big(4, \mathsf{Seq3}(11, x, z), \mathsf{Seq3}\big(9, \mathsf{Seq3}\big(3, \mathsf{Seq3}(11, y, x),$$
$$\mathsf{Seq3}(11, y, t)\big), y\big)\big), x\big)\big), z\big) \cup \big\{[3, t]\big\}\big)$$
$$\vee \big(s = \mathsf{Seq3}\big(9, \mathsf{Seq3}\big(10, \mathsf{Seq3}\big(9, \mathsf{Seq3}\big(4, \mathsf{Seq3}(11, y, u),$$
$$\mathsf{Seq3}\big(10, \mathsf{Seq3}\big(1, \mathsf{Seq3}(11, y, x), \mathsf{Seq3}(11, x, z)\big), x\big)\big), y\big), u\big), z\big)\big)$$
$$\vee \big(s = \mathsf{Seq3}\big(10, \mathsf{Seq3}\big(1, \mathsf{Seq3}\big(11, \mathsf{Seq2}\big(13, \mathsf{Seq2}(0, 29)\big)\big), u\big),$$
$$\mathsf{Seq3}\big(9, \mathsf{Seq3}\big(3, \mathsf{Seq3}(11, z, u), \mathsf{Seq3}\big(11,$$
$$\mathsf{Seq3}(13, \mathsf{Seq2}(0, 20), z) \cup \big\{[3, z]\big\}, u\big)\big), z\big)\big), u\big)\big)$$

$$\begin{aligned}
&\vee \big(s = \mathsf{Seq2}\big(5, \mathsf{Seq3}\big(10, \mathsf{Seq3}\big(1, \mathsf{Seq2}\big(5, \mathsf{Seq3}\big(8, x, \\
&\quad \mathsf{Seq2}\big(13, \mathsf{Seq2}(0, 29)\big)\big)\big)\big), \mathsf{Seq3}\big(9, \mathsf{Seq3}\big(3, \mathsf{Seq3}(11, y, x), \\
&\quad \mathsf{Seq3}\big(10, \mathsf{Seq3}\big(1, \mathsf{Seq3}(11, z, x), \mathsf{Seq3}(11, z, y)\big), z\big)\big), y\big)\big), x\big)\big)\big) \\
&\vee \big(s = \mathsf{Seq3}\big(9, \mathsf{Seq3}\big(4, \mathsf{Seq3}\big(12, \mathsf{Seq2}(0, 24), n\big), \mathsf{Seq3}\big(9, \\
&\quad \mathsf{Seq3}\big(3, \mathsf{Seq3}\big(2, \mathsf{Seq3}(11, x, n), \mathsf{Seq3}(8, x, n)\big), \mathsf{Seq3}\big(2, \\
&\quad \mathsf{Seq3}\big(8, x, \mathsf{Seq2}\big(13, \mathsf{Seq2}(0, 29)\big)\big), \mathsf{Seq3}\big(10, \mathsf{Seq3}\big(1, \\
&\quad \mathsf{Seq3}(11, y, x), \mathsf{Seq3}\big(12, \mathsf{Seq2}(0, 23), x\big) \cup \big\{[3, y]\big\}\big), y\big)\big)\big), x\big)\big), n\big)\big) \\
&\vee \big(s = \mathsf{Seq3}\big(9, \mathsf{Seq3}\big(4, \mathsf{Seq3}\big(13, \mathsf{Seq2}(0, 25), f\big), \mathsf{Seq3}\big(1, \mathsf{Seq3}\big(9, \\
&\quad \mathsf{Seq3}\big(3, \mathsf{Seq3}(11, x, f), \mathsf{Seq3}\big(10, \mathsf{Seq3}\big(8, x, \mathsf{Seq3}\big(13, \\
&\quad \mathsf{Seq2}(0, 21), y\big) \cup \big\{[3, z]\big\}\big), y\big) \cup \big\{[3, z]\big\}\big), x\big), \mathsf{Seq3}\big(9, \mathsf{Seq3}\big(3, \\
&\quad \mathsf{Seq3}\big(1, \mathsf{Seq3}\big(11, \mathsf{Seq3}\big(13, \mathsf{Seq2}(0, 21), x\big) \cup \big\{[3, y]\big\}, f\big), \\
&\quad \mathsf{Seq3}\big(11, \mathsf{Seq3}\big(13, \mathsf{Seq2}(0, 21), x\big) \cup \big\{[3, z]\big\}, f\big)\big), \\
&\quad \mathsf{Seq3}(8, y, z)\big), x\big) \cup \big\{[3, y], [4, z]\big\}\big)\big), f\big)\big) \\
&\vee \big(s = \mathsf{Seq3}\big(9, \mathsf{Seq3}\big(4, \mathsf{Seq3}\big(12, \mathsf{Seq2}(0, 26), f\big), \mathsf{Seq3}\big(1, \mathsf{Seq3}\big(12, \\
&\quad \mathsf{Seq2}(0, 25), f\big), \mathsf{Seq3}\big(10, \mathsf{Seq3}\big(1, \mathsf{Seq3}\big(12, \mathsf{Seq2}(0, 24), n\big), \\
&\quad \mathsf{Seq3}\big(9, \mathsf{Seq3}\big(4, \mathsf{Seq3}(11, x, f), \mathsf{Seq3}\big(10, \mathsf{Seq3}\big(1, \mathsf{Seq3}(11, m, n), \\
&\quad \mathsf{Seq3}\big(8, x, \mathsf{Seq3}\big(13, \mathsf{Seq2}(0, 21), m\big) \cup \big\{[3, y]\big\}\big)\big), y\big) \\
&\quad \cup \big\{[3, m]\big\}\big), x\big)\big), n\big)\big)\big), f\big)\big) \\
&\vee \big(s = \mathsf{Seq3}\big(9, \mathsf{Seq3}\big(4, \mathsf{Seq3}(8, a, b), Seq3\big(9, \mathsf{Seq3}\big(4, \mathsf{Seq3}(11, x, a), \\
&\quad \mathsf{Seq3}(11, x, b)\big), x\big)\big), a\big) \cup \big\{[3, b]\big\}\big) \\
&\vee \big(s = \mathsf{Seq3}\big(9, \mathsf{Seq3}\big(4, \mathsf{Seq3}\big(11, x, \mathsf{Seq3}\big(13, \mathsf{Seq2}(0, 20), a\big) \\
&\quad \cup \big\{[3, b]\big\}\big), \mathsf{Seq3}\big(2, \mathsf{Seq3}(8, x, a), \mathsf{Seq3}(8, x, b)\big) \cup \big\{[3, x], [4, a]\big\} \\
&\quad \cup \big\{[5, x]\big\}\big), x\big) \cup \big\{[3, a]\big\} \cup \big\{[4, b]\big\}\big) \\
&\vee \big(s = \mathsf{Seq3}\big(9, \mathsf{Seq3}\big(4, \mathsf{Seq3}\big(11, x, \mathsf{Seq3}\big(13, \mathsf{Seq2}(0, 22), a\big) \\
&\quad \cup \big\{[3, b]\big\}\big), \mathsf{Seq3}\big(2, \mathsf{Seq3}(11, x, a), \mathsf{Seq3}(11, x, b)\big) \cup \big\{[3, x]\big\} \\
&\quad \cup \big\{[4, a]\big\} \cup \big\{[5, x]\big\}\big), x\big) \cup \big\{[3, a]\big\} \cup \big\{[4, b]\big\}\big) \\
&\vee \big(s = \mathsf{Seq3}\big(9, \mathsf{Seq3}\big(8, \mathsf{Seq3}\big(13, \mathsf{Seq2}(0, 21), x\big) \cup \big\{[3, y]\big\}, \mathsf{Seq3}\big(13, \\
&\quad \mathsf{Seq2}(0, 20), \mathsf{Seq3}\big(13, \mathsf{Seq2}(0, 20), \mathsf{Seq3}\big(13, \mathsf{Seq2}(0, 20),
\end{aligned}$$

$$
\begin{aligned}
&\mathsf{Seq3}\big(13, \mathsf{Seq2}(0,20), y\big) \cup \big\{[3,y]\big\}\big) \cup \big\{[3,y]\big\}\big)\\
&\quad \cup \big\{\big[3, \mathsf{Seq3}\big(13, \mathsf{Seq2}(0,20), x\big) \cup \big\{[3,x]\big\}\big]\big\}\big)\\
&\quad \cup \big\{\big[3, \mathsf{Seq3}\big(13, \mathsf{Seq2}(0,20), x\big) \cup \big\{[3,x]\big\}\big]\big\}\big), x\big) \cup \big\{[3,y]\big\}\big)\\
&\vee \big(s = \mathsf{Seq3}\big(9, \mathsf{Seq3}\big(4, \mathsf{Seq3}\big(12, \mathsf{Seq2}(0,23), s\big) \cup \big\{[3,t]\big\},\\
&\quad \mathsf{Seq3}\big(9, \mathsf{Seq3}\big(4, \mathsf{Seq3}(11, x, t), \mathsf{Seq3}\big(2, \mathsf{Seq3}(11, x, s),\\
&\quad \mathsf{Seq3}(8, x, s)\big)\big), x\big)\big), s\big) \cup \big\{[3,t]\big\}\big)\big)\big)\big)\big).
\end{aligned}
$$

We may also want to include some large-cardinal axiom. We saw in our discussion of these axioms that multiple possibilities suggest themselves. Here is what is required for a formal statement of one of them.

$$
\begin{aligned}
\mathsf{Ord}(o) &\leftrightarrow \big(\forall x \in o, y \,\big|\, \big((y \in x) \to (y \in o)\big)\\
&\qquad \& \ \big((y \in o) \to (x = y \vee x \in y \vee y \in x)\big)\big)\\
\mathsf{As\_many}(s,t) &\leftrightarrow \big(\exists f \mid \mathsf{Svm}(f) \ \& \ \big(\forall y \in t \,\big|\, \big(\exists x \in s \mid [x,y] \in f\big)\big)\big)\\
\mathsf{Is\_cardinal}(o) &\leftrightarrow \mathsf{Ord}(o) \ \& \ \big(\neg\big(\exists x \in o \mid \mathsf{As\_many}(x,o)\big)\big)\\
\mathsf{Is\_regular\_cardinal}(o) &\leftrightarrow \big(\neg\big(\exists s, u \,\big|\, \big(\neg\mathsf{As\_many}(s,o)\big) \ \& \ \big(\forall y \mid (y \in u)\\
&\qquad \leftrightarrow (\exists w \in s \mid y \in w)\big) \ \& \ \big(\forall y \in s \,\big|\\
&\qquad\qquad \big(\neg\mathsf{As\_many}(y,o)\big)\big) \ \& \ \mathsf{As\_many}(u,o)\big)\big)\\
\mathsf{Is\_strong\_limit\_cardinal}(o) &\leftrightarrow \big(\forall x \in o \,\big|\, \big(\exists y \in o \mid \mathsf{As\_many}\big(y, Pow(x)\big)\big)\big)\\
\mathsf{Is\_inaccessible\_cardinal}(o) &\leftrightarrow \big(\mathsf{Is\_regular\_cardinal}(o)\\
&\qquad \& \ \mathsf{Is\_strong\_limit\_cardinal}(o)\big)\\
\mathsf{Large\_cardinal\_axiom\_1} &\leftrightarrow \big(\exists o, s \mid \mathsf{Is\_inaccessible\_cardinal}(o)\\
&\qquad \& \ \mathsf{As\_many}(s,o)\\
&\qquad \& \ \big(\forall x \in s \mid \mathsf{Is\_inaccessible\_cardinal}(x) \ \& \ x \in o\big)\big).
\end{aligned}
$$

The last formula in the group just shown asserts that there is an inaccessible cardinal $M$ which is the $M$th inaccessible cardinal. We saw in our earlier discussion of large-cardinal axioms that this is implied by the assumption that there exists a Mahlo cardinal. A somewhat weaker statement applies if we use $\mathscr{H}(M)$ as our model of set theory. In this case all the inaccessible cardinals in $M$ remain inaccessible, but now there are too many of them to constitute a set. The statement that applies is then

$$
\begin{aligned}
&\mathsf{Large\_cardinal\_axiom\_2} \leftrightarrow\\
&\quad \big(\big(\exists o \mid \mathsf{Is\_inaccessible\_cardinal}(o)\big) \ \&\\
&\quad \big(\neg\big(\exists s \,\big|\, \big(\forall x \mid x \in s \leftrightarrow \mathsf{Is\_inaccessible\_cardinal}(x)\big)\big)\big)\big).
\end{aligned}
$$

It results from our earlier discussion of set-theory models of the form $\mathcal{H}(n)$ that if the first set of large-cardinal axioms is assumed, it follows that there is a cardinal $M$ such that $\mathcal{H}(M)$ is a model for the set of axioms obtained by replacing Large_cardinal_axiom_1 with the weaker Large_cardinal_axiom_2.

The encodings of the large-cardinal axioms just stated constitute the set of large_cardinal axioms, whose formal definition is as follows. Note that we use the following codes for the function and predicate symbols which appear:

31: Ord,
32: As_many,
33: Card,
34: Is_regular_cardinal,
35: Is_strong_limit_cardinal,
36: Is_inaccessible_cardinal.

Note also that the encoded forms of the axioms listed above appear in what follows in the order definition of ordinal, of 'As_many', of 'Is_regular_cardinal', of 'Is_limit_cardinal', of 'Inacessible_cardinal', statement of Large_cardinal_axiom_1, of Large_cardinal_axiom_2.

Is_largeN_axiom($s$) $\leftrightarrow$

$$(\exists v, o, x, u, y, w, s, s_1, t, t_1, f, f_1 \mid o = \mathsf{Seq2}(0, v) \,\&\, x = \mathsf{Seq2}(0, u)$$
$$\&\, y = \mathsf{Seq2}(0, w) \,\&\, s = \mathsf{Seq2}(0, s_1) \,\&\, t = \mathsf{Seq2}(0, t_1) \,\&\, f = \mathsf{Seq2}(0, f_1)$$
$$\&\, \big((s = \mathsf{Seq3}\big(9, \mathsf{Seq3}\big(4, \mathsf{Seq3}\big(13, \mathsf{Seq2}(0, 31), o\big), \mathsf{Seq3}\big(9, \mathsf{Seq3}\big(3,$$
$$\mathsf{Seq3}(11, x, o), \mathsf{Seq3}\big(1, \mathsf{Seq3}\big(3, \mathsf{Seq3}(11, y, x), \mathsf{Seq3}(11, y, o)\big), \mathsf{Seq3}\big(3,$$
$$\mathsf{Seq3}(11, y, o), \mathsf{Seq3}\big(2, \mathsf{Seq3}\big(2, \mathsf{Seq3}(8, x, y),$$
$$\mathsf{Seq3}(11, x, y)\big), \mathsf{Seq3}(11, y, x)\big)\big)\big)\big), x\big) \cup \{[3, y]\}\big), o\big)\big)$$
$$\vee \big(s = \mathsf{Seq3}\big(9, \mathsf{Seq3}\big(4, \mathsf{Seq3}\big(13, \mathsf{Seq2}(0, 32), z\big) \cup \{[3, t]\}, \mathsf{Seq3}\big(10,$$
$$\mathsf{Seq3}\big(1, \mathsf{Seq3}\big(12, \mathsf{Seq2}(0, 25), f\big), \mathsf{Seq3}\big(9, \mathsf{Seq3}\big(3,$$
$$\mathsf{Seq3}(11, y, t), \mathsf{Seq3}\big(10, \mathsf{Seq3}\big(3, \mathsf{Seq3}(11, x, z), \mathsf{Seq3}\big(11, \mathsf{Seq3}\big(12,$$
$$\mathsf{Seq2}(0, 21), x\big) \cup \{[3, y]\}, f\big)\big), x\big)\big), y\big), f\big)\big), z\big) \cup \{[3, t]\}\big)\big)$$
$$\vee \big(s = \mathsf{Seq3}\big(9, \mathsf{Seq3}\big(4, \mathsf{Seq3}\big(13, \mathsf{Seq2}(0, 34), o\big), \mathsf{Seq2}\big(5, \mathsf{Seq3}\big(10,$$
$$\mathsf{Seq3}\big(1, \mathsf{Seq2}\big(5, \mathsf{Seq3}\big(13, \mathsf{Seq2}(0, 32), s\big) \cup \{[3, o]\}\big), \mathsf{Seq3}\big(1, \mathsf{Seq3}\big(9,$$
$$\mathsf{Seq3}\big(4, \mathsf{Seq3}(11, y, t), \mathsf{Seq3}\big(10, \mathsf{Seq3}\big(1, \mathsf{Seq3}(11, x, s),$$
$$\mathsf{Seq3}(11, y, x)\big), x\big)\big), y\big), \mathsf{Seq3}\big(1, \mathsf{Seq3}\big(9, \mathsf{Seq3}\big(3, \mathsf{Seq3}(11, y, s),$$
$$\mathsf{Seq2}\big(5, \mathsf{Seq3}\big(13, \mathsf{Seq2}(0, 32), y\big) \cup \{[3, o]\}\big)\big), y\big),$$
$$\mathsf{Seq3}\big(13, \mathsf{Seq2}(0, 32), t\big) \cup \{[3, o]\}\big)\big)\big), s\big) \cup \{[3, t]\}\big)\big), o\big)\big)$$

$$\begin{aligned}
&\vee \big(s = \mathsf{Seq3}\big(9, \mathsf{Seq3}\big(1, \mathsf{Seq3}(12, 35, o), \mathsf{Seq3}\big(9, \mathsf{Seq3}\big(3, \mathsf{Seq3}(11, x, o),\\
&\qquad \mathsf{Seq3}\big(10, \mathsf{Seq3}\big(1, \mathsf{Seq3}(11, y, o), \mathsf{Seq3}\big(13, \mathsf{Seq2}(0, 32), y\big)\\
&\qquad \cup \big\{[3, \mathscr{P}(x)]\big\}\big), y\big)\big), x\big)\big), o\big)\big)\\
&\vee \big(s = \mathsf{Seq3}\big(9, \mathsf{Seq3}\big(4, \mathsf{Seq3}\big(12, \mathsf{Seq2}(0, 36), o\big), \mathsf{Seq3}\big(1, \mathsf{Seq3}\big(12,\\
&\qquad \mathsf{Seq2}(0, 34), o\big), \mathsf{Seq3}\big(12, \mathsf{Seq2}(0, 35), o\big)\big)\big), o\big)\big)\\
&\vee \big(s = \mathsf{Seq3}\big(10, \mathsf{Seq3}\big(1, \mathsf{Seq3}\big(12, \mathsf{Seq2}(0, 36), o\big), \mathsf{Seq3}\big(1, \mathsf{Seq3}\big(13,\\
&\qquad \mathsf{Seq2}(0, 32), y\big) \cup \big\{[3, o]\big\}, \mathsf{Seq3}\big(9, \mathsf{Seq3}\big(3, \mathsf{Seq3}(11, x, y), \mathsf{Seq3}\big(1,\\
&\qquad \mathsf{Seq3}\big(12, \mathsf{Seq2}(0, 36), x\big), \mathsf{Seq3}(11, x, o)\big)\big)\big), x\big)\big)\big), o\big) \cup \big\{[3, y]\big\}\big)\\
&\vee \big(s = \mathsf{Seq3}\big(10, \mathsf{Seq3}\big(1, \mathsf{Seq3}\big(12, \mathsf{Seq2}(0, 36), o\big), \mathsf{Seq2}\big(5, \big(\mathsf{Seq3}\big(10,\\
&\qquad \mathsf{Seq3}\big(9, \mathsf{Seq3}\big(4, \mathsf{Seq3}(11, x, s), \mathsf{Seq3}\big(12,\\
&\qquad \mathsf{Seq2}(0, 36), x\big)\big)\big), s\big)\big)\big)\big), o\big)\big)\big)\big).
\end{aligned}$$

The slightly weakened large-cardinal axiom displayed above is encoded by the final clause of this last display.

We can now assert that a formula is an axiom if and only if it belongs to one of the three preceding groups of axioms, and go on to define the notions 'a sequence of statements is a proof', and finally our target '$f$ is provable'.

$$\begin{aligned}
\mathsf{Is_axiom}(f) &\leftrightarrow \big(\mathsf{Is_predicate_axiom}(f) \vee \mathsf{Is_ZF_axiom}(f) \vee \mathsf{Is_largeN_axiom}(f)\big)\\
\mathsf{Is_proof}(p) &\leftrightarrow \big(\mathsf{Is_seq}(p)\ \&\ \big(\forall y \in p \,\big|\, \big(\exists n, g \mid y = [n,\ g]\ \&\ \mathsf{Is_formula}(g)\ \&\\
&\qquad \big(\mathsf{Is_axiom}(g) \vee \big(\exists m \in n, h \,\big|\, \big([m,\ h] \in s\big)\\
&\qquad\quad \&\ \big(\exists v \mid g = \mathsf{Seq3}(9, v, h)\big)\\
&\qquad\quad \vee \big(\exists m \in n,\ k \in n, h \,\big|\, \big([m,\ h] \in s\big)\\
&\qquad\quad \&\ \big(\big[k,\ \mathsf{Seq3}(3, h, g)\big] \in s\big)\big)\big)\big)\big)\big)\big)\\
\mathsf{Pr}(f) &\leftrightarrow \big(\exists p, n \mid \mathsf{Is_proof}(p)\ \&\ [n,\ f] \in p\big).
\end{aligned}$$

Note in connection with the preceding that

$$\big(\exists v \mid g = \mathsf{Seq3}(9, v, h)\big)$$

states that $g$ arises from $h$ by a generalization step, and that

$$\big[k,\ \mathsf{Seq3}(3, h, g)\big] \in s$$

states that $g$ arises from $h$ and some preceding formula by a modus ponens step.

### 6.3.1 Statement of the Axioms of Reflection

Having now managed to include the 'provability' predicate that concerns us in an extension of the ZFC axioms in whose consistency we have some reason to believe, we can reach our intended goal by stating the axioms of reflection. These are simply all statements of the form

$$\mathsf{Pr}(`F\text{'}) \to F,$$

where $F$ is any syntactically well-formed formula of our set-theoretic language, and '$F$' is its syntax tree, encoded in the manner described above.

Potential uses of these axioms have been explained above. Of course, we only want to add axioms of reflection to our basic set if inconsistency does not result. We shall now prove that this must be true if we assume that there exists at least one inaccessible cardinal but do not include this assumption in the set of axioms which enter into the definition of the predicate Pr. More generally, consistency is ensured if we assume that there exists an inaccessible cardinal, but in the axioms which enter into the definition of the predicate Pr we include only a large-cardinality statement that is true for the set of all cardinals $M$ less than $N$.

So the setting in which we work is as follows. We let $N$ be an inaccessible cardinal, and let $\mathscr{U} = \mathscr{H}(N)$ be the set defined recursively by

$$\begin{aligned}\mathsf{H\_}(x) =_{\mathrm{Def}}\ & \textbf{if } x = \emptyset \textbf{ then } \emptyset \\ & \textbf{else } \bigcup\{\mathscr{P}(\mathsf{H\_}(y)) : y \in x\} \textbf{ end if}\end{aligned}$$

and

$$\mathscr{H}(N) =_{\mathrm{Def}} \bigcup\{\mathsf{H\_}(n) : n \in N\},$$

as in Chap. 2, so that, as shown there, all of the axioms of set theory remain valid if we restrict our universe of sets to $\mathscr{U}$. This statement makes reference to the set $\mathscr{U}$, hence to $N$, and so is a theorem of the extension $\mathrm{ZFC}^{+}$ of ZFC in which an axiom stating the necessary properties of $N$, for example stating that it is an inaccessible cardinal, is present.

For each syntactically well-formed formula $F$, we let $F^{\mathscr{U}}$ be the result of relativizing $F$ to $\mathscr{U}$ in the following way. We process the syntax tree of $F$, modifying quantifier nodes but leaving all other nodes unchanged. Each universal quantifier

$$(\forall x_1, \ldots, x_n \mid P)$$

is changed into

$$\big(\forall x_1, \ldots, x_n \mid (x_1 \in \mathscr{U} \ \& \cdots \& \ x_n \in \mathscr{U}) \to P\big).$$

Each existential quantifier

$$(\exists x_1, \ldots, x_n \mid P)$$

is changed into

$$(\exists x_1, \ldots, x_n \mid x_1 \in \mathcal{U} \;\&\cdots\&\; x_n \in \mathcal{U} \;\&\; P).$$

We let $A_0$ be the assignment which maps the collection of predicate and function symbols which appear in the chain of definitions leading up to the definition of the provability predicate Pr (or, more properly, maps the integers which encode these symbols) in the following way. (The symbols in question are: $=$, $\in$, $\{\cdot,\cdot\}$ (unordered pair), $[\cdot,\cdot]$ (ordered pair), $\cup$, Is_next, Is_integer, Svm, Is_seq, Seq2, Seq3, $\{\}$ (nullset), $\mathcal{P}$.)

$=$ is mapped into $\{[[x,y],\ \textbf{if}\ x=y\ \textbf{then}\ 1\ \textbf{else}\ 0\ \textbf{end if}\,] : x\in\mathcal{U}, y\in\mathcal{U}\}$
$\in$ is mapped into $\{[[x,y],\ \textbf{if}\ x\in y\ \textbf{then}\ 1\ \textbf{else}\ 0\ \textbf{end if}\,] : x\in\mathcal{U}, y\in\mathcal{U}\}$
$\{\cdot,\cdot\}$ is mapped into $\{[[x,y],\{x,y\}] : x\in\mathcal{U}, y\in\mathcal{U}\}$
$[\cdot,\cdot]$ is mapped into $\{[[x,y],[x,y]] : x\in\mathcal{U}, y\in\mathcal{U}\}$
$\cup$ is mapped into $\{[[x,y],x\cup y] : x\in\mathcal{U}, y\in\mathcal{U}\}$
Is_next is mapped into $\{[[x,y],\ \textbf{if}\ y=x\cup\{x\}\ \textbf{then}\ 1\ \textbf{else}\ 0\ \textbf{end if}\,] :$
$x\in\mathcal{U}, y\in\mathcal{U}\}$
Is_integer is mapped into $\{[x,\ \textbf{if}\ x\in\mathbb{N}\ \textbf{then}\ 1\ \textbf{else}\ 0\ \textbf{end if}\,] : x\in\mathcal{U}\}$
(where as usual $\mathbb{N}$ is the set of finite ordinals)
Svm is mapped into $\{[f,\ \textbf{if}$
$(\exists x\in\mathcal{U}, y\in\mathcal{U}, z\in\mathcal{U} \mid [z,x]\in f$
$\&\ [z,y]\in f\ \&\ x\neq y)$
$\vee(\exists z\in f \mid (\forall x\in\mathcal{U}, y\in\mathcal{U} \mid z\neq[x,y]))\ \textbf{then}\ 0$
$\textbf{else}\ 1\ \textbf{end if}\,] : f\in\mathcal{U}\}$
Is_seq is mapped into $\{[x,\ \textbf{if}\ \mathsf{Svm}(x)\ \&\ \mathsf{domain}(x)\in\mathbb{N}\ \textbf{then}\ 1$
$\textbf{else}\ 0\ \textbf{end if}\,] : x\in\mathcal{U}\}$
Seq2 is mapped into $\{[[x,y],\{[0,x],[1,y]\}] : x\in\mathcal{U}, y\in\mathcal{U}\}$
Seq3 is mapped into $\{[[x,y,z],\{[0,x],[1,y],[2,z]\}] : x\in\mathcal{U}, y\in\mathcal{U}, z\in\mathcal{U}\}$
$\mathcal{P}$ is mapped into $\{[x,\{y : y\subseteq x\}] : x\in\mathcal{U}\}$
$\{\}$ is mapped into $\emptyset$

The following lemma states the intuitively obvious property of this assignment that we need below.

**Lemma 6.1** (Evaluation lemma) *Let $N$, $\mathcal{H}(N)$, $\mathcal{U}$, $ZFC^+$, and $A_0$ be as above, and for each syntactically well-formed formula $F$ let $F^{\mathcal{U}}$ be as above, and let '$F$' denote the syntax tree of $F$. Given any list of variables $v_1,\ldots,v_n$ and an equally long list $x_1,\ldots,x_n$ of elements of $\mathcal{U}$ let $A_0(v_1\hookrightarrow x_1,\ldots,v_n\hookrightarrow x_n)$ be the assignment which maps each $v_j$ into the corresponding $x_j$.*

*Then if $x_1,\ldots,x_n$ is the list of free variables of $F$, and '$x_j$' designates the symbol naming the $j$th of these variables for each $j$ between 1 and $n$, it follows that*

$$\big(\forall x_1\in\mathcal{U},\ldots,x_n\in\mathcal{U} \,\big|\, (\mathsf{Val}(A_0(`x_1\text{'}\hookrightarrow x_1,\ldots,`x_n\text{'}\hookrightarrow x_n),`F\text{'})=1)\leftrightarrow F^{\mathcal{U}}\big)$$

*is a theorem of $ZFC^+$.*

**Lemma 6.2** (Evaluation lemma for terms) *Let $N$, $\mathcal{H}(N)$, $\mathcal{U}$, and $A_0$ be as above, and for each syntactically well-formed term $F$ let $F^{\mathcal{U}}$ be as above, and let '$F$' denote the syntax tree of $F$.*

*Then if $x_1, \ldots, x_n$ is the list of variables of $F$, and '$x_j$' designates the symbol naming the $j$th of these variables for each $j$ between 1 and $n$, it follows that*

$$\big(\forall x_1 \in \mathcal{U}, \ldots, x_n \in \mathcal{U} \mid \mathsf{Val}\big(A_0(\text{'}x_1\text{'} \hookrightarrow x_1, \ldots, \text{'}x_n\text{'} \hookrightarrow x_n), \text{'}F\text{'}\big) = F\big)$$

*is a theorem of ZFC$^+$.*

**Corollary 6.1** *Under the same hypotheses as above, suppose that the formula $F$ contains no free variables. Then*

$$\big(\mathsf{Val}(A_0, \text{'}F\text{'}) = 1\big) \leftrightarrow F^{\mathcal{U}}$$

*is a theorem of ZFC$^+$.*

We prove the evaluation lemmas by induction on the size of the syntax tree of $F$, starting with the evaluation lemma for terms. If a term is just a variable $x$, then

$$\mathsf{Val}\big(A_0(\text{'}x\text{'} \hookrightarrow x), \text{'}x\text{'}\big) = x$$

for each $x$, so the lemma holds in this case. If a term is formed directly from one of the primitives used above by supplying the appropriate number of variables as arguments to the primitive, as for example in '$\{x, y\}$', then we have

$$\begin{aligned}&\mathsf{Val}\big(A_0(\text{'}x\text{'} \hookrightarrow x_0, \text{'}y\text{'} \hookrightarrow y_0), \text{'}\{x, y\}\text{'}\big)\\ &\qquad = \big\{\big[[x, y], \{x, y\}\big] : x \in \mathcal{U}, y \in \mathcal{U}\big\}(x_0, y_0) = \{x_0, y_0\}\end{aligned}$$

for all $x_0$ and $y_0$ in $\mathcal{U}$, so the lemma holds in this case also. Similarly elementary observations cover all the other function symbols appearing in the list of symbols displayed above, namely $[\cdot, \cdot]$, $\cup$, $\mathsf{Seq2}$, $\mathsf{Seq3}$, and $\mathcal{P}$. The reader is invited to supply details.

Now suppose that the evaluation lemma for terms fails for some $F$, and, proceeding inductively, that it fails for no term having a syntax tree smaller than that of $F$. Then $F$ must have the form

$$f(t_1, \ldots, t_k),$$

where $f$ is one of the primitive function symbols appearing in the list displayed above and $t_1, \ldots, t_k$ are subterms. By definition we have

$$\begin{aligned}&\mathsf{Val}\big(A_0(v_1 \hookrightarrow x_1, \ldots, v_n \hookrightarrow x_n), \text{'}f(t_1, \ldots, t_k)\text{'}\big)\\ &\qquad = A_0(\text{'}f\text{'})\big(\mathsf{Val}\big(A_0(v_1 \hookrightarrow x_1, \ldots, v_n \hookrightarrow x_n), \text{'}t_1\text{'}\big), \ldots\\ &\qquad\qquad \ldots, \mathsf{Val}\big(A_0(v_1 \hookrightarrow x_1, \ldots, v_n \hookrightarrow x_n), \text{'}t_k\text{'}\big)\big).\end{aligned}$$

By inductive hypothesis, the statement

$$(\forall x_1 \in \mathcal{U}, \ldots, x_n \in \mathcal{U} \mid \mathsf{Val}\big(A_0(\text{`}x_1\text{'} \hookrightarrow x_1, \ldots, \text{`}x_n\text{'} \hookrightarrow x_n), \text{`}t_j\text{'}\big) = t_j\big)$$

is a theorem of $\mathrm{ZFC}^+$ for each $j$ from 1 to $k$, where $x_1, \ldots, x_n$ is the list of all free variables appearing in any of the terms $t_j$. Hence we have

$$\begin{aligned}(\forall x_1 \in \mathcal{U}, \ldots, x_n \in \mathcal{U} \mid \mathsf{Val}\big(&A_0(\text{`}x_1\text{'} \hookrightarrow x_1, \ldots, \text{`}x_n\text{'} \hookrightarrow x_n),\\ &\text{`}f(t_1, \ldots, t_k)\text{'}\big) = A_0(\text{`}f\text{'})(t_1, \ldots, t_k)\big).\end{aligned}$$

Now we need to consider the function symbols appearing in the list displayed above, namely $\{\cdot,\cdot\}$, $[\cdot,\cdot]$, $\cup$, $\mathsf{Seq2}$, $\mathsf{Seq3}$, and $\mathcal{P}$. The argument is much the same in all of these cases. For example, for the powerset symbol $\mathcal{P}$ we have

$$A_0(\text{`}\mathcal{P}\text{'})(t_1) = \big\{\big[x, \{y : y \subseteq x\}\big] : x \in \mathcal{U}\big\}(t_1) = \{y : y \subseteq t_1\} = \mathcal{P}(t_1),$$

so

$$(\forall x_1 \in \mathcal{U}, \ldots, x_n \in \mathcal{U} \mid \mathsf{Val}\big(A_0(\text{`}x_1\text{'} \hookrightarrow x_1, \ldots, \text{`}x_1\text{'} \hookrightarrow x_n), \text{`}\mathcal{P}(t_1)\text{'}\big) = \mathcal{P}(t_1)\big),$$

proving our claim in this case. The reader is invited to supply the corresponding details in the remaining cases, namely $\{\cdot,\cdot\}$, $[\cdot,\cdot]$, $\cup$, $\mathsf{Seq2}$, and $\mathsf{Seq3}$. Together, these prove the evaluation lemma for terms in all cases.

Next we prove the evaluation lemma for formulae, beginning with atomic formulae, whose lead symbols must be one of the predicate symbols appearing in the list above, namely $=$, $\in$, $\mathsf{Is\_next}$, $\mathsf{Is\_integer}$, $\mathsf{Svm}$, $\mathsf{Is\_seq}$. Consider for example the case of an atomic formula whose lead symbol is $\in$. This must have the form

$$t_1 \in t_2$$

where $t_1$ and $t_2$ are terms, and so by definition and using the evaluation lemma for terms we have

$$\begin{aligned}(\forall x_1 \in \mathcal{U}, \ldots, x_n \in \mathcal{U} \mid &\mathsf{Val}\big(A_0(\text{`}x_1\text{'} \hookrightarrow x_1, \ldots, \text{`}x_n\text{'} \hookrightarrow x_n), \text{`}t_1 \in t_2\text{'}\big)\\ &\leftrightarrow A_0(\text{`}\in\text{'})\big(\mathsf{Val}\big(A_0(\text{`}x_1\text{'} \hookrightarrow x_1, \ldots, \text{`}x_n\text{'} \hookrightarrow x_n), \text{`}t_1\text{'}\big),\\ &\qquad \mathsf{Val}\big(A_0\big(\text{`}x_1\text{'} \hookrightarrow x_1, \ldots, \text{`}x_n\text{'} \hookrightarrow x_n\big), \text{`}t_2\text{'}\big)\big)\big)\\ &= A_0(\text{`}\in\text{'})(t_1, t_2)\\ &= \big\{\big[[x, y], \textbf{if } x \in y \textbf{ then } 1 \textbf{ else } 0 \textbf{ end if}\big] : x \in \mathcal{U}, y \in \mathcal{U}\big\}(t_2, t_2)\\ &= \textbf{if } t_1 \in t_2 \textbf{ then } 1 \textbf{ else } 0 \textbf{ end if}\,.\end{aligned}$$

Hence

$$(\forall x_1 \in \mathcal{U}, \ldots, x_n \in \mathcal{U} \,\big|\, \big(\mathsf{Val}\big(A_0(\text{`}x_1\text{'} \hookrightarrow x_1, \ldots, \text{`}x_n\text{'} \hookrightarrow x_n), \text{`}t_1 \in t_2\text{'}\big) = 1\big) \leftrightarrow t_1 \in t_2\big),$$

proving our claim for atomic formulae whose lead symbol is $\in$. The reader is invited to supply the corresponding details in the remaining cases, namely $=$, Is_next, Is_integer, Svm, Is_seq. Together, these cover all atomic formulae.

General formulae are built from atomic formulae by repeated application of the propositional operators &, $\vee$, $\rightarrow$, $\leftrightarrow$, $\neg$, and the two predicate quantifiers. Inductive arguments like those just given apply in all these cases. For example, if $f$ has the form '$g$ & $h$', where $g$ and $h$ both satisfy the conclusion of the Evaluation Lemma, and our notations are as above, then

$$\begin{aligned}
&\big(\mathsf{Val}\big(A_0(\text{`}x_1\text{'} \hookrightarrow x_1, \ldots, \text{`}x_n\text{'} \hookrightarrow x_n), \text{`}g \,\&\, h\text{'}\big) = 1\big) \\
&\leftrightarrow \min\big(\mathsf{Val}\big(A_0(\text{`}x_1\text{'} \hookrightarrow x_1, \ldots, \text{`}x_n\text{'} \hookrightarrow x_n), \text{`}g\text{'}\big), \\
&\qquad \mathsf{Val}\big(A_0(\text{`}x_1\text{'} \hookrightarrow x_1, \ldots, \text{`}x_n\text{'} \hookrightarrow x_n), \text{`}h\text{'}\big)\big) = 1 \\
&\leftrightarrow \big(\mathsf{Val}\big(A_0(\text{`}x_1\text{'} \hookrightarrow x_1, \ldots, \text{`}x_n\text{'} \hookrightarrow x_n), \text{`}g\text{'}\big) = 1 \\
&\qquad \& \ \mathsf{Val}\big(A_0(\text{`}x_1\text{'} \hookrightarrow x_1, \ldots, \text{`}x_n\text{'} \hookrightarrow x_n), \text{`}h\text{'}\big)\big) = 1 \\
&\leftrightarrow \big(g^{\mathcal{U}} \,\&\, h^{\mathcal{U}}\big) \leftrightarrow (g \,\&\, h)^{\mathcal{U}} \leftrightarrow f^{\mathcal{U}}.
\end{aligned}$$

Next suppose that $f$ has the form

$$(\forall y_1, \ldots, y_k \mid g), \tag{6.4}$$

where $g$ satisfies the conclusion of the Evaluation Lemma. Since both $f^{\mathcal{U}}$ and $\mathsf{Val}(A'', f)$ (for any suitable assignment $A''$) are unchanged if variables $y_j$ not free in $g$ and repeated copies of variable are dropped from $y_1, \ldots, y_k$, we can suppose that there are none such. Hence, if the free variables of formula (6.4) are $x_1, \ldots, x_n$, then the free variables of $g$ are $x_1, \ldots, x_n, y_1, \ldots, y_k$. Therefore

$$\begin{aligned}
&\big(\mathsf{Val}\big(A_0(\text{`}x_1\text{'} \hookrightarrow x_1, \ldots, \text{`}x_n\text{'} \hookrightarrow x_n), \text{`}(\forall y_1, \ldots, y_k \mid g)\text{'}\big) = 1\big) \leftrightarrow \\
&\min\big(\mathsf{Val}(A_0', \text{`}g\text{'})\big),
\end{aligned}$$

where the minimum is extended over all assignments $A_0'$ which cover all the variables '$x_1$', ..., '$x_n$' and '$y_1$', ..., '$y_k$', and which agree with

$$A_0(\text{`}x_1\text{'} \hookrightarrow x_1, \ldots, \text{`}x_n\text{'} \hookrightarrow x_n)$$

except possibly on the variables '$y_1$', ..., '$y_k$'. That is,

$$\begin{aligned}
&\big(\mathsf{Val}\big(A_0(\text{`}x_1\text{'} \hookrightarrow x_1, \ldots, \text{`}x_n\text{'} \hookrightarrow x_n), \text{`}(\forall y_1, \ldots, y_k \mid g)\text{'}\big) = 1\big) \\
&\quad \leftrightarrow \min\big(A_0(\text{`}x_1\text{'} \hookrightarrow x_1, \ldots, \text{`}x_n\text{'} \hookrightarrow x_n, \text{`}y_1\text{'} \hookrightarrow y_1, \ldots, \text{`}y_k\text{'} \hookrightarrow y_k), \text{`}g\text{'}\big),
\end{aligned}$$

where now the minimum is extended over all possible values of $y_1, \ldots, y_k$, all belonging to $\mathcal{U}$. Hence, since by inductive assumption we have

$$\big(\forall x_1,\ldots,x_n,y_1,\ldots,y_k \,\big|\, \big(\mathsf{Val}\big(A_0(\text{`}x_1\text{'} \hookrightarrow x_1,\ldots,\text{`}x_n\text{'} \hookrightarrow x_n, \\ \text{`}y_1\text{'} \hookrightarrow y_1,\ldots,\text{`}y_k\text{'} \hookrightarrow y_k),\text{`}g\text{'}\big) = 1\big) \leftrightarrow g\big),$$

it follows that

$$\big(\mathsf{Val}\big(A_0(\text{`}x_1\text{'} \hookrightarrow x_1,\ldots,\text{`}x_n\text{'} \hookrightarrow x_n),\text{`}(\forall y_1,\ldots,y_k \mid g)\text{'}\big) = 1\big) \\ \leftrightarrow \big(\forall y_1,\ldots,y_k \mid \mathsf{Val}\big(A_0(\text{`}x_1\text{'} \hookrightarrow x_1,\ldots,\text{`}x_n\text{'} \hookrightarrow x_n, \\ \text{`}y_1\text{'} \hookrightarrow y_1,\ldots,\text{`}y_k\text{'} \hookrightarrow y_k),\text{`}g\text{'}\big) = 1\big) \\ \leftrightarrow (\forall y_1,\ldots,y_k \mid g),$$

verifying the Evaluation Lemma in this case also.

The reader is invited to supply the details of the remaining cases.

This concludes our proof of the Evaluation Lemma.

Next we note and will prove the following fact concerning the value $\mathsf{Val}(A_0, F)$ for every formula provable from the axioms of ZFC, as possibly extended by a collection of large-cardinal axiom like those displayed above. To avoid too much obscuring detail, we shall state and prove this fact using English in the normal way to abbreviate formal set-theoretic details.

**Lemma 6.3** *Let ZFC* be the collection of axioms of ZFC, possibly extended by a set of large-cardinal axioms like those displayed above. Let* Pr *be the proof predicate defined by these axioms in the manner detailed above. Let CFP all the function and predicate symbols that appear in the axioms ZFC*. Let* $\mathsf{Is\_assignment}(A,\mathscr{U})$ *be the set-theoretic formula which asserts that A is an assignment with universe* $\mathscr{U}$*, and let* $\mathsf{True\_on\_ax}(A)$ *be the formula which asserts that* $\mathsf{Val}(A,s) = 1$ *for the encoded form of every axiom of ZFC*. (The reader is invited to write out the details of these formulae.) Then*

$$\big(\forall s \,\big|\, \big(\mathsf{Pr}(s)\ \&\ \mathsf{Is\_assignment}(A_0,\mathscr{U})\ \&\ \mathsf{True\_on\_ax}(A_0) \\ \&\ \mathsf{domain}(A_0) \supseteq \big(\mathsf{Free\_vars}(s) \cup CFP\big)\big) \rightarrow \mathsf{Val}(A_0,s) = 1\big)$$

*is a theorem of ZFC.*

*Proof* Suppose not, so that there exist $A_0$, $\mathscr{U}$, and $s$ satisfying

$$\mathsf{Pr}(s)\ \&\ \mathsf{Is\_assignment}(A_0,\mathscr{U})\ \&\ \mathsf{True\_on\_ax}(A_0) \\ \&\ \mathsf{domain}(A_0) \supseteq \big(\mathsf{Free\_vars}(s) \cup CFP\big)\ \&\ \mathsf{Val}(A_0,s) = 0.$$

Using the definition of 'Pr', it follows that there exists a $p$ such that

$$\text{Is\_proof}(p) \,\&\, \text{Is\_integer}(n) \,\&\, [n, s] \in p \,\&\, \text{Is\_assignment}(A_0, \mathscr{U}) \,\&$$
$$\text{True\_on\_ax}(A_0) \,\&\, \text{domain}(A_0) \supseteq \big(\text{Free\_vars}(s) \cup CFP\big) \,\&\, \text{Val}(A_0, s) = 0.$$

The induction principle available in ZF set theory allows us to improve this last statement to

$$\text{Is\_proof}(p) \,\&\, \text{Is\_integer}(n) \,\&\, [n, s] \in p \,\&\, \text{Is\_assignment}(A_0, \mathscr{U})$$
$$\&\, \text{True\_on\_ax}(A_0)$$
$$\&\, \text{domain}(A_0) \supseteq \big(\text{Free\_vars}(s) \cup CFP\big) \,\&\, \text{Val}(A_0, s) = 0$$
$$\&\, \big(\forall m \in n, t \mid [m, t] \in p \rightarrow \big(\forall A_1 \,\big|\, \big(\text{Is\_assignment}(A_1, \mathscr{U}) \,\&\, \text{True\_on\_ax}(A_1)$$
$$\&\, \text{domain}(A_1) \supseteq \big(\text{Free\_vars}(t) \cup CFP\big)\big) \rightarrow \big(\text{Val}(A_1, t) = 1\big)\big)\big).$$

By the definition of Is_proof, we have

$$\text{Is\_axiom}(s) \vee \big(\big(\exists m \in n, h \mid ([m, h] \in p)\big) \,\&\, \big(\exists v \mid s = \text{Seq3}(9, v, h)\big)\big)$$
$$\vee \big(\big(\exists m \in n, k \in n, h \big|\big([m, h] \in p\big) \,\&\, \big(\big[k, \text{Seq3}(3, h, s)\big] \in p\big)\big)\big). \quad (6.5)$$

The alternative $\text{Is\_axiom}(s)$ of (6.5) is ruled out since in this case we have $\text{Val}(A_0, s) = 1$ from $\text{True\_on\_ax}(A_0)$. In the second case of (6.5) there exist $m$, $h$, and $v$ such that

$$m \in n \,\&\, [m, h] \in p \,\&\, s = \text{Seq3}(9, v, h).$$

It follows from '$m \in n$' that

$$\big(\text{domain}(A) \supseteq \big(\text{Free\_vars}(g) \cup CFP\big)\big) \rightarrow \big(\text{Val}(A, h) = 1\big)$$

for any assignment $A$ that agrees with $A_0$ on CFP. Since $s = \text{Seq3}(9, v, h)$, which states that the decoded version of $s$ has the form

$$(\forall v \mid d)$$

where $d$ is the decoded form of $h$, it follows that for each assignment $A'$ for which

$$\text{domain}(A') \supseteq \big(\text{Free\_vars}(s) \cup CFP\big)\big)$$

that agrees with $A_0$ on CFP we must have $\text{Val}(A', s) = 1$, since this is a minimum of values $\text{Val}(A, h)$, extended over assignments $A$ that agree with $A'$ on $\text{Free\_vars}(s) \cup CFP$. Hence $\text{Val}(A_0, s) = 0$ is impossible in the second case of (6.5) also. In the remaining case there exist formulae $h$ and $g$, and integers $m$ and $k \in n$, such that

$$[m, h] \in p \,\&\, [k, g] \in p \,\&\, m \in n \,\&\, k \in n \,\&\, g = \text{Seq3}(3, h, s).$$

It follows as above that

$$\big(\text{domain}(A) \supseteq \big(\text{Free\_vars}(g) \cup CFP\big)\big) \to \big(\text{Val}(A, h) = 1 \ \&\ \text{Val}(A, g) = 1\big),$$

for each assignment $A$ that agrees with $A_0$ on CFP. From this it follows that

$$\big(\text{domain}(A) \supseteq \big(\text{Free\_vars}(g) \cup CFP\big)\big) \to \big(\text{Val}(A, s)\big),$$

since $g = \text{Seq3}(3, h, s)$ states that the decoded form of $g$ is $e \to d$, where $e$ and $d$ are the decoded forms of $h$ and $s$, respectively. But any assignment $A'$ such that

$$\big(\text{domain}(A') \supseteq \big(\text{Free\_vars}(s) \cup CFP\big)\big)$$

can be extended to an assignment satisfying $\text{domain}(A) \supseteq (\text{Free\_vars}(g) \cup CFP)$ by defining it arbitrarily on the elements of the difference set $\text{Free\_vars}(g) \setminus \text{Free\_vars}(s)$, and plainly $\text{Val}(A', s) = \text{Val}(A, s)$ for any such assignment. Hence

$$\big(\text{domain}(A') \supseteq \big(\text{Free\_vars}(s) \cup CFP\big)\big) \to \big(\text{Val}(A, s')\big),$$

for each assignment $A$ that agrees with $A_0$ on CFP. This rules out the third alternative of (6.5) and so concludes our proof of the lemma. □

The following statement now follows easily from the lemmas proved above.

**Theorem 6.7** *Let ZFC$^+$ be the ZFC axioms of set theory, supplemented by an axiom stating that there exists at least one inaccessible cardinal $N$. Let $A_0$ be the model of set theory with universe $\mathcal{H}(N)$ described above. Then it is a theorem of ZFC$^+$ that $A_0$ is a model in which all the axioms of ZFC, plus all the reflection axioms*

$$\text{Pr}(`F\text{'}) \to F,$$

*where $F$ is any syntactically legal formula and 'Pr' means 'provable from the axioms of ZFC' (without the axiom of existence of an inaccessible cardinal) are true. Hence it follows from the axioms of ZFC$^+$ that this set of axioms is consistent.*

*Proof* The proof is simply as follows. Let $F$ be a syntactically legal formula without free variables. Corollary 6.1 tells us that

$$\big(\text{Val}(A_0, `F\text{'}) = 1\big) \leftrightarrow F^{\mathcal{U}}$$

is a theorem of ZFC$^+$, and Lemma 2 tells us that

$$\text{Pr}(`F\text{'}) \to \big(\text{Val}(A_0, s) = 1\big)$$

is a theorem of ZFC. Our theorem follows immediately from these two statements. □

The authors are indebted to Prof. Mark Fulk for suggesting the line of thought developed in this section. Prof. Luigia Carlucci Aiello and Richard Weyhrauch have explored similar ideas in [AW80].

## 6.4 A Digression Concerning Foundations

*Absolute, true, and mathematical time, of itself, and from its own nature flows equably without regard to anything external [· · · ] Absolute space, in its own nature, without regard to anything external, remains always similar and immovable.*

Isaac Newton, Principia, 1687

Much has been written about the broader significance of Gödel's results. The first Gödel theorem (undecidability) is best viewed as a special case of Chaitin's more general result, which states a general limit on the power of formal logical reasoning. Specifically, Chaitin exhibits a large class of statements which can be formalized but not formally proved. But why, in hindsight, should it ever have been expected that every statement which can be written in a formalism can also be proved in the formalism? There is plainly no reason why this should be so, and much prior mathematical experience points in the opposite direction (for example, few elementary functions have elementary integrals).

Gödel's theorems cast some light on the classical philosophical distinction between analytic (*a priori*) knowledge and the kind of inductive knowledge for which the scientist strives. The boundary lines drawn between these two realms of knowledge have shifted in the course of time. As illustrated by the famous nineteenth century changes in the dominant view of geometry, the analytic realm has steadily lost ground to the inductive realm. Originally the axioms of geometry were seen as statements about the physical universe, involving idealizations (e.g. consideration of points of zero extension and lines of zero thickness) which did not misrepresent physical reality in any significant way. Now the dominant view is that space is probably not Euclidean, and may not even be continuous. This means that classical geometry is but a crudely approximate model of some aspects of physical reality, and that the best evidence for the consistency of its traditional axioms is the fact that they have a formal set-theoretic model. Few will now include more than arithmetic, and perhaps abstract set theory, in the analytic realm. But if the theorems of arithmetic are analytic knowledge, but not knowledge of the physical world, what are they knowledge about? Perhaps they represent *a priori* knowledge about computation. Let us consider this possibility.

To use reasoning in a particular logical system as a surrogate for computation, we need only be certain that the logical system in which we reason should be consistent. But, since Gödel's second theorem tells us that formal proof of the consistency of a system $L$ requires use of a system different from $L$ and probably stronger than $L$, how can such certainty ever be achieved? One way in which such a belief, though of course no certainty, can arise is by the accumulation of experience with the objects of a certain realm, leading to formulation of statements concerning the entities of that realm. Generalized and formalized, these can subsequently become the axioms and theorems of a fully elaborated formal system. If experience then seems to show that the resulting formal system is consistent, this may be taken as evidence that its theorems are true statements about objects of some kind.

The hope of grounding mathematics, and hence the analytic truths which it may claim to embody, on a set of intuitions less tenuous than those available in a set theory incorporating Cantor's aggressive linguistic extensions has lent interest to various narrower formalisms. The most important of these is the pure theory of integers, in the form given it by Peano. Integers originally come into one's ken as the words 'zero, one, two, three, ...' of a kind of poem which, as a child, one learns to repeat, and with whose indefinite extensibility one becomes familiar. (The simplest, though not the most convenient, form of the number poem is its monadic version: 'one, one-and-one, one-and-one-and-one, ...') Experience with such collections of words leads to the following generalizations: (i) given any such word, there is a way of forming the very next word in the series; (ii) no word occurs twice in the series thereby generated; (iii) If one starts with any word in the sequence and repeatedly steps back from words to their predecessors, one will eventually reach zero.

Peano's axioms formalize these intuitions. They can be stated as follows:

1. (i) 0 is a natural number.
2. (ii) For every natural number $x$ there exists another natural number $x'$ called the successor of $x$.
3. (iii) $\neg(0 = x')$ for every natural number $x$ ($x'$ being the successor of $x$).
4. (iv) If $x' = y'$ then $x = y$.
5. (v) If $Q$ is a property of natural numbers and $x$ is a number such that $Q(0) \neq Q(x)$, then there exists a natural number $y$ such that $Q(y) \neq Q(y')$.

A compelling way of linking Peano's axioms to primitive physical experience is to regard them as statements about integers in monadic notation, i.e. sequences of marks having the form

$$/ \; // \; /// \; //// \cdots$$

(The empty sequence is allowed.) In physical terms, two such sequences are equal if their ends match when the sequences are set side by side. An extra mark can be added to the end of any such sequence, giving Peano's successor operation $x'$. If a sequence s is non-empty, we can erase one mark from its end, giving the 'Prev' operation. Experience indicates that $\mathsf{Prev}(x') = x$ (erasing a mark just added to $x$ restores $x$), and that if $x$ is not empty $\mathsf{Prev}(x)' = x$ (adding back a mark just removed from $x$ restores $x$). Peano's axioms (ii–iv) follow readily from these statements. Experience also indicates that if marks are repeatedly erased from the end of any such $x$ the empty string will eventually result. If $Q(x)$ is any stable property of such sequences of marks, this gives us a systematic way of searching for two successive integers $y$, $y'$ for which $Q(y)$ and $Q(y')$ are different, and so justifies Peano's axiom (v) of induction.

But the following objection can be raised to the universal quantification of these axioms. Physics tells us that sufficiently large sequences of marks need not behave in the same way as shorter sequences. For example, even if marks are stored in the most compact way likely to be feasible, as states of single atoms, it is probably not possible to store more than $10^{27}$ marks per kilogram of matter. $10^{57}$ marks would therefore have a mass roughly equal to that of the sun, and so could be expected to ignite a nuclear chain reaction spontaneously. The mass of our galaxy is unlikely to be more that $10^{13}$ times larger, so $10^{70}$ marks would have a mass larger than that of our galaxy. Compactly arranged, these marks would promptly disappear into a black hole. This makes it plain that integers larger than $2^{10^{70}}$ are fictive constructs, which can never be written out fully even in monadic notation. This suggests that denotations like $10^{10^{10^{10^{10}}}}$ of much larger integers should be viewed as logical specifications Exp(10, Exp(10, Exp(10, Exp(10, 10)))) of hypothetical computations that can in fact never be carried out. However, this does not make them useless, since we can reason about them in a system believed to be consistent, and such reasoning may lead us to useful conclusions about other, perfectly feasible, computations.

Note also that the direct evidence we have for the consistency of any logical system can never apply to proofs more than $10^{70}$ steps in length, since for the reasons stated above we can never expect to write out any such proof. Of course, this does not prevent us from reasoning about much longer proofs, but as above it may be best to regard such reasoning as the manipulation of marks in some formalized meta-logical system believed to be consistent.

Any attempt to move the consistency of Peano's full set of statements from 'belief' to 'certainty' would therefore seem to rest on a claim that there really exists a Platonic universe of objects, for example idealized integers, about which our axioms are true statements, and hence necessarily consistent. But how can truths about such Platonic universes be known reliably? Two methods, direct intuition and reasoning from consequences, suggest themselves. Claims concerning direct intuition are doubtful. If direct intuition is admitted as a legitimate source of knowledge, how can we decide between the rival claimants to direct intuition, if their claims differ? And, even if we can convince ourselves that all normal humans have the same intuition, why should the objective truth of this intuition be admitted? In biological terms the human differs little from the nematode, except for possessing limbs and an enlarged nervous system. Like the squid, we have a highly elaborated visual system. Beyond this, we have an ability to deal with language, and so to deal with abstract patterns. But, as work with visual illusions shows plainly, even stable, immediate, compelling, and universally shared perceptions about physical reality can be wrong. Even such immediate perceptions do not tell us what the world really contains, but only how our nervous systems react to that content. Why should the far more elusive mechanisms of logical intuition be more trustworthy? To move towards truth we must employ the patient and never conclusive methods of experimental science, and experience shows science to progress best when it tries actively to probe the limits of its own best current view.

A 'realist' or 'Platonist' view, reflecting the belief that the statements of mathematics are truths about some partly but progressively comprehended class of ideal objects can be stated as follows. Of all formally plausible axioms (for example, statements asserting the existence of various kinds of very large cardinal numbers) not provable from assumptions presently accepted, a growing and coherent collection, this view predicts, will prove to be particularly rich in consequences, including consequences for questions that can be stated in currently accepted terms, but not settled. These new axioms may be taken to hint at an underlying truth. The negatives of these progressively discovered axioms will prove to be unfruitful and so will gradually die out as dead ends.

In contrast, a more purely formalist view of the situation suggests that this may not prove to be the case, but that as collections of axioms rich in interesting consequences are found these collections will prove to be mutually contradictory and so not suggestive of any progressively revealed underlying truth. It further suggests that a useful path to progress may lie in the attempt to undercut existing axiom systems by looking for competing and incompatible systems identical with current systems only in areas covered by actual experience.

The theory of hereditarily finite sets presented in the preceding pages is logically equivalent to Peano's theory of integers, in the sense that (as we have shown) integers can be modelled within this restricted theory of sets, while conversely the hereditarily finite sets can be encoded as integers. However the theory of hereditarily finite sets has a considerably richer intuitive content. Peano's system captures only the process of counting, but without anything to count, or indeed any evident way of capturing the notion of 1-1 correspondence fundamental to the actual use of counting. The axiomatization of hereditarily finite sets given above is better in this regard, since it makes notions like mapping and function value more accessible.

Cantor's full theory of infinite sets goes beyond Peano's system, and is in fact strong enough to allow proof that Peano's system is consistent. However, in formal terms the step from the theory of hereditarily finite sets to the full Cantor theory is slight. Three changes suffice. First, an axiom of infinity (existence of at least one infinite set) must be added, and the subset induction principle abandoned in favour of the more limited principle of membership induction. Then the existence of the set of all subsets of a given set, which follows as a theorem in the theory of hereditarily finite sets, must be assumed as an axiom. Why do we assume that these changes leave set theory consistent?

The answer is in part historical. The application of set-theoretic reasoning in geometric and analytic situations dominated by the notion of the 'continuum' led to Cantor's theory of infinite sets. In Descartes' approach to geometry the real line is ultimately seen as the collection of all infinite decimals, which naturally introduces work with sets whose elements have no natural enumerated order. Further geometric and analytic studies of important point loci lead to work with increasingly general subsets of the real line. Out of such work the conviction grows that much of what can be said about infinite collections is entirely independent of the manner in which they are ordered, and so requires no particular ordering. This linguistic generalization was made systematically by Cantor, who then moved on to unrestrained discussions of sets, involving such notions as the set of all subsets of an infinite set. This led him to consider statements concerning sets which are (more and more) uncountably infinite. Of course, as such generalized language moves away from the areas of experience in which it originates, the evidence that what is being said is more than word-play destined to collapse either in self-contradiction or in collision with some more useful logical system, becomes increasingly tenuous. Fears of this kind certainly surrounded Cantor's work in its early decades, as indicated by his 1883 remark "[$\cdots$] I realise that in this undertaking I place myself in a certain opposition to views widely held concerning the mathematical infinite and to opinions on the nature of numbers frequently defended", and by Kronecker's remark that Cantor's new set theory was 'a humbug'. And in fact set theory, in the over-generalized form initially given it by Cantor, does lead to inconsistencies if pushed to the limit, as Cantor was pushing so many of his set-theoretic ideas. However, this fact did not lead to the collapse of the theory, but only to its repair. Such repair, in a manner preserving the validity of Cantor's general approach and all of his appealing statements concerning infinite sets, underlies the formalized set theory used in this book. It leads to a formalism that, as far as we know, is consistent, and that provides a good foundation for the now immense accumulation of work in mathematical analysis. Cumulatively this work gives evidence for the consistency of set theory that is just as compelling as the like evidence of the consistency of arithmetic. Only the existence of a set-theoretic proof that arithmetic is consistent, and of an arithmetic proof that no such proof is possible in pure arithmetic, would seem to justify a much greater degree of confidence in the consistency of the one rather than the other of these systems.

The remarks made in the preceding paragraphs suggest the following cautious view of the distinction between analytic and inductive knowledge. Inductive knowledge is the always uncertain knowledge of the physical universe gained by studying it closely and manipulating it in ways calculated to uncover initially unremarked properties of reality stable enough to be understood. Analytic knowledge is knowledge of an aspect of reality, specifically certain aspects of the behaviour of marks and signs (e.g. on paper or computer tape) limited enough for guessed generalizations to have a good chance of being correct. (It is in fact hard to do without these guesses, since the marks and signs to which they relate are the tools we use to reason in all other areas of science.) What we believe about these signs is that a certain way of manipulating them (by logical reasoning) that is somewhat more general than the standard process of automated computation seems to be formally consistent. Although inconsistencies, requiring some kind of intellectual repair, might possibly be found in still unexplored areas of the realm of these signs, we still have no idea of how to convert this suspicion into something useful.

## References


[AW80] Aiello, L., Weyhrauch, R.W.: Using meta-theoretic reasoning to do algebra. In: Bibel, W., Kowalski, R. (eds.) Proc. of the 5th Conference on Automated Deduction, Les Arcs, France. LNCS, vol. 87, pp. 1–13. Springer, Berlin (1980)

[SDDS86] Schwartz, J.T., Dewar, R.K.B., Dubinsky, E., Schonberg, E.: Programming with Sets: An Introduction to SETL. Texts and Monographs in Computer Science. Springer, Berlin (1986)

# Chapter 7
# A Self-contained Beginning for Ref's Main Proof Scenario

This chapter presents in full a group of formalized proofs that reaches in a small number of pages many results about ordinals, various properties of the transitive closure operation, transfinite induction, and then Zorn's lemma. We end with the proofs of a few basic facts concerning finite sets, including a finite induction principle.

## 7.1 Axioms of Set Theory

The *regularity* postulate and the *infinity* postulate are the only ones explicitly present in the THEORY 'Set_theory' underlying the proof-checker Ref. All other axioms typical of set theory—and, to some extent, even the two just recalled—, are built into the inferential machinery of Ref. We now recast the said postulates in the form of two theorems: citing them will thus become handier, because universal quantifiers are left understood.

THEOREM 0: [Global choice]
$\big(\mathsf{X} = \emptyset \ \&\ \mathbf{arb}(\mathsf{X}) = \emptyset\big) \vee \big(\mathbf{arb}(\mathsf{X}) \in \mathsf{X} \ \&\ \mathbf{arb}(\mathsf{X}) \cap \mathsf{X} = \emptyset\big)$. PROOF:
Suppose_not($x_0$) $\Rightarrow$
$$\textit{Stat0}:\ \neg\Big(\big(\mathsf{x}_0 = \emptyset \ \&\ \mathbf{arb}(\mathsf{x}_0) = \emptyset\big) \vee \big(\mathbf{arb}(\mathsf{x}_0) \in \mathsf{x}_0 \ \&\ \mathbf{arb}(\mathsf{x}_0) \cap \mathsf{x}_0 = \emptyset\big)\Big)$$
Assump $\Rightarrow$ $\textit{Stat1}:\ \big\langle \forall \mathsf{s} \,\big|\, \big(\mathsf{s} = \emptyset \ \&\ \mathbf{arb}(\mathsf{s}) = \emptyset\big) \vee \big(\mathbf{arb}(\mathsf{s}) \in \mathsf{s} \ \&\ \mathbf{arb}(\mathsf{s}) \cap \mathsf{s} = \emptyset\big)\big\rangle$
$\langle \mathsf{x}_0 \rangle \hookrightarrow \textit{Stat1}(\textit{Stat0}\star) \Rightarrow$ false; Discharge $\Rightarrow$ QED

In the statement of the following it would be easy, but pointless, to replace $\mathsf{s}_\infty$ by a new constant $\mathsf{s}'_\infty$ satisfying the stronger (more conventional) condition
$$\emptyset \in \mathsf{s}'_\infty \ \&\ \big(\mathsf{X} \in \mathsf{s}'_\infty \rightarrow \{\mathsf{X}\} \in \mathsf{s}'_\infty\big).$$

THEOREM 00: [Axiom of Infinity] $\mathsf{s}_\infty \neq \emptyset \ \&\ (\mathsf{X} \in \mathsf{s}_\infty \rightarrow \{\mathsf{X}\} \in \mathsf{s}_\infty)$. PROOF:
Suppose_not($x_0$) $\Rightarrow$ AUTO

J.T. Schwartz et al., *Computational Logic and Set Theory*,
DOI 10.1007/978-0-85729-808-9_7, © Springer-Verlag London Limited 2011

Assump ⇒ *Stat1* : $\langle \forall x \in s_\infty \mid \{x\} \in s_\infty \rangle$ & $s_\infty \neq \emptyset$

$\langle x_0 \rangle \hookrightarrow$ *Stat1* ⇒ false; Discharge ⇒ QED

## 7.2 Pairs and Maps

We now begin by making a trick, purely set-theoretic definition of the notion of *ordered pair*. We also give formal definitions of both ordered-pair component extractor functions. These definitions are shown only for completeness: all that really counts, about them, being that they enforce the 'unique retrieval' law

$$\langle \forall s, d \mid [s, d]^{[1]} = s \ \&\ [s, d]^{[2]} = d \rangle,$$

which could have been encapsulated inside a THEORY such as

THEORY ordPair( )
⇒ $(ordp_\Theta, fst_\Theta, snd_\Theta)$
$\langle \forall p, \ell, r \mid p = ordp_\Theta(\ell, r) \rightarrow fst_\Theta(p) = \ell \ \&\ snd_\Theta(p) = r \rangle$
END ordPair

and which, anyway, is built-in in the extended version of multilevel syllogistic encompassed by the most central among Ref's inference primitives, named ELEM.

DEF pairs · 0: [Ordered pair] $[L, R] =_{Def} \{\{L\}, \{\{L\}, \{\{R\}, R\}\}\}$

DEF pairs · 1: [1st component of ordered pair] $P^{[1]} =_{Def} \mathbf{arb}(\mathbf{arb}(P))$

DEF pairs · 2: [2nd component of ordered pair] $P^{[2]} =_{Def}$
$$\mathbf{arb}\big(\mathbf{arb}\big(\mathbf{arb}\big(P \setminus \{\mathbf{arb}(P)\}\big) \setminus \{\mathbf{arb}(P)\}\big)\big)$$

The following operations are usually applied to sets of ordered pairs, here called *maps*:

DEF maps · 1: [Map domain] $\mathbf{domain}(F) =_{Def} \{p^{[1]} : p \in F\}$

DEF maps · 2: [Map restriction] $F_{|A} =_{Def} \{p \in F \mid p^{[1]} \in A\}$

DEF maps · 3: [Value of single-valued function] $F \restriction X =_{Def} \mathbf{arb}\big(F_{|\{X\}}\big)^{[2]}$

It is convenient to summarize some of the key results about *maps* in auxiliary THEORYs, such as the following one, that ease their use. We focus here on maps of the form $\{[x, f(x)] : x \in s\}$, which are always single-valued.

THEORY fcn_symbol(f(X), g, s)
-- Contains some elementary lemmas about single-valued functions
$g = \{[x, f(x)] : x \in s\}$
END fcn_symbol

ENTER_THEORY fcn_symbol

Note: till we return from 'fcn_symbol' to set theory, we are reasoning within the theory, so $g = \{[x, f(x)] : x \in s\}$ is available as an axiom, and all theorems proved are added to the set of conclusions of the theory, rather than to the set of conclusions of the top-level set-theory. First we show that the domain of g is simply s.

THEOREM fcn_symbol · 1: [Mapformer domain] **domain**(g) = s. PROOF:
Suppose_not ⇒ $\textbf{domain}(g) \neq s$

For in the contrary case we would have $\{x^{[1]} : x \in \{[x, f(x)] : x \in s\}\} \neq s$ by definition, so there would exist an $x \in s$ such that $[x, f(x)]^{[1]} \neq x$, which is impossible.

Use_def(**domain**) ⇒ $\{x^{[1]} : x \in g\} \neq s$
Assump ⇒ $g = \{[y, f(y)] : y \in s\}$
EQUAL ⇒ $\{x^{[1]} : x \in g\} = \{x^{[1]} : x \in \{[y, f(y)] : y \in s\}\}$
ELEM ⇒ $\{x^{[1]} : x \in \{[y, f(y)] : y \in s\}\} \neq s$
SIMPLF ⇒ $\{[y, f(y)]^{[1]} : y \in s\} \neq \{x : x \in s\}$
Set_monot ⇒ $\{[y, f(y)]^{[1]} : y \in s\} = \{y : y \in s\}$
Discharge ⇒ QED

Next we show that $g \upharpoonright x = f(x)$ for any $x \in s$.

THEOREM fcn_symbol · 2: [Image by a mapformer] $X' \in s \rightarrow g \upharpoonright X' = f(X')$. PROOF:
Suppose_not(c) ⇒ $c \in s \;\&\; g \upharpoonright c \neq f(c)$

For suppose not, and let $c \in s$ be a counterexample, so that by definition of functional application (and map restriction) we would have

$$\textbf{arb}\left(\left\{[x, f(x)] : x \in s \,\middle|\, [x, f(x)]^{[1]} \in \{c\}\right\}\right)^{[2]} \neq f(c).$$

Use_def(↾) ⇒ $\textbf{arb}(g_{|\{c\}})^{[2]} \neq f(c)$
Use_def(|) ⇒ $\textbf{arb}(\{p \in g \mid p^{[1]} \in \{c\}\})^{[2]} \neq f(c)$
Assump ⇒ $g = \{[x, f(x)] : x \in s\}$
EQUAL ⇒ $\textbf{arb}(\{p \in \{[x, f(x)] : x \in s\} \mid p^{[1]} \in \{c\}\})^{[2]} \neq f(c)$
SIMPLF ⇒ $\textbf{arb}\left(\left\{[x, f(x)] : x \in s \,\middle|\, [x, f(x)]^{[1]} \in \{c\}\right\}\right)^{[2]} \neq f(c)$

|| We can simplify $\{[x, f(x)] : x \in s \mid [x, f(x)]^{[1]} \in \{c\}\}$ to $\{[x, f(x)] : x \in s \mid x \in \{c\}\}$, for if these sets were different there would be a $d \in s$ such that the conditions $[d, f(d)]^{[1]} \in \{c\}$ and $d \in c$ were inequivalent, which is impossible.

Suppose ⇒

$$\textit{Stat1}: \{[x, f(x)] : x \in s \mid [x, f(x)]^{[1]} \in \{c\}\} \neq \{[x, f(x)] : x \in s \mid x \in \{c\}\}$$

⟨d⟩↪*Stat1* ⇒ $d \in s \,\&\, \neg([d, f(d)]^{[1]} \in \{c\} \leftrightarrow d \in \{c\})$

Discharge ⇒ $\{[x, f(x)] : x \in s \mid [x, f(x)]^{[1]} \in \{c\}\} = \{[x, f(x)] : x \in s \mid x \in \{c\}\}$

|| But $\{[x, f(x)] : x \in s \mid x \in \{c\}\}$ simplifies in two steps to $\{[x, f(x)] : x \in \{c\}\}$, which is the same as $\{[c, f(c)]\}$. Hence if our theorem is false we would have **arb**$(\{[c, f(c)]\})^{[2]} \neq f(c)$, a contradiction proving the theorem.

Suppose ⇒ $\textit{Stat2}: \{[x, f(x)] : x \in s \mid x \in \{c\}\} \neq \{[x, f(x)] : x \in \{c\}\}$

⟨e⟩↪*Stat2* ⇒ $(e \in \{[x, f(x)] : x \in s \mid x \in \{c\}\} \,\&\, e \notin \{[x, f(x)] : x \in \{c\}\}) \vee$
$e \notin \{[x, f(x)] : x \in s \mid x \in \{c\}\} \,\&\, e \in \{[x, f(x)] : x \in \{c\}\}$

Suppose ⇒ $\textit{Stat3}: e \in \{[x, f(x)] : x \in s \mid x \in \{c\}\} \,\&$
$\textit{Stat4}: e \notin \{[x, f(x)] : x \in \{c\}\}$

⟨$e_1$⟩↪*Stat3* ⇒ $e = [e_1, f(e_1)] \,\&\, e_1 \in s \,\&\, e_1 \in \{c\}$

⟨$e_1$⟩↪*Stat4* ⇒ false; Discharge ⇒ $\textit{Stat5}: e \notin \{[x, f(x)] : x \in s \mid x \in \{c\}\} \,\&$
$\textit{Stat6}: e \in \{[x, f(x)] : x \in \{c\}\}$

⟨$e_2$⟩↪*Stat6* ⇒ $e = [e_2, f(e_2)] \,\&\, e_2 \in \{c\}$

⟨$e_2$⟩↪*Stat5* ⇒ false; Discharge ⇒
$\{[x, f(x)] : x \in s \mid x \in \{c\}\} = \{[x, f(x)] : x \in \{c\}\}$

SIMPLF ⇒ $\{[x, f(x)] : x \in \{c\}\} = \{[c, f(c)]\}$

EQUAL ⇒ $(\{[c, f(c)]\})^{[2]} \neq f(c)$

Discharge ⇒ QED

|| Our next theorem rounds out the preceding result by showing that $g\restriction x = \emptyset$ for $x \notin s$.

THEOREM fcn_symbol · 3: [Mapformer image in general]
$g\restriction X' =$ **if** $X' \in s$ **then** $f(X')$ **else** $\emptyset$ **fi**. PROOF:

Suppose_not(c) ⇒ $g\restriction c \neq$ **if** $c \in s$ **then** $f(c)$ **else** $\emptyset$ **fi**

|| For suppose not, and (as the possibility $c \in s$ gets readily discarded) let $c \notin s$ be a counterexample. Then by definition of functional application (and map restriction) the value **arb**$(\{[x, f(x)] : x \in s \mid [x, f(x)]^{[1]} \in \{c\}\})$ must be nonzero, and then—since **arb**$(\emptyset) = \emptyset$—so is the set $\{[x, f(x)] : x \in s \mid [x, f(x)]^{[1]} \in \{c\}\}$.

Suppose ⇒ $c \in s$

$\langle c\rangle \hookrightarrow$ *Tfcn_symbol* $\cdot 2 \Rightarrow$ $g\restriction c = f(c)$

Discharge ⇒ *Stat1* : $c \notin s \;\&\; g\restriction c \neq \emptyset$

Use_def($\restriction$) ⇒ $c \notin s \;\&\; \mathbf{arb}(g_{|\{c\}})^{[2]} \neq \emptyset$

Suppose ⇒ $\mathbf{arb}(g_{|\{c\}}) = \emptyset$

EQUAL ⇒ $\emptyset^{[2]} \neq \emptyset$

Use_def($\cdot^{[2]}$) ⇒ $\mathbf{arb}\big(\mathbf{arb}\big(\mathbf{arb}(\emptyset \backslash \{\mathbf{arb}(\emptyset)\}) \backslash \{\mathbf{arb}(\emptyset)\}\big)\big) \neq \emptyset$

TELEM ⇒ $\emptyset \backslash \{\mathbf{arb}(\emptyset)\} = \emptyset$

EQUAL ⇒ $\mathbf{arb}\big(\mathbf{arb}\big(\mathbf{arb}(\emptyset) \backslash \{\mathbf{arb}(\emptyset)\}\big)\big) \neq \emptyset$

$\langle \emptyset \rangle \hookrightarrow T0\ (\star) \Rightarrow$ $\mathbf{arb}(\emptyset) = \emptyset$

TELEM ⇒ $\mathbf{arb}(\emptyset) \backslash \{\mathbf{arb}(\emptyset)\} = \emptyset$

EQUAL ⇒ $\mathbf{arb}(\mathbf{arb}(\emptyset)) \neq \emptyset$

EQUAL ⇒ $\mathbf{arb}(\emptyset) \neq \emptyset$

EQUAL ⇒ false; Discharge ⇒ $\mathbf{arb}(g_{|\{c\}}) \neq \emptyset$

Use_def($|$) ⇒ $g_{|\{c\}} = \{p \in g \mid p^{[1]} \in \{c\}\}$

EQUAL ⇒ $\mathbf{arb}(\{p \in g \mid p^{[1]} \in \{c\}\}) \neq \emptyset$

Assump ⇒ $g = \{[x, f(x)] : x \in s\}$

EQUAL ⇒ $\mathbf{arb}(\{p \in \{[x, f(x)] : x \in s\} \mid p^{[1]} \in \{c\}\}) \neq \emptyset$

SIMPLF ⇒ *Stat2* : $\mathbf{arb}(\{[x, f(x)] : x \in s \mid [x, f(x)]^{[1]} \in \{c\}\}) \neq \emptyset$

$\langle \{[x, f(x)] : x \in s \mid [x, f(x)]^{[1]} \in \{c\}\} \rangle \hookrightarrow T0$ (*Stat2*$\star$) ⇒

*Stat3* : $\{[x, f(x)] : x \in s \mid [x, f(x)]^{[1]} \in \{c\}\} \neq \emptyset$

Hence there would exist a $d \in s$ such that $[d, f(d)]^{[1]} \in \{c\}$, implying $c \in s$, a contradiction which proves our assertion.

$\langle d \rangle \hookrightarrow$ *Stat3*() ⇒ *Stat4* : $d \in s \;\&\; [d, f(d)]^{[1]} \in \{c\}$

(*Stat1*, *Stat4*)Discharge ⇒ QED

ENTER_THEORY Set_theory

DISPLAY fcn_symbol

THEORY fcn_symbol(f(X), g, s)
-- Contains some elementary lemmas about single-valued functions
$g = \{[x, f(x)] : x \in s\}$
⇒
$\mathbf{domain}(g) = s$
$\langle \forall x' \mid x' \in s \rightarrow g\restriction x' = f(x') \rangle$
$\langle \forall x' \mid g\restriction x' = \mathbf{if}\ x' \in s\ \mathbf{then}\ f(x')\ \mathbf{else}\ \emptyset\ \mathbf{fi} \rangle$
END fcn_symbol

## 7.3 From Reachability to Transfinite Induction

### *7.3.1 Reachability in a Big Graph*

The following theory has two predicates, one monadic and the other dyadic, as arguments: these represent nodes (or 'vertices') and arcs (or 'edges') of a system. What we mean by 'system', following Aczel [Acz88], is a structure akin to a graph but whose nodes and arcs might form proper classes. Anyway, we insist that the immediate descendants of each node x must be included in a set (possibly a set which depends on x).

THEORY reachability$\big(\mathsf{V}(\mathsf{X}), \mathsf{E}(\mathsf{X}, \mathsf{Y})\big)$
$\big\langle \forall x \mid V(x) \rightarrow \big\langle \exists c, \forall y \mid E(x, y) \;\&\; V(y) \rightarrow y \in c \big\rangle\big\rangle$
END reachability

ENTER_THEORY reachability

Inside this THEORY 'reachability', we will now use Skolemization to associate with every node the set of its children in the system. For each node x, we own a set c comprising all the immediate descendants of x; hence separation enables us to form the set $ch = \{y \in c \mid E(x, y) \;\&\; V(y)\}$ of all nodes which are immediate descendants of x in the system. This set will be named children(x) by the subsequent application of Skolemization. When x is not a node, a forthcoming theorem will arrange things so that $\mathsf{children}(x) = \emptyset$.

THEOREM reachability · 0: [Every node has a set of children]
$\big\langle \exists ch, \forall y \mid E(X, y) \;\&\; V(X) \;\&\; V(y) \leftrightarrow y \in ch \big\rangle$. PROOF:
Suppose_not$(x_0)$ ⇒ *Stat0* : $\neg\big\langle \exists ch, \forall y \mid E(x_0, y) \;\&\; V(x_0) \;\&\; V(y) \leftrightarrow y \in ch \big\rangle$
Suppose ⇒ $\neg V(x_0)$
$\langle \emptyset \rangle \hookrightarrow$ *Stat0(Stat0⋆)* ⇒ *Stat1* : $\neg\big\langle \forall y \mid E(x_0, y) \;\&\; V(x_0) \;\&\; V(y) \leftrightarrow y \in \emptyset \big\rangle$
$\langle y \rangle \hookrightarrow$ *Stat1(Stat0⋆)* ⇒ false; Discharge ⇒ AUTO
Assump ⇒ *Stat2* : $\big\langle \forall x \mid V(x) \rightarrow \big\langle \exists c, \forall y \mid E(x, y) \;\&\; V(y) \rightarrow y \in c \big\rangle\big\rangle$
$\langle x_0 \rangle \hookrightarrow$ *Stat2(Stat0⋆)* ⇒ *Stat3* : $\big\langle \exists c, \forall y \mid E(x_0, y) \;\&\; V(y) \rightarrow y \in c \big\rangle \;\&\; V(x_0)$
$\langle k \rangle \hookrightarrow$ *Stat3(Stat3⋆)* ⇒ *Stat4* : $\big\langle \forall y \mid E(x_0, y) \;\&\; V(y) \rightarrow y \in k \big\rangle$
Loc_def ⇒ $kh = \big\{ y \in k \mid E(x_0, y) \;\&\; V(y) \big\}$
$\langle kh \rangle \hookrightarrow$ *Stat0(Stat4⋆)* ⇒ *Stat5* : $\neg\big\langle \forall y \mid E(x_0, y) \;\&\; V(x_0) \;\&\; V(y) \leftrightarrow y \in kh \big\rangle$
$\langle y_0 \rangle \hookrightarrow$ *Stat5(Stat3⋆)* ⇒ $E(x_0, y_0) \;\&\; V(y_0) \neq y_0 \in kh$
Suppose ⇒ *Stat6* : $E(x_0, y_0) \;\&\; V(y_0)$
(*Stat4⋆*)ELEM ⇒ *Stat7* : $y_0 \notin \big\{ y \in k \mid E(x_0, y) \;\&\; V(y) \big\}$
$\langle y_0 \rangle \hookrightarrow$ *Stat4(Stat6⋆)* ⇒ $y_0 \in k$

$\langle y_0 \rangle \hookrightarrow$ *Stat7(Stat6⋆)* ⇒ false; *(Stat4⋆)*Discharge ⇒

*Stat8* : $y_0 \in \{y \in k \mid E(x_0, y) \,\&\, V(y)\} \,\&\, \neg(E(x_0, y_0) \,\&\, V(y_0))$

$\langle\,\rangle \hookrightarrow$ *Stat8(Stat8⋆)* ⇒ false; Discharge ⇒ QED

‖ Skolemize this last statement, rewriting it in the form:

APPLY $\langle v1_{\Theta} : \text{children} \rangle$ Skolem⇒

THEOREM reachability · 1*a*: [Children lemma, 0]

$\langle \forall x, y \mid E(x, y) \,\&\, V(x) \,\&\, V(y) \leftrightarrow y \in \text{children}(x) \rangle$.

‖ Then recast the 'children lemma' just obtained in a form with tacit universal quantifiers.

THEOREM reachability · 1: [Children lemma] $E(X, Y) \,\&\, V(X) \,\&\, V(Y) \leftrightarrow Y \in \text{children}(X)$. PROOF:

Suppose_not(x, y) ⇒ AUTO

*Treachability* · 1*a* ⇒ *Stat1* : $\langle \forall x, y \mid E(x, y) \,\&\, V(x) \,\&\, V(y) \leftrightarrow y \in \text{children}(x) \rangle$

$\langle x \rangle \hookrightarrow$ *Stat1* ⇒ *Stat2* : $\langle \forall y \mid E(x, y) \,\&\, V(x) \,\&\, V(y) \leftrightarrow y \in \text{children}(x) \rangle$

$\langle y \rangle \hookrightarrow$ *Stat2* ⇒ false; Discharge ⇒ QED

‖ Now we start to prepare more closely for the proof of a preliminary version of the principle of transfinite induction by making an auxiliary definition: we introduce the set $\text{descs}_{\Theta}(s)$ of those x which either belong to s or are descendants of elements of s (i.e., children of s, children of children of s, and so on recursively). The construction of $\text{descs}_{\Theta}(s)$ will proceed in stages; as a preliminary, in fact, we define the sets descs_x(s, le) of all nodes that are reachable from s through paths of given 'length' le. In an intuitive discussion, we think that the length of a path is a natural number; but, as we do not own from the outset the set of all natural numbers, we exploit the basic infinite set $s_{\infty}$ as a convenient surrogate of this set.

DEF reachability · 0: [Recursively defined iterated children] $\text{descs\_x}(S, Le) =_{\text{Def}}$

**if** $Le = \mathbf{arb}(s_{\infty})$ **then** S **else**

$\{u : w \in \mathbf{arb}(\{\text{descs\_x}(S, y) : y \in Le \mid y \in s_{\infty}\}), u \in \text{children}(w)\}$

**fi**

Explanation: We know that $s_\infty$ is a nonnull set satisfying the property that $\{X\} \in s_\infty$ follows from $X \in s_\infty$. Hence $\mathbf{arb}(s_\infty) = a$, and $\{a\}$, $\{\{a\}\}$, … are members of $s_\infty$; and since each of them belongs to its immediate follower and membership does not form cycles (as one can deduce from regularity), they differ from one another and hence their supply is infinite. As natural numbers have not been introduced yet, we can exploit a in the role of 0, $\{a\}$ in the role of 1, $\{\{a\}\}$ of 2, etc. We have defined descs_x(S, Le) in such a way that when Le varies over a, $\{a\}$, $\{\{a\}\}$, … the sets descs_x(S, Le) come to form a sequence descs_x(S, a), descs_x(S, $\{a\}$), descs_x(S, $\{\{a\}\}$), … whose first component is S and hence is formed by the same elements as S, the second is formed by the children of elements of S, the third by the children of children of S, and so on. At the end, by forming the union of all components of this sequence (see our next definition), we obtain the set of all nodes reachable from S along paths formed by arcs of the system.

DEF reachability · 1: [Ultimate descendants of a node] $\text{descs}_\Theta(S) =_{\text{Def}}$

$$\{u : i \in s_\infty, u \in \text{descs\_x}(S, i)\}$$

The set just defined includes S; moreover, we will show that it is transitively closed under E. First we need the following simple lemma:

THEOREM reachability · 2: [Descendants indexed by the singletons in the basic infinite set] $X \in s_\infty \rightarrow$

$$\text{descs\_x}(S, \{X\}) = \{u : w \in \text{descs\_x}(S, X), u \in \text{children}(w)\}.$$

PROOF:
Suppose_not(x, s) ⇒ AUTO

Since $x \in s_\infty$, $\{x\} \neq \mathbf{arb}(s_\infty)$, and so descs_x(s, $\{x\}$) = $\{u : v \in \mathbf{arb}(\{\text{descs\_x}(s, y) : y \in \{x\}\}), u \in \text{children}(\{x\})\}$ by definition.

Use_def(descs_x) ⇒ $\text{descs\_x}(s, \{x\}) =$

$$\textbf{if } \{x\} = \mathbf{arb}(s_\infty) \textbf{ then } s \textbf{ else } \{u : w \in \mathbf{arb}(\{\text{descs\_x}(s, y) : y \in \{x\} \mid y \in s_\infty\}), u \in \text{children}(w)\} \textbf{ fi}$$

$\langle s_\infty \rangle \hookrightarrow T0(\star) \Rightarrow$ $\text{descs\_x}(s, \{x\}) =$

$$\{u : w \in \mathbf{arb}(\{\text{descs\_x}(s, y) : y \in \{x\} \mid y \in s_\infty\}), u \in \text{children}(w)\}$$

EQUAL ⇒ *Stat1* :

$$\{u : w \in \mathbf{arb}(\{\text{descs\_x}(s, y) : y \in \{x\} \mid y \in s_\infty\}), u \in \text{children}(w)\} \neq \{u : w \in \text{descs\_x}(s, x), u \in \text{children}(w)\}$$

The left-hand side of this inequality reduces to $\{u : w \in \text{descs\_x}(s, x), u \in \text{children}(w)\}$, which contradicts the initial hypothesis, and so proves our lemma.

Suppose ⇒ $\mathit{Stat2}: \{\mathsf{descs\_x(s,y)} : \mathsf{y} \in \{\mathsf{x}\} \mid \mathsf{y} \in \mathsf{s}_\infty\} \neq \{\mathsf{descs\_x(s,x)}\}$

Set_monot ⇒ $\{\mathsf{descs\_x(s,y)} : \mathsf{y} \in \{\mathsf{x}\} \mid \mathsf{y} \in \mathsf{s}_\infty\} \subseteq \{\mathsf{descs\_x(s,y)} : \mathsf{y} \in \{\mathsf{x}\}\}$

SIMPLF ⇒ $\{\mathsf{descs\_x(s,y)} : \mathsf{y} \in \{\mathsf{x}\}\} = \{\mathsf{descs\_x(s,x)}\}$

$(\mathit{Stat2}\star)$ELEM ⇒ $\mathit{Stat3}: \mathsf{descs\_x(s,x)} \notin \{\mathsf{descs\_x(s,y)} : \mathsf{y} \in \{\mathsf{x}\} \mid \mathsf{y} \in \mathsf{s}_\infty\}$

$\langle \mathsf{x} \rangle \hookrightarrow \mathit{Stat3}(\star)$ ⇒ false; Discharge ⇒

$\{\mathsf{descs\_x(s,y)} : \mathsf{y} \in \{\mathsf{x}\} \mid \mathsf{y} \in \mathsf{s}_\infty\} = \{\mathsf{descs\_x(s,x)}\}$

$\langle \{\mathsf{descs\_x}\}(\mathsf{s,x}) \rangle \hookrightarrow T0(\star)$ ⇒ $\mathbf{arb}(\{\mathsf{descs\_x(s,x)}\}) = \mathsf{descs\_x(s,x)}$

EQUAL $\langle \mathit{Stat1} \rangle$ ⇒ false; Discharge ⇒ QED

|| Now we can prove, for any set s, that $\mathsf{descs}_\Theta(\mathsf{s})$ includes s and is E-transitive.

THEOREM reachability · 3: [Stepwise reachability] $\mathsf{S} \subseteq \mathsf{descs}_\Theta(\mathsf{S})$ & $(\mathsf{X} \in \mathsf{descs}_\Theta(\mathsf{S})$ & $\mathsf{V(X)}$ & $\mathsf{V(Y)}$ & $\mathsf{E(X,Y)} \rightarrow \mathsf{Y} \in \mathsf{descs}_\Theta(\mathsf{S}))$. PROOF:

Suppose_not(s, x, y) ⇒ AUTO

|| Arguing by contradiction, we must consider the following alternative:

$\langle \mathsf{x,y} \rangle \hookrightarrow \mathit{Treachability} \cdot 1$ ⇒ $\mathsf{s} \nsubseteq \mathsf{descs}_\Theta(\mathsf{s}) \vee$
$(\mathsf{x} \in \mathsf{descs}_\Theta(\mathsf{s})$ & $\mathsf{y} \in \mathsf{children(x)}$ & $\mathsf{y} \notin \mathsf{descs}_\Theta(\mathsf{s}))$

|| The first of these cases is impossible, since an x′ in s but not in $\mathsf{descs}_\Theta(\mathsf{s})$ could not be in any of the sets descs_x(s, v) where v belongs to $\mathsf{s}_\infty$, contradicting the fact that $\mathbf{arb}(\mathsf{s}_\infty)$ belongs to $\mathsf{s}_\infty$, while $\mathsf{descs\_x}(\mathsf{s}, \mathbf{arb}(\mathsf{s}_\infty)) = \mathsf{s}$. Hence we need only consider the second case.

Suppose ⇒ $\mathit{Stat1}: \mathsf{s} \nsubseteq \mathsf{descs}_\Theta(\mathsf{s})$

$\langle \mathsf{x}' \rangle \hookrightarrow \mathit{Stat1}$ ⇒ $\mathsf{x}' \in \mathsf{s}$ & $\mathsf{x}' \notin \mathsf{descs}_\Theta(\mathsf{s})$

Use_def($\mathsf{descs}_\Theta$) ⇒ $\mathit{Stat2}: \mathsf{x}' \notin \{\mathsf{y} : \mathsf{v} \in \mathsf{s}_\infty, \mathsf{y} \in \mathsf{descs\_x(s,v)}\}$

$\langle \mathsf{s}_\infty \rangle \hookrightarrow T0(\star)$ ⇒ AUTO

$\langle \mathbf{arb}(\mathsf{s}_\infty) \rangle \hookrightarrow T0(\star)$ ⇒ $\mathbf{arb}(\mathsf{s}_\infty) \in \mathsf{s}_\infty$

$\langle \mathbf{arb}(\mathsf{s}_\infty), \mathsf{x}' \rangle \hookrightarrow \mathit{Stat2}$ ⇒ $\mathsf{x}' \notin \mathsf{descs\_x}(\mathsf{s}, \mathbf{arb}(\mathsf{s}_\infty))$

Use_def(descs_x) ⇒ $\mathsf{descs\_x}(\mathsf{s}, \mathbf{arb}(\mathsf{s}_\infty)) = \mathsf{s}$

$(\mathit{Stat1}\star)$Discharge ⇒ $\mathit{Stat4}: \mathsf{x} \in \mathsf{descs}_\Theta(\mathsf{s})$ & $\mathsf{y} \in \mathsf{children(x)}$ & $\mathsf{y} \notin \mathsf{descs}_\Theta(\mathsf{s})$

|| But in this case there must exist some d in $\mathsf{s}_\infty$ such that x in descs_x(s, d), and then descs_x(s, {d}) = {w : v ∈ descs_x(s, d), w ∈ v} must have y as a member. Since {d} is a member of $\mathsf{s}_\infty$, this contradicts the fact that $\mathsf{y} \notin \mathsf{descs}_\Theta(\mathsf{s})$, and so proves our theorem.

$\mathsf{Use\_def}(\mathsf{descs}_\Theta) \Rightarrow$ *Stat5* : $\mathsf{x} \in \{\mathsf{w} : \mathsf{v} \in \mathsf{s}_\infty, \mathsf{w} \in \mathsf{descs\_x}(\mathsf{S}, \mathsf{v})\}$
$\langle \mathsf{d}, \mathsf{w} \rangle \hookrightarrow$ *Stat5* $\Rightarrow$ *Stat6* : $\mathsf{d} \in \mathsf{s}_\infty$ & $\mathsf{x} \in \mathsf{descs\_x}(\mathsf{s}, \mathsf{d})$
$\langle \mathsf{d} \rangle \hookrightarrow T0 \Rightarrow \{\mathsf{d}\} \in \mathsf{s}_\infty$
$\mathsf{Use\_def}(\mathsf{descs}_\Theta) \Rightarrow$ *Stat7* : $\mathsf{y} \notin \{\mathsf{w} : \mathsf{v} \in \mathsf{s}_\infty, \mathsf{w} \in \mathsf{descs\_x}(\mathsf{s}, \mathsf{v})\}$
$\langle \{\mathsf{d}\}, \mathsf{y} \rangle \hookrightarrow$ *Stat7* $\Rightarrow \mathsf{y} \notin \mathsf{descs\_x}(\mathsf{s}, \{\mathsf{d}\})$
$\langle \mathsf{d}, \mathsf{s} \rangle \hookrightarrow$ *Treachability* $\cdot 2 \Rightarrow$ *Stat8* : $\mathsf{y} \notin \{\mathsf{u} : \mathsf{w} \in \mathsf{descs\_x}(\mathsf{s}, \mathsf{d}), \mathsf{u} \in \mathsf{children}(\mathsf{w})\}$
$\langle \mathsf{x}, \mathsf{y} \rangle \hookrightarrow$ *Stat8(Stat8, Stat6⋆)* $\Rightarrow$ *Stat9* : $\mathsf{y} \notin \mathsf{children}(\mathsf{x})$
$\langle \mathsf{x}, \mathsf{y} \rangle \hookrightarrow$ *Treachability* $\cdot 1 \Rightarrow$ false; Discharge $\Rightarrow$ QED

Transitivity of the reachability relation is proved next: if y is reachable from x and z is reachable from y, then z is reachable from x.

THEOREM reachability · 4: [Transitivity of reachability]
$\mathsf{Y} \in \mathsf{descs}_\Theta(\{\mathsf{X}\})$ & $\mathsf{Z} \in \mathsf{descs}_\Theta(\{\mathsf{Y}\}) \rightarrow \mathsf{Z} \in \mathsf{descs}_\Theta(\{\mathsf{X}\})$. PROOF:
$\mathsf{Suppose\_not}(\mathsf{y}_0, \mathsf{x}, \mathsf{z}) \Rightarrow$ AUTO

Assume that $\mathsf{y}_0$ is reachable from {x} and that z is reachable from $\{\mathsf{y}_0\}$; however, to start an argument by contradiction, assume that z is unreachable from {x}.

$\mathsf{Suppose} \Rightarrow \{\mathsf{s} \in \mathsf{s}_\infty \mid \mathsf{descs\_x}(\{\mathsf{y}_0\}, \mathsf{s}) \not\subseteq \mathsf{descs}_\Theta(\{\mathsf{x}\})\} = \emptyset$

It follows from the definition of the set $\mathsf{descs}_\Theta(\{\mathsf{y}_0\})$ of all sets reachable from $\{\mathsf{y}_0\}$ that at least one of the layers $\mathsf{descs\_x}(\{\mathsf{y}_0\}, \mathsf{i})$ (with $\mathsf{i} \in \mathsf{s}_\infty$) which compose $\mathsf{descs}_\Theta(\{\mathsf{y}_0\})$ has an element that is unreachable from {x}.

$\mathsf{Use\_def}(\mathsf{descs}_\Theta(\{\mathsf{y}_0\})) \Rightarrow$ AUTO
$\mathsf{ELEM} \Rightarrow$ *Stat1* : $\mathsf{z} \in \{\mathsf{u} : \mathsf{i} \in \mathsf{s}_\infty, \mathsf{u} \in \mathsf{descs\_x}(\{\mathsf{y}_0\}, \mathsf{i})\}$ & $\mathsf{z} \notin \mathsf{descs}_\Theta(\{\mathsf{x}\})$
$\langle \mathsf{i}, \mathsf{u} \rangle \hookrightarrow$ *Stat1* $\Rightarrow \mathsf{i} \in \mathsf{s}_\infty$ & $\mathsf{z} \in \mathsf{descs\_x}(\{\mathsf{y}_0\}, \mathsf{i})$ & *Stat2* :
$\mathsf{i} \notin \{\mathsf{s} \in \mathsf{s}_\infty \mid \mathsf{descs\_x}(\{\mathsf{y}_0\}, \mathsf{s}) \not\subseteq \mathsf{descs}_\Theta(\{\mathsf{x}\})\}$
$\langle \mathsf{i} \rangle \hookrightarrow$ *Stat2(Stat1⋆)* $\Rightarrow$ false; Discharge $\Rightarrow$ AUTO

So we can pick $\mathsf{s}_0 \in \mathsf{s}_\infty$ in such a way that $\mathsf{descs\_x}(\{\mathsf{y}_0\}, \mathsf{s}_0) \not\subseteq \mathsf{descs}_\Theta(\{\mathsf{x}\})$ whereas $\mathsf{descs\_x}(\{\mathsf{y}_0\}, \mathsf{s}) \subseteq \mathsf{descs}_\Theta(\{\mathsf{x}\})$ holds for all $\mathsf{s} \in \mathsf{s}_0 \cap \mathsf{s}_\infty$.

$\mathsf{Loc\_def} \Rightarrow \mathsf{s}_0 = \mathbf{arb}(\{\mathsf{s} \in \mathsf{s}_\infty \mid \mathsf{descs\_x}(\{\mathsf{y}_0\}, \mathsf{s}) \not\subseteq \mathsf{descs}_\Theta(\{\mathsf{x}\})\})$
$\langle \{\mathsf{s} \in \mathsf{s}_\infty \mid \mathsf{descs\_x}(\{\mathsf{y}_0\}, \mathsf{s}) \not\subseteq \mathsf{descs}_\Theta(\{\mathsf{x}\})\} \rangle \hookrightarrow T0(\star) \Rightarrow$ *Stat3* :
$\mathsf{s}_0 \in \{\mathsf{s} \in \mathsf{s}_\infty \mid \mathsf{descs\_x}(\{\mathsf{y}_0\}, \mathsf{s}) \not\subseteq \mathsf{descs}_\Theta(\{\mathsf{x}\})\}$ &

$$s_0 \cap \{s \in s_\infty \mid \mathsf{descs\_x}(\{y_0\}, s) \not\subseteq \mathsf{descs}_\Theta(\{x\})\} = \emptyset$$

$\langle\,\rangle \hookrightarrow \mathit{Stat3}(\star) \Rightarrow$ $\mathit{Stat4}$:

$$\mathsf{descs\_x}(\{y_0\}, s_0) \not\subseteq \mathsf{descs}_\Theta(\{x\}) \ \&\ s_0 \in s_\infty \ \&\ y_0 \in \mathsf{descs}_\Theta(\{x\})$$

The selected $s_0$ cannot coincide with $\mathbf{arb}(s_\infty)$, because $\mathsf{descs\_x}(\{y_0\}, \mathbf{arb}(s_\infty)) = \{y_0\}$, whose only element we have assumed to be reachable from $\{x\}$.

$\mathsf{Use\_def}(\mathsf{descs\_x}(\{y_0\}, s_0)) \Rightarrow$ AUTO

$\mathsf{Suppose} \Rightarrow$ $s_0 = \mathbf{arb}(s_\infty)$

$(\mathit{Stat4}\star)\mathsf{ELEM} \Rightarrow$ $\mathsf{descs\_x}(\{y_0\}, s_0) = \{y_0\}$

$(\mathit{Stat4}\star)\mathsf{Discharge} \Rightarrow$ $\mathsf{descs\_x}(\{y_0\}, s_0) =$

$$\{u : w \in \mathbf{arb}(\{\mathsf{descs\_x}(\{y_0\}, y) : y \in s_0 \mid y \in s_\infty\}), u \in \mathsf{children}(w)\}$$

But then, observe that the expression $\mathbf{arb}(\{\mathsf{descs\_x}(\{y_0\}, y) : y \in s_0 \mid y \in s_\infty\})$ occurring in the specification of $\mathsf{descs\_x}(\{y_0\}, s_0)$ designates a set of the form $a = \mathsf{descs\_x}(\{y_0\}, s_1)$, with $s_1 \in s_0 \cap s_\infty$. There must exist a child $u_0$ of an element $w_0$ of this set that is unreachable from $\{x\}$.

$\langle u_0\rangle \hookrightarrow \mathit{Stat4}(\mathit{Stat4}\star) \Rightarrow$ $\mathit{Stat5}$:

$$u_0 \in \{u : w \in \mathbf{arb}(\{\mathsf{descs\_x}(\{y_0\}, y) : y \in s_0 \mid y \in s_\infty\}), u \in \mathsf{children}(w)\}$$
$$\&\ u_0 \notin \mathsf{descs}_\Theta(\{x\})$$

$\langle w_0, u_1\rangle \hookrightarrow \mathit{Stat5}(\mathit{Stat5}\star) \Rightarrow$ $\mathit{Stat6}$:

$$w_0 \in \mathbf{arb}(\{\mathsf{descs\_x}(\{y_0\}, y) : y \in s_0 \mid y \in s_\infty\}) \ \&\ u_0 \in \mathsf{children}(w_0)$$

$\mathsf{Loc\_def} \Rightarrow$ $\mathit{Stat7}$: $a = \mathbf{arb}(\{\mathsf{descs\_x}(\{y_0\}, y) : y \in s_0 \mid y \in s_\infty\})$

$\langle\{\mathsf{descs\_x}(\{y_0\}, y) : y \in s_0 \mid y \in s_\infty\}\rangle \hookrightarrow T0\ (\mathit{Stat5}\star) \Rightarrow$ $\mathit{Stat8}$:

$$a \in \{\mathsf{descs\_x}(\{y_0\}, y) : y \in s_0 \mid y \in s_\infty\}$$

$\langle s_1\rangle \hookrightarrow \mathit{Stat8}(\mathit{Stat6}, \mathit{Stat7}, \mathit{Stat3}\star) \Rightarrow$ $\mathit{Stat9}$:

$$s_1 \notin \{s \in s_\infty \mid \mathsf{descs\_x}(\{y_0\}, s) \not\subseteq \mathsf{descs}_\Theta(\{x\})\}\ \&$$
$$s_1 \in s_0 \ \&\ s_1 \in s_\infty \ \&\ w_0 \in \mathsf{descs\_x}(\{y_0\}, s_1)$$

By the minimality of $s_0$, it turns out that $\mathsf{descs\_x}(\{y_0\}, s_1) \subseteq \mathsf{descs}_\Theta(\{x\})$, and therefore $w_0 \in \mathsf{descs\_x}(\{x_0\})$, holds. But then every child of $w_0$, including $u_0$, must belong to $\mathsf{descs}_\Theta(\{x\})$, as we know from Theorem reachability.1 that the children of any $w$ are the nodes directly accessible from $w$, ...

$\langle s_1\rangle \hookrightarrow \mathit{Stat9}(\mathit{Stat5}, \mathit{Stat6}\star) \Rightarrow$ $\mathit{Stat10}$: $w_0 \in \mathsf{descs}_\Theta(\{x\})$

$\langle w_0, u_0\rangle \hookrightarrow \mathit{Treachability}\cdot 1 \Rightarrow$ $E(w_0, u_0)\ \&\ V(w_0)\ \&\ V(u_0)$

‖ ...and this, with the aid of the previous Theorem reachability.3, leads us to a fact, $u_0 \in \mathsf{descs}_\Theta(\{x\})$, which blatantly conflicts with a fact established earlier.

$\langle \{x\}, w_0, u_0 \rangle \hookrightarrow \mathit{Treachability} \cdot 3 \Rightarrow$ AUTO

‖ This contradiction gives us the desired conclusion.

$(\mathit{Stat5}\star)\mathsf{Discharge} \Rightarrow$ QED

‖ Then we show that the set of all descendants of a set s is inclusion-minimal among all sets t that include s and are closed relative to the children-formation operation.

THEOREM reachability · 5: [Minimality of the reachability set]
$S \subseteq T \;\&\; \langle \forall x, y \mid x \in T \;\&\; E(x,y) \;\&\; V(x) \;\&\; V(y) \rightarrow y \in T \rangle \rightarrow \mathsf{descs}_\Theta(S) \subseteq T$. PROOF:
$\mathsf{Suppose\_not}(s,t) \Rightarrow$ *Stat1* :
$$\langle \forall x, y \mid x \in t \;\&\; E(x,y) \;\&\; V(x) \;\&\; V(y) \rightarrow y \in t \rangle \;\&\; s \subseteq t \;\&\; \mathsf{descs}_\Theta(s) \not\subseteq t$$

‖ Assume that $s \subseteq t$ and that every node which is directly accessible from a node in t belongs to t; however, to start an argument by contradiction, assume that not all sets reachable from s are in t.

$\mathsf{Use\_def}(\mathsf{descs}_\Theta(s)) \Rightarrow$ AUTO
$(\mathit{Stat1}\star)\mathsf{ELEM} \Rightarrow \mathit{Stat2} : \{u : i \in s_\infty, u \in \mathsf{descs\_x}(s,i)\} \not\subseteq t$

‖ It follows from the definition of the set $\mathsf{descs}_\Theta(s)$ of the descendants of s, that at least one of the layers $\mathsf{descs\_x}(s,i)$ (with $i \in s_\infty$) which compose $\mathsf{descs}_\Theta(s)$ is not included in t.

$\mathsf{Suppose} \Rightarrow \mathit{Stat3} : \{i \in s_\infty \mid \mathsf{descs\_x}(s,i) \not\subseteq t\} = \emptyset$
$\langle u_0 \rangle \hookrightarrow \mathit{Stat2}(\mathit{Stat2}\star) \Rightarrow \mathit{Stat4} : u_0 \in \{u : i \in s_\infty, u \in \mathsf{descs\_x}(s,i)\} \;\&\; u_0 \notin t$
$\langle i, u \rangle \hookrightarrow \mathit{Stat4}(\mathit{Stat4}\star) \Rightarrow i \in s_\infty \;\&\; \mathsf{descs\_x}(s,i) \not\subseteq t$
$\langle i \rangle \hookrightarrow \mathit{Stat3}(\mathit{Stat3}\star) \Rightarrow$ false; $\mathsf{Discharge} \Rightarrow$ AUTO

‖ So we can pick $i_0 \in s_\infty$ in such a way that $\mathsf{descs\_x}(s,i_0) \not\subseteq t$ whereas $\mathsf{descs\_x}(s,i) \subseteq t$ holds for all $i \in i_0 \cap s_\infty$.

$\mathsf{Loc\_def} \Rightarrow i_0 = \mathbf{arb}(\{i \in s_\infty \mid \mathsf{descs\_x}(s,i) \not\subseteq t\})$

$\langle\{\mathsf{i} \in \mathsf{s}_\infty \mid \mathsf{descs\_x}(\mathsf{s},\mathsf{i}) \not\subseteq \mathsf{t}\}\rangle \hookrightarrow T0(\star) \Rightarrow$ *Stat5*:

$$\mathsf{i}_0 \in \{\mathsf{i} \in \mathsf{s}_\infty \mid \mathsf{descs\_x}(\mathsf{s},\mathsf{i}) \not\subseteq \mathsf{t}\} \;\&\; \mathsf{i}_0 \cap \{\mathsf{i} \in \mathsf{s}_\infty \mid \mathsf{descs\_x}(\mathsf{s},\mathsf{i}) \not\subseteq \mathsf{t}\} = \emptyset$$

$\langle\,\rangle \hookrightarrow Stat5(Stat5\star) \Rightarrow$ *Stat6*: $\mathsf{i}_0 \in \mathsf{s}_\infty \;\&\; \mathsf{descs\_x}(\mathsf{s},\mathsf{i}_0) \not\subseteq \mathsf{t}$

Use_def$(\mathsf{descs_x}(\mathsf{s},\mathsf{i}_0)) \Rightarrow$ AUTO

The selected $\mathsf{i}_0$ cannot coincide with $\mathbf{arb}(\mathsf{s}_\infty)$, because $\mathsf{descs\_x}(\mathsf{s},\mathbf{arb}(\mathsf{s}_\infty)) = \mathsf{s}$, which we have assumed to be included in t.

Suppose $\Rightarrow$ $\mathsf{i}_0 = \mathbf{arb}(\mathsf{s}_\infty)$

$(Stat6\star)$ELEM $\Rightarrow$ *Stat7*: $\mathsf{descs\_x}(\mathsf{s},\mathsf{i}_0) = \mathsf{s}$

$(Stat7, Stat6, Stat1\star)$Discharge $\Rightarrow$ *Stat8*:

$$\{\mathsf{u} : \mathsf{w} \in \mathbf{arb}(\{\mathsf{descs\_x}(\mathsf{s},\mathsf{y}) : \mathsf{y} \in \mathsf{i}_0 \mid \mathsf{y} \in \mathsf{s}_\infty\}), \mathsf{u} \in \mathsf{children}(\mathsf{w})\} \not\subseteq \mathsf{t}$$

But then, observe that the expression $\mathbf{arb}(\{\mathsf{descs\_x}(\mathsf{s},\mathsf{y}) : \mathsf{y} \in \mathsf{i}_0 \mid \mathsf{y} \in \mathsf{s}_\infty\})$ occurring in the specification of $\mathsf{descs\_x}(\mathsf{s},\mathsf{i}_0)$ designates a set of the form $\mathsf{a} = \mathsf{descs\_x}(\mathsf{s},\mathsf{i}_1)$, with $\mathsf{i}_1 \in \mathsf{i}_0 \cap \mathsf{s}_\infty$. There must exist a child $\mathsf{u}_1$ of an element $\mathsf{w}_0$ of this set that does not belong to t.

$\langle \mathsf{u}_1\rangle \hookrightarrow Stat8(Stat8\star) \Rightarrow$ *Stat9*: $\mathsf{u}_1 \in$

$$\{\mathsf{u} : \mathsf{w} \in \mathbf{arb}(\{\mathsf{descs\_x}(\mathsf{s},\mathsf{y}) : \mathsf{y} \in \mathsf{i}_0 \mid \mathsf{y} \in \mathsf{s}_\infty\}), \mathsf{u} \in \mathsf{children}(\mathsf{w})\} \;\&\; \mathsf{u}_1 \notin \mathsf{t}$$

$\langle \mathsf{w}_0, \mathsf{u}_2\rangle \hookrightarrow Stat9(Stat9\star) \Rightarrow$

$$\mathsf{w}_0 \in \mathbf{arb}(\{\mathsf{descs\_x}(\mathsf{s},\mathsf{y}) : \mathsf{y} \in \mathsf{i}_0 \mid \mathsf{y} \in \mathsf{s}_\infty\}) \;\&\; \mathsf{u}_1 \in \mathsf{children}(\mathsf{w}_0)$$

Loc_def $\Rightarrow$ $\mathsf{a} = \mathbf{arb}(\{\mathsf{descs\_x}(\mathsf{s},\mathsf{y}) : \mathsf{y} \in \mathsf{i}_0 \mid \mathsf{y} \in \mathsf{s}_\infty\})$

$\langle\{\mathsf{descs\_x}(\mathsf{s},\mathsf{y}) : \mathsf{y} \in \mathsf{i}_0 \mid \mathsf{y} \in \mathsf{s}_\infty\}\rangle \hookrightarrow T0\ (Stat9\star) \Rightarrow$ *Stat10*:

$$\mathsf{a} \in \{\mathsf{descs\_x}(\mathsf{s},\mathsf{y}) : \mathsf{y} \in \mathsf{i}_0 \mid \mathsf{y} \in \mathsf{s}_\infty\}$$

$\langle \mathsf{i}_1\rangle \hookrightarrow Stat10(Stat9\star) \Rightarrow$ *Stat11*: $\mathsf{i}_1 \in \mathsf{i}_0 \;\&\; \mathsf{i}_1 \in \mathsf{s}_\infty \;\&\; \mathsf{w}_0 \in \mathsf{descs\_x}(\mathsf{s},\mathsf{i}_1)$

By the minimality of $\mathsf{i}_0$, it turns out that $\mathsf{descs\_x}(\mathsf{s},\mathsf{i}_1) \subseteq \mathsf{t}$, and therefore $\mathsf{w}_0 \in \mathsf{t}$, holds. But then every child of $\mathsf{w}_0$, including $\mathsf{u}_1$, must belong to t, as we know from Theorem reachability.1 that the children of any w are the nodes directly accessible from w, ...

$(Stat11, Stat5\star)$ELEM $\Rightarrow$ *Stat12*: $\mathsf{i}_1 \notin \{\mathsf{i} \in \mathsf{s}_\infty \mid \mathsf{descs\_x}(\mathsf{s},\mathsf{i}) \not\subseteq \mathsf{t}\}$

$\langle \mathsf{i}_1\rangle \hookrightarrow Stat12(Stat11\star) \Rightarrow$ $\mathsf{w}_0 \in \mathsf{t}$

$\langle \mathsf{w}_0, \mathsf{u}_1\rangle \hookrightarrow Treachability \cdot 1 \Rightarrow$ $\mathsf{E}(\mathsf{w}_0,\mathsf{u}_1) \;\&\; \mathsf{V}(\mathsf{w}_0) \;\&\; \mathsf{V}(\mathsf{u}_1)$

... and we have initially assumed that nodes directly accessible from t belong to t. This leads us into a contradiction, which gives us the desired conclusion.

$\langle w_0, u_1\rangle \hookrightarrow$ *Stat1(Stat9⋆)* $\Rightarrow$ false; Discharge $\Rightarrow$ QED

ENTER_THEORY Set_theory

DISPLAY reachability

THEORY reachability(V(X), E(X, Y))
$\langle \forall x \mid V(x) \rightarrow \langle \exists c, \forall y \mid E(x,y) \;\&\; V(y) \rightarrow y \in c\rangle\rangle$
$\Rightarrow (\mathrm{descs}_\Theta)$
$\langle \forall s, x, y \mid s \subseteq \mathrm{descs}_\Theta(s) \;\&\; \big(x \in \mathrm{descs}_\Theta(s) \;\&\; V(x) \;\&\; V(y) \;\&\; E(x,y) \rightarrow y \in \mathrm{descs}_\Theta(s)\big)\rangle$
$\langle \forall y, x, z \mid y \in \mathrm{descs}_\Theta(\{x\}) \;\&\; z \in \mathrm{descs}_\Theta(\{y\}) \rightarrow z \in \mathrm{descs}_\Theta(\{x\})\rangle$
$\langle \forall s, t \mid s \subseteq t \;\&\; \langle \forall x, y \mid x \in t \;\&\; E(x,y) \;\&\; V(x) \;\&\; V(y) \rightarrow y \in t\rangle \rightarrow \mathrm{descs}_\Theta(s) \subseteq t\rangle$
END reachability

### *7.3.2 Full Sets and Ordinals*

DEF powerset: [family of all subsets of a set] $\mathscr{P}X =_{\mathrm{Def}} \{y : y \subseteq X\}$
DEF unionset: [family of all members of members of a set]
$\bigcup X =_{\mathrm{Def}} \{u : v \in X, u \in v\}$

Our next theorem characterizes the powerset formation operation in more usable terms than the very definition of this construct. It also proves that no set can equal its own powerset (else it should belong to itself, against the acyclicity of membership).

THEOREM 1: [characterization of powerset; also: no set equals its own powerset]
$(X \supseteq Y \leftrightarrow Y \in \mathscr{P}X) \;\&\; X \neq \mathscr{P}X$. PROOF:
Suppose_not$(x_0, y_0) \Rightarrow$ AUTO

We begin by excluding the possibility that $x_0 = \mathscr{P}x_0$:

Use_def$(\mathscr{P}x_0) \Rightarrow$ AUTO
Suppose $\Rightarrow$ $x_0 = \mathscr{P}x_0$
ELEM $\Rightarrow$ *Stat0* : $x_0 \notin \{y : y \subseteq x_0\}$
$\langle x_0\rangle \hookrightarrow$ *Stat0* $\Rightarrow$ false; Discharge $\Rightarrow$ AUTO

Arguing by contradiction, if $x_0, y_0$ constituted a counterexample, then either one of the literals $x_0 \supseteq y_0$ and $y_0 \in \{y : y \subseteq x_0\}$ would be true and the other one would be false.

EQUAL $\Rightarrow$ *Stat1* : $x_0 \supseteq y_0 \not\leftrightarrow y_0 \in \{y : y \subseteq x_0\}$

If it is the second that is true then, via a substitution in the setformer, we would contradict the falsity of the first.

Suppose ⇒ *Stat2* : $y_0 \in \{y : y \subseteq x_0\}$
$\langle y_1\rangle \hookrightarrow$ *Stat2(Stat1⋆)* ⇒ false; Discharge ⇒ *Stat3* : $y_0 \notin \{y : y \subseteq x_0\}$

But then the literals $x_0 \supseteq y_0$ and $y_0 \notin \{y : y \subseteq x_0\}$ should hold together, which gives us a contradiction if we replace the bounded variable y of the setformer by $y_0$.

$\langle y_0\rangle \hookrightarrow$ *Stat3(Stat1⋆)* ⇒ false; Discharge ⇒ QED

Next we show that the union set of a set s is the set-theoretic 'upper bound' of all its elements, i.e. the smallest set which includes all these elements.

THEOREM 2: [Union set as an upper bound] $(X \in S \rightarrow X \subseteq \bigcup S)$ & $(\langle \forall y \in S \mid y \subseteq X\rangle \rightarrow \bigcup S \subseteq X)$. PROOF:
Suppose_not(t, s) ⇒ $(t \nsubseteq \bigcup s \;\&\; t \in s) \vee (\langle \forall y \in s \mid y \subseteq t\rangle \;\&\; \bigcup s \nsubseteq t)$

For if not, one of the two clauses of our theorem must be false. By definition of $\bigcup$, this cannot be the first clause, so it must be the second.

Use_def($\bigcup$s) ⇒ AUTO
Suppose ⇒ *Stat1* : $t \nsubseteq \bigcup s \;\&\; t \in s$
$\langle c\rangle \hookrightarrow$ *Stat1* ⇒ *Stat2* : $c \notin \{z : y \in s, z \in y\} \;\&\; c \in t$
$\langle t, c\rangle \hookrightarrow$ *Stat2* ⇒ false; Discharge ⇒ *Stat3* : $\bigcup s \nsubseteq t \;\&\; \langle \forall y \in s \mid y \subseteq t\rangle$

But a second use of the definition of $\bigcup$ shows that this case is also impossible, proving our theorem.

$\langle d\rangle \hookrightarrow$ *Stat3* ⇒ *Stat4* : $d \in \{z : y \in s, z \in y\} \;\&\; \langle \forall y \in s \mid y \subseteq t\rangle \;\&\; d \notin t$
$\langle b, a, b\rangle \hookrightarrow$ *Stat4* ⇒ false; Discharge ⇒ QED

One says that a set is *full*, or 'transitive', if any of its elements is also a subset of it; otherwise stated, a set is full if its members comprise all members of its members.

DEF fullness: [full, or 'transitive' set] Is_full(T) $\leftrightarrow_{\mathrm{Def}}$ $\{y \in T \mid y \nsubseteq T\} = \emptyset$

‖ Various alternative, more concise, characterizations of this 'fullness' notion, equivalent to one another, could be given, e.g., 'T is full if and only if $\bigcup T \subseteq T$'. We content ourselves with the following:

THEOREM 3: [Alternative characterization of a full set] $\mathsf{Is\_full}(T) \rightarrow T \subseteq \mathscr{P}T \;\&\; (X \in T \rightarrow X \subseteq T)$. PROOF:

$\mathsf{Suppose\_not}(t_0, x_0) \Rightarrow$ AUTO

$\mathsf{Use\_def}(\mathsf{Is\_full}) \Rightarrow$ *Stat1* : $\{y \in t_0 \mid y \not\subseteq t_0\} = \emptyset \;\&\; t_0 \not\subseteq \mathscr{P}t_0 \vee (x_0 \in t_0 \;\&\; x_0 \not\subseteq t_0)$

$\mathsf{Suppose} \Rightarrow$ *Stat2* : $t_0 \not\subseteq \mathscr{P}t_0$

$\langle e \rangle \hookrightarrow$ *Stat2* $\Rightarrow$ $e \notin \mathscr{P}t_0 \;\&\; e \in t_0$

$\langle e \rangle \hookrightarrow$ *Stat1* $\Rightarrow$ $e \subseteq t_0$

$\langle t_0, e \rangle \hookrightarrow T1 \Rightarrow$ false; $\mathsf{Discharge} \Rightarrow$ $x_0 \in t_0 \;\&\; x_0 \not\subseteq t_0$

$\langle x_0 \rangle \hookrightarrow$ *Stat1*(*Stat1*$\star$) $\Rightarrow$ AUTO

$\mathsf{Discharge} \Rightarrow$ QED

‖ The following is, in essence, the lemma

'every strict subset s of a full set t includes a set belonging to $t \backslash s$'

of [Ped62]. It readily yields (when $t = \emptyset$) that $\emptyset$ belongs to every nonnull full set.

THEOREM 4: [Full-set comparison lemma] $\mathsf{Is\_full}(T) \;\&\; S \subseteq T \;\&\; S \neq T \rightarrow \mathbf{arb}(T \backslash S) \in T \backslash S \;\&\; \mathbf{arb}(T \backslash S) \subseteq S$. PROOF:

$\mathsf{Suppose\_not}(t, s) \Rightarrow$ AUTO

‖ For if our assertion is false, t must have s as a proper subset, in which case Theorem 0 tells us that $a = \mathbf{arb}(t \backslash s)$ is a member of $t \backslash s$ disjoint from $t \backslash s$. Plainly a is also a member of the superset t of $t \backslash s$.

$\mathsf{Loc\_def} \Rightarrow$ $a = \mathbf{arb}(t \backslash s)$

$\langle t \backslash s \rangle \hookrightarrow T0\,(\star) \Rightarrow$ $a \in t \backslash s \;\&\; a \cap (t \backslash s) = \emptyset$

‖ But then, by definition of full set, a must be a subset of s, since it is disjoint from $t \backslash s$.

$\mathsf{Use\_def}(\mathsf{Is\_full}) \Rightarrow$ *Stat1* : $\{y \in t \mid y \not\subseteq t\} = \emptyset$

$\langle a \rangle \hookrightarrow$ *Stat1*$(\star) \Rightarrow$ false; $\mathsf{Discharge} \Rightarrow$ QED

DEF Is_ord: ['Is-an-ordinal' predicate] $\mathscr{O}(X) \leftrightarrow_{\mathrm{Def}}$
$\langle \forall x \in X \mid x \subseteq X \rangle \;\&\; \langle \forall x \in X, y \in X \mid x \in y \vee y \in x \vee x = y \rangle$

‖ The successor of an ordinal has a simple and very general definition:

DEF next: [successor (defined for any set, including ordinals and integers)]

$$\text{next}(X) =_{\text{Def}} X \cup \{X\}$$

THEOREM 5: [Ordinals are full] $\mathcal{O}(T) \rightarrow \text{Is\_full}(T) \,\&\, (Y \in T \rightarrow Y \subseteq T)$. PROOF:

Suppose_not($t_0, y_0$) ⇒ AUTO
  Use_def($\mathcal{O}$) ⇒ *Stat1* : $\langle \forall x \in t_0 \mid x \subseteq t_0 \rangle$
  $\langle y_0 \rangle \hookrightarrow$ *Stat1*(⋆) ⇒ $\neg \text{Is\_full}(t_0)$
  Use_def(Is_full) ⇒ *Stat2* : $\{y \in t_0 \mid y \not\subseteq t_0\} \neq \emptyset$
  Loc_def ⇒ $a_1 = \textbf{arb}(\{y \in t_0 \mid y \not\subseteq t_0\})$
  (*Stat2*)ELEM ⇒ *Stat3* : $a_1 \in \{y \in t_0 \mid y \not\subseteq t_0\}$
  $\langle\,\rangle \hookrightarrow$ *Stat3* ⇒ *Stat4* : $a_1 \in t_0 \,\&\, a_1 \not\subseteq t_0$
$\langle a_1 \rangle \hookrightarrow$ *Stat1*(*Stat4*⋆) ⇒ false; Discharge ⇒ QED

THEOREM 6: [Condition for a subset of an ordinal to be an ordinal]
$\mathcal{O}(T) \,\&\, S \subseteq T \,\&\, \langle \forall x \in S \mid x \subseteq S \rangle \rightarrow \mathcal{O}(S)$. PROOF:

Suppose_not(t, s) ⇒ AUTO
  Use_def($\mathcal{O}$(s)) ⇒ AUTO
  ELEM ⇒ *Stat1* : $\neg\langle \forall x \in s, y \in s \mid x \in y \vee y \in x \vee x = y \rangle \,\&\, s \subseteq t$
  $\langle b, c \rangle \hookrightarrow$ *Stat1* ⇒ $b, c \in s \,\&\, \neg(b \in c \vee c \in b \vee b = c)$
  Use_def($\mathcal{O}$) ⇒ *Stat3* : $\langle \forall x \in t, y \in t \mid x \in y \vee y \in x \vee x = y \rangle$
$\langle b, c \rangle \hookrightarrow$ *Stat3*(*Stat1*⋆) ⇒ false; Discharge ⇒ QED

Next we prove a first basic property of ordinals: any member of an ordinal is an ordinal.

THEOREM 7: [Members of ordinals are ordinals] $\mathcal{O}(T) \,\&\, S \in T \rightarrow \mathcal{O}(S)$. PROOF:

Suppose_not(t, s) ⇒ AUTO

We proceed by contradiction. If our theorem is false, there is an ordinal t having a member s which is not an ordinal.

  $\langle t, s \rangle \hookrightarrow T5$ ⇒ *Stat1* : $\mathcal{O}(t) \,\&\, s \in t \,\&\, s \subseteq t \,\&\, \neg\mathcal{O}(s)$
  $\langle t, s \rangle \hookrightarrow T6$ ⇒ *Stat2* : $\neg\langle \forall x \in s \mid x \subseteq s \rangle$
  Use_def($\mathcal{O}$) ⇒ *Stat3* : $\langle \forall x \in t, y \in t \mid x \in y \vee y \in x \vee x = y \rangle$

Hence, by the definition of ordinals, s must either have a member a not included in s, or a pair b, c of distinct members not related by membership. The latter possibility is ruled out by the preceding theorem; thus we need only consider the first case, in which a is a member but not a subset of s. In this case there plainly exists a d in a but not in s. Plainly a is a member of t, and thus a subset of t; so d is also a member of t.

  $\langle a \rangle \hookrightarrow$ *Stat2*(*Stat2*⋆) ⇒ *Stat4* : $a \not\subseteq s \,\&\, a \in s$

$\langle t, a\rangle \hookrightarrow T5\,(Stat1, Stat4\star) \Rightarrow \quad a \subseteq t$
$\langle d\rangle \hookrightarrow Stat4(Stat1\star) \Rightarrow \quad d \in a \;\&\; d \notin s \;\&\; d \in t$

|| By the definition of ordinals, it follows that d either equals s, is a member of s, or that s is a member of d. But all three of these cases are impossible, since any would imply the existence of a membership cycle. This contradiction proves our theorem.

$\langle d, s\rangle \hookrightarrow Stat3(Stat1\star) \Rightarrow \quad d \in s \vee s \in d \vee s = d$
$(Stat4\star)$Discharge $\Rightarrow$ QED

|| It is easy to show that the successor of a successor is an ordinal.

THEOREM 8: [Ordinals are closed under the successor operation] $S \neq \text{next}(S)$ & $\big(\mathcal{O}(S) \rightarrow \mathcal{O}\big(S \cup \{S\}\big) \;\&\; \mathcal{O}\big(\text{next}(S)\big)\big)$. PROOF:

Suppose_not$(s_0) \Rightarrow$ AUTO
Use_def(next) $\Rightarrow \quad \mathcal{O}(s_0) \;\&\; \neg\mathcal{O}\big(s_0 \cup \{s_0\}\big)$
Use_def$(\mathcal{O}) \Rightarrow \quad Stat1: \langle \forall x \in s_0, y \in s_0 \mid x \in y \vee y \in x \vee x = y\rangle$ &
$Stat2: \langle \forall x \in s_0 \mid x \subseteq s_0\rangle$
Use_def$\big(\mathcal{O}(s_0 \cup \{s_0\})\big) \Rightarrow$ AUTO
Suppose $\Rightarrow \quad Stat3: \neg\big\langle \forall x \in s_0 \cup \{s_0\} \mid x \subseteq s_0 \cup \{s_0\}\big\rangle$
$\langle x_0\rangle \hookrightarrow Stat3 \Rightarrow \quad x_0 \in s_0 \cup \{s_0\} \;\&\; x_0 \nsubseteq s_0 \cup \{s_0\}$
$\langle x_0\rangle \hookrightarrow Stat2(Stat3\star) \Rightarrow$ false; Discharge $\Rightarrow$
$Stat4: \neg\big\langle \forall x \in s_0 \cup \{s_0\}, y \in s_0 \cup \{s_0\} \mid x \in y \vee y \in x \vee x = y\big\rangle$
$\langle x_1, y_1\rangle \hookrightarrow Stat4 \Rightarrow$ AUTO
$\langle x_1, y_1\rangle \hookrightarrow Stat1 \Rightarrow$ false; Discharge $\Rightarrow$ QED

### 7.3.3 The Transitive Closure Operation

THEOREM act_reachability: [Activation of reachability] $\big\langle \forall x \mid \emptyset = \emptyset \rightarrow \langle \exists c, \forall y \mid y \in x \;\&\; \emptyset = \emptyset \rightarrow y \in c\rangle\big\rangle$. PROOF:

Suppose_not( ) $\Rightarrow \quad Stat1:$ AUTO
$\langle x\rangle \hookrightarrow Stat1(\star) \Rightarrow \quad Stat2: \neg\langle \exists c, \forall y \mid y \in x \;\&\; \emptyset = \emptyset \rightarrow y \in c\rangle$
$\langle x\rangle \hookrightarrow Stat2 \Rightarrow \quad Stat3: \neg\langle \forall y \mid y \in x \;\&\; \emptyset = \emptyset \rightarrow y \in x\rangle$
$\langle y\rangle \hookrightarrow Stat3 \Rightarrow$ false; Discharge $\Rightarrow$ QED

APPLY $\langle \text{descs}_\Theta : \text{trCl} \rangle$ reachability$\big(\text{V(X)} \mapsto \emptyset = \emptyset, \text{E(X,Y)} \mapsto \text{Y} \in \text{X}\big) \Rightarrow$

THEOREM 9*a*: [Recursively defined iterated members]

$\big\langle \forall \text{s}, \text{x}, \text{y} \mid \text{s} \subseteq \text{trCl(s)} \ \& \ \big(\text{x} \in \text{trCl(s)} \ \& \ \emptyset = \emptyset \ \& \ \emptyset = \emptyset \ \& \ \text{y} \in \text{x} \rightarrow \text{y} \in \text{trCl(s)}\big)\big\rangle \ \&$
$\big\langle \forall \text{y}, \text{x}, \text{z} \mid \text{y} \in \text{trCl}\big(\{\text{x}\}\big) \ \& \ \text{z} \in \text{trCl}\big(\{\text{y}\}\big) \rightarrow \text{z} \in \text{trCl}\big(\{\text{x}\}\big)\big\rangle \ \&$
$\big\langle \forall \text{s}, \text{t} \mid \text{s} \subseteq \text{t} \ \& \ \langle \forall \text{x}, \text{y} \mid \text{x} \in \text{t} \ \& \ \text{y} \in \text{x} \ \& \ \emptyset = \emptyset \ \& \ \emptyset = \emptyset \rightarrow \text{y} \in \text{t}\rangle \rightarrow \text{trCl(s)} \subseteq \text{t}\big\rangle.$

Now we can prove that, for any set s, trCl(s) includes s and is membership-transitive.

THEOREM 9: [Stepwise reachability of ultimate members]

$\text{S} \subseteq \text{trCl(S)} \ \& \ \big(\text{X} \in \text{trCl(S)} \ \& \ \text{Y} \in \text{X} \rightarrow \text{Y} \in \text{trCl(S)}\big)$. PROOF:

We proceed by contradiction. Suppose that our theorem is false, and let s, x, and y be a counterexample.

Suppose_not(s, x, y) $\Rightarrow$ AUTO

*T9a* $\Rightarrow$

*Stat1* : $\big\langle \forall \text{s}, \text{x}, \text{y} \mid \text{s} \subseteq \text{trCl(s)} \ \&$
$\big(\text{x} \in \text{trCl(s)} \ \& \ \emptyset = \emptyset \ \& \ \emptyset = \emptyset \ \& \ \text{y} \in \text{x} \rightarrow \text{y} \in \text{trCl(s)}\big)\big\rangle$

$\langle \text{s}, \text{x}, \text{y} \rangle \hookrightarrow$ *Stat1* $\Rightarrow$ false; Discharge $\Rightarrow$ QED

THEOREM 10: [Transitivity of iterated membership]

$\text{Y} \in \text{trCl}\big(\{\text{X}\}\big) \ \& \ \text{Z} \in \text{trCl}\big(\{\text{Y}\}\big) \rightarrow \text{Z} \in \text{trCl}\big(\{\text{X}\}\big)$. PROOF:

Suppose_not(y, x, z) $\Rightarrow$ AUTO

*T9a* $\Rightarrow$ *Stat1* : $\big\langle \forall \text{y}, \text{x}, \text{z} \mid \text{y} \in \text{trCl}\big(\{\text{x}\}\big) \ \& \ \text{z} \in \text{trCl}\big(\{\text{y}\}\big) \rightarrow \text{z} \in \text{trCl}\big(\{\text{x}\}\big)\big\rangle$

$\langle \text{y}, \text{x}, \text{z} \rangle \hookrightarrow$ *Stat1* $\Rightarrow$ false; Discharge $\Rightarrow$ QED

THEOREM 11: [Minimality of the set of ultimate members] $\text{S} \subseteq \text{T} \ \& \ \text{Is\_full(T)} \rightarrow \text{trCl(S)} \subseteq \text{T}$. PROOF:

Suppose_not(s, t) $\Rightarrow$ AUTO

*T9a* $\Rightarrow$ *Stat1* : $\big\langle \forall \text{s}, \text{t} \mid$
$\text{s} \subseteq \text{t} \ \& \ \langle \forall \text{x}, \text{y} \mid \text{x} \in \text{t} \ \& \ \text{y} \in \text{x} \ \& \ \emptyset = \emptyset \ \& \ \emptyset = \emptyset \rightarrow \text{y} \in \text{t}\rangle \rightarrow \text{trCl(s)} \subseteq \text{t}\big\rangle$

$\langle \text{s}, \text{t} \rangle \hookrightarrow$ *Stat1(Stat1⋆)* $\Rightarrow$

$\text{s} \subseteq \text{t} \ \& \ \langle \forall \text{x}, \text{y} \mid \text{x} \in \text{t} \ \& \ \text{y} \in \text{x} \ \& \ \emptyset = \emptyset \ \& \ \emptyset = \emptyset \rightarrow \text{y} \in \text{t}\rangle \rightarrow \text{trCl(s)} \subseteq \text{t}$

ELEM $\Rightarrow$ $\text{x} \in \text{t} \ \& \ \text{y} \in \text{x} \ \& \ \emptyset = \emptyset \ \& \ \emptyset = \emptyset \leftrightarrow \text{x} \in \text{t} \ \& \ \text{y} \in \text{x}$

EQUAL $\Rightarrow$ $\langle \forall \text{x}, \text{y} \mid \text{x} \in \text{t} \ \& \ \text{y} \in \text{x} \rightarrow \text{y} \in \text{t}\rangle \rightarrow \text{trCl(s)} \subseteq \text{t}$

ELEM $\Rightarrow$ *Stat2* : $\neg\langle \forall \text{x}, \text{y} \mid \text{x} \in \text{t} \ \& \ \text{y} \in \text{x} \rightarrow \text{y} \in \text{t}\rangle$

$\langle x, y \rangle \hookrightarrow Stat2 \Rightarrow \quad x \in t \,\&\, y \in x \,\&\, y \notin t$

$\langle t, x \rangle \hookrightarrow T3 \Rightarrow \quad$ false; Discharge $\Rightarrow$ QED

### 7.3.4 A Basic Form of the Principle of Transfinite Induction

Next we state a basic form of the principle of transfinite induction, which simply asserts that if there is any n satisfying a property P(X), there is a membership-minimal m such that P(m). We formulate this as a theory providing just one theorem.

THEORY transfinite_induction(n, P(X))
  P(n)
END transfinite_induction

ENTER_THEORY transfinite_induction

DEF transfinite_induction · 0: [Witness for transfinite induction argument]

$$\mathsf{mt1}_\Theta =_{\mathrm{Def}} \mathbf{arb}\big(\{m : m \in \mathsf{trCl}(\{n\}) \mid \mathsf{P}(m)\}\big)$$

THEOREM transfinite_induction · 1: [Transfinite membership induction]
  $\mathsf{P}(\mathsf{mt1}_\Theta) \,\&\, \big(K \in \mathsf{mt1}_\Theta \rightarrow \neg\mathsf{P}(K)\big)$. PROOF:

Suppose_not(k) $\Rightarrow \quad \neg\mathsf{P}(\mathsf{mt1}_\Theta) \vee \big(k \in \mathsf{mt1}_\Theta \,\&\, \mathsf{P}(k)\big)$

Proceed by contradiction, first noting that $\{m : m \in \mathsf{trCl}(\{n\}) \mid \mathsf{P}(m)\}$ cannot be null since n belongs to it.

Suppose $\Rightarrow \quad Stat1: \{m : m \in \mathsf{trCl}(\{n\}) \mid \mathsf{P}(m)\} = \emptyset$

Assump $\Rightarrow \quad \mathsf{P}(n)$

$\langle \{n\}, \mathrm{junk}, \mathrm{bunk} \rangle \hookrightarrow T9 \Rightarrow \quad n \in \mathsf{trCl}(\{n\})$

$\langle n \rangle \hookrightarrow Stat1 \Rightarrow \quad$ false; Discharge $\Rightarrow$ AUTO

The regularity axiom now tells us that there is an $\in$-minimal element $\mathsf{mt1}_\Theta$ of $\{m : m \in \mathsf{trCl}(\{n\}) \mid \mathsf{P}(m)\}$. This necessarily satisfies $\mathsf{mt1}_\Theta \in \mathsf{trCl}(\{n\}) \,\&\, \mathsf{P}(\mathsf{mt1}_\Theta)$.

$\langle \{m : m \in \mathsf{trCl}(\{n\}) \mid \mathsf{P}(m)\} \rangle \hookrightarrow T0 \Rightarrow$

$$\mathbf{arb}\big(\{m : m \in \mathsf{trCl}(\{n\}) \mid \mathsf{P}(m)\}\big) \in \{m : m \in \mathsf{trCl}(\{n\}) \mid \mathsf{P}(m)\} \,\&$$
$$\mathbf{arb}\big(\{m : m \in \mathsf{trCl}(\{n\}) \mid \mathsf{P}(m)\}\big) \cap \{m : m \in \mathsf{trCl}(\{n\}) \mid \mathsf{P}(m)\} = \emptyset$$

Use_def($mt1_\Theta$) ⇒ *Stat2* :

$mt1_\Theta \in \{u : u \in trCl(\{n\}) \mid P(u)\}$ & $mt1_\Theta \cap \{u : u \in trCl(\{n\}) \mid P(u)\} = \emptyset$

⟨$mt1_\Theta$⟩↪*Stat2* ⇒ $mt1_\Theta \in trCl(\{n\})$ & $P(mt1_\Theta)$

The negative of our theorem now tells us that there is a $k \in mt1_\Theta$ such that P(k); but such a k would clearly belong to {u : trCl({n}) | P(u)}, and so would contradict the minimality of $mt1_\Theta$. This contradiction proves our theorem.

⟨{n}, $mt1_\Theta$, k⟩↪*T9* ⇒ $k \in trCl(\{n\})$

Suppose ⇒ *Stat3* : $k \notin \{u : u \in trCl(\{n\}) \mid P(u)\}$

⟨k⟩↪*Stat3* ⇒ false; Discharge ⇒ $k \in \{u : u \in trCl(\{n\}) \mid P(u)\}$

Discharge ⇒ QED

ENTER_THEORY Set_theory

Now we have a preliminary form of the principle of transfinite induction, which is given by the following theory:

DISPLAY transfinite_induction

> THEORY transfinite_induction(n, P(X))
> P(n)
> ⇒ ($mt1_\Theta$)
> ⟨∀k | P($mt1_\Theta$) & (k ∈ $mt1_\Theta$ → ¬P(k))⟩
> END transfinite_induction

### 7.3.5 Some Basic Facts on Ordinal Numbers

Now we begin more serious development of the theory of ordinals, along von Neumann's line. Our first theorem uses induction to show that if one ordinal t is included in another ordinal s but not equal to s, then t must be a member of s, and in fact must be the smallest element of s\t.

THEOREM 12: [Ordinal comparison lemma] $\mathcal{O}$(S) & $\mathcal{O}$(T) & T ⊆ S →
T = S ∨ (T = **arb**(S\T) & T ∈ S\T). PROOF:

Suppose_not(s, t) ⇒ $\mathcal{O}$(s) & $\mathcal{O}$(t) & t ⊆ s & t ≠ s & ¬(t = **arb**(s\t) & t ∈ s)

For if our assertion is false, s must have as a proper subset t, in which case the regularity axiom tells us that s\t has an element **arb**(s\t) disjoint from s\t. Plainly **arb**(s\t) is also a member of the superset s of s\t. But then, by definition of ordinal, **arb**(s\t) must be a subset of $s \cap t$, since it is disjoint from s\t. Therefore **arb**(s\t) cannot include t, otherwise the initial assumption $t \neq$ **arb**(s\t) would be contradicted.

Loc_def ⇒ *Stat1* : a = **arb**(s\t)
⟨s⟩↪*T5*(⋆) ⇒ Is_full(s)
⟨s, t⟩↪*T4* ⇒ *Stat2* : $t \not\subseteq a \;\&\; a \in s \;\&\; \mathcal{O}(s) \;\&\; \mathcal{O}(t) \;\&\; t \subseteq s \;\&\; t \neq s$

Since **arb**(s\t) fails to include t, there must be some b in t but not in **arb**(s\t). By the definition of ordinals, this implies that **arb**(s\t) = b ∨ **arb**(s\t) ∈ b.

⟨b⟩↪*Stat2*(*Stat2*⋆) ⇒ $b \in t \;\&\; b \notin a$
Use_def($\mathcal{O}$) ⇒ *Stat3* : $\langle \forall x \in s, y \in s \mid x \in y \vee y \in x \vee x = y\rangle$
⟨a, b⟩↪*Stat3*(*Stat2*⋆) ⇒ $a \in b \vee a = b$

Using the definition of ordinals once more, this time for t, we see that b must be a subset of t, which rules out both **arb**(s\t) ∈ b and **arb**(s\t) = b, because either of these would yield **arb**(s\t) ∈ t, which is impossible. We have contradicted our original assumption, and so proved our theorem.

⟨t, b⟩↪*T5* (*Stat1*⋆) ⇒ $b \subseteq t$
(*Stat1*)Discharge ⇒ QED

THEOREM 13: [2nd ordinal comparison lemma; Boolean closure properties of $\mathcal{O}$]
$\mathcal{O}(\emptyset) \;\&\; \big(\mathcal{O}(S) \;\&\; \mathcal{O}(T) \rightarrow (S \subseteq T \vee T \subseteq S) \;\&\; \mathcal{O}(S \cap T) \;\&\; \mathcal{O}(S \cup T)\big)$. PROOF:
Suppose_not(s, t) ⇒ AUTO
Suppose ⇒ $\neg\mathcal{O}(\emptyset)$
Use_def($\mathcal{O}$) ⇒ *Stat0* : $\neg\langle \forall x \in \emptyset \mid x \subseteq \emptyset\rangle \vee \neg\langle \forall x \in \emptyset, y \in \emptyset \mid x \in y \vee y \in x \vee x = y\rangle$
⟨$x_2, x_1, y_1$⟩↪*Stat0* ⇒ false; Discharge ⇒ AUTO
Use_def($\mathcal{O}$) ⇒ *Stat1* : $\langle \forall x \in s \mid x \subseteq s\rangle \;\&\; \langle \forall x \in t \mid x \subseteq t\rangle$
Suppose ⇒ $\neg\mathcal{O}(s \cap t)$
⟨t, s ∩ t⟩↪*T6* ⇒ *Stat2* : $\neg\langle \forall x \in s \cap t \mid x \subseteq s \cap t\rangle$
⟨$x_0$⟩↪*Stat2*(*Stat2*⋆) ⇒ $x_0 \in s \cap t \;\&\; x_0 \not\subseteq s \cap t$
⟨$x_0, x_0$⟩↪*Stat1*(*Stat2*⋆) ⇒ false; Discharge ⇒ AUTO

Now we prove the related but slightly less elementary result that one of any pair of ordinals must include the other. For if not, neither of these ordinals is included in the other, so neither can equal the intersection of the two, which is an ordinal as just seen.

Suppose ⇒ $s \not\subseteq t \,\&\, t \not\subseteq s$

|| It now follows, using Theorem 12 twice, that $s \cap t$ is equal to both **arb**($s \backslash s \cap t$) and **arb**($t \backslash s \cap t$), and so, since neither of these sets is empty, is a member of both $s \backslash s \cap t$ and $t \backslash s \cap t$, which is impossible since the intersection of these two sets is empty. This contradiction proves our theorem.

⟨s, s ∩ t⟩↪*T*12 (⋆) ⇒ *Stat3* : $s \cap t \in s \backslash s \cap t$
⟨t, s ∩ t⟩↪*T*12 (⋆) ⇒ $s \cap t \in t \backslash t \cap s$
(*Stat3*⋆)Discharge ⇒ AUTO

|| We are now left with only one case to consider, namely that $\neg\mathcal{O}(s \cup t)$. Taking into account the facts already proved along the way, this case is settled easily, leading us the overall conclusion.

Suppose ⇒ $s \subseteq t$
ELEM ⇒ $s \cup t = t \,\&\, s \cap t = s$
EQUAL ⇒ false; Discharge ⇒ $s \cup t = s \,\&\, s \cap t = t$
EQUAL ⇒ false; Discharge ⇒ QED

|| Next we show that the class of all ordinals (we will see soon that this is not a set) is totally (and strictly) ordered by membership.

THEOREM 14: [Ordinal membership comparison] $\mathcal{O}(S) \,\&\, \mathcal{O}(T) \rightarrow S \in T \vee T \in S \vee S = T$. PROOF:
Suppose_not(s, t) ⇒ *Stat0* : $\mathcal{O}(s) \,\&\, \mathcal{O}(t) \,\&\, s \notin t \,\&\, t \notin s \,\&\, s \neq t$

|| For if we suppose the contrary, and note that by Theorems 13 and 12 one must include the other but not be equal to it, it follows (by the regularity axiom) that one must be a member of the other, a contradiction which proves our theorem.

⟨s, t⟩↪*T*13 ⇒ $s \subseteq t \vee t \subseteq s$
⟨s, t⟩↪*T*12 (*Stat0*, *Stat0*⋆) ⇒ $t \not\subseteq s$
⟨t, s⟩↪*T*12 (*Stat0*⋆) ⇒ false; Discharge ⇒ QED

|| Next we show that the class of ordinals is not a set.

THEOREM 15: [The class of ordinals is not a set] $\neg\langle \forall x \mid x \in OS \leftrightarrow \mathcal{O}(x)\rangle$. PROOF+:
Suppose_not(o) ⇒ *Stat1* : AUTO

For suppose the contrary, so that there is a set o consisting of all ordinals. But we can show that o must be an ordinal. Indeed, if it were not, then by the definition of ordinals there would exist a, b, c such that either a was a member but not a subset of o, or b and c are two members of o not related by membership.

Suppose ⇒ $\neg\mathcal{O}(o)$
Use_def($\mathcal{O}$) ⇒ $Stat2: \neg(\langle\forall x \in o \mid x \subseteq o\rangle \,\&\, \langle\forall x \in o, y \in o \mid x \in y \vee y \in x \vee x = y\rangle)$
$\langle a, b, c\rangle \hookrightarrow Stat2$ ⇒ $(a \in o \,\&\, a \nsubseteq o) \vee (b, c \in o \,\&\, \neg(b \in c \vee c \in b \vee b = c))$

In the second of these cases b and c are both plainly ordinals, so that this case is ruled out by Theorem 14. Hence only the first case need be considered.

Suppose ⇒ $b, c \in o \,\&\, \neg(b \in c \vee c \in b \vee b = c)$
$\langle b\rangle \hookrightarrow Stat1$ ⇒ $\mathcal{O}(b)$
$\langle c\rangle \hookrightarrow Stat1$ ⇒ $\mathcal{O}(c)$
$\langle b, c\rangle \hookrightarrow T14$ ⇒ false; Discharge ⇒ $Stat3: a \in o \,\&\, a \nsubseteq o$

In this case the set a, which must plainly be an ordinal, must have a member d which is not in o, and hence not an ordinal by Stat1 above, which is impossible, so our theorem is proved.

$\langle a\rangle \hookrightarrow Stat1$ ⇒ $\mathcal{O}(a)$
$\langle d\rangle \hookrightarrow Stat3$ ⇒ $d \in a \,\&\, d \notin o$
$\langle d\rangle \hookrightarrow Stat1$ ⇒ false; Discharge ⇒ $\mathcal{O}(o)$
$\langle o\rangle \hookrightarrow Stat1$ ⇒ false; Discharge ⇒ QED

Our next theorem shows that, for ordinals, inclusion is equivalent to the disjunction of identity and membership.

THEOREM 16: [Third ordinal comparison lemma] $\mathcal{O}(S) \,\&\, \mathcal{O}(T) \rightarrow (T \subseteq S \leftrightarrow T \in S \vee T = S)$. PROOF:
Suppose_not(s, t) ⇒ AUTO

For in the contrary case there must exist two ordinals s and t such that either t is a member but not a subset of s, or t is a subset of s but neither a member of, or equal to, s;

ELEM ⇒ $(t \nsubseteq s \,\&\, t \in s) \vee (t \subseteq s \,\&\, t \notin s \,\&\, t \neq s)$

but the first case is ruled out by definition of ordinal and the second case by Theorem 12, proving our theorem.

⟨s, t⟩↪*T5* ⇒ *Stat1* : $t \subseteq s$ & $t \notin s$ & $t \neq s$
⟨s, t⟩↪*T12* ⇒ false; Discharge ⇒ QED

|| It is sometimes convenient to use this theorem in the following modified form.

THEOREM 17: [Ordinal membership and comparison] $\mathcal{O}(S)$ & $\mathcal{O}(T) \rightarrow (T \notin S \leftrightarrow S \subseteq T)$. PROOF:
Suppose_not(s, t) ⇒ $\mathcal{O}(s)$ & $\mathcal{O}(t)$ & $t \notin s$ & $s \nsubseteq t$

|| Since $t \in s$ & $s \subseteq t$ is impossible, a counterexample to our assertion must satisfy $t \notin s$ & $s \nsubseteq t$. But by Theorems 14 and 13 we then have $s \subseteq t$, a contradiction which proves the present corollary.

⟨s, t⟩↪*T14* ⇒ $s \in t \vee s = t$
⟨t, s⟩↪*T13* ⇒ false; Discharge ⇒ QED

|| Our next lemma tells us that, for ordinals, membership in the successor of an ordinal s is equivalent to inclusion in s.

THEOREM 18: [Membership in the successor of an ordinal s] $\mathcal{O}(S) \rightarrow (T \in \text{next}(S) \leftrightarrow T \subseteq S$ & $\mathcal{O}(T))$. PROOF:
Suppose_not(s, t) ⇒ AUTO
Use_def(next) ⇒ *Stat1* : $\mathcal{O}(s)$ & $\neg(t \in s \cup \{s\} \leftrightarrow t \subseteq s$ & $\mathcal{O}(t))$
Suppose ⇒ *Stat2* : $t \in s \vee t = s$ & $\neg(t \subseteq s$ & $\mathcal{O}(t))$
Suppose ⇒ *Stat3* : $t = s$
EQUAL ⟨*Stat1*, *Stat3*⟩ ⇒ false; (*Stat4*)Discharge ⇒ *Stat5* : $t \in s$
⟨s, t⟩↪*T7* (*Stat1*, *Stat5*) ⇒ *Stat6* : $\mathcal{O}(t)$
⟨s, t⟩↪*T16* (*Stat1*, *Stat2*, *Stat5*, *Stat6*) ⇒ *Stat7* : false
(*Stat7*)Discharge ⇒ *Stat8* : $\neg(t \in s \vee t = s$ & $\neg(t \subseteq s$ & $\mathcal{O}(t)))$
⟨s, t⟩↪*T16* (*Stat1*, *Stat8*) ⇒ *Stat9* : false
(*Stat9*)Discharge ⇒ QED

THEOREM 19: [Membership of s in an ordinal t implies inclusion of next(s) in t] $\mathcal{O}(T)$ & $S \in T \rightarrow \text{next}(S) \subseteq T$. PROOF+:
Suppose_not(m, i) ⇒ $\mathcal{O}(m)$ & $i \in m$ & *Stat1* : $\text{next}(i) \nsubseteq m$
⟨j⟩↪*Stat1* ⇒ $j \in \text{next}(i)$ & $j \notin m$
Use_def(next) ⇒ $j \in i$
⟨j, m⟩↪*T16* ⇒ $m \nsubseteq j$

|| The following step exploits the fact, derived by means of proof-by-structure behind the scenes, that j is an ordinal. Indeed, since i belongs to m which is an ordinal, it is an ordinal in its turn and the same holds for next(i) and for j which belongs to it.

⟨m, j⟩↪*T17* ⇒ false; Discharge ⇒ QED

## 7.4 Zorn's Lemma

For subsequent use, we reformulate a few special cases of the principle of transfinite definition as THEORYs that can be applied internally within the proofs of theorems.

THEORY transfinite_def_0_params$\big(g(X), h_1(X')\big)$
END transfinite_def_0_params

ENTER_THEORY transfinite_def_0_params

DEF transfinite_def_0_params · 0*a*: [Function defined by a one-parameter transfinite recursion] $f_\Theta(X) =_{Def} g\big(\{h_1(f_\Theta(t)) : t \in X\}\big)$

THEOREM transfinite_def_0_params$_1$: [One-parameter transfinite recursive function definition] $f_\Theta(X) = g\big(\{h_1(f_\Theta(t)) : t \in X\}\big)$.

PROOF:
Suppose_not(x) ⇒ $f_\Theta(x) \neq g\big(\{h_1(f_\Theta(t)) : t \in x\}\big)$
Use_def($f_\Theta$) ⇒ $f_\Theta(x) = g\big(\{h_1(f_\Theta(t)) : t \in x\}\big)$
Discharge ⇒ QED

ENTER_THEORY Set_theory

DISPLAY transfinite_def_0_params

THEORY transfinite_def_0_params$\big(g(X), h_1(X')\big)$
⇒ $(f_\Theta)$
$\langle \forall x \mid f_\Theta(x) = g\big(\{h_1(f_\Theta(t)) : t \in x\}\big)\rangle$
END transfinite_def_0_params

Our next proof establishes a first, purely set-theoretic form of the well-known Zorn's Lemma. We prove that if t is any collection of sets such that every subfamily of t linearly ordered by inclusion admits an upper bound in t, then t has an element maximal for inclusion, i.e. not strictly included in any other element of t.

THEOREM 20: [Zorn's lemma]
$\big\langle \forall x \subseteq T \mid \langle \forall u \in x, v \in x \mid u \supseteq v \vee v \supseteq u\rangle \rightarrow \langle \exists w \in T, \forall y \in x \mid w \supseteq y\rangle\big\rangle \rightarrow$
$\big\langle \exists y \in T, \forall x \in T \mid \neg(x \supseteq y \;\&\; x \neq y)\big\rangle$. PROOF+:

Suppose_not(t) ⇒
*Stat1* : $\big\langle \forall x \subseteq t \mid \langle \forall u \in x, v \in x \mid u \supseteq v \vee v \supseteq u\rangle \rightarrow \langle \exists w \in t, \forall y \in x \mid w \supseteq y\rangle\big\rangle$ &
*Stat2* : $\neg\big\langle \exists y \in t, \forall x \in t \mid \neg(x \supseteq y \;\&\; x \neq y)\big\rangle$

For supposing the contrary, we can define a mapping of t into t which sends each element of t into a strictly larger element, and also a mapping of every subset of t linearly ordered by inclusion into an upper bound for it in t.

Loc_def ⇒ $\mathrm{larger} = \{[x, \mathbf{arb}(\{y \in t \mid y \supseteq x \ \& \ y \neq x\})] : x \in t\}$

APPLY ⟨ ⟩ fcn_symbol$(f(X) \mapsto \mathbf{arb}(\{y \in t \mid y \supseteq X \ \& \ y \neq X\}), g \mapsto \mathrm{larger}, s \mapsto t) \Rightarrow$

*Stat3* : $\langle \forall x \mid \mathrm{larger}\restriction x = \textbf{if } x \in t \textbf{ then } \mathbf{arb}(\{y \in t \mid y \supseteq x \ \& \ y \neq x\}) \textbf{ else } \emptyset \textbf{ fi}\rangle$

Loc_def ⇒ $\mathrm{upper\_bound} = \{[x, \mathbf{arb}(\{y \in t \mid \langle \forall u \in x \mid y \supseteq u\rangle\})] : x \in \mathscr{P}t\}$

APPLY ⟨ ⟩ fcn_symbol

$(f(X) \mapsto \mathbf{arb}(\{y \in t \mid \langle \forall u \in X \mid y \supseteq u\rangle\}), g \mapsto \mathrm{upper\_bound}, s \mapsto \mathscr{P}t) \Rightarrow$ *Stat4* :

$\langle \forall x \mid \mathrm{upper\_bound}\restriction x = \textbf{if } x \in \mathscr{P}t \textbf{ then } \mathbf{arb}(\{y \in t \mid \langle \forall u \in x \mid y \supseteq u\rangle\}) \textbf{ else } \emptyset \textbf{ fi}\rangle$

Now we use the functions 'upper_bound' and 'larger' to introduce the following (recursively defined) function, which we will then show maps each ordinal into t, and is strictly monotone increasing.

APPLY$\langle f_\Theta : \mathrm{Zo}\rangle$transfinite_def_0_params$(g(x) \mapsto \mathrm{larger}\restriction(\mathrm{upper_bound}\restriction x), h_1(x) \mapsto x) \Rightarrow$

*Stat5* : $\langle \forall x \mid \mathrm{Zo}(x) = \mathrm{larger}\restriction(\mathrm{upper\_bound}\restriction\{\mathrm{Zo}(y) : y \in x\})\rangle$

Suppose ⇒ *Stat6* : $\langle \exists x \mid \mathscr{O}(x) \ \& \ \mathrm{Zo}(x) \notin t \ \lor$

$\langle \exists u \in x \mid \neg(\mathrm{Zo}(x) \supseteq \mathrm{Zo}(u) \ \& \ \mathrm{Zo}(x) \neq \mathrm{Zo}(u))\rangle\rangle$

For if there exists some counterexample to this last assertion, then by transfinite induction there exists a smallest such counterexample c.

$\langle d\rangle \hookrightarrow$*Stat6* ⇒ $\mathscr{O}(d) \ \& \ \mathrm{Zo}(d) \notin t \lor \langle \exists u \in d \mid \neg(\mathrm{Zo}(d) \supseteq \mathrm{Zo}(u) \ \& \ \mathrm{Zo}(d) \neq \mathrm{Zo}(u))\rangle$

APPLY $\langle \mathrm{mt1}_\Theta : c\rangle$ transfinite_induction

$(n \mapsto d, P(x) \mapsto (\mathscr{O}(x) \ \& \ \mathrm{Zo}(x) \notin t \lor \langle \exists u \in x \mid \neg(\mathrm{Zo}(x) \supseteq \mathrm{Zo}(u) \ \& \ \mathrm{Zo}(x) \neq \mathrm{Zo}(u))\rangle)) \Rightarrow$

*Stat7* : $\langle \forall x \mid (\mathscr{O}(c) \ \& \ \mathrm{Zo}(c) \notin t \ \lor$

$\langle \exists u \in c \mid \neg(\mathrm{Zo}(c) \supseteq \mathrm{Zo}(u) \ \& \ \mathrm{Zo}(c) \neq \mathrm{Zo}(u))\rangle) \ \& \ (x \in c \rightarrow$

$\neg(\mathscr{O}(x) \ \& \ \mathrm{Zo}(x) \notin t \lor \langle \exists u \in x \mid \neg(\mathrm{Zo}(x) \supseteq \mathrm{Zo}(u) \ \& \ \mathrm{Zo}(x) \neq \mathrm{Zo}(u))\rangle))\rangle$

$\langle \emptyset\rangle \hookrightarrow$*Stat7* ⇒ $\mathscr{O}(c) \ \& \ \mathrm{Zo}(c) \notin t \lor \langle \exists u \in c \mid \neg(\mathrm{Zo}(c) \supseteq \mathrm{Zo}(u) \ \& \ \mathrm{Zo}(c) \neq \mathrm{Zo}(u))\rangle$

Suppose ⇒ *Stat8* : $\neg\langle \forall x \in c \mid$

$\neg(\mathscr{O}(x) \ \& \ \mathrm{Zo}(x) \notin t \lor \langle \exists u \in x \mid \neg(\mathrm{Zo}(x) \supseteq \mathrm{Zo}(u) \ \& \ \mathrm{Zo}(x) \neq \mathrm{Zo}(u))\rangle)\rangle$

$\langle x_0\rangle \hookrightarrow$*Stat8* ⇒ $x_0 \in c \ \& \ \mathscr{O}(x_0) \ \& \ \mathrm{Zo}(x_0) \notin t \ \lor$

$\langle \exists u \in x_0 \mid \neg(\mathrm{Zo}(x_0) \supseteq \mathrm{Zo}(u) \ \& \ \mathrm{Zo}(x_0) \neq \mathrm{Zo}(u))\rangle$

$\langle x_0\rangle \hookrightarrow$*Stat7* ⇒ false; Discharge ⇒ *Stat9* :

$\neg(\mathscr{O}(x) \ \& \ \mathrm{Zo}(x) \notin t \lor \langle \exists u \in x \mid \neg(\mathrm{Zo}(x) \supseteq \mathrm{Zo}(u) \ \& \ \mathrm{Zo}(x) \neq \mathrm{Zo}(u))\rangle)\rangle$

For this minimal counterexample c, the set {Zo(y) : y ∈ c} must be a collection of subsets of t and must be linearly ordered by inclusion.

$$\text{Suppose} \Rightarrow \quad \mathit{Stat10}: \mathrm{t} \not\supseteq \{\mathrm{Zo(y)} : \mathrm{y} \in \mathrm{c}\}$$
$$\langle \mathrm{x}_1\rangle \hookrightarrow \mathit{Stat10} \Rightarrow \quad \mathit{Stat11}: \mathrm{x}_1 \in \{\mathrm{Zo(y)} : \mathrm{y} \in \mathrm{c}\} \ \&\ \mathrm{x}_1 \notin \mathrm{t}$$
$$\langle \mathrm{y}_1\rangle \hookrightarrow \mathit{Stat11} \Rightarrow \quad \mathrm{y}_1 \in \mathrm{c} \ \&\ \mathrm{x}_1 = \mathrm{Zo(y_1)}$$
$$\langle \mathrm{y}_1\rangle \hookrightarrow \mathit{Stat9} \Rightarrow \quad \neg\left(\mathscr{O}(\mathrm{y}_1) \ \&\ \mathrm{Zo(y_1)} \notin \mathrm{t}\right) \ \&\ \mathscr{O}(\mathrm{y}_1)$$
$$(\mathit{Stat11})\text{Discharge} \Rightarrow \quad \mathrm{t} \supseteq \{\mathrm{Zo(y)} : \mathrm{y} \in \mathrm{c}\}$$
$$\text{Suppose} \Rightarrow \quad \mathit{Stat12}: \neg\langle \forall \mathrm{u} \in \{\mathrm{Zo(y)} : \mathrm{y} \in \mathrm{c}\}, \mathrm{v} \in \{\mathrm{Zo(y)} : \mathrm{y} \in \mathrm{c}\} \mid \mathrm{u} \supseteq \mathrm{v} \vee \mathrm{v} \supseteq \mathrm{u}\rangle$$
$$\langle \mathrm{a}, \mathrm{b}\rangle \hookrightarrow \mathit{Stat12} \Rightarrow \quad \mathit{Stat13}: \mathrm{a}, \mathrm{b} \in \{\mathrm{Zo(y)} : \mathrm{y} \in \mathrm{c}\} \ \&\ \neg(\mathrm{a} \supseteq \mathrm{b} \vee \mathrm{b} \supseteq \mathrm{a})$$
$$\langle \mathrm{o}_1, \mathrm{o}_2\rangle \hookrightarrow \mathit{Stat13} \Rightarrow \quad \mathit{Stat14}: \mathrm{o}_1, \mathrm{o}_2 \in \mathrm{c}$$
$$\&\ \neg\left(\mathrm{Zo(o_1)} \supseteq \mathrm{Zo(o_2)} \vee \mathrm{Zo(o_2)} \supseteq \mathrm{Zo(o_1)}\right) \ \&\ \mathscr{O}(\mathrm{o}_1) \ \&\ \mathscr{O}(\mathrm{o}_2)$$
$$\langle \mathrm{o}_1\rangle \hookrightarrow \mathit{Stat9} \Rightarrow \quad \mathit{Stat15}: \neg\langle \exists \mathrm{u} \in \mathrm{o}_1 \mid \neg\left(\mathrm{Zo(o_1)} \supseteq \mathrm{Zo(u)} \ \&\ \mathrm{Zo(o_1)} \neq \mathrm{Zo(u)}\right)\rangle$$
$$\langle \mathrm{o}_2\rangle \hookrightarrow \mathit{Stat9} \Rightarrow \quad \mathit{Stat16}: \neg\langle \exists \mathrm{u} \in \mathrm{o}_2 \mid \neg\left(\mathrm{Zo(o_2)} \supseteq \mathrm{Zo(u)} \ \&\ \mathrm{Zo(o_2)} \neq \mathrm{Zo(u)}\right)\rangle$$
$$\langle \mathrm{o}_1, \mathrm{o}_2\rangle \hookrightarrow T14 \Rightarrow \quad \mathrm{o}_1 \in \mathrm{o}_2 \vee \mathrm{o}_2 \in \mathrm{o}_1 \vee \mathrm{o}_1 = \mathrm{o}_2$$
$$\text{Suppose} \Rightarrow \quad \mathrm{o}_1 = \mathrm{o}_2$$
$$\text{EQUAL} \Rightarrow \quad \mathrm{Zo(o_1)} = \mathrm{Zo(o_2)}$$
$$(\mathit{Stat14})\text{Discharge} \Rightarrow \quad \mathrm{o}_1 \in \mathrm{o}_2 \vee \mathrm{o}_2 \in \mathrm{o}_1$$
$$\text{Suppose} \Rightarrow \quad \mathrm{o}_2 \in \mathrm{o}_1$$
$$\langle \mathrm{o}_2\rangle \hookrightarrow \mathit{Stat15} \Rightarrow \quad \text{false; Discharge} \Rightarrow \quad \mathrm{o}_1 \in \mathrm{o}_2$$
$$\langle \mathrm{o}_1\rangle \hookrightarrow \mathit{Stat16} \Rightarrow \quad \text{false; Discharge} \Rightarrow$$
$$\langle \forall \mathrm{u} \in \{\mathrm{Zo(y)} : \mathrm{y} \in \mathrm{c}\}, \mathrm{v} \in \{\mathrm{Zo(y)} : \mathrm{y} \in \mathrm{c}\} \mid \mathrm{u} \supseteq \mathrm{v} \vee \mathrm{v} \supseteq \mathrm{u}\rangle$$

Thus, by definition, {Zo(y) : y ∈ c} must have an upper bound cb which is a subset of t, and therefore, by the axiom of choice, upper_bound↾{Zo($z_1$) : $z_1$ ∈ c} must belong to t and include every element of {Zo(y) : y ∈ c}.

$$\langle \{\mathrm{Zo(z_1)} : \mathrm{z}_1 \in \mathrm{c}\}\rangle \hookrightarrow \mathit{Stat1} \Rightarrow \quad \mathit{Stat17}: \langle \exists \mathrm{w} \in \mathrm{t}, \forall \mathrm{y} \in \{\mathrm{Zo(z_1)} : \mathrm{z}_1 \in \mathrm{c}\} \mid \mathrm{w} \supseteq \mathrm{y}\rangle$$
$$\langle \mathrm{cb}\rangle \hookrightarrow \mathit{Stat17} \Rightarrow \quad \mathrm{cb} \in \mathrm{t} \ \&\ \langle \forall \mathrm{y} \in \{\mathrm{Zo(z_1)} : \mathrm{z}_1 \in \mathrm{c}\} \mid \mathrm{cb} \supseteq \mathrm{y}\rangle$$
$$\langle \{\mathrm{Zo(z_1)} : \mathrm{z}_1 \in \mathrm{c}\}\rangle \hookrightarrow \mathit{Stat4} \Rightarrow \quad \text{upper\_bound}\restriction\{\mathrm{Zo(z_1)} : \mathrm{z}_1 \in \mathrm{c}\} =$$
$$\textbf{if } \{\mathrm{Zo(z_1)} : \mathrm{z}_1 \in \mathrm{c}\} \in \mathscr{P}\mathrm{t}$$
$$\textbf{then arb}\left(\{\mathrm{y} \in \mathrm{t} \mid \langle \forall \mathrm{u} \in \{\mathrm{Zo(z_1)} : \mathrm{z}_1 \in \mathrm{c}\} \mid \mathrm{y} \supseteq \mathrm{u}\rangle\}\right) \textbf{ else } \emptyset \textbf{ fi}$$
$$\text{Suppose} \Rightarrow \quad \{\mathrm{Zo(z_1)} : \mathrm{z}_1 \in \mathrm{c}\} \notin \mathscr{P}\mathrm{t}$$
$$\langle \mathrm{t}, \{\mathrm{Zo(z_1)} : \mathrm{z}_1 \in \mathrm{c}\}\rangle \hookrightarrow T1\ (\mathit{Stat9}\star) \Rightarrow \quad \text{false; Discharge} \Rightarrow$$
$$\text{upper\_bound}\restriction\{\mathrm{Zo(z_1)} : \mathrm{z}_1 \in \mathrm{c}\} =$$
$$\textbf{arb}\left(\{\mathrm{y} \in \mathrm{t} \mid \langle \forall \mathrm{u} \in \{\mathrm{Zo(z_1)} : \mathrm{z}_1 \in \mathrm{c}\} \mid \mathrm{y} \supseteq \mathrm{u}\rangle\}\right)$$
$$\text{Suppose} \Rightarrow \quad \mathit{Stat19}: \{\mathrm{y} \in \mathrm{t} \mid \langle \forall \mathrm{u} \in \{\mathrm{Zo(z_1)} : \mathrm{z}_1 \in \mathrm{c}\} \mid \mathrm{y} \supseteq \mathrm{u}\rangle\} = \emptyset$$

$\langle cb\rangle \hookrightarrow Stat19 \Rightarrow$ false; Discharge $\Rightarrow$
$\{y \in t \mid \langle \forall u \in \{Zo(z_1) : z_1 \in c\} \mid y \supseteq u\rangle\} \neq \emptyset$
$\langle\{y \in t \mid \langle \forall u \in \{Zo(z_1) : z_1 \in c\} \mid y \supseteq u\rangle\}\rangle \hookrightarrow T0 \Rightarrow$
$\mathbf{arb}(\{y \in t \mid \langle \forall u \in \{Zo(z_1) : z_1 \in c\} \mid y \supseteq u\rangle\}) \in$
$\{y \in t \mid \langle \forall u \in \{Zo(z_1) : z_1 \in c\} \mid y \supseteq u\rangle\}$
$(Stat17)$ELEM $\Rightarrow$ $Stat20$ : upper_bound$\restriction\{Zo(z_1) : z_1 \in c\} \in$
$\{y \in t \mid \langle \forall u \in \{Zo(z_1) : z_1 \in c\} \mid y \supseteq u\rangle\}$
$\langle\,\rangle \hookrightarrow Stat20 \Rightarrow$ upper_bound$\restriction\{Zo(z_1) : z_1 \in c\} \in t$ & $Stat21$ :
$\langle \forall u \in \{Zo(z_1) : z_1 \in c\} \mid$ upper_bound$\restriction\{Zo(z_1) : z_1 \in c\} \supseteq u\rangle$

It follows by a second use of the axiom of choice that larger$\restriction$(upper_bound$\restriction\{Zo(z_1) : z_1 \in c\}) = Zo(c)$ is an element of t properly including every element of $\{Zo(y) : y \in c\}$. This refutes our earlier supposition, and so lets us conclude that Zo sends ordinals into t and is strictly monotone increasing.

$\langle$upper_bound$\restriction\{Zo(z_1) : z_1 \in c\}\rangle \hookrightarrow Stat3 \Rightarrow$
larger$\restriction$(upper_bound$\restriction\{Zo(z_1) : z_1 \in c\}) =$
$\mathbf{arb}(\{y \in t \mid y \supseteq$ upper_bound$\restriction\{Zo(z_1) : z_1 \in c\}$ &
$y \neq$ upper_bound$\restriction\{Zo(z_1) : z_1 \in c\}\})$
$\langle$upper_bound$\restriction\{Zo(z_1) : z_1 \in c\}\rangle \hookrightarrow Stat2 \Rightarrow$ $Stat22 : \neg\langle \forall x \in t \mid \neg(x \supseteq$
upper_bound$\restriction\{Zo(z_1) : z_1 \in c\}$ & $x \neq$ upper_bound$\restriction\{Zo(z_1) : z_1 \in c\})\rangle$
$\langle cu\rangle \hookrightarrow Stat22 \Rightarrow$ $cu \in t$ & $cu \supseteq$ upper_bound$\restriction\{Zo(z_1) : z_1 \in c\}$ &
$cu \neq$ upper_bound$\restriction\{Zo(z_1) : z_1 \in c\}$
Suppose $\Rightarrow$ $Stat23$ : $\{y \in t \mid y \supseteq$ upper_bound$\restriction\{Zo(z_1) : z_1 \in c\}$
& $y \neq$ upper_bound$\restriction\{Zo(z_1) : z_1 \in c\}\} = \emptyset$
$\langle cu\rangle \hookrightarrow Stat23 \Rightarrow$ false; Discharge $\Rightarrow$ $\{y \in t \mid y \supseteq$ upper_bound$\restriction\{Zo(z_1) : z_1 \in c\}$
& $y \neq$ upper_bound$\restriction\{Zo(z_1) : z_1 \in c\}\} \neq \emptyset$
$\langle\{y \in t \mid y \supseteq$ upper_bound$\restriction\{Zo(z_1) : z_1 \in c\}$ & $y \neq$ upper_bound$\restriction\{Zo(z_1) : z_1 \in c\}\}\rangle$
$\hookrightarrow T0 \Rightarrow$ $\mathbf{arb}(\{y \in t \mid y \supseteq$ upper_bound$\restriction\{Zo(z_1) : z_1 \in c\}$
& $y \neq$ upper_bound$\restriction\{Zo(z_1) : z_1 \in c\}\}) \in$
$\{y \in t \mid y \supseteq$ upper_bound$\restriction\{Zo(z_1) : z_1 \in c\}$
& $y \neq$ upper_bound$\restriction\{Zo(z_1) : z_1 \in c\}\}$
$(Stat20)$ELEM $\Rightarrow$ larger$\restriction$(upper_bound$\restriction\{Zo(z_1) : z_1 \in c\}) \in$
$\{y \in t \mid y \supseteq$ upper_bound$\restriction\{Zo(z_1) : z_1 \in c\}$
& $y \neq$ upper_bound$\restriction\{Zo(z_1) : z_1 \in c\}\}$
$\langle c\rangle \hookrightarrow Stat5 \Rightarrow$ $Stat24$ : $Zo(c) \in \{y \in t \mid y \supseteq$ upper_bound$\restriction\{Zo(z_1) : z_1 \in c\}$

$\& \ y \neq \text{upper\_bound} \lceil \{Zo(z_1) : z_1 \in c\}\}$

$\langle\,\rangle \hookrightarrow Stat24 \Rightarrow \quad Zo(c) \in t \ \& \ Zo(c) \supseteq \text{upper\_bound} \lceil \{Zo(z_1) : z_1 \in c\} \ \&$

$Zo(c) \neq \text{upper\_bound} \lceil \{Zo(z_1) : z_1 \in c\}$

$\text{ELEM} \Rightarrow \quad Stat25 : \langle \exists u \in c \mid \neg(Zo(c) \supseteq Zo(u) \ \& \ Zo(c) \neq Zo(u))\rangle$

$\langle cv\rangle \hookrightarrow Stat25 \Rightarrow \quad cv \in c \ \& \ \neg(Zo(c) \supseteq Zo(cv) \ \& \ Zo(c) \neq Zo(cv))$

$(Stat22)\text{ELEM} \Rightarrow \quad \text{upper\_bound} \lceil \{Zo(z_1) : z_1 \in c\} \not\supseteq Zo(cv)$

$\langle Zo(cv)\rangle \hookrightarrow Stat21 \Rightarrow \quad Stat26 : Zo(cv) \notin \{Zo(z_1) : z_1 \in c\}$

$\langle cv\rangle \hookrightarrow Stat26 \Rightarrow \quad \text{false}; \ \text{Discharge} \Rightarrow \quad Stat27 :$

$\neg\langle \exists x \mid \mathcal{O}(x) \ \& \ Zo(x) \notin t \vee \langle \exists u \in x \mid \neg(Zo(x) \supseteq Zo(u) \ \& \ Zo(x) \neq Zo(u))\rangle\rangle$

Thus Zo is a 1-1 map of all ordinals into the set t, a thing impossible. One way of seeing this is to consider the inverse zoInv of the restriction of Zo to the ordinals, extended arbitrarily so that all of its images are ordinal numbers. Then the set {zoInv(x) : x ∈ t} should coincide with the class of all ordinals, which is known to be a proper class.

$\text{Suppose} \Rightarrow \quad Stat30 : \neg\langle \forall y, \exists x \mid \mathcal{O}(x) \ \& \ Zo(x) = y \vee \neg\langle \exists x' \mid \mathcal{O}(x') \ \& \ Zo(x') = y\rangle\rangle$

$\langle y_2\rangle \hookrightarrow Stat30(Stat30\star) \Rightarrow \quad Stat31 :$

$\neg\langle \exists x \mid \mathcal{O}(x) \ \& \ Zo(x) = y_2 \vee \neg\langle \exists x' \mid \mathcal{O}(x') \ \& \ Zo(x') = y_2\rangle\rangle \ \& \ \mathcal{O}(\emptyset)$

$\text{Suppose} \Rightarrow \quad Stat32 : \langle \exists x' \mid \mathcal{O}(x') \ \& \ Zo(x') = y_2\rangle$

$\langle x_2\rangle \hookrightarrow Stat32 \Rightarrow \quad \text{AUTO}$

$\langle x_2\rangle \hookrightarrow Stat31(Stat31\star) \Rightarrow \quad \text{false}; \ \text{Discharge} \Rightarrow \quad \text{AUTO}$

$\langle \emptyset\rangle \hookrightarrow Stat31(Stat31\star) \Rightarrow \quad \text{false}; \ \text{Discharge} \Rightarrow$

$\langle \forall y, \exists x \mid \mathcal{O}(x) \ \& \ Zo(x) = y \vee \neg\langle \exists x' \mid \mathcal{O}(x') \ \& \ Zo(x') = y\rangle\rangle$

$\text{APPLY} \ \langle v1_\Theta : zoInv\rangle \ \text{Skolem} \Rightarrow \quad Stat33 :$

$\langle \forall y \mid \mathcal{O}(zoInv(y)) \ \& \ Zo(zoInv(y)) = y \vee \neg\langle \exists x' \mid \mathcal{O}(x') \ \& \ Zo(x') = y\rangle\rangle$

$\langle \{zoInv(x) : x \in t\}\rangle \hookrightarrow T15 \Rightarrow \quad Stat34 : \neg\langle \forall x \mid x \in \{zoInv(x) : x \in t\} \leftrightarrow \mathcal{O}(x)\rangle$

$\langle e\rangle \hookrightarrow Stat34(Stat34\star) \Rightarrow \quad e \in \{zoInv(x) : x \in t\} \neq \mathcal{O}(e)$

$\text{Suppose} \Rightarrow \quad Stat35 : e \in \{zoInv(x) : x \in t\}$

$\langle x_3\rangle \hookrightarrow Stat35(Stat34\star) \Rightarrow \quad x_3 \in t \ \& \ e = zoInv(x_3) \ \& \ \neg\mathcal{O}(e)$

$\langle x_3\rangle \hookrightarrow Stat33(Stat33, Stat33\star) \Rightarrow \quad \mathcal{O}(zoInv(x_3))$

$\text{EQUAL} \ \langle Stat35\rangle \Rightarrow \quad \text{false}; \ \text{Discharge} \Rightarrow \quad \text{AUTO}$

$\langle e\rangle \hookrightarrow Stat27(Stat34\star) \Rightarrow \quad Stat36 : e \notin \{zoInv(x) : x \in t\} \ \& \ \mathcal{O}(e) \ \& \ Zo(e) \in t \ \&$

$Stat37 : \neg\langle \exists u \in e \mid \neg(Zo(e) \supseteq Zo(u) \ \& \ Zo(e) \neq Zo(u))\rangle$

$\langle Zo(e)\rangle \hookrightarrow Stat36(Stat36, Stat36\star) \Rightarrow \quad e \neq zoInv(Zo(e))$

$\text{Suppose} \Rightarrow \quad Stat38 : \neg\langle \exists x' \mid \mathcal{O}(x') \ \& \ Zo(x') = Zo(e)\rangle$

$\langle e\rangle \hookrightarrow Stat38(Stat36\star) \Rightarrow \quad \text{false}; \ \text{Discharge} \Rightarrow \quad \text{AUTO}$

$\langle \mathrm{Zo(e)} \rangle \hookrightarrow$ *Stat33(Stat36⋆)* $\Rightarrow \quad \mathcal{O}(\mathrm{zoInv(Zo(e))})\ \&\ \mathrm{Zo(zoInv(Zo(e)))} = \mathrm{Zo(e)}$

$\langle \mathrm{e, zoInv(Zo(e))} \rangle \hookrightarrow$ *T14 (Stat36⋆)* $\Rightarrow \quad \mathrm{e} \in \mathrm{zoInv(Zo(e))} \vee \mathrm{zoInv(Zo(e))} \in \mathrm{e}$

Suppose $\Rightarrow \quad \mathrm{zoInv(Zo(e))} \in \mathrm{e}$

$\langle \mathrm{zoInv(Zo(e))} \rangle \hookrightarrow$ *Stat37(Stat36⋆)* $\Rightarrow$ false; Discharge $\Rightarrow$ AUTO

$\langle \mathrm{zoInv(Zo(e))} \rangle \hookrightarrow$ *Stat27(Stat34⋆)* $\Rightarrow$ *Stat39* : $\neg\langle \exists \mathrm{u} \in \mathrm{zoInv(Zo(e))} \mid$

$\neg(\mathrm{Zo(zoInv(Zo(e)))} \supseteq \mathrm{Zo(u)}\ \&\ \mathrm{Zo(zoInv(Zo(e)))} \neq \mathrm{Zo(u)})\rangle$

$\langle \mathrm{e} \rangle \hookrightarrow$ *Stat39(Stat36⋆)* $\Rightarrow$ false; Discharge $\Rightarrow$ QED

The following corollary of the preceding theorem shows that if s is any member of a family t of sets satisfying the hypotheses of that theorem, then s is contained in an element of t maximal in t.

THEOREM 21: [Zorn's lemma, generalized form]
$\langle \forall \mathrm{x} \subseteq \mathrm{T} \mid \langle \forall \mathrm{u} \in \mathrm{x}, \mathrm{v} \in \mathrm{x} \mid \mathrm{u} \supseteq \mathrm{v} \vee \mathrm{v} \supseteq \mathrm{u} \rangle \rightarrow \langle \exists \mathrm{w} \in \mathrm{T}, \forall \mathrm{y} \in \mathrm{x} \mid \mathrm{w} \supseteq \mathrm{y} \rangle\rangle \rightarrow$
$\langle \forall \mathrm{u} \in \mathrm{T}, \exists \mathrm{y} \in \mathrm{T} \mid \mathrm{y} \supseteq \mathrm{u}\ \&\ \langle \forall \mathrm{x} \in \mathrm{T} \mid \mathrm{x} \supseteq \mathrm{y} \rightarrow \mathrm{x} = \mathrm{y} \rangle\rangle$. PROOF:

Suppose_not(t) $\Rightarrow$ *Stat1* :

$\langle \forall \mathrm{x} \subseteq \mathrm{t} \mid \langle \forall \mathrm{u} \in \mathrm{x}, \mathrm{v} \in \mathrm{x} \mid \mathrm{u} \supseteq \mathrm{v} \vee \mathrm{v} \supseteq \mathrm{u} \rangle \rightarrow \langle \exists \mathrm{w} \in \mathrm{t}, \forall \mathrm{y} \in \mathrm{x} \mid \mathrm{w} \supseteq \mathrm{y} \rangle\rangle\ \&$

*Stat2* : $\neg\langle \forall \mathrm{u} \in \mathrm{t}, \exists \mathrm{y} \in \mathrm{t} \mid \mathrm{y} \supseteq \mathrm{u}\ \&\ \langle \forall \mathrm{x} \in \mathrm{t} \mid \mathrm{x} \supseteq \mathrm{y} \rightarrow \mathrm{x} = \mathrm{y} \rangle\rangle$

For suppose that u ∈ t contradicts the conclusion of our theorem, and consider the subset tt of all elements of t which contain u. It is clear that every collection of subsets of tt linearly ordered by inclusion has an upper bound in tt, and so by the preceding theorem tt contains an element ma inclusion-maximal among all the sets in tt.

$\langle \mathrm{u} \rangle \hookrightarrow$ *Stat2* $\Rightarrow \quad \mathrm{u} \in \mathrm{t}\ \&$ *Stat3* : $\neg\langle \exists \mathrm{y} \in \mathrm{t} \mid \mathrm{y} \supseteq \mathrm{u}\ \&\ \langle \forall \mathrm{x} \in \mathrm{t} \mid \mathrm{x} \supseteq \mathrm{y} \rightarrow \mathrm{x} = \mathrm{y} \rangle\rangle$

Loc_def $\Rightarrow \quad \mathrm{tt} = \{\mathrm{x} \in \mathrm{t} \mid \mathrm{x} \supseteq \mathrm{u}\}$

Suppose $\Rightarrow$ *Stat4* : $\mathrm{t} \not\supseteq \mathrm{tt}$

$\langle \mathrm{c} \rangle \hookrightarrow$ *Stat4* $\Rightarrow \quad \mathrm{c} \notin \mathrm{t}\ \&$ *Stat5* : $\mathrm{c} \in \{\mathrm{x} \in \mathrm{t} \mid \mathrm{x} \supseteq \mathrm{u}\}$

$\langle\ \rangle \hookrightarrow$ *Stat5* $\Rightarrow$ false; Discharge $\Rightarrow \quad \mathrm{t} \supseteq \mathrm{tt}$

Suppose $\Rightarrow$ *Stat6* :

$\neg\langle \forall \mathrm{x} \subseteq \mathrm{tt} \mid \langle \forall \mathrm{u} \in \mathrm{x}, \mathrm{v} \in \mathrm{x} \mid \mathrm{u} \supseteq \mathrm{v} \vee \mathrm{v} \supseteq \mathrm{u} \rangle \rightarrow \langle \exists \mathrm{w} \in \mathrm{tt}, \forall \mathrm{y} \in \mathrm{x} \mid \mathrm{w} \supseteq \mathrm{y} \rangle\rangle$

$\langle \mathrm{d} \rangle \hookrightarrow$ *Stat6* $\Rightarrow \quad \mathrm{d} \subseteq \mathrm{tt}\ \&\ \langle \forall \mathrm{u} \in \mathrm{d}, \mathrm{v} \in \mathrm{d} \mid \mathrm{u} \supseteq \mathrm{v} \vee \mathrm{v} \supseteq \mathrm{u} \rangle\ \&$ *Stat7* :

$\neg\langle \exists \mathrm{w} \in \mathrm{tt}, \forall \mathrm{y} \in \mathrm{d} \mid \mathrm{w} \supseteq \mathrm{y} \rangle$

$\langle \mathrm{d} \rangle \hookrightarrow$ *Stat1* $\Rightarrow$ *Stat8* : $\langle \exists \mathrm{w} \in \mathrm{t}, \forall \mathrm{y} \in \mathrm{d} \mid \mathrm{w} \supseteq \mathrm{y} \rangle$

$\langle \mathrm{wd} \rangle \hookrightarrow$ *Stat8* $\Rightarrow \quad \mathrm{wd} \in \mathrm{t}\ \&$ *Stat9* : $\langle \forall \mathrm{y} \in \mathrm{d} \mid \mathrm{wd} \supseteq \mathrm{y} \rangle$

Since u ∈ tt, d cannot be null, from which it is easily seen that wd must contain u, and so wd ∈ tt. Thus it follows by Theorem 20 that tt has an element ma maximal (for inclusion) in tt.

Suppose ⇒ $u \notin tt$
ELEM ⇒ *Stat10*: $u \notin \{x \in t \mid x \supseteq u\}$
$\langle\,\rangle \hookrightarrow$ *Stat10* ⇒ false; Discharge ⇒ $u \in tt$
Suppose ⇒ $d = \emptyset$
$\langle u\rangle \hookrightarrow$ *Stat7* ⇒ *Stat11*: $\neg\langle \forall y \in d \mid u \supseteq y\rangle$
$\langle a\rangle \hookrightarrow$ *Stat11* ⇒ false; Discharge ⇒ *Stat12*: $d \neq \emptyset$
$\langle b\rangle \hookrightarrow$ *Stat12* ⇒ $b \in d$
$\langle b\rangle \hookrightarrow$ *Stat9* ⇒ $wd \supseteq b$
ELEM ⇒ *Stat13*: $b \in \{x \in t \mid x \supseteq u\}$
$\langle\,\rangle \hookrightarrow$ *Stat13* ⇒ $wd \supseteq u$
Suppose ⇒ $wd \notin tt$
ELEM ⇒ *Stat14*: $wd \notin \{x \in t \mid x \supseteq u\}$
$\langle\,\rangle \hookrightarrow$ *Stat14* ⇒ false; Discharge ⇒ $wd \in tt$
$\langle wd\rangle \hookrightarrow$ *Stat7* ⇒ false; Discharge ⇒
$\big\langle \forall x \subseteq tt \mid \langle \forall u \in x, v \in x \mid u \supseteq v \vee v \supseteq u\rangle \rightarrow \langle \exists w \in tt, \forall y \in x \mid w \supseteq y\rangle\big\rangle$
$\langle tt\rangle \hookrightarrow$ *T20* ⇒ *Stat15*: $\big\langle \exists y \in tt, \forall x \in tt \mid \neg(x \supseteq y \;\&\; x \neq y)\big\rangle$
$\langle ma\rangle \hookrightarrow$ *Stat15* ⇒ $ma \in tt$ & *Stat16*: $\big\langle \forall x \in tt \mid \neg(x \supseteq ma \;\&\; x \neq ma)\big\rangle$

But it is easily seen that ma is maximal in the whole collection t, and so our theorem is proved.

$\langle ma\rangle \hookrightarrow$ *Stat3* ⇒ $\neg\big(ma \supseteq u \;\&\; \langle \forall x \in t \mid x \supseteq ma \rightarrow x = ma\rangle\big)$
ELEM ⇒ *Stat17*: $ma \in \{x \in t \mid x \supseteq u\}$
$\langle\,\rangle \hookrightarrow$ *Stat17* ⇒ $ma \supseteq u$
ELEM ⇒ *Stat18*: $\neg\langle \forall x \in t \mid x \supseteq ma \rightarrow x = ma\rangle$
$\langle e\rangle \hookrightarrow$ *Stat18* ⇒ $e \in t \;\&\; e \supseteq ma \;\&\; e \neq ma$
ELEM ⇒ $e \supseteq u$
Suppose ⇒ $e \notin tt$
ELEM ⇒ *Stat19*: $e \notin \{x \in t \mid x \supseteq u\}$
$\langle\,\rangle \hookrightarrow$ *Stat19* ⇒ false; Discharge ⇒ $e \in tt$
$\langle e\rangle \hookrightarrow$ *Stat16* ⇒ false; Discharge ⇒ QED

Next we note a special case common in applications of Theorem 21, namely that in which the union of any linearly ordered collection of elements of t is a subset of t.

THEOREM 22: [Zorn's lemma for union-closed collections]
$\big\langle \forall x \subseteq T \mid \langle \forall u \in x, v \in x \mid u \supseteq v \vee v \supseteq u\rangle \rightarrow \bigcup x \in T\big\rangle \rightarrow$
$\big\langle \forall u \in T, \exists y \in T \mid y \supseteq u \;\&\; \langle \forall x \in T \mid x \supseteq y \rightarrow x = y\rangle\big\rangle$. PROOF:

Suppose_not(t) $\Rightarrow$ *Stat1* : $\langle \forall x \subseteq t \mid \langle \forall u \in x, v \in x \mid u \supseteq v \vee v \supseteq u \rangle \rightarrow \bigcup x \in t \rangle$ &
$\neg \langle \forall u \in t, \exists y \in t \mid y \supseteq u \ \& \ \langle \forall x \in t \mid x \supseteq y \rightarrow x = y \rangle \rangle$

For given any subcollection of t linearly ordered by inclusion, $\bigcup$t plainly includes all the sets in t, and so our present assertion follows immediately from the preceding theorem.

*T21* $\Rightarrow$ *Stat2* : $\neg \langle \forall x \subseteq t \mid \langle \forall u \in x, v \in x \mid u \supseteq v \vee v \supseteq u \rangle \rightarrow$
$\langle \exists w \in t, \forall y \in x \mid w \supseteq y \rangle \rangle$
$\langle a \rangle \hookrightarrow$ *Stat2* $\Rightarrow$ $a \subseteq t \ \& \ \langle \forall u \in a, v \in a \mid u \supseteq v \vee v \supseteq u \rangle$ &
*Stat3* : $\neg \langle \exists w \in t, \forall y \in a \mid w \supseteq y \rangle$
$\langle a \rangle \hookrightarrow$ *Stat1* $\Rightarrow$ $\bigcup a \in t$
$\langle \bigcup a \rangle \hookrightarrow$ *Stat3* $\Rightarrow$ *Stat4* : $\neg \langle \forall y \in a \mid \bigcup a \supseteq y \rangle$
$\langle b \rangle \hookrightarrow$ *Stat4* $\Rightarrow$ $b \in a$ & *Stat5* : $\bigcup a \not\supseteq b$
$\langle b, a \rangle \hookrightarrow$ *T2* $\Rightarrow$ false; Discharge $\Rightarrow$ QED

## 7.5 Finiteness

Traditionally, finiteness is defined through the notion of cardinality of a set: a set is finite if its cardinality precedes the first infinite ordinal. As a shortcut, to begin developing an acceptable formal treatment of finiteness without much preparatory work, we adopt here the following definition (reminiscent of Tarski's 1924 paper [Tar24]): a set F is finite if every nonnull family of subsets of F owns an inclusion-minimal element. This notion can be specified very succinctly in terms of the powerset operator.

THEOREM 23: [Monotonicity of powerset] $S \supseteq X \rightarrow \mathscr{P}X \cup \{\emptyset, X\} \subseteq \mathscr{P}S$. PROOF:
Suppose_not($s_0, x_0$) $\Rightarrow$ AUTO
Set_monot $\Rightarrow$ $\{x : x \subseteq x_0\} \subseteq \{x : x \subseteq s_0\}$
Use_def($\mathscr{P}$) $\Rightarrow$ *Stat1* : $\emptyset \notin \{x : x \subseteq s_0\} \vee x_0 \notin \{x : x \subseteq s_0\}$
$\langle \emptyset, x_0 \rangle \hookrightarrow$ *Stat1* $\Rightarrow$ false
Discharge $\Rightarrow$ QED

DEF Fin: [Finiteness property] $\mathrm{Fin}(X) \leftrightarrow_{\mathrm{Def}}$
$\langle \forall g \in \mathscr{P}(\mathscr{P}X) \backslash \{\emptyset\}, \exists m \mid g \cap \mathscr{P}m = \{m\} \rangle$

THEOREM 24: [Monotonicity of finiteness] $Y \supseteq X \ \& \ \mathrm{Fin}(Y) \rightarrow \mathrm{Fin}(X)$. PROOF:
Suppose_not($y_0, x_0$) $\Rightarrow$ AUTO
$\langle y_0, x_0 \rangle \hookrightarrow$ *T23* ($\star$) $\Rightarrow$ $\mathscr{P}y_0 \supseteq \mathscr{P}x_0$
Use_def(Fin) $\Rightarrow$ *Stat1* : $\neg \langle \forall g \in \mathscr{P}(\mathscr{P}x_0) \backslash \{\emptyset\}, \exists m \mid g \cap \mathscr{P}m = \{m\} \rangle$ &

$\langle \forall g' \in \mathscr{P}(\mathscr{P}y_0)\backslash\{\emptyset\}, \exists m \mid g' \cap \mathscr{P}m = \{m\}\rangle$

$\langle \mathscr{P}y_0, \mathscr{P}x_0\rangle \hookrightarrow T23\ (\star) \Rightarrow \quad \mathscr{P}(\mathscr{P}y_0) \supseteq \mathscr{P}(\mathscr{P}x_0)$

$\langle g_0, g_0\rangle \hookrightarrow Stat1(Stat1\star) \Rightarrow \quad \neg\langle \exists m \mid g_0 \cap \mathscr{P}m = \{m\}\rangle \ \&\ \langle \exists m \mid g_0 \cap \mathscr{P}m = \{m\}\rangle$

Discharge ⇒ QED

THEORY finiteInduction$(s_0, P(S))$

Fin$(s_0)$ & P$(s_0)$

END finiteInduction

ENTER_THEORY finiteInduction

THEOREM finiteInduction$_1$. $\langle \exists m \mid \{s \subseteq s_0 \mid P(s)\} \cap \mathscr{P}m = \{m\}\rangle$. PROOF:

Suppose_not() ⇒ AUTO

Assump ⇒ Fin$(s_0)$ & P$(s_0)$

Use_def(Fin) ⇒ *Stat1* : $\langle \forall g \in \mathscr{P}(\mathscr{P}s_0)\backslash\{\emptyset\}, \exists m \mid g \cap \mathscr{P}m = \{m\}\rangle$

$\langle \{s \subseteq s_0 \mid P(s)\}\rangle \hookrightarrow Stat1 \Rightarrow \quad \{s \subseteq s_0 \mid P(s)\} \notin \mathscr{P}(\mathscr{P}s_0)\backslash\{\emptyset\}$

Suppose ⇒ *Stat2* : $s_0 \notin \{s \subseteq s_0 \mid P(s)\}$

$\langle s_0\rangle \hookrightarrow Stat2 \Rightarrow$ false; Discharge ⇒ $\{s \subseteq s_0 \mid P(s)\} \notin \mathscr{P}(\mathscr{P}s_0)$

Use_def($\mathscr{P}$) ⇒ *Stat3* : $\{s \subseteq s_0 \mid P(s)\} \notin \{y : y \subseteq \{z : z \subseteq s_0\}\}$

$\langle \{s \subseteq s_0 \mid P(s)\}\rangle \hookrightarrow Stat3 \Rightarrow \quad Stat4 : \{s \subseteq s_0 \mid P(s)\} \not\subseteq \{z : z \subseteq s_0\}$

$\langle s_1\rangle \hookrightarrow Stat4 \Rightarrow \quad Stat5 : s_1 \in \{s : s \subseteq s_0 \mid P(s)\} \ \&\ s_1 \notin \{z : z \subseteq s_0\}$

$\langle s, s_1\rangle \hookrightarrow Stat5(Stat5\star) \Rightarrow$ false

Discharge ⇒ QED

APPLY $\langle v1_\Theta : fin_\Theta\rangle$ Skolem⇒

THEOREM finiteInduction$_0$. $\{s \subseteq s_0 \mid P(s)\} \cap \mathscr{P}fin_\Theta = \{fin_\Theta\}$.

THEOREM finiteInduction$_2$: [Minimal finite set satisfying P]

$S \subseteq fin_\Theta \rightarrow s_0 \supseteq S \ \&\ Fin(S) \ \&\ (P(S) \leftrightarrow S = fin_\Theta)$. PROOF:

Suppose_not$(s_1)$ ⇒ AUTO

*T*finiteInduction$_0$ ⇒ $\{s \subseteq s_0 \mid P(s)\} \cap \mathscr{P}fin_\Theta = \{fin_\Theta\}$

ELEM ⇒ *Stat1* : $fin_\Theta \in \{s \subseteq s_0 \mid P(s)\}$

$\langle\,\rangle \hookrightarrow Stat1 \Rightarrow \quad fin_\Theta \subseteq s_0 \ \&\ P(fin_\Theta)$

Assump ⇒ Fin$(s_0)$

$\langle s_0, fin_\Theta\rangle \hookrightarrow T24 \Rightarrow \quad Fin(fin_\Theta)$

$\langle fin_\Theta, s_1\rangle \hookrightarrow T24 \Rightarrow \quad P(s_1) \neq s_1 = fin_\Theta$

Suppose ⇒ $s_1 = fin_\Theta$

EQUAL ⇒ false; Discharge ⇒ $s_1 \notin \{s \subseteq s_0 \mid P(s)\} \cap \mathscr{P}fin_\Theta \ \&\ P(s_1)$

Suppose ⇒ $s_1 \notin \mathscr{P}\mathrm{fin}_\Theta$

Use_def($\mathscr{P}$) ⇒ *Stat2* : $s_1 \notin \{y : y \subseteq \mathrm{fin}_\Theta\}$

$\langle s_1\rangle \hookrightarrow$ *Stat2* ⇒ false

Discharge ⇒ *Stat3* : $s_1 \notin \{s \subseteq s_0 \mid P(s)\}$

$\langle s_1\rangle \hookrightarrow$ *Stat3* ⇒ false

Discharge ⇒ QED

ENTER_THEORY Set_theory

DISPLAY finiteInduction

THEORY finiteInduction$(s_0, P(S))$
Fin$(s_0)$ & $P(s_0)$
⇒ $(\mathrm{fin}_\Theta)$
$\langle \forall s \mid s \subseteq \mathrm{fin}_\Theta \rightarrow s_0 \supseteq s \,\&\, \mathrm{Fin}(s) \,\&\, (P(s) \leftrightarrow s = \mathrm{fin}_\Theta)\rangle$
END finiteInduction

THEOREM 25: [Finiteness of the union of a finite set with a singleton]
$\mathrm{Fin}(F) \rightarrow \mathrm{Fin}(F \cup \{X\})$. PROOF:

Suppose_not$(f_0, x_0)$ ⇒ AUTO

Arguing by contradiction, suppose that $f_0$ and $x_0$ are such that $f_0$ is finite but $f_0 \cup \{x_0\}$ is not. A nonnull family $g_0$ of subsets of $f_0 \cup \{x_0\}$ must then exist none of whose elements is minimal. On the other hand $\{y\backslash\{x_0\} : y \in g_0\}$, which is also nonnull but consists entirely of subsets of $f_0$, must have a minimal element $m_0 = y_0\backslash\{x_0\}$, with $y_0 \in g_0$.

Use_def(Fin) ⇒ *Stat0* : $\neg\langle \forall g \in \mathscr{P}(\mathscr{P}(f_0 \cup \{x_0\}))\backslash\{\emptyset\}, \exists m \mid g \cap \mathscr{P}m = \{m\}\rangle$ &

*Stat1* : $\langle \forall h \in \mathscr{P}(\mathscr{P}f_0)\backslash\{\emptyset\}, \exists m \mid h \cap \mathscr{P}m = \{m\}\rangle$

$\langle g_0\rangle \hookrightarrow$ *Stat0(Stat0)* ⇒ *Stat2* : $\neg\langle \exists m \mid g_0 \cap \mathscr{P}m = \{m\}\rangle$ &

$g_0 \in \mathscr{P}(\mathscr{P}(f_0 \cup \{x_0\}))$ & $g_0 \neq \emptyset$

Loc_def ⇒ *Stat3* : $h_0 = \{y\backslash\{x_0\} : y \in g_0\}$

Suppose ⇒ $h_0 \notin \mathscr{P}(\mathscr{P}f_0)\backslash\{\emptyset\}$

Suppose ⇒ *Stat4* : $\{y\backslash\{x_0\} : y \in g_0\} = \emptyset$

$\langle \mathbf{arb}(g_0)\rangle \hookrightarrow$ *Stat4(Stat2, Stat2)* ⇒ false; Discharge ⇒ AUTO

Use_def($\mathscr{P}$) ⇒ *Stat5* : $h_0 \notin \{h : h \subseteq \{k : k \subseteq f_0\}\}$

$\langle h_0\rangle \hookrightarrow$ *Stat5(Stat5⋆)* ⇒ *Stat6* : $h_0 \not\subseteq \{k : k \subseteq f_0\}$

$\langle k_0\rangle \hookrightarrow$ *Stat6(Stat3⋆)* ⇒ *Stat7* : $k_0 \in \{y\backslash\{x_0\} : y \in g_0\}$ & $k_0 \notin \{k : k \subseteq f_0\}$

$\langle y_1, k_0\rangle \hookrightarrow$ *Stat7(Stat7⋆)* ⇒ $y_1 \in g_0$ & $y_1 \not\subseteq f_0 \cup \{x_0\}$

Use_def($\mathscr{P}$) ⇒ *Stat8*: $g_0 \in \{h : h \subseteq \{k : k \subseteq f_0 \cup \{x_0\}\}\}$

$\langle h_1 \rangle \hookrightarrow$ *Stat8(Stat7⋆)* ⇒ *Stat9*: $y_1 \in \{k : k \subseteq f_0 \cup \{x_0\}\}$

$\langle k_1 \rangle \hookrightarrow$ *Stat9(Stat7⋆)* ⇒ false

Discharge ⇒ AUTO

$\langle h_0, m_0 \rangle \hookrightarrow$ *Stat1(Stat3⋆)* ⇒ *Stat10*: $m_0 \in \{y \setminus \{x_0\} : y \in g_0\}$ & $h_0 \cap \mathscr{P} m_0 = \{m_0\}$

$\langle y_0 \rangle \hookrightarrow$ *Stat10(Stat10⋆)* ⇒ *Stat11*: $m_0 = y_0 \setminus \{x_0\}$ & $y_0 \in g_0$

We will reach the desired contradiction by showing that either $m_0$ or $y_0 = m_0 \cup \{x_0\}$ is minimal in $g_0$. We check first that $m_0$ itself must be minimal when $m_0 \in g_0$.

Suppose ⇒ $m_0 \in g_0$

$\langle m_0 \rangle \hookrightarrow$ *Stat2(Stat10⋆)* ⇒ *Stat12*: $g_0 \cap \mathscr{P} m_0 \nsubseteq \{m_0\}$

Use_def($\mathscr{P} m_0$) ⇒ AUTO

$\langle z_0 \rangle \hookrightarrow$ *Stat12(Stat3⋆)* ⇒

*Stat13*: $z_0 \in \{h : h \subseteq m_0\}$ & $z_0 \notin \{y \setminus \{x_0\} : y \in g_0\}$ & $z_0 \in g_0$

$\langle h_2, z_0 \rangle \hookrightarrow$ *Stat13(Stat11⋆)* ⇒ false

Discharge ⇒ AUTO

Suppose next that $m_0 \notin g_0$; we will reach a contradiction by showing that $y_0$ is minimal in $g_0$.

$\langle y_0, y_0 \rangle \hookrightarrow$ *T23 (Stat11⋆)* ⇒ $y_0 \in \mathscr{P} y_0$

$\langle y_0 \rangle \hookrightarrow$ *Stat2(Stat11⋆)* ⇒ *Stat14*: $g_0 \cap \mathscr{P} y_0 \nsubseteq \{y_0\}$

Use_def($\mathscr{P} y_0$) ⇒ AUTO

$\langle z_1 \rangle \hookrightarrow$ *Stat14(Stat11⋆)* ⇒ *Stat15*: $z_1 \in \{h : h \subseteq y_0\}$ & $z_1 \in g_0$ & $z_1 \setminus \{x_0\} \neq y_0 \setminus \{x_0\}$

EQUAL ⟨*Stat10*⟩ ⇒ $h_0 \cap \mathscr{P}(y_0 \setminus \{x_0\}) = \{y_0 \setminus \{x_0\}\}$

Suppose ⇒ $z_1 \setminus \{x_0\} \notin \mathscr{P}(y_0 \setminus \{x_0\})$

Use_def($\mathscr{P}$) ⇒ *Stat16*: $z_1 \setminus \{x_0\} \notin \{h : h \subseteq y_0 \setminus \{x_0\}\}$

$\langle z_1 \setminus \{x_0\} \rangle \hookrightarrow$ *Stat16(Stat16⋆)* ⇒ $z_1 \setminus \{x_0\} \nsubseteq y_0 \setminus \{x_0\}$

$\langle h_3 \rangle \hookrightarrow$ *Stat15(Stat16⋆)* ⇒ false; Discharge ⇒ AUTO

Suppose ⇒ *Stat17*: $z_1 \setminus \{x_0\} \notin \{y \setminus \{x_0\} : y \in g_0\}$

$\langle z_1 \rangle \hookrightarrow$ *Stat17(Stat15⋆)* ⇒ false; Discharge ⇒ $z_1 \setminus \{x_0\} \in h_0$

(*Stat15⋆*)Discharge ⇒ QED

THEOREM 26: [Finiteness of the union of two finite sets]

Fin(X) & Fin(Y) → Fin(X ∪ Y). PROOF:

$\mathsf{Suppose\_not}(x_0, y_1) \Rightarrow$ AUTO

Arguing by contradiction, suppose that $x_0$ and $y_1$ are finite sets whose union is not finite. Then finite induction enables us to take a minimal subset $y_0$ of $y_1$ for which $x_0 \cup y_0$ is not finite.

$\mathsf{APPLY}\ \langle \mathsf{fin}_\Theta : y_0 \rangle\ \mathsf{finiteInduction}\big(s_0 \mapsto y_1, \mathsf{P(S)} \mapsto \neg \mathsf{Fin}(x_0 \cup \mathsf{S})\big) \Rightarrow$

$\quad Stat1 : \big\langle \forall s \mid s \subseteq y_0 \rightarrow y_1 \supseteq s \;\&\; \mathsf{Fin}(s) \;\&\; \big(\neg \mathsf{Fin}(x_0 \cup s) \leftrightarrow s = y_0\big)\big\rangle$

$\langle y_0 \rangle \hookrightarrow Stat1(Stat1\star) \Rightarrow \quad \mathsf{Fin}(y_0) \;\&\; \neg \mathsf{Fin}(x_0 \cup y_0)$

$\mathsf{Loc\_def} \Rightarrow \quad a_0 = \mathbf{arb}(y_0)$

Since $y_0$ cannot be empty, the union $x_0 \cup y_0$ can be decomposed as $x_0 \cup (y_0 \setminus \{\mathbf{arb}(y_0)\}) \cup \{\mathbf{arb}(y_0)\}$, where $x_0 \cup (y_0 \setminus \{\mathbf{arb}(y_0)\})$ is finite by inductive hypothesis. But then $x_0 \cup y_0$ must also be finite, by the preceding theorem.

$\mathsf{Suppose} \Rightarrow \quad x_0 \cup y_0 = x_0$

$\quad \mathsf{EQUAL}\ \langle Stat1 \rangle \Rightarrow \quad \neg \mathsf{Fin}(x_0)$

$\mathsf{Discharge} \Rightarrow \quad Stat2 : y_0 \setminus \{a_0\} \neq y_0 \;\&\; x_0 \cup \big(y_0 \setminus \{a_0\}\big) \cup \{a_0\} = x_0 \cup y_0$

$\big\langle y_0 \setminus \{a_0\} \big\rangle \hookrightarrow Stat1(Stat1\star) \Rightarrow \quad \mathsf{Fin}\big(x_0 \cup \big(y_0 \setminus \{a_0\}\big)\big)$

$\big\langle x_0 \cup \big(y_0 \setminus \{a_0\}\big), a_0 \big\rangle \hookrightarrow T25\ (Stat2\star) \Rightarrow \quad \mathsf{Fin}\big(x_0 \cup \big(y_0 \setminus \{a_0\}\big) \cup \{a_0\}\big)$

$\mathsf{EQUAL} \Rightarrow \quad \mathsf{false}$

$\mathsf{Discharge} \Rightarrow$ QED

The proof of the following is left as an exercise for the reader: THEOREM 27: ["All that ends is short"] $\mathsf{Fin}(\emptyset)$.

## References


[Acz88] Aczel, P.: Non-Well-Founded Sets. CSLI Lecture Notes, vol. 14. CLSI, Stanford (1988)

[Ped62] Peddicord, R.: The number of full sets with *n* elements. Proc. Am. Math. Soc. **13**(5), 825–828 (1962)

[Tar24] Tarski, A.: Sur les ensembles fini. Fundam. Math. **VI**, 45–95 (1924)

# Index



J.T. Schwartz et al., *Computational Logic and Set Theory*,
DOI 10.1007/978-0-85729-808-9, © Springer-Verlag London Limited 2011